HIROSHIMA'S SHADOW

HIROSHIMA'S SHADOW

EDITED BY KAI BIRD AND LAWRENCE LIFSCHULTZ

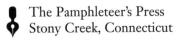

The Pamphleteer's Press
Stony Creek, Connecticut

10 9 8 7 6 5 4 3 2 1

Library of Congress Catalog Card Number
96-069657

ISBN 0-9630587-3-8 Hardcover
ISBN 0-9630587-4-6 Softcover

Design by Toki Design

Manufactured in the United States of America

THE PAMPHLETEER'S PRESS
P.O. Box 3374
Stony Creek, Connecticut 06405
Tel/Fax (203) 483-1429
Email: pamphpress@igc.apc.org
http: www.pamphleteers.com

A NOTE OF THANKS

THE EDITORS WISH TO THANK the contributors and the many friends and fellow workers who gave of their time, labor, and talent to make this book possible. The staff of the Pamphleteer's Press worked in a manner which is rarely found in modern publishing houses. They have crafted a book beautiful in its aesthetic balance which now houses the painful story of Hiroshima and Nagasaki. Danielle McClellan, managing editor of Pamphleteer's Press, is the person most responsible for finally bringing this book to publication. Her sensitive eye, penetrating intelligence, and sound judgment guided her editor's pen.

In terms of the labor involved, edited collections can be deceiving. When done with skill and care, they involve meticulous work. Many of the contributions to this volume are updated revisions of previously published articles or the fusion of several pieces by a single contributor. Each one had to be checked, rechecked, and confirmed.

Martha Cox directed a national and international search for executors of literary estates and the descendants of contributors. She followed leads to distant corners of the globe and into more than one dark alley in determined pursuit of every suspected executor or archivist on her "most wanted list."

We discovered the work of Michi Toki in a hauntingly beautiful book that she designed of Yoshuke Yamahata's photographs titled *Nagasaki Journey*. It has been our good fortune to work with her and her colleague, Lynn Coakley.

Jim Mooney brought a skilled professionalism to the task of copyediting. Thanks are also due to John Hill, who coordinated the scanning and preparation of the book's first set-up in pages, and to Fred Sinclair, John Kane, and Ellen Angus for their labor on the manuscript. Tim Young at Yale's Beinecke Library aided us in gaining access to John Hersey's still uncatalogued papers and provided wise technical counsel.

We wish to thank Shogo Yamahata for graciously allowing us access to his father's remarkable photographs. Carol Fouke of the National Council of Churches was of great assistance in tracing those who held the copyright of several contributions. John M. Staudenmaier, editor of *Technology and Culture*, provided us with the right contacts in the Jesuit community so we could learn about Edgar R. Smothers' history. Akio Yamaguchi, editor-in-chief of *Sekai*, was very helpful at the early stages of our work. We benefited immensely from the assistance of two skilled translators, Bruno Navasky and Sarah Frederick. Noah Doyle's facility with Japanese was also a valuable resource in our contacts with Japan.

Dr. Shutaro Hida and his memoir of the day Hiroshima disappeared reached our hands through the efforts of Jay Gould and Mike Tanzer. Dr. Zia Mian reminded us not to forget Lewis Mumford. Jharana Jhaveri in New Delhi assisted us in a detailed search in India's archives for comments by Gandhi and Nehru on the atomic bombings. We relied on Sanho Tree's expert knowledge of American archives to gather the documents collected in Part VI. Our thanks to Gar Alperovitz, Barton Bernstein, John Burroughs, John Dower, the late Stanley Goldberg, James Hershberg, William Lanouette, Uday Mohan, Martin Sherwin and numerous other historians who generously offered us advice on how to shape this volume. Susan Goldmark and Rabia Ali gave us the emotional and intellectual support to persevere. Finally, we wish to express our appreciation to Joseph Rotblat who a week after receiving the Nobel Peace Prize told us he had been waiting a very long time to write a preface to a book like *Hiroshima's Shadow*.

For Jamal and Joshua

WHEN A YOUNG MAN BORN IN HIROSHIMA on the A-bomb day was selected as the last runner to carry the Olympic flame, an American journalist—who has translated some Japanese literature and might be expected to understand Japan and the Japanese people—publicly stated his opinion that this was an unhappy choice because it reminded the Americans of the atomic bomb.

If the selected runner [at the 1964 Tokyo Olympic Games] had keloid scars or some other sign of radiation injury, that is, if he had been an unmistakable A-bomb casualty, then I would not object to the selection; [such] an A-bomb victim (if fortunate enough to have lived for these twenty years) would have been more representative of those born on the day of the atomic bombing. But the middle-distance runner actually chosen had a perfectly healthy body; we were impressed by his stamina as he ran at full speed in the huge stadium, with the smile of one free of all anxiety. . .

Still, the American journalist was displeased because the young man, born in Hiroshima on the atomic bombing day, reminded Americans of the atomic bomb. He preferred to erase all traces of Hiroshima from the American memory. Worse still, this preference occurs not only to the American mind. Do not all leaders and peoples who at present possess nuclear weapons also wish to erase Hiroshima from their memories?

On Human Dignity
Kenzaburo Oé

CONTENTS

VI. DOCUMENTS

EPILOGUE:

A SOCIAL
CONSCIENCE
FOR THE
NUCLEAR AGE

Joseph Rotblat
Recipient of the Nobel Peace Prize

Remember your humanity...
Albert Einstein and Bertrand Russell

THE BOMB DROPPED ON HIROSHIMA more than a half century ago heralded a new age. The nuclear age emerged as the creation of scientists, but it went sour on them from the very beginning. In total disregard of the basic tenets of science—openness and universality—the new age was conceived in secrecy and usurped, even before birth, by one state in order to gain political dominance. With such congenital defects, and being nurtured by an army of Dr. Strangeloves, it is no wonder that the creation grew into a monster: a monster with 70,000 heads, nuclear warheads; a monster that breathed fear and mistrust and threatened the continued existence of humankind on this planet.

The practical release of nuclear energy was the outcome of many years of experimental and theoretical research. It had great potential for the common good. But the first the general public learned about this discovery was the news of the destruction of Hiroshima by the atom bomb. A splendid achievement of science and technology had turned malign. Science became identified with death and destruction. We, scientists, have a great deal to answer for.

What is so sad about all this is that our intentions were good. Most of the scientists in England and America who initiated the atom bomb project were convinced that the bomb was needed in order that it not be used. The idea of the atom bomb occurred to a number of scientists soon after the discovery of fission of uranium, and it was an accident of history that this coincided with the outbreak of the Second World War, a war in which the survival of basic civilized values was at stake, a titanic struggle between democracy and the worst type of totalitarianism. The notion of using a scientific discovery to make a weapon of mass destruction would normally be anathema to a scientist, but coming at the time it did, it posed a hard dilemma for the scientists, a critical test of their social responsibility. On the one hand, developing an instrument of destruction goes against the basic ideals of science. On the other hand, these very ideals were in danger of being eradicated, if, by the scientists' refusal to make the bomb, a most vile regime were enabled to acquire world domination. As is usually the case with human behavior, the immediate danger took precedence. Nearly all of the scientists who faced the choice decided to go ahead with the research to establish the feasibility of the atom bomb.

The British and American scientists feared that German scientists would develop the bomb. When our calculations had shown that an atom bomb was feasible, it was natural for us to assume that the German scientists had reached the same conclusion. It was not until about five years later that we learned that the fear was groundless; that due to erroneous theoretical calculations and faulty experiments the atom bomb project in Germany, for all practical purposes, had folded up as early as 1942, even before the Manhattan Project started in earnest in the United States. However, we did not know this at the time. We feared that if Hitler acquired this weapon, it would enable him to win the war. It was this appalling prospect that convinced us to start the project. By that time we had worked out a rationale for making the bomb ourselves. The rationale is the same that is used to this day as a reason to keep nuclear arsenals: nuclear deterrence. The only way to deter Hitler from using the bomb against us would be if we too had it and threatened retaliation. We needed the bomb so that it would not be used. But as it turned out, we were wrong: the bomb was used; it was used as soon as it was made; it was used against the people of Hiroshima and Nagasaki.

More than a half century after these momentous events the question is still before us: Was the destruction of Hiroshima and Nagasaki necessary? The simple facts seemingly point to an affirmative answer to this question. On August 14, 1945, six days after the Nagasaki bomb, the war came to an end. Many lives among the military forces on both sides, which would have been lost if the war went on, were saved. The deaths in Hiroshima and Nagasaki were a necessary sacrifice to spare the lives of much larger numbers of others. Thus, the answer to this question, given to the children in their history lessons, is yes.

However, there is another version of the events. It is a version which makes people in the West very uncomfortable, so much so that it is being suppressed. When, in preparation for the fiftieth anniversary of the bomb, the Smithsonian Institution in Washington attempted to raise this question, it was met with such a vicious onslaught that the project had to be abandoned. But the American Legion and the Air Force Association, powerful as they are, cannot stop us asking questions. The evidence supporting the other version is too strong to be dismissed. The publication of *Hiroshima's Shadow: Writings on the Denial of History and the Smithsonian Controversy* is an important contribution toward guaranteeing that this suppression of history will not prevail.

To begin with, there is the nauseating argument about the relative losses of life in the two scenarios: ending the war with or without the atom bomb. Winston Churchill, the British Prime Minister, wrote in 1953 in his *History of the Second World War* that "to quell the Japanese resistance man by man...might well require the loss of a million American lives and half that number of British or more."[1] However, this figure is in stark contrast with the predictions of the Joint War Plans Committee about the casualties that might result from attempts to land American troops on the Japanese home islands. In a memorandum to President Truman in June

1945, they estimated the number of deaths that might result in three different landing operations. These vary from 25,000 to 46,000; far fewer deaths than in Hiroshima and Nagasaki. It is precisely the myths constructed around these familiar rationales that the essays in this volume demystify so convincingly. According to some historians, even the lower number of American lives would not have been lost, because the war could have ended earlier. Gar Alperovitz and Martin Sherwin, among others, have argued persuasively in this volume that Japan was militarily defeated before the atom bomb was manufactured, and was probably ready to surrender under conditions that were later actually accepted. Yet, Truman refused to negotiate.

Before analyzing the reasons for Truman's refusal, it should be emphasized that the atom bomb was not necessary to end the war with Japan. Winston Churchill stated: "It would be a mistake to suppose that the fate of Japan was settled by the atomic bomb. Her defeat was certain before the first bomb fell."[2] More telling is the postwar statement made by Dwight Eisenhower, who was at the time the Supreme Allied Commander: "I voiced...my grave misgivings, first on the basis of my belief that Japan was already defeated and that dropping of the bomb was completely unnecessary, and secondly because I thought that our country should avoid shocking world opinion by the use of a weapon whose employment was, I thought, no longer mandatory as a measure to save American lives."[3] Finally, after the bombs were dropped, Admiral William D. Leahy, the Chairman of the Joint Chiefs of Staff, expressed his strong feelings: "The Japanese were already defeated and ready to surrender. The use of this barbarous weapon at Hiroshima and Nagasaki was of no material assistance in our war against Japan. In being the first to use it we... adopted an ethical standard common to the barbarians of the Dark Ages. I was not taught to make war in that fashion."[4]

In view of these strong sentiments, why did President Truman accept the recommendations of his other advisers, to continue the war until the bombs were ready for use? There are solid grounds for the belief that the reason was not military but political, namely, that the bomb was from the beginning seen as a powerful instrument in the ideological struggle between the United States and the Soviet Union. A recent article in the *Bulletin of the Atomic Scientists* reminded us of the fact that Japan was the designated target for the atom bomb almost from the beginning of the Manhattan Project.[5] As far back as May 1943, a memorandum from the Military Policy Committee recommended that the target should be a Japanese fleet concentration. General Leslie Groves, the head of the Manhattan Project, said in April 1945, several months before the bomb was made: "The target is and was always expected to be Japan."[6]

However, the scientists who initiated the work never thought of Japan as the target. The deterrence argument, which was the main motivation for starting the project, did not apply to Japan because we had no evidence that Japan intended to make an atom bomb. Among the political leaders who advised President Truman to keep the war going until the bomb was ready was Secretary of State James Byrnes, who said that our possessing and demonstrating the bomb would make Russia more manageable.[7] General Groves was even more explicit about the purpose of the bomb. According to Groves, ". . . there was never from about two weeks from the time I took charge of this project any illusion on my part but that Russia was our enemy and that the project was conducted on that basis."[8] Thus, there is good reason to believe that the destruction of Hiroshima and Nagasaki was not so much the end of the Second World War as the beginning of the Cold War, the first step in a fateful chain of events, the start of an insane arms race that brought us very close to a nuclear holocaust and the destruction of civilization.

Most of the scientists on the Manhattan Project were unhappy about the course of events. One of the greatest scientists at the time, the Danish physicist Niels Bohr, actually predicted that this policy would lead to a nuclear arms race and foresaw its dire consequences. Long before the bomb was made, he put forward a plan to prevent the arms race, but his plan was rejected despite its sympathetic reception by President Roosevelt. When the bomb was nearly ready, scientists issued a memorandum, the Franck Report, strongly opposing the use of the bomb against civilian populations, and again warning that such use would lead to an arms race with grave consequences. This report was followed by a petition from Leo Szilard, opposing the use of the bomb on moral grounds.[9]

However, not all scientists supported this petition. One of those who opposed it was Edward Teller. Already in Los Alamos, well before the fission bomb was made, Teller was working on the hydrogen bomb. In reply to Szilard, he said, "Since our discussion I have spent some time thinking about your objections to an immediate military use of the weapon we may produce. I decided to do nothing....The accident that we worked out this dreadful thing should not give us the responsibility of having a voice in how it is to be used."[10] This view, that scientists should not have a say about the way the results of their work is applied, is unfortunately still common in the scientific community, although it is the height of hypocrisy that it should be voiced by the man who more than anyone else influenced the political and military leaders to continue to develop nuclear weapons.

It is a sad fact that many scientists, far from opposing the nuclear arms race, have played a leading role in maintaining its momentum, often simply to satisfy their own curiosity or as a challenge to their ingenuity in devising ever more sophisticated means of destruction. Theodore Taylor, who once was a chief designer of atom bombs in Los Alamos and is now an ardent supporter of the international Pugwash Movement of scientists which calls for the total elimination of nuclear weapons, aptly described this addiction of bomb designers. "The most stimulating factor of all," observed Taylor, "was simply the intense exhilaration that every scientist or engineer experiences when he or she has the freedom to explore completely new technical concepts and then bring them into reality." I am sure that the same applies to the scientists working in the nuclear establishments of Russia, Britain, France, China, Israel, Pakistan, and India. As I said, we scientists have a great deal to answer for.

It needs to be emphasized strongly, however, that there are many scientists in the West who from the beginning, and throughout the years, have campaigned against the misuse of science, and have made strenuous efforts to avert the dangers that arise from scientific discoveries, especially from the development of nuclear weapons. I want in particular to mention the ceaseless and valiant campaigns of the Federation of American Scientists, supported by the *Bulletin of the Atomic Scientists*. And, of course, in the international arena, we have the Pugwash Movement which was founded in 1957 and inspired by the Russell-Einstein manifesto of July 1955, which called upon scientists of all political persuasions to assemble in a conference to discuss the threat posed to civilization by the advent of thermonuclear weapons.

Scientists cannot live in isolation from other groups that together form the world community; they cannot ignore events that affect this community, particularly those which arise from their work as scientists. The ivory towers in which scientists once pretended to live had been crumbling for many years, and were finally demolished by the pressure and heat waves of the Hiroshima bomb. In this nuclear age, when the misuse of science can literally destroy the whole of our civilization, scientists can no longer evade their responsibility to society by hiding behind such precepts as: "science should be undertaken for its own sake"; "science is neutral"; "science has nothing to do with politics"; "science cannot be blamed for its misapplication"; and "scientists are just technical workers."

John Ziman, who has extensively studied the relation between science and society, convincingly demolished all these precepts, when he concluded: "There is great public concern about many of the effects of science upon society and upon humanity as a whole. Out of this concern there now flows the demand that scientists must be more careful, must be more responsible, in what they do, for it could bring us all to disaster....Whether or not they should be individually blamed for what they have collectively done for the world, not one of them can now cast off a personal responsibility to think about these matters and to act to make this disaster a little less probable." [11]

Consider the primary issue for a scientist: the nature of his work. John Ziman tells us that we must be responsible for the work we are doing and that we must take care that it will not lead to disastrous applications. A positive purpose of our research work was enunciated a long time ago by Francis Bacon, the father of modern science. "I would address one general admonition to all," declared Bacon, "that they consider what are the true ends of knowledge, and that they seek it not either for pleasure of the mind, or for contention...but for the benefit and use of life...that there may spring helps to man, and a line and race of inventions that may in some degree subdue and overcome the necessities and miseries of humanity." [12]

The work that we do as scientists should aim at improving the lot of mankind. A majority of us will say that this excludes work in military establishments, perhaps even in universities if they accept contracts involving the development of military devices. Some would go further and call for a definite pledge by scientists not to engage in this type of work; they call for a sort of a Hippocratic Oath, which implicitly—and sometimes explicitly—is a call to censure the scientists who work in such establishments.

Many of us are uneasy about such proposals because those who call for ethical conduct also prescribe its specific form. Among the workers in Los Alamos or Livermore there were scientists who genuinely believed that their work on weapons was of benefit to mankind, in the sense that it prevented the world being taken over by a Communist regime. No doubt, scientists in the Chelyabinsk or Arzamas laboratories used the same argument in reverse, protecting the world from capitalism. We may not agree with either of these views but we have to tolerate them if they are genuinely held. We may argue with these scientists, try to convince them to our way of thinking, but we have no right to condemn them or to ostracize them.

It is salutary to remind ourselves that among the scientists who started the Pugwash Movement, the prime movers were those who had developed the atom bomb. We were disciples of the Baconian principles, but nevertheless embarked on a project which was a denial of these principles. We believed that our work would prevent the use of the bomb by Hitler; we argued that the bomb was needed so that it would not be used. Events have proved us wrong. Many of us have since come to the conclusion that the whole concept of nuclear deterrence is flawed. Through our efforts we try to prevent such a situation occurring again; we attempt to persuade other scientists not to make the same mistake. But can we be sure ourselves that we have learned the lesson? There are no absolutes in human affairs; we cannot be one hundred percent sure that we will not behave in the same way should similar circumstances occur in the future.

All the same, there are scientists in the military establishments, perhaps the majority of them, who deserve to be condemned. It is those who do not give any thought whatsoever to the social implications of their work, the scientists who do it solely for the advancement of their careers, or worse still, who develop a passion for inventing ever more efficient or sophisticated means of destruction. Herbert York, former director of the Livermore Laboratory, described this phenomenon in the following way. "The various individual promoters of the arms race are stimulated sometimes by patriotic zeal, sometimes by a desire to go along with the gang, sometimes by crass opportunism," writes York. "...Some have been lured by the siren call of rapid advancement, personal recognition, and unlimited opportunity, and some have sought out and even made up problems to fit the solutions they have spent most of their lives discovering and developing." [13]

Here is a question: Should any scientist work on the development of weapons of mass destruction? A clear "no" was the answer given by Hans Bethe. Professor Bethe, a Nobel laureate, is the most senior of the surviving members of the Manhattan Project. On the occasion of the fiftieth anniversary of Hiroshima, Dr. Bethe issued a clear and categorical statement in this regard:

> As the Director of the Theoretical Division at Los Alamos, I participated at the most senior level in the World War II Manhattan project that produced the first atomic weapons. Now, at age 88, I am one of the few remaining such senior persons alive. Looking back at the half century since that time, I feel the most intense relief that these weapons have not been used since World War II, mixed with the horror that tens of thousands of such weapons have been built since that time—one hundred times more than any of us at Los Alamos could ever have imagined. Today we are rightly in an era of disarmament and dismantlement of nuclear weapons. But in some countries nuclear weapons development still continues. Whether and when the various nations of the world can agree to stop this is uncertain. But individual scientists can still influence this process by withholding their skills. Accordingly, I call on all scientists in all countries to cease and desist from work creating, developing,improving and manufacturing further nuclear weapons—and, for that matter, other weapons of potential mass destruction such as chemical and biological weapons. [14]

If all scientists heeded this call there would be no more new nuclear warheads; no new chemical and biological poisons. The arms race would be truly over. For me, of great importance would be the inclusion of courses in university curricula on the social impact and ethical consequences of the work of scientists. I would urge young scientists to study and think about these issues. As for the workers in the military establishments, I would implore them to ponder the implications of their work, and I would then leave it to their conscience to dictate their further conduct.

It has been a desideratum of the Pugwash Movement to be progressive, to foster new ways of thinking, to encourage pioneering ideas. Occasionally, this may bring us into conflict with the establishment; it may make us nonconformists, radicals, dissidents. Dissidence can be said to be part of our ethical code. We cannot be silent bystanders when the establishment—the nomenclatura, to use a term from the bygone age—behaves in a hypocritical manner. We cannot but protest against the manipulation or suppression of facts, particularly in areas in which we have expert knowledge. Our protest is often in the form of "whistle-blowing," when we bring to the notice of the public attempts by governments or industry to mislead by giving false information or by concealing misconduct. We encourage such acts of dissidence by scientists. Indeed, in line with our concept of societal verification, we would like to spur all members of the community to become involved in ensuring that international treaties are not violated. But in this too, things are not always simple. What are the criteria which determine whether an act of whistle-blowing is responsible or foolhardy? What is the difference between an eccentric and a freak? When is nonconformity laudable and when is it mischievous?

Let us not forget that deviation from accepted norms has played a vital role in the evolution of civilization. George Bernard Shaw expressed this in his inimitable style. "The reasonable man adapts himself to the world; the unreasonable one persists in trying to adapt the world to himself. Therefore, all progress depends on the unreasonable man." Bertrand Russell conveyed the same idea in different words, when he said, "Do not fear to be eccentric in opinion, because every opinion now accepted was once eccentric." Russell was the great dissident of this century: he was imprisoned during the First World War, for refusing on conscientious grounds to join the armed forces and, fifty years later, was sent to jail again for his campaign against the British hydrogen bomb. In between, he was persecuted and vilified for advocating views that are now accepted generally.

Progress may be contingent on nonconformity, but the established authority—the government, the church, the party—does not take kindly to deviations from the standard. Swimming against the current is not only strenuous but also dangerous, and sometimes fatal, as was the case, for example, with Giordano Bruno, who was burned at the stake for being iconoclastic. Nowadays, scientists are not put to death at the stake for heretical opinions but they are still severely punished. I have already mentioned Bertrand Russell. Another shining example of an intrepid dissident is Andrei Sakharov. He was fully aware of the danger he faced in taking on a brutal, mighty regime, but this did not stop him from exposing its hypocrisy and iniquity. There are not many capable of such bravery. Sakharov is revered for his heroic stand, for his integrity and steadfastness in his struggles for human rights and the survival of civilization.

We all know of other contemporary examples of whistle-blowing and its dangerous repercussions. Mordechai Vanunu is still lingering in prison, in solitary confinement, for disclosing that Israel has built up a nuclear arsenal. There has been a happier outcome for Vil Mirzayanov, the Russian chemist, who brought to public notice the fact that Russia was still manufacturing chemical and possibly biological weapons. He too was imprisoned, but was later released and all charges against him were dropped.

Although in both these cases whistle-blowing entailed a real or contrived transgression of national laws, the majority of independent scientists condoned these deeds, as evidenced by the numerous protests made against the imprisonments. But the reaction is different in the case of spies, such as Klaus Fuchs, who—while a member of the British team in Los Alamos—transmitted to the Soviet Union the design of the plutonium bomb. Documents recently released in Russia show that his contribution to the early Soviet effort was much greater than thought previously: the first Soviet bomb tested in August 1949 was an exact replica of the Nagasaki bomb.

After his trial and sentence in 1950 in England, people who knew him well thought that he regretted his deeds and had changed his political views, but when I met him accidentally much later, a few years before he died, I found him still to be an ardent communist, even a hard-liner. He was convinced until the end that he performed a noble deed. Some may find a justification for Fuchs' actions: he guessed that the main purpose of the Manhattan Project was to give the United States overwhelming military superiority over the Soviet Union and he decided to restore the balance.

I can testify from personal experience that his assessment of the main purpose of the Manhattan Project was largely true. In short, what happened was the following. In 1944, while working on the Manhattan Project at Los Alamos, I had occasion to dine with General Leslie Groves at the home of Professor James Chadwick. I was temporarily residing with the Chadwicks, and General Groves was an occasional dinner guest. During one memorable evening in March 1944, Groves remarked that the real purpose of building the bomb was to subdue the Soviets. This statement at the time was a shock to me. I was later to recall my encounter with Groves.

Although I had no illusions about the Stalin regime—after all, it was his pact with Hitler that enabled the latter to invade Poland—I felt deeply the sense of betrayal of an ally. Remember, this was said at a time when thousands of Russians were dying every day on the Eastern Front, tying down the Germans and giving the Allies time to prepare for the landing on the continent of Europe. Until then I thought our work was to prevent a Nazi victory, and now I was told that the weapon we were preparing was intended for use against the people who were making extreme sacrifices for that very aim. When it became evident, toward the end of 1944, that the Germans had abandoned their bomb project, the whole purpose of my being in Los Alamos ceased to be.[15]

Looked at from this angle, Klaus Fuchs could be considered a dissident. Yet, in my opinion, there is a big difference between spying and whistle-blowing. For one thing, in whistle-blowing the aim is to bring out into the open happenings about which the public should know. But what Fuchs did was to transmit information in secret to a regime notorious for its suppression of freedom of information. Many scientists on the Manhattan Project, primarily Niels Bohr, believed that the Soviet Union should be invited to participate in the control of the development of nuclear energy in both its peaceful and military applications.

When the war was over and Bohr returned to Copenhagen, he did talk with Soviet scientists about the bomb; this was in line with his basic philosophy about openness. Openness is a sine qua non in science; science could not exist unless its findings were shared by all, but the mechanism of detonating a bomb is not science. The Smyth Report, which was published immediately after the Hiroshima bomb, explained the principles on which it was based, but it was not a blueprint for making it. But this is exactly what Fuchs did; he did send the blueprint, and this cannot be condoned. Our aim is to eliminate nuclear weapons, not to make it easier for people to manufacture them. Openness has its limitations.

Even with whistle-blowing that does not entail spying, matters are not always straightforward. There may be reservations or limitations, for quite different reasons. I will illustrate this with another example from my own life. About forty years ago the hydrogen bomb was developed and begun to be tested. At that time the U.S. and U.K. governments encouraged the belief that this was a "clean" bomb, namely that while the blast and heat effects were a thousandfold greater than from the fission bombs, there was no significant increase in radioactivity. But, from an analysis of the radioactive fallout from the 1954 Bikini test, I came to the conclusion that the bomb had a three-stage structure: fission-fusion-fission, with an enormous increase in the production of radioactive materials. I considered it my duty to inform the public about the fallout hazard from testing such weapons. Despite an attempt by the British Government to stop me, I published a paper which was immediately picked up by the press and received much publicity.

I felt that by this act of whistle-blowing I performed a public duty. What I ignored at the time was that by the very act of defying the government I had considerably narrowed the possibilities of my influencing public opinion again. I have blotted my copybook with the establishment, and, even in a democracy like Britain, the establishment has powerful means to restrict dissident views. It was only recently that I came across documents showing that the British Government had issued a secret directive to the BBC to play down the effects of nuclear weapons. I was a victim of that directive: two planned programs were not broadcast.

The lesson from this is that we should carefully weigh the pros and cons of any action we contemplate, and assess the balance. In this specific case, and looking at it from the perspective of forty years, I believe that I did the right thing, but I should have arrived at this conclusion after careful consideration. The judgment of where the balance lies is of course highly subjective, and is greatly influenced by a multitude of factors. This explains why, even among those of us who support the elimination of all nuclear weapons, there are considerable differences of opinion about the ways to achieve it. Some feel that by being more circumspect they will have more credibility among decision-makers and thus be able to influence them in the right direction. For the same reason, some people stay in government posts even if they disagree with the official policy. In the Pugwash Movement we have retired generals, ex-ambassadors, former directors of weapons establishments; they feel free to express their real views only after retirement. In their judgment they have done more good by staying in their posts than by resigning in protest and being replaced by hawks. Social conscience can be multifaceted.

Coexistence of a variety of approaches and tolerance of different points of view is the essence of a democratic society. This applies particularly to dissidents and other nonconformists; they should not be too hasty in condemning those with a different philosophy. If you expect the community to listen to your views, which may appear heretical to them, you must allow different unorthodox views to be expressed by others. At the same time, we must avoid going to the other extreme.

Saying that we should not exclude anything does not mean that we should permit everything. Freedom does not mean anarchy; openness is not a license to obscenity. We want to have a society governed by ethical principles; a variation from these principles should be allowed, even encouraged, but the range of different views held by the majority should be fairly narrow; extremes should occur only rarely.

What applies to society at any point in time applies to individuals over a lifetime. Events may occur that cause a person to deviate from his normal behavior. For example, even though I recognized the mistake I made originally in working on the atom bomb, I cannot guarantee that I will not make the same mistake again. George Santayana said: "Those who cannot remember the past are condemned to repeat it." But I say that even if we remember the past, we may still be condemned to repeat it. My motto—a paradox in itself—is expressed in three words: "never say never." Nature is so immensely rich in its variety, with an infinite number of possibilities, that nothing can be excluded. Yes, I adhere passionately to humanitarian principles, I strongly support openness in all its aspects, I am an ardent champion of all freedoms for the individual, but I cannot guarantee that under certain circumstances I will not act contrary to these principles. My fervent hope is that these circumstances will not arise. Our aim must be to create a society in which large deviations from ethical norms will have a very low probability of occurrence.

The most frequent circumstance when an individual behaves in an abnormal way is wartime. As soon as war breaks out our standards break down. Moral principles go overboard, civilized behavior is forgotten. We develop murderous instincts—strongly encouraged by our government—against those designated as enemies, even though they have previously been our neighbors and friends.

For these and other reasons our ultimate aim must be the elimination of all war. Many will say that a war-free world is a utopian dream. Even the more limited objective of a nuclear-weapon-free world is seen as not achievable in the foreseeable future, even if desirable. But we are not utopians. We are not seeking Utopia, the perfect world of Thomas More. Our aim is more down-to-earth: a lasting world, a world in which civilization will continue, despite the peril that we scientists have created. We are fully cognizant of the problems facing us.

Our prime purpose may be basic: the survival of civilization, but if in the process we also create a finer world, a world in which people learn not only to resolve conflicts without fighting but also to collaborate for the enrichment of our culture, this will be an extra bonus, an additional incentive in our drive for the essential and the enjoyable; the practical and the beautiful. This is a worthwhile task for scientists and for all persons with a social conscience.

"Here then is the problem which we present to you, stark and dreadful and inescapable: Shall we put an end to the human race, or shall mankind renounce war?" This was the question posed in 1955 by Bertrand Russell and Albert Einstein in their manifesto.[16] It was put at that time because of the realization that with the development of the hydrogen bomb and ballistic missiles, the human species became an endangered species.

The chief characteristic of the nuclear age is that, for the first time in history, man has acquired the technical capacity to destroy his own species, and to accomplish it, willfully or accidentally, in a single action. It seems that the enormous significance of this situation is yet to sink in. We continue with our squabbles, which often lead to war, ignoring the danger that minor disputes may escalate into large-scale hostilities, and eventually to a nuclear confrontation with catastrophic consequences.

At present the danger of a nuclear confrontation is greatly reduced, but it is still there. The nuclear states still adhere to the deterrence policy, which is bound to lead to more countries seeking the security which the nuclear weapons states say that the possession of nuclear weapons provides. Unless there is a change in the basic philosophy, we will not see a reduction of nuclear arsenals to zero for a very long time, if ever. The present basic philosophy is nuclear deterrence. This was stated in the U.S. Nuclear Posture Review which concluded that the "post-Cold War environment requires nuclear deterrence." This view is echoed by other nuclear states. Nuclear weapons are kept as a hedge against some unspecified dangers.

We are told that the possession of nuclear weapons—in some cases even the testing of these weapons—is essential for national security. But this argument can be made by other countries as well. If the militarily most powerful and least threatened states need nuclear weapons for their security, how can one deny such security to countries that are truly insecure? The present nuclear policy of the nuclear weapons states is a recipe for proliferation. It is a policy for disaster. To prevent this disaster—for the sake of humanity—we must get rid of all nuclear weapons.

Achieving this goal will take time, but it will never happen unless we make a start. There is indeed a growing realization among the general public, as well as political and military leaders, of the need to create a nuclear-weapon-free world. Some essential steps towards it can be taken now. Several studies, and a number of public statements by senior military and political personalities, testify that—except for disputes between the present nuclear states—all military conflicts, as well as threats to peace, can be dealt with by using conventional weapons. This means that the only function of nuclear weapons, while they exist, is to deter a nuclear attack. All nuclear weapons states should now recognize that this is so, and declare in treaty form that they will never be the first to use nuclear weapons. This would open the way to the gradual, mutual reduction of nuclear arsenals, down to zero. It would open the way for a Nuclear Weapons Convention. This would be universal and it would prohibit the possession of nuclear weapons by any state.

The nuclear powers need to abandon the out-of-date thinking of the Cold War period. Above all, these states must be reminded of the long-term threat that nuclear weapons pose to humanity, and conditions must be created where action begins toward their total elimination. We have to convey to the peoples of the world the message that the safeguarding of our common property—humankind—calls for developing in each of us a new loyalty, a loyalty to mankind. Einstein and Russell appealed to us all: "Remember your humanity." [17]

At a time when the action of a single nation may endanger the whole of civilization, it is imperative to develop and recognize consciously, even formally, loyalty to the whole of mankind. We must learn to think of ourselves as citizens of the world. The survival of humankind can no longer be taken for granted. The protection and survival of humanity, threatened by nuclear war, should be our conscious goal as we approach the new millennium.

NOTES

1. Winston Churchill, *The Second World War: Triumph and Tragedy*, Vol. 6 (London: The Reprint Society, 1954), p. 508.

2. Churchill, p.514

3. Dwight D. Eisenhower, *Mandate for Change* (New York: Doubleday, 1963), pp. 312-313.

4. William D. Leahy, *I Was There* (New York: Whittlesey House, 1950), p. 441.

5. Arjun Makhijani, "Japan 'Always' the Target?," *The Bulletin of the Atomic Scientists*, May/June 1995, pp. 23–27.

6. Leslie Groves, "Memorandum to the Secretary of War: April 23, 1945," quoted in Makhijani, p. 23.

7. James Byrnes quoted in Spencer R. Weart and Gertrud Weiss Szilard, editors, *Leo Szilard: His Version of the Facts*, Vol. II (Cambridge: MIT Press, 1978), p. 184.

8. Leslie R. Groves, *In The Matter of J. Robert Oppenheimer* (Washington: U.S. Atomic Energy Commission, U.S. Government Printing Office, 1954), p. 173.

9. For a detailed account of Szilard's efforts see William Lanouette, "Three Attempts To Stop The Bomb," *Hiroshima's Shadow*, p. 99.

10. Szilard, pp. 208–209.

11. John Ziman, "Social Responsibility of Scientists: Basic Principles" in Joseph Rotblat, editor, *Scientists, The Arms Race and Disarmament* (Paris: UNESCO, 1982), pp. 177–178.

12. Francis Bacon, *Instauratio Magna* (1620)

13. Herbert York, *Race to Oblivion* (New York: Simon & Schuster, 1970), p. 234.

14. "Cease and Desist," a letter from Hans Bethe quoted in *The Bulletin of the Atomic Scientists*, November/December 1995, p. 3.

15. See Joseph Rotblat, "Leaving the Bomb Project," *Hiroshima's Shadow*, p.253.

16. See "The Peril of Universal Death" by Albert Einstein and Bertrand Russell, *Hiroshima's Shadow*, p. 485.

17. Einstein and Russell, p.487.

THE

LEGEND

OF

HIROSHIMA

Lawrence Lifschultz & Kai Bird

—I—

HOW DO WE KNOW, OR COME TO KNOW, what we know? Essentially, this question of epistemology pertains not only to one's self but also to the societies we inhabit. From the earliest days of human consciousness, mythical accounts of the past have guided entire peoples and nations. Myth and fact have been frequently united into narratives that ultimately become integral parts of the history of a person or a country. No society or individual is entirely free of this phenomenon. The narratives and myths we live with may often have great merit. They bind generations to one another and can establish a rich and textured context through which most people navigate difficult lives in harsh terrain. For many the tales of their ancestors provide security and even certainty in a world where there are few safe havens. Yet, the legends and stories of our past have at moments also blinded us to ourselves and have on more than one occasion become accessories to acts of willful and powerful destruction.

Certainly, one of the most enduring legacies of World War II is the legend associated with the advent of weapons of mass annihilation. In the great span of history from ancient times to the twentieth century, the destruction of entire cities in time of war had been a rather time-consuming process. Whether it took the form of sacking, siege, or burning—in Carthage, Jerusalem, Delhi, or Atlanta—the inefficient and incomplete character of the military techniques employed permitted much of the civilian population in most instances to find an exit or a refuge. Even when the Romans laid siege to Jerusalem and nearly the entire population starved to death, the Roman generals offered the fractured political leadership which led the city's doomed resistance the opportunity to surrender before mass starvation took its final toll.

At the end of the nineteenth century the first international conventions governing armed conflicts had formally guaranteed the protected status of civilian populations. By the mid–twentieth century, however, despite advances in international law the practice of mass annihilation was quietly advanced by military

strategists and wedded to powerful new technologies. The status of civilian populations was transferred from being "off limits" to being that of "primary target." In
his contribution to this volume, Murray Sayle, correspondent of the *New Yorker*
summarized the development and implementation of this concept in some detail:

> The doctrine of the knockout blow, first suggested by an Italian gen-
> eral, Giulio Douhet, in 1921, was the essential precursor to Hiroshima;
> between the two World Wars, it was generally accepted, without any
> real evidence, that a nation's will to fight could be broken by the right
> combination of high-explosive and incendiary bombs dropped on its
> cities. (Douhet added poison gas as well.). . .[I]n 1942 the British
> Royal Air Force, under an aggressive new commander, Air Marshal
> Sir Arthur T. Harris. . .began a campaign of what he termed "area"
> raids by night against Germany. . . .The same darkness that gave the
> British bombers some protection against German flak and fighters
> made it impossible for them to hit any but the biggest targets, like
> whole towns. Harris made a virtue of necessity, with the argument
> that "dehousing" the German workers would have much the same
> effect on their morale and efficiency as destroying war factories, with
> the difference that crowded working-class districts were easier to hit,
> and not as heavily defended. . . .
>
> . . .On the night of February 13, 1945, a force of seven hundred
> and ninety-six R.A.F. bombers attacked Dresden in two waves, three
> hours apart to harass or kill firefighters. The result was history's sec-
> ond major firestorm, stoked up the next day by three hundred and
> eleven American B-17s—the first such open collaboration by the
> Allied air forces in fire-raiding.* Between thirty-five thousand and
> a hundred thousand died, and possibly many more. Destroying the
> city did not help the Soviet advance; Hitler still ran his war from
> Berlin. Dresden confirmed one of the best-attested lessons of the
> Second World War: military leaders, themselves safe in bunkers, can
> take enormous civilian casualties without flinching. Dresden—
> and the very similar fire raid on Tokyo a month later—also marked
> the crossing, concealed from the public of the Allied nations, of an

---

* Editors' Note: The first firestorm occurred on July 25, 1943, following a midnight raid by seven hundred and twenty-eight R.A.F. aircraft and a daylight raid by the U.S. Eighth Air Force. According to
Sayle: "The Hamburg Fire Department's log, describing the scene, added a new word to the vocabulary of war: *Feuersturm*—firestorm. In just over an hour, four square miles of the city—equivalent to all
of Lower Manhattan from Madison Square to Battery Park—was a roaring inferno. People in basement
shelters heard a tornado howling outside, then saw boiling tar from the roads and lead melted from
roofs cascading down the stairs. Hundred-and-fifty-mile-an-hour winds uprooted trees, smashed doors,
and swept fleeing runners off their feet. A few made safety in the waterways; the rest died in the streets
or the shelters, as the fire replaced oxygen from the air with poisonous carbon monoxide. The firestorm
is not seen in nature. To achieve the effect, fires need to be started in many places, miles apart. Rising,
heated air draws in more air, which soon reaches gale force and links the fires together, killing by
asphyxiation, heat, and the collapsing of buildings. As the fire burns inward toward the center, escape
becomes all but impossible. Called, in the R.A.F. euphemism of the time, self-energized dislocation—
the target provides the fuel, the attacker only the lighter—the firestorm is the most one-sidedly efficient way yet discovered of killing human beings. Hiroshima, still two years away, would be destroyed
by a nuclear-ignited firestorm."

invisible moral line. . . .Moral qualms about wiping out whole cities had thus been silently overcome half a year before Hiroshima; the only question left was the ethically less troubling one of method. [1]

This book concerns the crossing of that invisible moral line and the legend in which it has been wrapped in the historical consciousness of the United States. Indeed, about one matter there can be little doubt—Hiroshima is an American legend. As the rationales for the atomic attacks have come under detailed historical scrutiny and the foundations underpinning much of the original justification have begun to erode, adherence to the legend of Hiroshima has intensified among those who believe the United States acted correctly, even morally.

In 1994–95, an effort to preserve the essential elements of the legend developed around the growing controversy over the Smithsonian Institution's plan to exhibit the *Enola Gay*, the plane which had dropped the first atomic bomb. A half-century had passed since the Second World War ended and the curators of America's principal national museum decided to commemorate the occasion with an exhibit that would have chronicled the origins of the war and its final act—the atomic bombings. The decision to include as part of the exhibition the fuselage of the *Enola Gay*, and the preparation of a script for the exhibit, soon led to a tangled, bitter, and revealing battle over the preservation of a legend that could no longer stand against historical facts.

As the controversy grew, the Secretary of the Smithsonian, I. Michael Heyman, sanctioned the effort by the Air and Space Museum's director, Martin Harwit, to negotiate with the American Legion over the text of the exhibit's script. When this attempt at what the historian Martin Sherwin called "historical cleansing" failed to satisfy the exhibit's orthodox critics, Heyman decided to cancel the original exhibit. The attempt at censorship and the cancellation will stand as one of the great intellectual scandals of American history. Among the items that critics of the exhibit wanted removed from the exhibit's script were the briefest references to the views of General Dwight D. Eisenhower and Fleet Admiral William D. Leahy. [2] The quotations which, in fact, were ultimately censored came from the memoirs both men published after the war.

Eisenhower had written of a war-time encounter in July 1945—a few weeks before the atomic bombings and just before the Potsdam conference—with Secretary of War, Henry Stimson: "I had been conscious of a feeling of depression," Eisenhower recalled, "and so I voiced to him my grave misgivings, first on the basis of my belief that Japan was already defeated and that dropping the bomb was completely unnecessary, and secondly, because I thought that our country should avoid shocking world opinion by the use of a weapon whose employment was, I thought, no longer mandatory as a measure to save American lives. It was my belief that Japan was, at that very moment, seeking some way to surrender with a minimum loss of 'face'." [3] Memoirs by definition represent a subjective form of historical evidence. However, those who censored the original *Enola Gay* script were content to retain highly dubious statements from President Truman's memoir, while Eisenhower's opinions were deleted precisely because they did not conform with the postwar legend of Hiroshima.

Admiral William Leahy, who had served as Chief of Staff to both Roosevelt and Truman (the equivalent to Chairman of the Joint Chiefs of Staff in the contemporary American military structure), had expressed similar views in his memoirs. "It is my opinion that the use of this barbarous weapon at Hiroshima and Nagasaki was of no material assistance in our war against Japan," wrote Leahy. "The Japanese were already defeated and ready to surrender. . . . My own feeling was that in being the first to use it, we had adopted an ethical standard common to the barbarians of the Dark Ages. I was not taught to make war in that fashion, and wars cannot be won by destroying women and children." [4] The Leahy view, once again, did not conform to the conventional historical understanding of why the United States had used atomic weapons.

The Smithsonian controversy was instigated by the lobbying efforts of two private organizations: the Air Force Association, a group that functions as a commercial lobby on behalf of corporations that are engaged in the highly profitable sale of nuclear-capable combat aircraft to the U.S. Air Force, and the American Legion. With the acquiescence of the Smithsonian's Secretary these two organizations accomplished the extraordinary act of censoring the opinions of two of the most prominent American military figures from World War II. According to Martin Sherwin, a member of the advisory committee of historians to the Smithsonian Institution for the Enola Gay exhibit, "The exhibit's critics. . . insisted upon something that was objectionable and unconscionable: The removal of all documents critical of the use of the atomic bombs. This blatant demand for *censorship* eliminated passages from the memoirs of Dwight D. Eisenhower and Admiral William D. Leahy among other texts." [5]

Throughout the Cold War, Americans routinely mocked the crude Stalinist revisions of history in which images of Trotsky or Bukharin, among others, could be removed from museums, books, and even photos where they had stood beside Lenin. Once done, a little historical cleansing could be followed by "new originals" from which the offending figures had been made to disappear. The censorship at the Smithsonian entered boldly and without shame into this ignominious intellectual terrain. This was not done without protest from a few isolated quarters within the American intelligentsia. Late in the controversy, an ad hoc group of 150 historians signed a letter objecting to historical cleansing. The Organization of American Historians issued a statement condemning the Smithsonian's actions, but otherwise, objections from the American intelligentsia were rather muted. No major literary or artistic figure protested the polishing of the Hiroshima legend with the dirty rag of censorship.

A public acknowledgment of the views of Eisenhower, Leahy, and a wide variety of other government officials, including the 155 scientists at the Manhattan Project who signed petitions raising moral questions about the prospective use of atomic weapons on Japanese cities, would clearly have opened the door to a great many unsettling questions. If it was not "necessary" to use the weapons to secure Japan's final surrender, then why were they used at all? When the prime target of a weapon of mass annihilation is a whole city, what is the moral significance of the frequently used phrase "it was necessary"? What alternatives existed to the first use of atomic weapons? If clear alternatives did exist, then why were they not pursued?

There also remained an even deeper moral issue regarding how targets were selected. John J. McCloy recorded in his diary that during a meeting on May 29,1945, General George Marshall, Army Chief of Staff, stated that "these weapons might first be used against straight military objectives such as a large naval installation and then if no complete result was derived from the effect of that, he [Marshall] thought we ought to designate a number of large manufacturing areas from which the people would be warned to leave. . . ."[6] However, the Interim Committee, which designated the targets, explicitly set "workers' housing" in an urban center as the specific target for destruction. Indeed, ground zero for both Hiroshima and Nagasaki was targeted for the center of each city and not for factories on the outskirts of these urban areas.

The defense of the bombing of Hiroshima and Nagasaki is often conducted against the emotive backdrop of Pearl Harbor. The Japanese air assault on Pearl Harbor remains for Americans "a date which will live in infamy."[7] The war between Japan and the United States opened with a surprise attack on an American military installation, but it would end with an atomic attack by the United States against two civilian population centers. This was a distinction that was not lost upon men like Marshall and Leahy. Of course, the Japanese leadership did not shrink from attacking noncombatants. Long before Pearl Harbor and America's entry into the war, Japan had ruthlessly targeted civilians in Nanjing and elsewhere in China. After indiscriminate incendiary air raids on Chongqing in May 1939 and the German destruction of the Dutch city of Rotterdam that killed 40,000 civilians a year later, the United States publicly excoriated both powers. As John Rawls has noted in his contribution, early in the war Franklin Roosevelt had appealed "to both sides not to commit the inhuman barbarism of bombing civilians."[8]

It was a principled position increasingly eroded in the last year of Roosevelt's life and obliterated in the first six months of Truman's presidency. Mark Selden's essay in this volume describes how the "fragile restraints on the bombing of noncombatants" that the United States had maintained until 1944 underwent a dramatic change in the last six months of the war:

> With respect to the uses of air power, the belief long persisted that the most cost-effective bombing strategies were those that pinpointed destruction of enemy forces and installations, factories, and railroads, not those designed to terrorize or kill non-combatants. Such a view guided U.S. bombing strategy prior to late 1944 or early 1945. . . . Throughout 1943–44 the U.S. Air Force proclaimed its adherence to precision bombing. However, as this approach proved futile not only in forcing surrender on either Germany or Japan but even in inflicting significant damage on their war-making capacity, as the sophistication, numbers and range of U.S. aircraft grew, as the technology of firebombing advanced with the development of napalm and more effective delivery methods, and as the Air Force sought to strengthen its position in inter-service rivalries and competition for resources, pressures mounted for a strategic shift. . . . In the final six months of the war, the U.S. threw the full weight of its air power into campaigns to bomb whole Japanese cities to the ground, and terrorize, incapacitate, and kill their virtually defenseless populations in an effort to force surrender. . . . Between January and July 1945, the United States firebombed and destroyed all but five Japanese cities.[9]

Although Leahy and others failed to object to the new firebombing tactics deployed against urban centers that began in 1943–44 with Hamburg and Dresden, to be followed by Tokyo and scores of other Japanese towns, the fact that a single atomic bomb could destroy an entire city did unsettle the minds of several senior officials.

As noted earlier, one of the most prominent of these officials was General Marshall who is clearly on the record as having stated that the use of the new weapon be confined in the first instance to a "straight" military target. In his May 29, 1945 memorandum of a conversation with Henry Stimson and General Marshall, John J. McCloy notes that Marshall also emphasized, "[E]very effort should be made to keep our record of warning clear. We must offset by such warning methods the opprobrium which might follow from an ill considered employment of such force."[10] (The key segments of McCloy's diary are reproduced in the document section of this volume.) Despite the views of Marshall and others, no warning of an atomic attack was given to either the Japanese authorities or the populations that had been targeted. There was never an opportunity for civilians to leave the target areas. This is a subject we shall return to in greater detail because it represents one of the most macabre of all the varied elements that went into the making of the Hiroshima legend.

Historians have searched the archives in vain for evidence at the presidential or cabinet level of some collective moment of thoughtful deliberation, sober reflection, or a careful weighing of alternatives commensurate with the impending use of an atomic weapon. To be sure, there is ample evidence that key figures such as Henry Stimson, John McCloy, James Byrnes, and Harry Truman understood that the atomic bomb was like nothing else, a primordial weapon. In those instances where such concerns were raised at the highest level, they were rarely discussed with any measure of sagacious insight into the nuclear peril that these men would shortly force their own and future generations to confront—and perhaps, one day, not survive. The decision to use atomic weapons in 1945 moved along in an atmosphere of incremental casualness and an obsession with a new technology fed by the secrecy that surrounded its development.

Only a handful of senior military officers and officials at the Under Secretary or Assistant Secretary level pressed for alternatives to the inflexible framework of "unconditional surrender," for the issuing of a clear warning, or for the careful targeting of an atomic attack on specifically non-civilian areas. Their individual haphazard efforts never crystallized into a focused and forceful lobby capable of imposing a serious policy debate at the presidential level. The high level of secrecy that surrounded the Manhattan Project obstructed the possibility of an open and visible debate over the use of the bomb. Nevertheless, there still remained forums where discussions could have come to grips with a full and integrated review of terms of surrender, Japanese negotiating initiatives, the effect of the impending Soviet entry into the war against Japan, alternative strategies to secure Japan's surrender, the exclusion of civilian targets, and clarity about warning procedures. And even if alternate strategies were consciously rejected after such discussions, Truman and his advisers could have designated an unambiguous military target for the atomic attack.

The only dynamic and tightly focused effort came from scientists within the Manhattan Project led by Leo Szilard, who directly sought to persuade Truman, and the future Secretary of State, James Byrnes, not to use atomic weapons on Japan. But these efforts were subverted by General Leslie Groves, director of the Project, and Robert Oppenheimer, Director of the Los Alamos Research Laboratory. The historical evidence indicates that Groves, who had been in direct communication with Secretary of War Stimson and the President during the Potsdam summit, deliberately delayed sending Szilard's petition to Truman. Instead, the petition was sent on a low priority basis for delivery to the White House while Truman was in Europe preparing to return. On the basis of existing documentary evidence it appears that the July 17th petition was only read by the President or members of his staff *after* the atomic bombings had already taken place. [11] It is doubtful, of course, that if the petition had been read by Truman, it would have altered his decision. Nevertheless, Groves was not taking any chances.

While General Dwight Eisenhower, Assistant Secretary of War John McCloy, Admiral William Leahy, Under Secretary of the Navy Ralph Bard, Secretary of the Navy James Forrestal, and other American officials had deep reservations about the nuclear juggernaut bearing down on Japan, Harry Truman and Winston Churchill appeared to be almost mystically enthralled by the destructive power of the new weapon as they learned of the successful July 16th Trinity test at Alamogordo, New Mexico. No longer a mere theoretical possibility, the weapon was instantly absorbed into a new calculus of political power. Truman and Churchill now had in hand what Secretary of War Henry Stimson had termed their "master card" in the emergent rivalry with the Soviet Union. A week after the Trinity test, Assistant Secretary of War John McCloy made the following entry in his diary: "Throughout it all the 'big bomb' is playing its part—it has stiffened both the Prime Minister [Churchill] and the President [Truman]. After getting Groves' report they went to the next meeting [with Stalin] like little boys with a big red apple secreted on their persons." [12] Evidently, it was not the prospect of using the weapon against Japan but the perception of the leverage it would afford them over the Soviet Union that excited the Allied leaders. Before Trinity, prescient men like the Nobel laureate, Niels Bohr, had warned that delusions of nuclear mastery would come to haunt the fathers of nuclear weapons, and after them, their children. In time, they would face the prospect of their own annihilation.

Yet, half a century later, any exploration of these issues in the Smithsonian exhibit was regarded as taboo by the guardians of the legend. The leadership of the American Legion presumed that all veterans of the Second World War shared a simple one-dimensional vision of history. Of course, the views of surviving veterans were as diverse and varied as those held by military, political, and scientific figures in the spring and summer of 1945. The Legion's leadership justifiably feared the prospect that Eisenhower's and Leahy's dissenting post-war opinions, along with those of Admiral Chester Nimitz, General Douglas MacArthur, and General Henry Arnold, would be displayed in a national museum exhibit attended by millions of visitors. The discovery of an unknown perspective so fundamentally at odds with the orthodox formulation could be sufficient to legitimize a critical reassessment of not only the bombing of Hiroshima, but America's continued reliance on nuclear deterrence and key assumptions about the origins of the Cold War.

Indeed, Stephen Rosenfeld, deputy editorial page editor for the *Washington Post*, understood the threat critics of Truman's Hiroshima decision posed to the broad conceptual architecture of America's post-war strategic doctrines. "The critics [of Truman's decision] have an agenda—not an ignoble agenda but one that goes well beyond instructing us to face up to our true history," wrote Rosenfeld. "It is to repudiate *the moral basis of nuclear weapons*. If their use in the one situation where they were actually employed can be shown to be unnecessary, illegitimate, and even depraved, then a powerful change will have been wrought in the political culture in which strategic decisions and historical judgments are made." [13] Although Rosenfeld never addresses what he perceives to be "the moral basis of nuclear weapons," he did recognize an essential fact. We live in a political culture that accepts the potential use of nuclear weapons directed against civilian targets as a "legitimate" weapon of war. This sense of legitimacy associated with our readiness to undertake, if "necessary," similar "strategic decisions" involving the use of nuclear weapons is intimately linked to our understanding, indeed our interpretation, of that original act which Wilfred Burchett in this volume has called "the first nuclear war."

In 1945, opinion polls indicated that upwards of 80 percent of all Americans approved of the atomic bombings. Yet, the country knew nothing of secret contacts with the Japanese regarding the prospect of a negotiated surrender or the view of many senior American military officials that surrender was possible without an invasion. Nevertheless, within days clear voices of dissent emerged from significant quarters. Among the harshest critics were many of the most distinguished theologians of the United States. The condemnation did not come from peripheral religious groups but from the mainstream Protestant and Catholic denominations. Indeed, the Federal Council of Churches quickly established a special commission to examine the question of atomic warfare in "light of the Christian faith."

Its report, reprinted in this volume in its entirety, was signed by twenty-two of the country's leading scholars in theological studies. Although this important document is barely known in modern America and fell into obscurity as the Hiroshima legend gained ideological paramountcy, its signatories included Reinhold and H. Richard Niebuhr of the Union Theological Seminary and Yale Divinity School; Henry Van Dusen, President of the Union Theological Seminary; B. Harvie Branscomb, Dean of Duke University's School of Religion; Roland Bainton of Yale Divinity School; and Benjamin Mays, President of Morehouse College. These men offered the following observation in the final document, entitled "Atomic Warfare and the Christian Faith," issued by the special commission of the Federal Council of Churches:

> We would begin with an act of contrition. As American Christians, we are deeply penitent for the irresponsible use already made of the atomic bomb. We are agreed that, whatever be one's judgment of the ethics of war in principle, the surprise bombings of Hiroshima and Nagasaki are morally indefensible. They repeated in a ghastly form the indiscriminate slaughter of non-combatants that has become familiar during World War II. They were loosed without specific warning, under conditions which virtually assured the deaths of 100,000 civilians. No word of the existence of atomic bombs was published before the actual blasting of Hiroshima. . . .[T]he peoples whose governments controlled the bomb were given no chance to weigh beforehand the moral and political consequences of its use.
>
> Nagasaki was bombed also without specific warning, after the power of the bomb had been proved but before the Japanese government and high command had been given reasonable time to reach a decision to surrender. Both bombings, moreover, must be judged to have been unnecessary for winning the war. Japan's strategic position was already hopeless, and it was virtually certain that she had not developed atomic weapons of her own. Even though use of

the new weapon last August may well have shortened the war, the moral cost was too high. As the power that first used the atomic bomb under these circumstances, we have sinned grievously against the laws of God and against the people of Japan. Without seeking to apportion blame among individuals, we are compelled to judge our chosen course inexcusable. . . .In light of present knowledge, we are prepared to affirm that the policy of obliteration bombing as actually practiced in World War II, culminating in the use of atomic bombs against Japan, is not defensible on Christian premises.[14]

Shortly after the bombings, James Martin Gillis, editor of the New York–based journal *Catholic World*, wrote: "I here and now declare that I think the use of the atomic bomb, in the circumstances, was atrocious and abominable; and that civilized peoples should reprobate and anathematize the horrible deed. . . .[L]et this opinion be recorded: the action taken by the United States Government was in defiance of every sentiment and every conviction upon which civilization is based."[15] A fortnight after the bombings, the Catholic journal *Commonweal* noted:

The name Pearl Harbor was a name for Japanese guilt and shame. The name Hiroshima, the name Nagasaki, are names for American guilt and shame. . . .[In June 1945] we said [regarding the fear that American forces might resort to poison gas]: "The time has come when nothing more can be added to the horror if we wish to keep our coming victory something we can use—or that humanity can use." Well, it seems that we were ridiculous writing that sort of thing. We will not have to write that sort of thing any more. Certainly, like everyone else, we will have to write a great deal about the future of humanity and the atomic bomb. But we will not have to worry any more about keeping our victory clean. It is defiled.[16]

What one realizes in reading these statements is how successful the legend of Hiroshima has been in obstructing from view the opinions of those who disagreed. If you ask an ordinary American whether he or she knew that General Eisenhower had opposed the use of the atomic bomb and considered that "awful thing" militarily "unnecessary," more than likely you will encounter surprise or disbelief. Eisenhower? Are you certain? And, if you should then cite the memoirs of Leahy, McCloy, Nimitz, Einstein, Szilard, and many others, explaining, if necessary, who each of these men were, then you might discover that your comments have disoriented or distressed your listener. Once the canon has been shaken, a mind may tremble.[17]

— II —

A HALF-CENTURY AFTER Hiroshima's destruction, the curators at the Smithsonian thought they could assemble an exhibit that would reflect modern scholarship. They did not realize that a modest attempt to present some of the complexity surrounding Truman's decision to use the bomb would threaten the established canon. The opponents of the original exhibit roused themselves into a highly organized

crusade in defense of the Hiroshima legend. By depicting the curators and historians as arrogant intellectuals, bent on inflicting a narrow-minded, "politically correct" version of history on the American people, the Air Force Association's public
relations men discovered that they were able to ignite a storm of resentment against
the Smithsonian. A new caricature was created to serve this purpose.

The museum's curators, "revisionist" historians, and intellectuals in general
became targets, and the Smithsonian was turned into another battlefield in the
country's on-going "culture wars." The exhibit's opponents tapped a deep vein
in American history which Richard Hofstadter, the late Columbia University
historian, wrote eloquently about in his Pulitzer Prize–winning volume, *Anti-
Intellectualism in American Life.* "Our anti-intellectualism is, in fact, older than our
national identity, and has a long historical background," observed Hofstadter.
"The common strain that binds together the attitudes and ideas which I call anti-
intellectual is a resentment and suspicion of the life of the mind and of those who
are considered to represent it; and a disposition constantly to minimize the value
of that life." [18]

Defenders of the Hiroshima legend were incensed that a group of mere
"historians" could question the decision to use the atomic bomb. Who were these
so-called "intellectuals" to cast doubt upon an action which the nation had been
told by its leaders had been "necessary" to ending the Second World War? After
all, Harry Truman had said there was no alternative to the bomb except for an invasion of Japan which inevitably would have resulted in more casualties to American
military forces than had been suffered during the entire conflict. The country had
accepted this explanation. Clearly, as one congressman put it, those who questioned this account were "biased" and reflected an "anti-American prejudice." [19]

Herman Harrington, an official of the American Legion's Internal Affairs
Division, wrote that his organization's interpretation of the role of the *Enola Gay*
at Hiroshima was "a history all of us can be proud of." He insisted that the Legion
had brought "the bright light of honesty" down upon the exhibit and thus "exposed
the mosaic that NASM [Smithsonian's National Air and Space Museum] and their
supporters hoped to create by their prostitution of history." Harrington did not
care to mention that the Legion had insisted during negotiations with the Smithsonian's curators that General Eisenhower and Admiral Leahy's condemnations of
the nuclear attack be removed from the exhibit in order to achieve "balance."
In his eyes, the Legion and the veterans were victims of an intellectual mugging by
a few historians attempting to pass off counterfeit history.

> We have earned the wrath of the revisionist historians. We have been
> accused of racism, bullying and political arm-twisting. We've been
> called the new McCarthyites. But the pips and squeaks of a few revi-
> sionist historians whose feelings are hurt. . .are, in my opinion, the
> best evidence that we are right. . . .Instead of a joyful mosaic celebrat-
> ing the end of the bloodiest calamity ever to befall this world, theirs
> was a mosaic of World War II that only they recognized. It was famil-
> iar to them because in their heart of hearts, that is how they see Amer-
> ica. They learned that their vision and our vision—the vision of the
> American Legion and, indeed, the American people—are irreconcil-
> able. Their vision is unrecognizable, because it is counterfeit. . . .We
> thank God for the *Enola Gay* and its crew—and for Harry Truman. [20]

For Harrington, the only acceptable history was a history Americans could be "proud" of, essentially a celebration of the past. What had worried those who first dissented from the idea of holding an exhibit in the first place was that it might appear as a glorification of the *Enola Gay* by Americans. On October 28, 1987, eight years before the exhibit was canceled, Admiral Noel Gayler attended an advisory committee meeting at the Smithsonian to discuss how the *Enola Gay* might be exhibited. Gayler had been a naval pilot during World War II and acquired a four-star rank before becoming commander-in-chief of U.S. military forces in the Pacific. He had also served as Director of the National Security Agency. Sitting together with the newly appointed director of the Air and Space Museum, Martin Harwit, and other members of the committee, Admiral Gayler expressed his anxieties over the proposed exhibit:

> Strategies of air warfare are certainly a most important historical subject, but this is quite a different one. This has to do with—and I am looking for a word stronger than "propriety"... the validity... of exhibiting the *Enola Gay* in this institution....The *[Enola Gay]* mission over Japan was not in any tactical or operational sense distinctive. The Japanese were essentially defeated. We were flying airplanes all over the Empire, at will. I was the operations officer of the task force at that time—with Japan and defined ports for us to strike. And except for accidents, we didn't lose any airplanes....The thing that made the mission distinctive was. . . that we used the nuclear weapon for the first time against human beings. . . .
>
> *[I]f we put that thing [the* Enola Gay *fuselage] on exhibit, we cannot fail to give the impression that we somehow are glorifying that mission or taking pride in it.* We can't reverse history; we can't change it, but we don't have to make it the forefront in the most important museum in the capital of our country. . . .I think that if we do that, [it] will tarnish the reputation of the Museum....There is a technology that, I think we would all agree around this table, can only be described as bad, and that is the technology of nuclear weapons. . . . I want to suggest that we do know the end of the story with respect to nuclear weapons. They will destroy us unless we do something about them.
>
> I will tell you why I know it; because there is a non-zero probability that in any given year there will be a nuclear war. And if you sum those up, the probability will become one some day. So, you know, there we are. [Exhibiting the *Enola Gay* would be] an act with incalculable consequences, no matter how you do it, no matter whether you surround it with symposia on what the effects were...and future nuclear wars might be....It could become a pilgrimage for the most radical right, or it could lead to a serious and constructive discussion of what is involved, and anything in between. [21]

Clearly, Admiral Gayler possessed a rather different vision of the *Enola Gay* mission than did Herman Harrington and his colleagues at the American Legion. Like Eisenhower and Leahy before him, Gayler did not view the Hiroshima mission as part of a "joyful mosaic." Attending that October 1987 meeting was

Robert McCormick Adams, Secretary of the Smithsonian Institution. According to the minutes of the advisory committee meeting, Adams replied to Admiral Gayler saying, "My own view would be that if we did move to exhibit the Enola Gay…it would have to be done with extraordinary sensitivity [and] that it could not be done without taking account of what happened as a result of that bombing, in other words, dealing with the devastation that at least that atomic bomb caused, rather than simply putting the aircraft itself on exhibit." [22]

However, Adams's successor, I. Michael Heyman, rather than guiding the controversy toward what Admiral Gayler called "a serious and constructive discussion of what is involved," yielded instead to the Smithsonian's critics and canceled an exhibit that had been seven years in the making. He also forced Martin Harwit, the Director of the Smithsonian Air and Space Museum to resign from his position. [23] The actor Charlton Heston, one of the original exhibit's most vociferous critics, recalled how this was accomplished: "Finally I had a meeting with Michael Heyman, the Secretary of the Smithsonian Institution. 'Well, what do you want, then?' he asked me. 'Mr. Harwit's head on a plate, to begin with,' I said. That's what we got…" [24] In one of his essays in this volume, John Dower, Professor of History at the Massachusetts Institute of Technology and author of *War Without Mercy*, describes Heyman's action as an act of "unconditional surrender" in the face of "this new McCarthyism."

> The director of the [Smithsonian] National Air and Space Museum resigned under pressure, and it is an open secret that morale among members of the Smithsonian's professional staff has been shattered. In this new McCarthyism, the catchall indictment is no longer "Communism" but rather "political correctness" or even just plain "revisionism." Few people in the media or among the general public seem to find the enforcement of a purely celebratory national history alarming. We praise other countries, especially those in the former Communist camp, for engaging in critical reappraisal of the past. We castigate the Japanese when they sanitize the war years and succumb to "historical amnesia." Yet at the same time, we skewer our own public historians for deviating from Fourth of July historiography. We are so besieged by polemics and sound bites that almost no one has time to dwell on the irony of demanding a pristine, heroic, official version of a war that presumably was fought to protect principled contention and the free play of ideas. [25]

Having capitulated, Heyman later unveiled exactly the sort of public exhibit that his predecessor, Robert Adams, had vowed the Smithsonian would never undertake. Under his orders, stacks of documents and photographs meticulously researched over seven years were locked away. A carefully prepared catalogue was embargoed. When a rump exhibit featuring the *Enola Gay*'s fuselage finally opened in late June 1995, Heyman was asked by the assembled reporters why the plane was being displayed without any reference either visual or textual to the attendant devastation that had descended upon Hiroshima. His reply reflected an essential distinction between the principles of rational inquiry and the dictates of political expediency. Heyman said that *what* had happened at Hiroshima and *why* it had happened ought to be left "more to the imagination." [26]

— III —

IN REFLECTING ON WHAT HE CALLED "the Great Inquisition of the 1950s," Richard Hofstadter argued that the real function of the McCarthyite witch hunt and its attack on American intellectuals who questioned the Cold War's prevailing paradigm was "not anything so simply rational as to turn up spies or prevent espionage (for which the police agencies presumably are adequate) or even to expose actual Communists, but to discharge resentments and frustrations, to punish, to satisfy enmities whose roots lay elsewhere than in the Communist issue itself." [27]

Robert Jay Lifton and Greg Mitchell in their penetrating work *Hiroshima in America* not only grasped Hofstadter's point but addressed another facet of the phenomenon which the Smithsonian controversy made apparent. Clearly, the discharge of "resentments and frustrations. . . whose roots lay elsewhere" masked a more troubling pathology that was specifically related to Hiroshima and Nagasaki.

> Few Americans know the full story of either the decision to use the bomb or its human effects. This is partly due to misleading official statements and government secrecy. But the most compelling reason for the failure to confront Hiroshima is our disinclination to do so— a collective form of psychic numbing. From the moment the American public learned of the use of the bomb and caught glimpses of its devastating power, we have been struggling with what to do with that knowledge and those images. . . .[W]e have not wished to permit Hiroshima to enter our psyches in ways that could affect our feelings. And we are greatly aided in our nonfeeling by the distancing technology of the Hiroshima attack.
>
> Hence we construct what Edith Wyschogrod calls a *"cordon sanitaire"* around Hiroshima—a barrier designed to prevent the spread of a threatening disease, the "illness" we block off in this case being what we did in Hiroshima. That *cordon sanitaire* was transmitted, as official policy, throughout American society. One was supposed to be numbed to Hiroshima. It became politically correct (before the expression existed) in the deepest sense to remain numbed toward Hiroshima—politically suspect if one was troubled or inclined to make a fuss about it. In that way, as a people, we developed a habit of numbing toward Hiroshima, a sustained tendency toward, one way or another, avoiding feeling in connection with what happened there. [28]

While the Smithsonian controversy and the fiftieth anniversary of the atomic bombings drew a new generation toward a difficult reexamination of their nation's history, the "habit of numbing" was also quite apparent. Professor Barton Bernstein was disinvited from a White House event commemorating the end of the war. Professor John Dower, the MIT historian, recalls how he was "disinvited" from two public meetings where the topic had been framed as a discussion on the reasons for the atomic bombings. According to Dower, the "disinvitations" were conveyed to him in a "genteel manner." He was simply told that the subject of the atomic bombings had become "too controversial." [29]

These small and less-noticed acts of censorship were the consequence of the assault by the opponents of the Smithsonian exhibit. Those who organized the attack on the Smithsonian's curators found their idiom in the language of violent accusation. It produced some extraordinary curiosities. One could almost hear the snarling whispers of an earlier era. Syndicated columnist George Will described the Smithsonian curators and historians as people who "obviously hate this country." [30] One of the most senior names in American broadcast journalism, David Brinkley of ABC News, declared, "What I don't understand is why a very strong element in the academic community seems to hate its own country and never passes up a chance to be critical of it." [31] ABC television commentator Cokie Roberts told a national television audience that "to rewrite history makes no sense." [32]

Brinkley, Will, and Roberts were reflecting the collective historical amnesia of many journalists for whom the legend of Hiroshima is an article of faith. Certainly, they seemed oblivious to the fact that critics of the legend were posing precisely the same questions that had been raised in 1945 by a number of American diplomats, military officers, Manhattan project scientists, and ordinary citizens. Essentially, a sober debate was precluded by those ideologically committed to the imperfect and untruthful rationales which have supported the legend for more than half a century. Thus, it was possible to sustain what has, in another context, been aptly described as a "discourse of avoidance" *(Vermeidungsdiskurs)*. [33]

In the service of concealing the issues within such a discourse, a polemic which bore no relationship whatsoever to the events of 1945 was developed. The sentiment of anti-intellectualism dormant in American life, described by Richard Hofstadter a generation earlier, was reawakened for the purpose of defending the bombings of Hiroshima and Nagasaki. The "subversive intellectual" who "hated his country" was seen to be on the prowl once again. In a society which had just lived through a Cold War for nearly forty years where "communists" were the familiar enemy, a new hateful caricature was launched called the "revisionist." In case the very sound of the word "revisionist historian" failed to evoke the visceral reaction that the term "communist" did for so long, the purported link was helpfully drawn between the two. As one media critic, Elliot Negin, observed in the Washington, D.C., weekly *City Paper*, a number of "columnists and reporters used the term 'revisionist' as an epithet synonymous with anti-American." Negin quotes Jonathan Yardley, a *Washington Post* columnist, as describing the historians as nothing but a "ragtag collection of academics and left-wing ideologues." Leaving aside the fact that some of America's most eminent historians of the Second World War had come to conclusions which fundamentally differed from the Hiroshima legend, Yardley dismissed such intellectuals as "the zealots of academe who prowl the liberal arts departments muttering against 'American imperialists'." [34]

Some writers advanced the notion that the real dispute over the depiction of events at Hiroshima and Nagasaki actually had more to do with sentiments linked to the Vietnam war than the decision to use atomic weapons in 1945. This curious thesis was advanced by another *Washington Post* reporter, Ken Ringle, who insisted that those who questioned Truman's action were essentially people "whose political sensibilities remain anchored in the anti-government, anti-war sentiments of the Vietnam era." Ringle used his considerable talents as a writer to attack in scathing terms one of the few documentaries to have appeared on American television that was not a rerun of the familiar clichés that had "informed" the American public for decades.

Produced by ABC's Peter Jennings, the program broke out of the confines of sophomoric discourse and gave expression to the views of those historians who for decades had been carefully researching the politics that lay behind the decision to use atomic weapons. In his review of the Jennings documentary Ringle declared, "Little of this, of course, is new. Some Vietnam-era historians have been insisting since the 1960s that the United States dropped the first atomic bombs on Japan for reasons other than speeding the end of World War II and saving American lives....Guiding Jennings along this road to generational second-guessing is a largely stacked deck of revisionist historians."[35] In a letter to the *Washington Post*, a former managing editor of the *Post*, William Greider, offered the following observation about the *Post's* coverage:

> Recently, I heard two distinguished historians from a leading university lament the impossibility of teaching American history to American students. You can teach the story of America as an unblemished icon for the world, they said. Or you can teach a radical version that demonizes America. But nothing in the culture equips young Americans to deal seriously with the "irreconcilable conflicts" embedded in America's past—the wrenching, ambiguous chapters that do not lead to easy moralisms. I was reminded of their complaint recently when Peter Jennings and ABC devoted ninety minutes to a brilliant documentary on "Hiroshima" and the U.S. decision to use the atomic bomb in 1945. It was a patient, sophisticated and, I thought, superbly balanced exposition of a profound political and moral dilemma.
>
> It taught our history whole—richly complicated and inescapably controversial. True patriotism, I believe, lies in facing and accepting the unresolved contradictions about ourselves. Instead of congratulating ABC, your reviewer, Ken Ringle, responded to this extraordinary project with patriotic indignation that sounded like bar talk at the Legion hall. Readers would be surprised to learn that the Boston Globe reviewer saw the same program and compared it—aptly—to the great tradition of Edward R. Murrow. Yours is a wonderful newspaper in numerous ways, but it can also be incredibly narrow-minded and nasty, even anti-intellectual, when it sets out to discipline nonconformist thinking. A serious newspaper would examine controversy and teach about the "irreconcilable" in the mature manner that ABC and Jennings have.[36]

The critique of Truman's decision, in fact, predates the Vietnam War by at least two decades, and many of those who first questioned the use of an atomic weapon were conservatives and senior military officers. Pre–Vietnam War–era critics of Hiroshima included General "Hap" Arnold, commander of the Army Air Force; *Time* magazine founder Henry Luce; David Lawrence, the conservative editor of what was to become *U.S. News & World Report*; and William F. Buckley's *National Review*. Perhaps Ringle might have wished that Eisenhower, Luce, and Lawrence had been men whose "political sensibilities" were "anchored in the anti-government, anti-war sentiments of the Vietnam era," but unfortunately the dates and chronology simply failed to match the paradigm. In a "discourse of avoidance" such facts simply did not fit in.

Indeed, what is distinctive about the critics of the Hiroshima and Nagasaki bombings is that they spanned familiar ideological boundaries. Socialists like Albert Einstein, Norman Thomas, and Bertrand Russell joined liberals like Reinhold Niebuhr and Norman Cousins, and conservatives such as Felix Morley and Herbert Hoover in condemning the first use of atomic weapons. The usual distinctions of "left" and "right" on economic and social issues were not reliable guides which could accurately predict what people thought about Hiroshima. Indeed, left-leaning publications like the *Nation* and *PM* were initially supportive of Truman's decision, while some of the harshest critics voiced their objections in conservative magazines like *Human Events* and the *National Review*. Many of those who condemned the bombings shared the view that a weapon of mass annihilation which inevitably, due to the very character of its design, made tens of thousands of civilians the prime target of an attack, was unquestionably immoral by any juridical or ethical standard in existence.

All of this was neatly forgotten by critics and commentators fifty years later in the midst of the Smithsonian controversy. The American Legion and other critics of the exhibit knew that there had *always* been controversy about Hiroshima. But if they were to be successful in their campaign to derail the exhibit, they had to suppress this fact. That is why the statements of Eisenhower and Leahy had to be censored from the museum's script. To be sure, the Smithsonian's critics came to the controversy with a variety of motives. The American Legion wanted a celebration on the fiftieth anniversary of the end of the war. They understandably wanted something that would remind people of the valor and sacrifices of the veterans who fought to defeat fascism in Europe and militarism in Asia. The Air Force Association, as Mike Wallace and Stanley Goldberg make clear in their essays, wanted a celebration of a specific airplane, the Air Force, and the aerospace industry—and ultimately they used the controversy as part of their power struggle to re-assert their influence over the Smithsonian's Air and Space Museum. Neither of these organizations wanted an exhibit cluttered with "irreconcilables." And neither did they wish to remind Americans of just how controversial the atomic bombings were fifty years ago.

Indeed, despite a carefully constructed official history of the atomic bombings, the American public a half-century after the bombings remained sharply divided over how the war had ended. A Gallup poll taken in November 1994—in the midst of the Smithsonian controversy—asked 1,026 Americans: "If the decision about dropping the atomic bomb had been yours to make, would you have ordered the bombs to be dropped, or would you have tried some other way to force the Japanese to surrender?" In response, 44 percent said they would have dropped the bomb. Another 49 percent said they would have "tried some other way." [37]

Obviously, many Americans continued to be quite troubled by the atomic bombings, despite everything they had been told over the years to justify the bombs. Quite aware of this latent ambiguity, critics of the Smithsonian understood the importance of eliminating any critical facts from an exhibit that might have opened the minds of millions of Americans and drawn them toward a substantive reconsideration of the official rationales underpinning the Hiroshima and Nagasaki attacks. Talk of the Vietnam War and historians who "hated their country" was an invidious method to suppress inquiry and doubt.

Ironically, those who utilized the phrase "revisionist historians" as a barbed epithet failed to recognize the important distinctions that have long existed within the so-called "revisionist" camp of historians who have studied the Hiroshima decision. J. Samuel Walker, the historian of the U.S. Nuclear Regulatory Commission, drew the following conclusion about those scholars who have, in the best tradition of historical scholarship, "revised" our understanding of why the atomic bombings occurred. It should be noted that Walker himself is a scholar who has never been vilified as being among the "revisionists." In his most recent work, *Prompt and Utter Destruction*, Walker came to this carefully worded conclusion:

> [B]y the late 1980s, specialists who studied the available evidence reached a broad, though hardly unanimous, consensus on some key issues surrounding the use of the bomb. One point of agreement was that Truman and his advisers were well aware of alternatives to the bomb that seemed likely, but not certain, to end the war within a relatively short time. Another was that an invasion of Japan would probably not have been necessary to achieve victory. A third point of general agreement in the scholarly literature on the decision to use the bomb was that the postwar claims that the bomb prevented hundreds of thousands of American combat deaths could not be sustained with the available evidence. Most students of the subject also concurred that political considerations figured in the deliberations about the implications of the bomb and the end of the war with Japan. On all of those points, the scholarly consensus rejected the traditional view that the bomb was the only alternative to an invasion of Japan that would have cost a huge number of American lives. At the same time, most scholars supported the claim of Truman and his advisers that the primary motivation for dropping atomic bombs on Hiroshima and Nagasaki was to end the war at the earliest possible moment—that is, for military reasons. [38]

Elsewhere, Walker has emphasized that it is hard to overstate the role of the federal government in creating the popular "collective memory" in which most Americans accept without any serious reservations such wholly inaccurate assertions as President George Bush's 1991 comment that the bombs "spared millions of American lives." Walker described how research by historians James Hershberg and Barton J. Bernstein had convinced a wide audience of historians that "former government officials consciously and artfully constructed the history of the decision." The first major step in this process was carried out by Henry Stimson— assisted by the young McGeorge Bundy—in his 1947 *Harper's* essay, which appears in this volume.

Bernstein's reconstruction of how the *Harper's* essay was written is a remarkable piece of historical detective work. His inquiry into how the contested terrain of early nuclear history was seized by the same men who took the decision to use the bomb is reproduced in this volume. Bernstein's essay—together with James Hershberg's biography of James Conant, President of Harvard and a prominent figure behind the Manhattan Project—reveals how one magazine article managed to popularize all the central myths of the Hiroshima legend.[39] As a result of this scholarship, Walker notes, there now exists a very broad consensus among historians who recognize that the legend surrounding the decision to use the bomb was a carefully crafted, official construct.

Yet, there exist significant differences among critical historians in their assessment of why Truman and his associates did use the bomb. If it was not done to save a half million (or a million) lives, why were these two cities destroyed? Gar Alperovitz's *The Decision to Use the Atomic Bomb* published in 1995 presents an exhaustive case that Truman and his advisers were well aware of the alternatives to ending the war without the atomic bomb and that they rejected these alternatives, largely for political and diplomatic—not military—reasons. Alperovitz's narrative emphasizes the deliberate and affirmative nature of the decision.

Barton Bernstein, another leading historian who is critical of the decision to bomb Hiroshima, takes a different perspective on the question of how "affirmative" a choice was made. While rejecting the official legend, Bernstein believes that Alperovitz unduly emphasizes the entire notion that there was a "decision" to use the bomb. "In 1945," Bernstein wrote in *Diplomatic History*, "American leaders were not seeking to avoid the use of the A-bomb. Its use did not create ethical or political problems for them. Thus, they easily rejected or never considered most of the so-called alternatives to the bomb. . . ." [40] As the historian Marilyn Young notes in a review essay in the *American Historical Review*, "Bernstein's approach suggested a conclusion that is, if anything, even harsher than Alperovitz's. So overwhelming was the assumption of use, that use was inevitable. It was not, however, necessary." [41]

Bernstein argues that no single alternative to the bomb was likely to have produced a surrender prior to November 1945. "But it does seem very likely, though certainly not definite, that a synergistic combination of guaranteeing the Emperor, awaiting Soviet entry, and continuing the siege strategy would have ended the war in time to avoid the November invasion," he writes. "And quite possibly, in the absence of a guarantee of the Emperor, the impact of the Soviet entry amid the strangling blockade and the heavy bombing of cities could have accomplished that goal without dropping the atomic bomb." [42]

Other scholars, such as Herbert Bix, have emphasized the Japanese side of the story and argue that "it was not so much the Allied policy of unconditional surrender that prolonged the Pacific war, as it was the unrealistic and incompetent actions of Japan's highest leaders." Bix has presented a detailed description of how the Japanese ruling class, faced with inevitable defeat, moved slowly and clumsily toward the prospect of a negotiated surrender. Bix argues that viewed through the eyes of Emperor Hirohito and his closest advisers, the decision to move haltingly toward surrender was based on the "overriding objective. . . to 'preserve the national polity (*kokutai*)'" and thus their continued dominance of Japan's existing social structure. Preserving the position of the Emperor after a surrender offered the best prospect of maintaining the prerogatives of the governing elite. [43]

By the spring of 1945, the Emperor and his more prescient advisers feared that the war-weary Japanese populace might soon take matters into their own hands. "The situation today," Bix quotes Prince Konoe telling Hirohito on July 12, 1945, "has reached a point where people hold a grudge against the imperial house." The Emperor reportedly responded that he "agreed completely." Bix is devastating in his critique of the cynicism and ineptitude of Japan's rulers as they moved forward toward negotiations at a snail's pace while their army and people were systematically destroyed. He argues how "Emperor Hirohito's reluctance to face the fait accompli of defeat, and then to act, positively and energetically, to end hostilities. . . prolonged the war." Yet, despite his revealing account of "Japan's delay in ending suicidal conflict," Bix concludes that political procrastination was "not sufficient cause for use of the bomb." [44]

Among those historians who study these issues, the differences between Alperovitz, Bernstein, Bix, Sherwin, and other specialists are obviously quite significant. However, to many readers the important distinctions drawn by these scholars pale in significance when set against the major tenets of the official legend. There have always been some historians who have vigorously defended Truman's decision to use nuclear weapons in 1945. These include reputable scholars such as Robert H. Ferrell, Alonzo L. Hamby, David McCullough, and Robert P. Newman who sharply differ with Truman's critics and generally stand well outside the broad consensus described by J. Samuel Walker. [45] In this volume, examples of this perspective are reflected in articles by Robert P. Newman and Paul Fussell. A selection of journalistic writing by Charles Krauthammer, Jonathan Yardley, Edwin M. Yoder, Jr., Albert R. Hunt, and Stephen Rosenfeld reflect the type of opinion that dominated the American press at the height of the Smithsonian controversy and defended America's use of nuclear weapons against Japan. [46]

—IV—

THE BRITISH HISTORIAN, ERIC HOBSBAWM, once observed that many "plain ordinary citizens" want to understand their history because they "want to know how the past turned into the present and what help it is in looking forward to the future." [47] In our search to understand the past, the ordinary citizen and the scholar alike confront visions of history that are not only disparate, but also stand in stark contradiction to one another. Clearly, the study of history does not follow a uniform methodology. Herman Harrington of the American Legion demands a singular historical methodology in relation to Hiroshima that would yield "a history all of us can be proud of." Of course, the phrase "all of us" begs the difficult question of perspective. If as William Greider argues we must teach "our history whole—richly complicated and inescapably controversial," then to make presumptions about who constitutes "all of us," inevitably denies history to others who may have stood in another place and seen another view at the same moment.

Several of the contributors to the *Shadows* section of this volume—such as Dr. Shuntaro Hida and Hideko Tamura Snider—write their history as individuals who personally witnessed and managed to survive "the day Hiroshima disappeared." Their words vividly remind us what happens when a single weapon of mass destruction is dropped on a whole city. Their stories of survival allow us to imagine what it was like on the ground, beneath the mushroom cloud. Many of us may be compelled to ask, "How could it have happened?" In William Greider's approach to history it is permissible to pose such a question, if only because Greider is prepared to deal with the possibility that the answer exists in "the 'irreconcilable conflicts' embedded in America's past—the wrenching, ambiguous chapters that do not lead to easy moralisms."

In his illuminating volume *What Is History?*, E.H. Carr noted that "the study of history is a study of causes." For many people a descriptive account of how an event happened or a sequence of developments took place is sufficient. More elaboration is neither necessary nor useful, and efforts to interpret a development in a broader context can in some quarters be considered a wrongful digression from the standards of empiricism. Yet, Carr regarded such a narrow approach to historical inquiry as a "functional" one that eschewed the most significant question a historian could pose:

> Some people. . . speak not of "cause" in history, but of "explanation" or "interpretation," or of "the logic of the situation," or of the inner logic of events, or reject the causal approach (why it happened) in favor of the functional approach (how it happened), though this seems inevitably to involve the question how it came to happen, and so leads us back to the question "why?". . . The study of history is a study of causes. The historian. . . continuously asks the question "why?" and so long as he hopes for an answer, he cannot rest. The great historian—or perhaps I should say more broadly, the great thinker—is the man who asks the question "why?" about new things or in new contexts. [48]

In light of the existing historical evidence, does the legend of Hiroshima satisfactorily explain *why* atomic bombs were used against Nagasaki and Hiroshima? If the legend is not true, then *why* were Hiroshima and Nagasaki bombed? Our purpose in *Hiroshima's Shadow* has been to draw together the most rigorous attempts to answer this question. Even if the decision to use atomic weapons was made rather haphazardly as we have suggested, there is still a need to identify as precisely as possible the various conflicting forces that existed among those responsible for the decision. If, indeed, many senior diplomatic and military officials in the Truman administration favored a clarification of the terms of "unconditional surrender" and were convinced that military strategies existed that might well secure Japan's defeat without an invasion, the question must be posed and a plausible answer advanced as to *why*, in such circumstances, atomic bombs were used.

Although the group of officials that unambiguously and strongly favored the use of atomic bombs was a distinct minority within Truman's entourage, clearly this group—centered around the newly appointed Secretary of State, James Byrnes, and the Manhattan Project's director, General Leslie Groves—did in the end prevail. Indeed, with Harry Truman as their happy passenger, Byrnes and Groves seem to have driven a truck right through the middle of the collective, albeit inadequately organized, position of McCloy, Forrestal, Eisenhower, Leahy, Bard, and Acting Secretary of State Joseph Grew. This latter group thought there was good reason to believe that the Japanese were essentially militarily defeated and that the war would end soon after Potsdam—either through the results of a new diplomatic initiative at Potsdam that included a clarification of the surrender terms, or by the shock of the Soviet Union's promised entry into the Pacific war, or both. In any case, they believed that the war could end before an invasion was launched in the autumn of 1945.

While the use of atomic weapons had been studied during 1944 and 1945, without the certainty that the "gadget" actually worked, its deployment remained essentially a theoretical question. By the spring of 1945, only Secretary of War Henry L. Stimson, Assistant Secretary John J. McCloy, and a handful of other officials had spent any time contemplating the consequences of the new weapon. It is clear from the Stimson and McCloy diaries that these two men understood that this was not a weapon like any other weapon. They worried about the post-war implications of living in a nuclear age. Stimson had actually made a point of briefing Truman on the "moral" implications of the weapon. "The world in its present state of moral advancement," Stimson told Truman on April 25, 1945, "compared with its technical development would be eventually at the mercy of such a weapon. In other words, modern civilization might be completely destroyed." [49]

Still, a war was raging, and even Stimson had little time to devote to a study of how to use the weapon—or whether to use it. Barely a week elapsed between the date of the Trinity test on July 16, 1945—the definitive confirmation that an operational weapon was available—and Truman's July 24th approval of the fateful order for the "S-1" to be used. It was also the week in which those who believed they had the firm agreement of Truman and Byrnes to include a crucial clarification to the Japanese in the text of the Potsdam Declaration discovered to their surprise that Byrnes had exercised his long-standing personal domination over Truman and had managed to talk the President into summarily dropping the critical offer. Byrnes, like Groves, was not interested in pursuing even the possibility of an alternative route to Japanese surrender. They were both in a hurry to use the weapon and they moved quickly. Those who might have spoken out against the new turn of events barely had a chance to catch their breath before the *Enola Gay* was in flight.

Why did Byrnes and Groves prevail upon Truman while Stimson and McCloy failed? It is the answer to this question that is likely to lead us—in E.H. Carr's sense—to a better understanding of the "causative factors" that lay behind the ultimate and fateful choice—mass annihilation by a single weapon targeted on a civilian zone without warning.

However, before we enter into such a discussion, it may be useful to analyze the key "articles of faith" that have sustained the Hiroshima legend for more than fifty years. The legend is built on four essential beliefs. First, Americans have been repeatedly told that the bomb saved a half-million, even a million, American lives or casualties. Second, the legend has led most Americans to believe that the citizens of Hiroshima and Nagasaki were given specific and ample warning of the impending attack upon their cities. Third, the official legend has persuaded defenders of the atomic bombings that Hiroshima and Nagasaki were legitimate military targets. Fourth, the legend frames Truman's decision as a stark choice between the use of atomic weapons to force Japan's early surrender and the grisly prospect of a costly military invasion of Japan.

These four "articles of faith" are the essential pillars of the official American rationale for the use of atomic weapons in 1945. Take them away and the Hiroshima legend collapses. "From the time of Hiroshima, Americans have assigned themselves the task of finding virtue in the first use of the most murderous device ever created," note Robert Lifton and Greg Mitchell. "We have felt the need to avoid at any cost a sense of moral culpability for this act. These efforts have taken us to the far reaches of moral argument, to the extent of creating something close to an Orwellian reversal." [50]

The essays in this volume by Barton Bernstein and Adam Goodheart carefully scrutinize the first "article of faith." [51] Bernstein concludes that the progressive inflation of casualty estimates was "a postwar creation" intimately linked to establishing a sense of justification in the popular mind or, in Lifton's phrase, "finding virtue in the first use." According to Goodheart, "In notes for his memoirs, Truman mentioned the figure of 250,000 American *casualties*—dead and wounded.

In the published version, he upped the number to half a million *dead*. He later told a historian that the bomb had saved a million American lives."[52] In 1991 the American President, George Bush, stated that "millions" of lives had been saved by America's use of atomic weapons in 1945.[53] Goodheart notes that "after carefully researched analysis of the planned attack [the historian John R.] Skates concludes that 'the large casualty figures for the invasion of Japan, cited by Truman, [Secretary of War] Stimson, and Churchill in their postwar writings were without basis in contemporary [military] planning'."[54]

Astonishingly, no high-level archival documents from the Truman period have been found to substantiate any of the estimates used by Truman or Stimson in their memoirs. To the contrary, the archives reveal that "most pre-Hiroshima military estimates ranged between about 20,000 and 46,000" military fatalities in the various battle plans for the invasion. As Bernstein notes, these are clearly "painful numbers" but all the battle scenario estimates "fell far short—by at least 454,000—of later claims of 500,000 American lives."[55] Certainly, none of the pre-Hiroshima estimates for an invasion reflected multipliers of five, ten, or twenty times the death toll of 100,000 deaths that American military forces suffered in the Pacific theater during the entire Second World War. Yet these exaggerated—essentially propagandistic numbers—remain an article of faith and the first pillar of the rationale that is the Hiroshima legend.[56]

The debate over casualty estimates has always been slightly surreal. It is, after all, a debate over casualty *estimates* for an invasion that never took place—and probably never would have taken place even if the atomic bomb had not been invented. In the view of historian Martin Sherwin, any attempt to frame the choices facing President Truman in the summer of 1945 as a bomb/invasion dichotomy is a fundamental distortion. Still, many defenders of the legend insist that Hiroshima was justified if it saved any American lives. In 1994, the National Commander of the American Legion, William Detweiler, observed, "Was it 30,000 or was it 500,000 potential invasion casualties? Does it matter? To the museum and historians, it seems to be of great importance in determining the morality of President Truman's decision. *To the American Legion it matters less, if at all.* The use of the weapon against a brutal and ruthless aggressor to save 30,000 American lives was as morally justifiable as to use it to save 500,000 lives."[57]

Is it reasonable, however, to characterize the civilian inhabitants of Hiroshima and Nagasaki "brutal and ruthless aggressor[s]"? In plain and simple language they were noncombatants. Ask the ordinary World War II veteran if he were prepared to deliberately kill a hundred noncombatants, including significant numbers of children, in order to destroy one enemy soldier and you will have few, if any, affirmative answers. As Dwight MacDonald put the issue in his contribution to this volume, "[T]here is really only one possible answer to the problem posed by Dostoyevsky's Grand Inquisitor: if all mankind could realize eternal and complete happiness by torturing to death a single child, would this act be morally justified?"[58]

John Rawls, the Harvard philosopher, makes a pertinent observation in his contribution to this volume:

> In the conduct of war, a democratic society must carefully distinguish three groups: the state's leaders and officials, its soldiers, and its civilian population. The reason for these distinctions rest on the

principle of responsibility: since the state fought against is not democratic, the civilian members of society cannot be those who organized and brought on the war. This was done by its leaders and
officials assisted by other elites who control and staff the state apparatus. They are responsible, they willed the war, and for doing that
they are criminals. But civilians, often kept in ignorance and swayed
by state propaganda, are not. . . .[I]n the case of Hiroshima many
involved in higher reaches of the [U.S.] government recognized the
questionable character of the bombing and that limits were being
crossed...Under the continuing pressure of war, such moral doubts
as there were failed to gain an express and articulated view... [T]here
was not sufficient prior grasp of the fundamental principles of just
war...practical reasoning justifies too much too easily, and provides a way
for a dominant power to quiet any moral worries that may arise.[59]

The second "article of faith" that sustains the Hiroshima legend among so
many Americans is the conviction that the citizens of Hiroshima and Nagasaki
were specifically warned that their cities would be bombed by a new type of
weapon. The depth of this conviction was evident in a collection of letters covering an entire page that appeared at the height of the Smithsonian controversy in
the *Washington Post*. The letters were a response to Kai Bird, one of the editors of
this volume, who wrote an article that appeared in the *Post* on July 7, 1995 entitled
"Enola Gay: 'Patriotically Correct'."

Bird noted that the censored remnant of the exhibit that was finally allowed
inside the Smithsonian's hall claimed as "fact" that "special leaflets were...dropped
on Japanese cities three days before a bombing raid to warn civilians to evacuate."
The very next sentence that followed this statement in the exhibit referred to the
bombing of Hiroshima—directly implying that the civilian inhabitants of
Hiroshima were given warning of an atomic attack. Bird stated in the *Post*, "This
is incorrect. No evidence has ever been uncovered that leaflets—issuing a warning
of either conventional or atomic attack—were dropped on Hiroshima."

The letters in response were revealing in a way their authors could not have
suspected. The argument about an advance warning secures a key psychological
touchstone critical to those Americans who justify the bombing and wish to believe
that civilians had been actually warned. It satisfies their sense of "fair play" and has
become an aid to living with the knowledge of Hiroshima. Bird was admonished
for failing to "temper his writing with better research."[60] In two letters to the
Washington Post attacking Bird, the authors—Leonard Nadler and William Jones—
recalled visits to peace museums in Hiroshima and Nagasaki where they saw "with
their own eyes" warning leaflets that had been dropped over the two cities. In their
view, this was clear evidence that Bird did not know his facts.

The truth about the atomic "warning" leaflets is macabre beyond belief—they
were dropped *after* both cities were destroyed. Sanho Tree, one of the contributors
to this volume, wrote to the *Post* to set the record straight:

> The July 18 letters attacking Kai Bird's July 7 op-ed contain serious
> factual errors that must not go uncorrected. . . .The leaflets Leonard
> Nadler and William P. Jones recall seeing in the Hiroshima museum
> in 1960 and 1970 respectively were dropped *after the bombing*.

This happened because the President's Interim Committee on the Atomic bomb decided on May 31, "that we could not give the Japanese any warning." Furthermore, the decision to drop "atomic" leaflets on Japanese cities was not made until August 7, the day *after* the Hiroshima bombing.

General Leslie Groves, the man in charge of the Manhattan Project, wrote in his memoirs *Now It Can Be Told*, "To exploit the psychological effect of the bombs on the Japanese, we had belatedly arranged for leaflets to be dropped on Japan proclaiming the power of our new weapon and warning that further resistance was useless. The first delivery was made on the ninth." The leaflet program was supervised by General Thomas F. Farrell and Lt. Colonel John F. Moynahan, both representatives of the Manhattan Project in the Marianas.

The leaflets were intended to notify 47 Japanese cities with populations of over 100,000 that the bombing of Hiroshima was atomic in nature and that more bombs would follow if they did not pressure their leaders to stop the war. Nagasaki, it should be noted, did not get leafleted until August 10—the day *after* it was bombed. In all, six million "atomic" leaflets were dropped and all of them *after* Hiroshima. [62] Furthermore, Nagasaki was the secondary target on August 9 and the primary target was Kokura (which was passed over due to cloud cover). Neither Kokura nor Niigata, the other city on the atomic bomb target list, received atomic warning leaflets....[W]e can say...that the residents of Hiroshima received no advance warning about the use of the atomic bomb. [61]

On June 1, 1945, a formal and official decision was taken during a meeting of the so-called Interim Committee *not to warn* the populations of the specific target cities. In attendance were Secretary of State-designate James Byrnes, Robert Oppenheimer, and General Leslie Groves among others. According to the records of the meeting, "Mr. Byrnes recommended and the Committee agreed, that the Secretary of War should be advised that, while recognizing that the final selection of the target was essentially a military decision, the present view of the Committee was that the bomb should be used against Japan as soon as possible... and that it be used *without prior warning*." Absent at that day's meeting was Secretary of War Henry Stimson, who had been displaying contradictory sentiments about how and when the bomb would be used. In any event, on July 24, a week after the Trinity test, Stimson passed on orders for the atomic attack despite his own declared views in favor of giving Japan "prior-warning" and "ample time" to respond diplomatically before using the weapon. [62]

If one hopes to find a thoughtful review of the profound issues inherent in the decision to use an atomic weapon, one will not find it in the deliberations of the Interim Committee. Indeed the degree of muddle-headedness, confusion, and contradictory positions taken by key personalities is remarkable. Stimson attended a Interim Committee session the day before the critical June 1st meeting. At one stage according to Oppenheimer, "[Stimson emphasized] the appalling lack of conscience and compassion that the war had brought about... the complacency, the indifference, and the silence with which we greeted the mass bombings of

Hamburg, of Dresden, of Tokyo... Colonel Stimson felt that, as far as degradation went, we had had it." [63] Of course, this was inaccurate. They had not "had it" all yet. The atomic bomb had not yet been dropped.

Despite Stimson's expressed qualms about area bombings, the minutes of the Interim Committee for May 31, 1945, report:

> After much discussion concerning various types of targets and the effects to be produced, the Secretary [Stimson] expressed the conclusion, on which there was general agreement, that we could not give the Japanese any warning; that we could not concentrate on a civilian area; but that we should seek to make a profound psychological impression on as many of the inhabitants as possible. At the suggestion of Dr. Conant, the Secretary agreed that the most desirable target would be a vital war plant employing a large number of workers and closely surrounded by workers' houses. [64]

Stimson's acceptance of the proposal made by James Conant, the President of Harvard University, that they "could not give the Japanese any warning" was diametrically opposite to Stimson's own July 2, 1945, memorandum to Truman arguing in favor of a "prior warning." [65] The contradictions were extraordinary. According to Richard Rhodes, Stimson "still insisted passionately that 'the objective was military damage... not civilian lives'." The muddle, the confusion, the self-delusion persisted throughout this decisive Interim Committee meeting. The self-deception was clearly evident from the fact that they were taking a decision to drop an atomic bomb in the center of a city and yet they could still say to themselves that they "could not concentrate [an atomic weapon] on a civilian area." [66]

According to Arthur Compton, the distinguished physicist who participated in the June 1st meeting, the members of the committee were told by Robert Oppenheimer that scientists at Los Alamos estimated that the death toll from the atomic attack would be 20,000 persons. [67] All sorts of fanciful assumptions were made. For example, it was assumed that Hiroshima's population would seek shelter when the attack began. But there had never been a devastating air attack carried out by a single plane and there was no shelter in existence adequate to protect the civilian population against a nuclear firestorm. Hiroshima's air defense network signaled an "all clear" when only a single plane was observed entering its air space. Much of the city's population was on their way to work or school when the bomb exploded at 8:15 in the morning. The actual death toll in Hiroshima was at least seven times the 20,000 Oppenheimer had conjured up with such authority. His speculative estimate represented only 14 percent of the actual casualties—a statistical disparity of 86 percent. The men of the Interim Committee did not have a clue as to the magnitudes involved in the atomic attack they were recommending.

Closely linked to the question of whether a warning of an atomic attack was given to the civilian populations of the target cities is the third "article of faith" that underpins the American legend of Hiroshima: the belief that Hiroshima and Nagasaki were military targets. The Headquarters of the Japanese Second Army was located in Hiroshima and approximately 20,000 men were stationed in the city of which about half, or 10,000, died in the atomic attack. In Nagasaki, there were almost no military units stationed in the city and it is estimated that "there were about 150 deaths among military personnel" in the city. [68] Thus, between the two cities, 4.4 percent of the total death toll was made up of military personnel. In short, more than 95 percent of the casualties were civilians. In Nagasaki, the military personnel who died represented *less than* two one-thousandths of one percent. "The first reports on August 6, 1945, described Hiroshima as a Japanese army base," writes Thomas Powers. "This fiction could not stand for long. The huge death toll of ordinary Japanese citizens, combined with the horror of so many deaths by fire, eventually cast a moral shadow over the triumph of ending the war with two bombs." [69]

McGeorge Bundy, who became National Security Adviser to John F. Kennedy, who as a young man had ghost-written Henry Stimson's *Harper's* magazine article justifying the atomic attacks, was pressed by Peter Jennings during a televised interview in 1995 to admit that Hiroshima and Nagasaki were indisputably *not* military targets. Bundy responded in a curious fashion. "It's not myth that it's [Hiroshima] a military target," said Bundy. And then, after a pregnant pause, he added, "It's a military target like New York." [70] For those who knew Bundy's dry sense of irony, it was evident that he was agreeing with Jennings. In his own book, *Danger and Survival*, Bundy addressed the issue directly: "Truman never chose, then or later, to grapple with this self-deception; indeed, he repeated to the end of his life that it was a purely military action against military targets. . . .Any target large enough to be thoroughly and shockingly destroyed by a single inaccurate bomb was also a target full of men, women, and children." [71] Clearly, a nuclear weapon used against an entire city obliterated all distinction between combatant and noncombatant, making civilians the prime target of attack.

In another sense, Bundy's comment to Jennings simply reflected the credo of a modern nuclear strategist, recalling the origin of the craft's first doctrinal sin. Like Hiroshima and Nagasaki, whole cities remain, to this day, "military targets" because the doctrine of nuclear "deterrence" requires that centers of civil society are to be annihilated in a nuclear war regardless of their actual military significance. In ancient times, the ordinary folk of Carthage and Jerusalem were given the opportunity to escape or managed to flee before their towns were laid to waste by the relatively inefficient methods of destruction then used. The nuclear option has placed us beyond Carthage. Although it counts for little in the ruling councils of the nuclear weapons states, it should be noted that under international conventions governing war and the 1996 World Court ruling on nuclear weapons, the deliberate targeting of civilians in the manner of Hiroshima and Nagasaki is considered to be a criminal act. [72]

The last key "article of faith" sustaining the Hiroshima legend is the belief that in order to achieve Japan's surrender the United States had no alternative to using the atomic bomb other than the prospect of a costly invasion of the Japanese home islands. When scholars such as Paul Fussell, a young soldier in 1945 and a contributor to this volume, offer their approval of the first use of atomic weapons, they do so with the firm conviction that their own deaths were the probable alternative. Yet, ordinary American military personnel and the American public were barely aware, if at all, of the debate that had been going on for months at the highest echelons of the American government. The historical record is replete with details that an alternative strategy to securing Japan's surrender *without an invasion* of the Japanese mainland was being recommended by a broad group of high-level advisers to the president.

Gar Alperovitz in his contribution to this volume reviews alternatives being recommended forcefully in Washington in order to secure Japan's negotiated surrender. Murray Sayle examines the same issue from the perspective of Tokyo during the critical months prior to August 1945. What were the conditions sought by the Japanese that might have facilitated an early surrender to Allied forces? Absent from the official legend of Hiroshima is the fact that for much of the late spring and early summer of 1945 a virtual majority of the President's closest advisers were persuaded that the Japanese were very close to surrender. The critical stumbling block, they believed, would be the future status of the Japanese Emperor. On May 28, 1945, John J. McCloy, Assistant Secretary of War, argued to Secretary of War Stimson that the phrase "unconditional surrender" be dropped altogether. "Unconditional surrender is a phrase," wrote McCloy, "which means loss of face and I wonder whether we cannot accomplish everything we want to accomplish in regard to Japan without the use of that term." [73]

A few days after McCloy had made his argument in favor of altering the inflexible formulation, the Office of Strategic Services (OSS) reported that on May 31, 1945, another Japanese peace feeler had been received through a Japanese diplomat posted in neutral Portugal. The OSS reported that he had stated that the "actual peace terms were unimportant so long as the term 'unconditional surrender' was not employed." [74] Acting Secretary of State Joseph Grew, a conservative diplomat who had served as Ambassador to Japan prior to the war, had been urging a clarification of the terms of surrender for many months. He believed that some form of guarantee for the future political status of the Emperor as a constitutional monarch was essential if the Japanese were not to fight to the last man and the door to a conditional surrender was to be opened.

Grew's views were shared by Navy Secretary James Forrestal, former President Herbert Hoover, Under Secretary of the Navy Ralph A. Bard, and a broad group of civilian and military officials. Although they regarded the decision to be a political one that had to be taken by Washington's civilian leadership, the country's key senior military officers favored a clarification of the Emperor's status. The main opposition to such a clarification came from James F. Byrnes. A former Senator from South Carolina, Byrnes had taken Harry Truman under his wing during their days together in the U.S. Senate. After Roosevelt's death Truman turned to his old mentor for support and guidance. Shortly after Truman was informed of the existence of the Manhattan Project he appointed Byrnes as his personal representative on the Interim Committee. By then, Truman had already decided to appoint Byrnes Secretary of State, a job the smooth-talking South Carolinian took over on July 3, 1945, only a month prior to the atomic bombings.

During the critical phase from December 1944 until July 1945 when Byrnes finally arrived, Joseph Grew had been in charge of the day-to-day activities of the State Department. Secretary of State Edward Stettinius had been spending long periods away from Washington in connection with the founding of the United Nations. As his deputy, Grew was essentially the Acting Secretary of State and referred to as such in Stettinius's absence. Thus, Grew's recommendations were those of a senior official. Only a month after Roosevelt's death, Grew met with Truman and made the following argument:

> The greatest obstacle to unconditional surrender by the Japanese is their belief that this would entail the destruction or permanent removal of the Emperor and the institution of the Throne. If some indication can now be given the Japanese that they themselves. . .

will be permitted to determine their own future political structure, they will be afforded a method of saving face without which surrender will be highly unlikely. [75]

Truman did not seem particularly opposed to the notion of providing some clarification regarding the Emperor. Indeed, Grew noted that the President had stated that "his own thoughts had been following the same line." Three weeks later, on June 18, 1945, Truman convened a meeting of his chief advisers to discuss the military's contingency plans for an invasion of the Japanese home islands—the first phase of which was to begin no earlier than November 1, 1945. There was no question that the planning for the invasion was being undertaken as a contingency. In his memoirs, Fleet Admiral William Leahy, the country's most senior military official, put it bluntly: "The invasion itself was never authorized." [76] The President and his advisers then drifted into a discussion of whether, in McCloy's words, "serious attention should be given to a political attempt to end the war." Stimson also told Truman, "I do think that there is a large submerged class in Japan who do not favor the present war and whose full opinion and influence have not yet been felt. . . I feel something should be done to arouse them and to develop any possible influence they might have before it became necessary to come to grips with them." [77]

During the same meeting Admiral Leahy expressed his skepticism regarding the necessity of a full-scale invasion of Japan. When asked directly by Truman for his opinion, Assistant Secretary of War McCloy said he thought the war had progressed to such a state that there was now a "question of whether we needed to get Russia in to help us defeat Japan." [78] McCloy was convinced that the Japanese had very nearly been defeated. The previous evening he had told Stimson that "there were no more cities to bomb, no more carriers to sink or battleships to shell; we had difficulty finding targets." When he was asked what he meant by a political solution, McCloy responded, "Some communication to the Japanese government which would spell out the terms that we would settle for." He said the United States needed to make an affirmation that "we would be quite prepared to permit Japan to continue to exist as a nation, as a viable nation, that we would permit them to choose their own form of government, including the retention of the Mikado [Emperor], but only on the basis of a constitutional monarchy." [79]

Historians are not entirely in agreement over what took place at the June 18th meeting. Incomplete minutes of this critical meeting report that there was a discussion of the need for the United States to make a political overture to the Japanese. The point is a crucial one. On it rests the implication that senior American policy makers did perceive *a plausible alternative to an invasion of the Japanese islands*. Until his death McCloy consistently claimed that he had specifically referred to the atomic bomb during this meeting and had urged that an explicit warning should be given as part of the overall political effort to end the war before an invasion could be launched.

McCloy published his account of the meeting in 1953 and none of the other participants in the meeting—most prominently Harry Truman and General George Marshall—disputed it then or later. Six years earlier McCloy had described the meeting to James Forrestal who wrote a detailed description of McCloy's account in his own diary of March 8, 1947. The segment of the Forrestal diary is reproduced in the document section of this volume. [80] The key point remains.

Truman was explicitly told by some of his most important advisers that in their opinion Japan was so close to defeat's door that a political overture regarding the future status of the Emperor might well open the door to surrender well before a costly invasion could be mounted.

Truman responded favorably to these suggestions, telling McCloy, "Well, that's just what I've been thinking about. . . . You go down to Jimmy Byrnes and talk to him about it."[81] Byrnes, however, was not receptive to McCloy's overture. He thought a clarification of the unconditional surrender terms was ill-advised politically. Byrnes evidently believed that the new bomb might be exploited as a weapon of diplomacy. A month earlier, on May 25th, Leo Szilard had been at the White House with a letter of introduction from Albert Einstein, his friend and colleague. Szilard had been instrumental in persuading Einstein to write to Franklin Roosevelt in 1939 about the military potential of nuclear fission and their fears concerning developments in German nuclear research. Six years later, Nazi Germany lay in ruins and, with it, the possibility of a German atomic bomb. Knowing that the Japanese militarists could not have built their own atomic weapon, Szilard now wanted to warn the new President of the preeminent dangers atomic weapons posed for the post-war world. If at all possible, Szilard hoped Truman could be persuaded not to authorize the use of this weapon against Japan.

At the White House, the President's staff told Szilard that Truman wanted him to proceed to South Carolina to meet James Byrnes. Szilard and his companions had no idea that in just over a month Byrnes would be named the new Secretary of State and become a key figure at the Potsdam Conference. Szilard took Harold Urey, a Manhattan Project chemist and Nobel laureate, and Walter Bartky, the associate director of the University of Chicago's Metallurgical Laboratory (Met Lab), with him to meet Byrnes. The encounter with the "Assistant President" was not what they expected. As described by William Lanouette in his contribution to this volume, the scientists were unsettled by Byrnes's preoccupation with the Soviet Union and his perception of the atomic bomb as a diplomatic weapon. "Mr. Byrnes did not argue that it was necessary to use the bomb against the cities of Japan to win the war," Szilard recalled. "Mr. Byrnes's. . . view [was] that our possessing and demonstrating the bomb would make Russia more manageable in Europe."[82]

Byrnes's thinking and the degree of his influence over Truman was at that stage still largely unknown to many others. Meanwhile, Roosevelt's men continued to pursue what they regarded to be the new agenda set during the June 18th meeting. Over the next six weeks, Stimson and McCloy at the War Department vigorously pursued the option of orchestrating a surrender of Japan by political means. The morning after the June 18th meeting the powerful Committee of Three met to begin drafting a definition of the surrender terms. Consisting of Secretary of War Stimson, Secretary of State Edward Stettinius, and Secretary of the Navy James V. Forrestal, with McCloy designated as recorder, this committee had rapidly become the venue for adjudicating some of the toughest issues facing policy makers during the remainder of the war.

On this occasion, Acting Secretary of State Joseph Grew argued that it was not even necessary to backtrack from a demand for unconditional surrender. "We must occupy Tokyo," Grew said. All that needed to be done was to explain "what we meant by unconditional surrender in such a way which might induce them to desist from further hostilities." Grew suggested that the Japanese should be notified that "they could determine for themselves the nature of the particular political structure they wanted for the future so long as it did not incorporate any of the militaristic elements." [83]

This position was further refined at another meeting of the Committee of Three on June 26. Stimson, Forrestal, Grew, and McCloy agreed that a clarification of the surrender terms should be issued well before an invasion and with "ample time to permit a national reaction to set in."[*] The participants in the June 26 meeting agreed that "Japan is susceptible to reason" and that there was every reason to avoid an outright invasion. McCloy was instructed to draft the actual language for what would become known as the Potsdam Declaration. As McCloy drafted it, the crucial "Paragraph 12" (or Article 12 as it is also known) specified that the post-war Japanese government "may include a constitutional monarchy under the present dynasty." McCloy acknowledged to Stimson that this was the "most controversial" point and might "cause repercussions at home." (A Gallup poll conducted during the first week of June 1945 indicated that 70 percent of the respondents favored some form of criminal proceedings against the Emperor.) However, if it were absent he noted, "those who seem to know most about Japan feel there would be very little likelihood of acceptance." [84]

Thus, only six weeks before the day the *Enola Gay* dropped an atomic bomb on Hiroshima, the consensus within the senior ranks of the Truman administration was that a negotiated surrender was within reach if the United States clearly specified acceptable terms regarding the Emperor's post-war status. What happened? At moments, history clearly turns on very small wheels and the capriciousness of men's souls.

In the six weeks after the June 26th meeting, the fate of Hiroshima and Nagasaki was sealed by a muted but profound conflict between a majority of Truman's advisers and the President's friend Byrnes. On July 3rd, slightly more than a week after that meeting, Byrnes took over as Secretary of State. Working under what they assumed were Truman's instructions, McCloy and others completed their draft of the Potsdam Declaration and the critical Article 12 regarding the Emperor. In fact, as we have noted, on June 18th Truman seemed receptive to the notion that the Japanese be offered a guarantee regarding the Emperor, telling McCloy "that's just what I've been thinking about." But it would soon be clear that Harry Truman was thinking many contradictory thoughts at the same time or casually altering his position without informing such key figures as Stimson, Grew, and McCloy.

Unknown to the authors of the Potsdam Declaration and Article 12, Truman was moving in quite the opposite direction, largely under the influence of Byrnes. All the evidence suggests that during the spring and summer of 1945 Byrnes influenced Truman to think of the atomic bomb as a diplomatic weapon, something that—as Truman himself wrote in his memoirs—"might well put us in a position to dictate our own terms at the end of the war." [85] As the new Secretary of State, Byrnes initiated a series of steps to ensure that McCloy's political overture to the Japanese, as embodied in Article 12, was eliminated.

---

[*] This view was ultimately set forth in a memo from Stimson to Truman dated July 2, 1945, which can be found in the document section of this volume. See *The Stimson Memo: Prior Warning with "Ample Time,"* p. 527.

On July 7, 1945, Truman left aboard the cruiser *Augusta*, bound for the fateful Potsdam conference where he would meet Stalin and Churchill. Accompanying him were a number of his Missouri poker-playing companions and Jimmy Byrnes. Four days earlier Byrnes had taken over the State Department and was now positioned to dominate Truman's staff at Potsdam. By the time they docked at Antwerp on July 15, Byrnes had persuaded Truman to cut the last sentence of Article 12, eliminating any assurance to the peace faction in Tokyo that the Emperor would be allowed to retain his throne as a constitutional monarch. This critical language—designed to clarify the surrender terms—had been thrown overboard enroute to Potsdam.

McCloy, Stimson, Forrestal, and others arrived at Potsdam by other routes to discover that the entire diplomatic plan on which they had been diligently working for the past month had suddenly been altered without any prior notice. The decision was allowed to stand even when additional evidence of a Japanese desire to surrender became available. As Truman and Byrnes were traveling toward Potsdam, Washington intercepted and decoded a July 13th cable from Japanese Foreign Minister Shigenori Togo to his Ambassador in Moscow that made Tokyo's intentions clear: "Unconditional surrender is the only obstacle to peace...." In another cable, Togo stated that "it is His Majesty's heart's desire to see the swift termination of the war." [86]

By the time Truman and his party arrived in Potsdam a new dynamic had taken hold. Stimson received an "eyes only" communication on July 16 informing him of "Trinity." The atomic bomb had been successfully tested that morning in New Mexico. Stimson was visibly jubilant. "The Secretary cut a gay caper," McCloy wrote in his diary, "and rushed off to tell the President and Jimmy Byrnes about it." McCloy, however, was decidedly more subdued by the news. A few days later, he wrote in his diary, "I hope it does not augur the commencement of the destruction of modern civilization. In this atmosphere of destruction and callousness of men and their leaders, the whole thing seems ominous." [87] The day after Trinity, Stimson made a final plea to Byrnes for an explicit warning regarding the capability of the bomb and a precise assurance to the Japanese that unconditional surrender did not mean an end to the Emperor. Byrnes cut him off and unequivocally rejected both ideas, saying he spoke for the President. The plausible alternative to both an invasion and the bomb was now dead at Potsdam.

Byrnes had the Soviet Union on his mind, and the manner of Japan's surrender would become a dramatic demarche in the opening phase of the post-war world. Sitting in his front parlor in Spartanburg, South Carolina, Byrnes had already shared his thoughts quite explicitly with an astonished Leo Szilard who recalled how Byrnes had indicated that demonstrating the bomb [on Japan] would make Russia more manageable in Europe. [88] The atom bomb for Byrnes was an instrument of diplomacy—*atomic diplomacy*. [89] His behavior at Potsdam indicated that once the operational capability of the weapon had been demonstrated he wanted the atomic bomb used before the Soviets launched their promised military offensive against Japanese positions in China. In a television interview twenty years after Hiroshima, Byrnes was unabashed about his views, "I cannot speak for the others but it was ever present in my mind that it was important that we should have an end to the war before the Russians came in...[N]either the President nor I were anxious to have them [the Soviets] enter the war after we had learned of this successful [atomic] test." [90]

The Potsdam conference had originally been conceived as a meeting designed to secure a final commitment from Stalin as to the exact date Soviet forces would enter the war against Japan. The Soviet Union had earlier committed itself to enter the Pacific war within three months of Germany's defeat. At Potsdam they confirmed they were prepared to open their front against Japan by mid-August. American intelligence assessments of the Japanese Army had determined that Soviet entry was the one action the Japanese military feared most. On the verge of defeat in the face of American advances, Japanese Army diehards were increasingly on the defensive and faced growing opposition within Japan's top echelons. Soviet entry would be a hammer blow. It would completely cut off their main units in China. According to the military historian Robert A. Pape:

> The Soviet invasion of Manchuria on August 9 raised Japan's military vulnerability to a very high level. The Soviet offensive ruptured Japanese lines immediately, and rapidly penetrated deep into the rear. Since the Kwantung Army was thought to be Japan's premier fighting force, this had a devastating effect on Japanese calculations of the prospects for home island defense....If their best forces were so easily sliced to pieces, the unavoidable implication was that the less well-equipped and trained forces assembled for [the last decisive home island battle] had no chance of success against American forces that were even more capable than the Soviets. [91]

But sitting in Potsdam, Byrnes was not so much concerned with the end of the war as with the next phase. Following the German defeat, America and its Western European allies had begun to encounter difficulties with the Soviet presence in Germany and throughout Eastern Europe. Two centers of world power were now emerging from the war. Although once allied against fascism, new rival spheres of influence had been established.

If the motivating factor underlying Byrnes's position on the use of an atomic weapon against Japan was to demonstrate the immensity of this new military power in order to make the Soviets "more manageable" and thereby attempt preemptively to subdue an emergent rival, we can perceive how the atomic bomb became a strategic element in the post-war reshuffle of imperial rivalries. It has been said that the atomic bombing of Hiroshima was not only the last act of the Second World War but also the first act of the Cold War. It is here that E.H. Carr's "causative factor" can be found. The bombing was not simply a final military tactic. By admission of its leading advocate its use was intimately tied to the determination of post-war spheres of influence.

Byrnes was anxious to avoid a situation where the United States would have to share authority with the Soviets in Japan or elsewhere in Asia as they were now compelled to do in Europe. On July 24, the day on which authorization was given to bomb Hiroshima, Byrnes's principal aide, Walter Brown, recorded in his diary entry at Potsdam that Byrnes was hoping that "after the atomic bomb Japan will surrender and Russia will not get in so much on the kill." [92] Only a day earlier, Churchill had dryly noted, "It is quite clear that the United States do not at the present time desire Russian participation in the war against Japan." [93]

In his preface and in his contribution to this volume, Joseph Rotblat, recipient of the 1995 Nobel Peace Prize, recalls the incident that led to his leaving the

Manhattan Project. Rotblat had joined the effort to build an atomic weapon because he, like many other scientists, feared that Nazi Germany might acquire a nuclear capability. When towards the end of 1944 it became clear that the Germans had abandoned their bomb project, Rotblat believed there was no purpose in building an atomic weapon. No atomic threat existed from the Japanese. His decision to leave the project was strongly influenced by a particular encounter that especially disturbed him. "While working on the Manhattan Project at Los Alamos," writes Rotblat, "I had occasion to dine with General Leslie Groves [chief of the Manhattan Project] at the home of Professor James Chadwick. I was temporarily residing with the Chadwicks and General Groves was an occasional dinner guest. During one memorable evening in March 1944, Groves remarked that the real purpose of building the bomb was to subdue the Soviets. This statement at the time was a shock to me."[94] It was also evidence that Groves and Byrnes were thinking alike.

It needs to be reemphasized that Byrnes's assumption (according to Leo Szilard) that "rattling the bomb might make Russia more manageable" was hardly the consensus among the American political and bureaucratic elite.[95] If it became necessary, conservatives like Stimson and McCloy believed the Soviets could be confronted by other measures. Indeed, their fear was that by using an atomic weapon Washington might provoke an atomic arms race that could someday render the United States vulnerable to nuclear attack. Niels Bohr and Leo Szilard, among others, had warned of precisely such an outcome.

In the midst of the Potsdam deliberations, McCloy received a report from Allen Dulles of the Office of Strategic Services (OSS) in Switzerland of yet another Japanese peace initiative. According to the Dulles report, Kojiro Kitamura, a senior Japanese official and director at the Bank for International Settlements in Switzerland, had approached Per Jacobsson, a Swede and economic adviser at the bank. Kitamura told Jacobsson that "he was anxious to establish immediate contact with American representatives and implied that the only condition on which Japan would insist with respect to surrender would be some consideration for the Japanese Imperial family."[96] The conversation between Kitamura and Jacobsson had taken place on July 13. McCloy, absolutely convinced that Article 12 held the potential key to a negotiated surrender, had Dulles flown post haste to Potsdam in order to report in person to Stimson. The pattern was clear. Initiatives by the Japanese had occurred in Moscow, Stockholm, Lisbon, and Bern. When combined with a daily reading of the Magic intercepts, it is only reasonable to conclude that Truman's men understood that a genuine option for a negotiated surrender existed.

On July 26th, U.S. signal intelligence had intercepted yet another message from Japanese Foreign Minister Shigenori Togo to his envoy in Moscow. Togo asked him to "communicate to the other party [the United States] through appropriate channels that we have no objection to a peace based on the Atlantic Charter."[97] This amounted to a significant signal to the United States since the Charter constituted a liberal statement of British and American war aims. Togo pleaded that it "was necessary to have them understand that we are trying to end hostilities by asking for very reasonable terms in order to secure and maintain our nation's existence and honor." Clearly, Togo was referring to the preservation of the Emperor's position. "Should the United States and Great Britain remain insistent on formality," Togo concluded, "there is no solution to this situation other than for us to hold out until complete collapse because of this point alone."[98]

On July 28th, Secretary of the Navy James Forrestal arrived uninvited at Potsdam, determined, in the words of one naval historian, to "'crash' the conference."[99] Along with his two top assistants, Ralph Bard and Admiral Lewis Strauss, Forrestal was convinced that "because of the bottling up of Japan, already effected by the Navy, an all-out invasion would not be necessary"—and like many of the high-ranking naval officers he supervised—that the tightening naval blockade had brought the Japanese to the point of surrender.[100] When he arrived at Potsdam in late July he made a point of bringing the transcripts of the latest Magic intercepts.[101]

Although Forrestal met Truman twice at Potsdam, he arrived four days after the President's authorization to proceed with an atomic attack and two days after the release of the July 26th Potsdam Declaration without the key wording in Article 12 that McCloy had drafted a month earlier.[102] Truman and Byrnes had set the timer on the bomb and Forrestal's eleventh-hour intervention would not stop what others had failed to prevent. According to his biographers, Townsend Hoopes and Douglas Brinkley, Forrestal's "overriding concern at this juncture was to develop strategic counterweights to what he foresaw as burgeoning Russian/Communist power in Asia." Yet, unlike Byrnes, Forrestal "may have feared that using the atomic bomb would aggravate the problems of Japan's recovery and produce hatred of America for years to come."[103]

At Potsdam, the standard bearer, if there was one, of the Grew–McCloy–Forrestal position was Henry Stimson who believed it to be a wholly reasonable proposition for the United States to clarify the terms of "unconditional surrender" and to respond to Japanese entreaties regarding a formal constitutional role for the Emperor. But at Potsdam, he was tired, his political skills were on the wane, and by comparison to Byrnes, his influence over the President was limited. Moreover, Stimson was a man of strong but inconsistent convictions. He had backed McCloy, his deputy, and supported the formulation of Article 12. Yet, just after arriving in Europe to attend the Potsdam conference, Stimson had reportedly disagreed with General Eisenhower over the possible use of a nuclear weapon against the Japanese. As noted earlier, Eisenhower claimed in his memoirs that there was no military reason which could justify the use of an atomic weapon. "[T]he Japanese were ready to surrender," Eisenhower told Newsweek in 1963, "and, it wasn't necessary to hit them with that awful thing."[104] Eisenhower reported that Stimson was annoyed and upset by his argument.

In an early draft of his famous 1948 memoirs, Stimson essentially accused Byrnes of indulging in atomic diplomacy. "In the State Department [that is, Byrnes] there developed a tendency to think of the bomb as a diplomatic weapon," he wrote. "Outraged by constant evidence of Russian perfidy, some of the men in charge of foreign policy were eager to carry the bomb for a while as their ace-in-the-hole…[they] were eager to browbeat the Russians with the bomb 'held rather ostentatiously on our hip.' "[105] And yet, who was Stimson to criticize Byrnes in this regard? Only two months prior to Potsdam, he confided to his diary that "over any such tangled web of problems [with the Soviets] the S-1 secret would be dominant." Looking ahead to the Potsdam conference, and noting that the bomb had yet to be tested, Stimson stated "it seems a terrible thing to gamble with such big stakes in diplomacy [vis-à-vis the Russians] without having your *master card* in your hand."[106]

At various times, Stimson both supported the inclusion of Article 12 in the Potsdam Declaration and simultaneously considered the atomic bomb to be a "master card" in dealing with the Soviets. Tired and inconsistent, he was a poor advocate at Potsdam of the view advanced by the Grew–McCloy–Forrestal circle. McCloy thought then and later that the decision to use the atomic bomb had been badly mishandled. He was disturbed by what he called the "atmosphere of rather deep suspicion" that pervaded the Potsdam conference. He thought Truman's closest advisers were neither "particularly intellectually-minded" nor "enlightened." In all the discussions he had heard at Potsdam, McCloy confided to his diary, "there was no clear evidence of an outstanding mind." This judgment stood for Truman as well. "He [Truman] always gives me the impression of too quick judgment," wrote McCloy, "a simple man, prone to make up his mind quickly and decisively, perhaps too quickly—a thorough American." But he was not a great President, "not distinguished at all. . . not Lincolnesque." [107]

There is no doubt that almost until the last moment senior American officials were aware of new Japanese efforts (post-Potsdam) to secure a negotiated peace. The recent discovery by Gar Alperovitz of an additional item in the diary of Walter Brown, Byrnes's special assistant, makes clear that on August 3rd, three days before the bombing of Hiroshima, a new report was received by the President as he crossed the Atlantic. Brown describes the following scene on the American ship *Augusta* after a rendezvous with the British vessel *Renown:* "Aboard *Augusta*—President, Leahy, JFB agreed Japs looking for peace. (Leahy had another report from Pacific.) President afraid they will sue for peace through Russia instead of some country like Sweden. JFB and Truman chide Leahy not to hold out news on atomic bomb. Leahy still doubtful. This was the subject of much conversation at the luncheon aboard the *Renown*." [108] The relevant excerpt of the Brown diary is reprinted in the document section of this volume.

As the years passed, McCloy questioned the morality of the Hiroshima decision. "I feel very strongly that if we had found a way to have a politically negotiated surrender, and had not dropped the bomb, we would today be in a stronger position morally," he said in a 1984 interview with an editor of this volume. "We should have given the Japanese a warning at least of what we had—in the postwar world it would have made an enormous difference." [109]

Following Japan's *conditional* surrender and American acceptance of a constitutional monarchy (precisely the position Grew had advocated to Truman in May 1945), McCloy visited Japan and flew over what remained of Hiroshima. One of his colleagues traveling with him described the scene: "We looked out and then gasped. . . [Hiroshima was] so flattened that nothing was left except red dust which lay feet deep. The color recalled Pompeii; the completeness of the ruin brought to mind the ancient prophecy that not one stone should be left standing on another. We were appalled and physically were sickened." [110] When invited to conduct an on-site inspection of the city, McCloy declined. Untouched by bogus rationales, McCloy, much better than others, understood how it had happened—a badly mishandled decision by two or three men among whom "there was no clear evidence of an outstanding mind." [111]

—V—

A YEAR AFTER THE BOMBS WERE DROPPED, Albert Einstein told a British newspaper that the decision to use the atomic bomb "was precipitated by a desire to end the war in the Pacific by any means before Russia's participation. I am sure that if President Roosevelt had still been there, none of that would have been possible." [112] During a discussion with Vannevar Bush, an advocate of making use of the bomb, Roosevelt, seven months before his death, had "raised the question of whether [the bomb] should actually be used against the Japanese or whether it should be used only as a threat with full-scale experimentation in this country." [113] Alexander Sachs, a Roosevelt adviser, similarly claimed that only a few months before his death in April 1945, Roosevelt told Sachs that he thought "a warning should be given before using the bomb and that it should be dropped on an area from which humans and animals were evacuated." [114]

Clearly, it is impossible to know what Roosevelt would have done had he lived another four months. The achievement of a diplomatic alternative required modest insight, a modicum of skilled diplomacy, and a determined commitment to answer and logically pursue Japanese requests for a clarification of surrender terms. Invariably, the question regarding whether or not an "alternative" to a nuclear weapon existed has been posed incorrectly. The *choice to use* a nuclear weapon negated existing alternatives. As has been demonstrated, the notion that a genuine alternative did not exist as a realistic possibility is factually inaccurate. Certainly, a negotiated surrender could not have been realized without having been seriously attempted. The choice *to use* was a choice *not* to seriously pursue a negotiated surrender.

Those who take refuge in the notion that sheer momentum swept the decision makers like a torrent down a river canyon need to be reminded that a choice between alternatives was actually exercised. Ineptly, almost casually, the fateful and final decision was taken that entailed executing a 180-degree turn away from a negotiated surrender. "[T]here is no doubt," writes Gar Alperovitz, "that it [the decision] was. . . an *active* choice." [115] Martin Sherwin insists that the "choice in the summer of 1945 was not between a conventional invasion or nuclear war. It was a choice between various forms of diplomacy and warfare. . . .While the decision that Truman made is understandable, it was not inevitable. It was even avoidable." [116] Would Roosevelt have chosen a different path at Potsdam? While it is easy to dismiss such a question as being purely speculative and impossible to answer, it remains useful to note where FDR did differ from Truman.

In this context, Alperovitz insists that one key factor would have been very different at Potsdam had Roosevelt lived until the summer of 1945:

> When Truman and Byrnes cut the critical assurances to the Emperor out of paragraph 12 of the draft Potsdam Proclamation, they did so against the recommendation of virtually the entire top American and British leadership. Truman and Byrnes had to reverse the thrust of a near-unanimous judgment that the terms should be clarified. Truman's journal also indicates that he understood that the proclamation in final form—without the key passage—was not likely to be accepted by Japan. If the Soviet option for ending the war was shelved for political/diplomatic reasons—and if the political reasons for not modifying the surrender formula no longer looked solid—is there any other explanation for why the Japanese were not told their Emperor would not be harmed, that he could stay on the throne in some innocuous position like that of the king of England?

> . . . [I]f anything the record suggests that he [Roosevelt] had considerable doubts about attacking a city. . . FDR's general approach to the Soviet Union also was both more subtle and more oriented to cooperation—and it is reasonable to assume that arguments against surprising and thereby indirectly threatening the Soviet ally might well have been more favorably received. The most important point...is the most obvious: *Had Roosevelt lived, James F. Byrnes would not have become Secretary of State.* Since by the time of Potsdam all of Roosevelt's civilian and military advisers (with Churchill) favored a clarification of the surrender terms—and since only Byrnes stood strongly in the way of the recommended policy—there is a reasonable likelihood that the assurances in paragraph 12 of the Potsdam Proclamation would not have been eliminated (and that the assurances it contained would have triggered the surrender process). [117]

The last foundation stone of the Hiroshima legend, namely the claim that no possible alternative existed to securing Japan's surrender other than a costly invasion or the use of nuclear weapons, is a belief without basis in the historical realities of the time. Indeed, the entire legend that has so persuasively gripped the American mind for over half a century is essentially a totem of bogus notions. The claim that an invasion of the Japanese home islands was necessary without the use of the atomic bomb is untrue. The claim that an "atomic warning" was given to the populace of Hiroshima and Nagasaki is untrue. And the claim that both cities were key military targets is untrue. Yet, the mythology of Hiroshima would have us believe otherwise.

Why do people and countries deceive themselves and deny what is in their past? This volume begins with a quotation from one of our contributors, the Japanese writer, Kenzaburo Oé, winner of the Nobel Prize for literature. In an essay entitled "On Human Dignity," Oé tells the story of a young man born in Hiroshima on the day the atomic bomb was dropped. During the Tokyo Olympic Games he was selected as the last runner to carry the Olympic flame. Oé recalls how an American journalist who knew Japanese and had translated Japanese literature and thus "might be expected to understand Japan" had objected to the selection of this young man "because it reminded the Americans of the atomic bomb." The American journalist, noted Oé, "preferred to erase all traces of Hiroshima from the American memory. Worse still, this preference occurs not only to the American mind. *Do not all leaders and peoples who at present possess nuclear weapons also wish to erase Hiroshima from their memories?*" [118]

In preparing this volume for publication we were reminded on several occasions that Hiroshima still evokes an instinct for denial. Although we had obtained permission to reprint Felix Morley's "The Return To Nothingness" from members of his family, we also approached the conservative journal *Human Events*, where the article had first appeared. Morley, a former editor at *The Washington Post*, had been a founding editor of *Human Events*. In a letter responding to our request, Thomas Winter, the journal's current editor, granted us permission to use both Felix Morley's article and Norman Thomas's "When Cruelty Becomes Pleasurable." "For the record," Winter wrote, "let it be noted that these articles represented the views of Mr. Thomas and Mr. Morley, not the views of *Human Events*—then or now." [119]

Having reviewed our table of contents for this volume Thomas Winter declared that this book—*Hiroshima's Shadow*—addressed the issue from "a leftist perspective." Winter was apparently indifferent to the rich legacy in both the conservative and liberal traditions where important voices forcefully condemned the atomic attacks. Indeed, Uday Mohan and Sanho Tree make this point very clearly in their contribution to this volume. "In the 1950s," they write, "challenges to the 'orthodox' view came from the right wing in publications like *National Review, The Freeman, and Human Events.*" [120] Together with such political figures as Dwight Eisenhower, Herbert Hoover, Henry Luce, John Foster Dulles, and George Kennan, these conservative publications took critical positions against the bombings.

Those who justify the bombings of Hiroshima and Nagasaki often go to great lengths to distance themselves from certain unsettling facts. How else can one explain Winter's declaration that Felix Morley's views were not the views of *Human Events* in 1945? When we showed Winter's letter to Felix Morley's son and grandson, both men were bemused. Jefferson Morley, now, like his grandfather before him, an editor at the *Washington Post*, told us:

> It is absolutely ridiculous to claim that my grandfather's opinion about Hiroshima was not the viewpoint of the editors of *Human Events*. My grandfather *was* Mr. *Human Events*. He was one of the magazine's founding editors. The rather ungrateful Mr. Winters would not have his job today if it weren't for Felix Morley. My grandfather, moreover, was as far from a "leftist perspective" as you can get. He was an economic libertarian and social traditionalist whose worldly philosophy was imbued with a family heritage of Quakerism. He saw no inconsistency in being both a conservative and also condemning the atomic bombings. In August 1945 he wrote, "Pearl Harbor was an indefensible and infamous act of aggression. But Hiroshima was an equally atrocious act of revenge." He observed that thousands of children attending Hiroshima's thirty-three schools were incinerated or crushed by collapsing buildings that day.
>
> "It was pure accident," he noted, "if a single person slain at Hiroshima had personal responsibility for the Pearl Harbor outrage." Writing just weeks after the bombing he already had occasion to lament the "miserable farce" of apologists who try "to reconcile mass murder of 'enemy children' with lip service to the doctrine that God created all men in his image." My grandfather would not be surprised that more than half a century later such views remain anathema to the custodians of the conventional wisdom in Washington. Although my grandfather wrote thousands of articles in his life and won a Pulitzer Prize for his *Post* editorials, it was his piece on Hiroshima, "The Return to Nothingness," published in *Human Events* in August 1945, of which he was most proud. [121]

Hiroshima was a man-made cataclysm. Thus, it may only be understandable human behavior when many otherwise intelligent and thoughtful people react by a willful desire "to erase Hiroshima from their memories." In the spring of 1995 a group of American historians approached the editors of the *Washington Post* and asked for a meeting to discuss the *Post*'s coverage of the Smithsonian controversy. "We are well aware that any piece of good reporting may necessarily involve subjective opinion. Reporters must make judgments all the time about how to tell a story. They also must weigh the reliability of their sources," wrote the co-chairs of the Historians Committee for Open Debate on Hiroshima. "But distortion is evident when a reader detects a consistent pattern in which certain sources are disparaged, ignored and otherwise distorted, and in which other sources to a controversy are repeatedly given a platform on which to frame the debate. This is what happened with the *Post*'s coverage of the *Enola Gay* controversy."

The editors and publisher of the *Post* refused to meet the Historians Committee—a group that included some of the most prominent historians of the Second World War. [122] In a letter that dismissed a carefully prepared and detailed critique of the *Post*'s coverage, Donald Graham, the publisher of *Washington Post*, wrote, "You appear to be propagandists who wish the *Post* would take your side." The committee's membership included John Dower of MIT, Stanley Hoffmann of Harvard, Gaddis Smith of Yale, Noam Chomsky of MIT, James Hershberg who is Director of the Wilson Center's Cold War History Project, Walter LaFeber of Cornell, Martin Sherwin of Tufts, Barton Bernstein of Stanford, and virtually all the historians who are contributors to this volume. The Historians Committee replied, "in the interest of civil discourse, we can only respond that in a face-to-face meeting you might discover that the last place to look for propaganda is in a roomful of historians." [123] Nevertheless, Graham and his editors declined to meet.

Ironically, Donald Graham appeared to lack any institutional memory regarding the *Washington Post*'s own position prior to the bombings of Hiroshima. Graham's grandfather, Eugene Meyer, was the publisher of the *Post* in the spring of 1945. Meyer played an important role in advancing the views of the group within the Truman administration who sought to clarify the "unconditional surrender" formulation, which in the opinion of Grew, Stimson, McCloy, and others remained an obstacle to an early and complete surrender by the Japanese. Less than a month after Roosevelt's death, the *Post* published on May 9, 1945, an editorial entitled "Now Japan."

> The impact on Japan of the unconditional surrender of Germany will be considerable. In following up the blow, political warfare should now be employed to the fullest extent. Specifically, Japan should be told her fate immediately so that she may be encouraged to throw in the sponge....What we are suggesting, to be sure, is conditional surrender. What of it? Unconditional surrender was never an ideal formula....The war in the Pacific is an Anglo-American affair, with the Americans doing the lion's share. It would not be difficult to get agreement on terms for Japan; in fact, agreement could be got overnight, so that the Japanese could be told without delay. We urge, therefore, that the task of compiling the terms for Japan and informing the Japanese of them should not be delayed....We must expand upon the Cairo agreement, which is the nucleus of peace with Japan, and spell out what we require of Japan as a condition of surrender....It is not a hard peace that we are interested in. It is an effective peace. In our view this means a Japan where, at the end of the road, we shall not find utter chaos, as we are finding in Ger-

many, but a going concern with a native administration still in operation within Japan. [124]

Ten days later the *Post* published an editorial entitled "Conditional Surrender":

> On May 9 an editorial on this page suggested that if full victory in
> the Far East and full realization of our war aims in the Pacific can be
> obtained by something short of the utter destruction of Japan, it
> would be the part of wisdom to obtain them by that method. This,
> as we admitted, was equivalent to suggesting conditional rather than
> unconditional surrender for the Japanese....We had suggested noth-
> ing more nor less than the destruction of Japanese militarism at the
> lowest possible cost in American lives....Washington grapevine
> reports to the effect that they are all but prepared to accept almost
> any terms that will permit them a continued national existence may
> or may not be well founded. But in any event the collapse of the mil-
> itarists who are responsible for the war in the Pacific is likely to be
> hastened by letting the Japanese people know the precise terms of
> the Allies in the Pacific. The important thing to remember is that in
> the Pacific, as indeed was the case in Germany, we are waging war
> not for its own sake but as the means to an end....To insist that a war
> be continued, after its purposes have been realized, is to make an end
> of the means, to make war for its own sake. This is militarism pure
> and simple, and it is a dangerous inversion of the racist superstition
> to suppose that only the Germans and the Japanese are biologically
> capable of militarism. [125]

After the war ended, Eugene Meyer published a pamphlet containing the
whole series of Post editorials that ran in the spring and early summer of 1945
arguing on behalf of conditional surrender. Meyer titled the pamphlet, *Psychological Warfare Against Japan: The Story of the Secret Weapon Which Had Japan Ready to
Yield Thirteen Days Before the Atomic Bomb Struck Hiroshima*. A short preface
revealed the *Post's* discreet links to the psychological warfare effort headed by
Captain Ellis Zacharias of the U.S. Navy. As part of an intelligence group located
in the Navy's Office of War Information, Zacharias had responsibility for directing Japanese language broadcasts to Japan's home islands. He was designated an
"official spokesman" for the American government and his broadcasts were considered to be an authoritative channel.

Throughout the spring and summer of 1945, Zacharias's broadcasts sought to
convince the Japanese political elite and the country's population as a whole that
the unconditional surrender of Japanese military forces would not mean the end of
the Japanese nation. The message to the Japanese—which Meyer's editorials in the
Washington Post effectively highlighted as authoritative—was that a reasonable surrender based on the Atlantic Charter was well within reach. Zacharias, like others,
did not anticipate that Secretary of State Byrnes would undermine and ultimately
manage to derail the effort to clarify the surrender terms with an assurance regarding the Emperor. (Zacharias would later bitterly condemn the way the Potsdam
Declaration was phrased and how its presentation was badly mishandled, saying it
"wrecked everything we had been working for. . . .")[126] Regardless of Byrnes's

untimely wrecking ball, Eugene Meyer was especially proud of the *Post*'s role as a newspaper during this period. The war, of course, ended shortly after Hiroshima and Nagasaki were bombed, but Meyer and his editors at the *Washington Post*—who knew nothing about the existence of the atomic bomb—clearly believed in the spring and summer of 1945 that the Pacific war might end without an invasion of the Japanese home islands. At the time, of course, they had yet to be "educated" in the legend of Hiroshima.

A half-century later, the reporters, editors, and publisher of the *Washington Post* would vilify, denigrate, and caricature historians and journalists who sought to make precisely the same point the *Post* had made in 1945. In an unsigned editorial, the *Post* stigmatized these critics as "narrow-minded representatives of a special-interest," a "ragtag collection of academics," "revisionists," "left-wing ideologues," "zealots"—and in Donald Graham's ultimately insulting phrase—"propagandists."[127] When Graham was sent a photocopy of the pamphlet his grandfather, Eugene Meyer, had published in 1946 under his own name and the *Washington Post*'s imprint, Graham replied with the silence of those who prefer, as Kenzaburo Oé writes, "to erase all traces of Hiroshima from the American memory."

With publications like the *Washington Post* and *Human Events* setting the tone, America's politicians jumped into the debate over the *Enola Gay* exhibit with memories that were equally selective. Newt Gingrich, the newly elected Speaker of the House of Representatives, said that he had found "a certain political correctness seeping in and distorting and prejudicing the Smithsonian's exhibits." Gingrich declared that the Smithsonian would not be permitted to become "a plaything for left-wing ideologies." A close associate of Gingrich on the Smithsonian's Board of Regents, Congressman Sam Johnson, indicated that his purpose was "to get patriotism back into the Smithsonian."[128] Republican Representative Peter Blute and twenty-three other House members condemned the museum for proposing an "anti-American" exhibit. Like the editors at the *Washington Post* and *Human Events*, Gingrich, Johnson, and Blute demonstrated an ignorance of their own party's history.

No modern Republican would acknowledge the fact that in the spring of 1945 Republican leaders were publicly and privately asking Truman to define precise and reasonable terms of surrender in order to achieve an early end to the Pacific war. The *New York Times* reported on July 3, 1945, "Senator [William] White of Maine, the minority [Republican] leader, declared that the Pacific war might end quickly if President Truman would state, specifically, in the upper chamber just what unconditional surrender means for the Japanese." White's statement was echoed on the same day by Senator Homer Capehart of Indiana who told a press conference, "It isn't a matter of whether you hate the Japs or not. I certainly hate them. But what's to be gained by continuing a war when it can be settled now on the same terms as two years from now?"[129] Uday Mohan and Sanho Tree note in their essay that the *New York Times* also reported on July 24, 1945, that "Republican Senator Kenneth S. Wherry had announced that 'a high military source' had passed on a letter to Truman asking that Truman stop the 'slaughter' in the Pacific by clarifying terms for Japan."

Wherry went on to claim that "his source had compiled a list of Japanese peace feelers and on that basis had suggested that the Japanese be allowed to keep their Emperor." In late May and early June 1945, former President Herbert Hoover wrote Truman a private memo listing all the factors that favored an early surrender. Furthermore, Hoover endorsed the notion of clarifying the surrender terms in order to make it clear that "the Allies have no desire to destroy either the Japanese people or their government, or to interference [sic] in the Japanese way of life." After meeting with Truman, Hoover conveyed these same views to a number of ranking Republican senators. [30]*

To a Republican leadership of the 1990s imbued, like many of their Democratic colleagues, with an ideology that regards nuclear weapons as "acceptable" and their first use as "justifiable," inconvenient facts about their own party's early "revisionist" and "politically incorrect" ideas were simply not to be mentioned. The contradictions between positions held in 1945 and the jingoistic posturing of 1995 were transparent for anyone who took the trouble to look. Of course, the preference in both major parties was to forget and deny. Faced with the prospect that millions of Americans might be exposed to a troubling historical narrative, the country's political leadership insisted that a publicly funded national museum had to be selective about the kind of history that its citizens would be permitted to see. The logical solution was simply to impose censorship on the Smithsonian.

The editor of *Human Events* denies that the views on Hiroshima of the founding editor of his journal ever reflected the standpoint of the magazine. The publisher of *Washington Post* calls historians "propagandists" for seeking some acknowledgment in the paper's coverage of views that the *Post* itself and the grandfather of the publisher once held. The leadership of the Republican Party denounced the Smithsonian for an historical exhibit that brought to light facts about the bombing of Hiroshima that leading Republicans in the late 1940s argued were true. This is more than bizarre behavior. It is a perilous illness at the heart of a society—an expression of a country gripped by a pathology of denial.

---

* In May 1949 at Secretary of Navy James Forrestal's funeral, Ralph Bard was approached by former President Herbert Hoover, a Republican. According to Bard, "Herbert Hoover came over to talk to me and said as a student of American history he wanted me to know how important he thought my recommendation had been, and how sorry he was it had not received the approval of the [Interim Committee]. He felt it would have been a great thing for this country if my advice had been followed." Bard, Under Secretary of the Navy and the Navy's representative on the Interim Committee, had dissented from use of the atomic bomb against Japan without a clear warning being given and explicit assurances regarding the Emperor's future position. Hoover, in a letter to John O'Laughlin, publisher of the *Army and Navy Journal*, declared that "the use of the atomic bomb, with its indiscriminate killing of women and children, revolts my soul." These were not facts the Republican leadership of the 1990s cared to acknowledge regarding the atomic bomb and eminent predecessors in the party. (See Gar Alperovitz, *The Decision to Use the Atomic Bomb* [New York, 1995], pp. 225, 391 & 459.)

Notes

For a detailed publication history of all the works cited in this introduction, and reprinted in *Hiroshima's Shadow*, see the Acknowledgements section.

1. Murray Sayle, "Did the Bomb End the War?," *Hiroshima's Shadow*, pp. 24-26.
2. Mike Wallace, "The Battle of the Enola Gay," *Hiroshima's Shadow*, p. 320.
3. Dwight D. Eisenhower, *Mandate For Change* (Garden City, 1963), pp. 312-313.
4. William Leahy, *I Was There: The Personal Story of the Chief of Staff to Presidents Roosevelt and Truman* (New York, 1950), p. 441.
5. Martin Sherwin, "Memory, Myth and History," *Hiroshima's Shadow*, p. 350. [Italics in original.]
6. John J. McCloy, "The McCloy Diary: Restrict First Use to Military Target," *Hiroshima's Shadow*, p. 511.
7. Ted Morgan, *FDR: A Biography* (New York, 1985), p. 618.
8. John Rawls, "Fifty Years After Hiroshima," *Hiroshima's Shadow*, p. 477.
9. Mark Selden, "The Logic of Mass Destruction," *Hiroshima's Shadow*, pp. 52, 53, 58.
10. John J. McCloy, "The McCloy Diary: General Marshall Argues Restrict First Use to Military Target," *Hiroshima's Shadow*, p. 511.
11. William Lanouette, "Note on the July 17th Petition," *Hiroshima's Shadow*, p. 559.
12. John J. McCloy, "The McCloy Diary: Warning, Surrender and Truman's 'Big Red Apple,'" *Hiroshima's Shadow*, p. 541.
13. Stephen Rosenfeld, "The Revisionists' Agenda," *Hiroshima's Shadow*, pp. 406-408. [Emphasis added.]
14. "Atomic Warfare and the Christian Faith," *Hiroshima's Shadow*, pp. 488-99.
15. James Martin Gillis, "Nothing but Nihilism," *Hiroshima's Shadow*, p. 277.
16. Editors of *Commonweal*, "The Horror and the Shame," *Hiroshima's Shadow*, p. 238.
17. Admiral Nimitz told his biographer, "It [the atomic bomb] is [an] indiscriminate killer and I am hopeful that it will be dropped as an inefficient weapon. Poison gas and bacteriological weapons are in the same category." See Gar Alperovitz, *The Decision to Use the Atomic Bomb* (New York, 1995), p. 330.
18. Richard Hofstadter, *Anti-Intellectualism in American Life* (New York, 1962), p. 6.
19. The reference to "bias" and "anti-American prejudice" can be found in correspondence from Congressman Peter Blute to the Secretary of the Smithsonian, Robert McCormick Adams, August 10, 1994. The letter was signed by twenty-four Members of the House of Representatives.
20. "History Upheld" by Herman G. Harrington, *The American Legion Magazine*, August 1995.
21. Martin Harwit, *An Exhibit Denied: Lobbying the History of Enola Gay* (New York, 1996), pp. 31-33. [Emphasis added.]
22. Harwit, *An Exhibit Denied*, pp. 31-32.
23. For a description of Heyman's abrupt demand for Harwit's resignation see Harwit's account in *An Exhibit Denied*, pp. 419-425.
24. Charlton Heston, Letter to the Editor, 'An Exhibit Denied,' *The New York Times Book Review*, December 7, 1997, p. 4.
25. John Dower, "How a Genuine Democracy Should Celebrate Its Past," *Hiroshima's Shadow*, p. 378.
26. Joel Achenbach, "*Enola Gay* Exhibit: Plane and Simple" *The Washington Post*, June 28, 1995, p. A1; Kai Bird and Lawrence Lifschultz, "Hiroshima's Shadow," *The Chicago Tribune*, August 13, 1996. Over the next year, an estimated 1.3 million visitors viewed the censored version of the *Enola Gay* exhibit.
27. Hofstadter, p. 7.
28. Robert Jay Lifton and Greg Mitchell, *Hiroshima in America*, (New York, 1995), pp. xiv, 338.
29. John Dower, "How a Genuine Democracy Should Celebrate Its Past," *Hiroshima's Shadow*, p. 377.
30. Lifton and Mitchell, p. 287.
31. Lyric Wallwork Winik, "A Voice of His Own," *The Washingtonian*, July 1995, p. 127.
32. *This Week with David Brinkley*, ABC Television, August 28, 1994, cited in Robert Jay Lifton and Greg Mitchell, *Hiroshima in America*, p. 287.
33. Daniel Jonah Goldhagen, *Hitler's Willing Executioners: Ordinary Germans and the Holocaust* (New York, 1997) p. 463. "The Afterword" in the 1997 Vintage edition should be consulted regarding *Vermeidungsdiskurs*.

34. Elliot Negin, "How the Bomb Was Spun," *Washington City Paper*, August 18, 1995.

35. Ken Ringle, "History Through a Mushroom Cloud" *The Washington Post*, July 27, 1995.

36. William Greider, "Irreconcilable Conflicts," *The Washington Post*, August 12, 1995.

37. Gallup Organization, File I.D. Gallup 94-N28-025, December 1994, Poll commissioned by *Cable News Network* and *USA Today*.

38. J. Samuel Walker, *Prompt and Utter Destruction: Truman and the Use of Atomic Bombs Against Japan* (Chapel Hill, N.C., 1997), pp. 105-106.

39. Barton J. Bernstein, "Seizing the Contested Terrain of Early Nuclear History," *Hiroshima's Shadow*, p. 163; James Hershberg, *James B. Conant: Harvard to Hiroshima and the Making of the Nuclear Age* (New York, 1993).

40. Barton J. Bernstein, "Understanding the Atomic Bomb and the Japanese Surrender," *Diplomatic History*, Spring 1995, p. 235.

41. Marilyn Young, *The American Historical Review*, Vol. 100, Number 5, December 1995, pp. 1515-1516.

42. Bernstein, "Understanding the Atomic Bomb," p. 254.

43. Herbert P. Bix, "Japan's Delayed Surrender: A Reinterpretation," *Diplomatic History*, Vol. 19, Number 2, Spring 1995, p. 223.

44. Bix, p. 223.

45. Robert P. Newman, *Truman and the Hiroshima Cult* (East Lansing, 1995); Robert James Maddox, *Weapons for Victory: The Hiroshima Decision Fifty Years Later* (Columbia, Mo., 1995); Thomas B. Allen and Norman Polmar, *Code-Name Downfall: The Secret Plan to Invade Japan and Why Truman Dropped the Bomb* (New York, 1995); Robert H. Ferrell, *Harry S. Truman: A Life* (Columbia, Mo., 1994); Alonzo L. Hamby, *Man of the People: A Life of Harry S. Truman* (New York, 1995); Edward J. Drea, *MacArthur's Ultra: Codebreaking and the War Against Japan, 1942-1945* (Lawrence, Kansas, 1992); Alonzo L. Hamby, untitled review essay, *Journal of American History*, Vol. 84, September 1997, pp. 609-614.

46. All page references are to *Hiroshima's Shadow*: Robert Newman, "What New Consensus?," pp. 390-393; Paul Fussell, "Thank God for the Atomic Bomb," pp. 211-222; Charles Krauthammer, "World War II, Revised Or, How We Bombed Japan Out of Racism and Spite," pp. 385-387; Jonathan Yardley, "Dropping a Bomb of an Idea," pp. 396-398; Edwin Yoder, Jr., "...Or Hiroshima 'Cult'?," pp. 401-402; Albert Hunt, "Truman Was Right in 1945," pp. 403-404; Stephen Rosenfeld, "The Revisionist's Agenda," pp. 406-408.

47. "Eric Hobsbawn: An Interview," Edited by MARHO, *Vision's of History* (New York, 1984), p. 32.

48. E.H. Carr, *What is History?* (Harmondsworth, 1982), p. 87.

49. Harwit, p. 229.

50. Lifton and Mitchell, p. 307.

51. Barton Bernstein, "A Postwar Myth: 500,000 U.S. Lives Saved," *Hiroshima's Shadow*, pp. 130-134; Adam Goodheart, "The Invasion That Never Was," *Hiroshima's Shadow*, pp. 135-40.

52. Goodheart, p. 139.

53. *The New York Times*, December 6, 1991.

54. Goodheart, p. 139.

55. Bernstein, "A Postwar Myth," p. 131.

56. For a contrary view see D.M. Giangreco, "Casualty Projections for the U.S. Invasions of Japan, 1945-1946: Planning and Policy Implications," *Journal of Military History*, 61, July 1997, pp. 521-581. Giangreco argues that Truman had received, prior to Hiroshima, high level estimates of one million U.S. casualties for the projected invasions of Japan. In fact, in his sixty-one page article, Giangreco could not cite a single pre-Hiroshima, high-level archival source that firmly substantiates his contention.

57. Brian D. Smith, "Rewriting *Enola Gay's* History," *The American Legion*, November 1994, p. 26. [Emphasis added.]

58. Dwight MacDonald, "The Decline to Barbarism," *Hiroshima's Shadow*, p. 265.

59. John Rawls, "Fifty Years After Hiroshima," *Hiroshima's Shadow*, pp. 474-479. It may be noted that many so-called "democratic states" who have fought "undemocratic states" have consistently violated the rules of war in declared and undeclared military operations. This extends from acts committed during nineteenth and twentieth century colonial wars to post-colonial operations (such as the "saturation carpet-bombing" of the Laotian Plain of Jars by the U.S. Air Force during the Third Indochina War.)

Furthermore, major violations of the Geneva and Hague Laws on armed conflict also occurred in conflicts fought between "democratic states". The First World War is only the most obvious example.

Despite the absence of a formal convention against chemical and poison weapons in 1914, the Hague Convention of 1899, and the Convention's unanimous adoption of the Martens Clause, declared that "the right of belligerents to adopt means of injuring the enemy is not unlimited."

60. *"Enola Gay* Revised," Letter by William P. Jones, July 18, 1995.

61. An abridged version of Sanho Tree's letter appeared in *The Washington Post* of August 7, 1995 under the title "After the Fact at Hiroshima." He was identified by the *Post* as Research Director for the Historians' Committee for Open Debate on Hiroshima. We have provided the full text of Tree's letter concerning the question of the atomic warning leaflets. The sections of the letter which addressed other issues has not been reproduced.

62. "The Stimson Memo: Prior Warning With 'Ample Time'," *Hiroshima's Shadow*, pp. 526-530.

63. Richard Rhodes, *The Making of the Atomic Bomb* (New York, 1986), p. 647.

64. Rhodes, p. 648.

65. "The Stimson Memo: Prior Warning with 'Ample Time'," *Hiroshima's Shadow*, pp. 526-30.

66. Rhodes, pp. 647-648.

67. Rhodes, p. 648.

68. *Hiroshima and Nagasaki: The Physical, Medical and Social Effects of the Atomic Bombings by the Committee for the Compilation of Materials on Damage Caused by the Atomic Bombs in Hiroshima and Nagasaki* (Tokyo, 1981), p. 367.

69 Thomas Powers, "Was It Right?," *Atlantic Monthly*, July 1995, p. 367.

70. Interview with McGeorge Bundy in "Hiroshima: Why the Bomb Was Dropped," Peter Jennings Reports/ABC News, July 27, 1995.

71. McGeorge Bundy, *Danger and Survival: Choices About the Bomb in the First Fifty Years* (New York, 1988), p. 80.

72. John Burroughs, *The Legality of the Threat or Use of Nuclear Weapons: A Guide to the Historic Opinion of the International Court of Justice* (Amsterdam: International Association of Lawyers Against Nuclear Arms, 1997). See also the discussion of the World Court's advisory opinion in the Epilogue of *Hiroshima's Shadow*.

73. McCloy to Stimson, May 28, 1945, Box WD 1, Folder 29, John J. McCloy Papers, Amherst College, Amherst, Mass.. Kai Bird, *The Chairman: John J. McCloy, The Making of the American Establishment* (New York, 1992), p. 243.

74. Charles S. Cheston, Acting Director, OSS, to President, May 31, 1945, Confidential Files, Harry S. Truman Library; Stimson diary, June 1, 1945, Library of Congress.

75. The Grew Memo, May 28, 1945, *Hiroshima's Shadow*, p. 505.

76. John J. McCloy, *The Challenge to American Foreign Policy* (Cambridge, 1953), p. 246; Gar Alperovitz, Atomic Diplomacy: Hiroshima and Potsdam (New York, 1965), p. 159; Bird, p. 246.

77. Gar Alperovitz, *The Decision To Use The Atomic Bomb* (New York, 1995), pp. 68-69; Bird, pp. 245-247.

78. Kai Bird, *The Chairman: John J. McCloy, the Making of the American Establishment* (New York, 1992), p. 246. Portions of this introductory essay, particularly the discussion of the preparations for the Potsdam Conference and the summit itself, are taken from Bird's biography of McCloy.

79. Alperovitz, *The Decision*, pp. 68-69.

80. "The Forrestal Diary: McCloy's Dissent on the Emperor and Prior Warning," *Hiroshima's Shadow*, p. 537.

81. Bird, p. 246. McCloy recalled that he went to see Byrnes, who was then working in the White House, and pitched the idea to him. But Byrnes dismissed the idea without explanation. "He said," recalled McCloy, "my proposal was not possible." McCloy left with the impression that Byrnes was angry about not having been invited to the meeting. (Kai Bird interview with McCloy, September 14, 1984.)

82. Leo Szilard, "A Personal History of the Atomic Bomb," University of Chicago Roundtable, No. 601, (September 25, 1949), pp. 14-15.

83. Bird, p. 247.

84. Bird, pp. 247-248; The polling data is cited by Alonzo L. Hamby in his review-essay, *The Journal of American History*, September 1997, p. 611.

85. Harry S. Truman, *Year of Decisions*, p. 87.

86. "The Magic Intercepts: Japanese Terms for Conditional Surrender," *Hiroshima's Shadow*, pp. 523-525. To be sure, other cables indicate that Togo was moving slowly and clumsily toward the difficult task of providing his emissaries with the kind of concrete surrender terms necessary to end the war. But it is nevertheless clear from Truman's own diary that even he read these cables as evidence that the Japanese were ready to "fold up" in a matter of weeks. [Truman diary, July 18, 1945]

87. McCloy diary, July 16/17 and July 23, 1945, DY Box 1, Folder 18, John J. McCloy Papers, Amherst College.

88. William Lanouette, "Three Attempts to Stop the Bomb," *Hiroshima's Shadow*, p. 104.

89. The most well known use of this phrase is attached to Gar Alperovitz's 1965 study, *Atomic Diplomacy*.

90. James F. Byrnes interview with Fred Freed for NBC Television, "The Decision to Use the Atomic Bomb," 1965, Herbert Feis Papers, Box 79, Manuscript Division, Library of Congress.

91. Robert A. Pape, "Why Japan Surrendered," *International Security* 18 (Fall 1993), pp. 178-79.

92. Alperovitz, *The Decision*, p. 266.

93. Bird, p. 695

94. Joseph Rotblat, "A Social Conscience for a Nuclear Age," *Hiroshima's Shadow*, p. xxii. See also Joseph Rotblat, "Leaving the Bomb Project," *Hiroshima's Shadow*, pp. 255-256; Joseph Albright and Marcia Kunstel, Bombshell: *The Secret Story of America's Unknown Atomic Spy Conspiracy* (New York, 1997), pp. 86-87, 100-103.

95. Spencer Weart and Gertrude Weiss Szilard, eds., *Leo Szilard: His Version of the Facts* (Cambridge, 1978), p. 184; William Lanouette, "Three Attempts to Stop the Bomb," *Hiroshima's Shadow*, p. 104.

96. Allen Dulles OSS cable, quoted in Alperovitz, *The Decision*, p. 27.

97. "Magic" Diplomatic Summary #121S, *Hiroshima's Shadow*, p. 524.

98. Bird, p. 257. Some historians interpret these Japanese intercepts less charitably. One of Truman's biographers, Alonzo L. Hamby, writes, "Just possibly, Truman and other American policy makers who read this and similar exchanges might have taken them as signals to offer some concessions, but it seems more plausible to read them as indications that Japan was determined to fight fanatically on to a bloody end." [Untitled review article, *Journal of American History*, September 1997, p. 611.]

99. Robert G. Albion and Robert H. Connery, *Forrestal and the Navy* (New York, 1962), pp. 176-77.

100. Alice K. Smith, "Behind The Decision to Use the Atomic Bomb," *Bulletin of the Atomic Scientists*, October 1958, p. 297.

101. "The Forrestal Diary: Japanese Peace Feelers," *Hiroshima's Shadow*, pp. 518-520; Bird, p. 257 and p. 696 (endnote # 89).

102. Herbert Bix describes the relevant terms and conditions issued at Potsdam as follows: "The Potsdam Declaration was issued on 26 July 1945 in the form of an ultimatum aimed at hastening Japan's surrender. The Japanese government was informed that if it fulfilled certain unilateral obligations ("our terms"), which the victorious powers would impose after the Japanese government had proclaimed 'the unconditional surrender of all Japanese armed forces' and furnished 'proper and adequate assurance of their good faith in such action.' Japan would then be allowed to retain its peace industries and resume participation in world trade on the basis of the principle of equal access to raw materials. 'The alternative for Japan,' the declaration concluded, 'is prompt and utter destruction.' Article 12 of the Declaration stated, 'The occupying forces of the Allies shall be withdrawn from Japan as soon as these objectives have been accomplished and there has been established in accordance with the freely expressed will of the Japanese people inclined and responsible government.' Deleted from this article was the phrase that Grew advised was necessary: "this may include a constitutional monarchy under the present dynasty." Consequently, the status of the Emperor was not guaranteed, and the policy of unconditional surrender remained intact." Herbert Bix, "Japan's Delayed Surrender," *Hiroshima in History and Memory*, edited by Michael J. Hogan (New York, 1996), pp. 90-91.

103. Townsend Hoopes and Douglas Brinkley, *Driven Patriot: The Life and Times of James Forrestal* (New York, 1992), p. 212.

104. "Ike on Ike," *Newsweek*, November 11, 1963, pp. 107-110.

105. This passage was eventually deleted from the published version of Stimson's memoirs. Bird, p. 697 (endnote #113). See the following correspondence: General George Marshall to McGeorge Bundy, Nov. 7, 1947; Nov. 19, 1947; McGeorge Bundy to George Kennan, Nov. 21, 1947; George Kennan to Bundy, Dec. 2, 1947; Bundy to Kennan, Dec. 4, 1947, Folder 17, Box 86, Marshall Papers, George C. Marshall Library, Lexington, Virginia.

106. "The Stimson Diary: The Soviets and the S-1 Master Card," *Hiroshima's Shadow*, pp. 549-550. [Emphasis added.]

107. Bird, pp. 256, 263.

108. "The Brown Diary: August 3rd Byrnes Acknowledges Japan 'Looking For Peace,' *Hiroshima's Shadow*, p. 546; Alperovitz, *The Decision*, p. 415. The original document can be found in

Walter Brown's diary, August 3, 1945, Folder 602, James F. Byrnes Papers, Clemson University Library, Clemson, South Carolina.

109. John J. McCloy interview with Kai Bird, September 14, 1984.

110. Bird, p. 264.

111. McCloy diary, July 28, 1945, DY Box 1, Folder 18, John J. McCloy Papers, Amherst College; Kai Bird, p. 256.

112. *Sunday Express* (London), August 18, 1946; *The New York Times*, August 19, 1946.

113. Alperovitz, *The Decision*, p. 661. Vannevar Bush to James Conant, September 23, 1944, Document 186, OSRD, S-1 Historical File, AEC Files, NA; reprinted in Michael Stoff, Jonathan Fanton and R. Hal Williams, eds., *The Manhattan Project* (Philadelphia, 1991), pp. 74-75. G. Pascal Zachary, *Endless Frontier: Vannevar Bush, Engineer of the American Century* (New York, 1997), pp. 213-217.

114. Alperovitz, *The Decision*, p. 662; Nat S. Finney, "How FDR Planned to Use the A-Bomb," *Look*, Vol. 14, No. 6 (March 14, 1950), pp. 23-27; John M. Blum, ed., *The Price of Vision*, pp. 499-500. On the other hand, in September 1944 at Hyde Park, Roosevelt signed a memorandum of understanding with Churchill stating that "when a 'bomb' is finally available, it might perhaps, after mature consideration, be used against the Japanese, who should be warned that this bombardment will be repeated until they surrender." Hyde Park Aide-Memoire, September 18, 1944, reprinted in Martin Sherwin, *A World Destroyed* (New York, 1975), p. 284.

115. Alperovitz, *The Decision*, p. 656.

116. Sherwin, p. xxiv.

117. Gar Alperovitz, "Historians Reassess: Did We Need To Drop The Bomb?," *Hiroshima's Shadow*, p. 14; Exact quote taken from Alperovitz, *The Decision*, pp. 662-663. [Emphasis in original.]

118. Kenzaburo Oé, *Hiroshima Notes* (London, 1995), pp. 108-109. [Emphasis added.]

119. Letter from Thomas S. Winter to Martha Cox, Editorial Department, The Pamphleteer's Press, Febuary 29, 1996.

120. Uday Mohan and Sanho Tree, "The Construction of Conventional Wisdom," *Hiroshima's Shadow*, p. 141.

121. Jefferson Morley interview with Lawrence Lifschultz, July 1997. See also letter to *The Washington Post* by Jefferson Morley, August 12, 1995.

122. Correspondence of Kai Bird and Martin Sherwin of the Historians Committee for Open Debate on Hiroshima with Donald Graham, Leonard Downie, Robert Kaiser, Karen DeYoung, Meg Greenfield and JoAnn Byrd of *The Washington Post* dated April 28, 1995; exchange and replies by Meg Greenfield, Editorial Page Editor to Bird and Sherwin, May 10, 1995; Donald Graham, Publisher, to Bird and Sherwin, undated; reply by Sherwin and Bird to Graham, May 24, 1995; Robert Kaiser, Managing Editor to Bird and Sherwin, June 14, 1995; reply from Bird to Kaiser, June 16, 1995; Kaiser to Bird, June 21, 1995.

123. Martin Sherwin and Kai Bird, Historian's Committee to Donald Graham, Publisher, *The Washington Post*, May 24, 1995.

124. Eugene Meyer, *Psychological Warfare Against Japan: The Story of the Secret Weapon Which Had Japan Ready to Yield Thirteen Days Before the Atomic Bomb Struck Hiroshima*, (*The Washington Post*, n.d.), pp. 9-10. The thirty-three page pamphlet is believed to have been published in 1946. Its cover page lists "Eugene Meyer—Editor and Publisher, *The Washington Post*" as the source of publication. A copy of "Psychological Warfare Against Japan" can be obtained from the Amherst College Archives in the John J. McCloy Papers.

125. Reprinted in Eugene Meyer, *Psychological Warfare Against Japan*, pp. 10-12.

126. Ellis M. Zacharias, "How We Bungled the Japanese Surrender," *Look* 14 (May 23, 1950), p. 21.

127. "The Smithsonian Changes Course," Editorial, *The Washington Post*, February 1, 1995, *Hiroshima's Shadow*, pp. 400-401; Elliot Negin, "How the Bomb Was Spun," *Washington City Paper*, August 18, 1995; Donald Graham letter to Kai Bird and Martin Sherwin, undated.

128. Mike Wallace, "The Battle of the Enola Gay," *Hiroshima's Shadow*, pp. 334-335.

129. *The Washington Post*, July 3, 1945. Cited by Alperovitz, *The Decision*, p. 228 and David Robertson, *Sly and Able: A Political Biography of James F. Byrnes* (New York, 1994), p. 415.

130. Uday Mohan and Sanho Tree, "The Construction of Conventional Wisdom," *Hiroshima's Shadow*, p. 148. Alperovitz, *The Decision*, pp. 43-44.

I

HIROSHIMA MYTHS VS. MODERN REALITY

During his [Secretary of War Henry Stimson's] recitation of the relevant facts, I had been conscious of a feeling of depression and so I voiced to him my grave misgivings: first, on the basis of my belief that Japan was already defeated and that dropping the bomb was completely unnecessary, and secondly, because I thought that our country should avoid shocking world opinion by the use of a weapon whose employment was, I thought, no longer mandatory as a measure to save American lives. It was my belief that Japan was, at that very moment, seeking some way to surrender with a minimum loss of "face." The Secretary was deeply perturbed by my attitude. . . .

General Dwight D. Eisenhower

It is my opinion that the use of this barbarous weapon at Hiroshima and Nagasaki was of no material assistance in our war against Japan. The Japanese were already defeated and ready to surrender. . . . My own feeling was that in being the first to use it, we had adopted an ethical standard common to the barbarians of the Dark Ages. I was not taught to make war in that fashion, and wars cannot be won by destroying women and children.

Fleet Admiral William D. Leahy
Chief of Staff to Presidents Roosevelt and Truman

HISTORIANS
REASSESS:
DID WE NEED
TO DROP
THE BOMB?

Gar Alperovitz

ASK THE AVERAGE PERSON why the United States exploded the atomic bomb over Hiroshima and Nagasaki and the answer will almost always be straightforward: "To save thousands of lives by making an invasion unnecessary at the end of World War II." American Broadcasting Corporation's correspondent Ted Koppel expressed such a view in a special broadcast a few years ago: "What happened over Japan . . . was human tragedy. . . . But what was planned to take place in the war between Japan and the United States would almost certainly have been an even greater tragedy." [1]

The only problem with this morally comforting explanation is that it is now known to be false. Any serious attempt to understand the depth of feeling the story of the atomic bomb still arouses must confront two critical realities. First, there is a rapidly expanding gap between what the expert scholarly community now knows and what the public has been taught. Second, a steady narrowing of the questions in dispute in the most sophisticated studies has sharpened some of the truly controversial issues in the historical debate.

Consider the following assessment:

> Careful scholarly treatment of the records and manuscripts opened over the past few years has greatly enhanced our understanding of why the Truman administration used atomic weapons against Japan. Experts continue to disagree on some issues, but critical questions have been answered. The consensus among scholars is that the bomb was not needed to avoid an invasion of Japan and to end the war within a relatively short time. *It is clear that alternatives to the bomb existed and that Truman and his advisers knew it.* [2]

The author of that statement is not a revisionist; he is J. Samuel Walker, chief historian of the U.S. Nuclear Regulatory Commission. Nor is he alone in that opinion. Walker is summarizing the findings of modern specialists in his literature review in the Winter 1990 issue of *Diplomatic History*. Another expert review, by University of Illinois historian Robert Messer, concludes that recently discovered documents have been "devastating" to the traditional idea that using the bomb was the only way to avoid an invasion of Japan that might have cost many more lives.[3]

Even allowing for continuing areas of dispute, these judgments are so far from the conventional wisdom that there is obviously something strange going on. One source of the divide between expert research and public understanding stems from a common feature of all serious scholarship: As in many areas of specialized research, perhaps a dozen truly knowledgeable experts are at the forefront of modern studies of the decision to use the atomic bomb. A second circle of generalists—historians concerned, for instance, with the Truman administration, with World War II in general, or even with the history of air power—depends heavily on the archival digging and analysis of the inner circle. Beyond this second group are authors of general textbooks and articles and, still further out, journalists and other popular writers.

One can, of course, find many historians who still believe that the atomic bomb was needed to avoid an invasion. Among the inner circle of serious experts, however, conclusions that are at odds with the official rationale have long been commonplace. Indeed, as early as 1946 the U.S. Strategic Bombing Survey, in its report *Japan's Struggle to End the War*, concluded that "certainly prior to December 31, 1945, and in all probability prior to November 1, 1945, Japan would have surrendered even if the atomic bombs had not been dropped, even if Russia had not entered the war, and even if no invasion had been planned or contemplated."[4]

Similarly, a top-secret April 1946 War Department study, *Use of Atomic Bomb on Japan*, declassified during the 1970s but brought to broad public attention only in 1989, found that "the Japanese leaders had decided to surrender and were merely looking for sufficient pretext to convince the die-hard Army Group that Japan had lost the war and must capitulate to the Allies." This official document judged that Russia's early-August entry into the war "would almost certainly have furnished this pretext, and would have been sufficient to convince all responsible leaders that surrender was unavoidable." The study concluded that even an initial November 1945 landing on the southern Japanese island of Kyushu would have been only a "remote" possibility and that the full invasion of Japan in the spring of 1946 would not have occurred.[5]

Military specialists who have examined Japanese decision making have added to the modern understanding that the bombing was unnecessary. For instance, political scientist Robert Pape's study, "Why Japan Surrendered," which appeared in the Fall 1993 issue of *International Security*, details Japan's military vulnerability, particularly its shortages of everything from ammunition to fuel to trained personnel: "Japan's military position was so poor that its leaders would likely have surrendered before invasion, and at roughly the same time in August 1945, even if the United States had not employed strategic bombing or the atomic bomb." In this situation, Pape stresses, "The Soviet invasion of Manchuria on August 9 raised Japan's military vulnerability to a very high level. The Soviet offensive ruptured Japanese lines immediately, and rapidly penetrated deep into the rear. Since the Kwantung Army was thought to be Japan's premier fighting force, this had a devastating effect on Japanese calculations of the prospects for home island defense." Pape adds, "If their best forces were so easily sliced to pieces, the unavoidable implication was that the less well-equipped and trained forces assembled for [the last decisive home island battle] had no chance of success against American forces that were even more capable than the Soviets."[6]

Whether the use of the atomic bomb was in fact necessary is, of course, a different question from whether it was believed to be necessary at the time. Walker's summary of the expert literature is important because it underscores the availability of the alternatives to using the bomb, and because it documents that "Truman and his advisers knew" of the alternatives.

Several major strands of evidence have pushed many specialists in the direction of this startling conclusion. The United States had long since broken the enemy codes, and the President was informed of all important Japanese cable traffic. A critical message of July 12, 1945—just before Potsdam—showed that the Japanese Emperor himself had decided to intervene to attempt to end the war.[7] In his private journal, Truman bluntly characterized this message as the "telegram from [the] Jap Emperor asking for peace."[8]

The Emperor wished to send a personal representative, Prince Konoye, to Moscow: "The mission . . . was to ask the Soviet Government to take part in mediation to end the present war and to transmit the complete Japanese case in this respect. . . . Prince Konoe [sic] was especially charged by His Majesty, the Emperor, to convey to the Soviet Government that it was exclusively the desire of His Majesty to avoid more bloodshed."[9]

Initial approaches to Russia can be traced as far back as 1944. The Emperor's personal initiative, however, was "real evidence" as Secretary of the Navy James Forrestal put it, of a determination to end the fighting. The intercepted cables also indicated that the main condition appeared to be an assurance that the Emperor could retain his title.[10]

Although the expert literature once mainly suggested that only one administration official—Undersecretary of State Joseph Grew—urged a change in the surrender formula to provide assurances for Japan's Emperor, it is now clear that with the exception of Secretary of State James Byrnes, the entire top echelon of the U.S. government in one way or another advocated such a change. By June 1945, in fact, Franklin Roosevelt's Secretary of State, Edward Stettinius, (who remained in office until July 3); the Undersecretary of State; the Secretary of War; the Secretary of the Navy; the President's Chief of Staff, Admiral William Leahy; and Army Chief of Staff General George Marshall—plus all the members of the Joint Chiefs of Staff (JCS)—had urged a clarification of the surrender formula.[11] So, too, had the British military and civilian leadership, including Prime Minister Churchill. Along with Grew, the Joint Chiefs in particular recommended that a statement be issued to coincide with the fall of Okinawa, on or around June 21.[12]

At that time, war crimes trials were being planned in Germany; the idea that the Emperor might be hanged was a possibility Tokyo could not ignore. Because the Japanese regarded the Emperor as a deity—more like Jesus or the Buddha than an ordinary human being—most top American officials deemed offering some assurances for the continuance of the dynasty an absolute necessity. The Joint Staff Planners, for instance, advised the Joint Chiefs in an April 25, 1945, report that "unless a definition of unconditional surrender can be given which is acceptable to the Japanese, there is no alternative to annihilation and no prospect that the threat of absolute defeat will bring about capitulation."[13] Secretary of War Henry Stimson took essentially the same position in a July 2 memorandum to Truman. Moreover, he judged that if the Japanese were offered such a definition, "I think the Japanese nation has the mental intelligence and versatile capacity in such a crisis to recognize the folly of a fight to the finish and to accept the proffer of what will amount to an unconditional surrender." [14] As University of Southern Mississippi military historian John Ray Skates has noted in his book, *The Invasion of Japan: Alternative to the Bomb*, "[General] Marshall, who believed that retention [of the Emperor] was a military necessity, asked that the members [of the Joint Chiefs of Staff] draft a memorandum to the President recommending that the Allies 'do nothing to indicate that the Emperor might be removed from office upon unconditional surrender.'" [15]

The other option that seemed likely to bring an end to the fighting concerned the Soviets. Joseph Stalin had promised to enter the war against Japan roughly three months after the May 8 defeat of Germany, which put the target date on or around August 8. Earlier in the war, the United States had sought Russia's help primarily to pin down Japanese armies in Manchuria and thus make a U.S. invasion of the home islands easier. By midsummer, however, Japan's position had deteriorated so much that top U.S. military planners believed the mere shock of a Red Army attack might be sufficient to bring about surrender and thus make an invasion unnecessary.

As early as February 1955, Harvard historian Ernest May, in an article in *Pacific Historical Review*, observed that the "Japanese die-hards . . . had acknowledged since 1941 that Japan could not fight Russia as well as the United States and Britain." May also observed that because Moscow had been an outlet for various Japanese peace feelers, when the Soviet declaration of war finally occurred it "discouraged Japanese hopes of secretly negotiating terms of peace." Moreover, in the end, "The Emperor's appeal [to end the war] probably resulted, therefore, from the Russian action, but it could not in any event, have been long in coming." [16]

The importance to U.S. leaders of the "Russian shock option" for ending the war—which was discussed even in the 1945 press—disappeared from most scholarly studies during the Cold War. We now know, however, that as of April 29, 1945 the Joint Intelligence Committee (JIC), in a report titled *Unconditional Surrender of Japan*, informed the JCS that increasing "numbers of informed Japanese, both military and civilian, already realize the inevitability of absolute defeat." The JIC further advised that "the increasing effects of air-sea blockade, the progressive and cumulative devastation wrought by strategic bombing, and the collapse of Germany (with its implications regarding redeployment) should make this realization widespread within the year." The JIC pointed out, however, that a Soviet decision to join with the United States and Britain would have enormous force and would dramatically alter the equation: "The entry of the USSR into the war would, together with the foregoing factors, convince most Japanese *at once* of the inevitability of complete defeat." [17]

By mid-June, Marshall advised Truman directly that "the impact of Russian entry [into the war] on the already hopeless Japanese may well be the decisive action levering them into capitulation at the time or shortly thereafter if we land in Japan."* [18] Again, Marshall's advice to Truman came almost a month before news

---

* Note especially the words "at the time." Throughout the summer the Russians were expected to attack in early August. Barton Bernstein mistakenly believes the "levering" could only take place if the United States actually landed in Japan (in November)—a logically contradictory reading of the

of the Emperor's personal intervention was received and four and a half months before even a preliminary Kyushu landing could have taken place. In July, the British General Sir Hastings Ismay, Chief of Staff to the Minister of Defense, summarized the conclusions of the latest U.S.–British intelligence studies for Churchill in this way: "[W]hen Russia came into the war against Japan, the Japanese would probably wish to get out on almost any terms short of dethronement of the Emperor." [19]

On several occasions, Truman made it abundantly clear that the main reason he went to Potsdam to meet Stalin was to make sure the Soviets would, in fact, enter the war. The atomic bomb had not yet been tested, and, as Truman later stated in his memoirs, "If the test [of the atomic bomb] should fail, then it would be even more important to us to bring about a surrender before we had to make a physical conquest of Japan." [20] Some of the most important modern documentary discoveries involve this point. After Stalin confirmed that the Red Army would indeed enter the war, the President's "lost" Potsdam journal (found in 1978) shows him writing: "Fini Japs when that comes about." [21] And the next day, in an exuberant letter to his wife (made public in 1982), Truman wrote that with the Soviet declaration of war "we'll end the war a year sooner now, and think of the kids who won't be killed!" [22]

It is also obvious that if assurances for the Emperor were put forward together with the Soviet attack, the likelihood of an early Japanese surrender would be even greater. The JIC recognized this in its April 29, 1945, report, observing that there first had to be a realization of the "inevitability of defeat," which the JIC judged a Soviet declaration of war would produce. Once "the Japanese people, as well as their leaders, were persuaded that absolute defeat was inevitable and that unconditional surrender did not imply national annihilation, surrender might follow fairly quickly." [23]

MANY MORE DOCUMENTARY FINDS support the view that top U.S. officials, including Truman, understood that use of the bomb was not required to end the war before an invasion. However, as Robert Messer observed in the August 1985 issue of *Bulletin of the Atomic Scientists*, the implications of Truman's diary and letters alone for the orthodox defense of the bomb's use are "devastating."

> If Soviet entry alone would end the war before an invasion of Japan, the use of atomic bombs cannot be justified as the only alternative to that invasion. This does not mean, of course, that having the bomb was not useful. But it does mean that for Truman the end of the war seemed at hand; the issue was no longer when the war would end, but how and on whose terms. If he believed that the war would end with Soviet entry in mid-August, then he must have realized that if the bombs were not used before that date they might well not be used at all. [24]

---

sentence in question given the expected timing of the Russian attack. See Barton Bernstein, "Understanding the Atomic Bomb and the Japanese Surrender," *Diplomatic History*, (Spring 1995), 224. See also General Lincoln to General Wedemeyer, July 10, 1945, Wedemeyer Folder, Box 5, Lincoln Papers, U.S. Military Academy Library, West Point, NY; and the extended discussion of "The Russian Option" in Alperovitz, *The Decision to Use the Atomic Bomb* (New York, 1995).

Minimally, the President's contemporaneous diary entries, together with his letters to his wife, raise fundamental questions about Truman's subsequent claims that the atomic bomb was used because it was the only way to avoid "a quarter million," "a half million" or "millions" of casualties.

The range of opinion even among expert defenders of Truman's decision is extraordinarily suggestive. For instance, McGeorge Bundy—who helped Stimson write a classic 1947 defense of the bombing, "The Decision to Use the Atomic Bomb" in *Harper's Magazine*—now holds that the necessity of bombing Hiroshima was "debatable," and the bombing of Nagasaki was "unnecessary." [25] In a *MacNeil/Lehrer* interview on the 40th anniversary of the bombing, Bundy went so far as to state that he was "not disposed to criticize the use of . . . the bomb to help to end the war, but it does seem to me, looking back on it, that there were opportunities for communication and warning available to the United States government which were not completely thought through by our government at that time." He added:

> In July and early August 1945, the United States government knew three things that the Japanese government did not. One was that the bomb was coming into existence, had been successfully tested. One was that the United States government was prepared to allow the Emperor to remain on his throne in Japan, and the third was that the Russians were coming into the war. And the question, it seems to me, that was not fully studied, fully presented to President Truman, was whether warning of the bomb and assurance on the Emperor could not have been combined in a fashion which would have produced Japanese surrender without the use of the bomb on a large city, with all of the human consequences that followed. [26]

Or consider the views of the late historian Herbert Feis, who was for decades the voice of orthodox historical opinion on the subject and a friend of Stimson's as well as an adviser to three World War II–era cabinet secretaries. It is rarely noted that Feis recognized—and emphasized—that by July 1945 there was a very good chance the war could have been ended without dropping the atomic bombs on Hiroshima and Nagasaki had the United States combined even the mere threat of a Soviet attack with assurances for the Emperor. He wrote in his 1961 work *Japan Subdued: The Atomic Bomb and the End of the War in the Pacific:* "I think it may be concluded that . . . the fighting would have continued into July at least, unless . . . the American and Soviet governments together had let it be known that unless Japan laid down its arms at once, the Soviet Union was going to enter the war. That, along with a promise to spare the Emperor, might well have made an earlier bid for surrender effective." [27]

Feis's only reservation was that Stalin might not have wanted to signal his willingness to join the war against Japan at this time, a rather odd idea that many documents now available show to be illusory. In addition, if a mere announcement of Soviet intentions might have forced a surrender, as the JIC pointed out, the reality of the attack would have been even more powerful.

Related to this is the fact that so many World War II military leaders are on record as stating that the bomb was not needed. Dwight Eisenhower, for instance, reported in his 1963 *Mandate for Change* that he had the following reaction when Secretary of War Stimson informed him the atomic bomb would be used:

During his recitation of the relevant facts, I had been conscious of a feeling of depression and so I voiced to him my grave misgivings, first on the basis of my belief that Japan was already defeated and that dropping the bomb was completely unnecessary, and secondly because I thought that our country should avoid shocking world opinion by the use of a weapon whose employment was, I thought, no longer mandatory as a measure to save American lives. It was my belief that Japan was, at that very moment, seeking some way to surrender with a minimum loss of "face." [28]

Historian Stephen Ambrose notes in his biography of Eisenhower that he also clearly stated that he personally urged Truman not to use the atomic bombs.[29] Eisenhower's opinion in other public statements in the early 1960's was identical: "It wasn't necessary to hit them with that awful thing." [30]

Admiral William Leahy, President Truman's Chief of Staff and the top official who presided over meetings of both the JCS and the U.S.–U.K. Combined Chiefs of Staff, also minced few words in his 1950 memoirs *I Was There*: "The use of this barbarous weapon at Hiroshima and Nagasaki was of no material assistance in our war against Japan. . . . [I]n being the first to use it, we . . . adopted an ethical standard common to the barbarians of the Dark Ages. I was not taught to make war in that fashion, and wars cannot be won by destroying women and children." [31] The Army Air Forces commander, General Henry "Hap" Arnold, put it this way in his 1949 *Global Mission*: "It always appeared to us that atomic bomb or no atomic bomb the Japanese were already on the verge of collapse." [32] Britain's General Ismay said in his memoirs that his initial reaction on hearing of the successful atomic test was one of "revulsion." He had previously observed: "for some time past it had been firmly fixed in my mind that the Japanese were tottering. . . ." [33]

Even as early as September 1944, General George C. Kenney, Commander of the Allied Air Forces Southwest Pacific Area, advised: "The situation is developing rapidly and there are trends which indicate that the Jap is not going to last much longer. His sea power is so badly depleted that it is no match for any one of several forces we could put into action. . . . Without the support of his sea power and air power his land forces cannot do anything except hold out in isolated, beleaguered spots all over the map until bombs, bullets, disease and starvation kill them off. . . ." [34] In April 1945, General Douglas MacArthur, commander of U.S. troops in the Pacific, reported that "the Japanese fleet has been reduced to practical impotency. The Japanese Air Force has been reduced to a line of action which involved uncoordinated, suicidal attacks against our forces. . . . Its attrition is heavy and its power for sustained action is diminishing rapidly." [35]

As the situation in Japan worsened, Japanese "peace feelers" began to erupt throughout Europe. On May 12, 1945, Office of Strategic Services Director William Donovan reported to President Truman that Shunichi Kase, Japan's minister to Switzerland, wished "to help arrange for a cessation of hostilities." He believed "one of the few provisions the Japanese would insist upon would be the retention of the Emperor." [36]

Truman received a similar report concerning Masutaro Inoue, Japan's counselor in Portugal, who, according to an Office of Strategic Services informant, "declared that actual peace terms were unimportant so long as the term 'unconditional surrender' was not employed. The Japanese, he asserted, are convinced that within a few weeks all of their wood and paper houses will be destroyed."[37] Though such feelers were not yet official, by mid-June 1945 Leahy, the President's Chief of Staff, concluded that "a surrender of Japan can be arranged with terms that can be accepted by Japan and that will make fully satisfactory provision for American defense against future trans-Pacific aggression." [38]

The strong language used by high-level military figures often comes as a shock to those not familiar with the documents, memoirs, and diaries now available. Defenders of the decision sometimes suggest that such views represent after-the-fact judgments, or are the result of interservice rivalry. However, not only are several assessments contemporaneous (as in Leahy's June 1945 observation), but in view of the traditional unwillingness of uniformed military officers to criticize their civilian superiors—and the extraordinary importance of the historic issue—it is difficult to explain the large number of statements, made with great force, on such grounds.

All of these judgments also bear on the question of the number of lives that might possibly have been lost if the atomic bombs had not been used. Over the last decade, scholars of very different political orientations, including Barton Bernstein, Rufus Miles Jr., and John Ray Skates, have all separately examined World War II U.S. military planning documents on this subject. These documents indicate that *if* an initial November 1945 Kyushu landing had gone forward, estimates of the number of lives that would have been lost (and therefore possibly saved by use of the atomic bombs) were in the range of 20,000 to 26,000. In the unlikely event a subsequent full-scale invasion had been mounted in 1946, the maximum estimate found in such documents was 46,000.[39]

Even these numbers, however, confuse the central issue: If the war could have been ended by clarifying the terms of surrender and/or allowing the shock of the Russian attack to set in, then no lives would have been lost in a November invasion. Fighting was minimal in August 1945 as both sides regrouped, and the most that may be said is that the atomic bombs might have saved the lives that would have been lost in the time required to arrange final surrender terms with Japan. That saving lives was not the highest priority, however, seems obvious from the choices made in July: If the United States really wished to end the war as quickly and surely as possible—and to save as many lives as possible—then as Marshall had pointed out as early as June, the full force of the Russian shock plus assurances for the Emperor could not be left out of the equation.

Moreover, if we accept Stimson's subsequent judgment that "history might find" that the decision to delay assurances for the Emperor "had prolonged the war," then, as historian Martin Sherwin noted in the October 10, 1981, *Nation*, the atomic bomb may well have cost lives. Why? Lives were lost during the roughly two-month delay in clarifying the surrender terms. Many historians believe the delay was caused by the decision to wait for the atomic test at Alamogordo, New Mexico, on July 16, and then, the bombs' use on Japan in early August. Several thousand American soldiers and sailors died between Grew's initial May 28 proposal to clarify the "unconditional" terms and the final surrender on August 14.

SOME OF THE BASIC QUESTIONS debated in the expert literature concern why alternatives for ending the war were not pursued. Little dispute remains about why the Russian option was discarded, however. Once the bomb was proven to work, the President reversed course entirely and attempted to stall a Red Army attack. A week after the Alamogordo test, for instance, Churchill observed that "it is quite clear that the United States do not at the present time desire Russian participation in the war against Japan."[40] Similarly, the diary of Secretary of Navy James Forrestal indicates that by July 28 Secretary of State Byrnes was "most anxious to get the Japanese affair over with before the Russians got in."[41] And the private journal of Byrnes' personal assistant, Walter Brown, confirms that Byrnes was now "hoping for time, believing [that] after [the] atomic bomb Japan will surrender and Russia will not get in so much on the kill, thereby being in a position to press claims against China."[42] Meanwhile, every effort was made to speed up the production and delivery of the weapon. These efforts were successful: Hiroshima was bombed on August 6, two days before the Soviet Union declared war on Japan. Nagasaki was bombed on the 9th.

A traditional argument as to why the surrender formula for Japan was not modified is that it was politically impossible for Truman to alter the "unconditional" language, that to do so would make him look soft on Japan. There is some evidence that some people felt this way, notably Roosevelt's ailing former Secretary of State Cordell Hull, and Assistant Secretaries of State Archibald MacLeish and Dean Acheson. There is some evidence (mainly from the period after the bombings) that Byrnes feared criticism if the rhetoric of unconditional surrender was abandoned. However, it does not appear that the President himself was much worried about such matters. Truman's views, as described in contemporaneous records, indicate that he generally seemed to favor altering the terms, and there is little evidence of concern about political opposition. Stimson's diary reports of July 24 and August 10, in particular, make it clear that neither Byrnes nor Truman were at all "obdurate" on the question. And, of course, a few days after the bombings the Japanese were given the assurances they sought: Japan would still have an Emperor.

Moreover, many leading newspapers at the time were pressing for—rather than resisting—a clarification of terms. The *Washington Post*, for instance, challenged the "unconditional surrender" formula head-on in a June 11, 1945, editorial titled "Fatal Phrase":

> President Truman, of course, has already stated that there is no thought of destroying the Japanese people, but such assurances, even from so high a source, are negated by that fatal phrase. . . [the two words] remain a great stumbling block to any propaganda effort and the perpetual trump card of the Japanese die-hards for their game of national suicide. Let us amend them; let us give Japan conditions, harsh conditions certainly, and conditions that will render her diplomatically and militarily impotent for generations. But also let us somehow assure those Japanese who are ready to plead for peace that, even on our terms, life and peace will be better than war and annihilation.[43]

Similarly, recent research has indicated that far from pushing the President to maintain a hard line, many leading Republicans urged him to modify the terms to get an early surrender, preferably before the Soviets entered the war. Former President Herbert Hoover, for instance, went to see Truman about the issue in late May, and on July 3 the *New York Times* reported that "Senator [Wallace] White [Jr.]

of Maine, the minority leader, declared that the Pacific war might end quickly if President Truman would state specifically in the upper chamber just what unconditional surrender means for the Japanese." [44]

Although White indicated he was speaking as an individual, the move by so important a political figure could hardly be ignored. Moreover, White's statement was immediately supported by Senator Homer Capehart of Indiana, who called a press conference the same day to state that "it isn't a matter of whether you hate the Japs or not. I certainly hate them. But what's to be gained by continuing a war when it can be settled now on the same terms as two years from now?" [45]

MARTIN SHERWIN HAS SUGGESTED that the atomic bomb was used because it was "preferred" to the other options. [46] Although it is sometimes thought that sheer momentum carried the day, there is no doubt that it was, in fact, an active choice. When Truman and Byrnes cut the critical assurances to the Emperor out of paragraph 12 of the draft Potsdam Proclamation, they did so against the recommendation of virtually the entire top American and British leadership. Truman and Byrnes had to reverse the thrust of a near-unanimous judgment that the terms should be clarified. Truman's journal also indicates that he understood that the proclamation in final form—without the key passage—was not likely to be accepted by Japan. [47]

If the Soviet option for ending the war was shelved for political/diplomatic reasons—and if the political reasons for not modifying the surrender formula no longer looked so solid—is there any other explanation for why the Japanese were not told their Emperor would not be harmed, that he could stay on the throne in some innocuous position like that of the king of England? Some historians, of course, continue to hold that the bomb's use was militarily necessary— or perhaps inevitable because of the inherited technological, bureaucratic, and military momentum that built up during the war. Others suggest that because huge sums were spent developing the new weapon, political leaders found it impossible not to use it. Still others have probed the intricacies of decision making through an analysis of bureaucratic dynamics.

Of greatest interest, perhaps, is another factor. The traditional argument has been that solely military considerations were involved in the decision to use the bomb; increasingly, however, the once controversial idea that diplomatic issues— especially the hope of strengthening the West against the Soviet Union—played a significant role in the decision has gained widespread scholarly acceptance. Although analysts still debate exactly how much weight to accord such factors, that they were involved is now well established for most experts. The bare chronology of events in 1945 itself raises questions about U.S. motives for dropping the bomb. Germany surrendered on May 8, and the Allied powers knew that Japan's situation was deteriorating rapidly. At the Yalta conference of Allied leaders in February, Stalin had agreed to declare war on Japan three months after the defeat of Germany—roughly August 8.

The *Enola Gay* dropped its world-shattering cargo over Hiroshima on August 6. On August 8, the Soviet Union informed Japan it was entering the war. The second atomic weapon exploded over Nagasaki on August 9. As noted, the first U.S. landing on Japan was still another three months off, and a full invasion was not expected to take place—even on paper—until the spring of 1946. Physicist Philip Morrison later testified that "a date near August tenth was a mysterious final date which we, who had the daily technical job of readying the bomb, had to meet at whatever cost in risk or money or good development policy." [48]

Nobel Prize-winning British physicist P.M.S. Blackett pointed out as long ago as 1948 how this sequence challenged the official rationale for the bombings. Was it really the case—with three months still to go before a U.S. landing—that American and British leaders saw no alternative except detonating the bomb?[49]

Modern research findings clearly demonstrate that from April 1945 on, top American officials calculated that using the atomic bomb would enormously bolster U.S. diplomacy vis-à-vis the Soviet Union in negotiations over both post-war Europe and the Far East. The atomic bomb was not, in fact, initially brought to Truman's attention because of its relationship to the war against Japan, but because of its likely impact on diplomacy. In late April, in the midst of an explosive confrontation with Stalin over the Polish issue, Secretary of War Stimson urged discussion of the bomb because, as he told Truman, it had "such a bearing on our present foreign relations and . . . such an important effect upon all my thinking in this field." [50]

Stimson, for his part, regarded the atomic bomb as what he called the "master card" of diplomacy towards Russia. However, he believed that sparring with the Soviet Union in the early spring, before the weapon was demonstrated, would be counterproductive. Before a mid-May meeting of a cabinet-level committee considering Far Eastern issues, Stimson observed that "the questions cut very deep and [were] powerfully connected with our success with S–1 [the atomic bomb]." [51] Two days later, he noted in his diary:

> I tried to point out the difficulties which existed and I thought it premature to ask those questions; at least we were not yet in a position to answer them. . . . it may be necessary to have it out with Russia on her relations to Manchuria and Port Arthur and various other parts of North China, and also the relations of China to us. Over any such tangled wave of problems the [atomic bomb] secret would be dominant and yet we will not know until after that time probably . . . whether this is a weapon in our hands or not. We think it will be shortly afterwards, but it seems a terrible thing to gamble with such big stakes in diplomacy without having your master card in your hand. [52]

Stimson's argument for delaying diplomatic fights with the Soviet Union was also described in another mid-May diary entry after a conversation with Assistant Secretary of War John McCloy:

> The time now and the method now to deal with Russia was to keep our mouths shut and let our actions speak for words. The Russians will understand them better than anything else. It is a case where we have got to regain the lead and perhaps do it in a pretty rough and realistic way. . . . This [is] a place where we really held all the cards. I called it a royal straight flush and we mustn't be a fool about the way we play it. They can't get along without our help and industries and we have coming into action a weapon which will be unique. Now the thing is not to get into unnecessary quarrels by talking too much and not to indicate any weakness by talking too much; let our actions speak for themselves. [53]

Stimson's files indicate that Truman had come to similar conclusions roughly a month after taking office. Quite specifically—and against the advice of Churchill, who wanted an early meeting with Stalin before American troops were withdrawn from Europe—the President postponed his only diplomatic encounter with the Soviet leader because he first wanted to know for certain that the still untested atomic bomb actually worked. Stimson's papers indicate the President's view was that he would have "more cards" later.[54] In a 1949 interview, Truman recalled telling a close associate before the test, "If it explodes, as I think it will, I'll certainly have a hammer on those boys" (meaning, it seemed clear, the Russians as well as the Japanese).[55] After another May 1945 meeting with Truman, Ambassador Joseph Davies's diaries also record:

> [t]o my surprise, he said he did not want it [the heads-of-government meeting] until July. The reason which I could assign was that he had his budget on his hands. . . . "But," he said, "I have another reason . . . which I have not told anybody." He told me of the atomic bomb. The final test had been set for June, but now had been postponed until July. I was startled, shocked and amazed.[56]

Evidence in the Stimson diaries suggests that the broad strategy was probably secretly explained to Ambassador Averell Harriman and British foreign minister Anthony Eden at this time.[57] Scientists in the field also got an inkling that there was a link between the Potsdam meeting with Stalin and the atomic test. J. Robert Oppenheimer, for instance, later testified before the U.S. Atomic Energy commission that "I don't think there was any time where we worked harder at the speed-up than in the period after the German surrender."[58]

The timing was perfect. The first successful atomic test occurred on July 16, 1945. Truman sat down for discussions with Stalin the very next day. Stimson's diary includes this entry after a full report of the test results was received:

> [Churchill] told me that he had noticed at the meeting of the [Big] Three yesterday that Truman was evidently much fortified by something that had happened and that he stood up to the Russians in a most emphatic and decisive manner, telling them as to certain demands that they absolutely could not have and that the United States was entirely against them. He said "Now I know what happened to Truman yesterday. I couldn't understand it. When he got to the meeting after having read this report he was a changed man. He told the Russians just where they got on and off and generally bossed the whole meeting."[59]

The July 23, 1945, diary entry of Lord Alanbrooke, Chairman of the British Chiefs of Staff Committee, provides a description of both Churchill's own reaction and further indirect evidence of the atomic bomb's impact on American attitudes:

> [The Prime Minister] . . . had absorbed all the minor American exaggerations and, as a result, was completely carried away. . . . We now had something in our hands which would redress the balance with the Russians. The secret of this explosive and the power to use it

would completely alter the diplomatic equilibrium which was adrift since the defeat of Germany. Now we had a new value which redressed our position (pushing out his chin and scowling); now we could say, "If you insist on doing this or that, well . . . And then where are the Russians!"[60]

THERE IS NO LONGER MUCH DISPUTE that ending the war with Japan before the Soviet Union entered it played a role in the thinking of those responsible for using the atomic bomb. Albert Einstein publicly voiced his suspicion early on that the bombing occurred because of "a desire to end the war in the Pacific by any means before Russia's participation. I am sure that if President Roosevelt had still been there, none of that would have been possible. He would have forbidden such an act."[61] There also is now important evidence that impressing the Russians was a consideration. Scholarly discussion of this controversial point has been heated, and even carefully qualified judgments that such a motive is "strongly suggested" by the available documents have been twisted and distorted into extreme claims. It is, nevertheless, impossible to ignore the considerable range of evidence that now points in this direction.

First, there are the diaries and other sources indicating that the President and his top advisers appear from late April on to have based their diplomatic strategy on the assumption that the new weapon, once demonstrated, would strengthen the U.S. position against the Soviet Union. A number of historians now agree that Truman, Stimson, and Byrnes were influenced, consciously or unconsciously, by this fact when they chose to reject other available options for ending the war. Like the language of others, Stimson's specific words to describe the new "master card" of diplomacy are also difficult to ignore:

> *Let our actions speak for words.* The Russians will understand them better than anything else. . . . we have got to regain the lead and perhaps do it in a pretty rough and realistic way. . . . *we have coming into action a weapon which will be unique. Now the thing is not . . . to indicate any weakness by talking too much; let our actions speak for themselves.*[62]

Particularly important has been research illuminating the role played by Byrnes. Although it was once believed that Stimson was the most important Presidential adviser on atomic matters, historians increasingly understand that Byrnes had the President's ear. Indeed, in the judgment of many experts, he fairly dominated Truman during the first five or six months of Truman's presidency. Byrnes, in fact, had been one of Truman's mentors when the young unknown from Missouri first came to the Senate. In selecting the then highly influential former Supreme Court Justice as Secretary of State, Truman put him in direct line of succession to the presidency.[63] By also choosing Byrnes as his personal representative on the high-level Interim Committee—which made recommendations concerning the new weapon—Truman arranged to secure primary counsel on both foreign policy and the atomic bomb from a single trusted adviser.

There is not much doubt about Byrnes's general view. In one of their very first meetings, Truman reports Byrnes told him that "in his belief the atomic bomb might well put us in a position to dictate our own terms at the end of the war."[64] Again, at the end of May, Byrnes met, at White House request, with atomic scientist Leo Szilard.* In his 1949 *A Personal History of the Atomic Bomb*, Szilard recalled, "Mr. Byrnes did not argue that it was necessary to use the bomb against the cities of Japan in order to win the war. . . . Mr. Byrnes's . . . view [was] that our possessing and demonstrating the bomb would make Russia more manageable in Europe." [65]

In a 1968 article in *Perspectives in American History*, Szilard wrote that "Russian troops had moved into Hungary and Rumania; Byrnes thought . . . that Russia might be more manageable if impressed by American military might." [66] Another excerpt from Ambassador Joseph Davies's diary records Byrnes's attitude at Potsdam, "[Byrnes] was still having a hard time. . . . The details as to the success of the Atomic Bomb, which he had just received, gave him confidence that the Soviets would agree. Byrnes' attitude that the atomic bomb assured ultimate success in negotiations disturbed me. . . . I told him the threat wouldn't work, and might do irreparable harm." [67]

Stimson's friend Herbert Feis judged a quarter century ago that the desire to "impress" the Soviets almost certainly played a role in the decision to use the atomic bomb.[68] On the basis of currently available information it is impossible to prove precisely to what extent Byrnes and the President were influenced by this consideration. Nevertheless, just as the discovery of new documents has led to greater recognition of the role of diplomatic factors in the decision, research on Byrnes's role—and the consistency of his attitude throughout this period—has clarified our understanding of this motive. Writing in the August 18, 1985, *New York Times*, Yale historian Gaddis Smith summarized this point: "It has been demonstrated that the decision to bomb Japan was centrally connected to Truman's confrontational approach to the Soviet Union." [69]

Quite apart from the basic judgment as to the necessity of and reasons for the bomb's use, the issue of why the public is generally ignorant of so many of the basic facts discussed in the expert literature remains. For one thing, the modern press has been careless in its reporting. During the 1995 *Enola Gay* controversy at the Smithsonian, few reporters even bothered to seriously consult specialist literature, or to present the range of specific issues in contention among the experts. Instead, historians who still remain unqualified defenders of the decision as dictated solely by military necessity were often cited as unquestioned authoritative sources. Many reporters repeated as fact the myth that "over a million" Americans would have perished or been wounded in an invasion of Japan. Only a handful wrote that among the many historians who criticized the Smithsonian for its "cleansing" of history were conservatives and others who disagreed about the specific issue, but begged for an honest discussion of the questions involved.

---

* Various scientists, upset that the bombing would proceed even though Germany had been defeated and Japan had been reduced to dire straits, attempted to head it off. New research has also given us a clearer picture of the many ways their efforts were blocked despite the intense efforts of men like Szilard. Peter Wyden, for instance, describes in his *Day One* how J. Robert Oppenheimer deftly sidetracked Chicago scientists opposed to using the atomic weapon. General Leslie Groves, the military leader of the Manhattan Project, and other top officials also simply delayed a petition to the President registering scientists' opposition until it was too late. See *Hiroshima's Shadow* p. 99, "Three Attempts to Stop the Bomb" by William Lanouette. See also p. 559, "A Note on the July 17th Petition" by William Lanouette.

Emotional issues were also at work. Time and again, the question of whether dropping the atomic bomb was militarily necessary has become entangled with the quite separate issue of anger at Japan's sneak attack and the brutality of its military. The Japanese people have an ugly history to confront, including not only Pearl Harbor but the bombing of Shanghai, the rape of Nanking, the forced prostitution of Korean women, the horror of the Bataan Death March, and the systematic torture and murder of American and other prisoners of war. Even so, the question of Hiroshima persists.

Americans also have often allowed themselves to confuse the discussion of the modern research findings on Hiroshima with criticism of American servicemen. This is certainly unjustified (as the comments of military leaders like Eisenhower, Leahy, and Arnold suggest). The Americans serving in the Pacific in 1945 were prepared to risk their lives for their nation; by this most fundamental test they can only be called heroes. This is neither the first nor the last time, however, those in the field were not informed of what was going on at higher levels.

Finally, we Americans clearly do not like to see our nation as vulnerable to the same moral failings as others. To raise questions about Hiroshima is to raise doubts, it seems to some, about the moral integrity of the country and its leaders. It is also to raise the most profound questions about the legitimacy of nuclear weapons in general. America's continued unwillingness to confront the fundamental questions about Hiroshima may well be at the root of the quiet acceptance that has characterized so many other dangerous developments in the nuclear era that began in 1945.

NOTES

A detailed treatment of the subjects covered in this summary essay can be found in my recent work, *The Decision to Use the Atomic Bomb and the Architecture of an American Myth* (New York, 1995).

1. ABC News, *Nightline*, "What if . . . We Hadn't Dropped the Bomb," (August 5, 1985), Transcript of the show No. 1096, p. 2.

2. J. Samuel Walker, "The Decision to Use the Bomb: A Historiographical Update," *Diplomatic History*, (Winter 1990), 97–114, cited material from p. 110. [Emphasis added]

3. Robert L. Messer, "New Evidence on Truman's Decision," *Bulletin of the Atomic Scientists*, (August 1985), pp. 50–56, cited material from p. 55.

4. United States Strategic Bombing Survey, *Japan's Struggle to End the War* (Washington, D.C.: United States Strategic Bombing Survey, Chairman's Office, 1946), p. 13.

5. Memorandum for Chief, Strategic Policy Section, S&P Group, OPD, Subject: Use of the Atomic Bomb on Japan, April 30, 1946, "Atom 471.6 (17 Aug. 1945), Sec. 7," Entry 421, RG 165, National Archives, Washington, D.C.

6. Robert A. Pape, "Why Japan Surrendered," *International Security*, (Fall 1993), 154–201, cited material from pp. 156, 178–79.

7. U.S. intelligence summaries of intercepted and decrypted Japanese diplomatic communications—otherwise known as "MAGIC" intercepts—were reported daily and designated "Eyes Only" for the very top political and military officials in the U.S. government. MAGIC—Diplomatic Summaries, No. 1205, July 13, 1945, Record Group 457, National Archives, Washington, D.C.

8. Harry S. Truman, *Off the Record: The Private Papers of Harry S. Truman*, edited by Robert H. Ferrell (New York, 1980, 1982), p. 53.

9. MAGIC, No. 1205, July 13, 1945, Record Group 457, National Archives, Washington, D.C.

10. MAGIC, No. 1218, July 26, 1945; No. 1163, June 1, 1945, Record Group 457, National Archives, Washington, D.C. See also the OSS reports to Truman of June 2 and July 7, reprinted in the U.S. State Department, *Foreign Relations of the United States* series, 1945, Vol. VI, (Washington, D.C., 1969), pp. 485–88.

11. For details on the recommendations of the various Presidential advisers and British officials, see Alperovitz, *The Decision to Use the Atomic Bomb and the Architecture of an American Myth* (New York, 1995), pp. 33–79, 224–38, and 297–301.

12. See SWNCC 149, "Immediate Demand For the Unconditional Surrender of Japan," June 9, 1945, "ABC 387 Japan (15 Feb. 45)," Entry 421, Record Group 165, National Archives, Washington, D.C.

13. JCS 924/15, "Pacific Strategy," April 25, 1945, p. 245, "ABC 384 Pacific (1–17–43) Sec. 9," Box 457, Entry 421, Record Group 165, National Archives, Washington, D.C.

14. Stimson to Truman, July 2, 1945, "White House Correspondence," Box 15, Stimson Safe File, Entry 74A, Record Group 107, National Archives, Washington D.C.

15. John Ray Skates, *Invasion of Japan: Alternative to the Bomb* (Columbia, SC, 1994), p. 238.

16. Ernest R. May, "The United States, the Soviet Union, and the Far Eastern War, 1941–1945," *Pacific Historical Review*, February 1955, 153–74, cited material from pp. 172–73.

17. Joint Chiefs of Staff Info Memo 390, "Unconditional Surrender of Japan," April 29, 1945, "ABC 387 Japan (15 Feb. 45)," Box 504, Entry 421, Record Group 165, National Archives, Washington, D.C. [Emphasis added]

18. U.S. Department of Defense, *The Entry of the Soviet Union into the War Against Japan: Military Plans, 1941–1945,* (Washington, D.C., 1955), p. 79.

19. John Ehrman, *Grand Strategy, Vol. VI: October 1944–August 1945* (London, 1956), p. 291.

20. Harry S. Truman, *Memoirs of Harry S. Truman, Vol. I: Year of Decisions* (New York, 1955), p. 417.

21. Truman, *Off the Record*, ed. Ferrell, p. 53.

22. Harry S. Truman, *Dear Bess: The Letters from Harry to Bess Truman, 1910–1959*, edited by Robert H. Ferrell (New York, 1983), p. 519.

23. Joint Chiefs of Staff Info Memo 390, "Unconditional Surrender of Japan," April 29, 1945, "ABC 387 Japan (15 Feb. 45)," Box 504, Entry 421, Record Group 165, National Archives, Washington, D.C.

24. Messer, "New Evidence on Truman's Decision," p. 55.

25. McGeorge Bundy, "Pearl Harbor Brought Peace," *Newsweek*, December 16, 1991, p. 8.

26. The *MacNeil/Lehrer NewsHour*, August 6, 1985, Transcript No. 2572.

27. Herbert Feis, *Japan Subdued: the Atomic Bomb and the End of the War in the Pacific* (Princeton, 1961), pp. 175–76.

28. Dwight D. Eisenhower, *Mandate for Change 1953–1956* (Garden City, 1963), pp. 312–13.

29. See Stephen E. Ambrose, *Eisenhower, Vol. I: Soldier, General of the Army, President-Elect, 1890–1952* (New York, 1983), pp. 425–26. For further discussion, see also Alperovitz, *The Decision to Use the Atomic Bomb*, footnote, p. 358.

30. "Ike on Ike," *Newsweek*, November 11, 1963, p. 107.

31. William D. Leahy, *I Was There: The Personal Story of the Chief of Staff to Presidents Roosevelt and Truman, Based on His Notes and Diaries Made at the Time* (New York, 1950), p. 441.

32. Henry H. Arnold, *Global Mission* (New York, 1949), p. 598.

33. Hastings Lionel Ismay, *Memoirs* (New York, 1960), p. 401.

34. Letter from Lt. General George C. Kenney to General Arnold, September 17, 1944, "McCormack Paper," Part 2, SRH–141, RG 457, National Archives, Washington, D.C.

35. U.S. Department of Defense, *The Entry of the Soviet Union Into the War Against Japan: Military Plans, 1941–1945* (Washington, D.C.: Government Printing Office, 1955), pp. 55–57.

36. Memorandum for the President from Donovan, May 12, 1945, "Rose Conway File," Paper of Harry S. Truman, Harry S. Truman Library, Independence, MO.

37. U.S. Department of State, *Foreign Relations of the United States: Diplomatic Papers, 1945,* Vol. VI, pp. 485–86.

38. Diaries of William D. Leahy, June 18, 1945, on microfilm at the Manuscripts Division of the Library of Congress.

39. Barton J. Bernstein, "A Post-war Myth: 500,000 U.S. Lives Saved," *Bulletin of the Atomic Scientists*, June–July 1986, 38–40; Rufus E. Miles, Jr., "Hiroshima: The Strange Myth of Half a Million American Lives Saved," *International Security*, (Fall 1985), 121–40; and Skates, *The Invasion of Japan*, pp. 76–83.

40. Ehrman, *Grand Strategy*, p. 292.

41. James V. Forrestal, *The Forrestal Diaries*, edited by Walter Millis (New York, 1951), p. 78.

42. "WB's Book," July 24, 1945, Folder 602, James F. Byrnes Papers, Robert Muldrow Cooper Library, Clemson University, Clemson, SC.

43. "Fatal Phrase," *Washington Post,* June 11, 1945, p. 8.

44. *New York Times,* July 3, 1945, p. 3.

45. *Washington Post,* July 3, 1945, p. 2.

46. See Martin J. Sherwin, "Hiroshima and Modern Memory," *Nation,* October 10, 1981, p. 352.

47. Truman, *Off the Record,* ed. Ferrell, p. 56.

48. Phillip Morrison, "Blackett's Analysis of the Issues," *Bulletin of the Atomic Scientists,* February 1949, 37–40, cited material from p. 40.

49. P.M.S. Blackett, *Fear, War, and the Bomb: Military and Political Consequences of Atomic Energy* (New York, 1949), p. 139.

50. Stimson to Truman, April 24, 1945, "White House Correspondence," Box 15, Stimson Safe File, Entry 74A, Record Group 107, National Archives, Washington, D.C.

51. Henry L. Stimson Diaries, May 13, 1945, Sterling Library, Yale University, New Haven, CT. Also on microfilm at the Library of Congress, Washington, D.C.

52. Stimson Diary, May 15, 1945.

53. Stimson Diary, May 14, 1945.

54. Stimson Diary, May 16, 1945.

55. Truman interview with Jonathan Daniels, November 12, 1949, "Research Notes Used in Connection with Writing *The Man of Independence,*" p. 67, Part I, Notes on Interviews, Daniels Papers, Harry S. Truman Library, Independence, MO.

56. "Journal," May 21, 1945 (11–2–50), Chrono File, Box 17, Joseph E. Davies Papers, Manuscripts Division, Library of Congress, Washington, D.C.

57. See Stimson Diary entries of May 10 and May 14, 1945.

58. Atomic Energy Commission, *In the Matter of J. Robert Oppenheimer; Transcript of Hearing before Personnel Security Board, Washington D.C., April 12, 1954 through May 6, 1954* (Washington, 1954), pp. 32–33.

59. Stimson Diary, July 22, 1945.

60. Arthur Bryant, *Triumph in the West: A History of the War Years Based on the Diaries of Field-Marshall Lord Alanbrooke, Chief of the Imperial General Staff* (Garden City, 1959), pp. 363–64.

61. Andre Labarthe, "The Atomic Bomb: The Future of Germany: The Peril of Another War," *The Sunday Express,* August 18, 1946.

62. Diary of Secretary of War Henry L. Stimson, Stimson Diary microfilm, Henry L. Stimson microfilms, Library of Congress, Manuscript Division. [Emphasis added]

63. The Presidential Succession Act of 1886 provided for transfer of the office to the Secretary of State. "Pending a change in the law," Truman later explained, "I felt it my duty to choose without too much delay a Secretary of State with proper qualifications to succeed, if necessary, to the presidency." Truman, *Year of Decisions,* p. 23.

64. Truman, *Year of Decisions,* p. 87.

65. Leo Szilard, "A Personal History of the Atomic Bomb," *University of Chicago Roundtable,* No. 601 (September 25, 1949), pp. 14–15.

66. Szilard, "Reminiscences," edited by Gertrud Weiss Szilard and Kathleen R. Winsor, *Perspectives in American History II* (1968), pp. 94–151, cited material from p. 128.

67. "Journal," July 28, 1945 (2–1–51) and "Diary" July 28, 1945, both in the Chrono File, Box 19, Davies Papers, Manuscripts Division, Library of Congress, Washington, D.C.

68. See Feis, *Japan Subdued,* p. 181.

69. Gaddis Smith, "Was Moscow Our Real Target?," *New York Times Book Review,* August 18, 1985, p. 16.

DID THE
BOMB END
THE WAR?

Murray Sayle

A
T EXACTLY FIFTEEN MINUTES PAST EIGHT in the morning, Japanese time, on August 6, 1995,—the moment when in 1945 an atomic bomb exploded over the city of Hiroshima—a single bong of the Peace Bell signaled a minute's silence. Mayor Takashi Hiraoka and other Japanese dignitaries made short speeches, followed by the flight of a thousand doves, which rose in a whirring cloud above our heads, circled the Memorial Cenotaph, the centerpiece of the Hiroshima Peace Memorial Park, and fluttered into nearby trees, to resume their everyday role as the park's resident pigeons. I have been coming to Hiroshima for twenty years. At first, I came out of simple curiosity: for my generation, children of the Second World War, the stunning news of the atomic bombs and, a few days later, the coming of peace will always be linked. Once, like everyone else, I thought that the atomic bombs had caused the surrender, ended the war, and saved many lives. Now I know that they did not. I began to doubt the official story on my first visit to Hiroshima. In the years since, I have been back many times, have read scores of books on the subject and talked with their authors, have discussed Hiroshima with everyone from my Japanese neighbors (we live in a small village near Tokyo) to officials of the Emperor's court, and have consulted the archives in Washington and Tokyo; and I have concluded that the debate over Hiroshima has been totally misconceived. To recover our moral bearings, we must examine anew the circumstances surrounding the dropping of the bomb and the Japanese surrender.

To the residents of Hiroshima, their history is a part of everyday life. Anyone connected with the bomb—the attendants in the Peace Memorial Museum, for instance; the gardeners who catch the park's pigeons in big bamboo nets the night before the annual ceremony; and the sellers of A-Bomb Dome paperweights, history books, and pigeon food—is cheerfully said to be in the *pikadon shōbai*, the "flash-bang game." Rebuilt Hiroshima has the cozy neighborliness of any provincial Japanese city, and its people gossip about things far less earthshaking than atomic bombs: the fortunes of the Hiroshima Carp, the hometown baseball team; the slowdown in the biggest local industry, the Mazda car plant, due to the ever-soaring yen; and the year's crop of Hiroshima oysters from the nearby Inland Sea, reckoned by gourmets to be the best in Japan. But these are not what draw a million-plus visitors here every year.

Hiroshima means "wide island," and the name well describes the city's site—on six low islands that are divided by seven branches of the Ota River delta and in few spots rise more than fifteen feet above water level, so offering no protection against an overhead blast. The many branches of the river, all natural firebreaks, were (along with the city's small size and relative unimportance) the main reason that Hiroshima had not already been firebombed, and thus was available as a target for the new weapon. The intimate, human scale of Hiroshima, derived from its setting amid green mountains rising directly from its outskirts, spares it from the usual Japanese urban wilderness of featureless suburbs; but those mountains, the target selectors reckoned, would concentrate both blast and radiation on the densely populated city center, and that is what happened. Right in the city center, like the dot in a bull's-eye, there was, and still is, a conspicuous bridge, shaped like the letter T, visible from five miles up. Colonel Paul Tibbets, the pilot of the *Enola Gay*, the B-29 that dropped the bomb, called it "the most perfect A.P."—aiming point—"I've seen in this whole damn war." In those days, the residential and business area around the bridge was built mostly of wood. As an A-bomb target, then, Hiroshima was, by ill luck, just about perfect.

Much of what was formerly the crowded city center is now the Peace Memorial Park. The park is set on a long, cleared axis, with the famous A-Bomb Dome—the skeleton of what was once the Industry Promotion Hall—across the river at one end; the cenotaph, sheltered by a kind of stone tent, in the middle; and the Peace Memorial Museum, recently doubled in size, at the other. The museum displays something of Hiroshima's past as a port of embarkation—an Oriental version of Oakland, California—for Japan's wars: against China, in 1894–95; against Russia, in 1904–5; and against the Allies in the early part of the Second World War. It also displays a full-size model of the atomic bomb—an ugly black cylinder about twelve feet long—and relics and memorabilia of the atomic attack: pots and pans melted by fire; the shadow left by a rare Japanese idler, vaporized as he lounged on the stone steps of a bank that never opened (the shadow was starting to fade a few years back, but a local artist found a way to preserve it); scraps of school uniforms very like the ones my own children wear to our village school; charred book bags; aluminum lunch boxes of long-dead pupils; rusty rifles; a photocopy of the order, in English, to drop the bomb on a list of target cities, headed by Hiroshima, "as soon as the weather will permit visual bombing after 3 August 1945"; a blast-crumpled sewing machine; a clock stopped at eight-fifteen; a model of the city with the bomb, shown as a blinking light, hanging over it (material of this kind was to have been displayed in the Smithsonian, but after protests by veterans' groups and others it was left out of the exhibit); and, most poignant of all, a diorama in which a mother and child stagger, ragged, blackened, and bleeding, through a realistic inferno.

This last scene has no caption. Its challenge is wordless: if you defend the atomic bomb, defend this. The diorama was for me when I first saw it a moment of revelation. Despite the omnipresence of the word "peace," there is nothing peaceful about the museum, the dome, or the Peace Park. The place is a cemetery—but not one like Gettysburg, where the dead of both sides are honored. Only one side fell here, unreconciled, its dead still bound together by the angry tribal solidarity of war. The evasive inscription on the cenotaph, composed by a professor at Hiroshima University—"Rest in peace, for the error will not be repeated"—defeats its own purpose. What error? The war? War in general? Pearl Harbor? The bomb? Who made the error? Japan? The United States? Was this a war crime, a military necessity, stern justice, harsh mercy, well-intentioned terror, the last act of a savage conflict? What is the message of the A-Bomb Dome, with a dent in its carefully preserved skeletal roof indicating the point in the sky, almost overhead, where the bomb exploded? The Peace Memorial Museum conspicuously gives no answers, and the exhibit in Washington, now scaled back to little more than part of the fuselage of the B-29 bomber *Enola Gay*, does not address these questions, either.

No longer does the Hiroshima bomb seem quite the triumph of science that it appeared to be at the time. War has not been abolished; there is no nuclear-enforced peace. Atomic weapons are under only the shakiest of international controls: China just tested one; France plans to resume testing, too. Electricity is not too cheap to meter, as was joyfully forecast; the once bright hopes of nuclear power seem to be dying an appropriately lingering death. Still, the facts are at last coming clear. All but a few of the documents have been declassified, some as recently as a few months ago. The official dead of Hiroshima have now been numbered at 186,940. The figure's precision hints at pious fraud, since it has long been impossible to connect any individual death to the bomb with any certainty, but the order of magnitude is right. Why did so many people have to die?

A CHILD'S DEATH BY FIRE

THE ROAD TO HIROSHIMA BEGAN, a clergyman once told me, under an apple tree in the Middle East. A more recent address is the East End of London, England, specifically 33 Cowper Road, Stoke Newington, where, on the night of May 31, 1915, the world's first strategic-bombing campaign claimed its first victim, Elsie Leggatt, aged three, who was killed by a bomb dropped from a German Navy airship, LZ 38; her sister, May, died a few days later. The German air attacks on England during the First World War, initially by zeppelins, then by primitive airplanes, are now largely forgotten, overshadowed by what came later. In eighty-four raids spread over almost four years, fewer than fourteen hundred civilians were killed, and British war production was mostly unaffected. Just the same, they made a deep impression; a new dimension had been added to war. Military visionaries prophesied that the next war would be fought by heavy bomber fleets smashing enemy cities; the only defense would be to get one's overwhelming blow in first. The doctrine of the knockout blow, first suggested by an Italian general, Giulio Douhet, in 1921, was the essential precursor to Hiroshima; between the two World Wars, it was generally accepted, without any real evidence, that a nation's will to fight could be broken by the right combination of high-explosive and incendiary bombs dropped on its cities. (Douhet added poison gas as well.) The generation that led and fought the Second World War lived under the shadow of the bomber; in its nuclear, ballistic-missile form, we are under it still.

Despite halfhearted attempts between the wars to forge an international agreement that would prohibit the bombing of cities, the knockout blow was tried several times before Hiroshima, with much loss of life but suspiciously little success. Unable to strike at the Axis any other way, in 1942 the British Royal Air Force, under an aggressive new commander, Air Marshal Sir Arthur T. Harris—Bomber Harris to the public, Chopper or Killer to his men—began a campaign of what he termed "area" raids by night against Germany. (The Germans called them "terror" raids.) The same darkness that gave the British bombers some protection against German flak and fighters made it impossible for them to hit any but the biggest targets, like whole towns. Harris made a virtue of necessity, with the argument that "dehousing" the German workers would have much the same effect on their morale and efficiency as destroying war factories, with the difference that crowded working-class districts were easier to hit, and not as heavily defended. Harris's raids led the British military theorist Basil Liddell Hart to a tart comment: "It will be ironical if the defenders of civilization depend for victory upon the most barbaric, and unskilled, way of winning a war that the modern world has seen." But Liddell Hart wrote this only for his diary. The people of Britain and its new ally, the United States, approved, and called for many more such raids.

Harris obliged with radically new tactics. By mid-1943, the Royal Air Force had made two breakthroughs in the world's first electronic war: a system for blinding radar defenses by dropping strips of aluminum foil, called Window; and a primitive airborne radar, H2S, that painted a crude picture of the terrain below. Hamburg, the second-largest city in Germany, was selected to try them out. Hamburg had many genuine military targets—aircraft factories, U-boat construction yards, and other war industries. By a trick of geography, these were all situated on canals on the southern side of the River Elbe. Hamburg's million and a half citizens lived for the most part in residential districts on the north side. Harris chose the north side for his experiment.

Just after midnight on July 25, 1943, the R.A.F. attacked with seven hundred and twenty-eight aircraft, showering the city with a mixture of high-explosive bombs, weighing between five hundred and eight thousand pounds, and clusters of incendiaries. The night was hot and dry; pilots saw many small fires linking up into a gigantic blaze. Two daylight raids by B-17s of the United States Eighth Air Force followed, aimed at the waterfront factories. Two nights later, seven hundred and eighty-seven R.A.F. bombers came back to refresh the fires north of the river. This time, Brigadier General Fred L. Anderson, United States Army Air Forces, flew as second pilot on a British bomber to witness a sight never seen in war before. Below him was, in the words of one witness, "a storm . . . a hurricane . . . a sea of fire." The Hamburg Fire Department's log, describing the scene, added a new word to the vocabulary of war: *Feuersturm*—firestorm. In just over an hour, four square miles of the city—equivalent to all of Lower Manhattan from Madison Square to Battery Park—was a roaring inferno. People in basement shelters heard a tornado howling outside, then saw boiling tar from the roads and lead melted from roofs cascading down the stairs. Hundred-and-fifty-mile-an-hour winds uprooted trees, smashed in doors, and swept fleeing runners off their feet. A few made safety in the waterways; the rest died in the streets or the shelters, as the fire replaced oxygen from the air with poisonous carbon monoxide.

The firestorm is not seen in nature. To achieve the effect, fires need to be started in many places, miles apart. Rising, heated air draws in more air, which soon reaches gale force and links the fires together, killing by asphyxiation, heat, and the collapsing of buildings. As the fire burns inward toward the center, escape becomes all but impossible. Called, in the R.A.F. euphemism of the time, self-energized dislocation—the target provides the fuel, the attacker only the lighter—the firestorm is the most one-sidedly efficient way yet discovered of killing human beings. Hiroshima, still two years away, would be destroyed by a nuclear-ignited firestorm.

Harris next tried to burn down Berlin, in the winter of 1943–44, and failed. It was too big, too spread out, too well defended. The R.A.F. lost a thousand and forty-seven bombers and their crews in the Berlin battle—more than its entire frontline strength when it began. Harris claimed that he could "produce in Germany by April 1st 1944, a state of devastation in which surrender is inevitable," but the date came and went without Germany's capitulation. If strategic air power alone was ever to win a war, the time had come, the air generals reasoned, to try terror, the theorists' knockout blow, "against the morale of the [German] High Command, the army and the civilian population," as Sir Charles Portal, Marshal of the R.A.F., put it. The result was the plan to destroy Dresden. Harris did not originate the idea. An Allied summit was due to meet at Yalta in February of 1945. Churchill called for dramatic proof to convince Stalin that his allies, bogged down in the West, were not leaving everything to him. Roosevelt, tired and ill, went along. Dresden, the "Florence on the Elbe," was a treasure-house of Baroque and rococo art and architecture. The normal population, some six hundred thousand, had been swollen to more than a million by hordes of refugees fleeing a Soviet tank army, reported to be seventy miles away. On the night of February 13, 1945, a force of seven hundred and ninety-six R.A.F. bombers attacked Dresden in two waves, three hours apart, to harass or kill firefighters. The result was history's second major firestorm, stoked up the next day by three hundred and eleven American B-17s—the first such open collaboration by the Allied air forces in fire-raiding. Between thirty-five thousand and a hundred thousand died, and possibly many more. Destroying the city did not help the Soviet advance; Hitler still ran his war from Berlin. Dresden confirmed one of the best-attested lessons of the Second World War: military leaders, themselves safe in bunkers, can take enormous civilian casualties without flinching.

Dresden—and the very similar fire raid on Tokyo a month later—also marked the crossing, concealed from the public of the Allied nations, of an invisible moral line. Air attacks on factories producing war supplies were generally considered defensible in a just war. Such factories were usually in or near cities; civilians inevitably suffered. Burning down the houses of the people who worked in such factories was still defensible, if barely so; able-bodied workers would go to air-raid shelters while the raids were in progress. But setting firestorms could have only one result—the mass killing of civilians, with no possibility of escape. Dresden was described as a communications center—as all big cities have to be. But United States Army Air Forces headquarters, in Washington, denied that Dresden marked any change in American bombing policy—which the Rutgers historian William L. O'Neill calls "an outright lie"—while the R.A.F. branded neutral reports that twenty to thirty-five thousand civilians had been killed in Dresden, far less than the real total, as Nazi propaganda. Moral qualms about wiping out whole cities had thus been silently overcome half a year before Hiroshima; the only question left was the ethically less troubling one of the method. With Dresden and downtown Tokyo destroyed by fire, the acceptability of wiping out Hiroshima with an atomic bomb was taken for granted by its makers.

Over the years since Americans dropped atomic bombs on Hiroshima and Nagasaki, it has been suggested—especially in Japan—that the bombs, even if they had been ready in time, would not have been used against Germans. This cannot be proved either way. However, given the stirrings of moral doubt about the fire-bombings in 1944 and 1945—"Are we beasts? Are we taking this too far?" Winston

Churchill said, on seeing the result of one raid—the difficulty of finding an undamaged German city after Dresden, and concern about the reaction of Americans of German descent, much more serious thought would have taken place first than was ever accorded to the atomic-bombing of Japan. Nazism was viewed as a thoroughly evil doctrine that held mostly decent, deceived people in bondage. But there was no such thing as a good Japanese; Japanese were all evil beyond redemption. Ernie Pyle, the G.I.s' favorite war correspondent, who was killed by a Japanese machine-gun bullet on the tiny island of Ie on April 18, 1945, wrote:

> In Europe we felt that our enemies, horrible and deadly as they were, were still people. But out here I soon gathered that the Japanese were looked upon as something subhuman or repulsive; the way some people feel about cockroaches or mice.

Resident Japanese aliens and Japanese-Americans alike had been interned, stripped of their property, denied legal rights. The idea that within fifty years a Japanese-American judge would be a household name in America would have seemed pure fantasy.

But, loathsome as they were, the Japanese were also terrifying, like any madmen ready to die for a cause; reasonable people would never have begun a war like theirs in the first place. They also seemed to have superhuman courage. On island after island, the Marines encountered a tenacity in defense that Americans had never before seen in war. Sheltered behind concrete bunkers and barriers of coconut logs, Japanese soldiers worked their machine guns until they died or were burned out by flamethrowers. They rarely surrendered, and then only in ones or twos, usually wounded. How, then, short of extermination, could they ever be defeated?

In fact, their military prowess was greatly exaggerated. By August of 1943, Japan had begun the long retreat from its sensational early victories against a poorly prepared United States and the ramshackle empires of the European colonial powers. Barely six months after the United States entered the war, four of the six aircraft carriers that Japan had sent against Pearl Harbor on December 7, 1941, were sunk at Midway, and they could not be replaced. By mid-1943, Guadalcanal, the first strong point of Japan's outer defense perimeter, had fallen to American Marines; Tarawa, in the Gilbert Islands, was next. But these places were far from Japan, the United States, or anywhere else, and were hard to find on a map. An American naval blockade had already drastically impaired Japan's ability to import oil it needed for the war; by April of 1945, the flow of oil would be cut off completely. Japan's eventual fate was sealed. Why did they fight on? Simple patriotism as Americans understood it seemed inadequate to explain what was usually described as the "fanatical courage" of individual Japanese, so attention turned to their military code, *Bushido*—literally, "the way of the gentry of the sword."

Bushido was the code of the Japanese samurai, the warrior caste that dominated Japan during its three and a half centuries of seclusion—a time, it should be noted, of all but unbroken peace. *Bushido* has points in common with the outlook of all military élites—and, for that matter, with the United States military's Code of Conduct—calling for obedience to orders, loyalty to comrades, death before dishonorable surrender. But it has many specifically Japanese elements. *Bushido* is not a realistic program for achieving victory at the lowest cost; it is a romantic cult of failure and death. Because it was the code of a self-conscious, arrogant minority, *Bushido* was not for the ordinary man, just as Nazism was not for every German. But enough Japanese were ready to die, freely or under manipulated moral pressure, to make them fearsome enemies.

How did Emperor Hirohito fit into this alarming pattern? His role, poorly understood even by most Japanese, baffled all but a few Americans. The Japanese monarchy had, and still has, a religious basis, nothing to do with war or the military caste. Hirohito himself was not a samurai, and did not share their ideals or their cult of death any more than the common people did.

Under Japan's constitution of 1889, which was current in the war years, the Emperor was a figurehead monarch not concerned with day-to-day politics. The same constitution, however, made him Commander-in-Chief—the supreme warlord, in theory, to whom every Japanese samurai-soldier owed obedience. Hirohito's "right of command" meant, in reality, the right of the military high command to issue orders in his name. Having tried to understand the enormous evil of Hitler, Americans could most easily interpret Japan as a branch office of Hitler's dictatorship, with Hirohito as a hereditary, all-powerful Führer—who also wore a small mustache.

Very few Americans knew enough about Japan to see that this reading was wrong. One who did was Joseph Grew, the Ambassador to Tokyo in the 1930s and subsequently Under-Secretary and Acting Secretary of State. Japanese and Americans who believed that Hirohito would order a fight to the bitter end were wrong, but only in the very last days of the war did a few Americans come to see that Hirohito was the only man who could actually prevent a suicidal last stand, and so save many lives. Grew was one of the first.

In September of 1944, with Germany's defeat near, Prime Minister Winston Churchill met with President Franklin D. Roosevelt at the President's home, in Hyde Park, New York, to confirm their understanding that the British-American monopoly of atomic energy would continue after the war. In the meantime, "when a 'bomb' is finally available, it might perhaps, after mature consideration, be used against the Japanese, who should be warned that this bombardment will be repeated until they surrender." These words occur in an aide-mémoire signed by both leaders—a reminder that the idea might be worth further study. This was not the first time that Japan had been mentioned as a possible nuclear target. As early as May of 1943, a Washington committee had thought about atom-bombing the Japanese fleet in Truk anchorage—a genuine military target. But Roosevelt died on April 12, 1945, before the first bomb was ready for testing; and in the press of events during the last weeks of the war no "mature consideration"—if the Churchillian-sounding adjective means unhurried and well informed—ever took place.

The most ominous question of all—whether the United States really wanted to lead the world down the unposted road to nuclear war—was never seriously discussed by the nation's politicians or the military chiefs of staff. Consciences had calloused. Destroying cities had by this time become routine; the atomic bomb was thought of as simply a more powerful explosive for the job.

When Saipan and Tinian, in the Mariana Islands, fell to an American assault in June of 1944—an assault that was dismayingly costly in terms of American lives—Tokyo and Japan's industrial belt on the Pacific coast came within B-29 range. But the results continued to be disappointing. When the B-29s flew high enough to avoid the Japanese flak and fighter defenses, they met a new and mysterious hazard, winds up to two hundred miles an hour (later to be called the jet stream), and overshot orthodox targets like aircraft factories and steel mills. Of the seventy-two bombers that attacked Nagoya in December of 1944, half failed to return.

In January of 1945, a new operational commander, Major General Curtis LeMay, a keen student of British bombing methods who had commanded the third division of the Eighth Air Force in Europe, took command of the strategic bombing of Japan. He introduced new tactics. Simply put, the XXI Bomber Command took over British techniques and, with them, British justifications, or rationalizations, for burning down entire cities. Tests on Japanese wood-and-paper houses, mocked-up in Utah, showed how well they would burn. LeMay ordered his B-29s prepared for incendiary raids in the style of the R.A.F. Guns and ammunition were left behind, to make possible the delivery of six-ton loads of incendiaries. The B-29s were, for the first time, to fly by night, in a loose stream, finding their targets individually and bombing from an altitude of five to seven thousand feet, instead of the previous twenty-five to thirty thousand.

THE GREAT FIRE

THE FIRST OF THE NEW-STYLE ATTACKS was delivered against downtown Tokyo, the most densely populated area in Japan, on the night of March 9–10, 1945. Three hundred and twenty-five B-29s were dispatched, with orders to bomb the general area between the Sumida and Ara Rivers—the oldest part of Tokyo. Airmen later joked that General Thomas Power, circling high overhead in the lead B-29, wore out a red pencil marking crosses on his map as the fires began. Within thirty minutes, the fires had joined into a sixteen-square-mile inferno, and its updraft tossed the big bombers around like paper airplanes. Their crews could smell burning flesh. The firestorm overwhelmed the primitive Japanese civil defenses—buckets of sand, shovels, and foot pumps. Most of the people in the target area were incinerated or suffocated. The next morning, the rivers were choked with bodies. The Tokyo police counted an implausibly precise eighty-three thousand seven hundred and eighty-three dead; the generally accepted figure is upward of a hundred thousand. General Power claimed after the war, "It was the greatest single disaster incurred by any enemy in military history. It was greater than the combined damage of Hiroshima and Nagasaki. There were more casualties than in any other military action in the history of the world." He may not have been exaggerating. "Properly kindled, Japanese cities will burn like autumn leaves," *Time* reported.

Mass death apart, what was achieved? Downtown Tokyo undoubtedly was an industrial area of sorts, as it is today. Japanese manufacturers have always relied on workers with tiny backyard factories and home workshops for many of their simpler components. But these small producers are easily replaced, and to put them all out of action would have taken the destruction of every city in Japan. Encouraged by his boss, the veteran chief of staff of the Army Air Forces, General Henry (Hap) Arnold, in Washington ("Congratulations . . . your crews have got the guts for anything"), LeMay energetically carried on the work.

Missions against Japan had become safer than training flights back in the United States, LeMay later reported. Eventually, of Japan's sixty-six biggest cities, fifty-nine had been mostly destroyed, and the seven others partly destroyed; a hundred and seventy-eight square miles of congested wooden houses had been burned out; upward of half a million Japanese civilians had been killed; more than twenty million were homeless. By the summer of 1945, only two Japanese cities with populations of more than a quarter of a million had not been firebombed—Kyoto and, for reasons given only to General LeMay, and to no one else in his command (knowledge, he later said, that stopped him from leading raids on Japan in person), Hiroshima. Defiantly, Japan fought on.

The firebomb campaign destroyed some forty percent of all urban housing in Japan. LeMay later claimed that his bombers alone might have brought Japan to surrender, but he conceded that he could offer no hard evidence—an echo of repeated claims made in Europe by Air Marshal "Bomber" Harris. In Japan, the national character has been offered as one explanation for Japan's perseverance. The country has a long history of natural disasters, stoically endured. Some hundred and forty thousand people were killed in the Tokyo-Yokohama earthquake of 1923, only a generation before the war; the memorial to the great fire raid is a simple annex to a shrine recalling the great earthquake.

But Japanese—and German and British—stoicism cannot be the complete explanation. There is something wrong with the theory of strategic bombing itself—particularly in the form of the knockout blow—which seems to rest on confusion about the meaning of "lowering morale." Bereavement, hunger, and homelessness depressed Japanese civilians, of course, as they would anyone. A handful of intellectuals began whispering about peace, in private, and some were arrested, but low spirits generally turned to anger, not against the Japanese government—as the theory predicted—but against the cruel enemy and his devilish bombers.

Over the years, dozens of Hiroshima and Nagasaki survivors have told me the same thing: even after the atomic bombs, they were ready to endure whatever had to be endured at the command of Emperor Hirohito, who was, they believed, directing Japan's war in person. How Hirohito actually viewed its opening move at Pearl Harbor is, like much about that tight-lipped monarch, not precisely known. Years later, however, his post-war Grand Chamberlain and confidant, Sukemasa Irie, told me that the Emperor considered America's terms for lifting the embargo on shipments of oil—Japan had to get out of both Indochina *and* China—"too severe." On being told about plans for a surprise attack on the American fleet at Pearl Harbor, Hirohito proposed that the Americans be given some warning. Since warnings tend to take the surprise out of surprise attacks, all that the military would agree to was breaking off diplomatic relations thirty minutes before the attack. In any event, the cipher clerks in the Japanese Embassy in Washington had trouble with the coded message from Tokyo, so the vague non-warning was delivered far too late.

Whether or not Hirohito was a closet pacifist on the eve of Pearl Harbor—probably not—he certainly became one, as Japan's never very rational hopes of victory faded. Japan still looked to Americans to be self-confident and supremely united—"a hundred million people with one heart," as Japanese propaganda broadcasts claimed. The real situation in Tokyo was very different. A peace party was tentatively forming as early as 1943, headed by no less a personage than Emperor Hirohito himself, universally seen by Americans—and by almost all Japanese as well—as a nearsighted, implacable warlord, still dreaming of world conquest. Hirohito could not, however, simply call off the war. Guided by the military, the Japanese nation was gripped by a solid official consensus to fight to the bitter end. Hirohito was not part of it, but the convention around his throne let him speak his mind with relative freedom to only one other person: a court official, Marquis Koichi Kido, Lord Keeper of the Privy Seal, a title that in practice translates less ornately as "household minister." Hirohito's real role was, like that of the British monarch, to track the day-to-day political process from an aloof distance, intervening only if it threatened to break down. For this, he needed inside information; his collector of political intelligence, and exerter of discreet influence, was Kido, a former education minister and the grandson of one of the founders of modern Japan. Kido kept a diary, and it, with other sources, lets us follow what happened.

As early as March of 1943, two months after the fall of Guadalcanal, Kido recorded an "unusually long" audience with Hirohito in which he warned the monarch that domestic Communism might flourish if the war went on. By January of 1944, Kido had developed a clear view—but only in his diary—of the future course of events; Japan should sue for peace, he wrote, while there was still time to stave off disaster; the initiative "should not coincide with the collapse of Germany," but should begin "prior to the time that the United States, Great Britain, and the U.S.S.R. unite in their hostility against Japan." In April of 1944, Japan launched its last offensive, Operation Ichigō (Priority), aimed at the final conquest of China, the war's original objective. Half a million troops attacked on a thousand-mile front; but Ichigō eventually petered out in China's crowded, endless distances. When Saipan fell, in June of 1944, the Cabinet of Prime Minister and General Hideki Tojo, who had launched the war with America, resigned. Japan had plainly lost its reckless gamble; the end was only a matter of time.

American observers expected that the new Prime Minister would put out feelers for peace. They reckoned without the labyrinthine, leisurely methods by which Japanese make and modify a national consensus—a process that still mystifies the rest of the world. The next Prime Minister was Kuniaki Koiso, governor-general of Japanese-occupied Korea. A serving lieutenant-general, Koiso was not about to recommend peace negotiations until the Japanese Army had won a last battle. The most favorable battlefield, the army planners claimed, would be the Japanese homeland itself. If Japan won the decisive battle, or lost it while inflicting many Allied casualties, they argued, the minimum condition for peace with military honor, preserving the throne of their Commander-in-Chief, Hirohito, might be achieved. What was essentially the Army's own interest was presented as patriotic loyalty to the throne—a self-serving maneuver that only Hirohito himself could defeat. The paradox baffled American analysts. An estimate prepared by the Office of Strategic Services, forerunner of the Central Intelligence Agency, in September of 1944, concluded, "The war will continue until the emperor says 'Cease!'" But no one in America could imagine how the Emperor, if he was indeed the captive of military "extremist groups," could possibly break free and say the magic word.

Meanwhile, the war went on. On February 4, 1945, President Roosevelt, Premier Joseph Stalin, and Prime Minister Churchill met at Yalta, on the Black Sea, to decide the future of Germany, which was tottering toward defeat, and for some haggling (between F.D.R. and Stalin, with Churchill excluded) over Stalin's price for joining the war against Japan and thus tying up Japanese troops. Stalin's asking price was high: the Kuril Islands, ports in China, rights on the railways linking the Trans-Siberian with the Chinese ports. In return, he agreed to enter the war against Japan within three months after the defeat of Germany. By mid-1945, Japanese ships had been driven off the high seas, and bringing Japanese troops home from China was impossible. Stalin's help was no longer needed, but he still wanted his triple reward.

WHO WAS GOING TO DEFEAT JAPAN?

AT THIS POINT, WITH GERMANY FINISHED, the three American services were vying for the post-war appropriations and prestige that would come with the inevitable victory over the last enemy. The Army hoped that an invasion of Japan would end the war; the Navy, that its blockade and carrier-based air attacks would suffice; the Air Forces, that strategic bombing, by fire and high explosives, would do the trick. The unknown factor, the atomic bomb, was still not ready. Beginning on April 1, 1945, the American noose around Japan tightened again; B-29s began mining the straits between the Japanese islands, choking off the last seaborne supplies, and the United States Army landed on Okinawa, regarded by the Japanese as part of the homeland. Four days later, a retired Japanese admiral, Baron Kantaro Suzuki, became the nation's last wartime Prime Minister. To outsiders, Suzuki seemed

a comical choice to lead Japan's last battle: he was seventy-seven and deaf, and walked with a limp—a reminder of four bullet wounds inflicted by ultra-nationalist Army officers who had tried to overthrow the government in 1936. In Japanese eyes, however, Suzuki's appointment, brokered by Kido, was not so strange. He had been Hirohito's Grand Chamberlain when he was wounded; his loyalty was beyond question. He was military but not Army; as Japan's situation became ever more hopeless, the weakening of Army influence had begun. Above all—and much to the confusion of American analysts, who found the elderly admiral's maneuverings utterly incomprehensible—Suzuki was a master of what the Japanese call *haragei*, or "stomach art": the skill of building, or changing, a consensus by unspoken communication.

The Japanese stomach artist's first priority is to keep his group together and functioning, often by proclaiming the old policy; then, imperceptibly, he introduces a new one. If there is still conflict, it may never be resolved, and any number of contradictory policies may be followed at once, or nothing may happen. If a new consensus emerges from hints and private talks, the master of stomach art graciously pretends to give way and abandons the old one; no one else needs to admit to a change of mind, and face is saved all round. Officially speaking, Japan already had a consensus, which Suzuki endorsed "without hesitation": fighting on to the end by mobilizing for total war. After this was confirmed in writing, the Army named General Korechika Anami, a veteran of the New Guinea fighting, who had once been Hirohito's aide-de-camp, as Minister of War. Further confusing American analysts, Shigenori Togo, the Foreign Affairs Minister at the time of Pearl Harbor, resumed his post, while Prime Minister Suzuki marked the imminent collapse of Germany by reaffirming Japan's improbable "faith in certain victory." From across the Pacific, the consensus for national suicide looked to be unbreakable.

Unlike the Soviets and the Americans, the Japanese got no secret information as they played out their lonely endgame in the war. American cryptanalysts had broken the Japanese diplomatic code—the so-called Purple code—and summaries of Japanese diplomatic traffic went every day to top officials in Washington, a group deliberately kept small to protect the source. Later the Japanese operational codes were broken as well. These intercepts were called Ultra, a reference to how secret they were, or Magic, a joke about how they were obtained. The Soviets, on their side, were kept posted on the progress of the American atomic bomb by various spies within the Manhattan Project: Klaus Fuchs, a German scientist with British nationality; Julius and Ethel Rosenberg; and others. But Japan's slender secret resources had long since dried up: they never got a hint, for instance, of the atomic bomb.

Japan's ambassador in Moscow, Naotake Sato, was, however, astute; he sensed that Stalin's neutrality, still guaranteed by treaty, could not be relied on. On May 9th, the day after Germany's defeat, Sato advised Foreign Affairs Minister Togo, in Tokyo, that the Soviet Union might well either join in the fighting or seek to broker a peace with substantial gains for itself—territorial or otherwise. Sato did not, of course, know that Stalin had already agreed to enter the war within three months of Germany's defeat, but the alert Japanese diplomat soon picked up hints. On May 23rd, he informed Togo in Tokyo that Japanese couriers maintaining surveillance on the Trans-Siberian Railroad had counted, in a seven-day span, almost two hundred trains headed east with troops, tanks, trucks, fighter aircraft, field guns, and bridging gear. A Japanese-Soviet crisis of some kind, Sato advised Tokyo the following day, was likely by August.

In Tokyo, complicated maneuvering was under way, but for what? On May 11, 1945—the same day that an ad-hoc Target Committee of scientists and military men in Los Alamos was selecting the best Japanese target for an atomic bomb—the Tokyo leadership met to consider Japan's options. The discussions, which lasted until the fourteenth, were restricted to the so-called Big Six—the Prime Minister, the Foreign Affairs Minister, the Minister of War, the Minister for the Navy, and the Army and Navy chiefs of staff—without any fanatical young aides or secretaries. The military men were at last ready to listen calmly to alternatives to their idea of a final battle, if there were any, although in public they continued preparations to fight on to the end.

The Army Chief of Staff reported the ominous Soviet troop movement east, and those who attended the meeting decided to seek negotiations with the Soviets, the objectives being (1) to keep the Soviet Union out of the war, (2) to persuade the Soviets to adopt a friendly policy, and (3) to seek Soviet mediation to end the war on terms acceptable to Japan. Noting that the Soviet Union was unlikely to consider "throwing in her lot with a nation tottering on the brink of defeat," Foreign Minister Togo suggested this payoff: the Soviet Union would regain the territories it lost in the Russo-Japanese War; Japan would keep Korea; and southern Manchuria, near the Soviet border, would be neutralized. The proposal was a fantasy—Japan was in no position to reward anyone—but its motivation was flexible enough to get the Army's agreement: Japan's approach to the Soviets was consistent either with fighting the last "decisive battle" and then suing for peace or with ending the war before it could be fought. Ambassador Yakov Malik, in Tokyo, the Soviet official they decided to approach, was noncommittal. Also in Tokyo, meanwhile, the Japanese Army unveiled its plans for the final, decisive battle. Japan's principal weapon was to be a national suicide pact—kamikaze planes, crash boats, human torpedoes, mines, and hand-carried anti-tank bombs.

This "fundamental policy" was formally submitted to Hirohito on June 8th. The Emperor scowled but said nothing. The next day, Suzuki introduced it to Japan's rubber-stamp parliament, and it was approved. Vice-Admiral Takajiro Onishi, the inventor of kamikaze tactics, spoke of twenty million suicide fighters for the final battle—another romantic fantasy. But Emperor Hirohito, Privy Seal Kido, and Foreign Affairs Minister Togo were all doing their best—a muddled, limited best—to see that the last battle was never fought.

While Japan was struggling with its intentions, the battle for Okinawa raged on. The island was invaded on April 1, 1945, and finally secured on June 22nd. In the sense that the stubborn Japanese resistance on Okinawa, without any air cover, resupply, or reinforcements, gave some credibility, on both sides, to the myth of Japan's decisive battle of the homeland, and so kept the war going until the bomb was ready, Okinawa made Hiroshima possible. Some writers have asserted that the Okinawa battle was badly handled by the American side and largely unnecessary, and that all conclusions based on it are suspect. The speculation about the number of American lives that, it is argued, Hiroshima may have saved are all extrapolations from, or interpretations of, the Okinawa casualties, which were heavy on both sides.

On June 22nd, the day Okinawa fell, Hirohito summoned the Big Six generals and politicians to a still standing annex of his burned-out palace and expressed the wish that they "study concrete means" for ending the war. For the first time, the Emperor mentioned peace directly to his military chiefs, but he proposed no terms of settlement—the essential point. Two weeks later, on July 7th, Hirohito suggested that Prime Minister Suzuki send Prince Fumimaro Konoe, a distant imperial relative, who had been the Prime Minister at the time Japan joined the Axis, to Moscow to seek peace terms from America and Britain, using the Soviets as intermediaries. Hirohito instructed Konoe to report directly back to the throne, adding that he himself would favor any peace that Konoe could negotiate. But Moscow, of course, had a more attractive deal on offer elsewhere.

Between July 11th and 14th, Foreign Minister Togo, in Tokyo, and Ambassador Sato, in Moscow, exchanged a series of messages, and these were decoded in Washington within hours. The Magic summary of this exchange was not declassified until 1993. Togo now wanted Sato to find out "the extent to which it is possible to make use of Russia in ending the war," without letting the Russians know his intentions. Japan, Togo said in subsequent messages, was ready to give up all territories occupied during the war but was not ready for unconditional surrender. The terms would have to be "virtually equivalent to unconditional surrender," Sato warned, and he added, "Unless we make up our own minds, there is absolutely no point in sounding out the views of the Soviet government." The only useful purpose of sending Konoe to Moscow was "to propose an armistice and peace." In a message of July 18th, however, Sato agreed on the importance of "preserving our national structure"—he meant the monarchy—to save from total destruction the traditional Japanese concept of the nation as an extended family. Soviet Foreign Affairs Commissar Vyacheslav Molotov, Sato reported, was about to leave for Potsdam and was too busy to receive him, Sato. Prince Konoe had not been invited to Moscow, either.

Meanwhile, in Washington, policy-makers were equally divided about what terms they wanted for the approaching peace. The United States Navy, eager to take credit for ending the war, believed that a combination of blockade and persuasion could preclude an invasion. On July 7th, Navy Captain Ellis Zacharias, in a broadcast to Japan, began explaining, in fluent Japanese, that "unconditional surrender" was "a technical term which refers to the form in which hostilities are terminated" and recalling the Atlantic Charter's promise of "the right of all peoples to choose the form of government under which they will live"—implying the preservation of the throne, if the Japanese freely chose it. Joseph Grew, who had been United States Ambassador in Tokyo for a decade before the war, and was then Acting Secretary of State, sought to turn the resulting rumors of a change in American war aims into some clarification of them. The Emperor, he argued, was the figurehead but not the source of Japanese militarism. With another State Department expert on Japan, Eugene Dooman, Grew wrote a first draft of what would become the Potsdam Declaration, calling for "the unconditional surrender of all the Japanese armed forces," but clearly leaving open the possibility of "a constitutional monarchy under the present dynasty." The draft warned that "the alternative for Japan is prompt and utter destruction." Conceding that "it was all guesswork," Grew showed his draft to Truman, and the President wanted it put on the agenda for the forthcoming Potsdam conference. A number of Administration officials—especially Secretary of War Henry Stimson and his assistants in the War Department—also found Grew's suggestion compelling. But by the time of the Potsdam conference, James F. Byrnes, Roosevelt's "assistant President," who had no special knowledge of Japan, had become Secretary of State. He disagreed, fearing a voter backlash in the United States, and, thanks to his influence, no discussions of the Emperor's future took place.

IN A HURRY TO DROP THE BOMB

MEANWHILE, THE MANHATTAN PROJECT MANAGERS were lobbying hard in the opposite direction. Their thinking converged on the idea of administering a "profound psychological shock" either to "the Japanese" in general or to "the Emperor and his military advisers." In nuclear disguise, this was simply the nightmarish interwar theory of the knockout blow all over again. The search for psychological shock narrowed the choice of target to a small, flat, previously undamaged city; the aiming point was changed from a "vital war plant . . . closely surrounded by workers' houses," as had been proposed by Dr. James Conant, the president of Harvard, to a city center. The effect of both changes was to maximize civilian casualties. J. Robert Oppenheimer, the scientific director of Los Alamos, estimated that twenty thousand might die. (He did not reckon on the firestorm lit by the bomb, which quadrupled the deaths—an early, unintended case of overkill.) As Secretary of State–designate, James Byrnes sat in on these meetings. Byrnes later told President Truman that a "military source" (probably General Leslie Groves, the head of the Manhattan Project, who gave Truman the same figure) estimated that the invasion of Japan might result in a million American casualties—a figure in the realm of fantasy, since the Japanese would have had to hold off the invading Americans for six months, until both Kyushu and the main island of Honshu had been invaded, and almost all the invaders then wiped out. By the time the last wartime summit convened, at Potsdam, on July 16, 1945, and, that same day, the successful test of the first atomic bomb was secretly reported to Truman—some historians have argued that Truman delayed the conference until the bomb was tested—its use was already a foregone conclusion. So was the first target city, Hiroshima.

Six days after the news of the successful explosion of a plutonium-type bomb at Alamogordo, New Mexico, reached Truman in Potsdam, he received a detailed report from Groves. On July 24th, Truman signed an order, previously drafted by Groves, authorizing the atomic-bombing of Japan. We now know that Truman had been misinformed about what he was agreeing to. The next day, he wrote in his diary, "This weapon is to be used against Japan between now and August 10. I have told the Sec of War, Mr. Stimson, to use it so that military objectives and soldiers and sailors are to be the target and not women and children. . . . The target will be a purely military one and we will issue a warning statement asking the Japs to surrender and save lives. I'm sure they will not do that, but we will have given them a chance."

On July 26th, the last day of the Potsdam conference, Truman's "warning statement" was issued jointly by the United States, Britain, and China. Revised by Secretary of State Byrnes, the Potsdam Declaration called for the "unconditional surrender of the Japanese armed forces," adding, "The alternative for Japan is prompt and utter destruction"—an alternative that the Japanese could, and did, take to mean continued firebombing. Neither of the new threats facing Japan—the atomic bomb and Soviet intervention, then just two weeks away—was mentioned. Stimson made a last try to persuade Truman to leave open the possibility that the Japanese dynasty might continue, if the people wanted it, but he failed, because, as he said later, "too many people [in America] were likely to cry shame." On July 28th, Prime Minister Suzuki told a press conference in Tokyo that his government had found nothing new in the declaration and would "Kill it with silence"—that is, ignore it. Some historians have seen in this rebuff the first stage of a typical Japanese negotiation, blank refusal; others have suggested that the atomic bombs were America's response to it. But the bombing had already been ordered.

How accurate, we may well wonder, was the knowledge on which the use of the bomb was based? Three information loops, kept rigidly separate by wartime secrecy, had influenced the Americans who contributed to the bombing decision. The first loop, those who knew the secret of the bomb itself, numbered perhaps a hundred people. Congress and the media, the normal shapers of public opinion, were rigorously excluded. So were the opinions of many of the scientists working on the Manhattan Project. The Magic intercepts showing that peace moves of some sort were under way in Tokyo were even more closely held by the second loop—understandably, to protect their source. Only a handful of Truman's closest advisers saw them. The third loop, those who knew something about Japan and the role of its Emperor, and suspected—correctly, as it turned out—that he might have a constructive part to play, then and in the future, numbered not more than half a dozen in all, and were far from the scene: Truman took no Japan experts with him to Potsdam. The key point is that no one fully belonged to all three loops: no decision-maker had all the facts; only by understanding the little that the decision-makers knew, or thought they knew, can one make sense of their decisions.

General Groves's motivation is transparent. By the summer of 1945, he headed what was in effect a new branch of the American armed services—a nuclear-strike command, with fifteen aircraft and, after July 24th, two atomic bombs. Having made the bombs, Groves saw it as his duty to have them used, so that, among other things, their future effectiveness as weapons could be judged. He hoped to make Japan's ancient capital, Kyoto, the first target. He said later, "It was large enough in area for us to gain complete knowledge of the effects of the bomb. Hiroshima was not nearly so satisfactory in this respect." Groves was told that Kyoto had a million people, and reasoned that "any city of that size in Japan must be involved in a tremendous amount of war work, even if there were but a few large factories." The fact is that there were none in the center of Kyoto, the intended aiming point, which is a collection of wooden shrines and temples; but there were none of any size in central Hiroshima, either.

Fearing that a premature end to the war would prevent a practical test of the bomb, Groves speeded up his preparations after Germany surrendered. When Oppenheimer, worried about the weather, asked for a postponement in the Alamogordo test, Groves allowed him only a risky hour and a half. Groves's intent, he later explained, was to hasten the Potsdam proceedings: "I knew the effect a successful test would have on the issuance and wording of the Potsdam ultimatum. . . . A delay in issuing the Potsdam ultimatum could result in a delay in the Japanese reaction, with a further delay in the atomic attack on Japan." But he was out of the Magic loop, and knew nothing of Japan's ambiguous peace moves, and not much about Japan.

Byrnes, who had been Secretary of State for two weeks, saw Magic at Potsdam, and read it with a plain man's misunderstanding. "So long as the enemy demands unconditional surrender, we will fight as one man against the enemy," he said years later, quoting from an intercepted message (before it was declassified) that had been sent by Foreign Minister Togo to Ambassador Sato in Moscow on July 21, 1945. Byrnes garbled the text, but the gist is correct, as far as it goes: Byrnes denied that the Emperor's fate was the only sticking point, and didn't mention that well before the bombs were dropped Togo had gone on to inform his ambassador that Japan had "no objection to a peace based on the Atlantic Charter." Stimson, the only adviser close to Truman who was even partly included in all three information loops—he saw Magic, knew about the bomb, and had at least visited Japan—had also hoped that an early surrender would deny the Soviets a zone of occupation. "If the Russians seek joint occupation after a creditable participation in the conquest of Japan, I do not see how we could refuse them at least a token occupation," he advised Truman. But even Stimson never once suggested that the bomb not be used at all.

THE DECISION TO DROP

NO ONE EVER MADE A POSITIVE DECISION to drop the bomb on Hiroshima, only a negative one: not to interfere with a process that had begun years before, in very different circumstances. Truman later described it as "not any decision that you had to worry about," but a decision implies a choice, and Truman never contemplated, or even heard suggested, any delay, or any alternative to the bomb's use on a Japanese city.

Some scholars—especially those not of the wartime generation—have found it hard to believe that the act that launched the world into nuclear war could have come about so thoughtlessly, by default. Equally, many have found it incredible that the Potsdam talks were almost exclusively taken up with conflicts over Germany and Poland, and that the still ongoing war against Japan was not mentioned in any of the main sessions but merely tacked on as an afterthought. Understandably, a hidden link has been suspected: that Hiroshima was in some sense intended as the opening blast of the Cold War. In 1948, the British Nobel physicist Patrick Blackett argued that the bomb was used in order to force Japan's surrender before the Soviets could intervene; a later version, offered in 1965 by Professor Gar Alperovitz, of the University of Maryland, was that the *primary* motive was not to end the war but to intimidate the Soviets. In his book, *The Decision to Use the Atomic Bomb*, he further develops his theme. The American-Soviet alliance was certainly cooling fast by the time of Potsdam, and few of the Americans at the conference still wanted Soviet help in the Far East. But to argue that the bomb was used in order to forestall Soviet intervention against Japan and the inevitable demand for a share in its occupation implies that *not* using it as soon as it was ready was ever considered; it was not.

Many threads, originally unconnected, met on that clear morning over Hiroshima. Hitler, by his persecutions, touched off a moral chain reaction that brought many brilliant minds to America, where they worked on the bomb. Originally intended to deter the Nazis, the bomb became at some point a bomb to be used—against Japan. Only thirty years separated the death of young Elsie Leggatt in London from the mass slaughter of the Second World War fire raids—three decades of scientific discovery so dizzying that the laws of war, painfully worked out over centuries, could only limp along behind, lost in a fog of half-truths and official euphemisms about "dehousing the industrial workers," which involved killing them; "self-energized dislocation," or setting firestorms; "the technical suitability of target systems," meaning houses made of wood and straw. Then, in a flash, the veil was ripped away, the real idea behind strategic bombing made as brutally simple as the scientists' equation $E=mc^2$ (and, indeed, its very first practical application): one plane + one bomb = minus one Japanese city.

Monday, August 6, 1945, began like any other wartime day in Japan. By 8 A.M. most Hiroshima office workers were at their desks, children were at school, soldiers were doing physical exercises, high-school students and civilian work gangs were busy pulling down wooden houses to clear more firebreaks. During the night, there had been two air-raid alerts—and then all-clears. At 7:09 A.M., there was another alert, as a B-29 on a last weather check approached the city, and, at 7:31 A.M., another all-clear as it turned away. Minutes after eight, watchers in the city saw two B-29s approaching from the northeast: these were an observation plane and the *Enola Gay*. (Colonel Paul Tibbets, the pilot, had only the day before named the bomber after his mother.) The *Enola Gay*, in the lead, held its course straight and level for ten miles; at eight-fifteen, it let fall its single bomb. Immediately, the other B-29 banked hard to the left, the *Enola Gay* to the right; both quit the scene. Released at thirty-one thousand six hundred feet, or nearly six miles, the bomb fell for forty-three seconds and was triggered (by a barometric switch) by heavily symbolic chance nineteen hundred feet directly above a small hospital that was two hundred and sixty yards from the aiming point, the T-shaped Aioi Bridge.

Atomic bombs achieve their effects by means different from those of conventional high explosives. The Hiroshima bomb's stated equivalent of eleven thousand five hundred to thirteen thousand five hundred tons of TNT is thus somewhat misleading. When the man-made nuclear chain reaction took place over Hiroshima, the bomb itself was instantly vaporized, at a temperature of several million degrees centigrade, creating a fireball and radiating immense amounts of heat. Heated air then expanded in a shock wave. The blast effect is rapidly attenuated by distance, however, so that in Hiroshima the overpressure at ground level was less than that of a near miss by a conventional one-ton bomb. This explains why the A-Bomb Dome, almost directly under the point of detonation, still stands, and why most of the reinforced-concrete buildings near the hypocenter, having been designed to resist earthquakes, survived the bombing, only to be gutted by the subsequent fire.

Human beings and their houses fared differently. Heat radiated by the bomb burned exposed skin more than two miles from the hypocenter; wood and straw roofs were charred at almost the same distance and started fires in the wreckage of wooden houses, most of which collapsed inside a radius of a mile and a half. Instantaneous fires lit over a wide area are the recipe for a firestorm; one developed within half an hour of the bomb's exploding, and by 5 P.M., when it began to die down, nearly five square miles of central Hiroshima had been burned out. About three percent of the bomb's energy was released as neutrons and gamma rays. These directly affected people who were exposed to them, set up residual radioactivity—which contaminated man-made materials, ground, and water—and caused fallout in a soot-stained "black rain" precipitated by the fires. From all these causes, between seventy thousand and eighty thousand people are estimated to have died on August 6th, with more deaths from radiation sickness spread over the ensuing days, months, and years.

Strictly military damage was insignificant. The headquarters of the Second General Army, responsible for the defense of Japan as far south as Kyushu, were in Hiroshima, but its commander, Field Marshal Shunroku Hata, had prudently established his personal command post on a mountainside a mile and a half away, where he survived, unhurt, to declare limited martial law in the city. His operations section, a mile from the hypocenter, was damaged but reparable. Some three thousand officers and men of the Hiroshima garrison, whose barracks were in the medieval Hiroshima Castle, were killed, along with (according to persistent reports) a small number of American prisoners of war. Altogether, around twenty thousand soldiers, in the city for one reason or another, may have died. But the city's rail service started up twenty-four hours later; the docks and the dock yards, protected by a low hill, were mostly undamaged; no significant war production was lost. The only effect that Hiroshima could possibly have had on the war was the psychological shock on the leaders in Tokyo, some four hundred miles away. They had to hear about it first.

The first specific news of what had happened reached Tokyo, ironically, from Washington. On the day of the bombing, the White House released a statement, drafted by Groves's office, that broke the long-kept secret. Addressing Americans, the release opened on a vengeful note. "The Japanese began the war from the air at Pearl Harbor. They have been repaid many fold. And the end is not yet." The bomb was atomic, the statement revealed, and even more powerful ones were being developed. Taxpayers' money had not been wasted: "We have spent two billion dollars on the greatest scientific gamble in history—we won." Thanks, the release added, to the United States Army, "which achieved a unique success in managing so diverse a problem in the advancement of knowledge in an amazingly short time." It ended with a threat: "We are now prepared to obliterate more rapidly and completely every productive enterprise the Japanese have above ground in any city.

We shall destroy their docks, their factories, their communications. . . . If they do not now accept our terms, they may expect a rain of ruin from the air, the like of which has never been seen on this earth." This was bluff. America had only one more bomb immediately available, and Japan had few functioning productive enterprises left.

The next day, the Japanese Cabinet set up an Atomic Bomb Counter-measure Committee. It met, inconclusively, in an atmosphere of rumor and contradictory reports. The Foreign Ministry sent a protest to Washington, via Switzerland, against the use of "an inhuman weapon." On August 8th, Foreign Affairs Minister Togo met with the Emperor and showed him preliminary reports on the bombing. Hirohito asked him to renew to Prime Minister Suzuki the imperial wish for a quick end to the war. Late on the same day, in Moscow, Ambassador Sato was at last granted his long-sought meeting with Foreign Affairs Commissar Molotov. Before Sato could ask for Soviet mediation, Molotov curtly told him to be seated and read out the Soviet declaration of war on Japan. Within a few hours, Soviet tanks and troops had crossed the Manchurian border in force.

The next morning, August 9th, Hirohito told his tireless legman, Lord Privy Seal Kido, that "now that the Soviets have entered the war with Japan, there is urgent need to resolve the problem of a cease-fire," and asked Kido to convey this message to Prime Minister Suzuki. Suzuki asked a military adviser about the state of the Manchurian defenses; on hearing that they were hopelessly inadequate to stop the Soviet invaders, he sighed and said, "Then the game is up." At 10:30 A.M., the Supreme Council for the Direction of the War, the Big Six, met in a bunker under the gutted Imperial Palace in Tokyo. But in the meeting that followed, the deadlock in the leadership continued. Prime Minister Suzuki proposed that Japan accept the Potsdam Declaration. Foreign Minister Togo suggested that only one condition be attached: a guarantee of the welfare of the imperial family. Minister of War Anami and the two service chiefs of staff wanted three more conditions: limitation of the area to be occupied, war criminals to be tried by Japan, and Japanese forces to disarm themselves. Togo responded that there was a better chance of getting the guarantee involving the Emperor accepted if it was the only condition proposed.

While the meeting was in progress, the B-29 *Bock's Car* dropped the second, plutonium-type bomb, on Nagasaki, at 11:02 A.M. A full air-raid warning was sounded before the bombing, but then scaled down to an alert, and only about four hundred people had remained in shelters. But, unlike the textbook perfection of Hiroshima, Nagasaki suffered the mishaps that mar most military operations: fuel was running low, the target was cloud-covered, and the bomb fell a mile and a half from the city center, destroying an outlying suburb, Urakami, which had the heaviest concentration of Christians and the biggest Catholic church in all Japan. No true firestorm broke out, but two arguably legitimate military targets, a foundry and a rolling mill, were wrecked. Between twenty thousand and thirty thousand people lost their lives that day.

Unable to agree (and with only confused, sketchy reports from Nagasaki), the Big Six adjourned at one o'clock, and the full Japanese Cabinet met between 3:30 P.M. and 10 P.M., with an hour out for dinner. Still there was no consensus: the civilians, with a couple of exceptions, were for accepting Potsdam, with a guarantee for the Emperor; most of the military leaders still wanted all four conditions attached. Suzuki and Togo, favoring a single-condition surrender, found a novel way out. For the first time in Japanese history, they asked for a conference with the Emperor in order to report not a unanimous decision but an unbreakable disagreement among the leadership. Hirohito agreed to receive the military chiefs and members of the Cabinet at midnight, in his air-raid shelter. There, for two hours, they reviewed the arguments of the afternoon. At 2 A.M., Suzuki approached the throne (Hirohito was actually sitting on a hard wooden chair behind a desk) and, apologizing for their failure to reach a new consensus, asked Hirohito for *his* opinion. "I agree with the proposal of the Foreign Minister," the Emperor said. "Now is the time to bear the unbearable." At 3 A.M., the Cabinet members reconvened: they agreed unanimously to attach only one condition. Togo hurried bleary-eyed to the Foreign Ministry to draft telegrams to the Allies accepting the Potsdam terms "with the understanding that the terms enumerated in the said Declaration do not include any demand for modification of the prerogatives of His Majesty as a sovereign ruler."

The war was not over yet—this was not unconditional surrender—but the events of August 9, 1945, were undoubtedly the crucial step in the peace process. The role the atomic bombs played in ending the war therefore rests on exactly what happened in Tokyo on that day. The part attributable to the Soviets' treachery (from the Japanese viewpoint: the Soviet-Japanese neutrality pact still had more than eight months to run) is clear; it forced the leadership to find a new peace policy. It is harder to say exactly what the atomic bombs contributed. Outside Japan, few knew of the approaches to Moscow, or of the political maneuverings and the desperate situation inside Japan, and therefore the sequence of events seemed clear: the second bomb was dropped on Nagasaki, and early the next day the Japanese were publicly suing for peace. In the day's news, the Soviet intervention was barely mentioned, overshadowed by the bomb, and its implications were not discussed. To those who had read the menacing White House statement released three days earlier and now learned of Japan's acceptance of the Potsdam terms, it seemed obvious that "the Japanese" had at last been terrorized into surrender. Seemingly self-evident, this was only a guess. To tie it down as a historical fact, the mechanism by which fear was translated into decision needs to be laid bare. Who, exactly, was shocked into submission by the bombs? A study of the day's events among the Tokyo leadership, the only people who could sue for peace, uncovers a cause-and-effect sequence fully capable of forcing the decision, without the bombs.

As early as twelve weeks before Hiroshima, the Big Six had agreed to seek peace. The issue then dividing them—a huge difference, to be sure, for the prospective American invaders—was whether to do so after winning the "battle of the homeland" (but not the war itself, for that was plainly lost) or immediately, by negotiation, which was what Hirohito and his civilian ministers wanted. No one, however, was ready for unconditional surrender. The consensus-saving compromise had been to send Prince Konoe to Moscow, leaving up to him the terms he could negotiate—and promising more wrangling in Tokyo, on whether to accept them.

This scenario, never very realistic, grew less so every day the Soviets stalled. The Soviet declaration of war and the invasion of Manchuria finally exploded it, and the uneasy consensus in the Tokyo leadership disintegrated. Even if Americans were war-weary, as some Japanese hoped, the Soviets plainly were not. The Soviet

moves meant that Japan now faced the world's best tank army, on open plains giving every advantage to the attacker; imminent defeat; invasion from a new direction; and (according to the precedent set in Germany) the partition and
Communization of at least a part of the Japanese home islands. A new consensus
had to be found, and quickly: with just about the entire world now in arms against
Japan, a direct approach to the country's enemies became, overnight, the only way
still open for continuing the peace overtures that in principle had already been
agreed on by the Japanese leadership.

The meeting of the Big Six on August 9, 1945, was called, on an indirect
suggestion that Hirohito had made the evening before, to discuss the reports of
the Hiroshima bombing. It might have considered surrender, but we will never
know. By the time the meeting took place, around 10:30 the next morning, the priority order of business had become how to respond to the Soviet entry into the
war. Yet neither the bombs nor the Soviet intervention, we now know, actually
broke the impasse; the Big Six were still divided, and, subsequently, so was the
full Cabinet. Why did Suzuki and Togo decide to take a divided Cabinet to
Hirohito? Because Kido told them that the Emperor desired some action. Why
had Hirohito, if he favored peace, not taken this step earlier? Because the Cabinet
had agreed on the ambivalent peace approach via Moscow, and that was a decision
the Emperor could not unilaterally reverse, according to his reading of the
Japanese constitution. Why did the Minister of War, General Anami, go along
with Hirohito's wishes when the Emperor at last voiced them? Because Hirohito
was his Commander-in-Chief. As long as Hirohito merely acquiesced in unanimous Big Six decisions, and the military controlled the Big Six, the armed forces
were the real rulers of Japan, in the Emperor's name. But when the Emperor
himself spoke directly to the Minister of War, who had once been his aide-de-
camp, the fiction suddenly became reality: Anami had been given a direct order.
Hirohito had followed the decision-making process set down in the constitution
as long as it worked; only when it broke down, and a crisis demanded action,
did he make his own wishes known—as he had done once before, when he
personally ordered the suppression of a junior officers' coup on February 26, 1936,
but only because he thought that the Prime Minister had been assassinated and
there was no regular government.

Which was the crisis that Hirohito and his divided Cabinet believed now
made the Emperor's personal decision necessary: the atomic bombs, Soviet intervention, or the worsening situation as a whole? Certainly the new bombs added
to Japan's woes—along with the ongoing sea blockade, "conventional" firebombing, burned-out cities, total enemy control of sea and air, the shelling of ports by
battleships close inshore, mass hunger, and the promise of a meager rice harvest.
A small provincial city had been largely destroyed by fire, and another partly
destroyed. But then so had Japan's capital, Tokyo, and the B-29s, still eliminating
such "productive enterprises" as Japan "had above ground," were doing so at least
as effectively as atomic bombs could. The war had continued despite the fire
raids; the new atomic weapon did not interfere with the Army chiefs' military
plans, or change their indifference to civilian casualties. The Soviet intervention,
however, demanded a new consensus, because it made the existing consensus
inoperative. And—a point implicit in much of the leadership's discussion—the
bombs promised only to kill more Japanese, whereas the Soviets, possibly allied
with local Communists, threatened to destroy the monarchy, which almost all

Japanese, and certainly those in the government, viewed as the soul of the nation. A surrender with some guarantee for the Emperor thus became the best of a gloomy range of options, and the quicker the better, because every day that passed meant more gains on the ground for the Soviets, and thus a likely bigger share of the inevitable occupation. Recognition that a surrender today will be more favorable than one tomorrow is the classic reason that wars end.

Togo's telegram meant that Japan's problem—the lack of consensus in Tokyo for surrendering without some guarantee of the monarchy's continuation—had now become America's. The sudden surrender offer was unexpected; Secretary of War Stimson had already packed for his vacation. Two reasons for his surprise stand out. The first is that, despite Truman's claims for the new weapon, the atomic bombs had yet to acquire their reputation as instant war-winners; in fact, American plans called for many more to be used in the planned invasion. The second reason is that the Magic intercepts were in many ways misleading: the Japanese had been maneuvering for peace in Moscow, so no one in Washington expected that Soviet intervention would drive Japan's rulers into the arms not of Stalin but of Harry Truman.

Faced with the surrender offer, Secretary of War Stimson was again one of the first to press the advantages, for the United States, of keeping Hirohito on his throne—for the time being, anyway. America, he said, would have to leave the Emperor on his throne at least long enough for him to order the surrender of Japanese armies scattered throughout Asia and the Pacific, "to save us from a score of bloody Iwo Jimas and Okinawas," since Hirohito's name was the only authority the Japanese military would accept. Failure to guarantee his position might also prolong the war, to the Soviets' advantage. "I felt it was of great importance to get the homeland into our hands before the Russians could put in any substantial claim to occupy and help rule it," Stimson wrote in his diary. The obstacle was America's demands for unconditional surrender, originally made to avoid negotiating with Hitler, then transferred without much thought to Japan. "Now they come to plague us," Stimson noted ruefully. As for Byrnes, he still feared a backlash among American voters over retaining the Emperor. "Now that the United States has the bomb," he said, "I do not see why we should retreat from our demand for unconditional surrender. . . . If any conditions are to be accepted, I want the United States and not Japan to state the conditions."

HIROHITO BREAKS THE DEADLOCK

ON AUGUST 11th, the Allies' reply to Togo's telegram was broadcast in Tokyo, and the next day Tokyo learned that Soviet troops had entered Korea, which was then a Japanese colony. The conventional bombing of Japanese cities continued. So did the deadlock in Tokyo. The Allies' reply did not guarantee the Emperor's position as "sovereign ruler"—the condition that the military chiefs had demanded—but said only that the Japanese might someday choose their own form of government. They might, of course, choose a monarchy, and even Hirohito as monarch—as they subsequently did—but their doing so would make the Emperor, and thus the Army, subject to the will of the people, invalidating the official Japanese theory of Hirohito's right to rule by divine descent. On August 13th, the Big Six, and then the Cabinet, met again; and they found that they were still split.

Overnight, seven B-29s dropped five million leaflets on Tokyo and four other cities, giving the texts of the Japanese offer to surrender and the Allies' reply. Privy Seal Kido read one, and feared that it would touch off a spontaneous uprising by troops determined to continue the war. Hirohito agreed to call a full imperial conference of the Cabinet, plus the top military commanders—the first since the conference on December 1, 1941, which had decided on Pearl Harbor—for 11 A.M. in his air-raid shelter.

Suzuki opened the conference by reporting that both the Cabinet and the Supreme Council for the Direction of the War (that is, the Big Six) were still split, and calling on the holdouts to speak. Minister of War Anami, displaying (for a Japanese general) deep emotion, said, "It would be better to fight on. We could still achieve something. If not to win, at least to end the war on better terms than these." Suzuki said, "There are no other views to present." Hirohito rose and said, "My mind is unchanged. I believe it is impossible to continue the war any longer. . . . The [Allied] reply is acceptable. . . . If the people, the land, and the imperial family survive, however, we can yet hope to rebuild the nation." Hirohito brushed a white-gloved hand across his eyes and then left the room. The Cabinet reconvened to vote unanimously to accept the Potsdam Declaration and to draft a rescript for the Emperor to record, to be broadcast at noon the next day, August 15th.

The rescript is an evasive document, written for immediate effect. It says, "We have decided to effect a settlement of the present situation," and adds—at Anami's insistence, to spare the Army's feelings—that "the war situation has developed not necessarily to Japan's advantage, while the general trends of the world have all turned against her interest." The latter statement must refer to the Soviet intervention, the only recent change in "general trends." Hirohito's rescript goes on, "Moreover, the enemy has begun to employ a new and most cruel bomb, the power of which to do damage is indeed incalculable, taking the toll of many innocent lives." This reference to the atomic bomb, it has been argued, establishes that it did indeed bring about Japan's surrender. However, Hirohito's rescript was addressed not to historians but to his subjects, and particularly to civilians, who had been told almost nothing about Hiroshima and Nagasaki. Responsibility for Japan's plight was shifted away from the Army and onto America: a cruel weapon has been used to kill the innocent. Hirohito's personal cease-fire order to the Japanese forces, issued the next day, gives an explanation, stressing fear of Soviet Communism, not of atomic bombs:

> The Soviet Union has now entered the war, and in view of the state of affairs both here and abroad, We feel that the prolongation of the struggle will merely serve to further the evil and may eventually result in the loss of the very foundation on which our Empire exists. Therefore, in spite of the fact that the fighting spirit of the Imperial army and navy are still high, We hereupon intend to negotiate a peace . . . for the sake of maintaining our glorious national polity.

Both documents explain the surrender, but the second was aimed at those who most needed persuading—Japan's military.

General Anami, as a samurai, was not about to surrender. Having voted with the Cabinet for peace, as Hirohito had commanded him, and then helped draft the rescript, he had done his duty to his sovereign. While Hirohito was recording the surrender broadcast, and more than a thousand American bombers were staging the last, heaviest conventional raids of the war, Anami went home and took a bath. His fanatical brother-in-law, Lieutenant Colonel Masahiko Takeshita, stopped by shortly after midnight hoping to persuade him to continue the war. He found the general drinking sake and working on a poem. Just before dawn, Anami slashed his stomach with a sword, and Takeshita, at his request, helped him thrust a dagger into his throat. He died hours later. His poem reads cryptically:

> *Having received great favors*
> *From His Majesty,*
> *When dying*
> *I have nothing to say.*

At noon on August 15, 1945, Hirohito's recording was broadcast. Many Japanese thought that he was exhorting them to fight on. Anami did not live to hear the Emperor read the words he had helped draft, or to suffer the disgrace of surrender. Torn between two inescapable loyalties—to his sovereign, who wanted peace, and to his closest subordinates, who wanted to continue the fight—the general had taken the samurai's way out, dying slowly, in agony, to show that he had chosen death not out of fear but to serve his master in a different way, as his poem indicates. Perhaps as many as two thousand officers and civilians killed themselves over the next few days—an indication of how comparatively thin the layer of last-ditch ultra-nationalism was when the day of reckoning arrived. With them died the ideology, and the political power, of the old Japanese Army; the present Japanese self-defense forces do not teach the samurai code and have little influence on Japanese politics.

THE ORPHAN CITY

OVER RUINED HIROSHIMA, a great silence descended. During the eighteen days of chaos between the peace announcement, on August 15th, and the formal surrender ceremony, on September 2nd, local Japanese Army commands distributed the remaining military stocks of rice and other materials, fearing that the occupiers would seize them. In Hiroshima, however, there were no more supplies to distribute. A Japanese hospital ship had been promised days after the bombing, but it never docked. Japanese soldiers and sailors from undamaged military facilities nearby arrived to burn or bury bodies in mass graves. Medical volunteers from neighboring cities, hampered by lack of supplies, gave whatever help they could; radiation burns, for instance, were treated with cooking or lubricating oil. For at least a week, the people of Hiroshima had no idea what had happened to them, and during that time a hundred and fifty thousand fled the ruins. Weeks later, modern medicines started to arrive: first from the International Red Cross, via the Swiss; then from the American Red Cross; and, finally, from the United States Army. The troops sent by General MacArthur to occupy the Hiroshima region were almost all Australians.

On August 20, 1945, *Life* published full-page aerial photographs of Hiroshima and Nagasaki; Americans saw for the first time the now familiar image of the mushroom cloud—the atomic bomb seen from the air. (The ground view is better known in Japan.) "We have sowed the whirlwind," Hanson Baldwin, the military commentator of the *Times* wrote the day after Hiroshima. Other quiet voices began to question the wisdom of the bomb, but what had actually happened on the ground remained an official secret for more than a year, with only one important leak.

On September 3, 1945, an enterprising Australian newsman, Wilfred Burchett, reporting for the London *Daily Express*, arrived in Hiroshima by train from Tokyo, alone and unescorted. Filed by Morse code from the Hiroshima office of the Japanese news agency *Domei*, his piece began:

> In Hiroshima, thirty days after the first atomic bomb destroyed the city and shook the world, people are still dying, mysteriously and horribly—people who were uninjured in the cataclysm from an unknown something which I can only describe as the atomic plague.

Burchett's piece ran in his paper two days later, and was picked up worldwide. He had stumbled on the ugliest secret of the atomic bomb—radiation sickness— which had been downplayed by its inventors, and not previously mentioned in either Japan or America. The atomic scientists, it emerged, had discovered not only the ideal weapon for achieving tactical surprise and fire-raiding in crowded wooden cities but also a new and still dimly understood way of dying—another terror for those threatened by war.

On September 10th, in Tokyo, General Douglas MacArthur had issued a Freedom of Speech and Press Directive: "The Supreme Commander for the Allied Powers has decreed that there shall be an absolute minimum of restrictions upon freedom of speech." On September 18th, he reimposed censorship on the Japanese press (which during the war years had, of course, been strictly controlled by the military regime) with a press code banning, among other things, anything that "might, directly or by inference, disturb public tranquillity," or convey "false or destructive criticism of the Allied Powers" or "destructive criticism of the Allied forces of Occupation . . . which might invite mistrust or resentment of those troops."

Hiroshima and Nagasaki soon vanished from the news in Japan, the United States, and the world. Japanese crews that photographed the ruined cities had their film confiscated. On the day the press code was issued, publication of the newspaper *Asahi* was suspended because it contained an article describing the atomic bomb as "a violation of international law and a war crime worse than an attack on a hospital ship or the use of poison gas." Japanese doctors were discouraged from studying the survivors in the two cities, and the scientific papers of any who did were suppressed. So were novels, and even poems, about the atomic bombs, on the ground that they would disturb public tranquillity and create ill will toward the United States. One research group was beyond the reach of the Tokyo censors. On the day of Japan's surrender, Truman ordered the United States Strategic Bombing Survey—a unit that had been established in 1944 by Roosevelt to investigate the results of bombing in Germany—to study the effects of conventional and atomic bombing in Japan. The Bombing Survey (commonly called Uss-busters), with more than a thousand researchers, economists, and interpreters, and with the President's backing, arrived a month after the surrender, toured the devastated islands, and interviewed members of the Japanese wartime government. From their report, released in Washington in June of 1946, this paragraph stands out:

Certainly prior to December 31, 1945, and in all probability prior to November 1, 1945 [the planned date of the Kyushu invasion], Japan would have surrendered even if the atomic bombs had not been dropped, even if Russia had not entered the war, and even if no invasion had been planned or contemplated.

The Uss-busters' report was long, technical, and mainly concerned with Japan's desperate economic plight, and it made no moral judgment on the atomic bombs; the officially sponsored version that they had terrified a fanatical military regime into surrendering was by then beyond challenge.

On August 31, 1946, the novelist and war correspondent John Hersey broke more than a year's silence on Hiroshima with a long article in the *New Yorker*. An account of six Hiroshima survivors, Hersey's article restored names and addresses to what had been mounds of anonymous dead in the news reports. The people of Hiroshima turned out, in his account, to be not unlike Americans. In many respects, Hersey could have been writing about Tokyo or Dresden—except that he described the appalling results of radiation, first mentioned briefly by Burchett, with a realism all the more heartrending for being quietly understated. Hersey's piece brought a quick rejoinder from the makers of the bomb.

One of the more sophisticated voices joining the debate was that of Dr. James B. Conant, the president of Harvard, who was himself a chemist. Conant was one of the important developers of poison gas in the First World War and of napalm and the atomic bomb in the Second. Writing late in 1946 to an old friend, the Boston lawyer Harvey H. Bundy (who had also worked on the bomb), Conant explained that he remained "quite unrepentant" about its use. Expressions like "the crime of Hiroshima and Nagasaki," Conant believed, were forms of "sentimentalism" that might "result in a distortion of history." To Bundy he complained of a widespread impression that the scientists who built the bomb had not been consulted about its use, though some of them had even participated in target selection: "I think it unfair for the scientists to try and dodge the responsibility for this decision, although of course they were not in a position to influence greatly whatever was done at Potsdam." Conant urged that "someone who can speak with authority" should make a clear-cut statement about the circumstances behind the decision to drop the bomb. The ideal authority, he felt, was the widely respected—and by then retired—Secretary of War Henry Stimson, who happened at that time to be working on his memoirs with the assistance of Harvey Bundy's son, McGeorge. The choice of Stimson was ironic; of all those closely connected with the bomb, he had agonized most over where its use might lead.

Pressured by Conant, Stimson reluctantly agreed to write an article along the lines suggested. "The history of it is that Jim Conant felt very much worried over the spreading accusation that it was entirely unnecessary to use the atomic bomb," he later explained to Justice Felix Frankfurter. "I have rarely been connected with a paper about which I have [had] so much doubt at the last moment. . . . I think the full enumeration of the steps in the tragedy will excite horror among friends who heretofore thought me a kindly-minded Christian gentleman but who will, after reading this, feel that I am cold-blooded and cruel." The article, largely drafted by McGeorge Bundy, was heavily rewritten by Conant. "The Decision to Use the Atomic Bomb," by Henry L. Stimson (the only author credited), was the cover story of *Harper's* for the issue of February, 1947. Though McGeorge Bundy later conceded that it was "not a piece of history," it was as reliable history that it was presented and, as such, was widely praised and lastingly influential.

Read in the light of what we know now, Stimson's article is filled with evasions and half-truths. The military use of the bomb, he wrote, was agreed on from the beginning: "If we should be the first to develop the weapon, we should have a great new instrument for shortening the war and minimizing destruction." But, during the war, Stimson had been a forceful opponent of saturation bombing. In 1945 he told Truman that he was trying to hold the Air Forces to the precision bombing of Japanese military targets, because he "did not want to have the United States get the reputation of outdoing Hitler in atrocities"—and precision bombing was, of course, impossible with the atomic bomb. In his private diary, which became available two decades later, Stimson deplored the firebombing of Dresden as "on its face terrible and probably unnecessary." Stimson's *Harper's* article noted that "the possible atomic weapon was considered to be a new and tremendously powerful explosive, as legitimate as any other of the deadly explosive weapons of modern war"—but he did not mention radiation sickness, which by 1947 had already cast much doubt on its legitimacy.

Stimson's article reported that Japan had made "tentative proposals to the Soviet government," and that "there was as yet no weakening in the Japanese determination to fight rather than to accept unconditional surrender"—but he did not say that the position of the Emperor, eventually conceded, was the only sticking point, as the Magic intercepts (still a closely held secret in 1947) must have made clear to those who saw them. He rightly claimed credit for keeping Kyoto off the target list, but called it "a target of considerable military importance," which by 1947 was known to be untrue. He cited an estimate of a million American lives saved by the bombs, but did not discuss the Strategic Bombing Survey's opinion, already published by then, that Japan would have surrendered before the Kyushu invasion.

Stimson's defense of the atomic bombs comes down to a familiar pair of propositions: (1) the atomic bombs caused the Japanese surrender, and (2) the surrender saved a large number of American lives. His version of what happened to end the war has long since hardened into dogma: "We believed that our [nuclear] attacks had struck cities which must certainly be important to the Japanese military leaders, both Army and Navy, and we waited for a result. We waited one day." Aside from his implications that the Japanese Army and Navy had somehow been intimidated by attacks on minor installations, his argument rests on the fallacy *post hoc, ergo propter hoc*—after, therefore because. But at the time Stimson wrote it was already known that the atomic bombs, in fact, had little effect on Japan's physical ability to continue the war. The target committee, in drawing up its list, did not consider the military importance of any of them. Above all, Stimson's article pretended that the issue of whether to drop the bomb was seriously studied; we know that it was not.

However, the sequence of events—Hiroshima, Nagasaki, surrender offer— is striking. Could it be that pure coincidence has clouded our understanding of the surrender for half a century? Indeed it could. By themselves, the dates prove nothing. In his article Stimson went further, not simply saying that the atomic bombs were intended to shorten the war, and thus save lives, which was no doubt true (and could be said of any action in any war), but arguing that they actually *did* end the war. This is the only defense he offers for their use—and the only defense seriously put forward by anyone since. This argument needs at least some supporting evidence; there is none.

THE RECKONING

ONE APPROACH TO THE MORALITY of the atomic bombs is to consider the consequences. In Japan (apart from those who lost their lives, families, and friends at the time), they have been contradictory. Japan has developed no nuclear weapons, and has shown a strong disinclination to participate in any new wars— Japan did not, for instance, send soldiers to Korea, Vietnam, or the Persian Gulf. On the other hand, meaningful examination by the Japanese of their own aggressive past tends to stop short when Hiroshima or Nagasaki is brought into the discussion; I have yet to find any Japanese who will agree that the bombs saved any Japanese lives, or American lives, either—although Americans visiting the bombed cities report sensing no hostility. Although radiation is known to induce mutations in all species exposed to it, the most recent studies of the children of atomic-bomb survivors have found no clear increase in stillbirths, deformities, or shortened life expectancy; the Japanese government has stopped adding them to the list of those needing special medical help. Physically, at least, the two cities have put the bombs behind them.

For Americans, the consequences of the atomic bomb have been more lastingly—if less obviously—traumatic. With peace proclaimed only days after the bombs were dropped, the Soviet intervention against Japan scarcely reported, and the complicated maneuverings in Tokyo concealed for years, it was assumed (except in Japan) that the bombs had subdued an enemy still full of fight, clearly achieving the victory for the knockout blow, as the air-power prophets had predicted. If there is such a process as military leaders being cowed into submission by air attacks, nuclear or otherwise, history has no clear example of it. Nevertheless, the United States' own defense and that of her allies, including, by proxy, Japan's, was based for many years on this unverified theory: immense resources have gone into nuclear weapons, for no benefit beyond self-perpetuating deterrence.

Unfortunately for Americans, the bomb also appeared, in 1945, to be the providential answer to an old problem, shared by all democracies. When peace broke out, millions of men and women in uniform suddenly wanted to go home, all at once. But the United States, as the world's strongest industrial power, undamaged by war, now had global responsibilities that might call for military action anywhere on the planet. The armed forces shrank to one and a half million; garrisons in what were judged to be far-off, unimportant places, like Korea, were withdrawn, leaving only handfuls of advisers. In 1947, the United States Air Force, now the glamour service, the presumed winner of the war, finally became independent, free to shape its own "air-atomic" strategy. When Stalin tested American resolve by cutting ground access to Berlin in 1948, Truman responded by sending B-29s to the same bases in England from which Germany had been bombed. The new Strategic Air Command, the successor of Groves's pioneer nuclear force, made plans to drop two atomic bombs on each of seventy Soviet cities. Diplomacy, and even strategy, had temporarily become superfluous, superseded by confidence in the miraculous, mindless knock-out blow.

In September of 1949, the dream turned to nightmare when the Soviets tested their own nuclear weapon. "Keep your shirt on," Oppenheimer advised his colleague Edward Teller, the "father" of the hydrogen bomb. Many Americans did not; any city in this country could now, at least in imagination, be another Hiroshima. The United States began a hunt for spies and traitors; atomic scientists began denouncing one another; Oppenheimer himself was subject to a political show trial, disguised as a public hearing over his security clearance, which was denied. These are totalitarian attitudes, imposed by the nature of the atomic bomb itself, and they surfaced most dramatically in the shameful McCarthy era.

Like the firebombings that cleared the moral path for them, nuclear weapons accept, without reflection, the doctrine that the nation is a kind of living organism, open to attack anyhow and anywhere, as opposed to the democratic principle that people are individually responsible for their actions. The use, or threat, of nuclear weapons presupposes omniscient supermen who can never make a mistake. Democracy accepts that our leaders are fallible human beings, like the people who elected them, who all too often, in the Biblical phrase, know not what they do—but who can be held to account, can have second thoughts, can put mistakes right. No one can put mass death right.

We ask Hiroshima to carry too many burdens. In August of 1945, the city suffered for Pearl Harbor, for Japan's fruitless alliance with Nazi Germany (the death camps, then newly opened, were all too well known), for the anti-rational, death-obsessed ideology of the Japanese officer corps, for the labyrinthine Japanese decision-avoiding process, for the ill-thought-out Allied demand for unconditional surrender, for the atrocities committed by Japanese soldiers against civilians and prisoners of war, for the presumed misdeeds of some (but not all) of the people actually in the city, for the monstrous, random cruelty of war itself. In the decades since, Hiroshima has had to carry the metaphorical weight of the Cold War, the morally arid balance of terror, and the sometimes frightening, sometimes perversely stabilizing nuclear standoff. Now these problems, never themselves solved, have transmuted into dangers more diffuse but not much less menacing. It is a heavy load for one unfortunate Japanese seaport to bear.

THE
LOGIC OF
MASS
DESTRUCTION

Mark Selden

HIS ESSAY EXPLORES THE LOGIC and the consequences—for its victims and for subsequent global patterns of warfare—of new technologies and strategies of mass destruction associated with the rise of air power and the obliteration of the distinction between combatant and non-combatant in World War II: from Japanese strafing of Shanghai in 1932 to Nazi bombardment of Guernica in 1937 through the initial stages of area bombing by German, British, Japanese and American forces in the years 1940–41, to the American leveling of Japanese cities culminating in the firebombing of Tokyo and the nuclear bombing of Hiroshima and Nagasaki in the final months of the war. The elimination of the distinction between combatant and non-combatant took many forms. The perfection of area bombing would shape subsequent wars including Korea, Vietnam, the Gulf War, and contemporary conflicts in the former Soviet Union and the former Yugoslavia.

The combatant—non-combatant distinction has always been at best fragile, even ephemeral, frequently providing little or no protection for those attacked. This mode of warfare, targeting for destruction entire communities, emerged most clearly in conflicts characterized by vast imbalances of technology and power and is well illustrated by the long history of religious and colonial wars. Nevertheless, certain constraints on barbarism did exist and affected the conduct of all sides in World War II. The assault on these norms in the context of new war-making technologies is among the legacies of the war.

Public debate in the United States, Japan and Europe has long pivoted on the ethical and political issues associated with the U.S. decision to drop the atomic bomb on Hiroshima and Nagasaki. Indeed, the dawn of the nuclear age has overshadowed a host of other important issues. This essay explores the systematic destruction of Japanese cities "before the bomb" as an important but neglected legacy of the war that has shaped American power and subsequent patterns of global conflict in the nuclear era.

The totalism of the Pacific war was established at the outset by American insistence that the only acceptable outcome of the conflict lay in unconditional surrender, a position that it maintained with respect to Japan until immediately after the atomic bombing of Hiroshima and Nagasaki, when it promptly softened its terms. Franklin Roosevelt's words delivered in his message to Congress a month after Pearl Harbor provide the classic moral-philosophical statement undergirding the total war position: "There never has been—there never can be—successful compromise between good and evil. Only total victory can reward the champions of tolerance, and decency, and faith."[1]

Ideological bases for the destruction of non-combatants defined as "the enemy" existed on all sides of the conflict from the outset, yet there were also constraints at work in the early years of the war. These constraints on policymakers derived in part from historically grounded moral strictures that placed limits (however fragile) on the bounds of warfare, for example those protecting women, children, and the elderly, from direct attack. More important than moral imperatives were well-grounded fears on all sides that the escalation of conflict by deliberate targeting of non-combatants for destruction would provoke devastating retaliation. The partial and imperfect restraints on the use of poison gas provide perhaps the best documented example of such fears.[2] With respect to the uses of air power, the belief long persisted that the most cost-effective bombing strategies were those that pinpointed destruction of enemy forces and installations, factories, and railroads, not those designed to terrorize or kill non-combatants. Such a view guided U.S. bombing strategy prior to late 1944 or early 1945, a point to which we return below.

The classic combat of World War I was trench warfare involving industrial nations of roughly comparable strength and technology. World War II was distinctive both for the growing importance played by the new weaponry, particularly air power and bombs, and the broadening of the theaters of war to include the colonial and semi-colonial zones as well as the industrial heartland.

The theoretical underpinnings for strategic or area bombing—the technical terms that mask the reality of the annihilation of civilians—were fully spelled out prior to and following World War I, particularly in the writings of the Italian General Giulio Douhet. By the early 1930s, U.S. General Billy Mitchell and others had already pinpointed Japan's wood and paper cities as prime targets for firebombing. Mitchell warned of the "yellow military peril" of a Japan bent on attacking both its possessions and the U.S. itself long before Pearl Harbor.[3]

In the course of the World War II, by stages, all major air powers—Germany, Britain, Japan and the United States—moved from sporadic and selective to systematic destruction, that is from attempts to destroy verifiable military and industrial objectives to the use of air power to terrorize and kill civilians.

In early instances, international protest, centered on the several thousand deaths, apparently contributed to a backing away from civilian bombing. The years 1939–40 constituted a second watershed. On May 3 and 4, 1939 Japanese incendiary raids on the Nationalist Chinese capital, Chongqing, took 5,400 lives.[4] The German destruction of central Rotterdam in May 1940 exacted 40,000 civilian lives and forced the Dutch surrender.[5] Up to this point, however, bombing of cities remained isolated and sporadic.

The decisive deployment of air power against cities came with the 1940–41 German-British conflict and with repeated Japanese attacks on Chongqing. These assaults constituted the most important prelude to the U.S. destruction of Japanese cities and the indiscriminate slaughter of civilians in the final half year of the war.

Roosevelt and his advisers, as well as a range of American writers and public figures from Ernest Hemingway to Herbert Hoover, bitterly denounced the most egregious instances of the bombing of civilian populations by Germany, Japan and Russia in the early war years.[6] To be sure, adversaries invariably demonized the enemy and cloaked their own mission in heroic garb, yet particularly where the adversary was a formidable military-industrial power with the capacity to retaliate, tacit rules limited the uses of air power. Not until late 1940 did German bombing attacks target London, killing approximately 40,000 people in a six-month period, and even then the primary targets were ostensibly military and military-related industry and infrastructure including bases, large factories and docks. By early 1941, however, Britain's Royal Air Force Bomber Command formalized what it had been doing in recent months, having abandoned all pretense of precision bombing of military and industrial targets in favor of bombing cities with the aim of killing workers and disrupting and demoralizing society. Both the British and the Germans shifted the focus of their attacks to night bombing.[7] Civilian populations, not bases or even factories, were the primary targets. In the final years of the war, Max Hastings observed, Churchill and his bomber commander Arthur Harris set out to concentrate "all available forces for the progressive, systematic destruction of the urban areas of the Reich, city block by city block, factory by factory, until the enemy became a nation of troglodytes, scratching in the ruins."[8]

The debate within U.S. military and political circles over the uses of air power in the years after Pearl Harbor is illuminating. While the air war in Europe was careening toward civilian bombing, throughout 1942 and 1943, Air Force strategists and generals insisted that tactical bombing of military and industrial targets was the most cost-effective use of air power. This view was reinforced by the fear that indiscriminate killing of civilians could strengthen enemy resolve, a phenomenon that had apparently occurred in both England and Germany under strategic bombing. Thus, at Casablanca in January 1943, the United States formally rejected British pressures to shift from daylight to night bombing and reaffirmed its intention to continue costly and largely ineffectual daylight precision bombing of German military and industrial targets. In practice, of course, U.S. air power complemented, and at times directly assisted, the equally ineffective British nighttime area bombing directed against civilian populations.[9]

Throughout 1943–44 the U.S. Air Force proclaimed its adherence to precision bombing. However, as this approach proved futile not only in forcing surrender on either Germany or Japan but even in inflicting significant damage on their war-making capacity—as the sophistication, numbers and range of U.S. aircraft grew, as the technology of firebombing advanced with the development of napalm and more effective delivery methods, and as the Air Force sought to strengthen its position in inter-service rivalries and competition for resources—pressures mounted for a strategic shift. In the early months of 1945, the remaining fragile restraints on the bombing of non-combatants dissolved just as the United States shifted its attention to the Pacific theater and as it gained the capacity to effectively attack the Japanese home islands from newly captured bases in the Pacific. In the final six months of the war, the U.S. threw the full weight of its air power into campaigns to burn whole Japanese cities to the ground and terrorize, incapacitate and kill their virtually defenseless populations in an effort to force surrender.

The techniques for firebombing cities, including nighttime and radar bombing that were honed by British and American fliers in the early 1940s against Germany and her European allies, were applied in the final months of the war in a series of attacks that began with Operation Thunderclap directed against Berlin.

In Europe, the culmination came on February 13–14, 1945 in the destruction of Dresden, a historic cultural center with no significant military industry or bases. At Dresden, by conservative estimate, 35,000 people were incinerated in a single raid led by British bombers with U.S. planes following up.[10] The American writer Kurt Vonnegut, then a young POW in Dresden, later recalled:

> They burnt the whole damn town down. . . . Every day we walked into the city and dug into basements and shelters to get the corpses out, as a sanitary measure. When we went into them, a typical shelter, an ordinary basement usually, looked like a streetcar full of people who'd simultaneously had heart failure. Just people sitting there in their chairs, all dead. A fire storm is an amazing thing. It doesn't occur in nature. It's fed by the tornadoes that occur in the midst of it and there isn't a damned thing to breathe.[11]

"Along with the Nazi extermination camps, the killing of Soviet and American prisoners, and other enemy atrocities," Ronald Schaffer observes, "Dresden became one of the moral causes célèbres of World War II." [12] Though far worse was in the offing, Dresden provoked the last significant public discussion of the bombing of women and children to take place during the war, and the city became synonymous with terror bombing by the U.S. and Britain. In fact, the debate was largely provoked not by the destruction wrought by the raids, which was already becoming commonplace, but by an Associated Press report widely published in the U.S. and British press stating explicitly that "the Allied air commanders have made the long-awaited decision to adopt deliberate terror bombing of the great German population centers as a ruthless expedient to hasten Hitler's doom." American officials quickly acted to neutralize the report, most effectively by pointing to the widely publicized great cathedral of Cologne, left standing after U.S. bombing as a symbol of American concern, and by reiterating U.S. adherence to principles restricting attacks to tactical bombing of military targets. In fact, in the midst of bombing on many fronts, and with a sense of victory in the air, U.S. public discussion, not to speak of protest, was minimal; in Britain there was slightly greater discussion. The bombing continued. Strategic bombing had passed its test in the realm of public reaction.

Curtis LeMay was appointed commander of the 21st Air Force Headquarters on January 20, 1945 just as a combination of circumstances placed Japanese cities within effective range of U.S. bombers with the capacity to inflict enormous damage on a Japanese nation whose depleted air and naval power left it virtually defenseless against air attack. If the bombing of Dresden produced a ripple of public debate, no discernible wave of revulsion, not to speak of protest, took place in the U.S. or Europe in the wake of the far greater destruction of Japanese cities and the slaughter of civilian populations on a scale that had no parallel in wartime bombing.

For thirty years General LeMay served as the most quotable spokesman for U.S. policies of putting enemy cities, villages and forests to the torch from Japan to Korea to Vietnam.[13] He would carry firebombing and napalming to new levels of technological sophistication and terror. Yet he was just a link in a chain of command that routinely sanctioned terror bombing extending upward through the Joint Chiefs to the president.[14] Every U.S. president from Franklin Roosevelt to

Bill Clinton has endorsed an approach to warfare that targets entire populations for annihilation, an approach that eliminates all vestiges of distinction between combatant and non-combatant, with often deadly consequences. The awesome power of the atomic bomb has obscured the fact that this policy and approach came fully of age in the U.S. firebombing of Japan.

U.S. RAIDS ON JAPANESE CITIES began with James Doolittle's solitary mission of April 18, 1942; this was widely hailed as the U.S. response to Pearl Harbor. Several of the B-25 bombers attempted to return to bases in China and were forced to land in Japanese-occupied territory. The Japanese captured eight American airmen, executing three and sentencing five to life imprisonment. The U.S. would make no further attempt to raid Japan's home islands for three years.[15] The full fury of firebombing and napalm was not unleashed on Japan until the night of March 9–10, 1945. LeMay sent 334 B-29s low over Tokyo from recently acquired bases in Guam, Saipan and Tinian. Their mission was to reduce the city to rubble with jellied gasoline and napalm. U.S. bombers carried two kinds of incendiaries: M47s, 100-pound oil-gel bombs, 182 per aircraft, each capable of starting a major fire, followed by M69s, 6-pound gelled-gasoline bombs, 1,520 per aircraft in addition to a few high explosives to deter firefighters.[16] The attack on an area that the U.S. Strategic Bombing Survey estimated to be 87.4 percent residential succeeded beyond the wildest dreams of air force planners. Whipped by fierce winds, flames detonated by the bombs leaped across Tokyo, generating immense firestorms that engulfed and killed tens of thousands of residents.

In contrast with Vonnegut's "wax museum" description of Dresden victims, accounts from inside the inferno that engulfed Tokyo chronicle scenes of utter carnage. We have come to measure the efficacy of bombing by throw weights and kill ratios. Here I would like to offer some perspectives drawing on the words of those who felt the wrath of the bombs.

Fleeing the flames, thousands plunged in desperation into the freezing waters of rivers, canals and Tokyo Bay:

> A woman spent the night knee-deep in the bay, holding onto a piling with her three-year-old son clinging to her back; by morning several of the people around her were dead of burns, shock, fatigue and hypothermia. Thousands submerged themselves in stagnant, foul-smelling canals with their mouths just above the surface, but many died from smoke inhalation, anoxia, or carbon monoxide poisoning, or were boiled to death when the fire storm heated the water. Others, huddling in canals connected to the Sumida River, drowned when the tide came in. . . . Huge crowds lined the gardens and parks along the Sumida, and as the masses behind them pushed toward the river, walls of screaming people fell in and vanished.[17]

Police cameraman Ishikawa Koyo described the streets of Tokyo as "rivers of fire. . . flaming pieces of furniture exploding in the heat, while the people themselves blazed like 'matchsticks' as their wood and paper homes exploded in flames. Under the wind and the gigantic breath of the fire, immense incandescent vortices rose in a number of places, swirling, flattening, sucking whole blocks of houses into their maelstrom of fire."

Father Flaujac, a French cleric, compared the firebombing to the Tokyo earthquake twenty-two years earlier, an event whose massive destruction had alerted some of the original planners of the Tokyo holocaust to the possibilities of destruction.

> In September 1923, during the great earthquake, I saw Tokyo burning for 5 days. I saw in Honjo a heap of 33,000 corpses of people who burned or suffocated at the beginning of the bombardment. . . . After the first quake there were 20-odd centers of fire, enough to destroy the capital. How could the conflagration be stopped when incendiary bombs in the dozens of thousands now dropped over the four corners of the district and with Japanese houses which are only match boxes? . . . In 1923 the fire spread on the ground. At the time of the bombings the fire fell from the sky. . . . Where could one fly? The fire was everywhere.[18]

Nature reinforced man's handiwork in the form of *akakaze*, the red wind that swept with hurricane force across the Tokyo plain and propelled firestorms across the city with terrifying speed and intensity. The wind drove temperatures up to eighteen hundred degrees Fahrenheit, creating superheated vapors that advanced ahead of the flames, killing or incapacitating their victims. "The mechanisms of death were so multiple and simultaneous—oxygen deficiency and carbon monoxide poisoning, radiant heat and direct flames, debris and the trampling feet of stampeding crowds—that causes of death were later hard to ascertain. . . ."[19]

The Strategic Bombing Survey, whose formation a few months earlier provided an important signal of Roosevelt's support for strategic bombing, provided a technical description of the firestorm and its effects on the city:

> The chief characteristic of the conflagration . . . was the presence of a fire front, an extended wall of fire moving to leeward, preceded by a mass of pre-heated, turbid, burning vapors. . . . The 28-mile-per-hour wind, measured a mile from the fire, increased to an estimated 55 miles at the perimeter, and probably more within. An extended fire swept over 15 square miles in 6 hours. . . . The area of the fire was nearly 100 percent burned; no structure or its contents escaped damage.

The survey concluded—plausibly, but only for events prior to August 6, 1945—that "probably more persons lost their lives by fire at Tokyo in a 6-hour period than at any time in the history of man." People died from extreme heat, from oxygen deficiency, from carbon monoxide asphyxiation, or from being trampled beneath the feet of stampeding crowds.

How many people died on the night of March 10 in what flight commander General Thomas Power termed without hyperbole "the greatest single disaster incurred by any enemy in military history?" The Strategic Bombing Survey estimated that 87,793 people died in the raid, 40,918 were injured, and 1,008,005 people lost their homes.[20] Rhodes, estimating the dead at more than 100,000 men, women, and children, suggested that probably a million more were injured and another million were left homeless. The Tokyo Fire Department estimated

97,000 killed and 125,000 wounded. The Tokyo Police offered a figure of 124,711 killed and wounded and 286,358 buildings and homes destroyed in the raid. With vast areas of Tokyo in ruins, more than one million residents fled the city. The figure of roughly 100,000 deaths, provided by Japanese and American authorities, both of whom for different reasons had an interest in minimizing the death toll, seems to me implausibly low in light of population density, wind conditions, and survivors' accounts.[21] With an average of 103,000 inhabitants per square mile and peak levels as high as 135,000 per square mile, the highest density of any industrial city in the world, and with firefighting measures ludicrously inadequate to the task, 15.8 square miles of Tokyo were destroyed on a night when fierce winds whipped the flames and walls of fire blocked tens of thousands fleeing for their lives.[22]

Following the attack, LeMay said that he wanted Tokyo "burned down—wiped right off the map" to "shorten the war." Tokyo did burn. Subsequent raids brought the devastated area of Tokyo to more than 56 square miles, provoking the flight of millions of refugees. No previous or subsequent conventional bombing raid ever came close to generating the death toll of the great Tokyo raid of March 10, yet the airborne destruction ground on relentlessly. According to Japanese police statistics, the 65 raids on Tokyo between December 6, 1944 and August 13, 1945 resulted in 137,582 casualties, 787,145 homes and buildings destroyed, and 2,625,279 people displaced.[23] The Tokyo raid initiated Japan's trial by fire. By July 1945, U.S. planes had dropped more than 41,000 tons of bombs on Japanese cities, killing hundreds of thousands and rendering an estimated fifteen million homeless.[24] LeMay's bombers were rapidly running out of targets to strike.

In July, U.S. planes blanketed the few remaining Japanese cities with an "Appeal to the People." "As you know," it read, "America, which stands for humanity, does not wish to injure the innocent people, so you had better evacuate these cities." Half the leafleted cities were firebombed within days of the warning. U.S. planes ruled the skies. In the spring of 1945, a gravely weakened Japan, its sea and air power virtually destroyed, bereft of oil (imports ceased from February 1945), facing acute food shortages as a result of declining production at home and the loss of vital imports, with its forces in full retreat across Asia and the Pacific, nevertheless revealed a defensive capacity to inflict the heaviest casualties of the war on the United States in its suicidal defense of Okinawa. Japan's offensive military capability had been virtually eliminated and the Soviet Union was preparing to enter the war.[25]

Following Japan's surrender, the Strategic Bombing Survey would bluntly—yet still skirting the issue of civilian deaths—state the premises of the air assault, as in the opening paragraph of this report on Japanese morale:

> The air attack on Japan was directed against the nation as a whole, not only against specific military targets, because of the contributions in numerous ways of the civilian population to the fighting strength of the enemy, and to speed the securing of unconditional surrender. The American attack against the "total target" was successful. In addition to enormous physical destruction, the strategic bombing of the home islands produced great social and psychological disruption and contributed to securing surrender prior to the planned war.[26]

Successful, yes, in producing "great social and psychological disruption," but the evidence suggests that just as in the German and British bombing of cities earlier, bombing which destroyed Japan's cities and exacted so terrible a death toll had no significant effect on securing surrender.

Between January and July 1945, the United States firebombed and destroyed all but five Japanese cities, deliberately sparing Kyoto, the ancient imperial capital, and four others from bombing. In the end, the Atomic Bomb Selection Committee selected Hiroshima, Kokura, Niigata, and Nagasaki to display the awesome power of the atomic bomb to Japan and the world. Michael Sherry compellingly describes the triumph of American technological fanaticism as the hallmark of the air war:

> The shared mentality of the fanatics of air war was their dedication to assembling and perfecting their methods of destruction, and . . . doing so overshadowed the original purposes justifying destruction. . . . The lack of a proclaimed intent to destroy, the sense of being driven by the twin demands of bureaucracy and technology, distinguished America's technological fanaticism from its enemies' ideological fanaticism.[27]

Technological fanaticism served to conceal the larger purposes of power both from military planners and the public. This wartime technological fanaticism in my view is best understood as a means of operationalizing an ideological package whose presuppositions included the legitimacy and benevolence of American global power and the perception of the Japanese as both uniquely brutal and inherently, or in John Dower's terms racially, inferior.

Between February and August 1945 the U.S. air war reached an intensity still unrivaled in the magnitude of technological slaughter directed against a people. That moment was a product of the combination of technological breakthroughs together with the erosion of moral and political restraints on the killing of civilians.

THE TARGETING FOR DESTRUCTION of entire populations, whether indigenous peoples, religious infidels, or others deemed inferior or evil, may be as old as human history, but the forms it takes are as new as the latest technologies of air power and nuclear weapons.[28] Among the most important ways in which World War II shaped the moral and technological tenor of mass destruction was the systematic targeting of civilian populations from the air. The ability to destroy an entire city and annihilate its population in a single bombing raid was not only far more "efficient" than previous methods of warfare, it also sanitized the process. Air power distanced victim from executioner, transforming the visual and tactile experience of annihilation. The bombardier never looks squarely into the eyes of a specified victim, nor does the act of destruction have the physical directness of decapitation by sword or even shooting with a machine gun. This is particularly useful when your principal victims are women, children and the elderly.

World War II is unrivaled in the scale of mass destruction. Nazi genocide, Japanese slaughter of Asian civilians, and Soviet losses during the German invasion exacted the heaviest toll in human lives. Each of the above-mentioned examples has its unique character and historical and ideological origins. All rested on dehumanizing assumptions concerning the "other" and produced large-scale slaughter of civilian populations. From the Rape of Nanjing to the bombing of Shanghai, Hankou, Chongqing and other cities, to the annihilation and pacification campaigns carried forward throughout the Chinese countryside, to the use of poison gas and the vivisection experiments conducted by Unit 731 to test and develop biological weapons, the death toll in the course of Japan's fifteen-year China war far exceeded that inflicted by U.S. bombing of Japan and probably surpassed the immense Soviet losses in the war that have conventionally been estimated at 20 million lives.[29] The war dead in Europe alone in World War II have been estimated in the range of 30 to 40 million, fifty percent higher than in World War I. To this we must add 25 to 30 million Asian victims, including 15 to 20 million Chinese, in the fifteen-year resistance war (1931–45), approximately three million Japanese, and millions more in Southeast Asia. Among the important instances of the killing of non-combatants, the U.S. destruction of Japanese cities is perhaps least known.

In World War I, ninety percent of the fatalities directly attributable to the war were military, nearly all of them Europeans and Americans. According to one estimate, approximately half of the dead in World War II in Europe were civilians and, when war-induced famine casualties are included, the civilian death toll for Asia was almost certainly substantially higher in both absolute and percentage terms.[30] The United States, its homeland untouched by war, suffered approximately 100,000 deaths in the entire Asian theater, a figure lower than that for the single Tokyo air raid of March 10, 1945, and lower than the death toll at Hiroshima. By contrast, Japan's three million war dead in the fifteen-year war, while thirty times the number of U.S. dead, was still only a small fraction of the toll suffered by the Chinese who resisted the Japanese military juggernaut throughout a fifteen-year war.[31]

The consequences of this shift in the nature of warfare between the world wars—from the military to civilian casualties, and a growing technological imbalance between warring parties—were profound. This pattern of imbalance of deaths in the Pacific War—twenty million Chinese, three million Japanese, one hundred thousand Americans—more closely resembled earlier colonial wars than World War I or the European theater in World War II.

World War II remains indelibly engraved in American memory as the "Good War" and in important respects it was. In confronting the war machines of Nazi Germany and Imperial Japan, the United States contributed to the defeat of some of the most brutal and aggressive foes of European and Asian peoples. It was also a war that fortuitously served American great power interests by weakening not only foes but also allies and other potential rivals whose industrial heartlands and cities were destroyed. For most Americans, it seemed a "Good War" in another sense: the U.S. entered and exited the war buoyed by absolute moral certainty borne of a mission to punish aggression in the form of a genocidal Nazi fascism and unbridled colonial aggression. The victory, propelling it to a hegemonic position which carried authority to condemn and punish war crimes committed by defeated nations, continues to constitute a major obstacle to a thoroughgoing reassessment of the United States' own wartime conduct in general and issues of mass destruction in particular.

World War II, building on and extending atavistic impulses deeply rooted in earlier civilizations and combining them with more destructive technologies, produced new forms of human depravity. Nazi and Japanese crimes have long been exposed and subjected to international criticism from the war crimes tribunals of the 1940s to the present. Most important, these have been the subject of reflection and self-criticism by significant groups within those countries, and in the case of Germany—but not yet Japan—of official recognition of the criminal conduct of genocidal and other barbaric policies as well as restitution to victims in the form of public apology and substantial reparations. And even in Japan, despite official intransigence, the war has been and remains a fiercely contested intellectual-political public issue.

In contrast to these responses to the war in Germany and Japan, and even to the ongoing debate in the United States about the uses of the atomic bomb, there has been virtually no awareness of, not to speak of critical reflection upon, the U.S. bombing of Japanese civilians in the half year prior to Hiroshima. The systematic American bombing of Japanese non-combatants must be added to a list of the horrific legacies of the war that includes Nazi genocide and a host of Japanese war crimes against Asian peoples.

The fiftieth anniversary of the end of World War II and the dawn of the nuclear age, coming on the heels of events that signal the end of the post-war era and the Cold War, offers an occasion for reflection on the American role in the mass destruction of non-combatants that is among the enduring legacies of the "Good War." The cancellation of the Smithsonian's *Enola Gay* exhibit, and the summary firing of the principal administrator associated with it in the absence of any significant public debate beyond the ranks of professional historians, illustrates the unwillingness on the part of much of the American public half a century later to come to grips with any facts that might require a reassessment of what we choose to remember.

NOTES

I am indebted to Noam Chomsky, Bruce Cumings, John Dower, Nikki Keddie, Hans Rogger, Michael Sherry, and to Kyoko and Yumi Selden for critical comments, sources, skepticism, and suggestions in response to earlier versions of this essay.

1. Quoted in Anne Armstrong, *Unconditional Surrender: The Impact of the Casablanca Policy Upon World War II* (New Brunswick, 1961), p. 17. In this as in so many other areas there was only partial congruence in the Japanese and American positions. While both sides claimed high moral justifications for their positions, only the Americans hewed to the unconditional surrender position. Japanese hopes, from the start of the conflict, indeed throughout the twentieth century, were pinned on a settlement with the United States and the European powers that would permit Japan to secure territories acquired in its invasions of China and Southeast Asia. The Japanese never seriously pursued the idea of subjugating the United States.

2. German, Japanese and American scientists, among others, conducted chemical and biological research throughout the war and after. Fear of retaliation restrained these nations from using these weapons against one another. The Japanese military felt no such compunctions, however, with respect to the use of such weapons against Chinese forces who were deemed unable to reply in kind. Japan used chemical weapons in China from 1938 forward, particularly making use of mustard gas against both Guomindang and Communist forces as well as against civilians. Cf. Chalmers Johnson, *Peasant Nationalism and Communist Power: The Emergence of Revolutionary China, 1937–1945* (Stanford, 1962),

p. 73; *Materials of Former Servicemen of the Japanese Army Charged with Manufacturing Bacteriological Weapons* (Moscow, 1950), pp. 23–25. Yuki Tanaka details Japanese use of chemical weapons against Chinese forces and in experiments on Chinese prisoners in "Poison Gas: The Story Japan Would Like to Forget," *Bulletin of the Atomic Scientists*, October 1988, pp. 10–19, and in his book *Shirarezaru*

Senso Hanzai (Unknown War Crimes) (Tokyo, 1993). An English edition of this book is forthcoming as *Hidden Horrors: Japanese War Crimes in the Second World War* (Boulder, 1995). On Japan's germ warfare experiments see Peter Williams and David Wallace, *Unit 731: Japan's Secret Biological Warfare in World War II* (New York, 1989) and John Powell, "Japan's Germ Warfare: The U.S. Cover-Up of a War Crime," *Bulletin of Concerned Asian Scholars*, Oct–Dec. 1980, pp. 2-17.

3. Michael Sherry, *The Rise of American Air Power: The Creation of Armageddon* (New Haven, 1987), pp. 23–28, pp. 57–59. Ronald Schaffer, *Wings of Judgment: American Bombing in World War II* (New York, 1985), pp. 20–30, 108–9. Mitchell's contradictory message, which became Air Force doctrine in 1926, was that air attack "was a method of imposing will by terrorizing the whole population . . . while conserving life and property to the greatest extent." Quoted in Sherry, *Air Power*, p. 30.

4. Gavan McCormack, "Remembering and Forgetting: The War, 1945–1995" (unpublished paper, 1995), p. 26.

5. Gordon Wright, *The Ordeal of Total War 1939–1945* (New York, 1968), p. 26. The figure of 40,000 civilian deaths, but not the civilian bombing itself, has been called into question. Anthony Cave-Brown offers a figure of 900 deaths. *Bodyguard of Lies* (New York: Harper and Row), p. 39.

6. Roosevelt sharply protested Japanese bombing of Shanghai in 1937–38 and subsequently of Chongqing, where the Guomindang had settled after being driven out of the coastal areas, as well as Soviet bombing of Helsinki and other cities following the 1939 Soviet attack on Finland. Schaffer, *Wings*, pp. 32–36; Sherry, *Air Power*, pp. 57–58, 95–96. It should be noted, however, that Roosevelt's public criticisms were never directed toward U.S. allies once the United States entered the war, or for that matter, toward U.S. bombing practice. Stewart Udall discusses a range of critics of civilian bombing in *The Myths of August: A Personal Exploration of Our Tragic Cold War Affair With the Atom* (New York, 1994), pp. 50–52.

7. Sherry, *Air Power*, pp. 93–96.

8. Max Hastings, *Bomber Command: The Myth and Reality of the Strategic Bombing Offensive* (New York, 1979), p. 139.

9. Sherry, *Air Power*, pp. 147–52; Schaffer, *Wings*, pp. 37–38.

10. Sherry describes the Dresden raids as "less the product of conscious callousness than of casual destructiveness." *Air Power*, p. 260. With much U.S. bombing already relying on radar, the distinction between tactical and strategic bombing had long been violated in practice and no orders from on high pointed to a new bombing strategy. The top brass, from George Marshall to Air Force chief Henry Arnold to Dwight Eisenhower, had all earlier given tacit approval for area bombing.

11. Interview quoted in Richard Rhodes, *The Making of the Atomic Bomb* (New York, 1986), p. 593.

12. Schaffer, *Wings*, p. 97; Sherry, *Air Power*, pp. 260–63.

13. Sherry, *Air Power*, pp. 272–73, 404–5. In December, 1950, following President Truman's threat to use nuclear weapons against China and North Korea, LeMay bid hard to conduct the operation, arguing that "his headquarters was the only one with the experience, technical training, and 'intimate knowledge' of delivery methods." Bruce Cumings, *The Origins of the Korean War: The Roaring of the Cataract, 1947–1950* (Princeton, 1990), p. 748.

14. Cf. Stewart Udall's discussion of responsibility for the U.S. shift to area bombing, centering on President Roosevelt, Secretary of War Henry Stimson, and Air Force Secretary Robert Lovett, and the difficulty of documenting responsibility for the policy shift. Sherry and Schaffer provide the most exhaustive study of the shift in U.S. bombing policy.

15. Sherry, *Air Power*, pp. 122-24. Sherry contrasts the Japanese attack on the U.S. fleet at Pearl Harbor with the U.S. bombing of populated urban areas in the Doolittle raid. While the attacks served notice of Japan's vulnerability, the damage was inconsequential.

16. Rhodes, *Atomic Bomb*, pp. 596–97.

17. Schaffer, *Wings*, pp. 134–35.

18. "Tokyo Under Bombardment, 1941–1945," *Bethanie Institute Bulletin* No. 5, trans. in General Headquarters Far East Command, Military Intelligence Section, *War in Asia and the Pacific* Vol. 12, *Defense of the Homeland and End of the War*, ed., Donald Detwiler and Charles Burdick (New York, 1980).

19. Sherry, *Air Power*, p. 276. A detailed photographic record, including images of scores of the dead, some burnt to a crisp and distorted beyond recognition, others apparently serene in death, and of acres of the city flattened as if by an immense tornado, is found in Ishikawa Koyo, *Tokyo daikushu no zenkiroku* (Complete Record of the Great Tokyo Air Attack) (Tokyo, 1992); Tokyo kushu o kiroku suru kai ed., *Tokyo daikushu no kiroku* (Record of the Great Tokyo Air Attack) (Tokyo, 1982), and *Dokyumento: Tokyo daikushu* (Document. The Great Tokyo Air Attack) (Tokyo, 1968).

20. The Survey's killed-to-injured ratio of better than two to one was far higher by most estimates than that at Hiroshima and Nagasaki where killed and wounded were approximately equal.

If accurate, it is indicative of the immense difficulty in escaping for those near the center of the Tokyo firestorm on that windswept night. The Survey's kill ratio has, however, been challenged by Japanese researchers who found much higher kill ratios at Hiroshima and Nagasaki, particularly when one includes those who died of bomb injuries months and years later. In my judgment, death figures for the Tokyo attack have been significantly understated in both Japan and the United States. The Committee for the Compilation of Materials on Damage Caused by the Atomic Bombs in Hiroshima and Nagasaki, *Hiroshima and Nagasaki: The Physical, Medical, and Social Effects of the Atomic Bombing* (New York, 1991), pp. 420–21; Cf. U.S. Strategic Bombing Survey, *Field Report Covering Air Raid Protection and Allied Subjects, Tokyo* (n.p., 1946), pp. 3, 79.

21. In contrast to the atomic bombing of Hiroshima and Nagasaki, which for fifty years have been the subject of intense research by Japanese, Americans and others, the most significant records of the Tokyo attacks are those compiled at the time by Japanese police and fire departments. In the absence of the mystique of the atomic bomb and the ongoing national and global focus on that event, there was no compelling reason to continue to monitor the results of firebombing attacks on Japanese cities following surrender. The U.S. Strategic Bombing Survey study of *Effects of Air Attack on Urban Complex Tokyo-Kawasaki-Yokohama* (n.p.,1947), p. 8, observes that Japanese police estimates of 93,076 killed and 72,840 injured in Tokyo air raids make no mention of the numbers of people missing. Surely, too, many classified as injured died subsequently of their wounds. In contrast to the monitoring of atomic bomb deaths over the subsequent five decades, the Tokyo casualty figures at best record deaths and injuries within days of the bombing at a time when the capacity of the Tokyo military and police to compile records had been overwhelmed.

22. Sherry, *Air Power*, p. 406; Rhodes, *Atomic Bomb*, pp. 591–96.

23. *Dokyumento. Tokyo daikushu*, pp. 168–73.

24. John Dower, "Sensational Rumors, Seditious Graffiti, and the Nightmares of the Thought Police," in *Japan in War and Peace* (New York, 1993), p. 117.

25. A good introduction to Japan's wartime agricultural and industrial production and consumption as well as labor power utilization is U.S. Strategic Bombing Survey, *The Japanese Wartime Standard of Living and Utilization of Manpower* (n.p., 1947); see also *Japanese War Production Industries* (n.p., 1945); and *The Effects of Strategic Bombing on Japan's War Economy* (n.p., 1946). The data highlight the astonishing gap in industrial power and war-making capacity between Japan and the United States, a gap that would widen immensely in the course of the war.

26. By "the planned war" the author meant the projected U.S. invasion of Japan, *The Effects of Strategic Power on Japanese Morale* (n.p. 1947), p. 1. Even in such direct statements, euphemisms like "great social and psychological disruption" mask the deaths of hundreds of thousands of non-combatants.

27. Sherry, *Air Power*, p. 253.

28. Cf. Dower's nuanced historical perspective on war and racism in American thought and praxis in *War Without Mercy: Race and Power in the Pacific War* (New York, 1986). In *Year 501: The Conquest Continues* (Boston, 1993) and many other works, Noam Chomsky emphasizes the continuities in Western ideologies that undergird practices leading to the annihilation of entire populations in the course of colonial and expansionist wars over half a millennium and more. Nikki Keddie notes that Christianity's slaughter of non-believers and heretics from the Crusades forward was on a scale without precedent among world religions (personal communication October 1, 1994).

29. I have explored the issues of Japan's China war and the Chinese resistance in *China in Revolution: The Yenan Way Revisited* (Armonk, 1995) and in Edward Friedman, Paul Pickowicz and Mark Selden, *Chinese Village, Socialist State* (New Haven, 1991). The most insightful discussion of Japanese war crimes in the Pacific War, locating the issues within a comparative context of atrocities committed by the U.S., Germany, and other military powers, is Tanaka's *Shirarezaru Senso Hanzai* and his forthcoming *Hidden Horrors: Japanese Crimes in World War II*. Daqing Yang surveys the contentious Chinese and Japanese literature on the rape of Nanjing in "A Sino-Japanese Controversy: The Nanjing Atrocity as History," *Sino-Japanese Studies*, (November 1990), pp. 14–35.

30. R.J.R. Bosworth, *Explaining Auschwitz and Hiroshima. History Writing and the Second World War 1945–1990* (London, 1993). Wide discrepancies and large lacunae remain with respect to World War II casualties and deaths, especially in Asia. Cf. John Dower's compilation and discussion of some of the basic data, *War Without Mercy*, pp. 295–300 and "Race, Language and War in Two Cultures," in *Japan in War and Peace*, p. 257.

31. The tenacity of the Chinese resistance is particularly striking in contrast to the relative ease with which Japanese forces suppressed resistance and consolidated their control over large areas of the Asia–Pacific region.

THE FIRST
NUCLEAR
WAR

Wilfred Burchett

I COULD HAVE HAD NO IDEA when I entered Hiroshima just four weeks after the city's incineration that this would become a watershed in my life, decisively influencing my whole professional career and world outlook. The "Occupation press corps" was a group of hand-picked American journalists flown out directly from Washington to report on the devastating power of America's new war-winning weapon. They were selected on the basis of their prestige, credibility, or expert knowledge to participate in a great cover-up conspiracy, although some of them may not have realized this at the time. They had been assured that they would be the first foreign journalists to enter Hiroshima—well ahead of their war correspondent colleagues who had covered the long and dangerous island-hopping operations and jungle battlefields which paved the way to Japan's defeat. A few were also veteran war correspondents, but the majority were being rewarded for faithful rewrites of the Washington headquarters' communiqués. In view of their officially guaranteed "scoop," they were chagrined to find an Australian rival wandering around in the Hiroshima rubble when they arrived.

The high-level public relations officers who were carefully shepherding them treated me with suspicion and hostility. Who was I and how did I get there? Their hostility seemed disproportionate to the usual frustrations of professional competition. My journey to Hiroshima—as will be related later—had been tough and dangerous, but my request for a lift back to Tokyo with their special U.S. Army plane was curtly refused. As was also my plea that they at least take a copy of my report to pass on to my *Daily Express* colleague at press headquarters. At the time I put this down to an excess of zeal by the senior press officer because he had not been able to keep the promise that "his" journalists would be the first to report from Hiroshima. (I learned later that some of his charges—colleagues from war reporting in the Pacific—protested at the cavalier way in which I was treated.) If the refusal to carry back my report was only an excess of zeal, I could afford to smile inwardly. By the time of our meeting and unknown to them, my report was being tapped out, letter by letter on a Morse handset from Hiroshima to Tokyo. But there was no certainty as to when it would arrive. And I had no inkling that in writing what I did, I was taking on the U.S. military and political establishment.

The most prestigious member of the U.S. journalist delegation was William L. Laurence, for many years the science writer for the *New York Times*. At the time of his Hiroshima visit, he was wearing two hats: one for the *New York Times*, the other as a member of the inner circle of the government's nuclear weapons directorate. Although at the time his favored official connections were obvious, few of his fellow journalists, much less his millions of readers, were aware of his real plenipotentiary status as the U.S. War Department's nuclear propagandist. Three months before Hiroshima he had been recruited by General Leslie R. Groves, the commander of the Manhattan Project, to act as a super public relations officer and news "manager." Given years of voluntary press censorship of any mention of atomic energy, and the general scientific ignorance of most wartime journalists, Laurence—precisely as Groves had intended—became a virtual oracle for Allied reporters. He alone had access to the Manhattan Project's super-secret plants and laboratories, and had been the sole journalist to observe the Alamogordo test of the prototype A-bomb used against Hiroshima. He had written the famous statement "from the President" announcing the destruction of Hiroshima, which Truman's Assistant Press Secretary Eban Ayers had read to astonished journalists on the morning of 6 August. His *New York Times* background pieces on the dawn of the nuclear era were syndicated worldwide, and on the morning of 10 August he flew in one of the three bombers which dropped "Fat Man," the plutonium-fueled bomb, on Nagasaki.[1] For these deeds, and his exultant descriptions of the "awesome beauty" of atomic genocide, Laurence later received both a Pulitzer Prize and a War Department commendation.

Laurence's arrival at Hiroshima, in the company of the Manhattan Project's deputy-commander, Brigadier-General Thomas D. Farrell, and the select party of house-trained reporters, was undoubtedly intended as a culminating coup in the official management of what had been described as "the biggest news story in the history of the world." It had not been anticipated that a maverick reporter, unvetted by the U. S. War Department or Project Manhattan, would have found the means to arrive at the dead city ahead of the Farrell party. Under these circumstances, and given the pre-rehearsed character of the Investigatory [*sic*] Group's "findings," it is no wonder that Laurence in the *New York Times*, and myself in the *London Daily Express*, ended up writing diametrically different reports. I reported what I had seen and heard, while Laurence sent back a prefabricated report reflecting the "official line."

THE ATOMIC PLAGUE: thus ran the *Daily Express* headline introducing my Hiroshima dispatch. The term "atomic radiation" was unknown to me—and most readers—at the time. But I knew that some terrible new malady had stricken the survivors of the original blast and fiery holocaust. I had seen some of them in what remained of a hospital and talked to the doctor in charge. The report took up most of the front page and the large part of an inside page of the September 5, 1945 edition. Laurence meanwhile preferred to take refuge behind Farrell. His first report in the *New York Times* appeared, unaccountably, only on September 13 under the following headlines:

No Radioactivity in Hiroshima Ruin
Army Investigators Also Report Absence
Of Ground Fusing—68,000 Buildings Damaged
By W. L. Laurence (Wireless to the New York Times)

Datelined Tokyo, September 12, his report starts:

> Brig. Gen. T. F. Farrell, chief of the War Department's atomic bomb
> mission, reported tonight after a survey of blasted Hiroshima that the
> explosive power of the secret weapon was greater even than its inven-
> tors envisaged, but he denied categorically that it produced a danger-
> ous, lingering radioactivity in the ruins of the town, or caused a form
> of poison gas at the moment of explosion. . . .
> He said his group of scientists found no evidence of continuing
> radioactivity in the blasted area on Sept. 9, when they began their
> investigations and said it was his opinion that there was no danger to
> be encountered by living in the area at present. . . .
> "The physical destruction in the target area was practically complete,"
> he reported. "The scene was one of utter devastation. The total num-
> ber of destroyed and damaged buildings was 68,000 or somewhere
> between 80 and 100 percent of all buildings in the city. . . ."

Another Laurence report from the Alamogordo test site where the first
A-bomb exploded had appeared in the *New York Times* the day prior to that from
Hiroshima. It was in relation to that report that the *New York Times* revealed that
Laurence was serving as a "special consultant" to the Manhattan Engineering
District, the War Department's special service for atomic development. His
Alamogordo dispatch was headlined:

U.S. Atom Bomb Site Belies Tokyo Tales
by William L. Laurence

> Atom bomb range, New Mexico, Sept. 9 (delayed)—This historic
> ground in New Mexico, scene of the first atomic explosion on earth
> and cradle of a new era in civilization, gave the most effective answer
> to Japanese propaganda that radiations were responsible for deaths
> even the day after the explosion, Aug. 6, and that persons entering
> Hiroshima had contracted mysterious maladies due to persistent
> radioactivity.
> To give the lie to these claims, the Army opened the closely-
> guarded gates of this area for the first time to a group of newspaper
> men and photographers to witness for themselves the readings on
> radiation meters carried by a group of radiologists and to listen to the
> expert testimony of several of the leading scientists who have been
> intimately connected with the atomic bomb project.
> The ground, visited for the first time by Maj. Gen. Leslie R.
> Groves, overall director of the atomic bomb project, since that
> historic morning on Monday, July 16, gave awesome testimony on
> a number of subjects. . . .

Having proved, at least to Laurence's satisfaction, that there was no radioactivity at the testing range where the A-bomb was detonated from a steel tower only 100 feet above ground, there was far less likelihood of any at Hiroshima or Nagasaki where, according to Laurence, the bombs were exploded at almost twenty times that altitude. He continued:

> This finding is borne out by a report just received by General Thomas F. Farrell, his next in command, who is now in Japan with a group of American scientists to study the effects of the bomb, on the scene.
>
> The studies of the American scientists are still in the preliminary stage, General Groves stated. But, he added that, according to General Farrell, Japanese sources now admitted that eleven days after the bomb had pulverized Hiroshima, the radiation there was much less than the tolerance dose which means, he added, "that you could live there forever."
>
> "The Japanese claim," General Groves added, "that people died from radiation. If this is true, the number was very small. However, any deaths from gamma rays were due to those emitted during the explosion, not to the radiations present afterwards. While many people were killed, many lives were saved, particularly American lives. It ended the war sooner. It was the final punch that knocked them out."
>
> "The Japanese are still continuing their propaganda aimed at creating the impression that we won the war unfairly and thus attempting to create sympathy for themselves and (obtain) milder terms, an examination of their present statements reveal." [2]

Like the fumbling and procrastination in replying to the Swiss Government's memorandum, there is something fishy about the correlation of dates in the activities of Farrell and Laurence.* Why did Laurence not file his own report from

---

* On August 11, 1945, the Swiss Legation in Tokyo, which looked after American interests in Japan, forwarded the following memorandum to the U.S. State Department. The contents were released twenty–five years later:

The Legation of Switzerland in charge of Japanese interests has received an urgent cable from the authorities abroad, requesting that the Department of State be immediately apprised of the following communication from the Japanese Government reading, in translation, as follows:
On 6 August 1945, American airplanes released on the residential district of the town of Hiroshima, bombs of a new type, killing and injuring in one second a large number of civilians and destroying a great part of the town. Not only is the city of Hiroshima a provincial town without any protection or special military installations of any kind, but also none of the neighboring region of this town constitutes a military objective.[3]
In a declaration President Truman has asserted that he would use these bombs for the destruction of docks, factories and installations for transportation.[4] However, this bomb, provided with a parachute, in falling has a destructive force of great scope as a result of its explosion in the air. It is evident, therefore, that it is technically impossible to limit the effect of its use to special objectives such as designated by President Truman, and the American authorities are perfectly well aware of this. In fact, it has been established on-the-scene that the

Hiroshima, or at least from Tokyo, where he presumably arrived back from the massacred city on September 3, or at latest the following morning? He had been in Hiroshima with the other correspondents on the same day as myself. Why the belated story from the atomic range?

Delay on a newspaper dispatch normally means a problem of transmission. It is hard to believe that the telephone lines and telegraph wires were not working between New Mexico and New York. And, in a story filed from Los Alamos on September 9, how was it possible that General Groves was able to quote Farrell for an on-the-spot report when Farrell only left for Hiroshima on that day, returning to Tokyo three days later? Above all, why the enormous effort to deceive the public into believing that there was no residual radioactivity in the A-bombed cities? With all modesty, I believe that I was partly the cause of all this.

When I stumbled out of a train at Tokyo station on the morning of September 7, after my harrowing journey to Hiroshima and back, my only thought was to get to a hotel and sleep in a bed for the first time in five days.

My return journey had been arduous, to say the least. At Kyoto station—about halfway in train-time those days between Tokyo and Hiroshima—I met some Australian POWs, pale ghosts of men who recognized by my suntan and general fitness that I was not one of them. When they realized that I was tangible confirmation of what had been rumors until then—that the war was really over—they begged me to leave the train, come to their camp, just show myself and tell their fellow POWs that the war was over and they would soon be on their way home. Our mates are dying every hour, they said. They've only got to see you and hear what you've told us and you'll save many lives.

I could not refuse despite the notes for follow-up stories on Hiroshima that were burning holes in my pocket. First I checked with the Kyoto branch of *Domei*

---

damage extends over a great area and that combatant and non-combatant men and women, old and young, are massacred without discrimination by the atmospheric pressure of the explosion as well as by the radiating heat which results therefrom. Consequently there is involved a bomb having the most cruel effects humanity has ever known, not only as far as the extensive and immense damage is concerned, but also for reasons of suffering endured by each victim.

It is an elementary principle of international public law that in time of war the belligerents do not have unlimited right in the choice of attack and that they cannot resort to projectile arms or any other means capable of causing the enemy needless suffering. . . .The bombs in question, used by the Americans, by their cruelty and by their terrorizing effects, surpass by far gas or any other arm, the use of which is prohibited. . . .

The Americans have effected bombardments of towns in the greatest part of Japanese territory, without discrimination massacring a great number of old people, women and children, destroying and burning down Shinto and Buddhist temples, schools, hospitals, living quarters, etc. This fact alone means that they have shown complete defiance of the essential principles of humanitarian laws, as well as international law. They now use this new bomb, having an uncontrollable and cruel effect much greater than any other arms or projectiles ever used to date. This constitutes a new crime against humanity and civilization. The government of Japan, in its own name and at the same time in the name of all of humanity and civilization, accuses the American Government with the present Note of an inhuman weapon of this nature, and demands energetically, abstinence from its use.

[For a full description of the American government's reply to the Swiss government see Wilfred Burchett, *Shadows of Hiroshima* (London, 1983), pp. 11–13.—*Editors*] (then the official Japanese news agency) to learn whether my report had got through to Tokyo. It was the *Domei* correspondent in Hiroshima who had tapped it out on his hand Morse set. A beaming employee confirmed that it had been received in the *Domei* office, then transferred to a *Daily Express* colleague. For the next few days and nights—I have never been able to work out how many—I toured all the POW camps in the Kyoto-Tsuruga area. My message was that the war was really over, a brief résumé of how the end had come, and that they should hang on for a few more days until arrangements were completed to free them and send them homeward.

An enthusiastic Japanese-speaking American POW said I must carry the same message to a big, mixed camp at Kobe-Osaka, where I soon had the local mayor on the mat, pledging to improve camp conditions immediately—a pledge I extracted from commanders of the half-dozen other camps I visited. With a .45 caliber pistol—loaned me by my *Daily Express* colleague who had arrived with General MacArthur's forces in Yokohama—strapped to my waist, I pretended to be an emissary sent by General MacArthur to ensure that the surrender conditions were being implemented.

Finally I arrived back at Tokyo station, clothes stiff with sweat, unwashed, unshaven, eyes red with train cinders and lack of sleep. When I had left Tokyo station what seemed ages ago, the capital had not yet been occupied. MacArthur's forces were concentrated in Yokohama, and Tokyo was about to be declared "off limits." Now it was full of smartly dressed American officers and troops. As I started to slink away from the station to the Dai Ichi Hotel where I had illegally (although I did not know it at the time) spent a night making arrangements to get to Hiroshima, a colleague hailed me—very dapper in his freshly-pressed war correspondent's uniform. "Burchett," he shouted, "you've just made it. Come with me to the Imperial Hotel. The top brass are giving a special briefing on Hiroshima."

"Impossible in the state I'm in," I replied. "All I want is a bath and a bed." "But," he argued, "the briefing is especially to deny your story about radiation sickness in Hiroshima." So I went. But on the way I learned that the *Daily Express* had not only "frontpaged" my story but had made it available world-wide *gratis*. The American nuclear big shots were furious.

The conference was nearly over when I arrived, but it was clear that its main purpose was to deny my dispatch from Hiroshima that people were dying from the after-effects of the bomb. A scientist in brigadier-general's uniform explained that there could be no question of atomic radiation or the symptoms I had described, since the bombs had been exploded at such a height as to avoid any risk of "residual radiation." [5]

There was a dramatic moment as I rose to my feet, feeling that my scruffiness put me at a disadvantage with the elegantly uniformed and bemedalled officers. My first question was whether the briefing officer had been to Hiroshima. He had not. I then described what I had seen and asked for explanations. He was very polite at first, a scientist explaining things to a layman. Those I had seen in the hospital were victims of blast and burn, normal after any big explosion. Apparently the Japanese doctors were incompetent to handle them, or lacked the right medication. He discounted the allegation that any who had not been in the city at the time of the blast were later affected. Eventually the exchanges narrowed down to my asking how he explained the fish still dying when they entered a stream running through the center of the city. "Obviously they were killed by the blast or overheated water."

"Still there a month later?"

"It's a tidal river, so they could be washed back and forth."

"But I was taken to a spot in the city outskirts and watched live fish turning their stomachs upwards as they entered a certain stretch of the river. After that they were dead within seconds."

The spokesman looked pained. "I'm afraid you've fallen victim to Japanese propaganda," he said, and sat down. The customary "Thank you" was pronounced and the conference was ended. Although my radiation story was denied, Hiroshima was immediately put out of bounds, and I was whisked off to a U.S. Army hospital for tests, which showed that my white corpuscle count was down.

The press corps picked this up and I soon received a gentle, admonitory cable from *Daily Express* foreign editor, Charles Foley, to the effect that the paper hoped they would not be scooped by rivals about my own disintegration. The drop in my white corpuscle count was written off by the hospital authorities as due to a knee infection which had been treated by antibiotics. Only later did I learn that the knee infection should have increased the number of white corpuscles battling against the infection on my behalf. A falling-off in white corpuscles, on the other hand, is a typical phenomenon of radiation sickness. By the time I left the hospital I found that my camera, with the historic pictures from Hiroshima still tucked away in its intestines, was missing; that General MacArthur had withdrawn my press accreditation; and that I was to be expelled from Japan for having gone "beyond the boundaries of 'his' occupation zone without permission." Later, I was to learn of a restriction placed on all Allied journalists seemingly as a direct result of my "misdemeanors."

On the day following the transmission of my Hiroshima dispatch from the Yokohama press headquarters, the following report was filed to the *New York Times:*

> Yokohama, Japan, Sept. 5. (By wireless to the *New York Times*) As units of the United States (Dismounted) Cavalry Division prepared for entry into Tokyo, Saturday, orders were repeated and enforced today for the withdrawal of all correspondents from the capital.
>
> When a correspondent asked the reason for this step, a spokesman for Gen. Douglas MacArthur replied: "It is not military policy for correspondents to spearhead the occupation." Meanwhile, general officers and other personnel from Allied Headquarters entered the city today to investigate the hotels where correspondents had been staying. These hotels will be taken over by headquarters which then will assign a hotel that was described by former Tokyo residents as third-rate. News from Japan's capital and news center now is being filed abroad entirely by the Japanese news agency *Domei*, while American correspondents are forced to remain on routine assignments a mile outside the city limits. . . .
>
> Forced to remain in Yokohama, correspondents belatedly receive handouts of translations from the Japanese press that are carefully edited and selected with a view to upholding the official Japanese line that: "We were defeated but we hope the Americans will be as good winners as we were losers. . . ."

As we will see later, there was method in this seeming MacArthur madness. The concentration of Allied newsmen into a sort of press ghetto and making them dependent on Japanese sources for all significant developments was preparatory to placing a total ban on Japanese journalists or scientists making any reports whatsoever about the fate of A-bomb survivors in Hiroshima or Nagasaki.

How I came to be in Hiroshima, what I saw there and how my report appeared in the *Daily Express* two days after my visit, is a long and complicated story. . . . [It was on Okinawa] while lining up for my hamburgers and mash at a U.S. Army canteen, that I heard snatches of a newscast, in which an excited announcer was talking about an enormously powerful new bomb that had just been dropped on a place called Hiroshima. Above the clatter of tin trays and plates, small talk about the previous night's movie or the Japanese infiltrator someone's unit had just shot, it was impossible to catch the details about the new bomb. As the cook's aide dumped my lunch onto the tray, I asked what the newscast was all about: "Ah," he said, "it's about some great new bomb we've just dropped on the Japs. A lotta good it'll do us here." And I shuffled on down the line none the wiser. (At the time it was taken for granted that the Okinawa operation which had been so costly—12,000 U.S. troops killed, 36,000 wounded, 34 Allied ships sunk and 368 damaged in almost three months of fighting—would be nothing in terms of human and material losses compared to the final assault on Japan.) In the comparative quiet of an officers' mess that evening, I learned that it was an A-bomb which had been dropped "on a place called Hiroshima" and I made a mental note that this would be my first goal if I made it to Japan.

I did make it, aboard the USS *Millette*, a freighter transformed into a troop transport, laden with Marines who were to be among the first landing party. Their job was to spike the enemy's guns and ensure security for the first waves of occupation troops. It was in Yokohama and not Tokyo that Henry Keys and I met for the first time since Melbourne. He had flown to Yokohama with an advance party from MacArthur's headquarters. Having picked up a few phrases of Japanese from a U.S. military manual within half an hour of landing at the Yokosuka naval base, I found that trains ran regularly between Yokosuka and Tokyo. Together with Bill McGaffin of the *Chicago Daily News*, an inseparable companion of many battlefields, we were soon on a Tokyo-bound train. Our Japanese fellow-passengers showed surprise, but not hostility. One of them, in good English, indicated at which station we should get out for the Dai Ichi Hotel—not far from the center of what was left of Tokyo after General LeMay's genocidal fire raids. After a mild altercation with the receptionist at the Dai Ichi, ending in our filling out a tourist-type form concerning "length of stay," "home address" and other irrelevancies, we booked in for the night, quickly discovering that cigarettes were an acceptable form of currency.

Next morning, while McGaffin strolled around taking notes for a piece on the atmosphere, I sought out *Domei* (today *Kyodo*), the official Japanese news agency. I was received with professional courtesy by someone on the foreign desk, to whom I explained my most ardent desire to get to Hiroshima as soon as possible and report exactly what had happened there. He gave me a startled look and said: "But no one goes to Hiroshima. Everyone is dying there." When I insisted that if this was the case it made my mission all the more urgent, he consulted with some colleagues and said: "There is a daily train leaving Tokyo at 6 A.M. which stops at Hiroshima. But no one can say at what time it stops there."

The upshot was that he agreed to buy me a return ticket in exchange for my taking some food and cigarettes to Nakamura-*san*, the *Domei* correspondent in Hiroshima. I asked if there was any chance of getting a message back to their Tokyo office through Nakamura-*san*. He replied: "It is an odd situation. He has a Morse handset and gets messages through to us. But he has no receiving apparatus so we cannot contact him. There are no radios in Hiroshima and the trains are not carrying newspapers there. Somehow he knows we get his messages, so he keeps on filing. If you like, we will give you a letter to Nakamura-*san* and ask him to help you. And please tell him how highly we value his services."

Back to the Dai Ichi hotel for a rendezvous with Bill McGaffin and the return trip to Yokosuka. McGaffin had come only to cover the *Missouri* surrender ceremony after which he was to return directly to Chicago. So it was no disloyalty to that highly-esteemed friend in not disclosing my secret plan. A friend at the Navy press center to whom I did divulge my project, delighted at the idea that it might be one of "their" correspondents who made it first into Hiroshima, provided me with adequate provisions including a huge chunk of beef for my *Domei* contact in Tokyo. All correspondents assembled that evening at a Yokohama hotel, temporarily designated as the Allied press headquarters, and I had an uproarious reunion with my compatriot-colleague, Henry Keys. Predictably there was a brief exchange of the hair-raising experiences we had each been through and—in view of the exceptionally high death-toll of correspondents—miraculously survived. The matter of division of labor for the following days we settled even more rapidly than when we had "split the Pacific up." Henry would cover the *Missouri* surrender ceremony and I would do my best to get to Hiroshima. He would do his utmost to maintain contact with *Domei* in Tokyo and in case the dubious miracle worked, would relay my report to London via the Yokohama press center.

We shared the same room that night, conscious of the necessity of absolute secrecy in relation to our colleagues. Fortunately they were all due to leave very early the following morning to be on the decks of the USS *Missouri* for the ceremony which would officially mark the end of the Second World War. Press officers came to wake us up and were appalled to discover that one of the fold was groaning on his bed with what appeared to be a bad case of diarrhea, his anxious colleague applying warm towels to his stomach. Nothing to be done, but abandon me to miss one of the "greatest moments of history." As Henry left to join his colleagues he wished me good luck and, saying: "You may need this," he thrust a Colt .45 automatic in my hand. He said he had "souvenired" it from one of the battlefields. I took it reluctantly, together with the webbing belt to which it was attached. War correspondents were not supposed to carry sidearms, but as the war was to be officially ended within a few hours, my scruples were short-lived. I tucked it into my haversack with my Hermes typewriter and provisions.

Less than an hour after the departure of the "six hundred," I was in *Domei's* Tokyo office, exchanging my chunk of beef for a return ticket to Hiroshima and a precious note to Nakamura-*san*. Precisely at 6 A.M., I was pushed into a terribly over-crowded train by some *Domei* colleagues who fervently expressed their hopes—with some misgivings, I felt—that all would go well.

ONE OF THE MOST HAZARDOUS PARTS of my venture was spent during the first eight or nine hours—I had been warned that the journey would last from fifteen to thirty hours. The train was overflowing with freshly demobilized troops and officers. The officers still wore their long swords with *samurai* daggers tucked into their belts. They occupied all the passenger compartments, while the ordinary troops were crammed onto the platforms separating the carriages. I had no alternative but to use my elbows and find standing space with them. They did not know what to make of me. I had shoved my very military-looking war correspondent's cap into the knapsack. Wearing marine jungle greens, I clutched an umbrella, hoping it would symbolize my civilian status.

The Japanese GIs, short, weary men, wearing leg puttees, were very sullen at first, chattering about me in what I sensed was a hostile way. When I handed round a packet of cigarettes, however, they brightened up. (I was soon to learn that the price of cigarettes had risen ten to twenty-fold since the news of the surrender was known.) In return I was offered a few swigs of *saki* with which the troops seemed to have filled their water canteens, and some bits of dried fish and hard-boiled eggs. After the first hour we were wartime buddies. They roared with laughter when I showed them scars around my right knee and a protruding bit of unremoved bullet, received from a Japanese fighter in Burma; I produced my typewriter to show that I was a journalist. Space was found for me to sit on one of the enormous bundles they all had and the *saki* flowed more freely. After demobilization, they had been allowed to help themselves to as much food and drink as they could carry, as well as their weapons—concealed among blankets (but that I discovered only later).

After the first five or six hours, my fellow platform-swingers, ruddy of face, bleary of eyes and glowing with *saki* started dropping off at the various stops, staggering away with their huge bundles. No salutes, I noted, for officers who got off at the same stops, no bows, no signs of recognition even. I managed to get a place in the seating compartment to which our platform gave access, grimy as I was from smoke and cinders. The hostility was total. An American in priest's clothes whom I approached with exuberance, not entirely due to *saki*, warned me in guarded language that the situation was very tense. Then I noticed that he had an armed escort and was very nervous. He said that a smile or handshake would be taken as gloating over the surrender, which was being signed at about that moment, and could cost us our lives. He warned about those "with the big sticks between their legs." He had been brought to Tokyo to broadcast to the Occupation troops as to how they should behave to avoid friction. Now he was being taken back to the camp in which he had been interned since Pearl Harbor.

Bothersome also was that for what seemed about half the time—and that is still the case today—the train plunged into long tunnels. The difference between then and today is that the train was blacked out and there was no lighting in the tunnels. Then we averaged about 40 kilometers per hour, today 220. To be decapitated by a saber in the dark was not a pleasant prospect but it seemed to me that my new fellow-travelers desired nothing more than to do just that, their hands constantly fumbling with the hilts of their swords and looking daggers at me.

Another problem was to know when I reached Hiroshima—all station signs were written exclusively in Japanese ideographs (today they are duplicated in English). The priest and his escort left the train at Kyoto and he informed me that I was about halfway to my journey's end. I had learned from my phrase book that *"Kono eki-wa nanti i meska"* meant: "What is the name of this station?" This saved me from uttering the name of what then seemed to be the immediate cause of the Japanese surrender. I had no interest in adding new fuel to the fire of the officers' outrage at my presence among them. It was only later that I understood that they were part of what were known as the "hotheads," ready to defy the emperor and continue the war. They were being bundled out of Tokyo to avoid incidents during the surrender ceremony and the first days of occupation. Seven or eight hours out of Kyoto, I started my ritual question. By that time the officers had thinned out, replaced by civilians. When someone replied: *"Kono eki-wa Hiroshima eki desu"* (This is Hiroshima station) I would leap out. At just 2 A.M., twenty hours after leaving Tokyo, the welcome reply came. The compartment by then was so crammed with sitting and standing passengers that I had to clamber out through the window, my knapsack handed me by my passenger-neighbor.

The station, formerly a brick building, seemed nothing but a roof propped up with poles. A rough barrier had been set up funneling passengers to two wooden gates at which tickets were collected. As I found later, it was about 2,000 meters from the epicenter (or ground zero as the Americans say) where the bomb exploded. When I passed through the ticket-control gate, I was grabbed by two black-uniformed, saber-carrying guards. Assuming I was an escaped POW, they escorted me to an improvised lockup and made me understand I was not to move. As it was almost twenty-four hours since I had left my Yokohama hotel room and was pitch dark, there was no point in trying to argue. I handed around some cigarettes and drank some hot water, offered with some chickpeas by a woman in the lock-up, settled into a rickety chair and went to sleep. At sunup I produced my precious letter to Nakamura-*san* and displayed my typewriter, trying to make the point that I was a professional colleague. My status had clearly improved and I was able to stroll over and have a closer look at what was left of the station. After a couple of hours, Mr. Nakamura turned up with a Canadian-born young Japanese woman who spoke excellent English.

At this point it is appropriate to pay a tribute to the courage, the integrity and internationalist outlook of Nakamura. He accepted me for what I was: a journalist who wanted to perform his professional duty. From the first moment it was clear that he did not consider me as an enemy. I told him that my concern was not just with the material destruction, the dimensions of which I could measure even from the state of the railway station. What did this monstrous new weapon do to human beings? If he could help me to discover the truth, I would report things as I saw them. He accepted my request at face value and promised to try to transmit whatever I wrote back to *Domei* in Tokyo. He was clearly delighted and moved by the letter I had brought with the confirmation that his reports were getting through and were highly appreciated.

We walked through the flattened rubble of the 68,000 buildings, which Brig. Gen. Thomas Farrell was so proudly to proclaim had been destroyed or damaged, to what was left of the eight-story Fukuoka department store, on the third floor of which the survivors of the city's police force had set up their headquarters. The police were extremely hostile and the atmosphere was tense, as Nakamura explained who I was and what I wanted. The more Nakamura explained the more the tension increased. There was some shouting by the police and the interpreter became pale as she translated my rare interventions. It was only thirty-five years later, at the *Kyodo* headquarters in Tokyo, that Nakamura explained what went on. A majority of the police officers were for shooting all three of us. In the end—of all people—it was the head of the dreaded "Thought Control Police," outranking the others, who accepted the explanations of Nakamura and myself. "Show him what his people have done to us," he said, obviously taking me for an American. He even arranged a police car to drive me through the rubble and ruins and on to the Communications Hospital, one of the city's two hospitals of which enough had survived to render what aid was possible for the A-bomb victims. (Nakamura, who seemed hale and hearty in May 1980, died a few months after our reunion: one of the many who survived the attack and its aftermath, then suddenly died for no apparent reason.)

As to my impressions, I can do no better than repeat them as they were published in the *Daily Express*, pounded out on my ancient Baby Hermes, as I sat on a chunk of rubble that had escaped pulverization at the very center of the explosion. I packed as much as possible into that one report, having no guarantee of getting another chance of instant transmission, and having no idea what awaited me on my return journey. Apart from some garbles in transmission and some insertions, apparently by the science editor, the story is as close to the original as possible. (The carbon copy of what I wrote disappeared in Tokyo at the same time as my camera, so I have no other record than what follows.)

> In Hiroshima, thirty days after the first atomic bomb destroyed the city and shook the world, people are still dying, mysteriously and horribly—people who were uninjured in the cataclysm from an unknown something which I can only describe as the atomic plague. Hiroshima does not look like a bombed city. It looks as if a monster steamroller has passed over it and squashed it out of existence. I write these facts as dispassionately as I can in the hope that they will act as a warning to the world. In this first testing ground of the atomic bomb I have seen the most terrible and frightening desolation in four years of war. It makes a blitzed Pacific island seem like an Eden. The damage is far greater than photographs can show.
>
> When you arrive in Hiroshima you can look around for twenty-five and perhaps thirty square miles you can see hardly a building. It gives you an empty feeling in the stomach to see such man-made destruction. I picked my way to a shack used as a temporary police headquarters in the middle of the vanished city. Looking south from there I could see about three miles of reddish rubble. That is all the atomic bomb left of dozens of blocks of city streets, of buildings, homes, factories and human beings. There is just nothing standing except about twenty factory chimneys—chimneys with no factories. A group of half a dozen gutted buildings. And then again nothing.
>
> The police chief of Hiroshima welcomed me eagerly [*sic*] as the first Allied correspondent to reach the city. With the local manager of *Domei*, the leading Japanese news agency, he drove me through, or perhaps I should say over, the city. And he took me to hospitals where the victims of the bomb are still being treated. In these hospitals I found people who, when the bomb fell suffered absolutely no injuries, but now are dying from the uncanny after-effects. For no apparent reasons their health began to fail. They lost appetite. Their hair fell out. Bluish spots appeared on their bodies. And then bleeding began from the ears, nose and mouth. At first, the donors told me, they thought these were the symptoms of general debility. They

gave their patients vitamin A injections. The results were horrible. The flesh started rotting away from the hole caused by the injection of the needle. And in every case the victim died. That is one of the after effects of the first atomic bomb man ever dropped and I do not want to see any more examples of it.

My nose detected a peculiar odor unlike anything I have ever smelled before. It is something like sulfur, but not quite. I could smell it when I passed a fire that was still smoldering, or at a spot where they were still recovering bodies from the wreckage. But I could also smell it where everything was still deserted. They believe it is given off by the poisonous gas still issuing from the earth soaked with radioactivity by the split uranium atom. And so the people of Hiroshima today are walking through the forlorn desolation of their once proud city with gauze masks over mouths and noses. It probably does not help them physically. But it helps them mentally.

From the moment that this devastation was loosed upon Hiroshima the people who survived have hated the white man. It is a hate, the intensity of which is almost as frightening as the bomb itself. The counted dead number 53,000. Another 30,000 are missing which means certainly dead. In the day I have stayed in Hiroshima, 100 people have died from its effects. They were some of the 13,000 seriously injured by the explosion. They have been dying at the rate of 100 a day. And they will probably all die. Another 40,000 were slightly injured.[6] These casualties might not have been as high except for a tragic mistake. The authorities thought this was just another Super-Fort raid. The plane flew over the target and dropped the parachute which carried the bomb to its explosion point. The American plane passed out of sight. . . . The all-clear was sounded and the people of Hiroshima came out from their shelters. Almost a minute later the bomb reached the 2,000-foot altitude at which it was timed to explode—at the moment when nearly everyone in Hiroshima was in the streets.

This version is quite different from that which Nakamura told me and which I included in my original story. It is possible that Nakamura preferred not to be quoted and omitted his account from that which he transmitted. "We had an alert early in the morning," he told me, "but only two aircraft appeared. We thought they were reconnaissance planes and no one took much notice. The all clear sounded and most people set off for work. Then at 8:20, one plane came back. I was just wheeling out my bicycle to ride to the office when there was a blinding flash—like lightning. At the same time. I felt scorching heat on my face and a tornado-like blast of wind. I fell to the ground and the house collapsed around me. As I hit the ground, there was a booming explosion as if a powerful bomb had burst alongside. When I peered out, there was a tremendous pillar of black smoke, shaped like a parachute, but drifting upward, with a scarlet thread in the middle. As I watched the scarlet core expanded, diffusing through the billowing cloud of smoke until the whole thing was glowing red. Hiroshima had disappeared and I realized that something new to our experience had occurred. I tried to phone the police and fire brigade to find out what had happened, but it was impossible even to raise the exchange." None of this precious on-the spot description from an experienced observer appeared in the *Daily Express*. The published account continued as follows:

> Hundreds upon hundreds of the dead were so badly burned in the terrific heat generated by the bomb that it was not even possible to tell whether they were men or women, old or young. Of thousands of others, nearer the center of the explosion, there was no trace. They vanished. The theory in Hiroshima is that the atomic heat was so great that they burned instantly to ashes—except that there were no ashes. If you could see what is left of Hiroshima, you would think that London had not been touched by bombs. The Imperial palace, once an imposing building is a heap of rubble three feet high, and there is one piece of wall. Roof, floors and everything else is dust. . .

(There follows several paragraphs which were obviously inserted by the paper's science editor and which could not possibly have been written by me. Statements like "almost every Japanese scientist has visited Hiroshima in the past three weeks. . ."—In fact the first two scientists had arrived the day before I did and were holding their first meeting at the time I was visiting the Communications Hospital. There is also reference to Nagasaki which I did not visit and so could not have written about, and to the fact that doctors believed the sickness was "due to radioactivity." In fact they had no idea what they were trying to cope with.)

An explanation of some inaccuracies and perhaps some omissions from my report comes indirectly from the autobiography of Arthur Christiansen, *Serving My Time*. He was the prestigious editor of the *Daily Express* for many years. Writing of the Hiroshima "scoop" he remarks that "poor Peter" (Burchett) was so overcome by the horror of it all that he had to take a hand in editing the story. The science editor clearly wanted to show his erudition on atomic matters, but it was highly unethical to do this under my name.

My only information as to the medical effects from atomic radiation came from Dr. Katsube, acting director and chief surgeon of the Communications Hospital, and from the physical aspects of the patients in his hospital. Dr. Katsube deserves the same credit as Mr. Nakamura. He took a great risk in personally escorting me through some of the hospital wards and his descriptions of the symptoms and effects of radiation sickness—although he did not call it that—have stood the test of time. His diagnoses were the more remarkable because there was no medical precedent on which to base them and the hospital was left without any equipment—not even a microscope. Everything had been destroyed in the blast and fiery holocaust which followed.

The reference to "hatred of the white man" in the *Daily Express* version came from the reactions of the patients and their relatives in the few wards I visited. Patients were laid out on *tatami* (sleeping mats made from woven swamp grass), heads to the wall and groups of family members kneeling around them. (It is a habit in Japan for some member of the family to move into a hospital and feed the patient. But in this case, *only* if family members could stay to perform minimum nursing tasks—changing bandages, keeping their relatives clean, feeding them, etc.—could survivors be admitted. 93 percent of the city's nurses had been killed or incapacitated in the first seconds of the blast.) I had to see the horrors for myself.

I had to look at the suppurating third-degree burns, the bleeding eyes and gums, the fallen-out hair which lay like black haloes around almost every head. The victims and their family members who looked at me with a burning hatred which cut into me like a knife. At one point Dr. Katsube spoke to me in English: "You must go. I cannot be responsible for your life if you stay any longer." And thus ended my visit to the hospital and my first meeting with Dr. Katsube. In fact the general attitude of the Hiroshima citizens in the streets was one of almost total apathy. They were still in a state of trauma. People walked alone or in groups of two or three. No one stopped to speak to anyone else. Even our little group, including a foreigner without a gauze mask, attracted no attention.

Dr. Katsube's final words to me were: "Please report on what you have seen and ask your people"—he naturally thought I was an American—"to send some specialists who know about this sickness, with the necessary medicines. Otherwise everyone here is doomed to die."

Despite errors of omission, transmission and insertions, I give great credit to Arthur Christiansen for using my "warning to the world" in the headlines and for retaining the essential point I wanted to make. Given the elation in the West that the Second World War was now definitely over and that the West had a monopoly of the war-winning weapon demonstrated against Hiroshima and Nagasaki, it was not easy for the editor of Britain's largest circulation daily to deflate the euphoria with such a warning.

The "lesson" of Hiroshima is, in my opinion, actually twofold. On the one hand, Hiroshima, like Auschwitz, asserts the existence of a will to genocidal, absolute destruction. We should never cease to meditate on the fact that there has already occurred a first nuclear war, and, because of this precedent, there is little reason to doubt the possibility of a second—particularly if the same constellation of class interests, will-to-power and mind-numbing rhetoric that authorized the exemplary immolation of Hiroshima and Nagasaki is again given pretext and opportunity. On the other hand, Hiroshima also represents the indestructibility of human resistance. Despite their ordeals, the cover-ups, even the ostracism from "normal" society, the *hibakusha* survivors have fought back, becoming the most stalwart and militant of peaceniks. Through them and their ongoing struggle, the *urgency* of Hiroshima is transmitted to all of us.

Notes

1. "Little Boy" was the name supposedly given "in honor" of Roosevelt while "Fat Man" was presumably to accord a similar "honor" to Churchill.

2. *New York Times*, September 12, 1945.

3. Hiroshima was, in fact, the headquarters of Japan's Southern Command. It had a garrison headquarters, but otherwise only minor military installations mainly connected with transport.

4. Truman's press statement of August 6, 1945, immediately after the attack on Hiroshima.

5. I discovered later that this was none other than Brig. Gen. Thomas Farrell, deputy-chief of the Manhattan Project.

6. These were provisional figures given by the police and later revised upwards of 130,000. At the time there was obviously no way of estimating how many victims lay under the ashes nor how many would die soon after from the effects of radiation.

THE DECISION

TO USE

THE BOMBS

P. M. S. Blackett*

THE ORIGIN OF THE DECISION to drop the bombs on two Japanese cities, and the timing of this event, both in relation to the ending of the Japanese war and to the future pattern of international relations, have already given rise to intense controversy and will surely be the subject of critical historical study in the future. The story has, however, great practical importance if one is to understand aright many aspects of American policy and opinion, and of the Russian reaction thereto.

The scientists on the Franck Committee, in a memorandum to the President in June 1945, strongly deprecated the first use of the bomb against Japanese cities, on the grounds chiefly that the gain resulting from the expected shortening of the war, would be offset by the inevitable worsening of international relations. Doubts have often been expressed as to the justification for using the bombs in the way they were used, and many American scientists undoubtedly felt morally distressed at finding the results of their brilliant scientific work used in a way which seemed to many of them to lack adequate moral or military justification. Before the bomb was used, most scientists probably felt that the only justification for its use against Japan would be one of overriding military necessity, and there seems definite evidence that, earlier in the summer of 1945, the American authorities did not anticipate such a situation arising. For instance, the Washington correspondent of the London *Times* wrote in the issue of August 8, 1945, as follows:

> The decision to use the new weapon was apparently taken quite recently and amounted to a reversal of previous policy. A correspondent in the *Baltimore Sun*, writing from an authority which seems unimpeachable, says that, until early in June, the President and military leaders were in agreement that this weapon should not

---

* Editors' Note: Recipient of the 1948 Nobel Prize in Physics, Blackett was the first writer to argue that the use of atomic weapons on Japan had more to do with the early stages of America's emerging Cold War with the Soviet Union than bringing about an early surrender by Japan. This essay was published in 1948.

be used, but a reversal of this High Command policy was made within the last sixty and, possibly the last thirty, days. There is, he says, much speculation about what caused this change of policy, but in the view of some highly placed persons those responsible came to the conclusion that they were justified in using any and all means to bring the war in the Pacific to a close within the shortest possible time.

It will be one of the objects of this analysis to elucidate the origin of this presumed change of policy. President Truman stated in a speech on August 9, 1945, three days after the first bomb was dropped: "We have used it in order to shorten the agony of war, in order to save the lives of thousands and thousands of young Americans." Then, on October 3rd, in a message to Congress, he said: "Almost two months have passed since the atomic bomb was used against Japan. That bomb did not win the war, but it certainly shortened the war. We know it saved the lives of untold thousands of American and Allied soldiers who otherwise would have been killed in battle."

In an article published in the *Atlantic Monthly*, in December 1946, under the title "If the Bomb Had Not Been Dropped," Dr. K. T. Compton gave his reasons for believing the decision to have been right. Dr. Compton writes: "I had, perhaps, an unusual opportunity to know the pertinent facts." At General MacArthur's H.Q., he learnt of the invasion plans and of "the sincere conviction of the best-informed officers that a desperate and costly struggle was still ahead. . . . Finally, I spent the first month after V-J Day in Japan, where I could ascertain at first hand both the physical and psychological state of the country. . . . From this background I believe with complete conviction that the use of the atomic bomb saved hundreds of thousands—perhaps several million—of lives, both American and Japanese; that without its use the war would have continued for many months." Dr. Compton quotes General MacArthur's staff as expecting 50,000 American casualties in the landing operations planned for November 1st, and a far more costly struggle later before the homeland was subdued. Dr. Compton's final views are as follows: "If the bomb had not been used, evidence like I have cited points to the practical certainty that there would have been many more months of deaths and destruction on an enormous scale."

On December 16th, President Truman wrote to Dr. Compton as follows:

Dear Dr. Compton,

Your statement in the *Atlantic Monthly* is a fair analysis of the situation except that the final decision had to be made by the President, and was made after a complete survey of the whole situation had been made. The conclusions reached were substantially those set out in your article. The Japanese were given fair warning, and were offered the terms which they finally accepted, well in advance of the dropping of the bomb. I imagine the bomb caused them to accept the terms.

Sincerely yours,

HARRY S. TRUMAN

The next contribution of importance was an article in *Harper's Magazine*, in February 1947, by Mr. Stimson, who in 1945 was Secretary of State for War.* This article is worthy of very close study. Mr. Stimson states that the President relied for advice on the "Interim Committee" under his Chairmanship and having, as scientific members, Vannevar Bush, K. T. Compton and J. B. Conant. This Committee was assisted in its work by a Scientific Panel whose members were A. H. Compton, Fermi, Lawrence and Oppenheimer. Mr. Stimson's article reads:

> On June 1, after discussions with the Scientific Panel, the Interim Committee unanimously adopted the following recommendations.
>
> (1) The bomb should be used against Japan as soon as possible. (2) It should be used on a dual target—that is, a military installation or war plant surrounded by or adjacent to houses and other buildings most susceptible to damage, and (3) It should be used without prior warning of the nature of the weapon. One member later changed his view and dissented from the recommendation (3).
>
> In reaching these conclusions the Interim Committee carefully considered such alternatives as a detailed warning or a demonstration in some uninhabited area. Both these suggestions were discarded as impracticable. They were not regarded as likely to be effective in compelling a surrender of Japan, and both of them involved serious risks. Even the New Mexico test would not give final proof that any given bomb was certain to explode when dropped from an airplane. Quite apart from the generally unfamiliar nature of atomic explosives, there was the whole problem of exploding a bomb at a predetermined height in the air by a complicated mechanism which could not be tested in the static test of New Mexico. Nothing would have been more damaging to our effort to obtain surrender than a warning of a demonstration followed by a dud—and this was a real possibility. Furthermore, we had no bombs to waste. *It was vital that a sufficient effort be quickly obtained with the few we had.*[1]

Later on in the article Mr. Stimson writes: "The two atomic bombs which we had dropped were the only ones we had ready, and our rate of production at that time was very small." Why this necessity for speed? What was it in the war plans of the Allies which necessitated rapid action? Mr. Stimson's article makes it clear that there was nothing in the American-British military plan of campaign against Japan which demanded speed in dropping the bombs in early August 1945.

Mr. Stimson describes the American war plans as follows:

> The strategic plans of our armed forces for the defeat of Japan, as they stood in July, had been prepared without reliance on the atomic bomb, which had not yet been tested in New Mexico. We were planning an intensified sea and air blockade and greatly intensified air-bombing, through the summer and early fall, to be

---

* Editors' Note: See p. 197 for the entire text of "The Decision to Use the Atomic Bomb" by Henry Stimson.

followed on November 1 by the invasion of the southern island of
Kyushu. This would be followed in turn by the invasion of the main
island of Honshu in the spring of 1946. We estimated that if we
should be forced to carry the plan to its conclusion, the major fighting would not end until the latter part of 1946 at the earliest. I was
informed that such operations might be expected to cost over a
million casualties to American forces alone.

Since the next major United States move was not to be until November 1,
clearly there was nothing in the Allied plan of campaign to make urgent the
dropping of the first bomb on August 6 rather than at any time in the next two
months. Mr. Stimson himself makes clear that, had the bombs not been dropped,
the intervening period of eleven weeks between August 6 and the invasion
planned for November 1 would have been used to make further fire raids with
B29s on Japan. Under conditions of Japanese air defense at that time, these raids
would certainly have led to very small losses of American air personnel.

Mr. Stimson's hurry becomes still more peculiar since the Japanese had
already initiated peace negotiations. In his own words: "Japan, in July 1945, had
been seriously weakened by our increasingly violent attacks. It was known to us
that she had gone so far as to make tentative proposals to the Soviet Government,
hoping to use the Russians as mediators in a negotiated peace. These vague
proposals contemplated the retention by Japan of important conquered areas and
were not therefore considered seriously. There was as yet no indication of
any weakening of the Japanese determination to fight rather than accept unconditional surrender."

On July 20, the Big Three Conference at Potsdam was in session, and an
ultimatum was sent to the Japanese Government on July 26. This was rejected by
the Premier of Japan on July 28 "as unworthy of public notice." Unfortunately,
Mr. Stimson does not give either the exact date or details of the Japanese approach
for mediation through Russia or the content of their proposals. So the exact relation between this *secret* approach for mediation and the *public* refusal of the Potsdam terms is not clear. At any rate, the reason for the immediate necessity of
dropping the bomb seems no clearer.

The solution of this puzzle of the overwhelming reasons for urgency in the
dropping of the bomb is not, however, far to seek. It is, in fact, to be found in
the omissions from both Dr. Compton's and Mr. Stimson's articles. As already
shown, both give a detailed account of the future plans for the American assault
on Japan planned for the autumn of 1945, and spring 1946. But neither makes any
reference in detail to the other part of the Allied plan for defeating Japan, that is,
the long-planned Russian campaign in Manchuria. We can, however, fill in this
information from other sources; for instance, from Mr. Elliott Roosevelt's book,
As He Saw It, published in 1946.

In the chapter on the Yalta Conference (February 1945) Mr. Elliott Roosevelt
writes: "But before the Conference broke up, Stalin had once more given the
assurance he had first volunteered in Teheran in 1943: that, within six months of
V-E Day, the Soviets would have declared war on Japan; then, pausing in thought,
he had revised that estimate from six months to three months." The European
war ended on May 8, so the Soviet offensive was due to start on August 8. This
fact is not mentioned either by Mr. Stimson or Dr. Compton in the articles from

which we have quoted. The first atomic bomb was dropped on August 6 and the second on August 9. The Japanese accepted the Potsdam terms on August 14.

The U.S.S.R. declared war on Japan on August 8, and their offensive started early on August 9. On August 24, the Soviet High Command announced that the whole of Manchuria, Southern Sakhalin, etc., had been captured and that the Japanese Manchurian army had surrendered. No doubt the capitulation of the home government on August 14 reduced the fighting spirit of the Japanese forces. If it had not taken place, the Soviet campaign might well have been more expensive; but it would have been equally decisive. If the saving of American lives had been the real objective, surely the bombs would have been held back until (a) it was certain that the Japanese peace proposals made through Russia were not acceptable, and (b) the Russian offensive, which had for months been part of the Allied strategic plan, and which Americans had previously demanded, had run its course.

In a broadcast to the American people on August 9, President Truman described the secret military arrangements between the Allies made at the Potsdam Conference. "One of those secrets was revealed yesterday when the Soviet Union declared war on Japan. The Soviet Union, before she had been informed of our new weapon, agreed to enter the war in the Pacific. We gladly welcome into this struggle against the last of the Axis aggressors our gallant and victorious ally against the Nazis."

Further details of the events which led up to the capitulation of Japan are given in the "Report on the Pacific War prepared by the United States Strategic Bombing Survey."

In the section significantly entitled "Japan's struggle to end the War," we read:

> By mid-1944, those Japanese in possession of basic information saw with reasonable clarity the economic disaster which was inevitably descending on Japan. Furthermore, they were aware of the disastrous impact of long-range bombing on Germany, and with the loss of the Marianas, could foresee a similar attack on Japan's industries and cities. Their influence, however, was not sufficient to overcome the influence of the Army which was confident of its ability to resist invasion.

The Report then outlines the Allied plan for the final defeat of Japan by staging a heavy air attack on Japan throughout the summer, to be followed by a large-scale landing on Kyushu in November 1945. The Report, however, states that "Certain of the United States commanders and the representatives of the Survey who were called back from their investigations in Germany in early June 1945, for consultation, stated their belief that by the coordinated impact of blockade and direct air attack, Japan could be forced to surrender without invasion." The Report continues:

> Early in May 1945, the Supreme War Direction Council (of Japan) began active discussion of ways and means to end the war, and talks were initiated with Soviet Russia seeking her intercession as mediator. The talks by the Japanese Ambassador in Moscow and with the Soviet Ambassador in Tokyo did not make progress. On June 20, the Emperor on his own initiative called the six members of the Supreme War Direction Council to a conference and said it was necessary to

have a plan to close the war at once, as well as a plan to defend the home islands. The timing of the Potsdam Conference interfered with a plan to send Prince Konoye to Moscow as a special emissary with instructions from the Cabinet to negotiate for peace on terms less than unconditional surrender, but with private instructions from the Emperor to secure peace at any price. . . .

Although the Supreme War Direction Council, in its deliberations on the Potsdam Conference, was agreed on the advisability of ending the war, three of its members, the Prime Minister, the Foreign Minister and the Navy Minister, were prepared to accept unconditional surrender, while the other three, the Army Minister and the Chiefs of Staff of both Services, favored continued resistance unless certain mitigating conditions were obtained. . . .

On August 6, the atomic bomb was dropped on Hiroshima and on August 9 Russia entered the war. In the succeeding meetings of the Supreme War Direction Council, the difference of opinion previously existing as to the Potsdam terms persisted as before. By using the urgency brought about by the fear of further bombing attacks, the Prime Minister found it possible to bring the Emperor directly into the discussion of the Potsdam terms. Hirohito, acting as the arbiter, resolved the conflict in favor of unconditional surrender. . . .

It seems clear that even without the atomic bomb attacks, air supremacy over Japan could have exerted sufficient pressure to bring unconditional surrender and obviate the need for invasion. . . . Based on a detailed investigation of all the facts, and supported by the testimony of the surviving Japanese leaders involved, it is the Survey's opinion that certainly prior to December 31, 1945, Japan would have surrendered even if the atomic bombs had not been dropped, even if Russia had not entered the war, and even if no invasion had been planned or contemplated.

General H. H. Arnold expressed the view that "without attempting to deprecate the appalling and far-reaching results of the atomic bomb, we have good reason to believe that its use primarily provided a way out for the Japanese Government. The fact is that the Japanese could not have held out long because they had lost control of the air. They could offer effective opposition neither to air bombardment nor to our mining by air and so could not prevent the destruction of their cities and industries and the blockade of their shipping."[2]

This account of the situation is, of course, based on information, much of which was available only after the surrender of Japan.[3] Thus some of it, for instance, the detailed instructions of the Emperor to Prince Konoye, could not have been known to the Allied Command at the time the decision to drop the first bombs was made.* It is also conceivable that in July 1945 the Allied High Command may have genuinely misjudged the real situation in Japan and have greatly overestimated the Japanese will to resist.[4] But all this information was

---

* Editors' Note: Blackett did not know, of course, that Stimson did indeed have this information through access to the Magic intercepts.

naturally available to Mr. Stimson when he wrote his articles justifying the dropping of the bombs.

As far as our analysis has taken us we have found no compelling military reason for the clearly very hurried decision to drop the first atomic bomb on August 6. But a most compelling diplomatic reason, relating to the balance of power in the post-war world, is clearly discernible.

Let us consider the situation as it must have appeared in Washington at the end of July 1945. After a brilliant, but bitterly-fought campaign, American forces were in occupation of a large number of Japanese islands. They had destroyed the Japanese Navy and Merchant Marine and largely destroyed their Air Force and many divisions of their Army: but they had still not come to grips with a large part of the Japanese land forces. Supposing the bombs had not been dropped, the planned Soviet offensive in Manchuria, so long demanded and, when it took place, so gladly welcomed (officially), would have achieved its objective according to plan. This must have been clearly foreseen by the Allied High Command, who knew well the great superiority of the Soviet forces in armor, artillery and aircraft, and who could draw on the experience of the European war to gauge the probable success of such a well-prepared offensive. If the bombs had not been dropped, America would have seen the Soviet armies engaging a major part of Japanese land forces in battle, overrunning Manchuria and taking half a million prisoners. And all this would have occurred while American land forces would have been no nearer Japan than Iwo Jima and Okinawa. One can sympathize with the chagrin with which such an outcome would have been regarded. Most poignantly, informed military opinion could in no way blame Russia for these expected events. Russia's policy of not entering the Japanese war till Germany was defeated was not only military common sense but part of the agreed Allied plan.

In this dilemma, the successful explosion of the first atomic bomb in New Mexico, on July 16, must have come as a welcome aid. One can imagine the hurry with which the two bombs—the only two existing—were whisked across the Pacific to be dropped on Hiroshima and Nagasaki just in time, but only just, to ensure that the Japanese Government surrendered to American forces alone. The long-demanded Soviet offensive took its planned victorious course, almost unheralded in the world sensation caused by the dropping of the bombs.

Referring to these events, a British military historian wrote:

> Two days later, Russia declared war on Japan; but so great an impression was made on the world by the first atomic bomb, that very few people took any notice of this important step. . . . The atomic bombs undoubtedly contributed to bring about the Japanese decision. So, also, to a lesser extent, did the swift and skillful over-running of Manchuria by the Russians. But it is impossible to hold that either, or both together, brought it about. The atomic bombs provided an excuse, a face-saving event that was seized upon to justify a surrender which was as abject as that of Germany and much less explicable.[5]

The last four words of this sentence cannot have been intended as a serious judgment. Of particular interest is the following quotation from the *New York Times* of August 15, 1945. Under the headline, "Chennault holds Soviet Forced

End: Russia's Entry Decided War with Japan despite Atomic Bomb, an Air General says," appears a report of an interview by the newspaper's Rome correspondent, containing the following passages:

> Russia's entry into the Japanese war was the decisive factor in speeding its end and would have been so, even if no atomic bombs had been dropped, is the opinion of Major-General Claire Chennault, who arrived *en route* home via Germany. The founder of the American Volunteer Group (Flying Tigers) and former Air Force Commander in China said that the Soviet armies had been alert for the invasion of Manchuria as far back as V-E Day. He added that their swift stroke completed the circle around Japan that brought the nation to its knees.

The special significance of this statement is that not only was it made by an expert on the Far Eastern war, on the basis of the then available evidence, but that it was made while the General was still in Europe and so was not so likely to appreciate the significance of Mr. Truman's statement on August 9 that "we have used it in order to shorten the agony of war, in order to save the lives of thousands and thousands of young Americans."

That this is no fanciful account of these events is seen in a clear picture of the relation between the dropping of the bomb and the planned Soviet Offensive given in an article by two American writers, Norman Cousins and Thomas K. Finletter, originally published in the *Saturday Review of Literature*, June 15, 1946. They refer in detail to the Report of the Committee under James Franck from which we have already quoted. "This report, not made public by the War Department at the time, is one of the most important American documents of recent years—even though it is virtually unknown to the American people." After analyzing and approving in general the arguments in the report against an initial use of bombs against Japan, and in favor of a demonstration to be witnessed by the United Nations, they write as follows:

> Why then did we drop it? Or, assuming that the use of the bomb was justified, why did we not demonstrate its power in a test under the auspices of the United Nations, on the basis of which an ultimatum would be issued to Japan—transferring the burden of responsibility to the Japanese themselves?. . .
>
> Whatever the answer, one thing seems likely: there was not enough time between July 16, when we knew at New Mexico that the bomb would work, and August 8, the Russian deadline date, for us to have set up the very complicated machinery of a test atomic bombing involving time-consuming problems of area preparations, etc. . . .
>
> No; any test would have been impossible if the purpose was to knock Japan out before Russia came in—or at least before Russia could make anything other than a token of participation prior to a Japanese collapse.
>
> It may be argued that this decision was justified; that it was a legitimate exercise of power politics in a rough-and-tumble world; that we avoided a struggle for authority in Japan similar to that we

have experienced in Germany and Italy; that, unless we came out of
the war with a decisive balance of power over Russia, we would be in
no position to checkmate Russian expansion.

This interpretation by Cousins and Finletter substantially confirms our own
analysis.[6] The hurried dropping of the bombs on Hiroshima and Nagasaki was a
brilliant success, in that all the political objectives were fully achieved. American
control of Japan is complete, and there is no struggle for authority there with
Russia.

Two other theories of the timing of the dropping of the bomb are worth a brief
notice. The first is that it was purely coincidental that the first bomb was dropped
two days before the Soviet offensive was due to start. This view explains Mr.
Stimson's statement, "It was vital that a sufficient effort be quickly obtained with
the few we had," as referring to the universal and praiseworthy desire to finish the
war as soon as possible. The difficulty about this view is that it makes the timing
of the dropping a supreme diplomatic blunder. For it must have been perfectly
clear that the timing of the dropping of the bombs, two days before the start of the
Soviet offensive, would be assumed by the Soviet Government to have the significance which we have assumed that it, in fact, did have. If it was not intended to
have this significance, then the timing was an error of tact, before which all the
subsequent "tactlessness" of Soviet diplomacy in relation to the control of atomic
energy pales into insignificance. That the timing was not an unintentional blunder
is made clear by the fact that no subsequent steps were taken to mitigate its effects.

The second view relates not to the timing, but to the choice of an unwarned
and densely populated city as target. This view admits that there was no convincing military reason for the use of the bombs, but holds that it was a political necessity to justify to Congress and to the American people the expenditure of the huge
sum of 2,000 million dollars. It is scarcely credible that such an explanation should
be seriously put forward by Americans, but so it seems to have been, and rather
widely. Those who espouse this theory do not seem to have realized its implications. If the United States Government had been influenced in the summer of 1945
by this view, then perhaps at some future date, when another 2,000 million dollars
had been spent, it might feel impelled to stage another Roman holiday with some
other country's citizens, rather than 120,000 victims of Hiroshima and Nagasaki,
as the chosen victims. The wit of man could hardly devise a theory of the dropping
of the bomb, both more insulting to the American people and providing greater
justification for an energetically pursued Soviet defense policy.

Let us sum up the three possible explanations of the decision to drop the
bombs and of its timing. The first, that it was a clever and highly successful move
in the field of power politics, is almost certainly correct; the second, that the
timing was coincidental, convicts the American Government of a hardly credible
tactlessness; and the third, the Roman holiday theory, convicts them of an equally
incredible irresponsibility. The prevalence in some circles for the last two theories
seems to originate in a curious preference to be considered irresponsible, tactless,
even brutal, but at all costs not clever.

There is one further aspect of the dropping of the bomb which must be mentioned. There were undoubtedly, among the nuclear physicists working on the
project, many who regarded the dropping of the bombs as a victory for the pro-
gressively minded among the military and political authorities. What they feared

was that the bombs would *not* be dropped in the war against Japan, but that the attempt would be made to keep their existence secret and that a stock-pile would be built up for an eventual war with Russia. To those who feared intensely this latter possible outcome, the dropping of the bombs and the publicity that resulted appeared, not unplausibly, as far the lesser evil. Probably those whose thoughts were on these lines, did not reckon that the bombs would be dropped on crowded cities.

The motives behind the choice of targets remains obscure. President Truman stated on August 9, 1945: "The world will note that the first atomic bomb was dropped on Hiroshima, a military base. That was because we wished in the first instance to avoid, in so far as possible, the killing of civilians." On the other hand, in the official *Bombing Survey Report* we read: "Hiroshima and Nagasaki were chosen as targets because of their concentration of activities and population." There seem here signs of a lack of departmental coordination.

So, in truth, we conclude that the dropping of the atomic bombs was not so much the last military act of the second world war, as the first act of the cold diplomatic war with Russia now in progress. The fact, however, that the realistic objectives in the field of Macht-Politik, so brilliantly achieved by the timing of the bomb, did not square with the advertised objective of saving "untold numbers" of American lives, produced an intense inner psychological conflict in the minds of many English and American people who knew, or suspected, some of the real facts. This conflict was particularly intense in the minds of the atomic scientists them-selves, who rightly felt a deep responsibility at seeing their brilliant scientific work used in this way. The realization that their work had been used to achieve a diplomatic victory in relation to the power politics of the post-war world, rather than to save American lives, was clearly too disturbing to many of them to be consciously admitted. To allay their own doubts, many came to believe that the dropping of the bombs had in fact saved a million lives. It thus came about that those people who possessed the strongest emotional drive to save the world from the results of future atomic bombs, had in general a very distorted view of the actual circumstances of their first use.

It can never be repeated often enough that the first maxim of the scientific study of current events is that one should not attempt to predict the future until one has attempted to understand the past. All attempts to control atomic energy involve predictions about the course of future events and, in particular, prediction of the probable part that atomic bombs will play in future wars. It is certainly necessary to make such estimates in order to approach the problem of their control in a rational manner. Inaccurate views as to the historical facts of their first use are a poor basis on which to plan for the future.

Perhaps the most important consequence of this situation, and of the inner personal conflicts to which it gave rise, is the firm belief amongst many Americans that it is certain that atomic bombs will be used against civilian populations at the outset of future wars as a matter of course and in all circumstances. Dr. J. R. Oppenheimer, with his characteristic clarity of expression, explains the origin of this view: "Every American knows that if there is another major war, atomic weapons will be used. We know this because in the last war, the two nations which we like to think are the most enlightened and humane in the world—Great Britain and the United States—used atomic weapons against an enemy which was essentially defeated." In the place of a rational attempt to understand in detail the part that atomic bombs are likely to play in future world affairs, and of the circumstances in which they would be likely to be used again, an atmosphere of imminent world destruction arose in which clear thinking was at a discount and emotion triumphant. The world became regaled with authoritative statements which departed wildly from the realm of probability. Of particular importance is the strand of thought represented by the well-known statement of Mr. Stimson, who wrote: "The future may see a time when such a weapon may be constructed in secret and used suddenly and effectively with devastating power by a willful nation or group against an unsuspecting nation or group of much greater size and material power. *With its aid even a very powerful and unsuspecting nation might be conquered within a very few days by a very much smaller one. . . ."* [7]

This view has two most important consequences. Firstly, it implies that an unsuspecting United States itself might be defeated in a few days by a very much smaller nation. The obvious result has been to stimulate a hysterical search for 100 percent security from such attack. Since there can be no such complete security for America, except through world hegemony imposed by America, Mr. Stimson's view, which is very widely accepted, justified a drive towards world hegemony by America in one form or another.

Secondly, the inescapable conclusion from the assumption that a small nation with atomic bombs could defeat a great nation without them in a few days, was that a great nation with bombs (America) could defeat another great nation (Russia) in a few hours, and consequently very cheaply. The justification for a cheap preventative war, of the "press-button" variety, became complete. The logic of the Irishman in the story was applied to the bomb. On seeing a stove advertised to save half one's fuel, he bought two to save it all! If two bombs could save a million American lives in a war with Japan, then a hundred would save them all in a war with Russia.

In all this discussion the question of the military effect of atomic bombs and their effect on warfare is of paramount importance; a full discussion has already been attempted in earlier chapters. From the point of view of the present discussion, the significant point is obvious. Atomic bombs will be used in future wars when the potential user estimates that the net gain, at any rate for some years, over the whole military, political and economic field is likely to be markedly positive. As has already been shown, this condition was fulfilled in the views of the American, and presumably also the British, statesmen in August 1945. But, this commonsense view shows up in its provocative nonsense such a remark as "If Russia had atomic bombs, they would already have been dropped on the United States." [8]

In the atmosphere created by such statements, the drive for one hundred percent security from atomic bombs becomes understandable, but nonetheless highly dangerous. For perfect security from any of the dangers besetting humanity is clearly not attainable. If one is a motor driver, complete security against the danger of being killed in a collision with another motor-car can only be attained by prohibiting anyone but oneself from driving a car—that is, by the abolition of road transport. It is to be noticed that there are strong tendencies in America today which strive for the illusionary goal of 100 percent security from atomic bombs, by attempting to prevent anyone else using atomic energy for any major purpose. [9]

The story behind the decision to drop the two atomic bombs on Hiroshima and Nagasaki, as far as it is possible to unravel it from the available published material, has been told in this chapter not with the intention of impugning motives of individuals or of nations, but for a much more practical reason. This is to attempt to offset as far as possible some of the disastrous consequences resulting from the promulgation of the official story, that the bombs were dropped from vital military necessity and did, in fact, save a huge number of American lives. For this story is not believed by well-informed people who therefore have to seek some other explanation. Since they reject the hypothesis that they were dropped to win a brilliant diplomatic victory as being too morally repugnant to be entertained, the only remaining resort is to maintain that such things just happen, and that they are the "essence of total war." Believing therefore that America dropped atomic bombs on Japan for *no compelling military or diplomatic reason*, the belief comes easily that other countries will, when they can, drop atomic bombs on America with equal lack of reason, military or diplomatic. This is a belief that provides the breeding ground for hysteria.

In decisive contrast are the consequences of believing what the writer holds to be the truth, that is, that the bombs were dropped for very real and compelling reasons—but diplomatic rather than military ones. For though the circumstances did then exist in which a great diplomatic victory could be won by annihilating the population of two cities, these circumstances were of a very special character and are not very likely to recur. If they did recur, few nations would perhaps resist the temptation to employ these means to attain such an end. But if we are right in supposing that a repetition of such special circumstances is unlikely, then the world is less in danger of more Hiroshimas than is generally believed.

NOTES

1. [Author's italics] A trial explosion at a predetermined height could of course equally well have been made over open country.

2. Dexter Masters and Katerine Way, eds., *One World or None* (New York, 1946), p. 28.

3. Paul Nitze, Vice-Chairman of the United States Strategic Bombing Survey, repeated the view in the Senate Committee Hearings (Senate Resolution 179, p. 530). "It is our opinion that Japan would have surrendered prior to November 1 in any case; the atomic bomb merely accelerated the date at which Japan surrendered."

4. It is not in dispute that had the invasion of Kyushu taken place as planned in November, and had the Japanese military forces fought as determinedly as they had previously, the American casualties would have been very heavy. All the available evidence suggests, however, that the Tokyo Government would have capitulated first.

5. Strategicus, *The Victory Campaign* (London, 1947), p. 242.

6. Particular interest attaches to these articles as one of the authors was later chosen by the President to be Chairman of "The Air Policy Committee." One can reasonably assume, therefore, that the authors of the article from which we have quoted were likely to be well-informed persons and with a reliable judgment of affairs. Quite recently Mr. Finletter has been appointed head of the Marshall Plan mission in London. *The Times*, May 26, 1948.

7. [Author's italics] *Bulletin of the Atomic Scientists*, February 3, 1947.

8. Mr. Bullitt, ex-Ambassador at Moscow, quoted by the *New Republic*, April 7, 1947. A still wilder expression of self-induced fear or deliberate provocation is Mr. Walter Winchell's remark, quoted by the *News Chronicle*, October 20, 1947. "Russia is going to make war on America. The cholera epidemic in Egypt is suspected of being the first Soviet experiment in mass killings by germs."

9. Dr. Oppenheimer has recently written: "In fact, it appears most doubtful if there are now any courses open to the United States which can give our people the sort of security they have known in the past. The argument that such a course *must* exist seems to be specious; and in the last analysis most current proposals rest on this argument."

NEW

EVIDENCE ON

TRUMAN'S

DECISION

Robert L. Messer

HE USE OF ATOMIC BOMBS ON JAPANESE CITIES at the end of World
War II is one of the most debated and analyzed events in history. This discussion is not an attempt to explain that event. Rather, to borrow a phrase from Senator Howard Baker during the Watergate hearings, the focus is upon what the president knew and when he knew it. My purpose is not to indict President Truman, but only to clarify his role in a larger process. The main source of information for such a clarification is not White House tape recordings, but something very nearly as candid and revealing—the president's own words. Not just his public statements, or his own writings on the subject after the fact, but Truman's private journal and letters written at the time he gave the bombing order.

The recent discovery of this evidence helps us to understand better at least some aspects of a 40-year-old issue. It reveals, for example, that contrary to his public justification of the bombings as the only way to end the war without a costly invasion of Japan, Truman had already concluded that Japan was about to capitulate. Whether or not he was correct in this estimate of when the war would end, the fact that he held this view at the time he made his decision to use the bomb is clearly set down in his own hand. This new evidence is not a "smoking gun" that settles the old issue of why the bomb was used. But it tells us more than we knew before about the timing of the bombings. It also tells us more than Harry Truman, for all his famous candor, ever told us.

In his first public statements regarding the use of the bomb, on August 6, 1945, Truman explained that this terrible new weapon represented an American victory in a life-and-death "race against the Germans." It had been dropped on a place called Hiroshima, which the president described as "a military base." It would continue to be used, he said, "until we have completely destroyed Japan's capacity to make war." Even then there were those, although in a distinct minority, who raised questions about the bombings. What relevance to its use against Japan, they asked, was the fear that Hitler might get the bomb first? Three months before the atomic bombs fell on Japanese cities, Germany had surrendered. Months before that, Allied scientists had concluded that the worst-case scenario, which had prompted the Anglo-American atomic bomb project, was overly pessimistic.

The Germans lagged far behind in the race for the bomb. Even more to the point, there had been no serious concern about a Japanese bomb. Was the bomb used then merely "because it was there," to justify its existence and its unprecedented expense?

Regarding the bomb's specific military justification, critics conceded that Hiroshima, as a major port and regional army headquarters, and Nagasaki, with its many war plants, contained legitimate military targets. We now know that those same targets could have been destroyed earlier by the sort of conventional bombing that had leveled just about every important military objective in Japan. In fact, the cities set aside as possible atomic targets were deliberately left "virgin," so as not to obscure the effects of the new weapon. It soon became clear, however, that the radius of destruction of even those first-generation 13-kiloton bombs far exceeded the size of any "military base." Casualty figures varied greatly, but all showed that the overwhelming majority of those killed and wounded were civilians in their homes, not soldiers or war workers on the assembly line. For having reversed the ratio of military and unavoidable or "incidental" civilian deaths, the Hiroshima and Nagasaki bombings were condemned, even at the time, by proponents of the principles of just war as "America's atomic atrocity."[1]

Such moral and religious outrage was confined almost exclusively to those who also had condemned conventional "obliteration" or "terror" bombing of civilians earlier in the war. By 1945 the technology of mass destruction had combined with the doctrine of total war to lower the moral threshold for all but a few dissenters. Many times brighter and hotter, the atomic fireballs over Hiroshima and Nagasaki were nonetheless dimmed when set against the precedents of the firestorms of Hamburg, Dresden, and Tokyo. The early critics also were at a disadvantage in assailing the broader military, political, and moral justification for the bombings. The bomb was used, said Truman, "to destroy Japan's capacity to make war." Few outside government could then know to what extent that war-making capacity had been destroyed before the use of atomic weapons. Certainly the Japanese surrender within days after Hiroshima and hours after Nagasaki were bombed seemed to leave no doubt in the minds of almost all Americans: This new bomb had ended history's greatest and most destructive war; without it the war might have dragged on for many months, even years.

In announcing the bombings the President had said that they were carried out in order to "shorten the agony of war" and save "thousands and thousands of American lives." Later he would be more specific, citing the estimated 250,000 Allied casualties expected to result from the planned invasion of Japan. Added to the Allied losses were the estimates of Japanese casualties in a prolonged war. These ranged from 500,000 to 5 million. Official U.S. estimates of Japanese killed in the atomic attacks totaled about 110,000. Thus, in saving more lives than they took, the atomic bombings were justified as the lesser of two evils. After the war Truman said that he had been told that the population of the target cities was about 60,000. Hiroshima's population was in fact more than 350,000 and Nagasaki's about 280,000. Of these, nearly 200,000 were killed and 150,000 injured.

At the time few could argue with such logic. Indeed, opinion polls taken immediately after the war showed that for every American who thought the bombs should not have been used (5 percent) more than four times as many (23 percent) were disappointed that more bombs had not been dropped before Japan had a chance to surrender. Predictably the majority of those polled (54 percent) backed

Truman's decision to use just two bombs on cities as the proper and prudent middle course.[2] Of course, none of these people knew then that the entire U.S. nuclear arsenal had been expended in as rapid succession as possible, without waiting for a response to the first of the only two bombs available.

It was not long, however, before critics of the bomb decision got what seemed authoritative support for their contention that Japan was already defeated by the summer of 1945 and that therefore the use of the bomb had been an unnecessary, wanton act. The U.S. Strategic Bombing Survey's official report on the Pacific War appeared less than one year after the Hiroshima and Nagasaki bombings and on the eve of a controversial series of atomic tests at Bikini atoll. The authors of this massive, authoritative study of Japan's war-making capability concluded that "the Hiroshima and Nagasaki atomic bombs did not defeat Japan, nor, by the testimony of the enemy leaders who ended the war, did they persuade Japan to accept unconditional surrender." Rather, the bombs, along with conventional air power, naval blockade, Soviet intervention, and other internal and external pressures acted "jointly and cumulatively" as "lubrication" of a peace-making machinery set in motion months before the atomic attacks. The Survey's analysts concluded that "certainly prior to December 31, 1945 and in all probability prior to November 1, 1945 Japan would have surrendered, even if the atomic bombs had not been dropped, even if Russia had not entered the war, and even if no invasion had been planned or contemplated."[3]

Responding to a resurgence of criticism based upon the Bombing Survey's findings, Truman moved quickly to preempt such second-guessing of his use of the bomb. The point man for the Administration's public counteroffensive was Henry L. Stimson, former Secretary of War and a key adviser on atomic matters at the time of the bomb decision. In responding to the president's urging that he "set the record straight" Stimson agreed on the need to get out in front of the issue nd "satisfy the doubts of that rather difficult class of the community . . . namely educators and historians."[4]

Sharing this concern about how future historians might judge the bomb decision, Truman lent his full support, during his years in the White House, to Stimson's writings on the subject and other such projects. After retiring to private life, he repeated—in private interviews, public statements, and his two-volume memoirs—that he had always regarded the bomb strictly as a weapon and had no doubt or regret, either at the time or in retrospect, about the necessity or wisdom of its use against Japan. Any speculation about how things might have been done differently was based upon hindsight. Truman frequently cut off any further discussion of the subject with the observation that "any schoolboy's afterthought is worth more than all the generals' forethought."[5]

In his off-the-record comments Truman was more blunt. To a correspondent who had questioned the propriety of the air of celebration surrounding the news of the bombings, the president responded with the observation: "When you have to deal with a beast you have to treat him as a beast." Similarly, Truman had no sympathy for anyone else who might have second thoughts. Even before Robert Oppenheimer publicly confessed to having "known sin" in helping to build the bomb, Truman dismissed him as typical of the "crybaby scientists" who thought they had blood on their hands. Even years after wartime passions had cooled, Truman remained unapologetic. When in the 1960s the makers of a television documentary suggested that he might travel to Japan as a goodwill gesture, the former president replied in classic Trumanesque language: "I'll go . . . but I won't kiss their ass." Perhaps fortunately for all concerned, the crusty old man never made the proposed trip to Hiroshima. Until his death in 1972 Truman held firm to his original justification for the bombings.[6]

The formulation by Truman, Stimson, and other official or "orthodox" defenders of the bomb decision established the terms of the debate and held the high ground of privileged sources and classified information for many years. That defense rested upon the military necessity and therefore the lesser-of-two-evils morality of the decision. The bomb had been dropped because not to do so risked prolonging the war. By ending the war the bomb saved lives, American and Japanese. The reason for using it was strictly military—to hasten the surrender of Japan. There had been no ulterior political motives: neither domestic, in justifying a very expensive weapons development project, nor international, in regard to any power other than Japan.

In the emerging Cold War between the United States and the Soviet Union the last point was perhaps the most important. The term "atomic diplomacy" had first appeared in *Pravda* within weeks after the end of the war. The charge that the Truman Administration was attempting to use the United States' atomic monopoly to intimidate the Soviet Union was picked up by political mavericks in the United States, such as Franklin Roosevelt's former vice-president, Henry Wallace, as well as by influential voices from abroad, such as British Nobel Prize laureate in physics P.M.S. Blackett, who pointed out that the invasion of Japan, the next major U.S. military action, was not scheduled to begin until November. However, the Soviet Union, under an agreement signed by the Big Three leaders at Yalta early in 1945, was scheduled to enter the war against Japan in August, three months before the planned invasion.

After Germany's defeat, the Soviets represented Japan's last hope for a negotiated peace, and American leaders knew of Japanese peace feelers in Moscow. Why then was there the rush to use the bomb before Moscow dashed Japan's hopes by declaring war? The impact of that major diplomatic and military blow might well have brought about surrender. Why not at least wait to find out? Blackett concluded that the timing and circumstances of the atomic bombings made sense only as an effort at atomic diplomacy directed at the Soviet Union. He put the "revisionist" case succinctly in his observation that "the dropping of the atomic bomb was not so much the last military act of the second World War, as the first major operation in the cold diplomatic war with Russia now in progress."[7]

The basic elements of the debate over the bomb decision remained essentially unchanged over the years. The revisionist hypothesis, largely deductive and circumstantial, won few converts beyond the left. Twenty years after the bombs fell on Japan, former State Department official-turned-historian Herbert Feis concluded that, even though we can say, with the advantage of hindsight, that the use of atomic bombs at that juncture probably was unnecessary to bring about Japan's surrender before the planned invasion, the decision-makers "ought not to be censured." Although perhaps mistaken, they acted in good faith. They sincerely believed, based upon the best evidence available to them at the time, that using this new weapon was the best, surest, and quickest way to end the war.[8]

Feis and other orthodox defenders of the faith in U.S. leaders dismissed New Left revisionist arguments on grounds of ideological preconceptions, selective use of evidence, and shoddy scholarship. Although in some cases deserved, such criticism of the revisionist challenge could not altogether offset the mounting evidence against the original orthodox defense. The declassification of government documents and presidential papers, and the release of privately held manuscript sources such as Stimson's private diary forced a revision if not a total refutation of accepted orthodoxy. Drawing upon this newly available primary source material, scholars put forth analyses that were more balanced, more penetrating, and more convincing than either extreme in the previous debate over the bomb.

In the 1970s the work of Martin Sherwin, Barton Bernstein, Gregg Herken, and others revealed the early and continuing connection U.S. leaders made between the bomb and diplomacy. Recent scholarship has stressed the continuity of atomic policy from Roosevelt to Truman. Concerning the motives or objectives of this policy, by the 1980s it was generally accepted that considerations of the bomb's effect on post-war Soviet behavior had been one of several factors contributing to what was in the end a virtually irresistible presumption in favor of using the bomb.[9]

While it is true that dropping the bomb was virtually a foregone conclusion, it does not follow that Truman was, as General Groves described him, merely "a little boy on a toboggan." Dependent upon his advisers and far from a free agent, he was still the ultimate decision-maker. He was the only person who had the final say—not only on whether the bomb would be used at all, but when and how it would be used. With the Soviet Union about to enter the war, the decision not to tell Stalin about the bomb and the decision to drop all the available bombs in advance of Soviet entry take on major implications for our understanding of the overall decision.

Until recently, the evidence of Truman's thinking at the moment he gave the order to deliver the bombs was largely circumstantial or indirect. Those "rather difficult" historians Stimson had worried about were able to reconstruct in detail the views of Truman's key advisers. We know, for example, that Truman's Secretary of State, James F. Byrnes, wanted to use the bomb to end the war before Moscow "could get in so much on the kill." It is clear from his diary entries at the time that Stimson saw the bomb as the United States' "master card" in dealing, not just with Japan, but with the Soviet Union as well.[10] But there did not seem to be comparable direct evidence about Truman's private thinking on the bomb at the time he made the decision.

The first batch of this new evidence on the bomb decision surfaced in 1979. It had been misfiled among the family records of Truman's press secretary at the Truman presidential library. This sheaf of handwritten notes made up Truman's private journal kept during his trip to the Big Three summit meeting at Potsdam outside Berlin in July 1945. During that trip Truman first learned of the successful test explosion of a plutonium device in New Mexico, gave the order for the Hiroshima and Nagasaki bombings, and, as he sailed home, received the news that his order had been carried out. The event, he said at the time, was "the greatest thing in history."

Four years after the discovery of Truman's Potsdam diary a second batch of new evidence of Truman's contemporary thinking on matters relating to the use of the bomb turned up among his widow's private papers. These letters, written during that same Potsdam trip, along with other private correspondence between Bess and Harry Truman had been presumed destroyed years earlier. But they had somehow survived. Taken together, these two sets of documents shed new light on how Truman came to grips with an entirely new force in human affairs and how he incorporated his understanding of the bomb into his thoughts about when, how, and on whose terms the war would end.

The first news of the successful test detonation in New Mexico reached Truman on the evening of July 16. The message gave no details about the size of the explosion. Although he makes no explicit reference to the bomb in his diary entry for that date, the news of its existence may have moved him to reflect upon the relation between technology and morality: "I hope for some sort of peace—but I fear that machines are ahead of morals by some centuries and when morals catch up perhaps there'll be no reason for any of it. I hope not. But we are only termites on a planet and maybe when we bore too deeply into the planet there'll [be] a reckoning—who knows?" Elsewhere in this diary, after the bomb's power had been made clear to him, Truman wondered if this new weapon might "be the fire [of] destruction prophesied in the Euphrates Valley Era, after Noah and his fabulous ark." A full report on the Trinity test, including vivid eye-witness accounts, arrived on the afternoon of July 21. Such apocalyptic visions, however, did not keep him from using what he recognized was "the most terrible bomb in the history of the world." Perhaps he reassured himself with the observation that "it seems the most terrible thing ever discovered, but it can be made the most useful."

On July 17, still without knowing any details about the bomb test, Truman met for the first time with Stalin. In his diary account of that meeting he noted that the Soviet leader's agenda items, which included the overthrow of Franco's fascist government in Spain, were "dynamite." To this observation Truman added: "but I have some dynamite too which I'm not exploding now." Whether or not he was thinking of the bomb as his diplomatic dynamite is unclear. But Truman then makes a very clear statement that goes to the heart of the issue of the bomb's necessity. Referring to the Soviet commitment to declare war on Japan three months after the defeat of Germany, Truman noted Stalin's reaffirmation of the agreement he had made with Roosevelt at Yalta: "He'll [Stalin] be in Jap War on August 15th." To this Truman added: "Fini Japs when that comes about." In these two brief sentences Truman set forth his understanding of how the war would end: Soviet entry into the war would finish the Japanese.

In writing to his wife the following day (July 18), the President underscored the importance of Soviet entry and its impact upon the timing of the war's end. "I've gotten what I came for—Stalin goes to war on August 15 with no strings on it. . . . I'll say that we'll end the war a year sooner now, and think of the kids who won't be killed! That is the important thing." The implications of these passages from Truman's diary and letters for the orthodox defense of the bomb's use are devastating: if Soviet entry alone would end the war before an invasion of Japan, the use of atomic bombs cannot be justified as the only alternative to that invasion. This does not mean, of course, that having the bomb was not useful. But it does mean that for Truman the end of the war seemed at hand; the issue was no longer when the war would end, but how and on whose terms. If he believed that the war would end with Soviet entry in mid-August, then he must have realized that if the bombs were not used before that date they might well not be used at all.

This relationship between the Soviet entry, the bomb, and the end of the war is set forth in Truman's diary account for July 18. "P[rime] M[inister Churchill] and I ate alone. Discussed Manhattan [the atomic bomb] (it is a success). Decided to tell Stalin about it. Stalin had told P.M. of telegram from Jap emperor asking for peace. Stalin also read his answer to me. It was satisfactory. [I] believe Japs will fold up before Russia comes in. I am sure they will when Manhattan appears over their homeland. I shall inform Stalin about it at an opportune time." Truman apparently believed that by using the bomb the war could be ended even before the Soviet entry. The bomb would shorten the war by days rather than months. Its use would not save hundreds of thousands of lives—but it could save victory for the Americans. The race with the Germans had been won. It was now a race with the Soviets.

Unaware of Soviet espionage, Truman assumed that Stalin did not know that such a race was underway. Despite his stated intention to tell Stalin about the bomb at an "opportune" time, Truman—apparently due to the urgings of Churchill and Byrnes—did not inform Stalin even of the bomb's existence, much less of the plans to use it on the eve of a major Soviet military offensive into Manchuria. We now know that Klaus Fuchs, among others, kept Stalin well informed about progress on the bomb. But at Potsdam, Truman believed he had succeeded in keeping Stalin in ignorance by a carefully staged charade, casually mentioning a "new weapon" without giving any details about it or its immediate use. Stalin showed no interest, and Truman was convinced he had fooled "Mr. Russia." The following day the order to deliver both bombs as soon as possible went out from Potsdam.

This cat-and-mouse game between the two leaders was apparently what the President had in mind when, in a letter to his wife at the end of the conference, Truman, an ardent poker player, commented on Stalin's stalling tactics: "He doesn't know it but I have an ace in the hole and another one showing—so unless he has two pairs (and I know he has not) we are sitting all right." It can be argued that ending the war sooner rather than later, even a few days later, by whatever means at his disposal was Truman's first responsibility. It also can be argued that limiting Soviet expansion in Asia, as a bonus to ending the war as soon as possible, was in the U.S. national interest and, therefore, also Truman's duty. But the point here is that the President, in publicly justifying his use of the bomb, never made those arguments.

It is in this light that the new evidence, in both the Potsdam diary and letters to his wife, calls for a reevaluation of the old issue: why were the only two bombs available used in rapid succession so soon after testing, and on the eve of the planned Soviet entry into the war? From this unique record, in Truman's own hand, we can understand better how this relatively inexperienced leader, who had only recently first heard the words "atomic bomb," grasped this new technology, and used it as a solution for a multitude of military, political, and diplomatic problems. The evidence of the Potsdam diary and letters does not close the book on the question why the bomb was dropped. Rather, it opens it to a previously unseen page. What appears there is by no means always clear or consistent. At times it is hard to know what to make of such statements as Truman's diary entry for July 25, in which he expresses his determination to use the bomb "so that military objectives are the target and not women and children." This extraordinary comment follows a very detailed and accurate description of the effects of the bomb test. Perhaps he really did believe that Hiroshima was just a "military base."

Elsewhere in these pages Truman seems to disprove the revisionist contention that he did not want "the Russians" in the war at all. In writing to his wife on July 18

Truman made it clear that his highest priority at the conference was getting the Soviet Union into the war against Japan. Two days later, after a "tough meeting" with Churchill and Stalin, the president noted that he had made his goals "perfectly plain" to both men: "I want the Jap War won and I want 'em both in it." The dual objectives of assuring Soviet entry while containing Soviet expansion apparently were not contradictory to Truman. As he put it a decade later, "One of the main objectives of the Potsdam Conference [was] to get Russia in as quickly as we could and then to keep Russia out of Japan—and I did it." [11] Although he saw the bomb as useful for ending the war before the Soviets could claim credit for the victory, Truman apparently wasn't ready to rely totally on the bomb until it was proven in combat. This lingering skepticism is revealed in his use of quotation marks in noting, on the same day he gave the bomb order, that "we 'think' we have found the way to cause a disintegration of the atom."

Truman's attitude toward "the Japs" seems clear enough in his diary references to them as "savages, ruthless, merciless and fanatic." Yet to a senator who, after the Hiroshima bombing, had urged continued attacks until the Japanese were brought "groveling to their knees," the president replied: "I can't bring myself to believe that, because they are beasts, we should ourselves act in the same manner." Indeed, after the Nagasaki bombing, Truman reportedly told his cabinet members that there would be no more such attacks because he could not bear the thought of killing "all those kids." [12]

While these new sources, as they relate to Truman's private perspective on the bomb, contribute to our understanding, they remain fragments which by no means complete the mosaic. [13] The point here is not that Truman single-handedly controlled the course of history. Rather, it is that as a major participant in that history his attempt to mold nuclear weapons policy at the beginning of the atomic era contributes to our understanding of an event the meaning and lessons of which, after 40 years, we still seek.

NOTES

1. Editorial, *Christian Century*, August 29, 1945, pp. 3–4.

2. "The Fortune Poll," *Fortune*, December 1945, p. 305.

3. "Japan's Struggle to End the War," p. 12, and "Summary Report" (Pacific War), p. 26, both dated July 1, 1946, in David MacIsaac, ed., *The United States Strategic Bombing Survey*, vol. 7 (New York, 1976).

4. Truman to Henry L. Stimson (Dec. 31, 1946), folder "Atomic Weapons, Use of," vertical file, part 2, Harry S Truman Papers, Harry S Truman Library (Independence, Mo.); Stimson to Truman (January 7, 1947), quoted in Martin J. Sherwin, *A World Destroyed: The Atomic Bomb and the Grand Alliance* (New York, 1975), p. 3.

5. Transcript of press conference (Aug. 14, 1947), folder "Atomic Bomb," box 4, Eban Ayers Papers, Harry S Truman Library.

6. Truman to Samuel Cavett (Aug. 11, 1945), folder 692 misc., Official File, Truman Papers; Nuell Pharr Davis, *Lawrence and Oppenheimer* (New York, 1968), p. 260; Merle Miller, *Plain Speaking* (New York, 1974), p. 248.

7. P. M. S. Blackett, *Fear, War and the Bomb* (New York, 1948), p. 139.

8. Herbert Feis, *The Atomic Bomb and the End of World War II* (Princeton, 1966), p. 200.

9. Martin J. Sherwin; *A World Destroyed: The Atomic Bomb and the Grand Alliance* (New York: Knopf, 1975); Barton J. Bernstein, "Roosevelt, Truman, and the Atomic Bomb, 1941–1945: A Reinterpretation," *Political Science Quarterly*, Spring 1975, pp. 23–69; Gregg Herken, *The Winning Weapon: The Atomic Bomb in the Cold War, 1945–1950* (New York, 1981).

10. Robert L. Messer, *The End of an Alliance: James F. Byrnes, Roosevelt, Truman and the Origins of the Cold War* (Chapel Hill, 1982), pp. 92, 105.

11. Truman's remark was made in an off-the-record session with staff members preparing his memoirs. The quotation did not appear in the published volumes. [See Acheson Interview (Feb. 17, 1955), p. 40, Post-Presidential Papers, Harry S Truman Library.]

12. Truman to Senator Richard Russell (Aug. 9, 1945), with attached telegram, Russell to Truman (Aug. 7, 1945), folder 197, misc., Official File, Harry S Truman Library; entry for Aug. 10, 1945 in John Morton Blum, ed., *Price of Vision: The Diary of Henry A. Wallace, 1942–1946* (Boston, 1973), p. 474.

13. The Potsdam diary and correspondence are reprinted in Robert H. Ferrell, ed., *Off the Record: The Private Papers of Harry S. Truman* (New York, 1980), pp. 48–60; and in Robert H. Ferrell, ed., *Dear Bess: The Letters from Harry to Bess Truman, 1910–1959* (New York, 1983), pp. 516–523.

THREE ATTEMPTS TO STOP THE BOMB

William Lanouette

B Y EARLY IN 1945, Leo Szilard had a place in the history of nuclear physics for his work in creating the world's first chain reaction. He was not sure, however, what role he could play in deciding how his invention would be used. Those decisions were being made by military and political leaders in Washington, not at the Metallurgical Laboratory at the University of Chicago, where Szilard worked, or at the secret Los Alamos site in New Mexico, where A-bombs were then being designed and built.

Isolated from both political and practical deliberations, Szilard had time to reflect on the admix of science, politics, and personality that had brought the United States into the atomic age. A dozen years earlier, the A-bomb had been little more than Szilard's private obsession. Now he was part of a $2 billion nationwide enterprise and found it necessary to argue, in a series of memoranda, for a research and development program for the "breeder" reactor he had invented "and the part that, given favorable conditions, I might be able to play in it." Believing that the breeder could yield abundant nuclear fuel, Szilard speculated about plentiful atomic energy in a post-war world and on ways to assure its control. As he later recalled:

> Initially we were strongly motivated to produce the bomb because we feared the Germans would get ahead of us and the only way to prevent them from dropping bombs on us was to have bombs in readiness ourselves. But now, with the war won, it was not clear what we were working for.[1]

Arthur Compton, the Met Lab director, shared Szilard's concern but, despite his access to the project's leaders in Washington, had no say about the A-bomb's use. Because the Manhattan Project's strict secrecy left no intermediate level in the government to consider these issues, Szilard concluded that "the only man with whom we were sure we were entitled to communicate was the president." Why not write to him?

In a memo on "Atomic Bombs and the Post-war Position of the United States in the World," Szilard warned President Franklin D. Roosevelt that the choice facing U.S. strategists was starkly simple: Strike an arms control agreement with the Russians or be forced to beat them in a nuclear arms race. With no direct knowledge of bomb-design work at Los Alamos, Szilard warned that "six years from now Russia may have accumulated enough [fissionable material] to make atomic bombs . . ." that would be so small they could be hidden in U.S. cities for later detonation. Worse, he said that ". . . after this war it is conceivable that it will become possible to drop atomic bombs on the cities of the United States from very great distances by means of rockets."

In a U.S.-Soviet nuclear arms race, Szilard wrote, the "greatest danger" is "the possibility of the outbreak of a *preventive war*. Such a war might be the outcome of the fear that the other country might strike first, and no amount of good will on the part of both nations might be sufficient to prevent the outbreak of a war if such an explosive situation were allowed to develop." Only a worldwide system of controls could avert this danger, Szilard warned: a system involving both Great Britain and the Soviet Union. By diluting and denaturing fissionable uranium and plutonium, the world powers could develop nuclear energy peacefully, free from the danger that this fuel might be diverted to weapons making.[2]

Finishing this visionary document on Monday, March 12, Szilard faced a practical problem. "Since I didn't suppose that he would know who I was, I needed a letter of introduction." He turned to his mentor and friend Albert Einstein.[3] His letters on Szilard's behalf had reached FDR in 1939 to initiate the bomb program and in 1940 to help move it along. So, on March 15, Szilard drafted a letter to the president that he hoped Einstein would sign and a memo to the Met Lab's associate director, Walter Bartky, about post-war controls of the A-bomb.

In the spring of 1945, Szilard was not the only person actively trying to influence the president's thinking about such post-war controls, but strict "compartmentalization" within the project kept like-minded individuals from sharing their thoughts. The same day that Szilard drafted the letter for Einstein, Secretary of War Henry L. Stimson met with FDR at the White House for lunch to review the need for policy decisions about international control of atomic energy.[4] A respected cabinet member to four presidents, Stimson posed two control strategies: a secret pact by the United States and Britain to share nuclear technology or an open international exchange of information. This issue had to be settled before the bomb was used, Stimson said, and he left the White House convinced that the president agreed with him.[5] Later in March, Danish physicist Niels Bohr, a consultant at Los Alamos, also sent FDR a follow-up letter to their August 1944 discussions on post-war controls.[6]

To prepare his approach to the president, Szilard arrived by train in Princeton on March 23 and walked the few blocks to the white clapboard house on Mercer Street where Einstein lived. The two friends met in the study, a sunny room that looked onto a back garden and lawn, and once Szilard explained his plight, Einstein agreed to sign the letter of introduction.

112 Mercer Street
Princeton, New Jersey
March 25, 1945

The Honorable Franklin Delano Roosevelt
The President of the United States
The White House
Washington, D.C.

Sir:

I am writing you to introduce Dr. L. Szilard who proposes to submit to you certain considerations and recommendations. Unusual circumstances which I shall describe further below induce me to take this action in spite of the fact that I do not know the substance of the considerations and recommendations which Dr. Szilard proposes to submit to you.

In the summer of 1939 Dr. Szilard put before me his views concerning the potential importance of uranium for national defense. He was greatly disturbed by the potentialities involved and anxious that the United States Government be advised of them as soon as possible. Dr. Szilard, who is one of the discoverers of the neutron emission of uranium on which all present work on uranium is based, described to me a specific system which he devised and which he thought would make it possible to set up a chain reaction in un-separated uranium in the immediate future. Having known him for over twenty years both from his scientific work and personally, I have much confidence in his judgment and it was on the basis of his judgment as well as my own that I took the liberty to approach you in connection with this subject. You responded to my letter dated August 2, 1939 by the appointment of a committee under the chairmanship of Dr. Briggs and thus started the Government's activity in this field.

The terms of secrecy under which Dr. Szilard is working at present do not permit him to give me information about his work; however, I understand that he now is greatly concerned about the lack of adequate contact between scientists who are doing this work and those members of your Cabinet who are responsible for formulating policy. In the circumstances I consider it my duty to give Dr. Szilard this introduction and I wish to express the hope that you will be able to give his presentation of the case your personal attention.

Very truly yours,

(A. Einstein)

After the two men had chatted awhile, Szilard's thoughts rushed on to his next task: drafting a new memorandum to send with Einstein's letter. In it Szilard warned FDR that "our 'demonstration' of atomic bombs will precipitate a race in the production of these devices between the United States and Russia and that if we continue to pursue the present course, our initial advantage may be lost very quickly in such a race." Szilard suggested delaying the A-bomb's use, called for a system of international controls, and asked that a cabinet-level committee meet to hear the scientists' views on atomic-energy issues.[7]

On the other hand, Szilard's second memo to FDR failed to mention the prospect of rockets delivering A-bombs, and most significantly, it omitted "the outbreak of a preventive war" as the "greatest danger" in a post-war world, substituting instead a nuclear arms race itself. Szilard recalled that in July 1943 an assistant to Eugene Wigner had managed to put complaints about the Hanford reactor project before the president by going through First Lady Eleanor Roosevelt; he now thought this approach worth a try and, with a note to her, enclosed a copy of Einstein's letter.[8]

Szilard could not know that on March 27, two days after he met with Einstein and drafted his memorandum, General Groves wrote a memo of his own, declaring that he expected the A-bomb to end the war in the Pacific, thereby justifying the project. Eleanor Roosevelt replied to Szilard in early April, proposing a meeting at her Manhattan apartment on May 8. Excited by this break, Szilard rushed to Compton's office and told him what he had done. Szilard was nervous as Compton slowly read the memo, expecting to be scolded for again working outside official channels. "I hope that you will get the president to read this," Compton said, and Szilard left the office elated. He was at his desk about five minutes later when he heard a knock on his office door. In walked Norman Hilberry, Compton's assistant, with news he had just heard on the radio. President Roosevelt had died.[9] Szilard's first attempt to stop the bomb had ended.

THAT AFTERNOON, Vice-President Harry S. Truman was sworn in as the thirty-third president of the United States, and after a brief meeting with the grief-stricken cabinet, Secretary of War Stimson told him in vague but ominous terms about a new explosive of unbelievable power. The next day, Truman learned more details from James F. Byrnes, a friend from the Senate who had served until recently as FDR's director of war mobilization.

"There I was now with my memorandum, and no way to get it anywhere," Szilard recalled. "At this point I knew I was in need of advice."[10] The Met Lab's associate director, Walter Bartky, suggested a talk with university chancellor Robert M. Hutchins. A man of independent views, Hutchins listened intently to Szilard, then asked what this situation might lead to. Szilard's answer was abrupt: A world under one government.

"Yes," Hutchins said, "I believe you are right." Despite their quick rapport, Hutchins was no help to Szilard at this, their first meeting. "I do not know Mr. Truman," he said.

Anxious days and nights passed as Szilard paced his room and the campus, groping for some way to reach Truman. The Met Lab was a large project, he reasoned. *Someone* there must come from Kansas City, Truman's political base. At Bartky's office, Szilard flipped through the lab's personnel files and found Albert Cahn, a young mathematician from Kansas City. Cahn agreed to help, telephoned home, and in two days—through the political machine of Tom Pendergast—Szilard had an appointment at the White House. But not until May 25, more than a month away.[11]

Truman learned more about the bomb by April 25, through a briefing by Groves and Stimson. Groves insisted that Japan had always been the target, and Stimson raised the long-range implications of the bomb, mentioned a possible nuclear arms race, warned about the horrors of a nuclear war, and urged international control. Szilard, the outsider, was struggling to give Truman similar advice, but "official" events were out-pacing him. On April 27, Groves's Target Committee, which included four military men and nine scientists (Oppenheimer among them), held its first meeting. To measure the new bomb's effectiveness, the committee sought targets that had suffered little damage from conventional weapons and picked seventeen cities, including Hiroshima and Nagasaki.

Stimson convened an Interim Committee of the bomb program "to study and report on the whole problem of temporary war controls and later publicity, and to survey and make recommendations on post war research, development and controls, as well as legislation necessary to effectuate them." The war in Europe ended on May 8, and the next day, the Interim Committee met for the first time. At the table with Stimson were Navy Under Secretary Ralph A. Bard, Assistant Secretary of State William L. Clayton, bomb-program executives Vannevar Bush and James Conant, James Byrnes, and Karl T. Compton, Arthur Holly's brother from MIT. At Conant's suggestion, the Interim Committee appointed a Scientific Panel, which included Oppenheimer, Ernest O. Lawrence, Enrico Fermi, and Arthur Compton.[12]

For his White House appointment on May 25, Szilard took along Bartky and Cahn. Matthew J. Connelly, Truman's appointments secretary, read Einstein's letter and Szilard's memo carefully. "I see now," Connelly said, "this is a serious matter. At first, I was a little suspicious, because this appointment came through Kansas City. The President thought that your concern would be about this matter, and he has asked me to make an appointment for you with James Byrnes, if you are willing to go down to see him in Spartanburg, South Carolina." Szilard and Bartky were surprised but said they were glad to go wherever the president directed them. Szilard asked if he might also bring Harold Urey, a Manhattan Project chemist and Nobel laureate, and Connelly agreed.

As their overnight train rolled south through the Virginia hills, Szilard, Bartky, and Urey wondered aloud why the president had sent them to Byrnes. He had been a U.S. representative and senator from South Carolina, becoming a budgetary expert during Roosevelt's New Deal legislative reforms. Named to the Supreme Court in 1941, Byrnes had resigned a year later to direct economic stabilization and, later, war mobilization. Now in his first weeks of retirement from government service, he seemed to have the president's ear. But why? Szilard suspected that Truman must be planning to appoint Byrnes to a new government post, perhaps to head atomic work after the war.[13]

During the train ride the three agreed to raise two points: First, they wanted to explore how the A-bomb would affect world affairs after the war and how America's role would change if it used the bomb to end the Pacific war. Second, they worried about the future of atomic energy and the need to plan post-war research.

Set in the mountains of northwestern South Carolina, Spartanburg was a small market and university town. From the tiny red-brick station the three walked past flat-front stores and beneath arching trees to Byrnes's bungalow, and once seated in the dark living room, Szilard handed him Einstein's letter to Roosevelt and his own memorandum. Byrnes glanced at the letter and studied the memo, but before he could finish reading, Szilard began a forceful lecture about the dangers of Russia's becoming an atomic power if the United States demonstrated the A-bomb's power and used it against Japan.

"General Groves tells me there is no uranium in Russia," Byrnes interrupted.

"Wrong," said Szilard. "There are rich ore deposits in Czechoslovakia, which Russia can obtain, and their own vast territory must contain some uranium."

Szilard then argued that the United States should not reveal the A-bomb's existence until the government had decided its post-war policy. Indeed, the United States should not even test the bomb, since its existence is its greatest secret.

"How would you get Congress to appropriate money for atomic energy research if you do not show results for the money which has been spent already?" Byrnes the politician replied.[14] He thought the war would be over in about six months, and his worry was Russia's post-war behavior. Russia had invaded Hungary and Rumania and wouldn't be persuaded to withdraw troops unless the United States demonstrated its military might. Szilard was "flabbergasted by the assumption that rattling the bomb might make Russia more manageable."

"Well," Byrnes added, "you come from Hungary—you would not want Russia to stay in Hungary indefinitely." This made Szilard furious. Byrnes had assailed Szilard's chief moral guide, his "sense of proportion," and his anger persists in an account written fifteen years later: "I was concerned at this point that . . . we might start an atomic arms race between America and Russia which might end with the destruction of both countries. I was *not* disposed at this point to worry about what would happen to Hungary."[15]

Szilard's anger turned to astonishment as the four men began to discuss the future of the Manhattan Project and Byrnes seemed indifferent. Only weeks later did Szilard learn that Byrnes was not in line to head the project but to become Truman's secretary of state.

Byrnes later wrote that Szilard's "general demeanor and his desire to participate in policymaking made an unfavorable impression on me. . . ." At the same time, Szilard became convinced that Byrnes did not grasp the importance of atomic energy, or much else.[16] The encounter left him frightened that if Byrnes had his way, a U.S.-Soviet nuclear arms race would be inevitable.

Byrnes tucked Szilard's letter and memo into his suit-coat pocket as he rose to bid his three visitors farewell, and Szilard later imagined that his memorandum stayed there—all the way to the dry cleaner. But an unsigned memorandum was found by historians among Byrnes's papers. In retrospect, Szilard thought their Spartanburg visit "fittingly naive," while Bartky concluded that it was "purely academic" and accomplished nothing.[17] As far as Szilard knew, his second attempt to stop the bomb had been as futile as his first.

"I was rarely as depressed as when we left Byrnes's house and walked toward the station," Szilard wrote later. "I thought to myself how much better off the world might be had I been born in America and become influential in American politics, and had Byrnes been born in Hungary and studied physics. In all probability there would have been no atomic bomb, and no danger of an arms race between America and Russia." At the station, Szilard, Urey, and Bartky boarded the next train for Washington.

EAGER TO INFLUENCE the Interim Committee, Szilard audaciously telephoned General Groves's Pentagon office on May 30 and had his secretary arrange a meeting there with Oppenheimer for later that morning.[18] But almost as soon as the two scientists sat down, they disagreed: first over plans to use the bomb, then over its post-war control.[19] It would be a serious mistake to use the bomb against Japanese cities, Szilard said.

"The atomic bomb is shit," Oppenheimer replied, surprising Szilard.

"What do you mean by that?" Szilard asked.

"Well, this is a weapon which has no military significance," said Oppenheimer. "It will make a big bang—a very big bang—but it is not a weapon which is useful in war."

Yet Oppenheimer did think it important to tell the Russians that we had an A-bomb and intended to use it on Japan's cities rather than taking them by surprise. Szilard knew Secretary of War Stimson shared this view, but he complained that while warning Russia was necessary, it was not sufficient.

"Well," said Oppenheimer, "don't you think that if we tell the Russians what we intend to do and then use the bomb in Japan, the Russians will understand it?"

"They'll understand it only too well," Szilard replied, no doubt with Byrnes's intentions in mind.[20]

When the Interim Committee met at the Pentagon on May 31, the four Scientific Panel members—Oppenheimer, Lawrence, Fermi, and Compton—attended, along with General George C. Marshall, there to hear firsthand the scientists' concerns. Oppenheimer echoed some of Szilard's ideas as he proposed an exchange of atomic information, with emphasis on peaceful uses. The goal of atomic energy, he said, should be the enlargement of human welfare, and America's moral position would be greatly strengthened if information were offered before the bomb were used.[21] What's more, Oppenheimer said, Russia had always been very friendly to science, and the United States should not prejudice its attitude toward cooperation. They would not have to await such cooperation, however, for Soviet spies had already informed Stalin of American progress.[22]

The Interim Committee agreed later that day that "the most desirable target [for the A-bomb] would be a vital war plant employing a large number of workers and closely surrounded by workers' houses." While Szilard could not attend this meeting, he was there in spirit, thanks to the anger of General Groves. Complaining about the "handling of undesirable scientists," Groves said that "the program has been plagued since its inception by the presence of certain scientists of doubtful discretion and uncertain loyalty." After the bomb becomes public, he vowed, there should be "a general weeding out of personnel no longer needed."[23]

Back in Chicago, Compton assured his Met Lab colleagues that Interim Committee members were receptive to the scientists' suggestions.[24] And, he said, they would welcome more advice at their next meeting at Los Alamos in two weeks. Compton offered to convey to the Scientific Panel any recommendations prepared by the time he left Chicago on June 14, and by Monday, June 4, the Met Lab scientists had seized this opportunity, forming committees on organization, research programs, education and security, production, and social and political implications.

Szilard was named chairman of the production group but declined in order to focus his energies as a member of the social and political committee that was headed by physicist James Franck.[25] Szilard quickly became its catalytic member and its conscience.[26] Eugene Rabinowitch, who drafted the Franck Committee report, recalled "many hours spent walking up and down the Midway with Leo Szilard arguing about these questions [and] sleepless nights when I asked myself whether perhaps we should break through the walls of secrecy and get to the American people the feeling of what was to be done by their government and whether we approved it. . . . " Rabinowitch credited Szilard with "the whole emphasis on the problem of the use of the bomb which really gave the report its historical significance—the attempt to prevent the use of the bomb on Japan." The report's "fundamental orientation," he said, was "due above all to Leo Szilard and James Franck. . . ." [27]

While Szilard and Rabinowitch were arguing along the green expanse of the Midway, Compton found himself again mediating between his scientists and the army. After Groves's assistant, Col. Kenneth D. Nichols, telephoned to ask about Szilard's visit to Byrnes, Compton admitted, "I have never been able to control Szilard's actions in matters such as this. . . ." Nevertheless, he wrote a thoughtful memorandum that stated eloquently the motives that would compel his colleagues to political action in the coming months. [28]

"The scientists have a very strong feeling of responsibility to society regarding the use of the new powers they have released," Compton wrote on June 4. "They first saw the possibility of making this new power available to human use . . ." and "have perhaps felt more keenly than others the enormous possibilities that would thus be opened for man's welfare or destruction." He continued:

> The scientists will be held responsible, both by the public and by their own consciences, for having faced the world with the existence of the new powers. The fact that the control has been taken out of their hands makes it necessary for them to plead the need for careful consideration and wise action to someone with authority to act. There is no other way in which they can meet their responsibility to society.

Compton noted that two approaches by the scientists, through official channels, had both failed to reach policymakers: Zay Jeffries's "Prospectus on Nucleonics" report and a November 1944 memo by Compton to Groves that summarized his colleagues' concerns. And Compton echoed Szilard's fear that U.S. negotiators needed to know about the A-bomb as they drafted the new UN Charter. Groves had told several Met Lab scientists that he discussed the bomb with "members of the State Department," but based on comments by Secretary of State Edward R. Stettinius after a briefing on the new weapons, Compton thought "his appreciation of the problem was so limited as possibly to serve as a hazard to the country's welfare." [29]

The Franck Committee report—with a recommendation that the A-bomb be demonstrated to Japan before use against its civilians—was finished in time for Compton to take it along as he boarded the train for Los Alamos on June 14, and when he arrived, he passed copies to Fermi, Lawrence, and Oppenheimer. But in a hasty session on Saturday, June 16, the four scientists concluded: "We can propose no technical demonstration likely to bring an end to the war; we see no acceptable alternative to direct military use." [30] With this "expert" advice by the Manhattan Project's respected Scientific Panel, the Interim Committee confidently rejected the Franck Committee's recommendations on June 21. Although he would not know it for several days, Szilard's third attempt to stop the bomb had just been shattered.

General Groves was angry with Szilard long before he read Compton's memo about the Byrnes visit and became even more angry about Szilard's other travels. "I understand that at frequently recurring intervals Dr. Szilard is absent from his assigned place of work at the Metallurgical Laboratory in Chicago," Groves wrote to Compton on June 29, "and further, that he travels extensively between Chicago, New York and Washington, D.C." He asked Compton for details on whether Szilard traveled on leave or on duty, what he was paid, whether the U.S. government financed these trips, what business he transacted, and whether his travels were cleared in advance. Demanding a "complete report" on all Szilard's activities for the project in the last six months, Groves also wanted to know "what positive contribution, if any, to the project he has made since July 1, 1943." Groves warned in closing that "these inquiries must not of course be discussed with Dr. Szilard either directly or indirectly."[31]

Groves even wrote to Lord Cherwell, Winston Churchill's science adviser and Szilard's former mentor at Oxford, seeking details of his meeting with Szilard more than a year earlier. "Frankly, Dr. Szilard has not, in our opinion, evidenced whole-hearted cooperation in the maintenance of security," Groves said. "In order to prevent any unjustified action, I am examining all of the facts which can be collected on Dr. Szilard. . . ."[32]

Groves would have been livid had he known what Szilard was actually doing then: bucking the army's chain of command to reach the commander in chief. "I knew by this time that it would not be possible to dissuade the government from using the bomb against the cities of Japan," Szilard wrote later. Having lost in the Interim Committee, "all that remained was for scientists to go unmistakably on record that they were against such an action."[33] Beginning on the first day of July, Szilard drafted and circulated a petition to the president, first around the Met Lab, then by colleagues who traveled to Oak Ridge and Los Alamos. "However small the chance might be that our petition may influence the course of events," Szilard wrote on July 4 to an Oak Ridge colleague, "I personally feel that it would be a matter of importance if a large number of scientists who have worked in this field went clearly and unmistakably on record as to their opposition on moral grounds to the use of these bombs in the present phase of the war."[34]

At Los Alamos, Ed Creutz delivered several copies to Edward Teller. But Teller was then striving ambitiously to promote a "super"—a "fusion" hydrogen bomb, expected to be hundreds of times more powerful than the "fission" bombs then nearing completion—and used Szilard's petition to gain political favor within the tight-knit and competitive Los Alamos community. Teller took the petition to Oppenheimer, knowing that he advocated immediate use of the bomb. Years later, Teller would write that he thought he could not circulate the petition without Oppenheimer's permission. But he also admitted to having "considerable respect for his opinion," and "I sincerely wanted to be on friendly terms with Oppie."

In Oppenheimer's office, Teller handed over the petition, saying it had come from a scientist "near Pa Franck." At once Oppenheimer criticized the Chicago scientists in general and Szilard by name. Scientists had no right to use their prestige to influence political decisions, Oppenheimer complained. In fact, while denying Szilard the right to influence policy, at the Interim Committee, Oppenheimer had advocated immediate bombing and had won the concurrence of his three reluctant colleagues by asserting his own status as lab director.[35]

Relieved that a decision about the petition had been taken from him, Teller nonetheless felt he owed his friend Szilard an answer. But the letter he wrote, which may have been drafted even before meeting Oppenheimer, was convoluted and disingenuous.[36] Teller complained that "no amount of protesting or fiddling with politics will save our souls" or clear their consciences for working on the bomb, although he knew that Szilard's motives had been purely defensive against Germany. Teller suspected that the A-bomb's "actual combat use might even be the best thing" to frighten the public about the weapon's horrors. But Teller's "main point," he said, siding with Oppenheimer, was that "the accident that we worked out this dreadful thing should not give us the responsibility of having a voice in how it is to be used." [37] Teller wrote this knowing that all mail was censored and that Oppenheimer was sure to see it, so, independently, he asked for his permission to send the letter to Szilard.[38]

Using physicist Ralph Lapp as a courier, Szilard sent eight sets of the petition to Los Alamos. "Of course, you will find only a few people on your project who are willing to sign such a petition," he wrote to Oppenheimer's brother Frank, to Teller, and to physicists Philip Morrison and Robert Wilson. "I am sure you will find many boys confused as to what kind of a thing a moral issue is." Admitting the futility of his petition to stop the bombing of Japan, Szilard said that

> from a point of view of the standing of the scientists in the eyes of the
> general public one or two years from now it is a good thing that a
> minority of scientists should have gone on record in favor of giving
> greater weight to moral arguments and should have exercised their
> right given to them by the Constitution to petition the President. . . .[39]

When Groves learned about Szilard's secret approach to the Los Alamos scientists and Teller's reply, the general at once feared that Szilard would some-how try to publicize the bomb. Suspecting the worst from Szilard, the lieutenant who reported on Szilard to Groves warned that army resistance to the petition might backfire: "Dr. Teller's attitude is rather interesting and might furnish Szilard with a new approach, i.e., to attempt to get fellow scientist [sic] to stop work." [40]

Szilard, for his part, had no time to think about organizing a scientists' boycott.[41] Independently, Groves's assistant, Colonel Nichols, asked Compton to check on the petition by confirming his colleagues' attitudes, and Compton asked Met Lab director Farrington Daniels to poll the scientists. On July 13, Daniels reported to Compton that a majority (72 percent) favored a military demonstration in Japan or a demonstration in the United States with Japanese representatives present." [42]

Szilard redrafted the petition during the second week in July but knew his time was running out when told that they were no longer permitted to telephone from the Met Lab to Los Alamos. "This could mean only one thing: Los Alamos must get ready to test the bomb, and the Army tried by this ingenious method to keep the news from the Chicago project." [43]

Another ingenious method to keep Szilard from public mischief came on July 15 when a Manhattan Project security officer arrived at the Met Lab with two copies of a secret document strapped to his body. With armed guards at the door, the captain sat Szilard and others in a university classroom to read galley proofs of chapters from a report by Henry DeWolf Smyth, chairman of the physics department at Princeton. To be released at the war's end, Smyth's "Atomic Energy for Military Purposes" described in a straightforward, nonscientific style the basic concepts in nuclear physics and how A-bombs were conceived, designed, and developed. The report credited Szilard and Fermi with devising the world's first reactor; mentioned Szilard and others for restricting their publications; credited Szilard and Wigner with prompting Einstein's letter to Roosevelt, with participating in the Uranium Committee, and with arranging government-sponsored research; and cited Szilard and Fermi for co-directing uranium research at Columbia University before the Federal Office of Scientific Research and Development (OSRD) and then the Manhattan Project were created. Smyth's report also revealed the project's scale and immense costs.

Asked to sign a receipt stating that he had read and approved the report, Szilard balked. The report gave away the important secret of "the general ideas and the knowledge of the methods that actually worked." This posed a problem beyond the war's end, Szilard feared, for once the bomb's secret was released, other powers would have no incentive to heed U.S. calls for international control. Refusing to agree with the report's release, Szilard scratched out "approved" and signed that he had "read" it.[44]

At 5:29.45 mountain war time on July 16, on a desert artillery range designated Trinity, near Alamogordo, New Mexico, the world's first nuclear explosive was tested successfully. A few hours later and unaware that the test had taken place, Szilard redrafted the petition, his last attempt to go on record against the weapon he had worked for years to create and for months to control. Szilard's final petition gained one hundred and fifty-five signatures. It read:

A PETITION TO THE PRESIDENT
OF THE UNITED STATES
July 17, 1945

Discoveries of which the people of the United States are not aware may affect the welfare of this nation in the near future. The liberation of atomic power which has been achieved places atomic bombs in the hands of the Army. It places in your hands, as Commander-in-Chief, the fateful decision whether or not to sanction the use of such bombs in the present phase of the war against Japan.

We, the undersigned scientists, have been working in the field of atomic power. Until recently we have had to fear that the United States might be attacked by atomic bombs during this war and that her only defense might lie in a counterattack by the same means. Today, with the defeat of Germany, this danger is averted and we feel impelled to say what follows:

The war has to be brought speedily to a successful conclusion and attacks by atomic bombs may very well be an effective method of warfare. We feel, however, that such attacks on Japan could not be justified, at least not until the terms which will be imposed after the war on Japan were made public in detail and Japan were given an opportunity to surrender.

If such public announcement gave assurance to the Japanese that they could look forward to a life devoted to peaceful pursuits in their homeland and if Japan still refused to surrender our nation might then, in certain circumstances, find itself forced to resort to the use of atomic bombs. Such a step, however, ought not to be made at any time without seriously considering the moral responsibilities which are involved.

The development of atomic power will provide the nations with new means of destruction. The atomic bombs at our disposal represent only the first step in this direction, and there is almost no limit to the destructive power which will become available in the course of their future development. Thus a nation which sets the precedent of using these newly liberated forces of nature for purposes of destruction may have to bear the responsibility of opening the door to an era of devastation on an unimaginable scale.

If after the war a situation is allowed to develop in the world which permits rival powers to be in uncontrolled possession of these new means of destruction, the cities of the United States as well as the cities of other nations will be in continuous danger of sudden annihilation. All the resources of the United States, moral and material, may have to be mobilized to prevent the advent of such a world situation. Its prevention is at present the solemn responsibility of the United States—singled out by virtue of her lead in the field of atomic power.

The added material strength which this lead gives to the United States brings with it the obligation of restraint and if we were to violate this obligation our moral position would be weakened in the eyes of the world and in our own eyes. It would then be more difficult for us to live up to our responsibility of bringing the unloosened forces of destruction under control.

In view of the foregoing, we, the undersigned, respectfully petition: first, that you exercise your power as Commander-in-Chief to rule that the United States shall not resort to the use of atomic bombs in this war unless the terms which will be imposed upon Japan have been made public in detail and Japan knowing these terms has refused to surrender; second, that in such an event the question whether or not to use atomic bombs be decided by you in the light of the consideration presented in this petition as well as all other moral responsibilities which are involved.[45]

Oppenheimer had banned an earlier draft of Szilard's petition at Los Alamos, but just as Teller had used it to curry favor with Oppenheimer, so Oppenheimer used this version to please Groves.[46] Franck persuaded several colleagues to sign Szilard's petition on condition that it be sent to Truman by official channels only. Szilard at first mistrusted this approach, fearing that Groves or his allies would intervene, but he finally agreed and handed the petition to Compton on July 19. He asked Compton to place the petition in an envelope addressed to the president and to seal the envelope before it left his office, keeping the signers' names secret. Compton agreed.[47]

After negotiating with Groves for a week—the general's way to stall Szilard's efforts—Compton sent the petition to Nichols, on July 24, noting that "since the matter presented in the petition is of immediate concern, the petitioners desire the transmission occur as promptly as possible." Compton also reported on Daniels's July 12 poll that the "strongly favored procedure" is to "give a military demonstration in Japan. . . ." This is Compton's own preference, he said, "and is, as nearly as I can judge, the procedure that has found most favor in all informed groups where the subject has been discussed."[48] Except, of course, at the highest levels of government, for the next day—in Potsdam with Truman, Stalin, and Churchill—Secretary of War Stimson approved the final orders to drop the A-bomb "after about August 3. . . ." [49]

When Nichols received Compton's memo and Szilard's petition on July 25, he added the amended versions that had been signed by 85 scientists at Oak Ridge. But then Nichols held these petitions for another week, and finally dispatched them to Groves by military police courier on July 30. In all, 156 Manhattan Project scientists had protested the imminent use of the bomb. Groves held the petition until August 1, when a telex from Tinian Island in the Pacific assured him that the A-bomb was ready for use.[50]

Having tried to reach the president, then having gone on record against use of the A-bomb, Szilard could only await nervously the disaster he was certain would occur. But for mischievous distraction—and to annoy the FBI agents who stalked him—Szilard joined Albert Cahn aboard a Braniff flight to Kansas City, met Cahn's parents, spent a night in the Phillips Hotel, and (according to an agent's report) the next morning returned to Chicago aboard a Santa Fe express train. Back at the Quadrangle Club, Szilard faced a new problem: eviction. His personal habits had annoyed the housekeeping staff during his years there: He seldom drained the bathtub or flushed the toilet; that was "maid's work, " he claimed, asserting his bourgeois European mentality in one of the few ways he could. The club's management had complained, and Szilard had refused to change his habits. Now he was asked to leave.[51]

President Truman's Potsdam Declaration on July 26 offered Japan "an opportunity to end this war" by urging the government "to proclaim now the unconditional surrender of all Japanese armed forces. . . ." The alternative for Japan, Truman and his allies said, is "prompt and utter destruction." [52] When Japan rejected the declaration two days later, Szilard grew more anxious than ever that the A-bomb would soon be used. To friends in Chicago he seemed disheartened and gloomy, as he had on the eve of the first chain-reaction experiment.

On August 1, worried that the bomb might soon be used and annoyed about his expulsion from the faculty club, Szilard stuffed his suitcases with papers and rumpled clothes and moved five blocks east, where he rented two back rooms from Dr. and Mrs. Paul A. Weiss in a three-story brick apartment house on South Blackstone Avenue. The view there was much less picturesque than Szilard enjoyed at the club; now he looked from large windows onto a back alley and garages instead of seeing through small leaded-glass panes the neo-Gothic spires of the Quadrangle and the divinity schools nearby.[53]

THE DAY OF SZILARD'S MOVE, Groves at last forwarded Szilard's petition to Stimson's office. But still in Potsdam with Truman, Stimson would not see the petition until his return later in August. Three U.S. B-29s lifted from the Tinian airstrip the morning of August 6, one bearing the uranium bomb nicknamed "Little Boy," one armed for aerial protection, and one along to photograph and film the mission. Over Hiroshima the single bomb fell to explode above the waking city at 8:15 A.M. A shock of light, a blast, heat, whirlwind firestorms. By sudden incineration and lingering death some 200,000 people died.[54] In a flash, the villains of the Pacific war became its greatest victims.

News of the single blast reverberated around the world. At a small cabin on Saranac Lake, in the Adirondack Mountains of New York, Albert Einstein's secretary heard a radio news item about the war in the Pacific that told of a new kind of bomb dropped on Japan. "Then I knew what it was," she recalled later, "because I knew about the Szilard thing in a vague way. . . . As Professor Einstein came down to tea, I told him, and he said, 'Oh, Weh' and that's that." To a newspaper reporter that day Einstein could only say, "Ach! The world is not ready for it."[55]

At Farm Hall, a seventeenth-century country house in England, ten eminent German scientists who the Allies thought had worked to build an A-bomb for the Führer were under house arrest: among them Otto Hahn, Werner Heisenberg, and Carl von Weizsäcker. Hahn, who was first to hear, was shattered by the news, said he felt responsible for the deaths of hundreds of thousands of people, and gulped several drinks to brace himself. Hahn's colleagues were incredulous, then suspicious.

"If the Americans have an uranium bomb," Hahn said to the others, "then you're all second-raters. Poor old Heisenberg." At first, Heisenberg thought the news a hoax. Their conversation, secretly taped by British intelligence, turned to moralizing.

After another radio announcement convinced the Germans that the bomb was real, they contemplated the magnitude of America's effort and their own failure. Heisenberg recalled a time, in early 1942, when "we had absolutely definite proof that it could be done." But Weizsäcker's excuse—though not shared by everyone—closed that speculation: "I believe the reason we didn't do it was because all the physicists didn't want to do it, on principles. If we had all wanted Germany to win the war we could have succeeded."

"I don't believe that," the gloomy Hahn replied, "but I am thankful we didn't succeed."[56]

In Chicago, Szilard "knew that the bomb would be dropped, that we had lost the fight," he recalled later. "And when it was actually dropped, my overall feeling was a feeling of relief. . . . Suddenly the secrecy was dropped and it was possible to tell people what this was about and what we were facing in this century."[57]

But first he had to tell someone special, and he sat down to write Trude Weiss. When she heard about the Hiroshima bombing on the radio, she later recalled, "Then I knew. Like a shock I knew. I was at my desk in New York, and I had to go home. Everything was suddenly out of proportion."[58] Szilard knew she was not prepared for the news that the A-bomb was her Leo's doing and needed to explain. Nervously he shifted from the matter-of-fact report that he had moved to a casual query about a party to rare self-confession. In English and German and English again. From past to present to future.

THE QUADRANGLE CLUB
CHICAGO

Monday, Aug. 6, 1945

Dear Ch,

I report my new address: 5816 Blackstone Ave., c/o Weiss. Telephone: MIDWAY 0545.

How are things with you? How was the Calderon party?

I suppose you have seen today's newspapers. Using atomic bombs against Japan is one of the greatest blunders of history.

—Both from a practical point of view on a ten-years scale and from the point of view of our moral position.—I went out of my way (and very much so) in order to prevent it but, as today's papers show, without success. It is very difficult to see what wise course of action is possible from here on. Maybe it is best to say nothing; this is what I suggest you do.

I hope you do not feel like a little mouse anymore. [This sentence is in German.] Maybe I'll come East for a visit soon, now that the cat is out of the bag.

Yours L.[59]

"I always thought it was his way of apologizing," Trude said after Leo's death. "It was one of the most important letters he ever wrote to me."[60] Relief at being free to discuss the bomb was tempered by Szilard's horror at early reports from Hiroshima, a horror that roused him to new thinking, writing, telephoning, buttonholing and berating his colleagues—and anyone else who would listen. For months he rushed around the campus, around the city, around the country, in a frenzy of activity.

His first stop on the day he heard about Hiroshima was Robert Hutchins's office because he needed a sympathetic person to talk to about the tragic news. He asked if the Met Lab staff might wear black mourning bands on their arms, but Hutchins thought the gesture "a little Hungarian" and suggested Szilard find some less dramatic way for the scientists to demonstrate their grief. A few days later, Szilard enlisted Hutchins to head a Chicago scientists' group to meet with President Truman, but this White House visit was never arranged.[61]

American B-29s took off from Tinian Island again on the morning of August 9, this time to drop a single plutonium bomb, nicknamed "Fat Man," on the port city of Nagasaki. The bomb killed only 70,000 because hills deflected the blast and radiation. "Dropping the bomb on Hiroshima was a tragic mistake," Szilard quoted his colleague Samuel K. Allison as saying. "Dropping the bomb on Nagasaki was an atrocity."[62]

On Saturday, August 11, Szilard asked a University of Chicago chaplain to hold a special prayer service for the dead of Hiroshima and Nagasaki and offered to transmit the prayer to the Japanese survivors.[63] Szilard's petition to the president three weeks earlier had been based on moral principles, and he was upset that political and religious leaders seemed to be silent about these concerns. Szilard enlisted philosophy professor Charles Hartshorne for a taxi ride uptown to call on

Chicago's Roman Catholic cardinal. When ushered into the churchman's presence, Szilard began at once to spout his views about the import and dangers of atomic energy. The cardinal listened patiently as Szilard demanded that the church confront the morality of the A-bomb, then replied briefly.

"God had locked up the energy in question so securely that only after thousands of years has it been unlocked," he intoned. "Surely there was a reason for this long delay."

"What *was* the reason?" Szilard demanded.

"The church will consider the matter and in due time will make a statement about it," the cardinal announced. End of discussion. Szilard and Hartshorne left disappointed and, riding back to campus, agreed they now wished the atom's energy had been locked up still more securely. Szilard called on other religious leaders but found them just as unconcerned.[64]

When a prayer service was held at the university's Rockefeller Chapel, Szilard attended with Met Lab physicist Alexander Langsdorf and his wife, Martyl—the artist who would design the "minutes to midnight" clock for the *Bulletin of the Atomic Scientists*. As the three walked out, Szilard noticed that he had forgotten his hat in the pew, and Langsdorf offered to fetch it.

"No, no," Szilard said. "General Groves will know where I am and it will get back to me." [65]

Groves may not have been watching Szilard quite so closely, but he did worry about any publicity he might create. Once Groves learned that Manhattan Project officers had agreed to allow Szilard to publicize the scientists' petition to Truman, the General ordered it reclassified "secret," blocking Szilard from releasing it to *Science* magazine. An army officer explicitly forbade Szilard from publishing the petition anywhere and threatened to fire him from the Met Lab if he did.[66] Quoting a letter sent to justify reclassification, Szilard complained to Hutchins how "the Manhattan District's definition of 'Secret' includes 'information that might be injurious to the prestige of any government activity,' which is, of course, very different from the definition adopted by Congress in the Espionage Act." [67]

He also complained directly to a Met Lab officer about what a "big mistake" it would be to publish the Smyth report. When it appeared, Szilard said, he would be known to the world as a "war criminal." Szilard insisted that for his own protection the army should furnish him with "a personal bodyguard and an automobile." This was ignored by the army but reported matter-of-factly by the FBI.[68]

In a memorandum for discussions with other Met Lab scientists, Szilard predicted that if A-bombs spread, U.S. cities "will be threatened by sudden annihilation within ten years. The outbreak of a preventive war will then hang over the world as a constant threat." He also fretted about other threats "for the large-scale extermination of human beings" from "biological methods," conceding that his latest speculation—city dispersal schemes—would be useless against this warfare. Only "moral inhibition" might work. And, he grieved, "Hiroshima shows that moral inhibitions can no longer be counted upon. . . ."[69]

Japan surrendered on Wednesday, August 15, a U.S. national holiday called V-J Day. Autos with their horns blaring paraded through cities and towns across the country, and the movie newsreels showed jitterbug dancing and a whirl of embraces. But Szilard appeared depressed that night when he visited Hartshorne's wood-frame house on East Fifty-seventh Street, near the university, and his spirits were little improved the next day, after the Smyth report's release. The press described Szilard's role in the early development of the bomb and pictured him along with Einstein, Fermi, and other well-known scientists. Good company, Szilard probably thought, but a sorry way to gain celebrity. Back at Hartshorne's for the family's traditional Friday afternoon tea, Szilard was still in a sour mood.

"Well," a young philosopher said to Szilard, referring to the Smyth report, "I hear you have become a great man."

"I've always been a great man," Szilard replied.[70]

Later that month, Szilard boarded an overnight train for Buffalo (tailed, as usual, by the FBI) and there met with his cousin, city planner Laszlo Segoe. Szilard wanted to know what dispersing urban centers—to defend against atomic attack—would cost: in land area, transportation, capital investment. Thanks to Segoe's advice, Szilard was able to spout elaborate statistics about city dispersal, although this line of pragmatic brainstorming seemed more fantastic with each telling.[71]

Japan formally signed documents of surrender on September 2, and to most Americans peace had come about because of the A-bomb. Without this weapon, they thought, the war would have dragged on for months. But recent scholarship suggests that Japan was about to surrender before the A-bombs were used and would have before the U.S. invasion planned for that fall.[72]

The United States was victorious and seemed invincible with its new weapon. Now the atom that had ended the war could also enrich the peace. Just after V-J Day a Scripps-Howard news service feature on the "Era of Atomic Energy" predicted that "no baseball game will be called off on account of rain" because atom-generated heat would dispel bad weather. Artificial "suns" would assure clear skies at resorts and heat "indoor farms," using uranium cores. "There is no reason why an internal combustion engine cannot be developed" using "tiny explosions of uranium 235."[73]

Such fantastic optimism was just what Groves and his engineers had hoped for during the weeks that followed Hiroshima and Nagasaki. But for the atomic scientists, who knew better and feared worse, the new technology they had created was still principally a weapon of mass destruction. Somehow, Szilard believed, something had to be done to stop the army from using it again. By the fall of 1945, the only solution he could imagine was to disarm the military and establish civilian control of the atom.

NOTES

1. Memorandum (March 6, 1944), Leo Szilard Papers, MSS 32, Mandeville Department of Special Collections, Central University Library, University of California, San Diego; Jane Wilson, ed., *All in Our Time: The Reminiscences of Twelve Nuclear Pioneers* (Chicago, 1975), pp. 122–123.

2. Spencer Weart and Gertrud Weiss Szilard, eds., *Leo Szilard: His Version of the Facts* (Cambridge, 1978), pp. 196–204.

3. Ibid., p. 181.

4. The meeting opened with Stimson addressing questions put to FDR in a March 3 memorandum by James F. Byrnes, his director of war mobilization, seeking results of the $2 billion secret program. Byrnes had admitted he knew little about it, and Stimson listed the eminent scientists engaged in the project, including four Nobel laureates. See Richard G. Hewlett and Oscar E. Anderson, *The New World, 1939/1946: A History of the United States Atomic Energy Commission* (Washington, D.C., 1972), p. 340.

5. Hewlett and Anderson, p. 340; cf. Alice K. Titus, "Collective Conscience: A Short Study of the Beginnings of the Scientists Movement," *Network*, p. 7; Henry L. Stimson, "The Decision to Use the Atomic Bomb," *Harper's Magazine*, February 1947, pp. 97–107.

6. Bohr to Roosevelt (March 24, 1945), Franklin D. Roosevelt Library, Hyde Park, New York.

7. Weart and Szilard, pp. 205–207.

8. Audio Disc Recording, "Leo Szilard: Inventor of the Atomic Bomb," George Garabedian Production, 1984, Leo Szilard Papers, 107; Weart and Szilard, p. 180; Hewlett and Anderson, pp. 203 and 681, n. 43; Conant to Bush (July 31, 1943), Manhattan Engineer District Records, National Archives, Washington, D.C., and Bush to Conant (September 22, 1944), Office of Scientific Research and Development Records, National Archives.

9. *U.S. News & World Report,* August 15, 1960, pp. 68–71.

10. Weart and Szilard, p. 182.

11. Richard Rhodes, *The Making of the Atomic Bomb* (New York, 1986), p. 636; Wilson, pp. 124–125; Weart and Szilard, pp. 182–183.

12. AEC Document 286, in Martin J. Sherwin, *A World Destroyed: The Atomic Bomb and the Grand Alliance* (New York, 1975), p. 169.

13. Hewlett and Anderson, p. 345.

14. Weart and Szilard, p. 184. Szilard later reversed his view. "I saw his point at the time, and in retrospect I see even more clearly that it would not have served any useful purpose to keep the bomb secret, waiting for the government to understand the problem and to formulate a policy; for the government will not formulate a policy unless it is under pressure to do so, and if the bomb had been kept secret there would have been no pressure for the government to do anything in this direction." Wilson, p. 127.

15. Weart and Szilard, p. 184; Wilson, p. 128.

16. Hewlett and Anderson, p. 355; James F. Byrnes, *All in One Lifetime* (New York, 1958), p. 284.

17. Hewlett and Anderson, p. 690, n. 38; Szilard's S-14 dictation (May 22, 1956) transcript p. 21, Leo Szilard Papers, 107; Walter Bartky interview with Alice K. Smith (July 8, 1957).

18. Groves diary (May 30, 1945), Manhattan Engineer District Records, 77, National Archives.

19. Audio Disc Recording, "Leo Szilard," Side D, Leo Szilard Papers, 107; Weart and Szilard, p. 185; Wilson, pp. 128–129.

20. Weart and Szilard, p. 185.

21. Hewlett and Anderson, p. 356; "Notes of the Interim Committee Meeting, May 31, 1945," Sherwin, Appendix L, pp. 295ff.

22. Sherwin, Appendix, pp. 295–304; Byrnes, p. 301. As the meeting's secretary recorded: "Mr. Byrnes expressed the view, which was generally agreed to by all present, that the most desirable program would be to push ahead as fast as possible in production and research to make certain that we stay ahead and at the same time make every effort to better our political relations with Russia."

23. This is based on notes of the meeting secretary and is not a direct quote from Groves.

24. Alice K. Smith, *A Peril and a Hope* (Cambridge, 1970), p. 41.

25. Szilard to Norman Hilberry (June 6, 1945), Leo Szilard Papers.

26. Herbert Feis, *The Atomic Bomb and the End of World War II* (Princeton, 1966), p. 50 n; Smith, p. 42. Other members of the Franck Committee were Thorfin R. Hogness, Donald Hughes, C. J. Nickson, Eugene Rabinowitch, Glenn T. Seaborg, and Met Lab director Joyce Stearns.

27. Feis, *The Atomic Bomb*, p. 51.

28. Compton to Nichols (June 4, 1945), MUC-AC-1306/7, Manhattan Engineer District Records, 201, Szilard, National Archives.

29. Ibid.

30. Barton J. Bernstein, in the introduction to *Toward a Livable World*, eds., Helen Hawkins, Allen Greb and Gertrud Weiss Szilard, (Cambridge, 1987); Stimson, "The Decision," pp. 97–107; Edward Teller, "Seven Hours of Reminiscences," *Los Alamos Sciences*, Winter/Spring 1983, p. 191; Sherwin, Appendix M.

31. Groves to Compton (June 29, 1945), Manhattan Engineer District Records, 201, Szilard, National Archives.

32. Groves to Cherwell (July 4, 1945), Frederick Alexander Lindemann (Cherwell) Papers, D. 35 and 49.3, Nuffield College, Oxford.

33. Wilson, p. 130.

34. Szilard to Waldo Cohen (July 4, 1945), Leo Szilard Papers.

35. Teller, p. 191.

36. Teller claims he dated the letter July 2 but actually wrote it days later. A more likely explanation is that he knew about the petition in advance and drafted his reply on the second, even before receiving a copy. Manhattan Engineer District Records, 201, Szilard, National Archives.

37. Teller to Szilard (July 2, 1945); Weart and Szilard, pp. 208–209.

38. Teller, p. 191.

39. Ralph E. Lapp interview (April 2, 1987); Weart and Szilard, pp. 212–213. See also Edward Creutz to Szilard (July 13, 1945), Manhattan Engineer District Records, 201, E. Creutz, National Archives.

40. Lieutenant Parish to Groves (July 9), with a copy of Szilard's July 4 letter to Teller, and Teller's reply, Manhattan Engineer District Records, National Archives; Ralph E. Lapp interview (April 2, 1987).

41. Weart and Szilard, p. 213.

42. The results of Daniels's poll, in votes and percentage, are as follows:

(1) Use the weapons in the manner that is from the military point of view most effective in bringing about prompt Japanese surrender at minimum human cost to our armed forces. (23, 15%)

(2) Give a military demonstration in Japan, to be followed by a renewed opportunity for surrender before full use of the weapons is employed. (69, 46%)

(3) Give an experimental demonstration in this country, with representatives of Japan present; followed by a new opportunity for surrender before full use of the weapons is employed. (39, 26%)

(4) Withhold military use of the weapons, but make public experimental demonstration of their effectiveness. (16, 11%)

(5) Maintain as secret as possible all developments of our new weapons, and refrain from using them in this war. (3, 2%)

DCN-55442, p. 9, Manhattan Engineer District Records, National Archives. See also Young to Szilard (January 31, 1961), Leo Szilard Papers.

43. Wilson, p. 130.

44. Szilard dictation (May 22, 1956), Leo Szilard Papers, 100; Claude C. Pierce, Jr. to Groves (November 26, 1947); Papers of Leslie R. Groves, Manhattan Engineer District Records, 200, entry 2, correspondence 1941–70, box 7, folder "P," National Archives. My thanks to Stanley Goldberg for this source.

45. Weart and Szilard, pp. 211–212.

46. Creutz to Szilard (July 13, 1945), and Szilard to Creutz (July 10, 1945), Manhattan Engineer District Records, 201, E. Creutz, National Archives.

47. Szilard to Compton, NDN-55430, Manhattan Engineer District Records, National Archives.

48. Compton to Nichols (July 24, 1945), Manhattan Engineer District Records, National Archives. For all versions of the petition, see Record Group 77, Harrison-Bundy Files, Box 153, Folder 76.

49. Groves directive, Manhattan Engineer District Records, 5E, National Archives.

50. Fletcher Knebel to Szilard (October 25, 1961), Leo Szilard Papers; Knebel and Bailey, Look, August 13, 1960, pp. 19–23; Wilson, p. 132, n. 57.

51. FBI Secret Report, p. 007, Leo Szilard Papers; Creutz to the author (October 22, 1986); George Weil interview (April 7, 1983).

52. Harry S. Truman, Year of Decisions (Garden City, 1955), p. 390ff.

53. FBI Secret Report, Leo Szilard Papers.

54. By the year's end, more than 130,000 had died, and latent effects claimed another 70,000 by 1950.

55. Jamie Sayen, Einstein in America (New York, 1985), pp. 151, 316, from an interview with Helen Dukas (November 9, 1977); Ralph E. Lapp, "The Einstein Letter That Started It All," New York Times Magazine, August 2, 1964, p. 54; R. W. Clark, Einstein: The Life and Times (New York, 1972), p. 708.

56. Leslie R. Groves, Now It Can Be Told (New York, 1962), pp. 333–336; Farm Hall Transcripts, Manhattan Engineer District Records, RG 77, box 163, National Archives.

57. Transcript for "The Mike Wallace Interview," February 27, 1961, Leo Szilard Papers, 40/22.

58. Leigh Fenly, "The Agony of the Bomb, and Ecstasy of Life with Leo Szilard," San Diego Union, November 19, 1978, pp. D-1, D-8.

59. (Copy in Leo Szilard Papers, original in Egon Weiss Papers, Cornwall-on-Hudson, New York.) Ironically, a War Department certificate dated August 6 and signed by Stimson soon came to Szilard. It read: "This is to Certify that Leo Szilard, University of Chicago, has participated in work essential to the production of the Atomic Bomb, thereby contributing to the successful conclusion of World War II. This certificate is awarded in appreciation of effective service."

60. Fenly, p. D-8.

61. Robert M. Hutchins, oral-history interview, November 21, 1967, p. 81, Columbia Oral History Research Office; Szilard to Hutchins, August 8, 1945, Leo Szilard Papers.

62. Szilard's May 22, 1956, dictation, transcript, p. 26, Leo Szilard Papers.

63. On August 13, Szilard drafted another letter to the White House urging President Truman to halt further atomic bombing, Leo Szilard Papers.

64. Hartshorne to the author (January 10, 1986); Hartshorne interview, April 10, 1986; Szilard's May 22, 1956, dictation, p. 26, Leo Szilard Papers, 107.

65. Langsdorf 1983 Questionnaire to L. Badesh, IGCC #1, p. 36. Martyl interview (Weiss and Patton), Leo Szilard Biography Project.

66. For details on Szilard's efforts to release the petition, see Capt. James S. Murray to Szilard (August 27 and 28, 1945), Leo Szilard Papers; Szilard to the editors of *Science* (August 18, 1945); Szilard to Hutchins (August 28, 1945), Leo Szilard Papers; Wilson, p. 133; Files on the petition are in Leo Szilard Papers, 40/15, 73/15, 73/16, and 89/6.

In rejecting Szilard's request, the army ruled that "[E]very paragraph . . . either contains some information or implies 'inside' information . . . which implies that internal dissention [*sic*] and fundamental differences in point of view disrupted the development and fruition of the District's work— an implication which you as well as I know is not founded on sober fact and which, if released at this time, might well cause 'injury to the interest or prestige of the nation or governmental activity.'" Murray to Szilard (August 27, 1945), Leo Szilard Papers. For Szilard's response to this ruling, see Szilard to Hutchins (August 28, 1945), Leo Szilard Papers and Manhattan Engineer District Records, 201, Szilard, National Archives.

67. Szilard to Hutchins (August 29, 1945), Leo Szilard Papers; Wilson, p. 133, n. 60.

68. FBI Secret Report, p. 12, Leo Szilard Papers.

69. Memorandum, First Version, Rough Draft (August 14, 1945) with September 13 and 17 revisions, Leo Szilard Papers; See also Lapp, "The Einstein Letter," p. 115.

70. FBI Secret Report, pp. 13, 53, and 241, Leo Szilard Papers; Hartshorne to the author (January 10, 1986).

71. FBI Report, December 23, 1946, p. 246, Leo Szilard Papers.

72. See, for example, papers prepared for "Round Table: Hiroshima and the End of World War II," The Society for Historians of American Foreign Relations, Seventeenth Annual Conference, June 19, 1991, Washington, D.C.

73. David Dietz, "Era of Atomic Energy: Man's Control of Weather Seen Possible in Future," *New York World Telegram*, Scripps-Howard, August 17, 1945, Leo Szilard Papers; Gertrud Weiss Szilard Scrapbook, No. 1, p. 48, Leo Szilard Papers.

RACING

TO THE

FINISH

Stanley Goldberg

I N 1995, THE YEAR WHICH MARKED A HALF-CENTURY since the
end of World War II, it was not surprising that there were many memorial ceremonies commemorating events of 1945 such as the meeting of Soviet and American forces at the Elbe, the end of the war in Europe, the deaths of Mussolini, of
Hitler, and of Eva Braun, the sinking of the *Indianapolis*, the battles for Iwo Jima
and Okinawa, and the fire-bombing of Tokyo. But the strongest interest of this
anniversary was undoubtedly focused on the atomic bombings of Hiroshima and
Nagasaki and the sudden ending of the war in the Pacific.

There has also been a revival of debate on issues surrounding the end of the
war. Much of this disputation is a byproduct of the controversy generated by the
Smithsonian's aborted exhibit, "The Last Act: The Atomic Bomb and the End of
World War II," which was to feature the fuselage of the B-29 which delivered the
atomic bomb that demolished Hiroshima.[1]

A number of these disputes place us in the realm of counterfactuals; they invite
us to speculate on events that never happened. Speculation on some of these questions has gone on ever since the end of World War II. For example: "If the atomic
bomb had not been used would the Japanese have surrendered without an Allied
invasion of their home islands?"[2] Some began before the end of the war: "If there
is an invasion, how many American and/or Japanese deaths will result?"[3] I will not
consider such questions here. I will argue that, invasion or not, General Leslie R.
Groves and his War Department superiors took all steps possible to ensure that the
atomic bomb played a role in bringing the war to an end.[4] Indeed, Groves and
those from whom he took orders were fearful that the war would end *before* the
atomic bomb was used.

Other motivations for using the bomb at the end of the war, it has been argued,
were to put the Russians on notice with regard to post-war adventurism and to end
the war before the Russians could get a firm foothold in the Pacific
theater. There is ample evidence that such a motivation played a role in the decision
to use the bomb. However, in this essay I will not address the relative strength of
these motivations. Instead, I will discuss first, the manner in which Groves pushed
to complete construction of the project's major industrial and laboratory facilities;

how he pressured the management of these installations to produce enough fission-able material as quickly as possible to insure that atomic bombs were ready for use; and how he then pressed his representatives on the island of Tinian to make haste to send the atomic bomb–carrying B-29s on their way to Hiroshima and Nagasaki.

One can identify two major streams in the historiography of the decision to drop the atomic bomb on Japan. On the one hand, the Feisians, after their spiritual leader Herbert Feis (*Japan Subdued*, 1961), argue and attempt to build an evidential base for the proposition that the major reason the bomb was used was to end the war as quickly as possible. The decision was motivated, the argument goes, to put an end to the bloodshed—to save lives. The second historiographic stream may be labeled the Alperovitzian, after Gar Alperovitz (*Atomic Diplomacy*, 1965). Alperovitz argues that the atomic bomb was used in order to end the war quickly to minimize Soviet involvement in the defeat of Japan, and to send a clear warning to the Russians concerning their post-war behavior and attitudes.

One of the curious features of the argument over why the atomic bomb was used on Japan has been that both historiographic camps have treated the question as if one had to choose between the two alternatives. The truth of the matter is that there is no reason why one could not have believed that the use of the bomb would result in a net saving of lives *and* that it would also serve the purpose of caging Soviet post-war ambitions. In fact, there were those who believed just that.[5]

However, there is convincing evidence that both of these motivations, while apparent, are far less important than three others: momentum (no one ever said "stop, it is not needed"); protection of the reputations of the civilian and military leadership of the project; and the personal ambitions of some, especially of General Groves.[6] These three factors were at play, almost from the beginning—the spring of 1941—when Vannevar Bush, who was essentially President Franklin D. Roosevelt's scientific advisor, was struggling with the question of whether or not to initiate an all-out, crash program to try to build an atomic bomb. Here I will concentrate on the latter two factors.

AS HAS BEEN ARGUED ELSEWHERE, Bush had to make a decision about uranium research.[7] It was becoming increasingly expansive and expensive. His budget, while large, had many demands on it. And he was being pressured by colleagues such as James B. Conant, who kept reminding him that they must only spend money on those projects which were likely to affect the outcome of "the upcoming conflict." Conant, among others, was skeptical that a practical uranium weapon could be developed over the short term. Others believed that the concept was nothing short of science fiction. And yet, persistent and seemingly creditable rumors filtered out of Germany that they were hard at work on building a uranium bomb and that success was assured. Bush decided that in spite of the uncertainties, and in spite of the slow progress to date, the United States had to make every effort to build its own atomic bomb. And so in the face of a serious lack of consensus among his advisors and colleagues, Bush manipulated an appearance of consensus and on October 9, 1941, recommended to the president that the project go forward with an all-out effort. It was estimated that the project would require $133 million. Bush and Roosevelt also decided to turn the project's administration over to the Army Corps of Engineers chiefly so that spending for the project could be easily buried in the now massive Corps budget. It was a way of keeping the existence of the project secret, even from Congress.[8]

Before the war was over, the cost was not $133 million, but almost twenty times that amount—$2 billion.[9] And Congress never knew. They knew something was going on, but every time serious efforts were made to find out, those efforts were thwarted either by aggressive demands from the secretary of war or by assuring House and Senate leadership that if they cooperated in not seeking justifications, all would be explained at war's end.[10] But as the costs mounted and the mystery deepened, Bush, Conant, Secretary of War Henry L. Stimson and Undersecretary of War Robert Patterson became increasingly nervous. Several times late in the war, Stimson or Patterson would preface notes to one another concerning Manhattan Project business with jokes about how, if the project was not successful, they would spend the rest of their lives testifying before Congress.[11] Time and time again, when the War Manpower Commission or War Production Board challenged the fact that the Manhattan Project had the very highest priorities, Stimson or Patterson would solemnly insist that the project was the most important of the war, more important than the bomber program, than bullets, than high-octane gasoline, than landing craft. All other programs had to give way, they insisted, in the struggle for scarce material and human resources.[12]

The effects of this on other war projects are not hard to discover. In mid-1944, the Manhattan Project ordered several thousand tons of fully fluorinated hydrocarbons (for use at Oak Ridge) from a New Jersey refinery. The requisition came with the highest possible priority (AAA) and was marked "Rush" and "Urgent." The manager of the refinery was apparently quite unnerved by this request. He called the Manhattan Project office from which the requisition had been sent. Fortunately there is a transcript of the conversation he had with the officer in charge which went something like this:

> Manager: *Who authorized you people to have AAA priority?*
> Major: *(quite used to this question) The President of the United States. I can send you a copy of his letter if you like.*
> Manager: *No, that is not necessary. You realize of course that if we honor this requisition, we will have to stop the manufacture of high octane airplane fuel for two weeks.*
> Major: *I am not surprised, but if you look at the priority list for ranking AAA requests you will see that the Manhattan Project is above high octane gasoline.*
> Manager: *Yes, I saw that. It is above everything. What is the Manhattan Project?*
> Major: *You don't have to know that.*
> Manager: *Just tell me one thing. Is it part of the war?*[13]

This type of exchange took place many times during the war at all levels of government and industry. One can barely imagine what the response of Congress and the public would have been at the end of the war had the atomic bomb not been used, that is, had it not been "part of the war." In fact, Undersecretary of War Patterson was so worried about that possibility that in January 1945 he sent a trusted civilian consultant, Jack Madigan, to examine the books of all major Manhattan Project installations.[14] According to General Groves, Madigan gave a harried and rushed Patterson an initial ten-second summary of his findings: "If the project succeeds there won't be any investigation. If it doesn't they won't investigate anything else."[15]

On March 3, 1945, as he was about to leave his post as head of the War Mobilization Board, James Byrnes sent a memo to President Roosevelt about the Manhattan Project. A troubled Byrnes told Roosevelt that although he did not know the project's purpose, Roosevelt should know that the project had spent upwards of two billion dollars with no end in sight. He warned Roosevelt that should there be no "product" before the war ended, the political consequences for Roosevelt and the Democratic party would be serious. His recommendation that an independent committee of scientists assess the project was vetoed by Stimson.[16]

THOUGH BUSH OFFICIALLY had turned the project over to the Army Corps of Engineers in June 1942, nothing much happened over the summer. The Corps of Engineers had appointed Colonel James Marshall to head the project. A solid administrator, Marshall was deliberate and not prone to moving quickly. He was also somewhat deferential to civilian authority. For example, when the War Production Board gave the Manhattan Project a AA-3 rating, which was high, but not nearly high enough to avoid long delays in obtaining crucial raw materials and machine tools, Marshall was not able to negotiate a reconsideration. And all summer long, he agonized over accepting the recommendation of the Corps real estate section, which stated that the best project location was a fifty-seven-square-mile reservation along the Clinch River in sparsely populated eastern Tennessee. It met all the requirements: remoteness, lots of water and plenty of power from nearby TVA. Finally in desperation and concern Bush demanded that the Army appoint someone else. That someone proved to be Colonel Leslie R. Groves, who had a reputation for efficiency in coordinating large projects done on time, but who also had a reputation for bravura, lack of tact, and lack of sensitivity.[17]

Groves was not pleased with the appointment. He had ambitions to be the General Patton of the Corps and had hoped for a command of a combat engineering regiment in the upcoming Africa campaign. However, when informed of his appointment to the Manhattan Project, he immediately realized that it was fait accompli and struggled no more.[18]

His first encounter with Vannevar Bush on September 17, 1942, was an unfortunate one. Groves in his usual bluff and sharp style made such a bad impression that after his departure, Bush shot a memo off to James Conant and Harvey Bundy fearing he said "that we are in the soup." He then called on Groves's superior, General Wilhelm Styer, and strongly suggested to Styer that Groves did not seem to be the right man for the job. What Bush feared most was that Groves's arrogance and lack of tact would alienate the scientists on whom the project was absolutely dependent. Styer assured Bush that he understood Bush's concerns but that having had a lot of experience with Groves, he felt confident that Groves would work out just fine.[19]

Within three days several things happened to reassure Bush. Immediately after leaving Bush's office, Groves had walked, unannounced, into the office of Donald Nelson, head of the War Production Board. He informed Nelson that he, Groves, was now head of the Manhattan Project and demanded immediate authorization to use AAA priority at his own discretion. Nelson laughed and started to walk away, at which point Groves said that he had been put in the unpleasant position of having to tell the president that his chief of war production did not agree with the president's assessment that the Manhattan Project was the most important single program in the war effort. Nelson stopped laughing. By 9:00 the next

morning, the letter which Groves had dictated to Nelson in Nelson's name, authorizing AAA priority for the Manhattan Project at Groves's discretion, was signed
and on Groves's desk.[20]

Three days later, there was a meeting to discuss the status of the project and
to introduce Groves to his superiors. Attending were the secretary of war, the
undersecretary of war, Chief of Staff James Conant, Vannevar Bush, and General
Brehon Somervell, commander of the umbrella organization which included the
Corps of Engineers. About thirty minutes into the meeting, to the astonishment
of all assembled, Groves suddenly stood up and announced that if no one had anything more important to say, he had to leave to catch a train to Tennessee to
inspect the recommended parcel of land along the Clinch River. Within twenty-
four hours, he had ordered the real estate section of the Corps of Engineers to
begin eminent domain proceedings.[21]

Groves's orders were to build the required factories and to stand in readiness
to provide the scientists with whatever they needed. But, whenever Groves was
asked, or when he thought it was important that a protagonist know what his
orders were, his rendering of them was "to build the atomic bomb in the shortest
time possible and thereby end the war."[22] In other words, if, by being ordered to
run this project he had gotten dumped off the fast track, he was going to make his
own fast track. Not only did Groves know how to get things done, he had immediately perceived what had escaped most of the leadership of the project. If this
effort was to succeed it would require an industrial plant on a scale which was
unprecedented. While Groves recognized that the contributions of the scientists
would be crucial he also realized that this was not, overall, a scientific project.
It was a far-flung, enormous industrial enterprise. To Groves, the scientists were
merely one cog in the machine; once they produced what was required of them,
they were expendable. Groves may not have known as much physics as the
scientists who were working for him, but he was a genius at running a large
organization. That genius can be summarized as "charisma by terror."

Groves began by convincing E. I. du Pont de Nemours and Company to agree
to build a semi-works—a step up from a pilot plant—at Oak Ridge, to chemically
separate plutonium from uranium. It was not a job that du Pont wanted. They had
no experience in the field, they were skeptical of the project's feasibility, and they
feared the physical operating hazards.[23] But Groves, speaking directly to the president of the company, Walter S. Carpenter, would not take no for an answer. "I...
made it clear . . . that the government considered the project to be of the utmost
national urgency and that this opinion was shared by President Roosevelt, Secretary Stimson and General Marshall. . . . He suddenly asked if I personally agreed.
Unhesitatingly, I told him that I did, and without any reservation." A letter of
understanding was signed on October 3.[24]

Soon after being appointed, Groves embarked on a series of visits to the laboratories at Columbia University, the University of Chicago, and the University of
California at Berkeley. Many of the scientists, especially a group at Chicago, were
infuriated by Groves's hostility toward abstract science and his defensiveness concerning his own knowledge. "I do know calculus," he would tell them, with some
hauteur. In fact, throughout the war, Groves had excellent tutoring from Conant
and Richard C. Tolman, dean of the graduate school at the California Institute of
Technology and a theoretical physicist. Groves was completely in command of the
project's physical principles.

He exasperated the Chicago scientists by making it clear that security and compartmentalization of knowledge would be rigidly enforced. Some of the scientists were convinced that they could manage the manufacturing phases of the project far more competently and efficiently than traditional industries. When they learned that du Pont would be given responsibility for building the reactors and plutonium separation facilities (eventually located at Hanford, Washington), the dismayed scientists complained that no industrial establishment had the necessary understanding of the science. They told Groves that they could do the job faster and better; they would only require a cadre of 50 to 100 junior engineers working under their direction.[25] This miscalculation can be better grasped if one considers that, during the peak of the Manhattan Project, in the summer of 1944, some 160,000 people were at work at more than 25 labs. The plutonium plant at Hanford, Washington, required the skills of 50,000 workers over the course of its construction—the Hanford construction camp was the largest ever assembled. For his part, Groves was astounded at the scientists' utter lack of understanding of the difference between bench-top and industrial processes.

This was a very large project. Ultimately, there were installations all across the United States and Canada and in all, before the end of the war, over half-a-million people cycled through as employees of one kind or another.[26] There were three major installations: Hanford Reservation, occupying 570 square miles in the south-central desert of Washington State, The 57-square-mile site at Oak Ridge, Tennessee, and Los Alamos, New Mexico. Groves's system of compartmentalization of information which the scientists despised and ridiculed was so effective on an industrial scale that no one in Congress ever suspected that the mysterious large operation in Washington State had anything at all to do with the other mysterious operation in eastern Tennessee. And, during the war, unlike the Soviets, no one in Congress ever knew of the existence of Los Alamos.

Of all the scientists, Leo Szilard's relationship with Groves was the most difficult. Groves's first direct encounter with Szilard took place at the Metallurgical Laboratory (Met Lab) in Chicago in October 1941. Szilard had played a crucial role initiating the Manhattan Project when he convinced in 1939 Albert Einstein to write to Franklin Roosevelt. Szilard's intent was to alert the highest levels of the U.S. government to the concern of the scientific community's that Nazi Germany had the potential capability of developing atomic weapons. According to Szilard's biographer, William Lanouette, "Einstein said later that he 'really only acted as a mailbox' for Szilard." In popular history his famous equation $E=MC^2$ and his letter to President Roosevelt are credited with starting the American effort to build atomic weapons. [27] Szilard, who must have perceived that control of the project was being lost to the army, was querulous and hostile. In a meeting with key Met Lab scientists, he publicly corrected Groves's technical errors of commission and omission, and when Groves made it clear that information exchange among scientists would be stringently controlled because of security risks, Szilard rose to announce to the assembly that, "You see, I told you we could not work with these people."

Groves perceived that Szilard represented a disruptive influence. Before he left Chicago, he told Met Lab Project Leader, Arthur Compton, that he would have to get rid of Szilard. Several days later, Compton, a man clearly caught in the middle, told Groves that removing the popular Szilard would lead to a revolt and indicated that "the situation had been stabilized." Meanwhile, Szilard continued peppering Compton, Vannevar Bush, James Conant, and anyone else who would listen, with diatribes against Groves's policy of compartmentalization.

Groves's next move was to draft a memo in the name of the Secretary of War Henry L. Stimson for the attorney general, directing that Szilard be interned for the duration of the war as a potentially dangerous alien. (Szilard had emigrated to America as a naturalized German citizen.) Secretary of War Stimson refused to send such a memo, and for the rest of the war Groves and Szilard parried and thrust at each other like two scorpions in a bottle. Groves had Szilard under constant surveillance and Szilard, knowing this, did everything he could to harass Groves. While Groves often said that what concerned him was his conviction that Szilard would betray the United States, what was really at issue was Groves's perception that Szilard's influence would distract scientists and engineers and slow the project down. It is instructive to contrast Groves's treatment of Szilard with his treatment of physicist J. Robert Oppenheimer.

The only bright spot in his long orientation trip had been his meetings with J. Robert Oppenheimer. They met briefly in Berkeley, and in Oppenheimer Groves found the only project leader who agreed with him that a separate laboratory would be needed to design and fabricate the "product" into a bomb. Oppenheimer joined Groves in Chicago on October 17 for the train ride back to New York, and he met with Groves two days later when Groves announced that such a laboratory would be created.

Compton had already brought Oppenheimer into the project at a relatively high level. But on their first meeting, Groves must have seen something in Oppenheimer that almost everyone who knew Oppenheimer well missed. All of the scientific leadership and consultants to the project, including Ernest Lawrence, Compton, Harold Urey, and I. I. Rabi, objected to the idea of appointing Oppenheimer to a position of administrative leadership at Los Alamos. They said Oppenheimer was a theoretician and this was an experimental lab; that he had never administered an organization of any size and he showed no obvious talents for such a task; and that he did not possess, as did the directors of all the other Manhattan Engineer District (MED) research laboratories, a Nobel Prize.

Groves persisted on the grounds that there was no one else to do the job. He needed Oppenheimer; he wanted Oppenheimer. Groves requested that Army Intelligence, G-2, give Oppenheimer security clearance. The head of G-2 Western Command, Boris Pash, reported back to Groves that not only could he not clear Oppenheimer to direct the new laboratory, Oppenheimer should not be given clearance to work on any phase of the project. It was undoubtedly information that Groves already knew, but he asked for details. Pash pointed out that Oppenheimer's wife, his brother, and his sometime mistress were, or had been, members of the Communist Party and that Oppenheimer himself had contributed to every fellow travelers' organization up and down the West Coast. When Groves tried to brush all this aside on the grounds that Oppenheimer was the only person to run the laboratory, Pash parried: Under the rules, should he, Pash, clear Oppenheimer, he would be subject to court-martial. Groves then ordered Pash to clear Oppenheimer on Groves's authority.

Pash was so concerned that he had an assistant, who was present at the meeting with Groves, draft a memo for the files which states that at this point in the discussion Pash asked Groves why he was so sure that Oppenheimer would not give information in his possession to Soviet agents or to Americans sympathetic to the Soviet cause. Groves responded that, in the first place, he had no doubt that, in spite of his leftist sympathies, Oppenheimer was a loyal American. Second, Groves continued, he was counting on Oppenheimer's ambition. Oppenheimer, Groves told Pash, was very troubled by the fact that those of lesser light within the scientific community had garnered honors and awards that had eluded him. He saw the successful completion of this project as his route to immortality. When it was convenient, Leslie R. Groves could be a very understanding and forgiving person.

FROM THE BEGINNING, Leslie Groves was in a race, not so much to outdo the Germans, though that certainly was an early consideration, but a race to complete and use the atomic bomb before the war was over.

Initially, Groves was thoroughly discouraged at the state in which he found things. The scientists seemed nowhere near to the solutions of the myriad puzzles which had to be solved, but they also did not seem to have any concept of the scope of the project.[28] Undaunted, he made a series of momentous go-for-broke decisions. Rather than following usual industrial practice—moving stepwise from bench top to pilot plant to semi-works to full scale—the project would move from bench top to full scale in one leap. When it came to the question of separating the different kinds of uranium, it was not clear which of two different techniques would be effective. Groves decided, in agreement with Conant's advice, not to choose, but to pursue both at the same time, full force. He also decided to make an all-out effort to produce plutonium. These were extremely expensive decisions. Furthermore, against the advice of most of the leadership of the project, Groves announced plans to build a special laboratory (Los Alamos) to design and build the bomb. The upshot was that by December 1942, Groves had sommitted, for what had been assumed to be a $133 million project, more than $500 million, with no end in sight. Some of his civilian colleagues admitted to being spooked, but also recognized that by now they were trapped.[29]

One of many major crises occurred in the summer of 1944. By that time, the construction of the reactors and chemical separation plants at Hanford, designed to produce fissionable plutonium, were nearing completion. The cost of construction alone had exceeded $400 million. Now, physicists at Los Alamos, working with tiny amounts of plutonium produced in an experimental reactor at Oak Ridge, realized that it would not be possible to design a plutonium bomb in the same way that the uranium bomb had been designed.[30] Groves faced the prospect of having committed the country to investing almost half-a-billion dollars to produce a worthless product. Within a week, the entire program at Los Alamos had been reorganized, the size of the staff would be increased by a full order of magnitude. A frenzied and ultimately successful program was undertaken to design a plutonium bomb based on a radically new and hitherto untried set of operations.

From the moment Groves learned that there would have to be two different types of bombs, whenever anyone suggested that the use of the atomic bomb would end the war, Groves would reply, "Not until we drop two bombs on Japan." [31] The implication is clear. One bomb justified Oak Ridge, the second justified Hanford.

But there were other, much more specific speed-ups. In January 1945, it was thought that the plutonium bomb being designed at Los Alamos would require five kilograms (about 11 pounds) of plutonium. Groves wrote the civilian manager of the plutonium works at Hanford (du Pont was the prime contractor) that he expected to receive one 11-pound lot of plutonium on June 1 and a second lot on July 1. The first of these was clearly for the plutonium bomb which was tested in the New Mexico desert on July 16, 1945. The second was for what became the bomb that obliterated Nagasaki. The manager protested. Meeting Groves's schedule would be impossible, he said. Groves would not take no for an answer. In his reply he informed the manager that he recognized that to meet Groves's demand, a great deal of uranium metal would have to be wasted, but, Groves continued, he was willing to waste up to 75 tons of the precious metal if that is what it would take to produce the needed plutonium by the dates Groves had set. Needless to say, the plutonium was delivered on schedule.[32]

Meanwhile, the uranium separation plants at Oak Ridge were just beginning to produce results in January 1945. Progress was exceedingly slow and in the end, in mid-July 1945, Oak Ridge was scoured for every drop of fissionable uranium.[33] There was barely enough for one bomb and there would not be enough for another uranium bomb before January 1946. Scientists were so sure that the mechanisms for exploding the uranium bomb would work, that the test, if test it be called, was the bomb that eradicated Hiroshima.

The delivery of the atomic bombs to Japan was to be from the island of Tinian in the Marianas, which had been turned into one big runway for the Twentieth Air Force. A special camp was constructed on Tinian to accommodate the Manhattan Project personnel. In the meantime, the Twentieth Air Force had been given orders not to fire-bomb four cities which had been chosen as candidates to receive the first atomic bombs. The cities were Hiroshima, Kokura, Nagasaki, and Niigata. The chief criteria for selection were that the cities have an industrial center surrounded by civilian dwellings and that the cities be large enough so that the effects of the bomb would run out within the city limits.[34] The original schedule, drafted by Groves, called for the first bomb to be dropped "after about August 3" and the second and subsequent bombs to be dropped at about ten-day intervals— matching the rate at which Hanford was now producing plutonium.[35] But this schedule did not satisfy Groves. Initially, both a uranium bomb and a plutonium bomb had been shipped to Tinian in late July. On July 24, Groves began pressing, by cablegram, for the Los Alamos team on Tinian to speed up the delivery to Japan of the second bomb, originally scheduled for August 11.[36] Against their own better judgment, the scientists and engineers suspended the tests originally planned and loaded the second bomb in the early morning hours of August 9.

It is doubtful that the United States would ever have had to invade Japan. But the point is a moot one, at best, a matter of counterfactual speculation. What the evidence does suggest is that the United States was determined to use the atomic bomb on Japan before the Japanese were given the chance to surrender. Prior to August 9, the U.S. position was that unconditional surrender was the only acceptable basis on which Japan would be permitted to give up. After the bombing of Hiroshima and Nagasaki, it no longer seemed to be so important. The United States now allowed that the Japanese might keep their emperor.

Some of President Harry S. Truman's advisors, as well as General Groves and some in the War Department, were probably very concerned that the Japanese might try to surrender before they could use both kinds of atomic bombs. Only then could they permit the Japanese to give up. As Martin J. Sherwin has suggested, the implication is that rather than shortening the war, the existence of the atomic bomb program probably lengthened it.[37]

In September 1945, in response to a congratulatory note from a close colleague, Groves stated: "I had to do some good hard talking at times. One thing is certain— we will never have the greatest congressional investigation of all times." [38] He was absolutely right.

NOTES

1. Stanley Goldberg, "Smithsonian Suffers Legionnaires Disease," *Bulletin of the Atomic Scientists* 51 (May/June 1995).

2. For a discussion of this issue see J. Samuel Walker, "The Decision to Use the Bomb: A Historiographical Update," *Diplomatic History* 14 (Winter 1990); Goldberg, "Smithsonian Suffers Legionnaires Disease."

3. For the U.S. Army's estimates in the spring and summer of 1945 see Martin J. Sherwin, *A World Destroyed: Hiroshima and the Origins of the Arms Race*, 2nd ed. (New York, 1985), app. U.

4. For a fuller, more detailed account of some of the issues discussed in this essay see, Stanley Goldberg, "General Groves and the Atomic West: The Making and the Meaning of Hanford," in Bruce Hevly and John Findlay, eds., *The Atomic West* (forthcoming).

5. On the use of the bomb to end the war quickly and save lives see Herbert Feis, *Japan Subdued: The Atomic Bomb and the End of the War in the Pacific* (Princeton, 1961). On the use of the bomb to warn the Soviets see Gar Alperovitz, *Atomic Diplomacy: Hiroshima and Potsdam: The Uses of the Atomic Bomb and the American Confrontation with Soviet Power*, 2nd ed. (1965; New York, 1985). Alperovitz has recently supplemented the argument with new evidence. See idem, "Why the United States Dropped the Bomb," *Technology Review* 93 (Aug./Sept. 1990) and Gar Alperovitz, *The Decision to Use the Atomic Bomb and the Architecture of an American Myth* (New York, 1996). It should be pointed out that not all historians are members of the Feisian or Alperovitz camp. For many years, historians Barton Bernstein and Martin J. Sherwin, for example, have advocated a more eclectic view. See Barton Bernstein, "The Atomic Bomb and American Foreign Policy, 1941–1945: An Historiographical Controversy," *Peace and Change* 2 (Spring 1974).

6. The relative strength of the various motivations is considered in Goldberg, *Fighting to Build the Bomb*.

7. Stanley Goldberg, "Creating a Climate of Opinion: Vannevar Bush and the Decision to Build the Bomb," *Isis* 83 (1992).

8. Stanley Goldberg, "Groves Takes the Reins," *Bulletin of the Atomic Scientists* 48 (December 1992).

9. Richard Hewlett and Oscar Anderson, *The New World 1939/1946: A History of the United States Atomic Energy Commission* (University Park, Pa., 1962), 1:723.

10. Goldberg, "General Groves and the Atomic West."

11. Ibid.

12. See memos between Assistant Secretary of Defense Patterson and Groves; Patterson and the chairman of the War Production Board, Donald Nelson; and Patterson and the chairman of the War Mobilization Commission, Paul V. McNutt, in folders 51 and 80, Harrison-Bundy Files, Entry 2, Papers of the Manhattan Engineer District, RG 77, National Archives and Record Administration, Washington, D.C.

13. "201 Groves, L. R. Lt. Gen. Telephone Messages," folder 86, Decimal Files, 1942–1948, Entry 5, Manhattan Engineer District, RG 77, National Archives.

14. Patterson to Madigan, folder 51, Harrison-Bundy Files, National Archives.

15. Leslie R. Groves, *Now it Can Be Told: The Story of the Manhattan Project* (New York, 1962), p. 360.

16. Byrnes to Roosevelt (Mar. 3, 1945), folder 8, Harrison-Bundy Files; Groves Memo to file (Apr. 7, 1945), tab. L, folder 20, General Groves's Secret Files, Entry 1, Manhattan Engineer District, RG 77, National Archives. For Stimson's reaction to the memo, see his own account of his discussion of the matter with Roosevelt in Henry L. Stimson and McGeorge Bundy, *On Active Service in Peace and War* (New York, 1971), pp. 615–16.

17. Goldberg, "Creating a Climate of Opinion"; idem, "Groves Takes the Reins."

18. Groves, p. 5.

19. Goldberg, "Groves Takes the Reins."

20. Nelson to Groves (Sept. 19, 1942), folder 221.3—General Styer's Manhattan Engineer District File, box 3451, The Army Adjutant General Classified Decimal File, 1946–1947, RG 407, National Archives. For Groves's account of his encounter (the first of many) with Nelson, see Groves, pp. 22–23. Cf. Stephane Groueff, *Manhattan Project: The Untold Story of the Making of the Atomic Bomb* (Boston, 1967), pp. 24–25. It should be noted that Groves's account is at odds with the account given by K. D. Nichols in "The Chronology of District X," a diary which Marshall and his second in command, Lt. Col. Kenneth Nichols, kept during the early days of the Manhattan Project. According to that account, entry for September 17: "I prepared a draft of a letter for Col. Groves which is to be signed, addressed to Donald Nelson, and signed by Gen. [George C.] Marshall. This procedure was subsequently modified to be a letter from Nelson to Col. Groves." The entry for September 19 notes that "Groves presented a brief letter on the subject of AAA priorities which Gen. Somervell was to get signed by Donald Nelson." "Miscellaneous," folder 6, Subseries II, "The Chronology of District X," General Groves Top Secret Files. Cf. K. D. Nichols, *The Road To Trinity: A Personal Account of How America's Nuclear Policies Were Made* (New York, 1987), pp. 49–50.

21. Groueff, p. 15–16. See especially the footnote on p. 15.

22. See, for example, the notes of British physicist Mark Oliphant taken at a meeting on September 13, 1943, in Groves's Office, "Notes on Conversations with Americans in Washington at the New War Department, On Monday September 13, 1943," AB 1/376, Public Records Office, London.

23. Groves, p. 46.

24. Ibid. The story is confirmed by Walter S. Carpenter. See, for example, "du Pont Stockholders Bulletin," Wilmington, Delaware, August 13, 1945.

25. Groves, pp. 448–49. See also, Eugene Wigner's angry memo to Arthur Compton, denouncing the du Pont agreement (Aug. 13, 1943), Manhattan Engineer District, Decimal File 080, National Archives.

26. Groves, p. 414.

27. William Lanouette, *Genius In the Shadows* (New York, 1992), p. 206.

28. Groueff, p. 7ff.

29. Conant to Groves (Dec. 9, 1942), folder 86, S-1, Bush-Conant Files, S-1, RG 227, National Archives. Conant was shocked to realize that in but two months, Groves had already committed the project to expenditures amounting to $500 million. A year earlier, the projected cost for the whole project was $133 million.

30. Lillian Hoddeson et al., *Critical Assembly: A Technical History of Los Alamos during the Oppenheimer Years, 1943–1945* (New York, 1993), p. 228ff.

31. See, for example, Groves, p. 228.

32. See the exchanges between Groves and Roger Williams, Manager of du Pont's Manhattan Project operations, January–March 1945, folder 5, General Groves Secret Files. Cf. Goldberg, "General Groves and the Atomic West."

33. Vincent C. Jones, *Manhattan: The Army and the Atomic Bomb* (Washington, D.C.: Center of Military History, United States Army, 1985), p. 144ff.

34. Goldberg, "General Groves and the Atomic West."

35. Handy to Marshall (July 24 1945), folder 64, Harrison-Bundy Files, Manhattan Engineer District, RG 77, National Archives.

36. "Minutes of the Meetings of the Special Project Technical Committee [on Tinian]," July 24 and 28, 1 Aug. 1945, Envelope A, Tinian Files, Entry 3, ibid. Cf. Derry to Kirkpatrick and Farrell, Envelope I, Tinian Files, ibid.

37. Author's communication with Martin J. Sherwin, January 6, 1995.

38. Groves to Styer (Oct. 12, 1945), folder "Stu-Sz," Correspondence 1940-1970, Entry 2, Papers of Leslie R. Groves, RG 200, National Archives.

A Post-war Myth: 500,000 U.S. Lives Saved

Barton J. Bernstein

"I wanted to save a half million boys on our side. . . .
I never lost any sleep over my decision." [1]
Harry S. Truman, 1959

MORE THAN FIVE DECADES after the dropping of atomic bombs on Hiroshima and Nagasaki, many question whether these bombings were necessary, why the two terrible weapons were used, and whether opportunities were missed to end the war without them. Such questioners tend to regard with skepticism President Truman's post-war claims, now embedded in popular lore, that the atomic bombs saved a half million American lives. [2] Actually, there is no evidence that any top military planner or major American policymaker ever believed between May 1945 and Hiroshima that an invasion would cost that many lives. Indeed, there is solid evidence, in declassified files in Washington, that military planners seven weeks before Hiroshima had placed the number at 46,000 and sometimes as low as about 20,000 American lives.

The claim of a half million American lives was a post-war creation. Shortly after the Nagasaki bombing, Winston Churchill declared that the atomic bombings had saved well over 1,200,000 Allied lives, including about a million American lives. General Leslie Groves, commanding general of the wartime atomic bomb project who was proud of the bombings of Hiroshima and Nagasaki, suggested that Churchill's number was "a little high" and seemed to wish for an estimate of slightly under a million. [3] During Truman's years in the White House, the president usually placed the number at about a quarter of a million lives, and occasionally at only 200,000. [4] But after leaving the White House, he began raising this number. His memoir writers stated in their first draft, "half a million [U.S. and Allied] casualties with at least 300,000 dead." But by the time Truman's book came out in 1955, they had increased the number to "half a million American lives" saved and cited General George C. Marshall, wartime army chief of staff, as having given that estimate to Truman shortly before Hiroshima. That is the number that Truman often used publicly in his post-presidential years.[5]

At first glance, such claims may seem plausible—especially to a generation that recalls the brutal war and to the next two generations of Americans who have often heard that their fathers, grandfathers, or uncles might well have died in the planned U.S. invasions of Japan. World War II had been vicious; the island warfare in the Pacific seemed especially bloody. In five weeks in February and March 1945, on the tiny (eight square miles) island of Iwo Jima, where 80,000 American troops engaged in the battle, 6,281 died and another 19,000 were wounded when nearly the entire garrison of 21,000 Japanese fought to the death. Between March 1, 1944, and May 1, 1945, 13,742 Americans died in land war in the Pacific while killing about 310,000 Japanese. At Okinawa, in the bloodiest major battle of the Pacific, stretching from mid-April to mid-June and involving more than 170,000 U.S. troops, about 13,000 were killed, and almost 36,000 others wounded, while killing about 70,000 Japanese military personnel and an estimated 80,000 Okinawa residents.

Yet, none of these painful numbers—when carefully examined and extrapolated—support the claim that 500,000 Americans might have been killed in the invasion of Japan. In fact, in June 1945, while the Okinawa battle was winding down, U.S. military planners estimated that, at most, 46,000 might die in the various possible invasions of Japan. On June 15, 1945, four weeks before the atomic bomb test at Alamogordo and seven weeks before Hiroshima was bombed, the Joint War Plans Committee (JWPC), a high-level advisory group to the Joint Chiefs of Staff, concluded that about 40,000 Americans would die in the likely two-stage assault on Japan: southern Kyushu (operation "Olympic") beginning on November 1, 1945, and, if necessary, the Tokyo plain (operation "Coronet") starting on about March 1, 1946. The Kyushu campaign, the JWPC stressed, "may well prove to be the decisive operation which will terminate the war." In that event, according to JWPC estimates, many fewer Americans would die, perhaps under 20,000.[6]

The JWPC acknowledged that it was impossible to make an "accurate estimate," since experience with the Japanese varied widely, from the four-day battle in November 1943 at Tarawa, where 1,000 marines died and about 2,300 were wounded while killing 4,700 Japanese, to the "unopposed landing" at Lingayen Gulf in the Philippines in January 1945, where 175,000 American troops easily established themselves in what one historian later called a "walkover." Despite this mixed pattern of the immediate past, the JWPC were reasonably comfortable in offering what they called an "educated guess."

The JWPC's June 15 educated guesses projected three different invasion scenarios. The most likely was an attack on southern Kyushu followed by an assault on the Tokyo plain. This contingency plan estimated American casualties at about 40,000 dead, 150,000 wounded, and 2,500 missing. The second scenario, which was also considered less likely, was an attack on southern Kyushu, followed by north-western Kyushu. Casualties were estimated at 25,000 Americans dead, 105,000 wounded, and 2,500 missing. The third battle scenario projected an attack on south-ern Kyushu, followed by northwestern Kyushu and then the Tokyo plain. American casualties for this attack plan were estimated at 46,000 dead, 170,000 wounded, and 4,000 missing in action. Clearly, all these estimates fell far short—by at least 454,000—of later claims of 500,000 American lives. In fact, in early June 1945, when a layman suggested such a high number as a half million dead, army planners bluntly replied in a secret report: "[such an] estimated loss . . . is entirely too high." Studying this planners' report, General George C. Marshall, army chief of staff, agreed with their assessment and so informed Secretary of War Henry L. Stimson.[7]

It was not simply most top military men in Washington but also General Douglas MacArthur, U.S. commander in the Pacific, who believed that the casualties and deaths would not be as high as the rate at Normandy and Okinawa. MacArthur's plans for the first stage, the November invasion of southern Kyushu, apparently estimated total casualties (dead plus wounded) in the first three months at well under 100,000. When he discovered that some of his staff, in putting together "purely academic" estimates, had forecast possibly 118,000-125,000 American casualties, he cabled Marshall on June 18, "I do not anticipate such a high rate of loss."[8] Later that day, at a White House meeting, Marshall informed President Truman "that the first 30 days in Kyushu should not exceed the price [of 31,000 casualties] we have paid in Luzon," where 156,000 Japanese were killed or surrendered. Even the more pessimistic Admiral William Leahy, military aide to the president, exaggerating U.S. losses at Okinawa, anticipated that the casualties at Kyushu would not be worse than the 35 percent he incorrectly ascribed to Okinawa. (Actually, the Okinawa rate was about 29 percent.) Leahy, using the wrong data, suggested that total casualties at Kyushu might run as high as 230,000.[9]*

At this June 18 meeting, Marshall had not explained the "general conclusions" that his advisers had reached. "The highest casualty rate occurs during the assault phase of an amphibious operation." The first thirty days could be the worst. After that, as MacArthur's estimates also showed, the rate of U.S. wounded and killed would undoubtedly decline. Three weeks after this White House meeting, on July 9, the Joint Staff Planners (JSP), another advisory group to the JCS, roughly reaffirmed Marshall's June 18 conclusions. Leahy's highest estimates were disregarded in that July 9 report.[10] The JSP were also optimistic about the low level of U.S. casualties if the March 1 invasion of the Tokyo plain became necessary. According to this report, the Japanese would not be able to concentrate their forces at the plain, because of the "number and extent of beaches suitable for [the United States'] amphibious assault. . . . The terrain permits us to exploit our superiority in maneuver and in equipment." In summary, "this invasion of the Tokyo Plain should be relatively inexpensive."

When Truman approved the order of July 24 to use atomic bombs, he had never received a high-level report suggesting half a million or even a quarter million U.S. dead. All the estimates, especially those presented by Marshall, whom the president greatly trusted, were considerably lower in the months before Japan's surrender. Of course, these were all pre-Hiroshima estimates, and often did not take full account of the growing build-up of Japanese troops on Kyushu after June 1945.

But soon after Hiroshima and Nagasaki, U.S. military leaders, writing in private and thus having no reason to distort estimates, agreed that any claim of 500,000 American lives saved was exorbitant. In September 1945, even though some U.S. military leaders feared that the Japanese were conducting "an intensive propaganda campaign concerning the bombing of their cities" to make the United

---

* Editors' Note: On June 18, Leahy recorded in his diary: "General Marshall is of the opinion that such an effort will not cost us in casualties more than 63,000 of 190,000 combatant troops estimated as necessary for the [Kyushu] operation." See "The Leahy Diary: Prospect of a Negotiated Surrender," *Hiroshima's Shadow*, p. 515.

States seem bloodthirsty, top generals in Washington argued that the invasions of Japan, if carried out, would have cost fewer than 200,000 American lives and maybe only "tens of thousands." Such were the post-war estimates of Lt. General John E. Hull, assistant chief of the Army's operations division, and of Lt. General Ira C. Eaker, deputy commander of the Air Force, and endorsed by General Henry ("Hap") Arnold, commander of the Air Force.[11]

The myth of 500,000 American lives saved thus seems to have no basis in fact. No U.S. military planner between May 1945 and the Hiroshima bombing, or even after Hiroshima that year, would have put the number over 200,000, and many placed it much lower—near 40,000. The destruction of this myth does not resolve the pressing question of whether using the atomic bombs on Japan was morally justified or not. But at least recognizing that most pre-Hiroshima military estimates ranged between about 20,000 and 46,000 may help Americans understand the thinking of their leaders who, in 1945, welcomed the use of the bomb on Japanese cities in what was clearly a campaign of terror bombing. Perhaps in the aftermath of Hiroshima and Nagasaki, Truman developed a need to exaggerate the number of U.S. lives that the bombs might have saved by possibly helping render the invasions unnecessary. It is probably true, as he contended repeatedly, that he never lost any sleep over his decision. Believing ultimately in the myth of 500,000 lives saved may have been a way of concealing ambivalence, even from himself. The myth also helped deter Americans from asking troubling questions about the use of the atomic bombs. The destruction of this myth should reopen these questions.

NOTES

1. Quoted in Alfred Steinberg, *The Man From Missouri* (New York, 1962), p. 259.

2. This article is a revised version of "The Myth of Lives Saved by A-Bombs," *Los Angeles Times*, July 28, 1985, sec. 4, pp. 1, 2. Rufus Miles, "Hiroshima: The Strange Myth of Half a Million Lives Saved," *International Security* (Fall 1985), pp. 121–140, came to somewhat similar conclusions without using the relevant archival sources. Miles argues, substantially on the basis of inference, that Truman's military advisers believed before Hiroshima that the Kyushu invasion would cost only 7,000–8,000 U.S. lives; Miles concluded that the number would "probably [have been] less than 15,000 [and] almost surely . . . not more than 20,000." He seems naively to believe admit that an invasion of Honshu (which he was sure would not have been necessary) could have cost 50,000–250,000 U.S. lives, based on what he uncritically seems to believe Gen. Marshall told Truman before Hiroshima. Miles almost entirely disregarded archival sources, relied heavily on inference for his 7,000–20,000 for Kyushu, and strangely trusted Truman's January 1953 claim about what Marshall had allegedly said before Hiroshima—that the Honshu invasion would cost 250,000–1,000,000 American casualties. Miles translated this estimate into 50,000–250,000 U.S. dead. Much of Miles's article argues that U.S. policymakers should have pursued various alternatives to the atomic bomb and that any single alternative would have ended the Pacific war before November 1, the date of the Kyushu invasion. Parts of this argument are reminiscent of Gar Alperovitz, *Atomic Diplomacy* (New York, 1965, rev. 1985).

3. Winston Churchill, cited by Gen. Leslie Groves in Senate Special Committee on Atomic Energy, *Atomic Energy: Hearings*, 79th Cong., 1st sess., p. 39.

4. *Public Papers of the Presidents: Harry S. Truman, 1947* (Washington, D.C., 1962), p. 381; ibid., *1948*, p. 859; ibid., *1949*, p. 200.

5. Memoir draft 1, p. 249; draft 2, p. 683; draft 3, p. 804, Post-Presidential Papers, Harry S. Truman Library (Independence, Mo.); Harry S. Truman, *Memoirs*, vol. 1, *Year of Decisions* (Garden City, 1955), p. 417.

6. Joint War Plans Committee, 369/1, June 15, 1945, file 384 Japan (5–3–44), Records of the Army Staff, RG 319, National Archives.

7. Marshall to secretary of war (June 7, 1945), with Handy to Hull (June 1, 1945) and attachment, file OPD 336 TS; Truman to secretary of war, n.d., with Herbert Hoover, "Memorandum on Ending

the Japanese War," file OPD 704 TS, Records of War Department General Staff, RG 165, National Archives, Washington, D.C.

8. MacArthur to Marshall, June 18, 1945, file OPD 704 TS, War Department General Staff Records.

9. Minutes of June 18, 1945, meeting in Department of State, *Foreign Relations of the United States: Berlin (Potsdam)* (Washington, D.C., 1960), pp. 904–909; for unprinted parts, see file CCS 381 Japan (6–14–45), Records of the Joint Chiefs of Staff, RG 218, National Archives.

10. Joint Staff Planners, 697/2 (July 9, 1945), file 384 Japan (5–3–44), War Department General Staff.

11. J. E. Hull to Ira Eaker (Sept. 13, 1945); Eaker to Hull (Sept. 14, 1945); Arnold to Far Eastern Air Force (Sept. 14, 1945), all in file OPD 704 PTO, War Department General Staff.

THE
INVASION
THAT
NEVER WAS

Adam Goodheart

X-DAY: NOVEMBER 1, 1945. Chevrolet Beach. The Battle of Ariake Bay. Had events not taken an unexpected turn, these words might be as familiar as D-Day, Omaha Beach and the invasion of Normandy. As it is, they are merely a footnote to the history of World War II. Although it never occurred, the invasion of Japan was one of the most intricately plotted campaigns of World War II. Yet it was never looked at in depth until John Ray Skates, a historian at the University of Southern Mississippi, published a book on the subject in 1994.

Skates's book, *The Invasion of Japan*, recounts that as early as May 1942 some American strategists were projecting an eventual attack on Japan's home islands. By August 1945, when atomic bombs fell on Hiroshima and Nagasaki, the Allied forces were preparing for an all-out assault. A million weary American veterans of the war against Germany braced themselves for redeployment to the western Pacific; one infantry division fresh from Europe was already en route to the Philippines when news of Japan's surrender came. Air attacks on Japanese coastal defenses were set to begin within a week. At ports in California and throughout the Pacific, soldiers and longshoremen loaded cargo ships with weapons and supplies—and stacks of white crosses.[1]

On the Japanese side, the preparations that summer were equally intense. A final mobilization drafted every able-bodied man left in the country, bringing the number of troops defending the home islands to more than two million. Entire squadrons of kamikaze pilots, both volunteers and conscripts, studied how to inflict the most damage when crashing their bomb-laden planes into American ships. Volunteers dug tank traps and set barbed wire along the beaches. Schoolgirls pulled up pine stumps from forests already stripped of timber; the resin would be used to make aviation fuel. In the absence of firearms, civilian defense squads of women, children and the elderly practiced close combat with knives, bamboo staves—even carpenter's awls, according to *Valley of Darkness*, Thomas Havens's history of wartime Japan.[2] "One hundred million die proudly," went one slogan meant to harden the resolve of the Japanese people.[3]

Operation Olympic was set for November 1, 1945, designated "X-Day" in the top-secret military plans. Its chief architects, including Generals Douglas

MacArthur and George C. Marshall, saw it as a final step in the process of "island hopping" that had brought U.S. forces from remote Guadalcanal in 1942 to Okinawa, at the southern gateway to Japan, by the spring of 1945. In the attack on Japan's home islands, the two previously separate American thrusts across the Pacific—MacArthur's from the south, and Admiral Chester Nimitz's from the east—would converge, with MacArthur and Nimitz sharing the command. The invasion was to have two stages. First, the Americans would seize the lower third of Kyushu, the southernmost island of Japan. Here they would build naval bases and huge airfields that would allow them to tighten their sea blockade and launch unrelenting bombing raids against Japanese troops and civilians. If the enemy did not surrender after the invasion of Kyushu, a second wave of Allied landings was scheduled to begin on March 1, 1946. Operation Coronet would strike at the industrial heart of Japan on the main island of Honshu. The Allies planned to seize Tokyo, Yokohama and other cities.

X-Day was to be preceded by air and naval bombardments of unprecedented ferocity, according to Skates. Beginning in mid-August of 1945, American pilots would be sent to destroy Japan's remaining ships and planes, as well as key bridges, roads and fortifications. Before the troops went ashore, more than 500 warships would pound Kyushu's coast. Meanwhile, American bombers would continue their attacks on Japanese civilians. Over the previous months, they had killed more than 300,000 people and reduced many of Japan's major cities to ashes; they were now turning to smaller cities, preferably those with high "congestion and inflammability." [4]

As they awaited the invasion, American GIs had only the vaguest sense of their destination. The Pentagon brass, however, knew exactly who would land where, and they had carefully selected which troops would bear the heaviest burdens. The assault on southern Kyushu would be spearheaded by MacArthur's Sixth Army, which had led the drive across New Guinea and the Philippines. Three of the Army's toughest and most experienced infantry divisions would make the first landings on Kyushu's east coast. From the south, the 11th Corps, fresh from the fighting in the Philippines, would attack the heavily defended beaches of Ariake Bay. Other infantry and Marines would land at several beach areas to the west. The hardest task would fall to the Fifth Marine Amphibious Corps, veterans of Iwo Jima: They would fight their way up the Satsuma Peninsula, along narrow corridors through the mountains. In all, according to Skates, about 600,000 men would participate in the landings—nearly twice as many as had landed at Normandy. [5]

In at least one respect the American strategists displayed amazing, if unwitting, foresight. On the top-secret invasion maps, the landing beaches were code-named after makes of automobiles. Thus, one of the first landings would happen at Chevrolet Beach. Other troops would come ashore at Buick Beach, Cadillac Beach, Oldsmobile Beach, and Studebaker Beach. [6] Could the planners ever have guessed that although their invasion would never come off, the United States and Japan would later fight fierce battles over this very terrain?

While the Americans were naming beaches after cars, the Japanese had no time for rhetorical flourishes. They named the defense of their homeland simply *ketsu-go*, or "decisive operation." [7] Its aim, the strategists revealed to American interviewers after the war, was not to achieve total victory, but to inflict heavy casualties on the invaders at any cost. Eventually, it was hoped, the Americans would mitigate their demand that Japan surrender unconditionally. [8] Many Japanese believed that this was their only hope of keeping the Emperor in power, perhaps even their only hope of preventing his execution for war crimes—a horror nearly equivalent to deicide in the eyes of some of his subjects.

The Allies planned an elaborate deception to convince the enemy that they intended to invade northern Japan from the Aleutians.[9] But the Japanese saw through the ruse, they later told the American interviewers, and planned to use their remaining resources defending Kyushu. By August 1945 they had more than 200,000 troops in the southern part of the island.[10] According to military documents discovered by the American occupation force after the war, the local Japanese commanders had been ordered to ready a defense "at the water's edge."[11] As the Americans disembarked, they would find themselves face to face with Japanese soldiers. The battle lines on the beaches would be so confused that U.S. planes and warships would have to cease-fire lest they massacre their own men.[12] Meanwhile, Americans waiting at sea in crowded transports would face wave after wave of kamikaze attacks. Although its navy was nearly gone, Japan still had more than 5,000 planes, most of which would fly on suicide missions early in the invasion. Manned torpedoes and suicide boats would also be sent against American troopships. Infantrymen with explosives strapped to their backs would hurl themselves under advancing American tanks.[13]

But even with the Japanese throwing everything they had at the invasion force, it is unlikely they could have held the Kyushu coast for long. Because of shortages of steel and concrete, most of their fortifications were constructed of earth and logs (as Americans who toured the area after the war discovered).[14] Radios and telephones on Kyushu were few and primitive, and the chaos of battle would have further hampered Japanese coordination. The pre-invasion U.S. bombardments and air raids, which were to be the heaviest of the war, would have blocked many roads, preventing the arrival of reinforcements. Most of the kamikaze planes and boats would probably have been destroyed. Ammunition, even assuming none was captured or destroyed, would not have lasted much more than six weeks, according to post-war assessments of the stockpiles by American military historians.[15]

Kyushu is an island roughly the size of Maryland. The rugged terrain in the south would have been the Japanese commanders' most formidable ally. Steep hills backed all the invasion beaches, and the few flat areas were often wet rice paddies, where movement by troops and heavy equipment would be slow or impossible. Farther inland, an American intelligence report described "the cliff-like terrace fronts, the commanding heights surrounding all lowland areas, and the rugged mountains full of tortuous narrow defiles."[16] Caves were everywhere. The landscape was perfect for the Japanese tactics of concealment and ambush that had caused heavy American losses on Okinawa. There the Japanese created a kind of "land battleship," writes George Feifer in *Tennozan*, his recent history of the battle. Small groups of soldiers hid in bunkers, caves and tunnels awaiting the perfect moment to strike. They almost always died, but they almost always killed Americans in the process.[17]

Unwilling to endure a larger-scale Okinawa, the American generals made plans to clear the caves and tunnels with chemical weapons—something that has gone nearly unreported for half a century. In his description of the invasion plans, Skates reveals that as the Americans prepared to assault Kyushu, they secretly stockpiled not just napalm and flame-throwing tanks, but bombs, grenades and mortar rounds filled with lethal gas. Throughout the war, both Allies and Axis had refrained from using gas for fear of retaliation. President Roosevelt had been particularly firm in his opposition to chemical warfare. But by the late spring of 1945, Roosevelt was dead, Germany was defeated and Japan's chemical warfare capability was all but eliminated. Gas was an option again. General Marshall was a strong advocate. At a meeting with the secretary of war in late May, according to a contemporary memorandum, he spoke in favor of using chemical weapons to eliminate "pockets of resistance which had to be wiped out but had no other military significance."

By July, the War Department's Chemical Warfare Service reported that it had tested chemical weapons against caves and found them extremely effective. Several types of gas would pool like water in the caves, then expand to produce concentrations strong enough to kill even masked soldiers. On August 13, Marshall reported to the Joint Chiefs that ample chemical stocks would be ready in time for the invasion. Had Japanese troops on Kyushu held out like those on Okinawa, Skates concludes, it is likely that they would have been gassed.[18] Once Kyushu fell, Japan's situation would have been hopeless. The once-fearsome imperial armies in China, Manchuria and Korea would be stranded by the Allies' naval blockade and under attack by the Soviets. The forces left to defend the homeland were mostly untrained and virtually unarmed. And despite the old women training with bamboo spears, Japanese commanders never seriously planned to encourage civilians to fight. In fact, defense plans found after the war called for their evacuation from combat zones.[19] The invasion of Honshu, had it come to that, would likely have been quick and relatively free of American casualties.

While the soldiers landing on Kyushu would have all been American, the second stage of the invasion would have included British, Canadians, French and Australians. (The question of Soviet participation was still unresolved at war's end.) The other Allied nations jostled to get in on the landings so that they could play a part in the final victory over Japan. The American generals reluctantly agreed to give them a role, albeit a secondary one.[20] "We were resolved to share the agony," Winston Churchill later declared. "To quell the Japanese resistance man by man and conquer the country yard by yard might well require the loss of a million American lives and half that number of British." [21]

In fact, not even the most pessimistic Allied casualty estimates in 1945 remotely approached such figures. Marshall's staff estimated that the invasion of Kyushu would result in about 31,000 American casualties, including 7,000 to 8,000 dead. MacArthur, who time and again had shown a remarkable ability to forecast a battle's toll of dead and wounded, predicted fewer than 50,000 casualties in the first month of fighting on Kyushu, and an additional 50,000 or so if the campaign dragged on for another two months. Assuming a situation similar to Okinawa, where one American was killed for every four wounded, this meant that about 20,000 Americans would have died had the fighting on Kyushu lasted until February 1946. Such a rate approximates that of the Normandy campaign. Although there were no formal projections for the invasion of Honshu, that campaign was generally expected to be far less costly in American lives.[22]

Far more Japanese would have died if the invasion had occurred. On Okinawa, for every American who died, 10 Japanese soldiers were killed—about 100,000 in all.[23] The ratio on Kyushu might have been even higher. Throughout Japan, tens of thousands of civilians probably would have perished under the continuing rain of incendiary bombs dropped by American planes.

In the years after 1945, Allied leaders, especially Harry Truman, insisted that American deaths alone would have surpassed the number of Japanese killed at Hiroshima and Nagasaki. In the notes for his memoirs, Truman mentioned the figure of 250,000 American *casualties*—dead and wounded. In the published version, he upped the number to half a million *dead*. He later told a historian that the bomb had saved a million American lives.[24] These figures, along with the notion of fanatical civilian resistance, have been widely accepted by historians and ordinary Americans. (William Manchester wrote in *The Glory and the Dream* that an American invasion would have been opposed "by every member of the civilian population old enough to carry a hand grenade.")

But after carefully researched analysis of the planned attack, Skates concludes that "the large casualty figures for the invasion of Japan, cited by Truman, [Secretary of War] Stimson, and Churchill in their post-war writings, were without basis in contemporary [military] planning." Skates also discovered a "what-if" study of the invasion prepared eight months after Japan's surrender by U.S. Army intelligence experts. It concluded that even without the atomic bombs, Operation Olympic would never have been launched, since the Soviet invasion of Manchuria on August 8 would have added urgency to the Japanese peace overtures already under way. In the unlikely event that an invasion had proved necessary, the experts wrote, it would have ended successfully within two months.[25]

Maybe so, but in the summer of 1945 nearly every American—civilian or soldier—believed there was a long and bloody struggle ahead. The jaunty bravado of the song lyrics, "Good-bye, Mama, I'm off to Yokohama," did little to mask the fears of millions. When news of the bomb came, American soldiers in the Pacific had little doubt that it had saved their lives. "We whooped and yelled like mad, we downed all the beer we'd been stashing away," recalled one Marine veteran of Okinawa. "We shot bullets into the air and danced between the tent rows, because this meant maybe we were going to live." [26]

NOTES

1. John Ray Skates, *The Invasion of Japan: Alternative to the Bomb* (Columbia, 1994), pp. 68–69, 175.

2. Thomas Havens, *Valley of Darkness: The Japanese People and World War Two* (New York, 1978), pp. 188–190.

3. George Feifer, *Tennozan: The Battle of Okinawa and the Atomic Bomb* (New York, 1992), p. 576.

4. Skates, pp. 3–7, 48.

5. Ibid., pp. 67, 167–177, 189.

6. "Diagram of Beach Designations for Operations Against Kyushu," map in COMPHIBSPAC OP Plan A11–45 (August 10, 1945).

7. U.S. Army Japan/U.S. Army Forces Far East, "Japanese Monograph No. 17," p. 62.

8. Herbert Feis, *The Atomic Bomb and the End of World War II* (Princeton, 1966), pp. 119–120.

9. Skates, pp. 163–164.

10. "Japanese Monograph No. 17," pp. 126–127; "Japanese Monograph No. 45," pp. 205–206.

11. Skates, p. 104.

12. "Japanese Monograph No. 17," p. 127.

13. Skates, pp. 109, 114.

14. "Japanese Monograph No. 17," p. 32; Skates, p. 127.

15. "Japanese Monograph No. 17," pp. 136–137.

16. Skates, p. 151

17. Feifer, p. 233.
18. Skates, pp. 93–97.
19. Ibid., p. 130.
20. Ibid., pp. 219, 227, 229.
21. Feifer, p. 577.
22. Skates, pp. 74–82.
23. Feifer, p. 572.
24. Skates, p. 77.
25. Ibid., pp. 244, 256.
26. Feifer, p. 567.

THE
CONSTRUCTION OF
CONVENTIONAL
WISDOM

Uday Mohan & Sanho Tree

MANY OF TODAY'S JOURNALISTS covering the atomic bombings of World War II write their stories as if President Harry S. Truman's endgame with Japan in the months before August 1945 entailed only two choices: bomb or invasion. In this scenario Truman's use of the bombs against Hiroshima and Nagasaki was necessary to secure Japanese capitulation and prevent a bloody invasion. While this framework lends itself to a tidy, uncluttered narrative, it omits the crucial months prior to the bombings when a confluence of events might well have brought about a very different termination of the war.

In the spring and summer of 1945, before the world knew of the existence of the atomic bomb, the American media engaged in extensive speculation and debate about the best means for bringing an end to the war with Japan. The media reported on, and also helped put into play, possible alternatives to the bomb for successfully concluding the Pacific War.

The media discussed four key issues before the bomb was dropped: the impact on Japan of possible Russian entry into the Pacific War; the importance of clarifying terms of surrender for Japan; the significance of Japanese peace feelers; and the rapid deterioration of the war-making capacity of Japan. Many in the media appeared to believe that this constellation of factors would bring about an early end to the war. But once Truman announced that the United States had used an atomic bomb against Japan, the media by and large discarded the rich historical process they had commented on in favor of Truman's narrow public interpretation. The media helped to put aside, as a result, the historical understanding in which civil society could fully ground its response to the use of an unprecedented weapon of war, a weapon that held the potential for global destruction, as commentators at the time understood.[1] Remaining, instead, was the official account, which further legitimized use of the bomb by articulating a narrow understanding of the historical process leading to the bomb's use. Rather than being remembered as the ultimate weapon of mass destruction, the bomb became for many of that generation an icon of salvation: "Thank God for the Atom Bomb," as Paul Fussell later would write.[2]

Although the official explanation that the bombs were needed to obviate a bloody invasion was challenged by a few mainstream dissenters and religious commentators in the 1940s, the right wing in the 1950s, and then the left in the 1960s, the overall legacy of post-Hiroshima reporting and official explanation has led to a virtually immutable popular history of the end of World War II, resistant to the findings of modern scholarship. The media coverage of the recent controversy over the Smithsonian's *Enola Gay* exhibit illustrated all too well this wide and difficult-to-bridge gap between scholarly and public understanding of Truman's decision.

Most historians who have analyzed the news media's response to Hiroshima have generally treated the media as reflectors of public opinion. These scholars have suggested that wartime culture, official censorship, and a belief in American exceptionalism were largely responsible for the lack of dissenting commentary in the media.[3] While these are important issues to keep in mind, viewed only in this way, the media become reflectors rather than shapers, as well, of popular opinion. According to this view, the media had not the means or reason to challenge the official line. This approach also suggests why studies of the media and Hiroshima do not continue beyond the 1940s. Once Hiroshima becomes a settled matter of public opinion, there appears to be little reason for media behavior to change, thus making further analysis of media coverage unwarranted.

There are four problems with this approach. It contributes to the notion, regardless of scholarly intention, that the Hiroshima question is settled as far as Truman's decision is concerned; it fails to explore the choices available to the media concerning the ending of the war; it minimizes the media's role in reflecting the government position, as opposed to reflecting public opinion generally. Finally, it overlooks the growing gap between media and scholarship, especially in the last two decades, during which scholars reached a consensus that the bomb was not dropped to avoid an invasion of Japan, though it was used to end the war quickly and, many agree, for political reasons.[4] As we shall see, taken together, media reporting before the bomb was dropped provided an understanding for the decision to use the bomb that is broadly similar to the one available in current scholarship.

Before the bomb was dropped, the major newspapers and leading popular and reflective magazines surveyed the progress of the war and often noted several positive trends: the existence, confirmed and unconfirmed, of Japanese peace feelers; the break between Russia and Japan and the impact of a possible Russian entry into the war; and the rapid deterioration of the Japanese economy and military in relation to overwhelming American military superiority. Most importantly, publications debated the issue of unconditional surrender, generally suggesting clarification of surrender terms as a way of bringing Japan closer to capitulation. While the ideological positions of publications sometimes affected their war policy choices, the significance and interpretation of the evidence the policy choices were based on remained remarkably consistent across the ideological spectrum.

Japan's "desperate situation" was commented on as early as April 1945 by a number of publications.[5] The influential Protestant weekly, *Christian Century*, saw the reshuffling of the Japanese government to include more moderate elements and the contemporaneous naval suicide runs that resulted in the loss of Japan's last large battleship as possible signs that "surrender" "may be" near. It also noted that "Russia's abrogation of her neutrality pact with Japan is likely to strengthen the peace party [in Japan]."[6] The popular press echoed these assessments. In *Newsweek*, for example, a headline of April 16 read, "Lost Battles, Slap From Moscow Shake

Props of Jap Ruling Clique: Shift in Tokyo Government Smoothes Way for Peace Feelers, Cuts Power of Army Group."[7] Similarly, the liberal *Nation* saw the apparent elimination of militarists from recent Japanese cabinets as a sign that the Japanese were intending to pave the way for peace in order to save Japan from the destruction that had been visited upon Germany. But the editorial writer of the *Nation* cautioned that the cabinet replacements, mainly from the business community, had cooperated with the militarists "in their expansion program." The same editorial noted "the elimination of the Japanese fleet as an effective force and the decimation of the Japanese air force," as well as the military importance of the date of Russian entry into the war.[8]

Also in mid-April, the *New York Times* reported that due particularly to Japanese cabinet changes and "Russian denunciation of the Soviet-Japanese neutrality pact," military and naval officials increasingly believed "that the Japanese [would] sue for peace before [the United States was] in a position to 'Germanize' their country." The *Times* added that American officials regarded "the possibility of Japanese peace overtures" as an extremely delicate matter and were making an effort to discourage any discussion of such issues.[9] A month later a *Times* editorial summed up Japan's bleak situation: Japan had been dislodged from most of its colonial gains, its navy had been rendered "almost impotent" and its air force reduced to tactical capability, substantial portions of its army had been isolated, Japan was squeezed economically by a blockade, and its cities were in ruins. The government of Premier Suzuki Kantaro no longer "promise[d] victory, but offer[ed] only a pledge to fight to the last," though it did appear to welcome a change in unconditional surrender terms.[10] These and other articles clearly suggested that Japan seemed to be helpless and interested in exploring an end to the war.

Although Russian intentions had not been announced publicly, speculation existed in the press about a Russian declaration of war in the Pacific, because this would amount to a major military blow against Japan.[11] As Harry Howard observed in an early May edition of *Christian Century*, "Soviet airforces are already far superior to Japanese, and Japan is hopelessly vulnerable from contiguous Russian territory."[12] Two weeks earlier, *Newsweek* had been even more blunt about the issue: "Last week the Russians denounced [the Russian-Japanese neutrality pact]. . . . For Japan the news was pure disaster. . . . And war with Russia would deal a fatal blow to the plans of the Japanese generals to carry on the struggle in Asia even if the home islands are themselves invaded."[13] The article went on to note that the formation of the Suzuki government meant a defeat for the army, albeit a qualified defeat, and that peace proposals would probably be forthcoming.

In the following month, on May 21, *Newsweek* reported the existence of the peace feeler it had predicted: "Reports that at least one peace feeler has been made are well founded." The magazine noted, however, the Japanese unwillingness "to meet unconditional surrender terms."[14] Harry Howard elaborated on perhaps the same peace feeler in the left-wing journal, the *Progressive*: "On May 9, the *Washington Post* made public the Japanese Government's proffer of surrender— a story known for weeks to a number of well-informed persons in Washington, but bound by secrecy and personal confidence."[15] Howard described the peace feeler and noted that it "virtually accepts the demands . . . laid down at the Cairo Conference." The *Christian Century*, scrutinizing recent press coverage of peace feelers reported by reputable correspondents, characterized the number of feelers as a "flood." It added that a Chicago paper had reported another feeler that went beyond the terms laid out in the *Post*.

The Catholic weekly *Commonweal* described a peace feeler some days later as coming from "certain industrialists" and "addressed to the Allies through Russian good offices shortly after VE-day." The writer added that the "rejected offer was not comprehensive enough," and that surrender terms needed to be clarified: "Terms that are stern, definite but acceptable are the immediate need." [16]

One can thus see a fairly consistent picture emerging across a number of publications: the Japanese military was deteriorating rapidly; the installation of the Suzuki government meant that non-militarists were beginning to seize the initiative (as the *Christian Century* stated, "most commentators suspect [the Suzuki cabinet] has been formed to put out peace feelers"); the Japanese had reason to fear Russian entry into the war, which remained a looming possibility; and peace feelers had begun to emerge.[17]

That there was some momentum in the press toward negotiating an end to the war can be gauged by reactions in the more hawkish press. The *New York Times* and the *Nation*, for example, read the signs of a weakening Japan as a signal to prosecute the war more intensely. Editorials in the *Nation*, for example, criticized the recent "intimations from various quarters [in the press and officialdom] concerning" a possible conditional peace for Japan. Such a peace would leave intact the industrialists who supported the militarists.[18] The *New York Times* in its editorials generally warned against false hopes for peace and the relaxation of the war effort. The *Times* editorial of June 9 noted that "People are beginning to talk comfortably of a Japanese surrender 'before we know it,' or certainly before the first of next year." [19] The news division of the *Times*, however, reported many peace feelers. For example, part of a June 16 story on Japanese peace feelers, subtitled "Efforts to Conclude War Said to Be Intensified With Growing Defeats," stated that prominent Japanese officials in Stockholm "have made what are described as strenuous efforts to communicate with Allied diplomatic circles to propose a negotiated peace." [20]

The editorial concerns of the popular and reflective press highlighted what was perhaps the major issue in the media debate about the conclusion of the war: unconditional surrender. Should Japan be forced to surrender unconditionally as demanded by the Allies at the Casablanca Conference in 1943? Or should its surrender be conditional, given its apparent willingness to fight to the end while the policy of unconditional surrender continued to threaten the existence of the divine emperor? It was not uncommon for commentators to urge that a Japan with its military in tatters, seemingly seeking a way out, should be offered tough terms but not unqualified unconditional surrender.

President Franklin D. Roosevelt's slogan of "unconditional surrender" had been a useful domestic rallying cry in the beginning of 1943 when the close of the war seemed far away as did the attendant requirement of defining what form of surrender and post-war government the Allies would impose on the Axis powers. But what was a convenient soundbite for inspiring the home front also proved to be a bonanza for the Axis propagandists—particularly toward the end of the war. The leaders of both Germany and Japan frightened their citizens into more spirited resistance by claiming that unconditional surrender would translate into a host of horrifying consequences: slavery, torture, rape, national dissolution, extermination and for the Japanese the most unthinkable outcome—the prosecution and execution of the Emperor.

Some of the most forceful and sophisticated arguments for clarifying surrender terms came from the *Washington Post.*[21] On May 9, the day after V-E Day, when Truman first began to vaguely define unconditional surrender, the *Post* wrote:

> Japan should be told her fate immediately so that she may be encouraged to throw in the sponge. . . . What we are suggesting, to be sure, is conditional surrender. What of it? Unconditional surrender was never an ideal formula. . . . We urge, therefore, that the task of compiling the terms for Japan and informing the Japanese of them should not be delayed. . . . It is not a hard peace that we are interested in. It is an effective peace.[22]

Commenting on Truman's speech to Congress in an editorial of June 3, the *Washington Post* wrote:

> We still hope that this stepped up [military] offensive will be accompanied by a vigorous attack in the sphere of political warfare. President Truman again held out to the Japanese people the assurance that "we have no desire or intention to destroy or enslave" them. But he also repeated the vague demand for "unconditional surrender." We think that the price the Japanese must pay . . . should be made much more definite than that. The winning powers should tell the Japanese in simple and positive terms what they must do to stop the slaughter of their people and the destruction of their homeland. Those terms must necessarily include, as we have previously noted, stripping Japan of her gains by conquest as well as complete demilitarization of that country. But millions of Japanese are likely to prefer these harsh terms to utter destruction. We should encourage them to throw off at the earliest possible moment the military rule that is leading them to their doom, and thus avoid paying a higher price than necessary for the kind of victory that is essential to future peace in the Pacific.[23]

Three days later the *Washington Post* again reiterated the point:

> Every Japanese in authority must have read the President's account of our war preparations with a sinking feeling about the future of Japan. The lesson must be rubbed in. But it cannot lead to surrender unless we spell out our war aims against Japan. We feel strongly that for the next six months our main target in Japan should be its leaders, with our political warriors in charge of the campaign.[24]

Again on June 11, the *Post* editorialized:

> But the same two words [unconditional surrender] remain a great stumbling block to any [U.S.] propaganda effort and the perpetual trump card of the Japanese die-hards for their game of national suicide. Let us amend them: let us give Japan conditions, harsh conditions certainly, and conditions that will render her diplomatically

and militarily impotent for generations. But also let us somehow assure the Japanese who are ready to plead for peace that, even on our terms, life and peace will be better than war and annihilation.[25]

The next day the *Post* affirmed the importance of the emperor in the debate: "The Emperor is both god and *paterfamilias*. He is thus of the utmost significance in our war with Japan. One word from him . . . and millions of Japanese would lay down their arms tomorrow."[26] On July 13, the *Washington Post* again hammered away at the importance of surrender terms:

The defeat of Japan is now certain, but how many more lives we must sacrifice, what further privations we must endure to achieve our further purposes, is something we cannot know until we know what our further purposes are. If these purposes are clear in the minds of our statesmen they are nevertheless masked under the purely rhetorical and meaningless phrase, "unconditional surrender."[27]

Another vociferous contingent of critics of unconditional surrender came from the reflective or religious journals. The *Christian Century* put it this way on May 9: "Japan is beaten. She has lost all of her key bases. . . . There is nothing left of her fleet that can hold up the American advance. . . . the outcome of the war is certain. Yet it seems likely that the war will go on." The magazine suggested that it was time to clarify the terms on which Japan's defeat could be accepted. Only then could the Japanese understand what they had to do to prevent the horror that was to come.[28] A month later the magazine was still urging Truman to clarify terms, suggesting that this might end the war far sooner than Truman's public speculations gave "any basis for hoping." The magazine interpreted a Suzuki speech to the Diet as an indication of Japanese desire to negotiate an end to the war.[29]

Throughout May, June, and July, journals such as *Christian Century* and Reinhold Niebuhr's *Christianity and Crisis* maintained a steady drumbeat through editorials and massive petition campaigns urging Truman to clarify surrender terms. *Christianity and Crisis* pleaded for making explicit the "economic and political consequences of surrender for the Japanese people." Doing so might help non-militarist forces to gain ascendancy in Japan. The statement was signed by most of the members of the magazine's editorial board, including Niebuhr.[30] The editors noted in a later issue that the statement received considerable attention (apparently unlike the petition mentioned below in *Christian Century*) in the religious and secular press.[31]

Commonweal added its voice to this virtually unanimous chorus. Norman Thomas counseled that "Not to try now for a reasonable peace . . . is a crime of the first magnitude against the men who endure the anguish of jungle warfare."[32] The editors stated that to insist on unqualified unconditional surrender "is to condemn all hands to fight on in a war of mutual extinction."[33]

Christian Century noted that its petition released on June 18 by sixty Christian ministers urging Truman to state American war aims regarding Japan was either ignored or criticized by most of the press.[34] The magazine printed the petition, asking its readers to send in their names. The petition was meant to be a compromise on the issue of unconditional surrender. Japan would surrender unconditionally, but then be subject to the conditions of the petition. By mid-July the magazine reported that thousands of signatures had been received by their office and more came by "the thousand daily." [35] Eventually 15,000 signatures were collected and were to be given to Truman on his return from Potsdam. Attempts were made before Truman left for Potsdam to at least apprise him of the contents of the petition.[36] In promoting its petition *Christian Century* brought the debate to a new level by arguing that clarifying terms was not only strategically smart, but also *morally necessary*:

> What moral right have we to ask our soldiers to die needlessly, or their families to sustain the awful losses of further unnecessary fighting? What moral right have we to inflict even more awful losses upon the Japanese, simply because we keep hidden from them the nature of the peace which we intend to impose? [37]

Although Japan's military, economic, and political decline was abundantly evident, a central question still remained: When does a hopeless *military* situation translate into a *political* capitulation? This simple point, long misunderstood over the years, was addressed by Captain Ellis Zacharias and others involved in psychological warfare in World War II via radio broadcasting to and leafleting in Japan.[38] On July 20, Zacharias, working simultaneously for the Office of War Information and the Office of Naval Intelligence's psychological warfare branch, broadcast a statement to the Japanese getting around the issue of unconditional surrender by offering "unconditional surrender with its attendant benefits as laid down by the Atlantic Charter." [39] This broadcast was reported in newspapers and magazines around the country.[40] The *Washington Post* had urged on July 21 an even clearer definition of terms:

> The Japanese people who are running from bombs and wondering where their next meal is coming from will not have the time or means to look up the Atlantic Charter and the many declarations laying down the conditions on which Japan is asked to surrender. Let them be restated clearly and emphatically, with the gaps appropriately bridged.[41]

The response to the Zacharias broadcast from *Dōmei*, the official Japanese news agency, appeared on the front page of the *New York Times* four days later under the headline "Tokyo Radio Appeals to U.S. For a More Lenient Peace: Hints Militarists Would Call Off the War if Punitive Demands Were Softened— Asks Sincerity on Atlantic Charter Terms." *Dōmei* replied to Zacharias:

> Should America show any sincerity of putting into practice what she preaches, as for instance in the Atlantic Charter, excepting its punitive clause, the Japanese nation, in fact the Japanese military, would automatically, if not willingly [several words missing] follow in the stopping of the conflict.[42]

Official Japanese radio's general acceptance of the Atlantic Charter as a beginning for peace occurred almost two weeks before the dropping of the atomic bombs.[43] The sequence of events in the news created optimism among the editors of *Christian Century*. They were unfazed by the initial statements from Tokyo that the fighting would continue. The editors saw this as public bluster that did not preclude quiet efforts by peace-minded elements to begin an end to the war, perhaps through Moscow.[44] Other publications warned that a failure to end the war quickly would only benefit the Soviet Union. The *Catholic World* felt Japan was "at our mercy." The question for the Paulist monthly was whether unconditional surrender was worth the American lives it would take to procure it—the same question raised often but privately by conservatives like Undersecretary of State Joseph C. Grew and his friend Herbert Hoover. *Catholic World*, like the conservatives, answered no, not only would American lives be wasted but a delay in the war's end would only benefit the Russians if they were to enter the war.[45]

The secular press was not unanimous on the subject, sometimes not even within a particular publication. Such was the case with the *New York Times*. The paper's editorial page called for unconditional surrender, but Hanson Baldwin, its military affairs editor, noted that:

> Japan is seeking a way out of the holocaust of flame and death to which her own policies have brought her. . . . Bombs and bullets must be supplemented by a clear and positive statement of our own—and Allied—aims in the Orient, a program of "do's" as well as "don'ts." Unconditional surrender is not enough.[46]

Contrast Baldwin's title, "Ideas Can Fight Japan," with the closing line of an editorial a day earlier: "the sword must speak."[47] For the *New York Times* editors, there was no reason to treat Japan differently than Germany. Even though the end of the Japanese empire could be "forecast with mathematical certainty," and American lives hung in the balance, anything short of unconditional surrender would inaugurate a precarious peace. The editors saw "uncertainty" and "confusion" in the deviations from unconditional surrender, much as they had detected exhaustion in June when discussion turned to peace feelers and clarification of surrender terms.[48]

On July 24, the *New York Times* printed a story about another call for clarification of unconditional surrender. Republican Senator Kenneth S. Wherry had announced that a "high military source" had passed on a letter to Truman asking that Truman stop the "slaughter" in the Pacific by clarifying terms for Japan. According to Wherry, his source had compiled a list of Japanese peace feelers and on that basis had suggested that the Japanese be allowed to keep their emperor.[49] The *Times* dismissed this the next day in an editorial stating that Japanese militarism had to be wiped out completely and that Allied hesitancy in prosecuting the war would only encourage Japanese resistance.[50]

Two days after the Potsdam Proclamation, July 28, a *New York Times* headline read, "Japanese Cabinet Weighs Ultimatum: Dōmei Says Empire Will Fight to the End—[Speaker of the House Sam] Rayburn Reports Tokyo Has Made Peace Bids." Part of the story indicated that Japanese embassy officials in Moscow were "in a state of excitement" over the "surrender ultimatum." On the editorial page, however, this information was translated into: "Tokyo announces that Japan will ignore the Potsdam ultimatum." The editorial also pointed to the imprecise terms the proclamation mentioned. In reference to the point about the elimination of the "authority and influence of those who have deceived and misled the people of Japan," the *New York Times* wrote, "This is a broad phrase. It is broad enough to include not only the military caste but, though he is not mentioned by name, the 'God-Emperor' whose authority and influence have been used at every stage to lead the Japanese people to conquest." [51]

Some other commentators in the secular press echoed Baldwin's call for clarification rather than the relative inflexibility of the *New York Times* editorial writers. Walter Lippmann, for example, had urged two weeks earlier that "the minimum terms which are certainly necessary, rather than the maximum terms which may be desirable," should be pursued. It was best to let the Japanese determine their own democratic course, rather than impose a solution. Thus Lippmann accepted retention of the Emperor. [52]

Both *Time* and *Life* magazines called for statesmanship and clarification of surrender terms in this critical stage of the war. On July 16 *Time* had noted that a redefinition of unconditional surrender

> has not yet been formulated. Or if it has, it is still a deep secret. U.S. military policy is clear: blow upon blow until all resistance is crushed. But the application of shrewd statesmanship might save the final enforcement of that policy—and countless U.S. lives. [53]

On that same day, a *Life* editorial began in much the same tone. It stated that "The big problem confronting the U.S. with regard to Japan [was] no longer a military problem; it [was] . . . essentially a problem in statesmanship." [54] As we have seen, this logic echoed in the religious press as did *Life*'s clarification of surrender terms. Essentially, the Japanese were to be responsible for their own affairs. *Life* suggested that Japan be demilitarized and shorn of its colonies, its war criminals tried, and a legitimately elected government recognized after a brief U.S. occupation. *Life* followed this up in another editorial three weeks later, noting, as had the editors of *Christian Century*, the sequence of positive diplomatic events culminating in the Potsdam Proclamation. [55] *Life* remained optimistic about negotiations despite initial Japanese ambiguity regarding the Potsdam Proclamation. Moreover, *Life* noted that unlike its proposal for terms, which allowed the Japanese to choose to keep their emperor, the Potsdam Proclamation had remained silent on the question.

For the *United States News* (later *U.S. News & World Report*), the Zacharias broadcasts and Potsdam Proclamation had created a momentum that appeared to guarantee an early end to the war: "Japan definitely and desperately is trying at this time to get out of the war." The magazine added that American "officials are convinced that Japan's present attempt to end the war is real and is not a subterfuge." The same article went on to speculate about the timing of the surrender:

> Pressure inside Japan is strongly in the direction of surrender. The next few weeks should show whether that pressure can be checked by Japanese military leaders who stand to lose their necks after surrender or whether it will overwhelm them. Odds in official appraisals are beginning to swing toward surrender at some point short of invasion or very soon after invasion. [56]

Unlike the *New York Times*, *United States News* was optimistic despite Japanese hesitation. The subheading to the article read, "Slow Move Toward Our Terms, Even While Ultimatum Is Rejected."

Newsweek's coverage throughout July was fairly upbeat. The possibility that the Russians might enter the conflict meant an early end to the war and the saving of thousands of Allied lives.[57] Essentially the Japanese had a choice, between surrender, once the terms had been more clearly defined, and annihilation.[58] The war, in late July, had "entered the next to the last stage" as Japan was finally ringed in.[59] An issue of *Time* also in late July noted that, "In Congress, clamor for a clear definition of U.S. policy toward a defeated Japan would not down [*sic*]." [60] The magazine went on to note that Undersecretary of State Joseph Grew was aware of "indirect, unofficial Japanese peace feelers," which he felt the United States should respond to only in connection with "a major military blow." As Grew phrased it, and the media understood it, a major military blow at that point could have meant Russian entry.[61] In the same article, "To the Enemy," *Time* added that a statement was being prepared for the Japanese that included the following: "If the Japanese choose to keep the Emperor, the throne must be so remodeled that it can never again become the keystone of a military structure." [62]

Though many in the media did not overtly challenge the policy of unconditional surrender, the policy offered the main ground on which questions about the war's prosecution arose. The clarity about the treatment of the emperor in the *Time* article, for example, was missing from the Potsdam Proclamation, which only mentioned the need for free elections in Japan. And yet *Time* failed to ask why the Allies could not have been clearer at Potsdam, or before, since the United States eventually left the throne intact.

At the end of July a *Newsweek* column also urged clarification of surrender terms, suggesting that this and the retention of the emperor might hasten surrender.[63] The same issue noted the existence of a Japanese peace feeler sent through the Russians as well as a message sent by Japan, through a Swedish diplomat, that requested clarification of surrender terms. The article added that "it seemed as if Japan at last had begun preparing its people for defeat." Just before the atomic bomb was dropped, *Time* assured its readers that although American officials denied the existence of definite Japanese peace proposals, "Japanese officialdom was thinking of peace, discussing the possibilities, and seeing to it that this state of mind was made known to Washington, Moscow, London." The insider tone, similar to that in the business-press accounts noted below, suggested that the reporter had access to more than press handouts. The article continued: "Nobody expected the Japanese to answer 'Yes' as soon as they saw the Potsdam terms. Truman's statesmanlike move was intended to recapture the political initiative, not to win the war in an afternoon." [64]

Also on August 6, *Time* described the efforts of several military officers who were calling on Japan to surrender by "talking tough." The object of their "word war" was to "persuade the enemy to surrender now" (before the "complications" of Russian entry). By surrendering, the enemy could avoid the "harsh alternative." "Words are weapons," as the title of the article stated, implying that the war did not have to be fought solely with military might. In the August 6 issue of *Time*, another article emphasized that there were only two alternatives: unconditional surrender or "utter devastation of the Japanese homeland," as stated by the Potsdam Proclamation. *Time* did suggest, however, that the emperor's fate depended "on how the throne's influence is exerted." [65]

Interestingly, some of the most sophisticated reporting came from a small-circulation business newsletter. The business community estimates of the date of surrender were crucial, for entire fortunes could be made or lost in the ensuing rush for economic reconversion to a civilian economy. The *Kiplinger Washington Letter* was particularly frank in its assessment of the diplomatic situation. On July 21 it advised its readers:

> Our military men do NOT think in terms of an early Jap end. They say it will take at least a year more, and perhaps even longer. But they talk only of MILITARY operations for outright DEFEAT, whereas current peace moves involve DIPLOMATIC operations for SURRENDER. Note the distinction when you read the news, the rumors, the denials.[66]

On August 4, after the Japanese government stated that it would ignore the Potsdam Proclamation, the *Kiplinger Washington Letter* concluded with this estimate:

> As for Jap surrender, the impression left by news headlines is that the Japanese government has flatly rejected our peace terms. True, that's the formal front of the situation. . . . But behind that formal front the Japs are studying the terms, instituting inquiries through channels, asking for "clarifications." This is going on right now, and without getting into the published news. May be only "feelers". . . but feelers are usual forerunners of diplomatics. May be only a "trick". . . but we have some very good reasons for believing that Japanese leaders are really considering surrender . . . CONSIDERING.[67]

This sampling of pre-bomb reporting and commentary suggests that a rich basis existed for a critique of the decision to drop the bomb. Once the bomb was dropped, however, the media generally discarded the pre-bomb understanding of a Japan seeking a way out of the war in favor of the official position that the Japanese were refusing to surrender and that use of the bomb had prevented a costly future invasion of Japan.

Generally, if the pre-bomb understanding was carried forward at all, it was stated in a neutral tone or used to browbeat the Japanese. For example, *Time* magazine's concern that the Japanese may not easily submit to a U.S. occupation led it to say that:

> Japanese (and U.S.) emphasis on the atomic bomb as a decisive surrender factor did not help matters. There was danger that the Japanese would attribute defeat to a single scientific advance, fail to realize that they were beaten before Hiroshima dissolved. The occupation authorities, or a future Japanese government, would have to tell the people that Tokyo in July had secretly asked Moscow to mediate for peace.[68]

The liberal *New Republic* was more neutral:

> Just what part the atomic bomb played in Japan's plea for peace we do not yet know. Even before the first one was dropped on Hiroshima,

it seemed certain that the Japanese could not hold out very much longer. The entry of Russia into the war would itself have been enough to bring the final act of the drama appreciably nearer. Yet the atomic bomb must have been an important factor.[69]

There were, however, an important minority of dissenters who questioned or criticized Truman's decision after the war, including Norman Cousins, editor of the *Saturday Review*, Henry Luce, David Lawrence, editor of *United States News*, and Hanson Baldwin, military affairs editor of the *New York Times*, as well as many religious commentators. David Lawrence, a staunch conservative, wrote shortly after the bomb: "Yet we had already been winning the war against Japan. Our highest officials have known for some time that Russia was planning to enter the war in the Far East. . . . The surrender of Japan has been for weeks inevitable."[70] A few weeks later he added, "Spokesman of the Army Air Forces say it wasn't necessary anyway and that the war had been won already. Competent testimony exists to prove that Japan was seeking to surrender many weeks before the atomic bomb came."[71]

Norman Cousins, who supported the air war at least through 1944, argued along with his co-author Thomas Finletter (later to become a secretary of the Air Force) that the tight time frame after the bomb was successfully tested in New Mexico precluded a non-lethal demonstration of the bomb to the Japanese, "if the purpose was to knock Japan out before Russia came in."[72] Henry Luce, in a speech in Milwaukee in 1948, stated, "If instead of our doctrine of 'unconditional surrender,' we had all along made our conditions clear, I have little doubt that the war with Japan would have ended no later than it did—without the bomb explosion that so jarred the Christian conscience."[73]

Hanson Baldwin elaborated on the same theme in his criticism. In an article for *Atlantic* he stated that "Our only warning to a Japan already militarily defeated and in a hopeless situation was the Potsdam demand for unconditional surrender . . . when we knew Japanese surrender attempts had started." Baldwin added that after the bomb was dropped, "our unconditional surrender demand was made conditional as [Secretary of War Henry L.] Stimson had originally proposed we should do."[74] In the same year, Baldwin wrote critically of the bomb decision in his book *Great Mistakes of the War*:

> We dropped the bomb at a time when Japan already was negotiating for an end of the war but before those negotiations could come to fruition. We demanded unconditional surrender, then dropped the bomb and accepted conditional surrender, a sequence which indicates pretty clearly that the Japanese would have surrendered, even if the bomb had not been dropped, had the Potsdam Declaration included our promise to permit the Emperor to remain on his imperial throne.[75]

In the 1950s, challenges to the "orthodox" view came from the right wing in publications like *National Review*, *The Freeman*, and *Human Events*. Using mostly the limited secondary sources available in this period, these commentators generally combined a moral and geopolitical critique. For the most part they believed that Truman could have ended the war earlier by modifying unconditional surrender terms and thus prevented Soviet entry into the war. In doing so, the Americans and not the Red Army would have taken the Japanese surrender in Manchuria. Thus, the argument went, the "Reds" would not have overrun China in 1949 and the Korean War could have been averted.[76] Forrest Davis, for example, wrote in *The Freeman* that:

> In the interval between May 29 and July 26, when the door finally was opened to Japan's surrender, the order was issued to drop A-bombs on Hiroshima and Nagasaki; a deed which given the supposed willingness of Japan to capitulate, comes little short of being a high crime and one that may return unmercifully to plague us.[77]

Harry Elmer Barnes's May 1958 article in *National Review* said that the atomic bomb was unnecessary, that the Japanese were already defeated and making bids for peace. Barnes also made quite clear his view that the real target of the bomb was not Japan but Russia. Barnes stated that "Stalin took this view and, many date the origins of the Cold War from the time he received news of the bombing shortly after the Potsdam Conference." If this is true, Barnes reasoned, "the tens of thousands of Japanese who were roasted at Hiroshima and Nagasaki were sacrificed not to end the war or save American and Japanese lives but to strengthen American diplomacy vis-à-vis Russia."[78] A few years later this iconoclastic position taken in the conservative *National Review* would be labeled as "left-wing revisionism" and would remain thus to this day.

In the 1960s and early 1970s, Gar Alperovitz and historians on the "new left" questioned the decision to use the bomb from a different perspective. These so-called "revisionists" saw the use of the bomb as an implied threat against the Soviet Union and an early shot in the Cold War, rather than an act of military necessity. It is in this period that a significant split emerged between accumulating scholarly evidence and the media's elaboration of a popular history in its coverage of Hiroshima-related anniversaries.

The media coverage of the early 1990s shows an almost irreconcilable difference between contemporary news media and recent scholarly examinations of Hiroshima. In August 1990, the forty-fifth anniversary of Hiroshima, for example, the approximately 150 newspaper and magazine items that mentioned the atomic bombing of Hiroshima essentially avoided acknowledging even the existence of a historical debate about the dropping of the bomb.[79] In 1991, when President George Bush during Pearl Harbor Commemoration Week bluntly stated that Truman's decision "was right because it spared the lives of millions of American citizens," only three of the approximately 130 print and television stories and op-eds surveyed that mentioned Hiroshima acknowledged in the briefest of phrases alternatives to his view.[80]

Contemporary scholarship enters the news media almost solely in the form of an extremely infrequent op-ed. It almost never shapes news coverage of Hiroshima-related anniversaries or controversies, unless historians themselves make the news, as they did when a group of historians publicly challenged the Smithsonian in mid-November of 1994 for caving in to veterans groups.

From surveying half a century of coverage on the end of the Pacific War, it becomes clear that the so-called "conventional wisdom" on the bomb decision was shaped *after* the fact—it did not evolve from the popular understanding of the war in the spring and summer of 1945. As we have seen from the pre-bomb understanding of likely scenarios for ending the war, it can be argued that the amnesia-ridden version of events offered by Truman, and repeated by much of the press as well as "orthodox" historians, represents the original attempt at "revisionist" history.[81]

NOTES

1. The advent of the atomic bomb was generally seen as an unprecedented historic event. As Bruce Bliven wrote in the *New Republic*, "There is no doubt that [the coming of the atomic bomb] is, in its potentialities, the most significant event in the history of mankind for many generations. At last it seems literally true that humanity as a whole must either learn to live at peace or face destruction on a grotesquely vast scale." Later in his essay he called the bomb an "appalling weapon." See "The Bomb and the Future," *New Republic*, Aug. 20, 1945, pp. 210–12. See Paul Boyer, *By the Bomb's Early Light* (New York, 1985), for a record of similar reactions.

2. Paul Fussell, *Thank God for the Atom Bomb* (New York, 1988).

3. The two main studies of Hiroshima and the American media/public opinion are Boyer, *By the Bomb's Early Light*, and Michael Yavenditti, "American Reactions to the Use of Atomic Bombs on Japan, 1945–1947" (Ph.D. diss., University of California, Berkeley, 1970).

4. J. Samuel Walker, "The Decision to Use the Bomb: A Historiographical Update," *Diplomatic History* 14 (Winter 1990). This scholarly consensus also showed that Truman had greatly exaggerated the casualty estimates of an invasion that was not inevitable.

5. Editorial, *Christian Century*, Apr. 18, 1945.

6. Ibid.

7. *Newsweek*, Apr. 16, 1945, p. 56.

8. "Looking to the Pacific," *Nation*, May 12, 1945.

9. "Talk of Tokyo Bid Rife in Washington," *New York Times*, Apr. 11, 1945.

10. "Fortress Japan," ibid., June 11, 1945.

11. Press speculation occurred even after an urgent appeal from General George C. Marshall and Admiral Ernest J. King via the Office of Censorship to editors and publishers on April 5, and again on May 8. It was feared that speculation about future Soviet hostilities toward Japan might trigger preemptive actions against the Soviets by the Japanese before the Soviet forces had been built up. See "Miscellany (Nov. 19, 1943–Dec. 1945)," item 11, Exec. 2, OPD Executive File, entry 422, RG 165, National Archives, Washington, D.C.

12. Harry P. Howard, "America, Japan and Russia," *Christian Century*, May 2, 1945.

13. "Lost Battles, Slap from Moscow Shake Props of Jap Ruling Clique," *Newsweek*, Apr. 16, 1945.

14. "The Periscope," ibid., May 21, 1945.

15. Harry Howard, "Is Japan Trying to Surrender?" *Progressive*, May 28, 1945.

16. "Definite Terms for Japan," *Commonweal*, June 15, 1945.

17. "After Okinawa, What?" *Christian Century*, May 9, 1945. A study by the Office of Strategic Services (the forerunner of the CIA) mirrored this sentiment. The study stated that "Admiral Suzuki's appointment strongly suggests that Japan is laying the groundwork for a peace offensive." Memorandum for information, Apr. 15, 1945, folder 696: "Japan—Cabinet," box 57, Entry 136, RG 226, National Archives.

18. Editorials in the *Nation*, for example, criticized the recent "intimations from various quarters [in the press and officialdom] concerning" a possible conditional peace for Japan. Such a peace would leave intact the industrialists who supported the militarists. The *Nation* added that "advocates of a negotiated peace have sought to capitalize on anti-Soviet feeling by circulating wild stories about supposed Russian ambitions on the Asiatic continent." "Soft Peace for Japan?" and Freda Kirchwey, "Russia and the West," both in *Nation*, June 23, 1945.

19. The *Times* editorial of June 9 noted that "People are beginning to talk comfortably of a Japanese surrender 'before we know it,' or certainly before the first of next year." The *Times* added that the country began to relax in February, "when victory in Europe was assured," and that feeling is again apparent because victory over Japan is "assured." "No doubt the current diffusion of interest at home is an interlude between an exhausting victory in Europe and the final deployment of strength in the Far East five or six months hence." Thus the *Times* editors portrayed the talk of peace feelers and a defeated Japan as American exhaustion rather than as an opportunity to end the war.

20. "Stockholm Hears Tokyo Peace Tale," *New York Times*, June 16, 1945.

21. The Navy's psychological warfare branch, called Op-16-W, enjoyed a special covert relationship with the *Washington Post*. Ladislas Farago, then a member of Op-16-W working with Capt. Ellis Zacharias (see below), would later recall, "The editor of the *Washington Post* was Herbert Elliston. He was my friend. I used to go to his small inner sanctum from time to time to 'inspire' editorials about Japan." Ladislas Farago, *Burn After Reading: The Espionage History of World War II* (New York, 1961), p. 296. After the war (ca. 1946) the *Washington Post* would publish a pamphlet boasting about its role in "The story of the secret weapon [psychological warfare] which had Japan ready to yield thirteen days before the atomic bomb struck Hiroshima." The pamphlet, found in the John J. McCloy Papers, Amherst College Archives, Amherst, Mass. (file WD6:34), was entitled "Psychological Warfare Against Japan" and mostly consisted of reprinted *Washington Post* editorials from the spring and summer of 1945 urging clarification of surrender terms for Japan. Perhaps in a lapse of institutional memory the *Washington Post* today dismisses historians who take the view that was held by the *Post* in the 1945–46 period as "revisionist." See "The Smithsonian Changes Course" (editorial), *Washington Post*, Feb. 1, 1995: "Narrow-minded representatives of a special-interest and revisionist point of view attempted to use their inside track to appropriate and hollow out a historical event that large numbers of Americans alive at that time and engaged in the war had witnessed and understood in a very different—and authentic—way." In a later editorial the *Post* agreed that it was a "bad idea" to mix "50-year commemorative anniversary ceremonies" with "hotly contested revisionist analysis." "Smithsonian: After the Shouting," *Washington Post*, May 7, 1995.

22. "Now Japan," *Washington Post*, May 9, 1945.

23. "Writing on the Wall," ibid., June 3, 1945.

24. Ibid., June 6, 1945.

25. "Fatal Phrase," ibid., June 11, 1945.

26. "Inside Japan," ibid., June 12, 1945.

27. "Mr. Grew on Peace," ibid., July 13, 1945.

28. "After Okinawa, What?" *Christian Century*, May 9, 1945.

29. "Peace Maneuvers in the Pacific," ibid., June 20, 1945.

30. "A Statement on Our Policy Toward Japan," *Christianity and Crisis*, June 25, 1945. Niebuhr initiated his journal in 1941 "to combat pacifism and neutralism within the churches," according to Lawrence Wittner. See Wittner, *Rebels Against War: The American Peace Movement, 1933–1983* (Philadelphia, 1984), p. 16.

31. "Editorial Notes," *Christianity and Crisis*, Aug. 6, 1945.

32. Norman Thomas, "Our War with Japan," *Commonweal*, Apr. 20, 1945.

33. "Define Terms for Japan," ibid., June 15, 1945.

34. "Ministers Ask for Statement of Japanese War Aims," *Christian Century*, June 27, 1945.

35. "Why Korea Isn't Named in the Petition," ibid., July 18, 1945.

36. "Terms for Japan," ibid., Aug. 8, 1945.

37. "A Petition to the President," ibid., June 27, 1945.

38. The efforts of Zacharias and the Army and Navy psychological warfare experts was similarly taken up within the Truman administration by Secretary of War Henry L. Stimson, Assistant Secretary of War John J. McCloy, Acting Secretary of State Joseph C. Grew, Secretary of the Navy James V. Forrestal, Undersecretary of the Navy Ralph A. Bard, former President Herbert Hoover and others. See Gar Alperovitz, *The Decision to Use the Atomic Bomb and the Architecture of an American Myth* (New York, 1995).

39. "Japan is Warned to Give Up Soon," *New York Times*, July 22, 1945. This was the twelfth in a series of broadcasts to Japan which began on V-E Day. Before each broadcast, Zacharias (who spoke fluent Japanese) was introduced as an "official spokesman."

40. It even showed up in intercepted and decrypted Japanese diplomatic communications. See "MAGIC Diplomatic Summaries," July 26, 1945, RG 457, National Archives.

41. "Surrender Terms," *Washington Post*, July 21, 1945.

42. *New York Times*, July 26, 1945. The article noted that several words appeared to be missing from the broadcast.

43. For more on this crucial broadcast see the following works by Ellis Zacharias: *Secret Missions: The Story of an Intelligence Officer* (New York, 1946); "Eighteen Words that Bagged Japan," *Saturday Evening Post*, Nov. 17, 1945; "We Did Not Need to Drop the A-bomb," *Look*, May 23, 1950; "How We Bungled the Japanese Surrender," ibid., June 6, 1950.

44. "Terms for Japan," *Christian Century*, Aug. 8, 1945.

45. "Why Prolong the War Against Japan?" *Catholic World*, August 1945.

46. Hanson Baldwin, "Ideas Can Fight Japan," *New York Times*, July 20, 1945.

47. "The Peace Rumors," ibid., July 19, 1945.

48. "Terms for Japan," ibid., July 23, 1945.

49. "Terms to End War Urged on Truman," ibid., July 24, 1945.

50. "Bargaining With Japan," ibid., July 25, 1945.

51. "Japanese Cabinet Weighs Ultimatum" and "The Ultimatum," (editorial) ibid., July 28, 1945.

52. Walter Lippmann, "Terms for Japan," *New York Herald Tribune*, July 12, 1945.

53. "Power v. Statesmanship," *Time*, July 16, 1945.

54. "Japan—An Opportunity for Statesmanship," *Life*, July 16, 1945.

55. "Japan: The Opportunity for Bringing Classic Statesmanship to Bear on Tokyo Still Exists," ibid., Aug. 6, 1945.

56. "Is Japan Ready to Quit? New Denials, New Overtures," *United States News*, Aug. 3, 1945.

57. "The Ring Tightens Around Japan as Lend-Lease Pours into Siberia," *Newsweek*, July 9, 1945.

58. Ernest Lindley, "The Jap Does Have a Choice," ibid., July 16, 1945.

59. "Naval Bombardment of Jap Soil Warns Foe Final Blow Is Near," ibid., July 23, 1945.

60. "To the Enemy," *Time*, July 23, 1945.

61. Little did the magazine know that Grew had recommended clarification of surrender terms back in May, after massive fire bombing raids against Tokyo, to provide "surrender-minded elements in the Government . . . a valid reason and the necessary strength to come to an early and clear-cut decision." Joseph C. Grew, *Turbulent Era: A Diplomatic Record of Forty Years 1904–1945*, 2 vols. (Boston, 1952), 2:1429–34. See also Grew to Stimson, Feb. 12, 1947, Atomic bomb file, box 2, Papers of Eugene Dooman, Hoover Institution, Stanford University, Stanford, Calif. Dooman (former State Department Far Eastern expert) and Grew corresponded on the issue of the atomic bomb after Stimson's article defending the decision to drop the bomb appeared in *Harper's* in February 1947. The two friends were appalled by Stimson's attempt to rewrite history and Grew decided to keep a file of notes and articles that he might one day use to vindicate his position.

62. "To the Enemy," *Time*, July 23, 1945.

63. Ernest Lindley, "The Decision We Face on Japan," *Newsweek*, July 30, 1945.

64. "Attention, Tokyo!" *Time*, Aug. 6, 1945.

65. Ibid.

66. *Kiplinger Washington Letter*, July 21, 1945.

67. Ibid., Aug. 4, 1945.

68. "The Harvest," *Time*, Aug. 27, 1945.

69. Bliven, *New Republic*, Aug. 20, 1945.

70. David Lawrence, "What Hath Man Wrought," *United States News*, Aug. 17, 1945.

71. David Lawrence, "The Right to Kill," ibid., Oct. 5, 1945.

72. Norman Cousins and Thomas Finletter, "A Beginning for Sanity," *Saturday Review of Literature*, June 15, 1946.

73. Robert T. Elson, *The World of Time Inc.*, 3 vols. (New York, 1973), 2:137.

74. Hanson Baldwin, "Our Worst Blunders in the War," *Atlantic*, February 1950.

75. Hanson Baldwin, *Great Mistakes of the War* (New York, 1950), p. 92.

76. For a sample of right-wing positions from the 1950s see Forrest Davis, "Did Marshall Prolong the Pacific War?" *The Freeman*, Nov. 19, 1951; Anthony Kubek, "How We Lost the Pacific War," *Human Events*, Dec. 1, 1958; Harry Elmer Barnes, "Hiroshima: Assault on a Beaten Foe," *National Review*, May 10, 1958; Elizabeth Churchill Brown, *The Enemy at His Back* (New York, 1956).

77. Davis, "Did Marshall Prolong the Pacific War?"

78. Barnes, "Hiroshima."

79. The articles were retrieved through the Nexis database of newspapers and magazines (and NPR and ABC news transcripts) by searching for all items that mentioned both "Hiroshima" and "bomb."

80. Bush's remarks appeared in an interview with David Brinkley. See transcript, ABC's *This Week with David Brinkley*, Dec. 1, 1991.

81. A comparison of pre- and post-bomb reporting suggests that the summer of 1945 itself was contested terrain regarding Hiroshima: the media chose to put aside what it had recently reported. This choice helped set the stage for Henry Stimson's success in capturing the interpretive ground for understanding Truman's decision with his article in *Harper's* in February 1947. See, for example, Barton J. Bernstein, "Seizing the Contested Terrain of Early Nuclear History: Stimson, Conant, and Their Allies Explain the Decision to Use the Atomic Bomb," *Diplomatic History* 17 (Winter 1993). Bernstein views 1947 as a critical moment in the shaping of popular understanding without placing that moment in the context of the news reporting of the summer of 1945.

II

THE EARLY CONTROVERSY

Mr. Byrnes did not argue that it was necessary to use the bomb against the cities of Japan in order to win the war. . . Mr. Byrnes's view [was] that our possessing and demonstrating the bomb would make Russia more manageable in Europe.

Leo Szilard

I cannot speak for the others but it was ever present in my mind that it was important that we should have an end to the war before the Russians came in. . . . [N]either the President nor I were anxious to have them [the Soviets] enter the war after we had learned of this successful [atomic] test.

James Byrnes
Secretary of State 1945-47

[The use of the atomic bomb] was precipitated by a desire to end the war in the Pacific by any means before Russia's participation. I am sure that if President Roosevelt had still been there, none of that would have been possible.

Albert Einstein

Seizing the Contested Terrain of Early Nuclear History

Barton J. Bernstein

[My] article ["The Decision to Use the Atomic Bomb"] has also been intended to satisfy the doubts of that rather difficult class of the community which will have charge of the education of the next generation, namely educators and historians, I have therefore gone into a good deal of detail to show the care that we all took to get the best advice . . . .
— Henry L. Stimson to President Harry S. Truman, January 7, 1947

[Your] article will play an important part in accomplishing the . . . goal [of international control], for I believe that if the propaganda against the use of the atomic bomb had been allowed to grow unchecked, the strength of our military position by virtue of having the bomb would have been correspondingly weakened, and with this weakening would have come a decrease in the probabilities of an international agreement for the control of atomic energy.
— James B. Conant to Henry L. Stimson, January 22, 1947

I N THE LATE AUTUMN and early winter of 1946–47, more than a year after the atomic bombings of Japan, as the Baruch Plan for international control of atomic energy was going down to defeat in the nascent United Nations, two influential articles appeared in respected national magazines justifying the 1945 attacks on Hiroshima and Nagasaki. In the December 1946 *Atlantic Monthly*, physicist Karl T. Compton, MIT's president and a wartime atomic-energy adviser, published "If the Atomic Bomb Had Not Been Used." Two months later, in February 1947, a more extended treatment of the issues appeared in *Harper's Magazine* as "The Decision to Use the Atomic Bomb," under the authorship of Henry L. Stimson, the wartime secretary of war who had helped to guide America's use of the two bombs.[1]

Despite differences in emphasis and length, these two articles seemed deeply informed, honest and open, and generally persuasive. They were ventures by respected Americans to examine the wartime use of the bombs, to describe the care andconsiderations leading to those decisions, to explain why alternatives would not have worked and were rejected, and to show that the bombings had been necessary to end the Pacific war and save lives. Appearing at a time when most Americans continued to endorse the atomic bombings,[2] and when few mistrusted their government or questioned the major wartime decisions, these essays confirmed popular beliefs. Compton's article seemed to be mostly a revealing history with some calm advocacy. Stimson's was an even richer history, disclosing new documents, and seemed largely to eschew advocacy for candor. Taken together, these two articles affirmed, and emphasized, the rectitude of American leaders and of the A-bomb decisions.

The essays, and especially Stimson's, would become leading sources for history. Lay people, journalists, political scientists, and historians comfortably treated both, but particularly Stimson's, as accurate and valuable revelations of the inner workings of the government. Few analysts wondered why these essays had been written, whether their appearance at virtually the same time might be more than serendipity, or whether they were conceived with some larger purposes in mind.

Indeed, there was a rich and revealing history behind the creation and publication of these two A-bomb defenses. The ventures were conceived, and urged, by James B. Conant, Harvard's president and a wartime atomic policymaker. Fearful of doubts emerging in America about the A-bomb decisions, Conant wanted to shape popular understanding and demolish the wrong kind of thinking, hoping thereby to bar a return to prewar isolationism and to promote international control of atomic energy. His was a bold program, springing from hope and fear, and one in which he was able to enlist powerful associates.[3] It was history with a purpose. And yet, Conant's aim was to conceal much of the purpose, to avoid having the A-bomb essays seem argumentative, and thus to have the history—especially Stimson's essay—appear largely as matter-of-fact narration. The most powerful way to persuade, as Conant knew, was to provide guided description, not explicit argument.

The present study is an analysis, resting heavily upon Stimson's own correspondence files and also upon the related materials by Conant, Compton, and others, to examine the history of these early articles on the A-bomb decision. In doing so, the purposes are to uncover an important part of early nuclear history, to show how a part of the American elite sought to shape popular understanding, and to raise questions for latter-day analysts about the use of memoirs and similar sources in understanding, and writing, history. Thus, this is an analysis of "The Decision to Use the Atomic Bomb" and Stimson's 1948 expansion (explicitly with McGeorge Bundy) of that essay for Stimson's memoir-book, *On Active Service in Peace and War*,[4] and also a briefer study of "If the Atomic Bomb Had Not Been Used," as a way of examining how history is constructed by memoirists.

Among other themes, the present essay emphasizes that key members of America's policy elite—Conant, Stimson, Compton, Justice Felix Frankfurter, President Harry S. Truman, and others—recognized that history was valuable contested terrain. Creating the right history could be essential to gaining popular support for the right policy. That enterprise, linked so intimately to ending isolationism and defending the A-bomb decision, also involved a young man, then unknown to the American public—McGeorge Bundy, who was the concealed wordsmith of Stimson's 1947 essay but the acknowledged co-author for the ex–secretary of war's 1948 book-memoir.

Bundy, a talented young scholar, served as the hidden co-writer of the important "Decision" article. Enlisting as Stimson's "scribe," as Bundy later phrased his role, he helped promote the retired secretary of war's view that the A-bomb was used *only* after "a searching consideration of alternatives." But forty-one years later, looking back on the A-bomb decisions again, Bundy's own judgment changed. Informed by more sources and undoubtedly chastened after living for over four decades with nuclear weapons, sometimes himself as an influential policymaker, Bundy, by 1988, recognized that the 1945 A-bomb decision did not, unfortunately, involve an effort "as long or wide or deep as the subject deserved." Put bluntly, Stimson had "claimed too much for the process of consideration" in 1945 leading to Hiroshima and Nagasaki.[5]

Bundy's own recent analysis, presented at the end of his seventh decade, has helped to inspire this essay, which focuses primarily on Stimson, who was then nearing the end of his eighth decade, and secondarily on Conant, who was then in his sixth. All are men who understood the power of authority and prestige, who held important appointive offices in government, and who generally eschewed the hurly-burly of electoral politics and preferred to shape policy in the councils of the executive branch. Their purview involved foreign policy and weapons policy, and they worried deeply about the problems of creating, and maintaining, popular support for elite-formulated programs.

IN SEPTEMBER 1946, thirteen months after the atomic bombings of Hiroshima and Nagasaki, Harvard president James B. Conant, one of the architects of America's World War II nuclear policy, read a disturbing editorial criticizing America's use of the A-bomb on Japan. What upset Conant was a September 14 *Saturday Review of Literature* editorial by Norman Cousins, who welcomed the recent publication of John Hersey's "Hiroshima."[6] In praising Hersey's powerful essay, Cousins spoke of "the crime of Hiroshima and Nagasaki." A few months earlier, Cousins had contended that the atomic bombings had been unnecessary and suggested that the weapon had been dropped to stop the Soviets from grabbing territory in Asia and to "checkmate Russian expansion." In his September 14 editorial, he deplored that Americans had failed to ask their World War II leaders why they had not first given Japan a demonstration of the bomb combined with a surrender ultimatum. This question was important, Cousins argued, because "we have learned . . . that Japan was ready to quit even before Hiroshima," and therefore there was no merit to the contention that the atomic bombings were necessary to save American lives.[7]

Conant, a strong, pre-Hiroshima proponent of using the bomb on Japan, had also become a vigorous post-war defender of that action. Earlier in 1946, when the Federal Council of Churches had publicly condemned the use of the bomb on Japanese cities, Conant privately criticized theologian Reinhold Niebuhr for signing that statement. In his letter to Niebuhr, Conant argued that the council's statement was deeply flawed, because it did not take adequate account of the mass conventional bombing of Japan's cities and thus treated the atomic bombings as ethically distinctive. Why, Conant asked, should the American people not "be equally penitent" for the firebombing of Tokyo and other cities? Conant claimed that he had been equally involved in the decisions regarding each method of destruction, and that he thus could view these issues impartially. Neither method should be condemned, Conant contended, and he wondered how Niebuhr, as the author of the fiercely realistic *Children of Light and Children of Darkness*, could have abandoned such thinking to oppose the 1945 use of the atomic bomb.[8]

In a letter dated March 11, 1946, Niebuhr replied that the council's statement was inadequate, but he emphasized that its crucial point was that American leaders had decided to drop the bomb on Japan without a forceful, dramatic warning. "We would have been in a stronger moral position had we published the facts about this instrument of destruction, made a demonstration of its effects over Japan in a non-populated area, and threatened the use of the bomb if the Japanese did not surrender." [9] Thus, Niebuhr presented two unsettling implications: America had acted immorally by not issuing a substantial prior warning; and America may have missed an opportunity to end the war without using the bomb. In a September 1945 article, Niebuhr had raised a related criticism: The United States should not have demanded Japan's unconditional surrender. Niebuhr's themes of a missed opportunity, of the unnecessary brutality of the war, and of the questionable insistence on unconditional surrender would continue to appear in the critiques by A-bomb opponents.[10]

During 1946, Conant became more attentive to, and more worried by, criticisms of that decision. He seemed not to notice that the objectors were few, that the decision was unchallenged by most Americans, and that the support for the decision was overwhelming. Instead, he became more exercised when,[11] in mid-1946, a well-publicized book, *While Time Remains*, appeared in which journalist Leland Stowe, while criticizing America for failing to achieve international control of atomic energy, framed a *single* paragraph condemning the A-bombing of Japan.[12] Instead of first providing a non-combat demonstration as a warning to Japan, according to Stowe, President Truman "listened to certain U.S. Army generals" and dropped the bombs on Japanese cities. Stowe's indictment was harsh: "The United States became morally guilty of being the first nation to inflict mass murder, on a scale of horror hitherto unknown, through an atomic weapon." American leaders, he insisted, could not argue in rebuttal that a test-demonstration would not have produced an early surrender, because that was not the ethical issue. "History's stark record simply reads that America's leaders were not humane enough to make the attempt." [13]

Stowe's condemnation, Cousins's recent editorial, probably Hersey's essay, and possibly the Federal Council's criticisms outraged and alarmed Conant. Poring over his worries, he wrote in September 1946 to a prominent Boston attorney and wartime associate, Harvey H. Bundy, who had been Secretary of War Henry L. Stimson's close aide, to complain that these criticisms were "increasing in recent days." The problem, Conant explained in his three-page letter of the twenty-third, was that the criticisms were not just coming from "professional pacifists and . . . certain religious leaders" but from others, including "non-religious groups and people taking up the same theme." The dangers, he said, were considerable:

> This type of sentimentalism . . . is bound to have a great deal of influence on the next generation. The type of person who goes into teaching, particularly school teaching, will be influenced a great deal by this type of argument. We are in danger of repeating the fallacy which occurred after World War I [when] it became accepted doctrine among a group of so-called intellectuals who taught in our schools and colleges that the United States made a great error in entering World War I. . . . A small minority, if it represents the type of person who is both sentimental and verbally minded and in contact with our youth, may result in distortion of history.[14]

As an architect of the bomb's use in Japan and a proponent of international control, Conant had both a recent past to defend and a general program to advance. Doubts about the use of the bomb, he suggested, could spill over into a new isolationism. That was a fear that he shared with many World War II-era policymakers, who did not want their general purposes, or America's conduct, in that great but terrible war challenged. They were eager, and anxious, to shape the public's understanding of the recent American past.[15]

CONANT HIMSELF, WITH SCIENTIST-ADMINISTRATOR VANNEVAR BUSH, had helped to persuade President Roosevelt to embark upon the expensive, and daring, project that had culminated in the atomic bombings.[16] In 1943, Conant had actually hoped that the bomb would prove impossible. "Civilization would then be, indeed, fortunate—atomic energy for . . . destruction an impossibility." [17] More visionary, and more fearful, than many in the upper levels of the wartime government about the bomb, by early 1944 he had started thinking about the need for international control of atomic energy. The choices, he thought, were international control ("a scheme to remove atomic energy from the field of conflict") or a "race between nations and in the next war destruction of civilization." [18] By late 1944, with Bush's help, Conant sought to tutor Secretary of War Stimson on the need to deal with the problem of international control, and Conant's efforts not only compelled Stimson to think about this problem but to create in the spring of 1945 the high-level group, the Interim Committee, to give advice on how to handle the atom.[19]

Anticipating in May 1945 the midsummer use of the atomic bomb on Japan, Conant had continued to think about the future. He was suspicious of scientists' requests, coming in that spring from the secret Chicago laboratory of the Manhattan Project, for continued funding. "We are to spend our money and our scientific manpower on a feverish race but when we have the ultimate what do we do with it?" Unsure himself about how to produce a safe future, Conant was willing, in May, both to back "an all-out research program" for a hydrogen bomb and also to push for international control.[20]

In a secret May 1945 memorandum to Bush, Conant had revealed his own thinking about weaponry, military victory, and peace. "Supposing it were possible to wipe out a city suddenly . . . , so what of it? Will [that] nation surrender?" No, Conant concluded—as "the evidence in this war indicates." "The essence of war is not slaughter but *impressing your will upon the enemy.*" [21] But such slaughter, he knew, could *help* win the war for America. Such thinking apparently led him, on May 31, 1945, at the Interim Committee meeting to recommend, and Stimson agreed, in the paraphrased words of the minutes, *"that the most desirable target [for the A-bomb in Japan] would be a vital war plant employing a large number of workers and closely surrounded by workers' houses."* Stripped of euphemisms, that of course meant the massive killing of non-combatants. Compton and Bush, with the other committee members, apparently concurred.[22]

Six weeks later, on July 16, while Stimson was in Germany for the Potsdam Conference, Conant was at Alamogordo for the "Trinity" test—the first atomic detonation. There, as he wrote in a secret memorandum the next day, the results had been stunning and alarming. "The enormity of the light. . . . My instantaneous reaction was that something had gone wrong and that the thermal nuclear transformation of the atmosphere [a gigantic burning up] had actually occurred." It had been "like the end of the world," he emphasized. He followed with these apocalyptic, and alarming, words: "Perhaps my impression was only premature on a time scale of years." [23] Yet this experience did not lead him to reconsider the forthcoming atomic bombing of Japan. Conant never graphically commented, in prospect or in retrospect, on what the bomb would, and did, mean when its power reached human skin and bone, blood and marrow. But the July 16 test, and the later atomic bombings, did further persuade him of the dangers of atomic weapons, of the perils to America and to civilization, and of the need for international control.

In his private September 1946 letter to Harvey Bundy, written thirteen months after the atomic bombings and when the Baruch Plan did not yet seem doomed to total rejection, Conant insisted—perhaps too much, and unconvincingly—that he felt no guilt over the use of the bomb on Japan.[24] He clearly recalled, he said in this letter, that he had recommended the bomb's use "on the grounds (1) that I believed it would shorten the war against Japan, and (2) that unless it was actually used in battle there was no chance of convincing the American public and the world that it should be controlled by international agreement." There was nothing in the emerging evidence, he contended, that would change his opinion about how America should have acted, in 1945, to speed the end of the Pacific war. A test- demonstration would not have been "realistic" for this purpose, he stressed. And it was simply "Monday morning quarterbacking [that Japan] would have surrendered anyway." [25]

Conant's September 1946 letter undoubtedly expressed a theme that he preferred not to make public: a powerful pre-Hiroshima reason, at least for himself, to use the bomb on Japan was that the dramatic detonation would make America and the world face the facts and move to international control. Phrasing matters loosely, he left unclear whether this facing-the-facts theme had been an additional, a coequal, or the controlling reason for using the atom bomb. Put somewhat differently, had the aim to end the war been necessary and sufficient for his recommendation to use the bomb? [26]

It was essential, Conant stressed in his letter to Bundy, that someone with great moral authority should publicly and persuasively defend the use of the bomb. After discussing this matter with Vannevar Bush, his World War II associate on nuclear policy, Conant strongly concluded that they could specify the ideal person: former Secretary of War Henry L. Stimson. In this letter to Bundy, who was Stimson's friend and admirer, there was no need to explain at length why the former secretary, widely admired for his integrity, was the ideal author in this venture. A lifelong Republican who had served as secretary of war under both Roosevelt and Truman, Henry L. Stimson had also been Hoover's secretary of state and Taft's secretary of war. His public career spanned nearly a half century, and his "boys" included such notables as John J. McCloy, Robert P. Patterson, and Robert A. Lovett. Stimson was the pillar of the "establishment" long before the term was coined.[27]

According to Conant, Stimson should write a short article "clarifying what actually happened with regard to the decision" to use the bomb. Conant hoped that Harvey Bundy and insurance executive George Harrison, who like Bundy had served Stimson as a wartime aide and adviser on nuclear policies, would convince the retired seventy-nine-year-old secretary of war to write such an essay for publication. It should, among other themes, according to Conant, show that, while some working scientists had opposed the use of the A-bomb, the major scientific leaders, including physicists J. Robert Oppenheimer, Enrico Fermi, Arthur H. Compton, and Ernest O. Lawrence, had supported the use of the weapon, met with the special Interim Committee, and been present for the "discussion of the actual target to be chosen." It was "unfair for the scientists by implication to try to dodge the responsibility for the decision," wrote Conant, who had been a noted chemist before becoming president of Harvard.[28]

SUCH CONCERNS ALSO APPARENTLY PROPELLED the fifty-three-year-old Conant, probably aided by Bush, to ask MIT president Karl T. Compton, a well-known physicist who had served on the Interim Committee with Conant and Bush, to write a similar article on the A-bomb. Because Conant and Bush had frequently been mistrusted by the Manhattan Project working scientists, neither man was a suitable author for such an essay, and any publication on the subject under their name might well have provoked hostility and direct rebuttals. That was exactly what Conant and presumably Bush desired to avoid, and Karl Compton was likely to have far more support among the Manhattan Project alumni.[29]

Karl Compton was glad to comply with Conant's request and sent a draft of his article to the Harvard president on October 15, saying that he had followed the latter's "suggestions."[30] Conant replied, "I think it excellent. I have no suggestions or comments, only applause." Conant added that he looked forward to its prompt publication, and he hoped that the *Atlantic* would also publicize it.[31]

That article, with minor revisions,[32] appeared in the December 1946 *Atlantic*. Printed under the name of a prominent university president and respected scientist, who had served as wartime atomic-energy adviser and later had traveled to Japan after the fateful August 1945 bombings, the article possessed great authority. Calm, apparently informed, and not defensive, it undoubtedly seemed persuasive to most readers. Its argument appeared rather straightforward: The atomic bombings undoubtedly prevented the costly invasion of Japan, produced a speedy surrender that was otherwise unlikely, and saved many American and Japanese lives. To Compton, the A-bombing itself was ethically no different from the earlier firebombings of Japan's cities. Its great value was that it "strengthened the hands" of the peace forces in Japan's government and "provided a face-saving argument for those [Japanese leaders] who had hitherto advocated continuing war." "It was not one atomic bomb, or two, which brought surrender," Compton asserted. "It was the experience of what an atomic bomb will actually do, *plus* the dread of many more, that was effective."[33]

Upon close scrutiny, Compton's brief article, "If the Atomic Bomb Had Not Been Used," might have raised unintended questions and challenges. If, for example, the firebombing of Japan's cities had been immoral (Compton assumed it was not), then the atomic bombing was equally immoral. Or, why did the Potsdam Declaration, issued by the United States, Great Britain, and China (but not the Soviet Union) on July 26, not guarantee maintenance of the emperor and include the Soviet signature? And how exactly had the decision to use the bomb been made, and who had made it? Compton had mentioned that the Interim Committee had been "called together by Secretary of War Stimson to assist him in plans for [the bomb's] test, use, and subsequent handling," and generally implied that Stimson, General George C. Marshall, the army chief of staff, "and their associates" (not specified) had made the decision. But what had been the role of President Harry S. Truman?[34]

When Karl Compton sent Truman the published article in mid-December, the President praised it, calling it "the first sensible statement I have seen on the subject," but he also emphasized a point that Compton had omitted: The President himself had made the decision. "It was made," Truman insisted in his December 16 letter to Compton, "after a complete survey of the whole situation." [35] Truman added, incorrectly, that "the Japanese were given fair warning and were offered the terms, which they finally accepted, well in advance of the dropping of the bomb." Truman's version, and possibly his memory, was flawed. The Potsdam Declaration had not guaranteed continuation of the Emperor, but Japan's conditional surrender of August 10 (after the Nagasaki bombing) had required an American guarantee of the Emperor, and the American reply had *implied* (but intentionally not promised) fulfillment of this single condition. [36]

In February 1947, when the *Atlantic Monthly* proudly published part of Truman's brief letter, most Americans had forgotten the important details of July and August 1945 involving America's surrender demands, Japan's significant condition on maintaining the Emperor, and the final resolution of that issue. Indeed, the hatred of Hirohito and of Japan's imperial system, a hatred widespread in America into August 1945, had quickly faded in the victory and had never become a political issue in the post-war United States.

IN AN UNPUBLISHED PARAGRAPH of his letter to Compton, Truman also said that he had asked Stimson "to assemble the facts" on the A-bomb decision. [37] Compton may well have known what the President himself probably did not: that the impetus for Stimson's effort, like Compton's own article, had come from James Conant. Indeed, by early autumn 1946 the former secretary and his young co-author, McGeorge Bundy, the able son of Harvey Bundy, were hard at work on this essay. Stimson had chosen the twenty-seven-year-old McGeorge Bundy, a Harvard junior fellow, a former Yale mathematics major and ex-World War II army officer, to assist him in preparing his memoir. [38] The article on the atomic bomb, though spurred by Conant, would deal with a subject that Bundy and Stimson had planned to treat in the book-memoir. Their task, at Conant's recommendation, was to get the essay speedily into shape as a freestanding article (initially separate from the book) to defend the A-bomb decision without appearing defensive.

In his discussions with young Bundy, during the summer of 1946, Stimson had already sketched the lines of his explanation and defense of the use of the A-bomb: It saved "so many million casualties," and only killed "a little over 100,000," a number which should be placed in the perspective of bloody tragedies like Gettysburg. "I think a pretty heavy burden lies on the person who would say we ought to be chastised because we didn't do it another way in an effort to save more," Stimson told Bundy in July 1946. [39]

The problem was to fashion this line of explanation into a compelling essay, one that would be historically informed, respectful of continuing secrecy restrictions, seem authoritative, and be persuasive. This required work in Stimson's own substantial wartime diaries and correspondence (which Stimson held), access to the Washington-based files of the secretary of war and related offices, help from a government historian (War Department historian Rudolph Winnacker eagerly assisted) in checking the details, and interviews with some other participants (Harvey Bundy and George Harrison shared their recollections). In addition, to assist, and to help shape the final product, General Leslie Groves, commanding general of the wartime Manhattan Project, R. Gordon Arneson, secretary of the Interim Committee, and Harvey Bundy all submitted drafts of a possible A-bomb defense.[40]

The most powerful draft, heavily shaping the final essay, was by Harvey Bundy. Dated September 25, 1946, two days after Conant wrote his plea for Stimson's essay, Harvey Bundy's version may well have been designed somewhat earlier to help his son and the former secretary of war put together the A-bomb events for the book-memoir. Harvey Bundy's draft stressed that the bomb, from 1941 on, was conceived as a legitimate weapon to be used in war against the enemy; that Stimson, in discussions with President Roosevelt and others, assumed that it would be used; that the Interim Committee had "discussed intensively whether the bomb should be used at all," considered various alternatives including a test-demonstration, but recommended that the bomb should be used; that top-level scientist-advisers in 1945 endorsed the combat use of the bomb on Japan; and that there was no persuasive evidence, even in 1946, that Japan would otherwise have surrendered without an invasion. The decision to use the bomb "was based primarily on the belief that the use would save American lives by terminating the war as rapidly as possible," and the final decision, according to Harvey Bundy's draft, was made by President Truman and Prime Minister Winston Churchill at Potsdam after consulting with the military chiefs.[41]

In Harvey Bundy's version, Stimson and the Interim Committee had rejected targets "where the destruction of life and property would be greatest so as to have the most complete impact on the course of the war," and therefore they had instead selected targets "primarily military in character but where the nature of the building construction would show completely the devastating effect of the bomb." [42] This rather benign view of 1945 target criteria was followed by Bundy's incorrect claim that the bomb had been detonated high in the air in order to "minimize radioactive poisoning . . . to avoid any contention that poison gases were being used." [43] Noting that some working scientists on the Manhattan Project had opposed the prospective use of the bomb, Bundy also wrote—again in error—that their petition "was discussed by the Secretary with the President." [44]

Two paragraphs from Harvey Bundy's draft, raising important issues later lost in the final Stimson version, warrant full quotation:

> In the minds of at least some of the Interim Committee and possibly in the minds of the executive authorities in Potsdam was the thought that unless the bomb were used it would be impossible to persuade the world that the saving of civilization in the future would depend on proper international control of atomic energy.
>
> The time of the dropping of the bomb had been set tentatively early in the year 1945 and was in no way dependent on the Russian commitments to enter the War. The time was not set with reference to any attempt to keep Russia from entering the War in the Far East. No doubt those in executive authority saw large advantages to winning the Japanese War without the aid of Russia, but the time schedule was set by the military with sole reference to using the earliest moment that all preparations would be ready for the effective use of the weapon.[45]

In early November 1946, Groves sent to Harvey Bundy two possible drafts for Stimson's essay—one by Arneson, and the other one revised by Groves from Arneson's and some other materials. These two drafts, though providing more information about pre-Hiroshima dissent by scientists, did not significantly reach beyond Harvey Bundy's September version. Borrowing from Harvey Bundy's version, Groves's draft included, verbatim, the same paragraph about using the bomb on Japan "to persuade the world" of the need for international control.[46]

Because the likely number of American lives saved was a central part, in early post-war America, of a compelling justification for the use of the A-bomb, Stimson needed the specific data, presumably that had been available to him shortly before Hiroshima, on the army's plans for the invasion of Japan, the estimated American casualties and fatalities, and the size of Japan's forces. He and McGeorge Bundy were informed by War Department historian Rudolph Winnacker that total Japanese forces (including about two million in Japan) had been estimated at about five million, that total U.S. Army troops to be deployed to the Pacific by mid-1946 would have been 2.6 million, that the number of U.S. Army forces killed in the war against Germany had been 142,000, and that total U.S. Army casualties (dead, wounded, and missing) in the entire Pacific war (through V-J Day) were 160,000.[47] Strangely, the War Department, in 1946, did not send Stimson and McGeorge Bundy any information—probably known to Stimson in mid-1945—that Joint Chiefs of Staff committees in June and July 1945 had estimated American *fatalities* between about twenty-five thousand (if just the Kyushu invasion had been required) and about forty-six thousand (if the later Honshu invasion had also proved necessary). Before Hiroshima, those estimates had been translated into about 132,500 to 220,000 *casualties* (fatalities, wounded, and missing).[48] At some point, presumably based on Winnacker's numbers and not the actual pre-Hiroshima estimates, McGeorge Bundy and Stimson produced a highly questionable sentence for Stimson's article: "I was informed that [the two invasions] might be expected to cost over a million casualties, to American forces."[49]

In meeting with Winnacker in early November to discuss his needs for data and to outline his analysis, Stimson provided the themes that would shape much of his article: The bomb had to "force Japanese surrender before invasion; for this [the bomb] must impress upon [the] Emperor the hopelessness of [the] military situation; he alone could make Japanese troops stop fighting all over Asia. . . . If [the] atomic bomb works, [it] might save hundred thousands of American lives." In that discussion, however, Stimson also included a theme—similar to one phrased earlier, in Conant's September 23 letter, in Harvey Bundy's September 25 draft, and in Groves's early November draft—that would *not* appear in the final article: "Full demonstration of the power of [the] new weapon [on Japan] might convert nations to accept peaceful solution of conflicts in the future."[50]

BY LATE NOVEMBER, when a draft of Stimson's essay was ready, Conant, who had originally urged the venture, went over it in detail, apparently made many minor revisions, and also offered some general advice to McGeorge Bundy, the co-author. Perhaps most important was the Harvard president's recommendation about tone and tactics: "Eliminate all sections in which the Secretary appears to be arguing his case or justifying his decision [because] Mr. Stimson's position is such that it is quite unnecessary for him to take an argumentative line." What Conant wanted was an article that would be "a mere recital of the facts," one that would speak "for itself." As he told McGeorge Bundy, "it will be very hard for anyone on the other side to challenge this article if [it] deals almost entirely with facts." [51]

Conant also wanted Stimson to deal, at some length, with the American decision not to provide a warning or a test-demonstration before actual combat use. Conant recommended that the essay should emphasize that the bomb's success was not definite before Hiroshima (the uranium bomb had never been tested), but that there was "only a matter of probability" that it would explode. "Nothing would have been more disastrous than a prior warning followed by a dud, and this was a very real possibility." In addition, Conant proposed that Stimson should delete the discussion about retention of the emperor and that he should point out the "similarity in destruction" between the Tokyo firebombing and the atomic bombings. Conant even offered some sentences for the article: "The atomic bomb seemed an ideal weapon for giving exactly that shock to the Japanese which was required to bring about surrender before the bitter fighting of invasion should commence. The damage done would be commensurate with the fire raids over Tokyo, but since one plane and not many hundreds would be involved in the attack, it would be clear to the Japanese that defense against such a raid or even a conventional air raid warning were not possible." Conant also strongly suggested deletion of everything in the manuscript "dealing with the problem of controlling the bomb in the future"—the very issue that had commanded Conant's attention since 1944 and that had helped to spur him to propose that Stimson write an article on the A-bomb decision. [52]

All of these major revisions, with the exception of the pre-Hiroshima thinking about guaranteeing the Emperor, were apparently incorporated into the next draft. [53] Even then, Stimson was unsure whether he wanted to publish the article, and he anxiously turned for advice to Supreme Court Justice Felix Frankfurter, a longtime friend and former assistant, to Secretary of War Robert Patterson, another longtime friend and Stimson's World War II under secretary, and again to Conant.

Stimson explained to Frankfurter that the article had been inspired by Conant's worries "over the spreading accusation that it was unnecessary to use the atomic bomb at all, particularly among the class of citizens whom he described as 'verbal-minded'—citizens . . . influential among the coming generations of . . . teachers or educators." The Secretary, acknowledging that the essay "is the product of many hands," seemed in sincere anguish. "I have rarely been connected with a paper about which I have so much doubt at the last moment. I think the full enumeration of the steps in the tragedy [the atomic bombing of Japan] will excite horror among friends who theretofore thought me a kindly minded Christian gentleman but who will, after reading this, feel I am cold blooded and cruel." Perhaps instead of publishing it separately, Stimson suggested, the essay should be held up until his book-memoir, where he (and Bundy) could also discuss the growing horror of war in the twentieth century, especially with the Nazis. [54]

Frankfurter's enthusiastic response may have quickly eased Stimson's anxiety. Speedily, the justice, who had long endorsed the use of the bomb, telegraphed Stimson: "Article proves that clear thinking, duty to restrict losses, and wise courage dictated [the] decision." [55] In a follow-up letter the same day, December 16, Frankfurter urged prompt publication: "The longer a sentimentally appealing error is allowed to make its way, the more difficult it is to overtake it." There was great need, Frankfurter emphasized, to prevent "sloppy sentimentality" in the national understanding of the A-bomb decision. Stimson was the right man and this essay, with some minor revisions, the right way to make "the facts . . . known." [56] Patterson welcomed the article, which "being source material and in the form of a narrative, will be of the greatest worth in firming up public opinion." [57] Conant, having inspired the article, assured Stimson that its publication "will accomplish a great deal of good." "You are the only one," Conant stated, "who can [correct the dangerous misinterpretations,] and I am delighted that you propose to publish the article." [58]

With such strong support from good friends who could be sharp critics, Stimson eagerly accepted the offer by Harper & Brothers, which had the contract for his book-memoir, to publish the essay in the firm's respected magazine. Frankfurter had initially suggested *Life* magazine because of its large circulation, but Conant strongly preferred *Harper's Magazine* because it was not splashy but rather staid.[59] Harper's board chairman, Cass Canfield, informed Stimson that his magazine had a circulation of nearly 150,000, was probably read by about three times that number, and reached "a substantial proportion of the educated public." To guarantee even more attention for this important article, *Harper's*, with Stimson's approval, allowed other magazines, as well as newspapers, to reprint it without charge.[60]

TO ADD TO THE DESIRED PUBLICITY, Stimson himself, despite his poor health, sought to meet with Henry Luce, also a Yale graduate and the influential publisher of *Time* and *Life*, to lobby for substantial coverage. When that meeting could not be arranged, presumably because of Luce's ill health, Stimson sent him a copy of the essay, explaining that it was conceived as "a full account of the way in which our [A-bomb] decision was reached" in order to counter "a good deal of rather slapdash criticism" that had appeared.[61]

Sending a preprint in mid-January to Karl Compton, Stimson emphasized, "The purpose of this article is to help in [s]laying the same ghosts as those to which you gave such skillful attention in your *Atlantic* article." Complaining that "uninformed and damaging criticism [of the A-bomb decision] has been so widespread," Stimson stated, "I hope that together we may have done something to bring it to an end." [62] Curiously, he made no mention of Conant's efforts, and perhaps the former secretary of war did not know that Conant had also enlisted Compton in this campaign to shape public understanding.

To Conant, Frankfurter, Harvey Bundy, George Harrison, Arneson, and Winnacker, Stimson also sent preprints in mid-January of "The Decision to Use the Atomic Bomb," along with words of gratitude for their "own constructive assistance." This essay, he added, "has given me as much trouble as any piece of work that I can remember, but I find myself more and more pleased with the final result. . . . I hope that it will serve the purpose that we had in mind." [63] Presumably all of them knew what the public would not learn when the essay appeared as the featured article in the February 1947 *Harper's* and was subsequently widely reprinted, reaching millions of homes in America and abroad: that McGeorge Bundy was the co-author.[64]

Summarized briefly, Stimson's eleven-page article asserted that American leaders since 1941 had assumed that the bomb was a "legitimate" weapon to be used against the enemy; that no leader had dissented from the belief that the bomb was used to save American and Japanese lives; that the decision was "carefully considered," that major scientist-advisers had agreed, and that a test-demonstration or a warning had been deemed too risky and "impractical"; and that there had been no alternative to the bomb that could have ended the war (with "the complete surrender of Japan") as quickly with as small a loss of American lives. He emphasized that speedy victory, not use or avoidance of the bomb, had been the controlling factor.[65]

The article's tone was not one of celebration or enthusiasm, but rather of necessity and of duty—to select "the least abhorrent choice." Patriotism and, yes, humanity, he seemed to be saying, had created the grim necessity of killing "over a hundred thousand Japanese" at Hiroshima and Nagasaki to end the war. "It stopped the fire raids, and the strangling blockade; it ended the ghastly specter of a clash of land armies." Such vast death, he stressed, was further evidence of how war in this century "has grown steadily more barbarous, more destructive, more debasing in all its aspects." [66]

The atomic bombings, Stimson wrote, had ended the dreadful war and "also made it wholly clear that we must never have another war. This is the lesson men and leaders everywhere must learn. . . . There is no other choice." Such horatory and frighteningly apocalyptic words were designed to inspire the establishment of peace. But nowhere in his essay did he acknowledge that such hopes and fears had helped to influence his decision to use the atomic bomb.[67] Stimson's article also excluded other evidence that might have both enriched understanding and raised unsettling questions: that the wartime A-bomb project had been systematically kept secret from the Soviet Union; that some advisers had believed that the bomb's use might well render the Soviets more tractable; and that the bomb's likely influence on the Soviet Union had often helped to shape policy and been the subject of deliberations. Only a very careful, and cynical, reader might have gleaned some of these themes peeking through a few scattered phrases about America's wartime nuclear policy of secrecy.[68]

Contrary to the implications of Stimson's discussion of the Interim Committee, that group had not been created to consider *whether* to use the atomic bomb on Japan. In considering *how* to use the bomb, the committee had discussed an advance warning but, contrary to Stimson's statement, it had *not* "carefully" examined the possibility of a test-demonstration. That option had received only passing attention, probably briefly at one lunch before the Interim Committee had defined the criteria for the A-bomb targets.[69] Nor had the essay dwelled on whether a guarantee of the emperor, if issued well before Hiroshima, might have produced a surrender without the A-bomb or an invasion. Politely concealing the July-August dispute between Stimson (who had wanted such a guarantee) and Secretary of State James F. Byrnes (who had opposed it), the article did not address this tantalizing "what might have been." [70]

Stimson also chose not to deal directly with the July 1946 summary report by the United States Strategic Bombing Survey: "that certainly prior to December 31, 1945, and in all probability prior to November 1, 1946, Japan would have surrendered even if the atomic bombs had not been dropped, even if Russia had not entered the war, and even if no invasion had been planned or contemplated." [71] Nor did he reveal that in 1945, well before Hiroshima, he had been pained by— and even had tried to stop—the mass killing of non-combatants by American bombers. His likening of the Hiroshima and Nagasaki bombings to the Tokyo firebombings might have raised unsettling issues if readers had known about his pre-Hiroshima efforts and anxieties. Readers would have discovered that, months before Hiroshima, Stimson had uneasily concluded that his own nation, and the army air forces theoretically under him in his position as secretary of war, were violating the ethics of warfare in the mass bombing of Japan's cities.[72]

With such matters concealed or at least not discussed, the article, appearing in the February 1947 *Harper's*, was remarkably effective. Calm, authoritative, and often seeming matter-of-fact, it was a skillful brief presented as a virtual narrative of events. It seemed honest and open, and never defensive. And, very importantly, it appeared to be written only by Henry L. Stimson, a respected statesman and famous Republican.

STIMSON'S ESSAY undoubtedly satisfied most American readers, probably silenced some critics, and greatly pleased Truman, Conant, Karl Compton, and other current or former officials involved in nuclear policy, including former Under Secretary of the Navy Ralph Bard (who had dissented from the Interim Committee recommendation and wanted a pre-Hiroshima warning of the A-bomb) and former Vice President Henry A. Wallace (who, McGeorge Bundy had feared, would be an unfriendly critic).[73]

Reporting on responses from Boston, co-author McGeorge Bundy wrote to Stimson in mid-February 1947 that "the *Harper's* article has been read by everyone I meet, and it seems to have covered the subject so well that I find no follow-up work needed. This is of particular interest in the case of one or two of my friends who certainly fall in Mr. Conant's unkindly classification of the 'verbal-minded'—I think we deserve some sort of medal for reducing these particular chatterers to silence."[74] Providing more accolades, Karl Compton, who was undoubtedly delighted to have such a prestigious ally in this campaign, congratulated Stimson for having written "one of the most important statements made" by a public servant. "Certainly no one can read your article and not be tremendously impressed by the care, thoughtfulness, and high-minded consideration which led to the atomic bomb decisions." In Compton's view, the essay "was a highly needed finishing touch" to end the criticisms of the atomic bombings.[75]

In a letter to Stimson, Truman praised the article for clarifying the situation "very well." Disregarding the article's potentially unsettling admission that the particular targets for the A-bomb had been "a military installation or war plant surrounded by or adjacent to houses and other buildings most susceptible to damage," the President could continue to cling tenaciously to his false belief that the two A-bomb cities had been "entirely" or "almost exclusively" devoted to war work.[76] By not fully describing these cities, the essay failed to acknowledge that substantial parts of their economies, and industries, were *not* engaged in war work.

Stimson sincerely hoped that the article would end the criticism of the atomic bombings by liberal radio commentator Raymond Gram Swing. Seeking to move the discussion beyond the A-bomb decision, Stimson wrote privately to Swing that the criticism of that decision had usually been based "on the notion that it is the bomb and not war which must be outlawed." "This seems to me," Stimson said, "a wholly incorrect appreciation of the problem since it is clear to me that neither the bomb nor any other weapon can be banished until we are reasonably free of the fears and ambitions which threaten the peace."[77]

Swing did not note, in his reply, that Stimson had appeared to reverse himself in just eleven months. In March 1946 the retired secretary had published in *Harper's* a plea for international control as a way of eliminating the menace of the bomb, building confidence and trust among nations, and paving the way ultimately for peace. In that March 1946 analysis, the bomb had been the pressing threat, and Stimson's solution then—international control with America giving up its monopoly—had required prompt action.[78] Amid the chilling Cold War, with rancorous disputes over Germany, Eastern Europe, Japan, and the bomb, Stimson had shifted his analysis since March 1946.[79]

Agreeing with Stimson's 1947 position, Swing replied, "the problem is to end war rather than to stop the use of the bomb." But Swing also still wanted to discuss the 1945 decision to use the weapon on Japan. His own criticism, he acknowledged, had the "benefit of hindsight"—the evidence, overwhelming in his judgment, by the Strategic Bombing Survey—that Japan in 1945 would have surrendered without the bomb or the invasion. "But if I had been in your position," Swing stressed, "knowing what you knew then, I am sure I should have inclined to decide as you did." [80]

Ironically, Swing lamented that insufficient "weight was given the effect on the future of using such a weapon." "By using it," he argued, "the United States lost any moral power to prevent its use against this country or the use of any weapon of mass destruction. . . . In using the bomb we became the most ruthless nation in warfare on earth." [81]

Swing could not know—and Stimson's article had largely concealed—that he, Conant, and others in 1945 had given great weight to the effect of the bomb, and its use, on the future. Before Hiroshima and Nagasaki, they had believed that the A-bomb would help to solve many of the problems with the Soviet Union. After the atomic bombings, Stimson had begun to split from Secretary of State Byrnes and President Truman and came to believe that America's A-bomb monopoly might sour the peace and provoke Soviet fear and suspicion. In Stimson's last cabinet meeting, on September 21, 1945, he tried to persuade the administration to approach the Soviets directly and promptly in order to seek international control of atomic energy. In September 1945, Stimson had urged control of the bomb in order to improve international relations and to get on a better footing with the Soviet Union.[82]

But by late 1946 he had decided, like Swing, that it was not the bomb that was the problem. On February 4, 1947, replying to Swing, Stimson expanded on his earlier letter and on the theme, placed toward the end of his February *Harper's* article, that the growth of terrible technologies, culminating in the A-bomb, required the elimination of war itself. He told Swing:

> It thus will take a revolutionary shock and change in men's thinking
> to get at the root of the growing evil which is likely to destroy our
> civilization altogether. President Conant has written to me that one
> of the principal reasons he had for advising me that the bomb must
> be used was that was the only way to awaken the world to the neces-
> sity of abolishing war altogether. No technological demonstration,
> even if it had been possible under the conditions of war—which it
> was not—could take the place of the actual use with its horrible
> results. I think he was right and I think that was one of the main
> things which differentiated the eminent scientists who concurred
> with President Conant from the less realistic ones who didn't.[83]

Stimson, in his private letter to Swing, could not accept the radio commentator's conclusion that both the bomb and the invasion had been unnecessary. Despite the Strategic Bombing Survey's contentions, Stimson maintained that no adequate evidence had appeared that compelled him to revise his judgment. He did not confront and criticize the survey's speculative argument. He just disregarded it. In 1945, as well as in early 1947, Stimson argued, the bomb and the invasion had been the *two* painful choices. The bomb, he insisted, had avoided "the much greater horrors" of the invasion.[84]

ALTHOUGH STIMSON HAD MOVED TO FOCUS primarily on war, and not on its deadly technology, Conant continued to worry about the bomb itself and to believe that Stimson's essay might actually help force the Soviets to accept the American proposal (the Baruch Plan) for international control of atomic energy. According to Conant's analysis, unless the arguments against the use of the bomb on Japan were demolished as Stimson had done in his narrative, the power of the American nuclear monopoly would have been undercut by popular doubts about the weapon and the chances for international control would therefore have been reduced. In a private letter of January 22, 1947, Conant further explained his thinking to Stimson:

> I am firmly convinced that the Russians will eventually agree [even after their December 1946 rejection at the United Nations] to the American proposals for the establishment of an atomic energy authority of world-wide scope, *provided* they are convinced that we would have the bomb in quantity and would be prepared to use it without hesitation in another war. Therefore, I have been fearful lest those who have been motivated by humanitarian considerations in their arguments against the bomb were as a matter-of-fact tending to accomplish exactly the reverse of their avowed purpose.[85]

Despite Conant's efforts to advance his quasi-official version of the A-bomb history, by enlisting both Karl Compton and Henry Stimson, the Harvard president feared that he was still being foiled. In March 1947, after reading Stimson's article, one of Conant's longtime friends, a well-to-do Chicago attorney, still remained unconvinced of the morality of the A-bombing of Japanese cities and, further, told Conant that many of the scientists agreed with this criticism.[86] Why, asked Conant's friend, could not a test-demonstration on an uninhabited area, preceded by a warning, have first been tried to propel a Japanese surrender? The use of the bomb on heavily populated cities violated "every human instinct of many civilized people." He added a telling criticism: "Whatever might be said for dropping the first bomb on Hiroshima, I don't think that even Mr. Stimson makes a case for having dropped it on Nagasaki." The Chicago attorney's moral judgment was harsh, excoriating the use of both bombs: "I am sorry to say I still believe that the only justification for our action is our complete acceptance of the Nazi philosophy which supposedly we were fighting against, and which asserts that anything, no matter how brutal, and whether directed against non-combatants or not, is justified if it helps to win a war." [87]

In anguish, Conant asked another friend, a wartime and post-war associate, J. Robert Oppenheimer, the former director of Los Alamos, to check on whether this lawyer (unnamed in the letter) was correct about the scientists' attitudes. "As you know," Conant emphasized, "I feel that a great deal turns on this point in regard to the future." [88] Oppenheimer's response, if there was one, seems lost to history. Undoubtedly, if he replied, he told Conant what the Harvard president both knew and feared: Criticism of the A-bomb decision among scientists, including Albert Einstein, Leo Szilard, James Franck, and Eugene Rabinowitch, was frequent, but they were a minority, albeit a vocal one.[89]

To add to the evidence of continuing criticism among scientists, Conant undoubtedly had seen the recent editorial in the *Bulletin of the Atomic Scientists*, by Eugene Rabinowitch, who had co-authored the unsuccessful June 1945 Franck report opposing the combat use of the bomb on Japan. "The predicted race of atomic armaments, as the Franck report had warned, is upon us," wrote Rabinowitch in February 1947. "So is the predicted wrangling over international control, in an atmosphere of distrust and suspicion." Such words were undoubtedly designed as a rebuke to Truman, Conant, and Stimson for their 1945 decision.[90]

Stimson himself apparently received only a few letters criticizing his article, and they were generally from plain citizens he did not know. Nevertheless, their attacks—unfriendly and moralistic—may have seemed cruel blows to the retired statesman as he approached his eightieth birthday. Born in the aftermath of Appomattox, well before the airplane seemed possible to Americans, Stimson was now being condemned for the weapons dropped by the *Enola Gay* and *Bock's Car*.

"We assailed Germany for initiating poison gas in the first World War," argued one minister, but after "Hiroshima and Nagasaki it is simply a case of the pot calling the kettle black."[91] Stimson's essay, like earlier American government pronouncements on the atomic bombings, the minister continued, was "an unsuccessful effort at self-justification." [92] The bombs were used, another critic contended, to end the war before the Soviets could "claim parts of the spoils." And furthermore, the same writer argued, Japan was already near surrender and "there was no military necessity whatever to use the bombs." "The decision to use the bombs was indefensible, as indeed was the policy to prepare them." To clinch this point, the letter writer quoted the strong words by MIT mathematician Norbert Wiener to explain why, after Hiroshima and Nagasaki, he would no longer share his research with the American government: "The experience of the scientists who have worked on the atomic bomb has indicated that in any investigation of this kind the scientist ends by putting unlimited powers in the hands of the people whom he is least inclined to trust with their use." [93]

In letters criticizing Stimson and his essay,[94] the speculative counterclaims by the U.S. Strategic Bombing Survey occasionally popped up. That report probably helped inspire the nine-page February 1947 letter from former Under Secretary of State Joseph Grew chiding Stimson for not having adequately treated what Grew believed had been a likely missed opportunity to end the war: guaranteeing the emperor in May or June 1945. Looking back, Grew stressed that he had urged such a policy but been rebuffed by others. The ideal time to offer such a guarantee, he told Stimson, would have been shortly after the firebombing of Tokyo in late May 1945, because the surrender-minded elements in the Japanese government might well have triumphed before August. The war would have ended without the bomb and without Soviet entry, Grew concluded, and "the world would have been the gainer." [95]

In the effort to end doubts about the use of the A-bomb, Stimson, as well as Conant and Compton, received new assistance from a minor ally, War Department historian Rudolph Winnacker. In late 1946, Winnacker had assisted Stimson and McGeorge Bundy by checking Washington files and supplying needed data on the 1945 war in the Pacific. He had read, and suggested some rephrasing of, at least one draft of the *Harper's* article.[96] When it appeared in print, he enthusiastically wrote to Stimson: "From now on all reasonable people have the facts with which to confound the wishful thinking of foggy idealists who have held the center of the stage for too long." [97]

Winnacker himself joined the public campaign for the Stimson–Compton–Conant position with a brief article, "The Debate about Hiroshima," published in the pro-military journal, *Military Affairs*.[98] A professional magazine for military buffs, official historians and their academic cohorts, and retired and on-duly officers from the services, it had planned to reprint Stimson's "Decision" article but been scooped by a rival. As a result, Winnacker agreed to fill the allotted space with a pro-bomb article, which he allegedly put together in two evenings by heavily quoting from the defenders and, to a lesser extent from the critics.[99] His strategy was to lay out many of the basic issues, to summarize quite briefly the critics' views, and then to plump for the Stimson version, with heavy reliance upon quotations from the "Decision" article. Winnacker extolled Compton and Stimson for making known the basic facts, and declared that there was no "important new material" likely to change views.[100]

"We have been most fortunate," Winnacker asserted in his essay, because "Secretary Stimson has stated fully the reasons" for the use of the bomb. Like Stimson, Winnacker emphasized "the careful consideration which was given to the problem." But unlike Stimson, Winnacker dealt, albeit briefly, with the Strategic Bombing Survey's contention that the A-bombing had probably been unnecessary. "To what extent should our government have been guided by such an estimate," Winnacker shrewdly asked, "in view of the proven inaccuracy of similar optimistic opinions for Germany and the ever increasing Japanese resistance as our armed forces approached the home islands?" [101] To force Japan to surrender without the invasion, he argued in quoting Stimson's article, "the atomic bomb was an eminently suitable weapon." Ironically, it was Winnacker himself, in December, who had helped to cast that pungent sentence when the "Decision" article was still in draft. He omitted such information from his essay—as he did any information that he had done research, provided advice, and commented on at least one draft of the Stimson article, which, he knew, had been co-authored by McGeorge Bundy.[102]

Echoing Stimson's position, Winnacker wrote in his own essay: "We can kill in war and still disapprove of killing. This is the necessary compromise we have to make for the survival of our civilization." Winnacker urged readers to be "realistic idealists," and to join the ex-infantryman, who had recently said, "History will not scorn us for our last-resort use of this most horrible of all weapons to end finally, and completely, the most horrible of all wars. But we will be damned as barbarians without vision or heart if we do not feel the deepest sadness at the necessity for authorizing such cruelty."[103] Winnacker's essay, like Stimson's, relied ultimately on the "lesser evil" argument. Privately, he wrote to Stimson, "I wish I had more time to think through the philosophical problem in the debate." [104]

This brief literary effort by an official War Department historian undoubtedly added to the legitimation of Stimson's article, though Winnacker's essay did not play a substantial role in the public debate. Had he taken the opposite position in the quasi-official *Military Affairs*, or had he chosen to reveal information about the complicated authorship of Stimson's "Decision" and Winnacker's own role in that venture, then "The Debate" essay might have some significant impact. But Winnacker, loyal to Stimson and sincerely supportive of the A-bomb decision, had no desire to chip away at the authority of Stimson or his *Harper's* article.

Undoubtedly, no official War Department historian, even if he had private doubts about the A-bomb decision, would have published them so soon after the war. The subtle but powerful dictates of official history would not have allowed a War Department historian to criticize Groves, Stimson, and Truman on the important matter of the decision to use the atomic bombs.

AFTER THE APPEARANCE of Winnacker's supportive article, Stimson, who had been on vacation for a time, finally got around, in June 1947, to responding privately to Grew's February criticisms. Strangely, in this reply, Stimson misconstrued Grew's argument and did not address the retired under secretary of state's main objections. The result was a curiously oblique letter—perhaps out of Stimson's sincere confusion and perhaps out of his desire to avoid confronting an unpleasant matter. In his private letter, Stimson stated that he had not sought in his article to claim primary credit for recommending a pre-Hiroshima official statement on keeping the Emperor (the issue of credit had not been Grew's objection), that Stimson and others had vetoed such a statement in late May 1945 because the costly Okinawa campaign made "us . . . afraid that any public concession at that time might be taken as an indication of [American] weakness," but that "in the end the right policy was pursued . . . and your insight and advocacy were of the greatest service" in helping to produce that policy—a guarantee of the Emperor.[105]

What Stimson's letter failed to acknowledge was that the American guarantee of the emperor *followed* (not preceded) Hiroshima and Nagasaki, that the July 1945 Potsdam Declaration had omitted such a guarantee, and that Stimson's own pre-Hiroshima pleadings for such a statement had been overridden.[106] Basically, Grew had argued in his February 1947 letter that an American guarantee, if issued well before August 1945, might have produced a surrender *without the dropping of the atomic bomb*. Stimson did not rebut or even acknowledge that claim; he simply sidestepped it.[107]

Grew's criticism probably did influence Stimson and McGeorge Bundy, when expanding their treatment of the A-bomb for *On Active Service in Peace and War* (1948), to mention the Under Secretary's May 1945 efforts and also to emphasize Stimson's later attempts to have Truman issue such a guarantee of the Emperor. The book said, "only on this question did he [Stimson] later find . . . that the United States, by its delay in stating its position, had [possibly] prolonged the war." In this book-memoir, Stimson did not claim, or even imply, that he had sought this guarantee *in order* to avoid the use of the bomb—and, indeed, he had not. Nor was Stimson willing, in the book, to be explicit, as Grew had been in his 1947 chiding letter, by stating that the bombing might have been unnecessary.[108] Stimson preferred to leave that implicit in this brief, uneasy addition to the article.

That lament, with its important implications, went largely unnoticed in 1948, when the book first appeared. So did this new passage (added after the *Harper's* article), which tried to defend the A-bomb decision from critics:

[An] error, made by critics after the war, in Stimson's view, was their assumption that American policy was, or should have been, controlled or at least influenced by a desire to avoid use of the atomic bomb. In Stimson's view this would have been as irresponsible as the country's course of guiding policy by a desire to ensure the use of the bomb. Stimson believed, both at the time and later, that the dominant fact of 1945 was war, and that therefore, necessarily, the dominant objective was victory. If victory could be speeded by using the bomb, it should be used; if victory must be delayed in order to use the bomb, it should *not* be used. So far as he knew, this general view was shared by the President and all his associates.[109]

In other ways, too, the book sought further to legitimize the A-bomb decision. More than in the 1947 article, the memoir implied that the Interim Committee had been established, among other purposes, to decide *whether* the bomb should be used on Japan. The book stated, incorrectly, that "the first and greatest problem was the decision on the use of the bomb—should it be used against the Japanese?"[110] In fact, that was never the question on the Interim Committee agenda. Nor was it a real question in 1945. The questions were actually how and where in Japan the bomb would be dropped, not whether.

Unlike the 1947 article, the book revealed far more about the connections in 1945 official thinking between the A-bomb and the Soviet Union. But these themes were not dealt with in the chapter on the use of the bomb (entitled "The Atomic Bomb and the Surrender of Japan"). They came up instead in a separate chapter ("The Bomb and Peace with Russia"), thereby implying that the *use* of the weapon was in no way connected with the Soviet problem. The separation of issues may well have had the effect, in 1948 and well into the early 1960s, of undermining theories (first suggested by Norman Cousins) that the use of the bomb had an anti-Soviet purpose—or even the related theme (stated privately by Conant and Stimson in 1946) that the bomb had been dropped on Japan partly to persuade the world of the need to control the atom and avoid war.

In an important statement, generally disregarded by reviewers in 1948, the book noted "it was already apparent [by April 1945] that the crucial questions in American policy toward atomic energy would be directly connected with Soviet Russia." Just a few sentences later, in discussing the changing estimates of the need for Soviet entry into the Pacific war, the memoir stated: "Even the immediate tactical discussion about the bomb involved the Russians." When the dramatic news of the successful July 16 Alamogordo test reached Potsdam, the book said, it was "clear to the Americans that further diplomatic efforts to bring the Russians into the Pacific war were largely pointless."[111] The implication was that the bomb, no longer a prospect but suddenly a reality, had rendered speedy, and perhaps any, Soviet entry unnecessary. But that did not necessarily mean that the bombing and Soviet entry were viewed as interchangeable ways of ending the war. Nor that the bomb was being used in order to avoid Soviet entry.[112]

Yielding part way to critics and further developing a theme that Stimson's article had briefly treated, the memoir-book also stressed that Stimson had acceded, in 1945, to the very obliteration bombing that he had ethically reviled and wished to prevent. The new passage expressed the pain and anguish, as well as the hope, that Stimson had felt in 1945, and the regrets and sense of grim necessity that he felt in 1945 and continued to feel in 1947:

> As soldier and Cabinet officer he had repeatedly argued that war itself must be restrained within the bounds of morality. As recently as June 1 [1945] he had sternly questioned his Air Force leader [General Henry A. Arnold] wanting to know whether the apparently indiscriminate bombings of Tokyo were absolutely necessary. . . . Now in the conflagration bombings by massed B-29s he was permitting a kind of total war he had always hated, and in recommending the use of the atomic bomb he was implicitly confessing that there could be no significant limits to the horror of modern war. The decision was not difficult, in 1945, for peace with victory was a prize that outweighed the payment demanded. But Stimson could not dodge the meaning of his action.[113]

His defense in this memoir, as in his earlier article, was that the atomic bombings had saved lives—primarily Americans and also Japanese—and ended the terrible war. The bomb, as he had also stated in the article, might force people and leaders to seek peace, because the awful alternative, atomic war, was too frightening.

TOTALLY HIDDEN FROM VIEW, and actually removed from the book-draft, were some important sentences on high-level, post-Nagasaki thinking within the Truman administration about the diplomatic power of the bomb in handling the Soviets. Those deleted—and, hence, never published—sentences might well have raised unnerving insights for careful readers, buttressed post-war Soviet charges of American "atomic diplomacy," and even suggested troubling connections between the decision to drop the bomb on Japan and the hopes for the diplomatic uses of the bomb in the post-war world in dealing with the Soviet Union.

In a draft of the book chapter on "The Bomb and Peace with Russia," which dealt mostly with post-Nagasaki matters, Bundy had included, verbatim, Stimson's two memorandums of September 11, 1945, which the Secretary had submitted to Truman on the twelfth. Those two papers had pleaded with Truman in September 1945 to approach the Soviets speedily and directly with an effort at international control of atomic energy, lest the American nuclear monopoly otherwise frighten the Soviets, provoke an American-Soviet nuclear arms race, and ruin the hard-won peace. Stimson's pleading had actually reflected the counsel, first delivered by Conant and Bush in 1944, for the need to work out a way with the Soviets in order to avoid a post-war atomic race.[114]

Stimson, who had hoped before Hiroshima that the A-bomb monopoly would provide powerful leverage in dealing with the Soviets, had sharply changed his position while on vacation in the three weeks after the atomic bombings. Shifting his analysis in that post-Nagasaki period, he had begun drafting a paper on his new position and lining up support in the administration for his new view.[115] Despite the seeming support of a few influential associates, however, he lost—mostly because of the opposition of Secretary of State James F. Byrnes, who was backed by President Truman. To explain Stimson's defeat on this important issue in the early post-war Truman administration, Bundy had cast in the draft some very revealing—

indeed, strikingly arresting—sentences about post-war official "atomic diplomacy" thinking: "In the State Department there developed a tendency to think of the bomb as a diplomatic weapon. Outraged by constant evidence of Russian perfidy, some of the men in charge of foreign policy were eager to carry the bomb for a while as their ace-in-the-hole. . . . [Stimson's September 11 papers were] presented at a time when American statesmen were eager for their country to browbeat the Russians with the bomb 'held rather ostentatiously on our hip'." [116]

These statements, a close paraphrase of Stimson's post-Nagasaki diary of August and early September 1945, referred to Secretary of State Byrnes but did not name him. Stimson's private diary, unlike the memoir-draft, was blunt about Byrnes's hopes for using the bomb as an implied threat in dealing with the Soviets:

> He [Byrnes] quite radically opposed . . . any approach to Stalin [on control of atomic energy]. He was on the point of departing for the foreign ministers' meeting [in London in September 1945] and wished to have the implied threat of the bomb in his pocket during the conference. [117]

> [On September 4] I found that Byrnes was very much against any attempt to cooperate with Russia. His mind is full of his problems with the coming meeting of foreign ministers and he looks to having the presence of the bomb in his pocket, so to speak, as a great weapon to get through the thing. [118]

Before publishing the draft chapter on Russia and the bomb, as well as others on the World War II period and the immediate aftermath, Bundy and Stimson checked with General George C. Marshall, who by 1947 had replaced Byrnes as Truman's secretary of state. Bundy and Stimson asked Marshall in late October 1947 to read the wartime and post-war sections of the draft memoir for historical accuracy and judgment and to make sure that Marshall, as the former wartime chief of staff and now as secretary of state, was not troubled by any statements. Bundy and Stimson were especially concerned that the book's words not compromise Marshall's efforts in Cold War diplomacy. [119]

In early November 1947, Marshall quickly read most of the chapters, made a few small suggestions, and expressed his gratitude for the praise that Stimson (often with Bundy's pen) had lavished on him for wartime leadership. But Marshall added that he was still giving "careful consideration" to the crucial chapter on the Soviet Union and the bomb "because the question of its publication at the present time is a very critical matter." [120] Reserving final judgment on that chapter, Marshall requested that it be sent for review to George Kennan, the recent author of the already famous "X" containment article and the head of the State Department's Policy Planning Staff. [121]

Reading the draft, Kennan was shocked and offended by the Bundy–Stimson statements about post-war American atomic diplomacy. In vigorous but polite language, George Kennan—though he in late 1946 had actually recommended use of implicit atomic threats to push the Soviets to accept the Baruch Plan—insisted that the draft was profoundly wrong: No significant American official had contemplated atomic diplomacy in 1945. Kennan warned that this draft, if published, would embarrass the Truman administration and Secretary Marshall by confirming Soviet charges of atomic diplomacy. Kennan's brisk statement merits partial quotation:

I am sure . . . that the responsible heads of the [State] Department did not hold the views described [in this draft chapter];
and these views were emphatically not shared by those of us
in the Department and Foreign Service. . . . I am afraid that if
these statements were now to appear in an official biography
of Mr. Stimson, a part of the reading public might conclude
that the hope of influencing Russia by the threat of atomic attack
had been, and probably remained, one of the permanently
motivating elements of our foreign policy. Such an impression
would play squarely into the hands of the Communists who
so frequently speak of our "atomic diplomacy" and accuse us
of trying to intimidate the world in general by our possession of
the bomb.[122]

Kennan added that he believed that Marshall had similar misgivings about the offending sentences in the draft chapter. Bundy, with privileged access to Stimson's own diary, knew that his draft was historically accurate and that John J. McCloy, Stimson's wartime assistant secretary, had also discussed these issues in early September 1945 with Byrnes and could confirm Stimson's diary record. Bundy may not have known that McCloy had also made a diary record of his own discussion with Byrnes, noting on September 2, 1945 that Byrnes believed that the Soviets "were cognizant of the power of this bomb, and with it in his hip pocket he felt he was in a far better position [in the London conference]."[123]

In dealing with Kennan's criticisms of this draft chapter, Bundy and Stimson understood that the real issue was not historical accuracy but the need for political correctness: The truth would embarrass the United States. Therefore, Stimson quickly deleted the offending passages.[124] Promising these revisions, Bundy assured Kennan that "we do not want to play into the hands of the Kremlin's hired liars."[125] The recast version, designed to protect the American government, avoided any hint of official atomic diplomacy in the post-war period.[126] Acting as loyal citizens with deep affection for Truman and Marshall, and probably concluding that they had no right or duty to publish still-secret information about Byrnes's actions, Stimson and Bundy chose to suppress the unpleasant information.[127]

Had those deleted passages been printed, they might also have raised questions—through a process of *possible* inference—about the decision to drop the atomic bomb on Japan. If Byrnes had embraced the general tactics of atomic diplomacy so soon after Hiroshima and Nagasaki, as the draft asserted, some readers might have wondered whether these anti-Soviet aims had antedated the atomic bombings and possibly even influenced the decision to drop the bomb on Japan. If so, readers could have wondered and worried whether an anti-Soviet motive had been a primary, secondary, or confirming impulse for using the bombs. Such suspicions were largely avoided by the deletion, and recasting, of those revealing passages before *On Active Service* was published in 1948. Corrosive doubts, cynical suspicions, and demanding questions were blocked.[128]

Yet, significantly, in an initial act of blunt honesty, Stimson and Bundy had intended, before yielding to Marshall and Kennan, to disclose information that could have undercut Conant's purposes and Stimson's own similar goal: to persuade Americans that the A-bomb decisions had been judiciously conceived, morally inspired, and undoubtedly necessary. Marshall and Kennan, for their own reasons, had protected Stimson and Bundy from undermining Stimson's and Conant's efforts to legitimize the 1945 decision to use atomic bombs on Japan.

IN THE LATE 1940s, AND IN THE DECADE OR MORE thereafter, Stimson's explanation of the use of the bomb, and possibly his own 1946–1948 hopes for the future, helped to block a probing dialogue, among plain citizens and foreign policy analysts too, about why the bombs were dropped, whether their use was ethically justified, and what role the bombs' use and America's related policy had on the Cold War. But Stimson's attempts to stifle the small controversy of 1946–47, one that had so alarmed Conant, ultimately failed. Ironically, the wartime files these two men had helped to produce, when examined by new interpreters, would often provoke unsettling interpretations of Hiroshima and Nagasaki. The decision to use the atomic bomb, to borrow the title of Stimson's 1947 article, would become a rich area of dispute and controversy [129] in the mid-1960s and afterward as Americans of a new generation, often asking new questions about their nation's purposes and values, would challenge the orthodoxy that Stimson and Conant, with the help of the two Bundys, Karl Compton, and Winnacker, as well as Bush, Frankfurter, Kennan, and Marshall, among others, had created.

In examining the process, including the drafts and private correspondence, leading to the promulgation of such history, this essay has also noted, at some points, the post-Nagasaki claims, especially by Conant, Stimson, and Harvey Bundy, of the influence of their desire for world peace after victory in the Pacific war in leading them to endorse the prospective use of the A-bomb on Japan. Such thinking did indeed exist before Hiroshima for at least some of these men, and undoubtedly also for others. But it would be a mistake to interpret such desires as simply anti-Soviet motives or to define such desires as the primary or essential, rather than a confirming, reason for using the bomb on Japan in August 1945. [130]

By 1945 these men had long lived with the prospect of the bomb. They had initially endorsed its development in what was believed to be a deadly atomic race with Germany, and they were undoubtedly prepared, in 1943 or 1944, to use the bomb against Hitler's Germany, and possibly on its cities with their many noncombatants. But the bomb was not ready until the summer of 1945, and by then Germany had already surrendered. This general schedule had been foreseen by late 1944, and the planning in the Roosevelt administration had thus easily shifted to the use of the weapon on Japan.

In thinking about the prospective use of the bomb, American leaders, especially Stimson, had anticipated that its use on Japan might well also intimidate the Soviet Union and help to compel a change of Soviet behavior and move toward some form of international control of atomic energy. In 1945, for Stimson, as well as for Byrnes and undoubtedly Truman, anti-Soviet aims helped confirm the long-run assumption, inherited from the Roosevelt years, that the bomb would be used. The prospect, savored before Hiroshima, that the use of the bomb on Japan might well help to cement the peace, was a tasty bonus. It was an *added* reason for American leaders to implement in August 1945 the long-held assumption that the weapon would be employed on a hated enemy.

Such expectations of a bonus, the hope of cementing the peace in the process of punishing and pummeling Japan into victory, may have had the subtle effect, probably unrecognized by American leaders of the time, of giving these men additional reasons for not taking risks and seeking to avoid the use of the bomb on Japan. In that way, U.S. policymakers differed profoundly from scientists Leo Szilard, Eugene Rabinowitch, and other signatories of the June 1945 Franck report, who had pleaded against the use of the bomb and warned that its use might well intimidate the Soviets, unleash a post-war nuclear arms race, and ruin the hopes for peace. That shrewd warning ran contrary to the hopes, and expectations, of American leaders before Hiroshima. If they had shared such fears, then—perhaps only then—they might have searched for alternatives to the use of the bomb, or approached the Soviets with some notion of international control. The sense of missed opportunities should not be conflated, however, with the argument that anti-Soviet purposes were essential to propel American leaders in 1945 to use the bomb on Japan. Such an interpretation errs by failing to understand the long-run momentum for the use of the bomb, the willingness to punish the Japanese, and the desires to end the war speedily without dangerous concessions, to avoid the dreaded invasion, and to save American (and Allied) lives.

THE EFFORT TO UNDERSTAND, AND TO EXPLAIN, the dropping of the atomic bomb has engaged various analysts—whether memoirists, journalists, plain citizens, scientists, or other scholars—for nearly one half century. The subject has been ethically and intellectually compelling, the drama significant, and the meanings of the events powerful. That process of study has raised issues about evidence and interpretation, and about the purposes and assumptions of many authors.

Strangely, in that process, as so often in the efforts to unravel the nation's recent past, there has often been a generally trusting attitude in using many of the main memoirs on the subject. Among the influential sources in this enterprise have been Stimson's 1947 essay and his 1948 book-memoir chapters. Most often, these sources have not been treated essentially as interpretations but, instead, substantially as descriptions of fact. Surprisingly, analysts have seldom even noticed some crucial differences between the 1947 and 1948 published versions, and virtually no one has focused on these differences or considered the reasons for, and the significance of, the revisions.[131]

Indeed, virtually none of the analysts has explored the political reasons for Stimson's essay or Conant's crucial role in that venture.[132] Nor have they generally recognized that Stimson's defense of the A-bomb decision was designed to help shape Americans' self-conceptions and their conceptions of their leaders, their morality, and their uses of secrecy and of state power. For Stimson, as a successful attorney and leader of the American bar, knew that the best defense, and offense, on these occasions—in his 1947 and 1948 publications—was not forceful, explicit argument but seemingly matter-of-fact narration. That was, of course, largely the strategy that Conant recommended and Patterson applauded.

Undoubtedly, in 1947, as well as afterward, many Americans would have been dismayed by Conant's own views of schoolteachers, professors, and other educators. Viewing himself as tough-minded and undoubtedly as realistic, the Harvard president feared that "sentimentality" and doubt might triumph. Not only were they the wrong attitudes for Americans, he believed, but those attitudes in his view might also cripple the American effort to secure Soviet approval of the Baruch Plan. His was a convoluted argument, arising from a curious personal brew of strained optimism (that the Soviets might accept) and unwarranted cynicism (that many Americans would doubt their government on the A-bomb decision).

In their minds, Conant and Stimson, and undoubtedly Karl Compton and Felix Frankfurter too, would not have said that they were seeking to distort history. Rather, they were seeking to reveal enough of the past, and to present it in a framework, that it would justify recent decisions on the A-bomb, advance American policy, and maintain calm patriotism.

It is tempting to speculate whether these efforts, for Stimson and Conant and possibly Compton too, also came partly out of an uneasy conscience. Helping to make decisions that killed over one hundred thousand of the enemy, even in the last stages of a very bloody war, was a responsibility that could later bear heavily upon such men. Perhaps even Harry S. Truman, who welcomed the writings by Compton and Stimson and apparently did not know of Conant's pivotal influence, seemed at times, despite his frequent protests, to view his decision as a burden after the Nagasaki bombing.[133]

Such themes may help guide efforts to understand the decision to use the atomic bomb, and such efforts should also be guided by a carefully critical use—informed by other materials and tested against them—of "The Decision to Use the Atomic Bomb." To fail to be carefully critical in relying upon this source, or on other so-called primary materials—whether memoirs, interviews, or other similar post-facto documents—may mean that the latter-day analyst is unknowingly, and perhaps even naively, enrolling in a policymaker's own campaign. That can mean history with a purpose—but it may not even be recognized by the latter-day trusting analyst.

The history of Stimson's 1947 and 1948 publications on the A-bomb decisions underscores the perils for analysts in relying trustingly on memoir sources and similar post-facto evidence. Henry L. Stimson, in a double meaning that he probably did not intended, offered sage advice in 1948: "History is often not what actually happened but what is recorded as such." Those words, apparently crafted by his own pen, appeared in his personal introduction to On Active Service,[134] the account of his public life written largely by McGeorge Bundy.

That book, like the related "Decision" essay the year before, was shaped, in explaining the A-bomb decision, by Stimson's "fervor [as] a great advocate," as Bundy recently acknowledged.[135] Stimson's impressive feat, aided by Bundy and Conant, among others, was to conceal that great fervor and thus to present his version of the facts as the history. Recognizing that the past was valuable contested terrain, Henry L. Stimson had easily seized the high ground. For many years, his triumph endured—virtually unchallenged.[136]

NOTES

The author is grateful for the counsel of McGeorge Bundy, Alexander Hammond, James Hershberg, David Holloway, William Tuttle, and Martin Sherwin; for help with sources from Eric Alterman, Larry Bland, Mark Kleinman, Chase Madar, and Michael Salman; and for assistance from the MacArthur Foundation, the Stanford Center for International Security and Arms Control (CISAC), and the NSF History of Science Program. Seminars based partly on this paper were the subject of separate sessions at Stanford University of the Nuclear History group and the Peace Studies Program, and many of the ideas were worked out in my Stanford courses on the nuclear age, in seminars with the Coe Fellows, and in sessions with the Stanford Engineering Executives Program.

1.   Karl T. Compton, "If the Atomic Bomb Had Not Been Used," *Atlantic Monthly*, December 1946, pp. 54–56; Henry L. Stimson, "The Decision to Use the Atomic Bomb," *Harper's Magazine*, February 1947, pp. 97–107.

2.   The available polls on the A-bomb decision are from mid-August and late November 1945. A mid-August Gallup poll indicated 85 percent support for the atomic bombing and only 10 percent opposition. A November 30 *Fortune* poll, which offered more alternatives, found that 4.5 percent opposed the use of the bomb, and another 13.8 percent thought that a test-demonstration should have first been made on Japan; but 53.5 percent approved the use of the bombs, and another 22.7 percent thought that more than two atomic bombs should have been used. See AIPO poll in *Public Opinion Quarterly* 9 (Fall 1945): 385; and "Fortune Survey: Use of the Atomic Bomb," *Fortune*, December 1945, p. 305. For other studies of responses to the atomic bombings see Michael Yavenditti, "The American People and the Use of the Atomic Bombs on Japan: The 1940s," *Historian* 36 (February 1974): 224–247; and Paul Boyer, *By the Bomb's Early Light: American Thought and Culture at the Dawn of the Atomic Age* (New York, 1985), pp. 1–287.

3.   James B. Conant to Harvey H. Bundy (September 23, 1946), and Conant to Karl T. Compton (October 26, 1946), Conant Presidential Papers, Pusey Library, Harvard University, Cambridge, Mass.; Compton to Conant (October 15, 1946), Karl T. Compton MIT Presidential Papers, MIT Library, Cambridge, Mass.

4.   Henry L. Stimson and McGeorge Bundy, *On Active Service in Peace and War* (New York, 1948), pp. xi, 673–677.

5.   McGeorge Bundy, *Danger and Survival: Choices about the Bomb in the First Fifty Years* (New York, 1988), pp. 92–93. See ibid., pp. 54–97, on the A-bomb decision.

6.   Conant to Harvey Bundy (September 23, 1946), Conant Presidential Papers.

7.   Norman Cousins, "The Literacy of Survival," *The Saturday Review of Literature*, September 14, 1946, p. 14, citing Hersey's magazine-length essay in the *New Yorker*, which Knopf soon issued as a well-publicized book. For Cousins's anti-Soviet theory see Cousins and Thomas K. Finletter, "A Beginning for Sanity," *The Saturday Review of Literature*, June 15, 1946, pp. 7–9, 38–40. Because the Norman Cousins Papers at the UCLA Library, Los Angeles, Calif., are not well organized, it is impossible to determine whether Finletter actually agreed with this theme of an anti-Soviet motive for using the A-bomb on Japan. Indirect evidence—Finletter's 1947 visits with Stimson and Finletter's own later career as Truman's air force secretary—suggests that this anti-Soviet explanation was largely, if not entirely, framed by Cousins. For responses to Hersey's article and book see Michael Yavenditti, "John Hersey and the American Conscience: The Reception of 'Hiroshima'," *Pacific Historical Review* 42 (February 1974): 24–49.

8.   Conant to Reinhold Niebuhr (March 6, 1946), Reinhold Niebuhr Papers, Library of Congress, Washington, D.C. The council's statement was excerpted and also reported in the *New York Times*, March 6, 1946.

9.   Niebuhr to Conant (March 12, 1946), Niebuhr Papers. Also see Niebuhr, in editorial note, *Christianity and Crisis*, April 1, 1946, p. 2.

10. Niebuhr, "Our Relations to Japan," *Christianity and Crisis*, September 17, 1945, pp. 5–7. Apparently Niebuhr did not finally sign the Federal Council's report. Niebuhr to Robert Calhoun (March 13, 1946), Niebuhr Papers. In 1945 journalist David Lawrence has raised similar objections to the atomic bombings. See Lawrence to Stimson (October 4, 1945), Stimson Papers, Yale University Library, New Haven, CT.

11. Conant to Bundy, (September 23, 1946), Conant Presidential Papers.

12. Leland Stowe, *While Time Remains* (New York, 1946), p. 14.

13. Ibid.

14. Conant to Bundy (September 23, 1946), Conant Presidential Papers.

15. See, for example, Robert P. Patterson to Troyer Anderson (December 16, 1945), Anderson to Patterson (December 17, 1945), and Anderson to Patterson (January 24, 1946), Robert Patterson Papers, Library of Congress.

16. Conant remains a rather elusive figure, and his memoir, *My Several Lives: Memoirs of a Social Inventor* (New York, 1970), describes most matters skimpily and reveals little of the man. That source aided Sam Bass Warner, Jr., *Province of Reason* (Cambridge, Mass., 1970), pp. 213–247, to offer a brief interpretation. More useful are William Tuttle, "James B. Conant, Pressure Groups, and the National Defense, 1933–1945" (Ph.D. diss., University of Wisconsin, 1967); and James Hershberg, "James B. Conant and the Atomic Bomb," *Journal of Strategic Studies* 8 (March 1985): 78–92; and idem, " 'Over My Dead Body': James B. Conant and the Hydrogen Bomb," in *Sociology of the Sciences Yearbook*, vol. 12, *Science, Technology and the Military*, ed. Everett Mendelsohn, M. R. Smith, and P. Weingart (Dordrecht, Netherlands, 1988), pp. 379–430.

17. Conant, "A History of the Development of the Atomic Bomb, Part II: The Reorganization of S-1 Committee December 1941," 17, Offices of Scientific Research and Development Records, Bush-Conant Files, RG 227, National Archives, Washington, D.C.

18. Conant, "Some Thoughts on International Control of Atomic Energy" (May 4, 1944), Bush-Conant Files, RG 227.

19. See, for example, Bush and Conant to Stimson, "Salient Points Concerning Future Handling of Atomic Bombs" (September 30, 1944), and Conant to Bush, "Supplementary Memorandum giving further details concerning military potentialities and the need for international exchange of information" (September 30, 1944), Manhattan Engineer District Records, Harrison-Bundy Files 69, RG 77, National Archives; and Conant to George Harrison (May 9, 1945), Harrison-Bundy Files 20, RG 77.

20. Conant to Bush (May 9, 1945), Bush-Conant Files, RG 227.

21. Ibid. (emphasis in original). In this memorandum, Conant was discussing the issue of Germany, but there were obviously significant implications for Japan.

22. Interim Committee minutes (May 31, 1945), Harrison-Bundy Files 100, RG 77 (emphasis in original).

23. Conant, "Notes on the 'Trinity' Test" (July 17, 1945), Bush-Conant Files, RG 227. The word in this statement may not be thermal; Conant's handwriting is very difficult to decipher.

24. The suggestion of possible guilt over the atomic bombing was stated—too strongly, I think—in Barton J. Bernstein, "The H-Bomb Decisions: Were They Inevitable?" in *National Security and International Stability*, ed. Bernard Brodie, M. Intriligator, and R. Kolkowicz (Cambridge, Mass., 1983), p. 332; and the judgment was softened in Peter Galison and Bernstein, "In Any Light: Scientists and the Decision to Build the Superbomb, 1942–1954," *Historical Studies in the Physical and Biological Sciences* 19 (1989): 292. The notion of guilt is disputed by Hershberg, "'Over My Dead Body': Conant," pp. 392–400; and Hershberg's judgment can be sustained by a *literal* (but not an imaginative) reading of Conant's words on the atomic bombings, including even a 1974 interview with Conant by John Landers, "The Manhattan Project as seen by Dr. Conant . . ." (1974), James Conant Papers (not the Harvard Presidential collection), Pusey Library. The present essay does not rest significantly on the matter of whether or not Conant in 1946 was impelled *partly* by guilt.

25. Conant to Harvey Bundy (September 23, 1946), Conant Presidential Papers.

26. This facing-the-facts motive did not appear for Conant in the available documents until *after* Hiroshima, when Conant agreed, in mid-August 1945, that this had been his motive. See Conant to Grenville Clark (August 17, 1945), and Clark to Conant (August 13, 1945), Grenville Clark Papers, Dartmouth College, Hanover, N.H. Strangely, Conant, in this letter, did not mention ending the war with Japan and saving lives as motives. On saving lives see Conant to Dr. Frank Whitmore (August 24, 1945), Bush-Conant Files, RG 227.

27. Stimson appears as a powerful influence (even in memory) in Walter Isaacson and Evan Thomas, *The Wise Men: Six Friends and the World They Made* (New York, 1986), a richly evocative but not especially analytical book. Stimson has never received a probing biography. His memoir with Bundy revealed a few warts, and Richard Current, *Secretary Stimson: A Study in Statecraft* (New Brunswick, N.J., 1954), is unduly harsh. Elting E. Morison, *Turmoil and Tradition: A Study of the Life and Times of Henry Stimson* (Boston, 1960), is a subsidized, adulatory study; and Godfrey Hodgson, *The Colonel: The Life and Wars of Henry L. Stimson, 1867–1950* (New York, 1990), is really an extended essay based on limited archival research and drawing heavily upon previous books about Stimson.

28. Conant to Harvey Bundy (September 23, 1946), Conant Presidential Papers.

29. Conant to George Harrison (May 9, 1945), Harrison-Bundy Files 20, RG 227; W. Higinbotham to Irving Kaplan (February 11, 1946), Federation of American Scientists Papers, Regenstein Library, University of Chicago, Chicago, Ill. On Bush's urging Compton to write the A-bomb article see George Russell Harrison, "Karl Taylor Compton: A Biography" (n.d.), p. 375, File MC 105, MIT Library.

30. Karl Compton to Conant (October 15, 1946), Compton MIT Presidential Papers.

31. Conant to Compton (October 26, 1946), Conant Presidential Papers.

32. The draft, by the same title, is in the Conant Presidential Papers.

33. Compton, "If the Atomic Bomb Had Not Been Used," pp. 55, 56.

34. Ibid., pp. 54–56.

35. Truman to Karl Compton (December 16, 1946), Harry S. Truman Papers, Official File, 692A, Truman Library, Independence, Mo.

36. Barton J. Bernstein, "The Perils and Politics of Surrender: Ending the War with Japan and Avoiding the Use of the Third Atomic Bomb," *Pacific Historical Review* 46 (February 1977): 1–27.

37. Truman to Compton (December 16, 1946), and Stimson to Karl Compton (December 16, 1946), Stimson Papers. The February *Atlantic Monthly* had only published part of Truman's letter, but perhaps it did not know—it certainly did not indicate—that the published version was an excerpt.

38.   Harvey Bundy and War Department historian Rudolph Winnacker were involved in the search to find Stimson a memoir writer and aide. Harvey Bundy to Stimson (April 1, 1946) and n.d. [June 1946], Winnacker to Stimson (March 14 and May 1 and 7, 1946), and Cass Canfield to Arthur Page (June 10, 1946), all in Stimson Papers. For Stimson's earlier attention to McGeorge Bundy's career and desire for combat see Stimson Diary (February 12, 1945).

39.   "Atomic Energy" (a rough transcript of Stimson's responses on the subject) (July 9, 1946), p. 11, Stimson Papers.

40.   The drafts are in Top Secret Documents Files of Interest to General Groves 20, RG 77, National Archives.

41.   "Notes on the Use by the United States of the Atomic Bomb" (September 25, 1946), marked #3, presumably for draft 3. The upper right bears the typed initials HHB, and thus the conclusion of Harvey H. Bundy's authorship, as is indirectly confirmed in Groves to Harvey Bundy (November 6, 1946), Top Secret Documents File 20, RG 77, National Archives.

42.   This strained interpretation is not supported by the Interim Committee minutes (May 31 and 1 June 1945), Harrison-Bundy Files 100, RG 227, National Archives.

43.   There is no evidence—in the target committee minutes (three meetings) or in other documents—that there was any effort to minimize the impact of radioactive poisoning. See "Notes on Initial Minutes of Target Committee," n.d. (probably April 27–28, 1945), Major D. A. Derry and N. F. Ramsey to Groves, "Summary of Target Committee Meetings on May 10 and 11, 1945," and L. E. Seeman, "Minutes of Third Target Committee Meeting—Washington, May 28, 1945," all in Top Secret Documents File 5, RG 77, National Archives. General Leslie Groves, *Now It Can Be Told: The Story of the Manhattan Project* (New York, 1962), p. 269, later offered a similar interpretation that the bombs had been detonated to avoid radiation on the ground. That claim is undercut, in part, by the contents of transcripts for two conversations between Groves and Lieutenant Colonel Rea, a physician at Oak Ridge, on August 25, 1945, file 201, Groves, RG 77, National Archives. For an interpretation of 1945 thinking about radiation see Barton J. Bernstein, "An Analysis of 'Two Cultures': Writing about the Making and the Using of the Atomic Bombs," *Public Historian* 12 (Spring 1990): 104.

44.   There is no support for this contention in the Stimson Diary, the Stimson Papers, the Manhattan Engineers District Records, Truman's "Potsdam Diary" at the Truman Library, or in the Secretary of War Records, RG 107, National Archives.

45.   Bundy, "Notes on the Use by the United States of the Atomic Bomb."

46.   Groves to Harvey Bundy (November 6, 1946), with "Decision to Use the Atomic Bomb Against Japan" (marked as Arneson original), and "Decision to Use the Atomic Bomb Against Japan" (marked as revised Arneson draft and thus, presumably, Groves's revision).

47.   Winnacker to Stimson (November 12, 1946), with five enclosures, Winnacker to Stimson (November 14, 1946), with enclosure, Winnacker to Stimson (November 18, 1946), with enclosure, all in Stimson Papers.

48.   Marshall to secretary of war (June 7, 1945), with Handy to Hull (June 1, 1945), War Department General Staff Records, RG 165, OPD 336 file, National Archives; G. A. L. [George A. Lincoln] staff paper, attached to Marshall to Stimson (June 15, 1945), Secretary of War Records, RG 107, Safe File, National Archives. On pre-Hiroshima estimates also see Stimson Diary (June 11, 1945). For other sources and the additional evidence see Barton J. Bernstein, "A Post-war Myth: 500,000 Lives Saved," *Bulletin of the Atomic Scientists* 42 (June/July 1986): 38–40.

49.   Stimson, "The Decision to Use the Atomic Bomb," p. 102. Interestingly, years later, Bush recalled a lower number—"a hundred thousand or more casualties," See Bush in transcript of 1965 interview, "Looking Back on the Bomb," 2, Bush Papers, MIT.

50.   Item V ("Japanese Surrender and the Atomic Bomb"), attached to Winnacker to Stimson (November 12, 1946), Stimson Papers.

51.   Conant to McGeorge Bundy (November 30, 1946), Stimson Papers.

52.   Ibid. For Conant's interest in international control see Conant to Grenville Clark, Bush Papers, box 27, Library of Congress, and Conant, "Diary of Moscow Trip" (December 10–26, 1945), and his fears about Secretary of State James F. Byrnes's commitment, in Conant Papers.

53.   This draft of late November is not available; apparently Conant returned it to McGeorge Bundy, but it is not in the Stimson Papers. Conant to McGeorge Bundy (November 30, 1946), Stimson Papers.

54.   Stimson to Felix Frankfurter (December 12, 1946), Stimson Papers. Unfortunately, this draft cannot be located—in the Frankfurter Papers, Library of Congress, or in the Stimson Papers—and it was apparently returned to Stimson.

55. Frankfurter to Stimson (telegram, December 16, 1946), Stimson Papers. For Frankfurter's earlier dismay and even contempt for criticisms of the A-bomb use see Frankfurter Diary (November 6, 1946), Frankfurter Papers.

56. Frankfurter to Stimson (December 16, 1946), Frankfurter Papers. Strangely, the copy in the Stimson Papers is missing the last two pages.

57. Patterson to Stimson (December 17, 1946), Patterson Papers. After reading a draft of my essay, McGeorge Bundy commented that Stimson's *Harper's* article did not conceal its argumentative purpose and that the average reader understood that the article was an argument. Bundy to Bernstein (November 29, 1991). For powerful suggestive evidence to the contrary see Patterson to Stimson (December 17, 1946), Patterson Papers; and Conant to Harvey Bundy (September 23, 1946), and Conant to McGeorge Bundy (November 30, 1946), Stimson Papers.

58. Conant to Stimson (December 14, 1946). In a letter to McGeorge Bundy on (December 13, 1946), Winnacker provided minor suggestions. In a sentence, based partly on Conant's November 30 suggestion, the December version stated: "For such a purpose the atomic bomb was an ideal weapon." Winnacker urged that this be rephrased to say "uniquely suitable." In a letter of December 13 to Stimson, Winnacker called the essay "one of the great state papers of our time." Both letters in Stimson Papers.

59. Frankfurter to Stimson (December 20, 1946 and January 6, 1947), McGeorge Bundy to Frankfurter (January 2, 1947, misdated as 1946), and Frankfurter to McGeorge Bundy (January 4, 1947), Frankfurter Papers.

60. Cass Canfield to Stimson (December 13 and 16, 1946), Stimson Papers.

61. Stimson to Henry Luce (January 20, 1947), Stimson Papers.

62. Stimson to Karl Compton (January 20, 1947), Stimson Papers.

63. Stimson to Conant (January 20, 1947), with note on file copy of "same letter to" H. Bundy, Frankfurter, Harrison, Ameson, and Winnacker, in Stimson Papers.

64. In his November 29, 1991 letter to me, responding to a draft of my study, Bundy stressed that his role in preparing the *Harper's* article was like that of a law clerk in serving a judge, that there was no effort at concealing this role, that he and Stimson would have acknowledged it if queried on the subject, that it would have been cumbersome to mention his role as co-author in the article, and that it might also have seemed as if he was seeking such recognition and being pushy. Many of these points have considerable merit. But where Bundy and I seem basically to disagree is on the political functions of the article appearing *only* as Stimson's work, because that is the conclusion that most readers and commentators reached then—and that most teachers and advanced Stanford undergraduates, to whom I have often taught this essay, conclude now. The claim of Stimson's exclusive authorship bestowed greater prestige on the article; explicit shared authorship would probably have diluted that authority and prestige—and undercut Conant's aim. In 1947, when Stimson was inclined to place *only* McGeorge Bundy's name as author on what was later published as Stimson's "memoir," Harper publisher Cass Canfield energetically and successfully persuaded Stimson to list his own name also. See Canfield to Stimson (November 7 and 11, 1947), Stimson Papers, and Frankfurter to Bundy (November 12, 1947), Frankfurter Papers.

65. Stimson, "The Decision to Use the Atomic Bomb," pp. 98–101. Stimson's essay did not note that, on at least two occasions, President Roosevelt had implied that the A-bomb might not be used on Japan. Probably Stimson did not know of one occasion (a September 22, 1944, Roosevelt conversation including Bush but not Stimson), and Stimson may well have forgotten the other (secret aide-mémoire at Hyde Park on September 19, 1944, between Roosevelt and Churchill), because the normal assumption in late 1944 was, indeed, use against Japan when the bomb was ready. Bush to Conant (September 23, 1944), AEC Doc. 186, Department of Energy Historical Office, Germantown, Md.; and aide-mémoire reprinted in various places including Margaret Gowing, *Britain and Atomic Energy, 1939–1945* (London, 1964), p. 447. Stimson may not have learned of this aide-mémoire until June 1945. See Stimson Diary (June 25, 1945). After the war, financier Alexander Sachs, who seems less than reliable, claimed that Roosevelt, in a November 1944 meeting with Sachs, had endorsed the conception of a test-demonstration as a warning before use. Sachs to Robert Patterson (June 28, 1946), Sachs Papers, box 56, Franklin D. Roosevelt Library, Hyde Park, N.Y. Sachs's claim is also reported in Henry A. Wallace Diary (October 24, 1945), Wallace Papers, University of Iowa Library, Iowa City, Iowa; and in Nat Finney's unduly trusting "How FDR Planned to Use the A-Bomb," *Look*, March 14, 1950, p. 23. On September 30, 1944, Conant and Bush, in a memorandum to Stimson, mentioned the possibility of a test-demonstration and warning before actual use. See Bush and Conant to Stimson (September 30, 1944), AEC Doc. 282, Department of Energy Historical Office. It is quite likely that Stimson, as well as Conant and Bush, forgot this suggestion well before Hiroshima. Thus, there is no implication intended in the

present essay that Stimson or Conant willfully suppressed this information after the war or that it was therefore intentionally omitted from Stimson's 1947 *Harper's* article.

66. Stimson, "The Decision to Use the Atomic Bomb," pp. 106–107.

67. Ibid., p. 107.

68. Ibid., pp. 98–100.

69. Interim Committee minutes, esp. May 9 and 31 and June 1 and 21, 1945, Harrison-Bundy Files, RG 77, National Archives; Arthur Compton, *Atomic Quest* (New York, 1956), pp. 238–239; Ernest Lawrence to Karl Darrow (August 17, 1945), Ernest Lawrence Papers, Bancroft Library, University of California, Berkeley, California. After the Franck committee report of mid-June, and after the four-man Scientific Advisory Panel recommended against a test-demonstration, the Interim Committee on June 21, 1945 reaffirmed its earlier decision on use; Barton J. Bernstein, "Four Physicists and the Bomb: The Early Years, 1945–1950," *Historical Studies in Physical Sciences* 18 (1988): 234–239; and idem, "Roosevelt, Truman, and the Atomic Bomb, 1941–1945: A Reinterpretation," *Political Science Quarterly* 90 (Spring 1975): 37–41.

70. Bernstein, "Roosevelt, Truman, and the Atomic Bomb," pp. 53–57.

71. United States Strategic Bombing Survey, *Summary Report (Pacific War)* (Washington, 1946), p. 26. Winnacker had earlier sent Bundy and Stimson a copy of this report. See Winnacker to Stimson (November 14, 1946), and Stimson to Winnacker (November 20, 1946), Stimson Papers.

72. See Stimson Diary (June 1, 1945); Stimson, "Memorandum of Conversation with the President" (June 6, 1945), Stimson Papers; Bernstein, "An Analysis of 'Two Cultures,'" pp. 95–97; and Stimson and Bundy, *On Active Service*, p. 632. When Stimson's pre-Hiroshima concerns about mass conventional bombings of non-combatants were revealed in his 1948 memoir, reviewers did not note this theme. Admittedly, reviewers were discussing a long book about an eventful, important life, and they seldom even focused on the A-bomb issues.

73. See McGeorge Bundy to Stimson (February 18, 1947), Ralph Bard to Stimson (February 7, 1947), and Henry A. Wallace to Stimson (February 5, 1947), Stimson Papers.

74. McGeorge Bundy to Stimson (February 18, 1947), Stimson Papers.

75. Karl Compton to Stimson (January 28, 1947), Stimson Papers.

76. Truman to Stimson (February 4, 1947), Truman Papers, President's Secretary's File, Truman Library. Truman's statements about the targets are from Truman to Stimson (November 13 and December 31, 1946), Truman Papers, President's Secretary's File. For Truman's July 1945 views see Truman, "Potsdam Diary" (July 25, 1945), Truman Library; and Bernstein, "An Analysis of 'Two Cultures,'" pp. 98–99.

77. Stimson to Raymond Gram Swing (January 20, 1947), Stimson Papers. Swing criticisms are in Swing, transcript, radio broadcast, ABC, (April 5, May 17, July 12, August 23, and December 13, 1946), Raymond Gram Swing Papers, box 31, Library of Congress; and in Swing, *In the Name of Sanity* (New York, 1946), which suggested an anti-Soviet motive for using the bomb. When Stimson retired in 1945, Swing had praised him for his leadership. Swing to Stimson (September 21, 1945), with excerpt of September 19 broadcast, Stimson Papers.

78. Swing to Stimson (January 31, 1947), Stimson Papers. See Stimson, "The Bomb and the Opportunity," *Harper's Magazine*, March 1946, p. 204, which was actually based upon Stimson's September 11, 1945 memorandum to Truman and then drafted into an article by Gordon, probably at the behest of Stimson's wartime aide, George Harrison. See Harrison to Stimson (January 4, 1946), Stimson Papers, on the background of the article. The September 11 memorandum is printed, among other places, in Stimson and Bundy, *On Active Service*, pp. 642–646. Cass Canfield, of Harper publishers, told Stimson that the magazine was printing "your clear and impressive statement." See Canfield to Stimson (January 21, 1946), Stimson Papers. It is unclear whether Canfield knew, or cared, that it had been drafted by someone else; that was not unusual for famous men both in office and out, but undoubtedly most readers did not realize that there was often a hidden co-authorship. Stimson sent his September 11 memorandum to the U.S. atomic energy negotiator Bernard Baruch. See Stimson to Baruch (May 28, 1946), and Stimson to John J. McCloy (May 28, 1946), Stimson Papers.

79. Stimson's odyssey reached a further point in mid-1947. Stimson to George Roberts (June 11, 1947), Stimson Papers.

80. Swing to Stimson (January 31, 1947), Stimson Papers.

81. Ibid.

82. Stimson Diary (September 21, 1945); John J. McCloy Diary (September 2, 1945), Amherst College Library, Amherst, Mass.; Bernstein, "The Quest for Security: American Foreign Policy and International Control of Atomic Energy, 1942–1946," *Journal of American History* 60 (March 1974): 1012–1023.

83. Stimson to Swing (February 4, 1947), Stimson Papers.

84. Ibid.

85. Conant to Stimson (January 22, 1947), Stimson Papers. Actually, even in autumn 1947, Conant continued to hold out hope for a Soviet-American agreement on international control, though he also feared the coming of a period when both nations would have many nuclear weapons. See Conant, "The Atomic Age: A Preview 1947 Edition," October 1947 speech at National War College, in 1916–52 File, Dwight D. Eisenhower Library, Abilene, Kans.; Bush to Conant (October 21, 1947), Bush Papers, Library of Congress; and Conant to J. Robert Oppenheimer (November 1, 1947), and Oppenheimer to Conant (October 29, 1947), J. Robert Oppenheimer Papers, box 27, Library of Congress.

86. "Dear Jim" (signatory concealed) (March 7, 1947), attached to Conant to Oppenheimer (March 14, 1947), Oppenheimer Papers, box 27, Library of Congress.

87. Ibid.

88. Conant to Oppenheimer (March 14, 1947), Oppenheimer Papers, box 27, Library of Congress. See also V. F. Weisskopf to Conant (March 24, 1947), Conant Presidential Papers.

89. On Szilard, for example, see Leo Szilard to [Trude Weiss] (August 6, 1945), Leo Szilard Papers, University of California, San Diego, California; and Szilard's 1947 call for a crusade (quite different from Conant's strategy) for improving Soviet-American relations, "Calling for a Crusade," *Bulletin of the Atomic Scientists* 3 (March 1947): 102–106, 125. On Franck see Szilard's article, "The Social Task of the Scientist," ibid. 4 (March 1947): 70, which dwelled on issues of secrecy and the scientist's responsibility. Scattered evidence of Franck's criticisms is in the Franck Papers, Regenstein Library, University of Chicago.

90. "The Decision to Use the Atomic Bomb," *Bulletin of the Atomic Scientists* 3 (February 1947): 33, 68. This editorial is quite probably by Rabinowitch, but my efforts to check in the Papers of the *Bulletin of the Atomic Scientists* at the Regenstein Library were not successful. No substantial interpretation rests upon whether or not the author was Rabinowitch. The January 1947 *Bulletin*, p. 31, had reprinted mathematician Norbert Wiener's *Atlantic Monthly* article on his refusal to share his work with the military, because of his mistrust of the military, the nation-state's disregard of scientists' advice, and the atomic bombings. Surprisingly, many Manhattan Project scientists who opposed the atomic bombing before Hiroshima seem not to have continued, or not to have publicized, their opposition after V-J Day. On pre-Hiroshima doubts or opposition see the scientist petitions, especially those of July 17, 1945, with over 130 signatories from the Chicago and Clinton laboratories, in Harrison-Bundy Files 76, RG 77, National Archives.

91. E. Marcellus Nesbitt, First Presbyterian Church, Beaver, Pa., to Stimson (January 28, 1947), Stimson Papers.

92. Nesbitt to Elizabeth Neary, secretary to Stimson (February 19, 1947), Stimson Papers.

93. R. D. Van Deman to Stimson (February 15, 1947), Stimson Papers.

94. The Stimson Papers, by my count, include only four letters by plain citizens objecting to the A-bomb decision and responding to Stimson's essay. It is quite possible that other hostile letters were not retained in the files, and thus that they are lost.

95. Grew to Stimson (February 12, 1947), Joseph Grew Papers, Houghton Library, Harvard University. For Grew's 1945 efforts and Stimson's 1945 concerns see Stimson Diary (May 29 and June 19 and 24, 1945).

96. Winnacker to McGeorge Bundy (December 13, 1946), and Stimson to Winnacker (December 13, 1946), Stimson Papers.

97. Winnacker to Stimson (February 5, 1947), Stimson Papers.

98. Winnacker, "The Debate about Hiroshima," *Military Affairs* 11 (Spring 1947): 25–30.

99. Winnacker to Stimson (May 16, 1947), Stimson Papers.

100. Winnacker, "The Debate about Hiroshima," p. 25.

101. Ibid., pp. 26, 29.

102. Winnacker to McGeorge Bundy (December 13, 1946), Stimson Papers. In his November 29, 1991, comments to me on this section, Bundy contended that it is unfair to criticize Winnacker on these matters, because one should not expect any official historian to mention in his own work the aid he gave a former boss. At root between Bundy's and my opinions on this point may be fundamentally different conceptions about the relationship of seemingly independent scholarship to the standards for official historians. Winnacker's set of omissions strikes me as significant—and I, unlike Bundy and possibly other former government officials, do think that scholars, and even journalists, should in some way acknowledge the kind of conflict of interest that Winnacker did not disclose. That conflict, in my judgment, reached beyond the evident fact that he was an official historian and

presumably, therefore, less than free to disagree in print with his former boss, especially when Win-nacker's new boss, Patterson, was Stimson's friend, his former undersecretary, and also a supporter of the A-bomb decision.

103. Winnacker, "The Debate about Hiroshima," p. 30, quoting from the *Washington Post*, November 13, 1946.

104. Winnacker to Stimson (May 16, 1947).

105. Stimson to Grew (June 19, 1947), Grew Papers. Curiously, John J. McCloy, who had served Stimson during the war as assistant secretary, apparently never received a draft of the *Harper's* essay, but McCloy's post-war criticisms of U.S. policy leading to Hiroshima were similar to Grew's. See James Forrestal Diary (March 8, 1947), Naval Archives, Washington, D.C. After the war, McCloy claimed to recall his own counsel on these matters at the June 18, 1945, White House meeting, but, despite the trusting judgment by James Reston, Kai Bird, and others, there is good reason to question some of McCloy's claims about his advice in that June 18 meeting. See McCloy Diary (June 18, 1945); Forrestal Diary (June 18, 1945); "McCloy on the A-bomb," in James Reston, *Deadline: Memoirs* (New York, 1991), pp. 501–509; and Kai Bird, *The Chairman: John J. McCloy: the Making of the American Establishment* (New York, 1992), pp. 244–252, 262–264. Apparently, neither Stimson's correspondence nor McCloy's, in the Stimson Papers or in the McCloy Papers, contains any criticism of Stimson's essay by McCloy from 1946 to 1949.

106. Bernstein, "Perils and Politics of Surrender," pp. 3–8.

107. Grew to Stimson (February 12, 1947), Grew Papers.

108. Stimson and Bundy, *On Active Service*, p. 629.

109. Ibid.

110. Ibid., p. 617.

111. Ibid., pp. 636–637. Virtually alone among reviewers, Harold Laski in the *New Statesman and Nation* 37 (June 1949): 618–619, raised prickly questions involving the connection between the A-bomb and the Soviet Union. McGeorge Bundy privately responded to Laski. See Bundy to Frank-furter (July 14, 1949), with attachment of Bundy to Laski (July 13, 1949), and Frankfurter to Bundy (December 16, 1949), in Frankfurter Papers.

112. The conception that the bomb and Soviet entry were viewed as interchangeable in their capacity to end the war speedily (a proposition that is quite different from the view that the bomb made Soviet entry less important but that Soviet entry had not generally been foreseen as decisive or even powerful in its psychological impact on Japan's government) is one of the underpinnings for conclusions in Gar Alperovitz, *Atomic Diplomacy*, rev. ed. (New York, 1985), which has been criticized in, among other places, Barton J. Bernstein, "Eclipsed by Hiroshima and Nagasaki: Early Thinking about Tactical Nuclear Weapons," *International Security* 15 (Spring 1991): 168–170 and esp. n. 70. For an exchange on this subject and related issues on the use of the A-bomb see Gar Alperovitz and Robert Messer, "Marshall, Truman, and the Decision to Drop the Bomb," and Bernstein's rejoinder, in *International Security* 16 (Winter 1991/92): 204–221.

113. Stimson and Bundy, *On Active Service*, pp. 632–633.

114. Stimson to Truman (September 11, 1945), and Stimson, "Memorandum for the President: Proposed Action for Control of Atomic Bomb" (September 11, 1945), Stimson Papers (reprinted in Stimson and Bundy, *On Active Service*, pp. 642–646).

115. Stimson Diary (August 12–September 3, 1945).

116. Quoted in George Kennan to McGeorge Bundy (December 2, 1947), George C. Marshall Papers, Pentagon Office, Selected, box 86, George C. Marshall Library, Lexington, Va. Unfortu-nately, the chapter draft is not available but important parts can be determined from Kennan's critical letter.

117. See Stimson Diary (August 12–September 3, 1945), reporting McCloy's conversation with Byrnes; and McCloy Diary (September 2, 1945).

118. Stimson Diary (September 4, 1945).

119. Bundy to secretary [Marshall] (October 31, 1947), and Bundy to secretary (November 10, 1947), both in Marshall Papers.

120. Marshall to Bundy (November 7, 1947), Marshall Papers.

121. Ibid. (November 19, 1947), Marshall Papers.

122. Kennan to Bundy (December 2, 1947), Marshall Papers, Pentagon Office, Selected, box 86. On Kennan's 1946 proposal for compelling Soviet acceptance of the Baruch Plan see Franklin Lindsay to staff (November 12, 1946), Bernard Baruch Papers, Princeton University Library, Prince-ton, N.J.

123. McCloy Diary (September 2, 1945).

124. Bundy to Kennan (December 8, 1947), Marshall Papers.

125. Ibid. (December 4, 1947), Marshall Papers.

126. The revised segments appear in Stimson and Bundy, *On Active Service*, p. 641 (with the first deletion following the sentence "the War Department civilian staff was thinking long and painful thoughts about the atomic triumph") and on p. 647 (where the key noun in the sentence about "some American statesmen were eager" was transformed into "some Americans"). There also had been a third criticism by Kennan on whether or not Byrnes and the American government, by making a vague December 1945 offer to the Soviets for future negotiations on international control, had actually followed Stimson's September counsel for a prompt, direct effort with the Soviets. Bundy had softened Stimson's complaint about the American failure to follow Stimson's September counsel, and the revised version appears in *On Active Service*, p. 647. See Kennan to Bundy (December 2, 1947), Bundy to Kennan (December 4, 1947), Bundy to Kennan (December 8, 1947), Kennan to Bundy (December 19, 1947), Bundy to Kennan (December 22, 1947), and Kennan to secretary [Marshall] (December 16, 1947), with Marshall's "I concur" to approve the changes, all in Marshall Papers.

127. For salient literature on whether there was post-war atomic diplomacy, and its meaning, motives, and nature, see Barton J. Bernstein, ed., *The Atomic Bomb: The Critical Issues* (Boston, 1976), pp. 121–142; Alperovitz, *Atomic Diplomacy*, pp. 236–273; Thomas Hammond, "'Atomic Diplomacy' Revisited," *Orbis* 19 (Winter 1976): 1403–1422; and McGeorge Bundy, "The Unimpressive Record of Atomic Diplomacy," in *The Choice: Nuclear Weapons Versus Security*, ed. Gwin Prins (London, 1984), esp. p. 44.

128. For distress among Kennan and other policymakers and associates when Alperovitz's *Atomic Diplomacy* appeared see "Memo of Telecon: George Kennan and W. A. Harriman" (February 2, 1968), and "Kennan Notes," n.d. (probably 1967), both in W. Averell Harriman Papers, box 867, Library of Congress.

129. The substantial literature on the use of the atomic bomb is critically examined in Barton J. Bernstein, "The Atomic Bomb and American Foreign Policy, 1941–1945: A Historiographical Controversy," *Peace and Change* 2 (Spring 1974): 1–16; and J. Samuel Walker, "The Decision to Use the Bomb: A Historiographical Update," *Diplomatic History* 14 (Winter 1990): 97–114.

130. This general analysis is developed more fully in Bernstein, "Roosevelt, Truman, and the Atomic Bomb," pp. 23–62; and briefly in Bernstein, "Eclipsed by Hiroshima and Nagasaki," esp. pp. 168–170. This analysis is challenged by Alperovitz and Messer, "Marshall, Truman, and the Decision to Drop the Bomb," pp. 204–214, with a brief rejoinder by Bernstein, pp. 214–221.

131. For an unduly brief treatment of these changes see Bernstein, ed., *The Atomic Bomb*, pp. 2–3; and Bernstein, "The Atomic Bomb and American Foreign Policy," pp. 3–4.

132. Conant's role was mentioned, briefly, in Bernstein, ed., *The Atomic Bomb*, p. 1; and in Hershberg, "James B. Conant and the Atomic Bomb," p. 80. Martin J. Sherwin, *A World Destroyed* (New York, 1987), p. 3, as well as in his original 1975 edition, perceptively opened with a quotation from Stimson to Truman (January 7, 1947), briefly mentioning the political purpose of Stimson's "Decision" essay. In 1986, Sherwin, "Scientists, Arms Control, and National Security," in *The National Security: Its Theory and Practice, 1945–1960*, ed. Norman Graebner (New York, 1986), p. 117, briefly mentioned Conant's influence and quoted a passage from Conant's November 30, 1946 letter to McGeorge Bundy.

133. Truman, in Wallace Diary (August 10, 1945); Truman to Stimson (November 13, and December 31, 1946), Stimson Papers. The present essay does not rest, in any important way, upon this possible motive of a guilty conscience *after* the two atomic bombings.

134. Stimson in Stimson and Bundy, *On Active Service*, p. xi. For an earlier draft see Bundy to Frankfurter, n.d. (after November 14, 1947), with draft of "Forward," Stimson Papers.

135. Bundy, *Danger and Survival*, p. 92.

136. See Bernstein, "Writing, Righting, or Wronging the Historical Record: President Truman's Letter on His Atomic-Bomb Decision," *Diplomatic History* 16 (Winter 1992), 163–173. For a related analysis of a well-known memoir-statement on another major U.S. decision, Robert Kennedy's *Thirteen Days*, which may also have had a concealed author (Sorensen), see Bernstein, "Reconsidering the Missile Crisis: Dealing with the Problems of the American Jupiters in Turkey," in *The Cuban Missile Crisis Revisited*, ed. James Nathan (New York, 1992), pp. 55–128.

THE
DECISION
TO USE
THE ATOMIC
BOMB

Henry L. Stimson

IN RECENT MONTHS there has been much comment about the decision to use atomic bombs in attacks on the Japanese cities of Hiroshima and Nagasaki. This decision was one of the gravest made by our government in recent years, and it is entirely proper that it should be widely discussed. I have therefore decided to record for all who may be interested smy understanding of the events which led up to the attack on Hiroshima on August 6, 1945, on Nagasaki on August 9, and the Japanese decision to surrender, on August 10. No single individual can hope to know exactly what took place in the minds of all of those who had a share in these events, but what follows is an exact description of our thoughts and actions as I find them in the records and in my clear recollection.

It was in the fall of 1941 that the question of atomic energy was first brought directly to my attention. At that time President Roosevelt appointed a committee consisting of Vice President Wallace, General Marshall, Dr. Vannevar Bush, Dr. James B. Conant, and myself. The function of this committee was to advise the President on questions of policy relating to the study of nuclear fission which was then proceeding both in this country and in Great Britain. For nearly four years thereafter I was directly connected with all major decisions of policy on the development and use of atomic energy, and from May 1, 1943, until my resignation as Secretary of War on September 21, 1945, I was directly responsible to the President for the administration of the entire undertaking; my chief advisers in this period were General Marshall, Dr. Bush, Dr. Conant, and Major General Leslie R. Groves, the officer in charge of the project. At the same time I was the President's senior adviser on the military employment of atomic energy.

The policy adopted and steadily pursued by President Roosevelt and his advisers was a simple one. It was to spare no effort in securing the earliest possible successful development of an atomic weapon. The reasons for this policy were equally simple. The original experimental achievement of atomic fission had occurred in Germany in 1938, and it was known that the Germans had continued their experiments. In 1941 and 1942 they were believed to be ahead of us, and it was vital that they should not be the first to bring atomic weapons into the field of battle. Furthermore, if we should be the first to develop the weapon, we should have a great new instrument for shortening the war and minimizing destruction. At no time, from 1941 to 1945, did I ever hear it suggested by the President, or by any other responsible member of the government, that atomic energy should not be used in the war. All of us of course understood the terrible responsibility involved in our attempt to unlock the doors to such a devastating weapon; President Roosevelt particularly spoke to me many times of his own awareness of the catastrophic potentialities of our work. But we were at war, and the work must be done. I therefore emphasize that it was our common objective, throughout the war, to be the first to produce an atomic weapon and use it. The possible atomic weapon was considered to be a new and tremendously powerful explosive, as legitimate as any other of the deadly explosive weapons of modern war. The entire purpose was the production of a military weapon; on no other ground could the wartime expenditure of so much time and money have been justified. The exact circumstances in which that weapon might be used were unknown to any of us until the middle of 1945, and when that time came, as we shall presently see, the military use of atomic energy was connected with larger questions of national policy.

The extraordinary story of the successful development of the atomic bomb has been well told elsewhere. As time went on it became clear that the weapon would not be available in time for use in the European Theater, and the war against Germany was successfully ended by the use of what are now called conventional means. But in the spring of 1945 it became evident that the climax of our prolonged atomic effort was at hand. By the nature of atomic chain reactions, it was impossible to state with certainty that we had succeeded until a bomb had actually exploded in a full-scale experiment; nevertheless it was considered exceedingly probable that we should by midsummer have successfully detonated the first atomic bomb. This was to be done at the Alamogordo Reservation in New Mexico. It was thus time for detailed consideration of our future plans. What had begun as a well-founded hope was now developing into a reality.

On March 15, 1945 I had my last talk with President Roosevelt. My diary record of this conversation gives a fairly clear picture of the state of our thinking at that time. I have removed the name of the distinguished public servant who was fearful lest the Manhattan (atomic) project be "a lemon"; it was an opinion common among those not fully informed.

> The President ... had suggested that I come over to lunch today. ... First I took up with him a memorandum which he sent to me from ———— who had been alarmed at the rumors of extravagance in the Manhattan project. ———— suggested that it might become disastrous and he suggested that we get a body of "outside" scientists to pass upon the project because rumors are going around that Vannevar Bush and Jim Conant have sold the President a lemon on the subject and ought to be checked up on. It was rather a jittery and nervous memorandum and rather silly, and I was prepared for it and I gave the President a list of the scientists who were actually engaged on it to show the very high standing of them and it comprised four Nobel Prize men, and also how practically every physicist of standing was engaged with us in the project. Then I outlined to him the future of it and when it was likely to come off and told him how important it was to get ready. I went over with him the two schools

of thought that exist in respect to the future control after the war of this project, in case it is successful, one of them being the secret close-in attempted control of the project by those who control it now, and the other being the international control based upon freedom both of science and of access. I told him that those things must be settled before the first projectile is used and that he must be ready with a statement to come out to the people on it just as soon as that is done. He agreed to that. . . .

This conversation covered the three aspects of the question which were then uppermost in our minds. First, it was always necessary to suppress a lingering doubt that any such titanic undertaking could be successful. Second, we must consider the implications of success in terms of its long-range post-war effect. Third, we must face the problem that would be presented at the time of our first use of the weapon, for with that first use there must be some public statement.

I did not see Franklin Roosevelt again. The next time I went to the White House to discuss atomic energy was April 25, 1945, and I went to explain the nature of the problem to a man whose only previous knowledge of our activities was that of a Senator who had loyally accepted our assurance that the matter must be kept a secret from him. Now he was President and Commander-in-Chief, and the final responsibility in this as in so many other matters must be his. President Truman accepted this responsibility with the same fine spirit that Senator Truman had shown before in accepting our refusal to inform him.

I discussed with him the whole history of the project. We had with us General Groves, who explained in detail the progress which had been made and the probable future course of the work. I also discussed with President Truman the broader aspects of the subject, and the memorandum which I used in this discussion is again a fair sample of the state of our thinking at the time.

MEMORANDUM DISCUSSED WITH PRESIDENT TRUMAN APRIL 25, 1945

(1) Within four months we shall in all probability have completed the most terrible weapon ever known in human history, one bomb of which could destroy a whole city.

(2) Although we have shared its development with the U.K., physically the U.S. is at present in the position of controlling the resources with which to construct and use it and no other nation could reach this position for some years.

(3) Nevertheless it is practically certain that we could not remain in this position indefinitely.

a. Various segments of its discovery and production are widely known among many scientists in many countries, although few scientists are now acquainted with the whole process which we have developed.

b. Although its construction under present methods requires great scientific and industrial effort and raw materials, which are temporarily mainly within the possession and knowledge of U.S. and U.K., it is extremely probable that much easier and cheaper methods of production will be discovered by scientists in the future, together with the use of materials of much wider distribution. As a result, it is extremely probable that the future will make it possible for atomic bombs to be constructed by smaller nations or even groups, or at least by a larger nation in a much shorter time.

(4) As a result, it is indicated that the future may see a time when such a weapon may be constructed in secret and used suddenly and effectively with devastating power by a willful nation or group against an unsuspecting nation or group of much greater size and material power. With its aid even a very powerful unsuspecting nation might be conquered within a very few days by a very much smaller one. . . .*

(5) The world in its present state of moral advancement compared with its technical development would be eventually at the mercy of such a weapon. In other words, modern civilization might be completely destroyed.

(6) To approach any world peace organization of any pattern now likely to be considered, without an appreciation by the leaders of our country of the power of this new weapon, would seem to be unrealistic. No system of control heretofore considered would be adequate to control this menace. Both inside any particular country and between the nations of the world, the control of this weapon will undoubtedly be a matter of the greatest difficulty and would involve such thoroughgoing rights of inspection and internal controls as we have never heretofore contemplated.

(7) Furthermore, in the light of our present position with reference to this weapon, the question of sharing it with other nations and, if so shared, upon what terms, becomes a primary question of our foreign relations. Also our leadership in the war and in the development of this weapon has placed a certain moral responsibility upon us which we cannot shirk without very serious responsibility for any disaster to civilization which it would further.

(8) On the other hand, if the problem of the proper use of this weapon can be solved, we would have the opportunity to bring the world into a pattern in which the peace of the world and our civilization can be saved.

(9) As stated in General Groves's report, steps are under way looking towards the establishment of a select committee of particular qualifications for recommending action to the executive and legislative branches of our government when secrecy is no longer in full effect. The committee would also recommend the actions to be taken by the War Department prior to that time in anticipation of the post-war problems. All recommendations would of course be first submitted to the President.

---

* A brief reference to the estimated capabilities of other nations is here omitted; it in no way affects the course of the argument.

The next step in our preparations was the appointment of the committee referred to in paragraph (9) above. This committee, which was known as the Interim Committee, was charged with the function of advising the President on the various questions raised by our apparently imminent success in developing an atomic weapon. I was its chairman, but the principal labor of guiding its extended deliberations fell to George L. Harrison, who acted as chairman in my absence. It will be useful to consider the work of the committee in some detail. Its members were the following, in addition to Mr. Harrison and myself:

> James F. Byrnes (then a private citizen) as personal representative of
> the President.
> Ralph A. Bard, Under Secretary of the Navy.
> William L. Clayton, Assistant Secretary of State.
> Dr. Vannevar Bush, Director, Office of Scientific Research and
> Development, and president of the Carnegie Institution of
> Washington.
> Dr. Karl T. Compton, Chief of the Office of Field Service in the
> Office of Scientific Research and Development, and president
> of the Massachusetts Institute of Technology.
> Dr. James B. Conant, Chairman of the National Defense Research
> Committee, and president of Harvard University.

The discussions of the committee ranged over the whole field of atomic energy, in its political, military, and scientific aspects. That part of its work which particularly concerns us here relates to its recommendations for the use of atomic energy against Japan, but it should be borne in mind that these recommendations were not made in a vacuum. The committee's work included the drafting of the statements which were published immediately after the first bombs were dropped, the drafting of a bill for the domestic control of atomic energy, and recommendations looking toward the international control of atomic energy. The Interim Committee was assisted in its work by a Scientific Panel whose members were the following: Dr. A. H. Compton, Dr. Enrico Fermi, Dr. E. O. Lawrence, and Dr. J. R. Oppenheimer. All four were nuclear physicists of the first rank; all four had held positions of great importance in the atomic project from its inception. At a meeting with the Interim Committee and the Scientific Panel on May 31, 1945 I urged all those present to feel free to express themselves on any phase of the subject, scientific or political. Both General Marshall and I at this meeting expressed the view that atomic energy could not be considered simply in terms of military weapons but must also be considered in terms of a new relationship of man to the universe.

On June 1, after its discussions with the Scientific Panel, the Interim Committee unanimously adopted the following recommendations:

> (1) The bomb should be used against Japan as soon as possible.
> (2) It should be used on a dual target—that is, a military installation
> or war plant surrounded by or adjacent to houses and other buildings
> most susceptible to damage, and
> (3) It should be used without prior warning [of the nature of the
> weapon]. One member of the committee, Mr. Bard, later changed his
> view and dissented from recommendation (3).

In reaching these conclusions the Interim Committee carefully considered such alternatives as a detailed advance warning or a demonstration in some uninhabited area. Both of these suggestions were discarded as impractical.* They were not regarded as likely to be effective in compelling a surrender of Japan, and both of them involved serious risks. Even the New Mexico test would not give final proof that any given bomb was certain to explode when dropped from an airplane. Quite apart from the generally unfamiliar nature of atomic explosives, there was the whole problem of exploding a bomb at a predetermined height in the air by a complicated mechanism which could not be tested in the static test of New Mexico. Nothing would have been more damaging to our effort to obtain surrender than a warning or a demonstration followed by a dud—and this was a real possibility. Furthermore, we had no bombs to waste. It was vital that a sufficient effect be quickly obtained with the few we had.

The Interim Committee and the Scientific Panel also served as a channel through which suggestions from other scientists working on the atomic project were forwarded to me and to the President. Among the suggestions thus forwarded was one memorandum which questioned using the bomb at all against the enemy. On June 16, 1945, after consideration of that memorandum, the Scientific Panel made a report, from which I quote the following paragraphs:

> The opinions of our scientific colleagues on the initial use of these weapons are not unanimous: they range from the proposal of a purely technical demonstration to that of the military application best designed to induce surrender. Those who advocate a purely technical demonstration would wish to outlaw the use of atomic weapons, and have feared that if we use the weapons now our position in future negotiations will be prejudiced. Others emphasize the opportunity of saving American lives by immediate military use, and believe that such use will improve the international prospects, in that they are more concerned with the prevention of war than with the elimination of this special weapon. We find ourselves closer to these latter views; *we can propose no technical demonstration likely to bring an end to the war; we see no acceptable alternative to direct military use.* [Italic mine]
>
> With regard to these general aspects of the use of atomic energy, it is clear that we, as scientific men, have no proprietary rights. It is true that we are among the few citizens who have had

---

* Editors' Note: Stimson's claim that the Interim Committee rejected "a detailed advance warning…as impractical" appears inconsistent with a statement he made a month after the June 1st committee session that had recommended the atomic bomb be "used on a war plant surrounded by workers' homes…without any prior warning." In reproducing his July 2, 1945 memorandum to the President within the text of the *Harper's* article (p. 204), Stimson made a curious omission. He failed to include a crucial part of the July 2 memorandum—his cover letter to Truman. "I am enclosing herewith a memorandum to you on the matter of the proposed warning to Japan, a subject which I have heretofore discussed with you…," wrote Stimson, "You will note that it is written without special relation to the employment of any new weapon. *Of course, it would have to be revamped to conform to the efficacy of such a weapon if the warning were to be delivered, as would almost certainly be the case, in conjunction with its use.* (Emphasis added.) The cover letter and the text of the memorandum is reproduced in its entirety in the document section of *Hiroshima's Shadow*, p. 527.

occasion to give thoughtful consideration to these problems during the past few years. We have, however, no claim to special competence in solving the political, social, and military problems which are presented by the advent of atomic power.

The foregoing discussion presents the reasoning of the Interim Committee and its advisers. I have discussed the work of these gentlemen at length in order to make it clear that we sought the best advice that we could find. The committee's function was, of course, entirely advisory. The ultimate responsibility for the recommendation to the President rested upon me, and I have no desire to veil it. The conclusions of the committee were similar to my own, although I reached mine independently. I felt that to extract a genuine surrender from the Emperor and his military advisers, they must be administered a tremendous shock which would carry convincing proof of our power to destroy the Empire. Such an effective shock would save many times the number of lives, both American and Japanese, that it would cost. The facts upon which my reasoning was based and steps taken to carry it out now follow.

THE PRINCIPAL POLITICAL, SOCIAL, and military objective of the United States in the summer of 1945 was the prompt and complete surrender of Japan. Only the complete destruction of her military power could open the way to lasting peace. Japan, in July 1945, had been seriously weakened by our increasingly violent attacks. It was known to us that she had gone so far as to make tentative proposals to the Soviet government, hoping to use the Russians as mediators in a negotiated peace. These vague proposals contemplated the retention by Japan of important conquered areas and were therefore not considered seriously. There was as yet no indication of any weakening in the Japanese determination to fight rather than accept unconditional surrender. If she should persist in her fight to the end, she had still a great military force.

In the middle of July 1945, the intelligence section of the War Department General Staff estimated Japanese military strength as follows: in the home islands, slightly under 2,000,000; in Korea, Manchuria, China proper, and Formosa, slightly over 2,000,000; in French Indo-China, Thailand, and Burma, over 200,000; in the East Indies area, including the Philippines, over 500,000; in the bypassed Pacific islands, over 100,000. The total strength of the Japanese Army was estimated at about 5,000,000 men. These estimates later proved to be in very close agreement with official Japanese figures. The Japanese Army was in much better condition than the Japanese Navy and Air Force. The Navy had practically ceased to exist except as a harrying force against an invasion fleet. The Air Force had been reduced mainly to reliance upon Kamikaze, or suicide, attacks. These latter, however, had already inflicted serious damage on our seagoing forces, and their possible effectiveness in a last ditch fight was a matter of real concern to our naval leaders.

As we understood it in July, there was a very strong possibility that the Japanese government might determine upon resistance to the end, in all the areas of the Far East under its control. In such an event the Allies would be faced with the enormous task of destroying an armed force of five million men and five thousand suicide aircraft, belonging to a race which had already amply demonstrated its ability to fight literally to the death.

The strategic plans of our armed forces for the defeat of Japan, as they stood in July, had been prepared without reliance upon the atomic bomb, which had not yet been tested in New Mexico. We were planning an intensified sea and air blockade, and greatly intensified strategic air bombing, through the summer and early fall, to be followed on November 1 by an invasion of the southern island of Kyushu. This would be followed in turn by an invasion of the main island of Honshu in the spring of 1946. The total U.S. military and naval force involved in this grand design was of the order of 5,000,000 men; if all those indirectly concerned are included, it was larger still.

We estimated that if we should be forced to carry this plan to its conclusion, the major fighting would not end until the latter part of 1946, at the earliest. I was informed that such operations might be expected to cost over a million casualties, to American forces alone. Additional large losses might be expected among our allies, and, of course, if our campaign were successful and if we could judge by previous experience, enemy casualties would be much larger than our own.

It was already clear in July that even before the invasion we should be able to inflict enormously severe damage on the Japanese homeland by the combined application of "conventional" sea and air power. The critical question was whether this kind of action would induce surrender. It therefore became necessary to consider very carefully the probable state of mind of the enemy, and to assess with accuracy the line of conduct which might end his will to resist. With these considerations in mind, I wrote a memorandum for the President, on July 2, which I believe fairly represents the thinking of the American government as it finally took shape in action. This memorandum was prepared after discussion and general agreement with Joseph C. Grew, Acting Secretary of State, and Secretary of the Navy Forrestal, and when I discussed it with the President, he expressed his general approval.

July 2, 1945
MEMORANDUM FOR THE PRESIDENT
PROPOSED PROGRAM FOR JAPAN

(1) The plans of operation up to and including the first landing have been authorized and the preparations for the operation are now actually going on. This situation was accepted by all members of your conference on Monday, June 18.

(2) There is reason to believe that the operation for the occupation of Japan following the landing may be a very long, costly, and arduous struggle on our part. The terrain, much of which I have visited several times, has left the impression on my memory of being one which would be susceptible to a last ditch defense such as has been made on Iwo Jima and Okinawa and which of course is very much larger than either of those two areas. According to my recollection it will be much more unfavorable with regard to tank maneuvering than either the Philippines or Germany.

(3) If we once land on one of the main islands and begin a forceful occupation of Japan, we shall probably have cast the die of last ditch resistance. The Japanese are highly patriotic and certainly

susceptible to calls for fanatical resistance to repel an invasion. Once started in actual invasion, we shall in my opinion have to go through with an even more bitter finish fight than in Germany. We shall incur the losses incident to such a war and we shall have to leave the Japanese islands even more thoroughly destroyed than was the case with Germany. This would be due both to the difference in the Japanese and German personal character and the differences in the size and character of the terrain through which the operations will take place.

(4) A question then comes: Is there any alternative to such a forceful occupation of Japan which will secure for us the equivalent of an unconditional surrender of her forces and a permanent destruction of her power again to strike an aggressive blow at the "peace of the Pacific"? I am inclined to think that there is enough such chance to make it well worthwhile our giving them a warning of what is to come and a definite opportunity to capitulate. As above suggested, it should be tried before the actual forceful occupation of the homeland islands is begun and furthermore the warning should be given in ample time to permit a national reaction to set in.

We have the following enormously favorable factors on our side—factors much weightier than those we had against Germany:
• Japan has no allies.
• Her navy is nearly destroyed and she is vulnerable to a surface and underwater blockade which can deprive her of sufficient food and supplies for her population.
• She is terribly vulnerable to our concentrated air attack upon her crowded cities, industrial and food resources.
• She has against her not only the Anglo-American forces but the rising forces of China and the ominous threat of Russia.
• We have inexhaustible and untouched industrial resources to bring to bear against her diminishing potential.
• We have great moral superiority through being the victim of her first sneak attack.

The problem is to translate these advantages into prompt and economical achievement of our objectives. I believe Japan is susceptible to reason in such a crisis to a much greater extent than is indicated by our current press and other current comment. Japan is not a nation composed wholly of mad fanatics of an entirely different mentality from ours. On the contrary, she has within the past century shown herself to possess extremely intelligent people, capable in an unprecedentedly short time of adopting not only the complicated technique of Occidental civilization but to a substantial extent their culture and their political and social ideas. Her advance in all these respects during the short period of sixty or seventy years has been one of the most astounding feats of national progress in history—a leap from the isolated feudalism of centuries into the position of one of the six or seven great powers of the world. She has not only built up powerful armies and navies. She has maintained an honest and effective national finance and respected position in many of the sciences in which we pride ourselves. Prior to the forcible seizure of power over her government by the fanatical military group in 1931, she had for ten years lived a reasonably responsible and respectable international life.

My own opinion is in her favor on the two points involved in this question:

a. I think the Japanese nation has the mental intelligence and versatile capacity in such a crisis to recognize the folly of a fight to the finish and to accept the proffer of what will amount to an unconditional surrender; and

b. I think she has within her population enough liberal leaders (although now submerged by the terrorists) to be depended upon for her reconstruction as a responsible member of the family of nations. I think she is better in this last respect than Germany was. Her liberals yielded only at the point of the pistol and, so far as I am aware, their liberal attitude has not been personally subverted in the way which was so general in Germany.

On the other hand, I think that the attempt to exterminate her armies and her population by gunfire or other means will tend to produce a fusion of race solidity and antipathy which has no analogy in the case of Germany. We have a national interest in creating, if possible, a condition wherein the Japanese nation may live as a peaceful and useful member of the future Pacific community.

(5) It is therefore my conclusion that a carefully timed warning be given to Japan by the chief representatives of the United States, Great Britain, China, and, if then a belligerent, Russia by calling upon Japan to surrender and permit the occupation of her country in order to insure its complete demilitarization for the sake of the future peace.

This warning should contain the following elements:

• The varied and overwhelming character of the force we are about to bring to bear on the islands.

• The inevitability and completeness of the destruction which the full application of this force will entail.

• The determination of the Allies to destroy permanently all authority and influence of those who have deceived and misled the country into embarking on world conquest.

• The determination of the Allies to limit Japanese sovereignty to her main islands and to render them powerless to mount and support another war.

• The disavowal of any attempt to extirpate the Japanese as a race or to destroy them as a nation.

A statement of our readiness, once her economy is purged of its militaristic influence, to permit the Japanese to maintain such industries, particularly of a light consumer character, as offer no threat of aggression against their neighbors, but which can produce a sustaining economy, and provide a reasonable standard of living. The statement should indicate our willingness, for this purpose, to give Japan trade access to external raw materials, but no longer any control over the sources of supply outside her main islands. It should also indicate our willingness, in accordance with our now established foreign trade policy, in due course to enter into mutually advantageous trade relations with her.

The withdrawal from their country as soon as the above objectives of the Allies are accomplished, and as soon as there has been established a peacefully inclined government, of a character representative of the masses of the Japanese people. I personally think that if in saying this we should add that we do not exclude a constitutional monarchy under her present dynasty, it would substantially add to the chances of acceptance.

(6) Success of course will depend on the potency of the warning which we give her. She has an extremely sensitive national pride and, as we are now seeing every day, when actually locked with the enemy will fight to the very death. For that reason the warning must be tendered before the actual invasion has occurred and while the impending destruction, though clear beyond peradventure, has not yet reduced her to fanatical despair. If Russia is a part of the threat, the Russian attack, if actual, must not have progressed too far. Our own bombing should be confined to military objectives as far as possible.

It is important to emphasize the double character of the suggested warning. It was designed to promise destruction if Japan resisted, and hope, if she surrendered. It will be noted that the atomic bomb is not mentioned in this memorandum. On grounds of secrecy the bomb was never mentioned except when absolutely necessary, and furthermore, it had not yet been tested. It was of course well forward in our minds, as the memorandum was written and discussed, that the bomb would be the best possible sanction if our warning were rejected.

THE ADOPTION OF THE POLICY OUTLINED in the memorandum of July 2 was a decision of high politics; once it was accepted by the President, the position of the atomic bomb in our planning became quite clear. I find that I stated in my diary, as early as June 19, that "the last chance warning . . . must be given before an actual landing of the ground forces in Japan, and fortunately the plans provide for enough time to bring in the sanctions to our warning in the shape of heavy ordinary bombing attack and an attack of S-1." S-1 was a code name for the atomic bomb.

There was much discussion in Washington about the timing of the warning to Japan. The controlling factor in the end was the date already set for the Potsdam meeting of the Big Three. It was President Truman's decision that such a warning should be solemnly issued by the U.S. and the U.K. from this meeting, with the concurrence of the head of the Chinese government, so that it would be plain that *all* of Japan's principal enemies were in entire unity. This was done, in the Potsdam ultimatum of July 26, which very closely followed the above memorandum of July 2, with the exception that it made no mention of the Japanese Emperor. On July 28 the Premier of Japan, Suzuki, rejected the Potsdam ultimatum by announcing that it was "unworthy of public notice." In the face of this rejection we could only proceed to demonstrate that the ultimatum had meant exactly what it said when it stated that if the Japanese continued the war, "the full application of our military power, backed by our resolve, will mean the inevitable and complete destruction of the Japanese armed forces and just as inevitably the utter devastation of the Japanese homeland."

For such a purpose the atomic bomb was an eminently suitable weapon. The New Mexico test occurred while we were at Potsdam, on July 16. It was immediately clear that the power of the bomb measured up to our highest estimates. We had developed a weapon of such a revolutionary character that its use against the enemy might well be expected to produce exactly the kind of shock on the Japanese ruling oligarchy which we desired, strengthening the position of those who wished peace, and weakening that of the military party.

Because of the importance of the atomic mission against Japan, the detailed plans were brought to me by the military staff for approval. With President Truman's warm support I struck off the list of suggested targets the city of Kyoto. Although it was a target of considerable military importance, it had been the ancient capital of Japan and was a shrine of Japanese art and culture. We determined that it should be spared. I approved four other targets including the cities of Hiroshima and Nagasaki.

Hiroshima was bombed on August 6, and Nagasaki on August 9. These two cities were active working parts of the Japanese war effort. One was an army center; the other was naval and industrial. Hiroshima was the headquarters of the Japanese Army defending southern Japan and was a major military storage and assembly point. Nagasaki was a major seaport and it contained several large industrial plants of great wartime importance. We believed that our attacks had struck cities which must certainly be important to the Japanese military leaders, both Army and Navy, and we waited for a result. We waited one day.

Many accounts have been written about the Japanese surrender. After a prolonged Japanese cabinet session in which the deadlock was broken by the Emperor himself, the offer to surrender was made on August 10. It was based on the Potsdam terms, with a reservation concerning the sovereignty of the Emperor. While the Allied reply made no promises other than those already given, it implicitly recognized the Emperor's position by prescribing that his power must be subject to the orders of the Allied Supreme Commander. These terms were accepted on August 14 by the Japanese, and the instrument of surrender was formally signed on September 2, in Tokyo Bay. Our great objective was thus achieved, and all the evidence I have seen indicates that the controlling factor in the final Japanese decision to accept our terms of surrender was the atomic bomb.*

The two atomic bombs which we had dropped were the only ones we had ready, and our rate of production at the time was very small. Had the war continued until the projected invasion on November 1, additional fire raids of B-29's would have been more destructive of life and property than the very limited number of atomic raids which we could have executed in the same period. But the atomic bomb was more than a weapon of terrible destruction; it was a psychological weapon. In March 1945 our Air Force had launched its first great incendiary raid on the Tokyo area. In this raid more damage was done and more casualties were inflicted than was the case at Hiroshima. Hundreds of bombers took part and hundreds of tons of incendiaries were dropped. Similar successive raids burned out a great part of the urban area of Japan, but the Japanese fought on. On August 6 one B-29 dropped a single atomic bomb on Hiroshima. Three days later a second bomb was dropped on Nagasaki and the war was over. So far as the Japanese could know, our ability to execute atomic attacks, if necessary by many planes at a time, was unlimited. As Dr. Karl Compton has said, "it was not one atomic bomb, or two, which brought surrender; it was the experience of what an atomic bomb will actually do to a community, *plus the dread of many more*, that was effective."

The bomb thus served exactly the purpose we intended. The peace party was able to take the path of surrender, and the whole weight of the Emperor's prestige was exerted in favor of peace. When the Emperor ordered surrender, and the small but dangerous group of fanatics who opposed him were brought under control, the Japanese became so subdued that the great undertaking of occupation and disarmament was completed with unprecedented ease.

IN THE FOREGOING PAGES I HAVE TRIED to give an accurate account of my own personal observations of the circumstances which led up to the use of the atomic bomb and the reasons which underlay our use of it. To me they have always seemed compelling and clear, and I cannot see how any person vested with such responsibilities as mine could have taken any other course or given any other advice to his chiefs.

Two great nations were approaching contact in a fight to a finish which would begin on November 1, 1945. Our enemy, Japan, commanded forces of somewhat over 5,000,000 armed men. Men of these armies had already inflicted upon us, in our breakthrough of the outer perimeter of their defenses, over 300,000 battle casualties. Enemy armies still unbeaten had the strength to cost us a million more. *As long as the Japanese government refused to surrender,* we should be forced to take and hold the ground, and smash the Japanese ground armies, by close-in fighting

---

* Report of United States Strategic Bombing Survey, "Japan's Struggle to End the War;" "If the Atomic Bomb Had Not Been Used," by K.T. Compton, *Atlantic Monthly*, December 1946; unpublished material of historical division, War Department Special Staff, June 1946. [Editors' Note: In fact, the U.S. Strategic Bombing Survey stated: "The Hiroshima and Nagasaki atomic bombs did not defeat Japan, nor by the testimony of the enemy leaders who ended the war did they persuade Japan to accept unconditional surrender.... Based on a detailed investigation of all the facts and supported by the testimony of surviving Japanese leaders involved, it is the Survey's opinion that certainly prior to 31 December 1945, and in all probability prior to 1 November 1945, Japan would have surrendered even if the atomic bombs had not been dropped, even if Russia had not entered the war, and even if no invasion had been planned or contemplated." See "Japan's Struggle to End the War," U.S. Strategic Bombing Survery, *Hiroshima's Shadow*, p. 501.]

of the same desperate and costly kind that we had faced in the Pacific islands for nearly four years.

In the light of the formidable problem which thus confronted us, I felt that every possible step should be taken to compel a surrender of the homelands, and a withdrawal of all Japanese troops from the Asiatic mainland and from other positions, before we had commenced an invasion. We held two cards to assist us in such an effort. One was the traditional veneration in which the Japanese Emperor was held by his subjects and the power which was thus vested in him over his loyal troops. It was for this reason that I suggested in my memorandum of July 2 that his dynasty should be continued. The second card was the use of the atomic bomb in the manner best calculated to persuade that Emperor and the counselors about him to submit to our demand for what was essentially unconditional surrender, placing his immense power over his people and his troops subject to our orders.

In order to end the war in the shortest possible time and to avoid the enormous losses of human life which otherwise confronted us, I felt that we must use the Emperor as our instrument to command and compel his people to cease fighting and subject themselves to our authority through him, and that to accomplish this we must give him and his controlling advisers a compelling reason to accede to our demands. This reason furthermore must be of such a nature that his people could understand his decision. The bomb seemed to me to furnish a unique instrument for that purpose.

My chief purpose was to end the war in victory with the least possible cost in the lives of the men in the armies which I had helped to raise. In the light of the alternatives which, on a fair estimate, were open to us I believe that no man, in our position and subject to our responsibilities, holding in his hands a weapon of such possibilities for accomplishing this purpose and saving those lives, could have failed to use it and afterwards looked his countrymen in the face.

As I read over what I have written, I am aware that much of it, in this year of peace, may have a harsh and unfeeling sound. It would perhaps be possible to say the same things and say them more gently. But I do not think it would be wise. As I look back over the five years of my service as Secretary of War, I see too many stern and heartrending decisions to be willing to pretend that war is anything else than what it is. The face of war is the face of death; death is an inevitable part of every order that a wartime leader gives. The decision to use the atomic bomb was a decision that brought death to over a hundred thousand Japanese. No explanation can change that fact and I do not wish to gloss it over. But this deliberate, premeditated destruction was our least abhorrent choice. The destruction of Hiroshima and Nagasaki put an end to the Japanese war. It stopped the fire raids, and the strangling blockade; it ended the ghastly specter of a clash of great land armies.

In this last great action of the Second World War we were given final proof that war is death. War in the twentieth century has grown steadily more barbarous, more destructive, more debased in all its aspects. Now, with the release of atomic energy, man's ability to destroy himself is very nearly complete. The bombs dropped on Hiroshima and Nagasaki ended a war. They also made it wholly clear that we must never have another war. This is the lesson men and leaders everywhere must learn, and I believe that when they learn it they will find a way to lasting peace. There is no other choice.

THANK GOD

FOR THE

ATOM BOMB

Paul Fussell

MANY YEARS AGO IN NEW YORK I saw on the side of a bus a whiskey ad I've remembered all this time. It's been for me a model of the short poem, and indeed I've come upon few short poems subsequently that exhibited more poetic talent. The ad consisted of two eleven-syllable lines of "verse," thus:

In life, experience is the great teacher.
In Scotch, Teacher's is the great experience.

For present purposes we must jettison the second line (licking our lips, to be sure, as it disappears), leaving the first to register a principle whose banality suggests that it enshrines a most useful truth. I bring up the matter because, writing on the forty-second anniversary of the atom-bombing of Hiroshima and Nagasaki, I want to consider something suggested by the long debate about the ethics, if any, of that ghastly affair. Namely, the importance of experience, sheer, vulgar experience, in influencing, if not determining, one's views about that use of the atom bomb.

The experience I'm talking about is having to come to grips, face to face, with an enemy who designs your death. The experience is common to those in the marines and the infantry and even the line navy, to those, in short, who fought the Second World War mindful always that their mission was, as they were repeatedly assured, "to close with the enemy and destroy him." *Destroy,* notice: not hurt, frighten, drive away, or capture. I think there's something to be learned about that war, as well as about the tendency of historical memory unwittingly to resolve ambiguity and generally clean up the premises, by considering the way testimonies emanating from real war experience tend to complicate attitudes about the most cruel ending of that most cruel war.

"What did you do in the Great War, Daddy?" The recruiting poster deserves ridicule and contempt, of course, but here its question is embarrassingly relevant, and the problem is one that touches on the dirty little secret of social class in America. Arthur T. Hadley said recently that those for whom the use of the A-bomb was "wrong" seem to be implying "that it would have been better to allow

211

thousands on thousands of American and Japanese infantrymen to die in honest hand-to-hand combat on the beaches than to drop those two bombs." People holding such views, he notes, "do not come from the ranks of society that produce infantrymen or pilots." And there's an eloquence problem: most of those with first-hand experience of the war at its worst were not elaborately educated people. Relatively inarticulate, most have remained silent about what they know. That is, few of those destined to be blown to pieces if the main Japanese islands had been invaded went on to become our most effective men of letters or impressive ethical theorists or professors of contemporary history or of international law. The testimony of experience has tended to come from rough diamonds—James Jones is an example—who went through the war as enlisted men in the infantry or the Marine Corps. Anticipating objections from those without such experience, in his book *WWII* Jones carefully prepares for his chapter on the A-bombs by detailing the plans already in motion for the infantry assaults on the home islands of Kyushu (thirteen divisions scheduled to land in November 1945) and ultimately Honshu (sixteen divisions scheduled for March 1946). Planners of the invasion assumed that it would require a full year, to November 1946, for the Japanese to be sufficiently worn down by land-combat attrition to surrender. By that time, one million American casualties was the expected price. Jones observes that the forthcoming invasion of Kyushu "was well into its collecting and stockpiling stages before the war ended." (The island of Saipan was designated a main ammunition and supply base for the invasion, and if you go there today you can see some of the assembled stuff still sitting there.) "The assault troops were chosen and already in training," Jones reminds his readers, and he illuminates by the light of experience what this meant:

> What it must have been like to some old-timer buck sergeant or staff sergeant who had been through Guadalcanal or Bougainville or the Philippines, to stand on some beach and watch this huge war machine beginning to stir and move all around him and know that he very likely had survived this far only to fall dead on the dirt of Japan's home islands, hardly bears thinking about.

Another bright enlisted man, this one an experienced marine destined for the assault on Honshu, adds his testimony. Former Pfc. E. B. Sledge, author of the splendid memoir *With the Old Breed at Peleliu and Okinawa*, noticed at the time that the fighting grew "more vicious the closer we got to Japan," with the carnage of Iwo Jima and Okinawa worse than what had gone before. He points out that

> what we had *experienced* [my emphasis] in fighting the Japs (pardon the expression) on Peleliu and Okinawa caused us to formulate some very definite opinions that the invasion . . . would be a ghastly blood-letting. . . . It would shock the American public and the world. [Every Japanese] soldier, civilian, woman, and child would fight to the death with whatever weapons they had, rifle, grenade, or bamboo spear.

The Japanese pre-invasion patriotic song, "One Hundred Million Souls for the Emperor," says Sledge, "meant just that." Universal national kamikaze was the point. One kamikaze pilot, discouraged by his unit's failure to impede the

Americans very much despite the bizarre casualties it caused, wrote before diving his plane onto an American ship, "I see the war situation becoming more desperate. All Japanese must become soldiers and die for the Emperor." Sledge's First Marine Division was to land close to the Yokosuka Naval Base, "one of the most heavily defended sectors of the island." The marines were told, he recalls, that

> due to the strong beach defenses, caves, tunnels, and numerous Jap suicide torpedo boats and manned mines, few Marines in the first five assault waves would get ashore alive—my company was scheduled to be in the first and second waves. The veterans in the outfit felt we had already run out of luck anyway. . . . We viewed the invasion with complete resignation that we would be killed—either on the beach or inland.

And the invasion was going to take place: there's no question about that. It was not theoretical or merely rumored in order to scare the Japanese. By July 10, 1945, the pre-landing naval and aerial bombardment of the coast had begun, and the battleships *Iowa*, *Missouri*, *Wisconsin*, and *King George V* were steaming up and down the coast, softening it up with their sixteen-inch shells.

On the other hand, John Kenneth Galbraith is persuaded that the Japanese would have surrendered surely by November without an invasion. He thinks the A-bombs were unnecessary and unjustified because the war was ending anyway. The A-bombs meant, he says, "a difference, at most, of two or three weeks." But at the time, with no indication that surrender was on the way, the kamikazes were sinking American vessels, the *Indianapolis* was sunk (880 men killed), and Allied casualties were running to over 7,000 per week. "Two or three weeks," says Galbraith. Two weeks more means 14,000 more killed and wounded, three weeks more, 21,000. Those weeks mean the world if you're one of those thousands or related to one of them. During the time between the dropping of the Nagasaki bomb on August 9 and the actual surrender on the fifteenth, the war pursued its accustomed course: on the twelfth of August eight captured American fliers were executed (heads chopped off); the fifty-first United States submarine, *Bonefish*, was sunk (all aboard drowned); the destroyer *Callaghan* went down, the seventieth to be sunk, and the Destroyer Escort *Underhill* was lost. That's a bit of what happened in six days of the two or three weeks posited by Galbraith. What did he do in the war? He worked in the Office of Price Administration in Washington. I don't demand that he experience having his ass shot off. I merely note that he didn't.

Likewise, the historian Michael Sherry, author of a recent book on the rise of the American bombing mystique, *The Creation of Armageddon*, argues that we didn't delay long enough between the test explosion in New Mexico and the mortal explosions in Japan. More delay would have made possible deeper moral considerations and perhaps laudable second thoughts and restraint. "The risks of delaying the bomb's use," he says, "would have been small—not the thousands of casualties expected of invasion but only a few days or weeks of relatively routine operations." While the mass murders represented by these "relatively routine operations" were enacting, Michael Sherry was safe at home. Indeed, when the bombs were dropped he was going on eight months old, in danger only of falling out of his pram. In speaking thus of Galbraith and Sherry, I'm aware of the offensive implications *ad hominem*. But what's at stake in an infantry assault is so entirely unthinkable to those without the experience of one, or several, or many, even if they possess very wide-ranging imaginations and warm sympathies, that experience is crucial in this case.

In general, the principle is, the farther from the scene of horror, the easier the talk. One young combat naval officer close to the action wrote home in the fall of 1943, just before the marines underwent the agony of Tarawa: "When I read that we will fight the Japs for years if necessary and will sacrifice hundreds of thousands if we must, I always like to check from where he's talking: it's seldom out here." That was Lieutenant (j.g.) John F. Kennedy. And Winston Churchill, with an irony perhaps too broad and easy, noted in Parliament that the people who preferred invasion to A-bombing seemed to have "no intention of proceeding to the Japanese front themselves."

A remoteness from experience like Galbraith's and Sherry's, and a similar rationalistic abstraction from actuality, seem to motivate the reaction of an anonymous reviewer of William Manchester's *Goodbye Darkness: A Memoir of the Pacific War* for the *New York Review of Books*. The reviewer naturally dislikes Manchester's still terming the enemy Nips or Japs, but what really shakes him (her?) is this passage of Manchester's:

> After Biak the enemy withdrew to deep caverns. Rooting them out became a bloody business which reached its ultimate horrors in the last months of the war. You think of the lives which would have been lost in an invasion of Japan's home islands—a staggering number of Americans but millions more of Japanese—and you thank God for the atomic bomb.

Thank God for the atom bomb. From this, "one recoils," says the reviewer. One does, doesn't one? And not just a staggering number of Americans would have been killed in the invasion. Thousands of British assault troops would have been destroyed too, the anticipated casualties from the almost 200,000 men in the six divisions (the same number used to invade Normandy) assigned to invade the Malay Peninsula on September 9. Aimed at the reconquest of Singapore, this operation was expected to last until about March 1946—that is, seven more months of infantry fighting. "But for the atomic bombs," a British observer intimate with the Japanese defenses notes, "I don't think we would have stood a cat in hell's chance. We would have been murdered in the biggest massacre of the war. They would have annihilated the lot of us."

The Dutchman Laurens van der Post had been a prisoner of the Japanese for three and a half years. He and thousands of his fellows, enfeebled by beriberi and pellagra, were being systematically starved to death, the Japanese rationalizing this treatment not just because the prisoners were white men but because they had allowed themselves to be captured at all and were therefore moral garbage. In the summer of 1945 Field Marshal Terauchi issued a significant order: at the moment the Allies invaded the main islands, all prisoners were to be killed by the prison-camp commanders. But thank God that did not happen. When the A-bombs were dropped, van der Post recalls, "This cataclysm I was certain would make the Japanese feel that they could withdraw from the war without dishonor, because it would strike them, as it had us in the silence of our prison night, as something supernatural."

In an exchange of views not long ago in the *New York Review of Books*, Joseph Alsop and David Joravsky set forth the by now familiar argument on both sides of the debate about the "ethics" of the bomb. It's not hard to guess which side each chose once you know that Alsop experienced capture by the Japanese at Hong Kong early in 1942, while Joravsky came into no deadly contact with the Japanese: a young, combat-innocent soldier, he was on his way to the Pacific when the war ended. The editors of the *New York Review* gave the debate the tendentious title "Was the Hiroshima Bomb Necessary?" surely an unanswerable question (unlike "Was It Effective?") and one precisely indicating the intellectual difficulties involved in imposing *ex post facto* a rational and even a genteel ethics on this event. In arguing the acceptability of the bomb, Alsop focuses on the power and fanaticism of War Minister Anami, who insisted that Japan fight to the bitter end, defending the main islands with the same techniques and tenacity employed at Iwo and Okinawa. Alsop concludes: "Japanese surrender could never have been obtained, at any rate without the honor-satisfying bloodbath envisioned by . . . Anami, if the hideous destruction of Hiroshima and Nagasaki had not finally galvanized the peace advocates into tearing up the entire Japanese book of rules." The Japanese plan to deploy the undefeated bulk of their ground forces, over two million men, plus 10,000 kamikaze planes, plus the elderly and all the women and children with sharpened spears they could muster in a suicidal defense makes it absurd, says Alsop, to "hold the common view, by now hardly challenged by anyone, that the decision to drop the two bombs on Japan was wicked in itself, and that President Truman and all others who joined in making or who [like Robert Oppenheimer] assented to this decision shared in the wickedness." And in explanation of "the two bombs," Alsop adds: "The true, climactic, and successful effort of the Japanese peace advocates . . . did not begin in deadly earnest until *after* the second bomb had destroyed Nagasaki. The Nagasaki bomb was thus the trigger to all the developments that led to peace." At this time the army was so unready for surrender that most looked forward to the forthcoming invasion as an indispensable opportunity to show their mettle, enthusiastically agreeing with the army spokesman who reasoned early in 1945, "Since the retreat from Guadalcanal, the Army has had little opportunity to engage the enemy in land battles. But when we meet in Japan proper, our Army will demonstrate its invincible superiority." This possibility foreclosed by the Emperor's post-A-bomb surrender broadcast, the shocked, disappointed officers of one infantry battalion, anticipating a professionally impressive defense of the beaches, killed themselves in the following numbers: one major, three captains, ten first lieutenants, and twelve second lieutenants.

David Joravsky, now a professor of history at Northwestern, argued on the other hand that those who decided to use the A-bombs on cities betray defects of "reason and self-restraint." It all needn't have happened, he says, "if the U.S. government had been willing to take a few more days and to be a bit more thoughtful in opening up the age of nuclear warfare." I've already noted what "a few more days" would mean to the luckless troops and sailors on the spot, and as to being thoughtful when "opening up the age of nuclear warfare," of course no one was focusing on anything as portentous as that, which reflects a historian's tidy hindsight. The U.S. government was engaged not in that sort of momentous thing but in ending the war conclusively, as well as irrationally Remembering Pearl Harbor with a vengeance. It didn't know then what everyone knows now about leukemia and various kinds of carcinoma and birth defects. Truman was not being sly or coy when he insisted that the bomb was "only another weapon." History, as Eliot's "Gerontion" notes,

> . . . *has many cunning passages, contrived corridors*
> *And issues, deceives with whispering ambitions,*
> *Guides us by vanities. . . .*
> *Think*
> *Neither fear nor courage saves us.*
> *Unnatural vices*
> *Are fathered by our heroism. Virtues*
> *Are forced upon us by our impudent crimes.*

Understanding the past requires pretending that you don't know the present. It requires feeling its own pressure on your pulses without any *ex post facto* illumination. That's a harder thing to do than Joravsky seems to think. The Alsop-Joravsky debate, reduced to a collision between experience and theory, was conducted with a certain civilized respect for evidence. Not so the way the scurrilous, agitprop *New Statesman* conceives those justifying the dropping of the bomb and those opposing. They are, on the one hand, says Bruce Page, "the imperialist class-forces acting through Harry Truman" and, on the other, those representing "the humane, democratic virtues"—in short, "fascists" as opposed to "populists." But ironically the bomb saved the lives not of any imperialists but only of the low and humble, the quintessentially democratic huddled masses—the conscripted enlisted men manning the fated invasion divisions and the sailors crouching at their gun-mounts in terror of the Kamikazes. When the war ended, Bruce Page was nine years old. For someone of his experience, phrases like "imperialist class forces" come easily, and the issues look perfectly clear.

He's not the only one to have forgotten, if he ever knew, the unspeakable savagery of the Pacific war. The dramatic post-war Japanese success at hustling and merchandising and tourism has (happily, in many ways) effaced for most people the vicious assault context in which the Hiroshima horror should be viewed. It is easy to forget, or not to know, what Japan was like before it was first destroyed, and then humiliated, tamed, and constitutionalized by the West. "Implacable, treacherous, barbaric"—those were Admiral Halsey's characterizations of the enemy, and at the time few facing the Japanese would deny that they fit to a T. One remembers the captured American airmen—the lucky ones who escaped decapitation—locked for years in packing crates. One remembers the gleeful use of bayonets on civilians, on nurses and the wounded, in Hong Kong and Singapore. Anyone who actually fought in the Pacific recalls the Japanese routinely firing on medics, killing the wounded (torturing them first, if possible), and cutting off the penises of the dead to stick in the corpses' mouths. The degree to which Americans register shock and extraordinary shame about the Hiroshima bomb correlates closely with lack of information about the Pacific war.

And of course the brutality was not just on one side. There was much sadism and cruelty, undeniably racist, on ours. (It's worth noting in passing how few hopes blacks could entertain of desegregation and decent treatment when the U.S. Army itself slandered the enemy as "the little brown Jap.") Marines and soldiers could augment their view of their own invincibility by possessing a well-washed Japanese skull, and very soon after Guadalcanal it was common to treat surrendering Japanese as handy rifle targets. Plenty of Japanese gold teeth were extracted—some from still living mouths—with Marine Corps Ka-Bar knives, and one of E. B. Sledge's fellow marines went around with a cut-off Japanese hand. When its smell grew too offensive and Sledge urged him to get rid of it, he defended his possession of this trophy thus: "How many Marines you reckon that hand pulled the trigger on?" (It's hardly necessary to observe that a soldier in the ETO would probably not have dealt that way with a German or Italian—that is, a "white person's"— hand.) In the Pacific the situation grew so public and scandalous that in September 1942, the Commander in Chief of the Pacific Fleet issued this order: "No part of the enemy's body may be used as a souvenir. Unit Commanders will take stern disciplinary action. . . ."

Among Americans it was widely held that the Japanese were really subhuman, little yellow beasts, and popular imagery depicted them as lice, rats, bats, vipers, dogs, and monkeys. What was required, said the Marine Corps journal *The Leatherneck* in May 1945, was "a gigantic task of extermination." The Japanese constituted a "pestilence," and the only appropriate treatment was "annihilation." Some of the marines landing on Iwo Jima had "Rodent Exterminator" written on their helmet covers, and on one American flagship the naval commander had erected a large sign enjoining all to "KILL JAPS! KILL JAPS! KILL MORE JAPS!" Herman Wouk remembers the Pacific war scene correctly while analyzing Ensign Keith in *The Caine Mutiny*: "Like most of the naval executioners of Kwajalein, he seemed to regard the enemy as a species of animal pest." And the feeling was entirely reciprocal: "From the grim and desperate taciturnity with which the Japanese died, they seemed on their side to believe that they were contending with an invasion of large armed ants." Hiroshima seems to follow in natural sequence: "This obliviousness of both sides to the fact that the opponents were human beings may perhaps be cited as the key to the many massacres of the Pacific war." Since the Jap vermin resist so madly and have killed so many of us, let's pour gasoline into their bunkers and light it and then shoot those afire who try to get out. Why not? Why not blow them all up, with satchel charges or with something stronger? Why not, indeed, drop a new kind of bomb on them, and on the un-uniformed ones too, since the Japanese government has announced that women from ages of seventeen to forty are being called up to repel the invasion? The intelligence officer of the U.S. Fifth Air Force declared on July 21, 1945, that "the entire population of Japan is a proper military target," and he added emphatically, *"There are no civilians in Japan."* Why delay and allow one more American high school kid to see his own intestines blown out of his body and spread before him in the dirt while he screams and screams when with the new bomb we can end the whole thing just like that?

On Okinawa, only weeks before Hiroshima, 123,000 Japanese and Americans *killed* each other. (About 140,000 Japanese died at Hiroshima.) "Just awful" was the comment on the Okinawa slaughter not of some pacifist but of General MacArthur. On July 14, 1945, General Marshall sadly informed the Combined Chiefs of Staff—he was not trying to scare the Japanese—that it's "now clear . . . that in order to finish with the Japanese quickly, it will be necessary to invade the industrial heart of Japan." The invasion was definitely on, as I know because I was to be in it.

When the atom bomb ended the war, I was in the Forty-fifth Infantry Division, which had been through the European war so thoroughly that it had needed to be reconstituted two or three times. We were in a staging area near Rheims, ready to be shipped back across the United States for refresher training at Fort Lewis, Washington, and then sent on for final preparation in the Philippines. My division, like most of the ones transferred from Europe, was to take part in the invasion of Honshu. (The earlier landing on Kyushu was to be carried out by the 700,000 infantry already in the Pacific, those with whom James Jones has sympathized.) I was a twenty-one-year-old second lieutenant of infantry leading a rifle platoon. Although still officially fit for combat, in the German war I had already been wounded in the back and the leg badly enough to be adjudged, after the war, 40 percent disabled. But even if my leg buckled and I fell to the ground whenever I jumped out of the back of a truck, and even if the very idea of more combat made me breathe in gasps and shake all over, my condition was held to be adequate for the next act. When the atom bombs were dropped and news began to circulate that "Operation Olympic" would not, after all, be necessary, when we learned to our astonishment that we would not be obliged in a few months to rush up the beaches near Tokyo assault-firing while being machine-gunned, mortared, and shelled, for all the practiced phlegm of our tough façades we broke down and cried with relief and joy. We were going to live. We were going to grow to adulthood after all. The killing was all going to be over, and peace was actually going to be the state of things. When the *Enola Gay* dropped its package, "There were cheers," says John Toland, "over the intercom; it meant the end of the war." Down on the ground the reaction of Sledge's marine buddies when they heard the news was more solemn and complicated. They heard about the end of the war

> with quiet disbelief coupled with an indescribable sense of relief. We thought the Japanese would never surrender. Many refused to believe it. . . . Sitting in stunned silence, we remembered our dead. So many dead. So many maimed. So many bright futures consigned to the ashes of the past. So many dreams lost in the madness that had engulfed us. Except for a few widely scattered shouts of joy, the survivors of the abyss sat hollow-eyed and silent, trying to comprehend a world without war.

These troops who cried and cheered with relief or who sat stunned by the weight of their experience are very different from the high-minded, guilt-ridden GIs we're told about by J. Glenn Gray in his sensitive book *The Warriors*. During the war in Europe, Gray was an interrogator in the Army Counterintelligence Corps, and in that capacity he experienced the war at Division level. There's no denying that Gray's outlook on everything was admirably noble, elevated, and responsible. After the war he became a much-admired professor of philosophy at Colorado College and an esteemed editor of Heidegger. But *The Warriors*, his meditation on the moral and psychological dimensions of modern soldiering, gives every sign of error occasioned by remoteness from experience. Division headquarters is miles—*miles*—behind the line where soldiers experience terror and madness and relieve those pressures by crazy brutality and sadism. Indeed, unless they actually encountered the enemy during the war, most "soldiers" have very little idea what "combat" was like. As William Manchester says, "All who wore uniforms are called veterans, but more than 90 percent of them are as uninformed about the killing zones as those on the home front." Manchester's fellow marine E. B. Sledge thoughtfully and responsibly invokes the terms *drastically* and *totally* to underline the differences in experience between front and rear, and not even the far rear, but the close rear. "Our code of conduct toward the enemy," he notes, "differed drastically from that prevailing back at the division CP." (He's describing gold-tooth extraction from still-living Japanese.) Again he writes: "We existed in an environment totally incomprehensible to men behind the lines . . . ," even, he would insist, to men as intelligent and sensitive as Glenn Gray, who missed seeing with his own eyes Sledge's marine friends sliding under fire down a shell-pocked ridge slimy with mud and liquid dysentery shit into the maggoty Japanese and USMC corpses at the bottom, vomiting as the maggots burrowed into their own foul clothing. "We didn't talk about such things," says Sledge. "They were too horrible and obscene even for hardened veterans. . . . Nor do authors normally write about such vileness; unless they have seen it with their own eyes, it is too pre-posterous to think that men could actually live and fight for days and nights on end under such terrible conditions and not be driven insane." And Sledge has added a comment on such experience and the insulation provided by even a short distance: "Often people just behind our rifle companies couldn't understand what we knew." Glenn Gray was not in a rifle company, or even just behind one. "When the news of the atomic bombing of Hiroshima and Nagasaki came," he asks us to believe, "many an American soldier felt shocked and ashamed." Shocked, OK, but why ashamed? Because we'd destroyed civilians? We'd been doing that for years, in raids on Hamburg and Berlin and Cologne and Frankfurt and Mannheim and Dresden, and Tokyo, and besides, the two A-bombs wiped out 10,000 Japanese troops, not often thought of now, John Hersey's kindly physicians and Jesuit priests being more touching. If around division headquarters some of the people Gray talked to felt ashamed, down in the rifle companies no one did, despite Gray's assertions. "The combat soldier," he says,

> knew better than did Americans at home what those bombs meant in suffering and injustice. The man of conscience realized intuitively that the vast majority of Japanese in both cities were no more, if no less, guilty of the war than were his own parents, sisters, or brothers.

I FIND THIS CANTING NONSENSE. The purpose of the bombs was not to "punish" people but to stop the war. To intensify the shame Gray insists we feel, he seems willing to fiddle the facts. The Hiroshima bomb, he says, was dropped "without any warning." But actually, two days before, 720,000 leaflets were dropped on the city urging everyone to get out and indicating that the place was going to be (as the Potsdam Declaration has promised) obliterated. Of course few left.

Experience whispers that the pity is not that we used the bomb to end the Japanese war but that it wasn't ready in time to end the German one. If only it could have been rushed into production faster and dropped at the right moment on the Reich Chancellery or Berchtesgaden or Hitler's military headquarters in East Prussia (where Colonel Stauffenberg's July 20 bomb didn't do the job because it wasn't big enough), much of the Nazi hierarchy could have been pulverized immediately, saving not just the embarrassment of the Nuremberg trials but the lives of around four million Jews, Poles, Slavs, and gypsies, not to mention the lives and limbs of millions of Allied and German soldiers. If the bomb had only been ready in time, the young men of my infantry platoon would not have been so cruelly killed and wounded.

All this is not to deny that like the Russian Revolution, the atom-bombing of Japan was a vast historical tragedy, and every passing year magnifies the dilemma into which it has lodged the contemporary world. As with the Russian Revolution, there are two sides—that's why it's a tragedy instead of a disaster—and unless we are, like Bruce Page, simple-mindedly unimaginative and cruel, we will be painfully aware of both sides at once. To observe that from the viewpoint of the war's victims-to-be the bomb seemed precisely the right thing to drop is to purchase no immunity from horror. To experience both sides, one might study the book *Unforgettable Fire: Pictures Drawn by Atomic Bomb Survivors*, which presents a number of amateur drawings and watercolors of the Hiroshima scene made by middle-aged and elderly survivors for a peace exhibition in 1975. In addition to the almost unbearable pictures, the book offers brief moments of memoir not for the weak-stomached:

> While taking my severely wounded wife out to the river bank. . . ,
> I was horrified indeed at the sight of a stark naked man standing in
> the rain with his eyeball in his palm. He looked to be in great pain
> but there was nothing that I could do for him. I wonder what became
> of him. Even today, I vividly remember the sight. I was simply
> miserable.

These childlike drawings and paintings are of skin hanging down, breasts torn off, people bleeding and burning, dying mothers nursing dead babies. A bloody woman holds a bloody child in the ruins of a house, and the artist remembers her calling, "Please help this child! Someone, please help this child. Please help! Someone, please." As Samuel Johnson said of the smothering of Desdemona, the innocent in another tragedy, "It is not to be endured." Nor, it should be noticed, is an infantryman's account of having his arm blown off in the Arno Valley in Italy in 1944:

> I wanted to die and die fast. I wanted to forget this miserable world.
> I cursed the war, I cursed the people who were responsible for it,
> l cursed God for putting me here . . . to suffer for something I never
> did or knew anything about.

(A good place to interrupt and remember Glenn Gray's noble but hopelessly one-sided remarks about "injustice," as well as "suffering.")"For this was hell," the soldier goes on,

> and I never imagined anything or anyone could suffer so bitterly. I
> screamed and cursed. Why? What had I done to deserve this? But no
> answer came. I yelled for medics, because subconsciously I wanted to
> live. I tried to apply my right hand over my bleeding stump, but
> I didn't have the strength to hold it. I looked to the left of me and
> saw the bloody mess that was once my left arm; its fingers and palm
> were turned upward, like a flower looking to the sun for its strength.

The future scholar-critic who writes *The History of Canting in the Twentieth Century* will find much to study and interpret in the utterances of those who dilate on the special wickedness of the A-bomb-droppers. He will realize that such utterance can perform for the speaker a valuable double function. First, it can display the fineness of his moral weave. And second, by implication it can also inform the audience that during the war he was not socially so unfortunate as to find himself down there with the ground forces, where he might have had to compromise the purity and clarity of his moral system by the experience of weighing his own life against someone else's. Down there, which is where the other people were, is the place where coarse self-interest is the rule. When the young soldier with the wild eyes comes at you, firing, do you shoot him in the foot, hoping he'll be hurt badly enough to drop or mis-aim the gun with which he's going to kill you, or do you shoot him in the chest (or, if you're a prime shot, in the head) and make certain that you and not he will be the survivor of that mortal moment?

It would be not just stupid but would betray a lamentable want of human experience to expect soldiers to be very sensitive humanitarians. The Glenn Grays of this world need to have their attention directed to the testimony of those who know, like, say, Admiral of the Fleet Lord Fisher, who said, "Moderation in war is imbecility," or Sir Arthur Harris, director of the admittedly wicked aerial-bombing campaign designed, as Churchill put it, to "de-house" the German civilian population, who observed that "War is immoral," or our own General W. T. Sherman: "War is cruelty, and you cannot refine it." Lord Louis Mountbatten, trying to say something sensible about the dropping of the A-bomb, came up only with "War is crazy." Or rather, it requires choices among crazinesses. "It would seem even more crazy," he went on, "if we were to have more casualties on our side to save the Japanese." One of the unpleasant facts for anyone in the ground armies during the war was that you had to become pro tem a subordinate of the very uncivilian George S. Patton and respond somehow to his unremitting insistence that you embrace his view of things. But in one of his effusions he was right, and his observation tends to suggest the experiential dubiousness of the concept of "just wars." "War is not a contest with gloves," he perceived. "It is resorted to only when laws, which are rules, have failed." Soldiers being like that, only the barest decencies should be expected of them. They did not start the war, except in the terrible sense hinted at in Frederic Manning's observation based on his front-line experience in the Great War: "War is waged by men; not by beasts, or by gods. It is a peculiarly human activity. To call it a crime against mankind is to miss at least half its significance; it is also the punishment of a crime." Knowing that unflattering truth by experience, soldiers have every motive for wanting a war stopped, by any means.

The stupidity, parochialism, and greed in the international mismanagement of the whole nuclear challenge should not tempt us to misimagine the circumstances of the bomb's first "use." Nor should our well-justified fears and suspicions occasioned by the capture of the nuclear-power trade by the inept and the mendacious (who have fucked up the works at Three Mile Island, Chernobyl, etc.) tempt us to infer retrospectively extraordinary corruption, imbecility, or motiveless malignity in those who decided, all things considered, to drop the bomb. Times change. Harry Truman was not a fascist but a democrat. He was as close to a genuine egalitarian as anyone we've seen in high office for a long time. He is the only President in my lifetime who ever had experience in a small unit of ground troops whose mission it was to kill people. That sort of experience of actual war seems useful to presidents especially, helping to inform them about life in general and restraining them from making fools of themselves needlessly—the way Ronald Reagan did in 1985 when he visited the German military cemetery at Bitburg containing the SS graves. The propriety of this visit he explained by asserting that no Germans who fought in the war remain alive and that "very few . . . even remember the war." Reagan's ignorance or facile forgetfulness are imputed by Arthur Schlesinger to his total lack of serious experience of war—the Second World War or any other. "Though he often makes throwaway references to his military career," says Schlesinger, "Mr. Reagan in fact is the only American president who was of military age during the Second World War and saw no service overseas. He fought the war on the film lots of Hollywood, slept in his own bed every night and apparently got many of his ideas of what happened from subsequent study of the *Reader's Digest.*"

Truman was a different piece of goods entirely. He knew war, and he knew better than some of his critics then and now what he was doing and why he was doing it. "Having found the bomb," he said, "we have used it. . . . We have used it to shorten the agony of young Americans." The past, which as always did not know the future, acted in ways that ask to be imagined before they are condemned. Or even simplified.

HIROSHIMA

AND

MODERN

MEMORY

Martin J. Sherwin

N O ONE WHO LOOKS CLOSELY AT THE ARGUMENTS related to
the atomic bombings of Hiroshima and Nagasaki will fail to recognize
that there is more than a matter of military history at stake. Hiroshima not only
introduced the nuclear age to the world but it also served as the symbolic coronation of American global power. The atomic bomb, as contemporary cartoonists
depicted it, was our scepter, and its use contributed to the image of our international authority.

But power was not the only foundation for that authority. "The position of
the United States as a great humanitarian nation" was also important, Under Secretary of the Navy Ralph Bard wrote to the Secretary of War on June 27, 1945.[1]
Urging that the Japanese be warned several days prior to the attack, Bard sought
to modify the decision made a month earlier by the Interim Committee:

> After much discussion concerning various types of targets and the
> effects to be produced [the minutes of the May 31 meeting read], the
> Secretary [of War] expressed the conclusion, on which there was
> general agreement, that we could not give the Japanese any warning;
> that we could not concentrate on a civilian area; but that we should
> seek to make a profound psychological impression on as many of the
> inhabitants as possible. At the suggestion of Dr. [James] Conant the
> Secretary agreed that the most desirable target would be a vital war
> plant employing a large number of workers and closely surrounded
> by workers' houses.*[2]

Bard's advice went unheeded, however, and the initial irony of Hiroshima was
that the very act symbolizing our wartime victory was quickly turned against our

---

* The leaflets dropped on Hiroshima and numerous other cities prior to August 6 did not provide the
residents of those cities with a relevant warning, as Fussell erroneously claims. They only informed
them of the terms of the Potsdam Declaration of July 26, which called for Japan to surrender unconditionally or face "the utter devastation of the Japanese homeland."

peacetime purposes. At the 1946–48 Tokyo War Crimes Trials, which, like the
Nuremberg trials, were a symbolic expression of our moral authority, Justice
Rabhabinod Pal of India cited Hiroshima and Nagasaki as evidence against our
claim to rule in Asia by right of superior virtue. The atomic bombings, he wrote
in a dissenting opinion, were "the only near approach [in the Pacific War] to the
directive . . . of the Nazi leaders during the Second World War."[3]

Addressing the issues of just cause and morality that Pal raised, the earliest
explanations for the bombings of Hiroshima and Nagasaki aimed at convincing
"a candid world" that our actions had been morally justified. "We have used
[the atomic bomb]," President Truman stated publicly, "in order to shorten the
agony of war, in order to save the lives of thousands and thousands of young
Americans."[4] His private explanation, written on August 11, 1945, in response to
criticism of the atomic bombings from none other than John Foster Dulles, was
more revealing:

> Nobody is more disturbed over the use of atomic bombs than I am
> but I was greatly disturbed over the unwarranted attack by the Japan-
> ese on Pearl Harbor and their murder of our prisoners of war. The
> only language they seem to understand is the one we have been using
> to bombard them. When you have to deal with a beast you have to
> treat him as a beast. It is most regrettable but nevertheless true."[5]

*Hiroshima and Nagasaki: The Physical, Medical, and Social Effects of the Atomic
Bomb* was researched by the Committee for the Compilation of Materials on
Damage Caused by the Atomic Bombs in Hiroshima and Nagasaki, and translated
by Eisei Ishikawa and David L. Swain. It was published simultaneously in the
United States, Britain and Japan on August 6, 1981, the anniversary of the bombing of Hiroshima. The book is an encyclopedic summary of the devastation experienced by the "beasts" who inhabited those cities. Its findings are presented in
four parts. Part One describes "the Physical Aspects of Destruction," such as damage to buildings, and its chapters assess the blast effects and the physical behavior
and properties of the radiation released. Part Two, "Injury to the Human Body,"
is the most gruesome but also the most important section, for the studies summarized there deal with the impact of radiation on human beings over time. The
third section, "The Impact on Society and Daily Life," carries the study into the
areas of psychology, sociology and even politics. And Part Four, "Toward the Abolition of Nuclear Arms," contains chapters on medical care afforded the victims,
on government policies toward them, on efforts of researchers to document the
damage and on the cities' peace education programs.

In the appendix there is a useful chronology of events, "Atomic Bomb Damages, 1945-1978"; a list of the thirty-four Japanese scientists, medical personnel and
social scientists responsible for the study; and, I assume, the most complete bibliography available in English of the medical and scientific literature in English and
Japanese related to the atomic bombings. All told, it is a most important reference
work, which is also to say that it is a book whose message will be discussed by
many, but whose pages will be read by few.

The concerns behind the publication of *Hiroshima and Nagasaki* are self-
consciously historical in the sense that the authors want to insure that the
experience of having suffered the first two atomic holocausts shall not have been in

vain. "The A-bomb catastrophe has become more remote with each passing year," the mayors of Hiroshima and Nagasaki write in the foreword.

> Thus, it is clear that we must make a renewed effort to keep alive the A-bomb experience. . . . Hiroshima and Nagasaki have joined in the publication of this comprehensive compilation of the findings that are so far scientifically confirmed; and we have done so out of the conviction that, in the present state of international policy in regard to nuclear arms, there is not a moment to lose.

But it may be that "the moment" is lost, and was lost, even before August 6, 1945, when Franklin Roosevelt and Winston Churchill rejected steps that might have led to the international control of atomic energy. And it may be that at some level we recognize that such a moment, if indeed it ever existed, is now beyond our grasp.

The American public's sense of powerlessness before a monster its own government created and used may be the single most important reason behind the easy acceptance of the idea that only nuclear superiority can guarantee our national security. Even here, the debate over the atomic bombings of Hiroshima and Nagasaki is relevant, for it is of paramount importance to those who wish to rely increasingly upon nuclear weapons that these weapons not be tarnished with a sense of guilt that could inhibit their use as an instrument of diplomacy.

However, the least obvious impact of Hiroshima and Nagasaki may be the most important: the subtle conversion of tens of millions of people over the course of thirty-six years of nuclear arms racing to the idea that nuclear war is inevitable. The button exists and someday someone will push it; nothing can prevent that. Technology has altered our confidence in free will. Kurt Vonnegut suggests this intellectual metamorphosis in *Slaughterhouse Five*, a book which attempts to come to grips with his Hiroshima-like experience as a prisoner of war in Dresden when that city was pulverized by a massive British-American bombing raid that killed 35,000 people on February 13–15, 1945.

"'How does the universe end?'" Billy Pilgrim asks his omniscient Trafalmadorian captors, who have shuttled him to their planet through a time warp.

> "We blow it up, experimenting with new fuels for our flying saucers. A Trafalmadorian test pilot presses a starter button, and the whole Universe disappears."
>
> "If you know this," said Billy, "isn't there some way you can prevent it? Can't you keep the pilot from pressing the button?"
>
> "He has *always* pressed it, and he always *will*. We *always* let him and we always *will* let him. The moment is *structured* that way." So it goes.[6]

And so it went at Hiroshima, and quite properly so, according to Paul Fussell in "Hiroshima: A Soldier's View," who argues that the President made his decision in Washington for the same reasons he (Fussell) celebrated that decision in Europe. A professor of English at Rutgers University and author of *The Great War and Modern Memory*, Fussell, like Vonnegut, was profoundly affected by the conflict. Their experiences were somewhat different, however. Vonnegut was a captured enlisted man who lived through a veritable holocaust initiated by the Allies; Fussell was a second lieutenant who had been wounded by one enemy, but not seriously enough to be denied orders to the Pacific to participate in an invasion planned for March 1946 into the homeland of another.

"Experience whispers that the pity is not that we used the bomb to end the Japanese war," he says from his precarious vantage point, "but that it wasn't ready earlier to end the German one." To be dropped on Dresden, perhaps. As Vonnegut notes, "World War Two certainly made everybody very tough." [7]

Well, not exactly everybody, in Fussell's view. "In life" he argues, "experience is the great teacher." And it was only combat experience that taught soldiers what Hiroshima and Nagasaki were all about. If you were holding a rifle and a set of orders designating you an American kamikaze, you thanked God—as William Manchester did in *Goodbye Darkness: A Memoir of the Pacific War*—for the atomic bomb. Fair enough. It is well to be reminded that in any war, soldiers in trenches may justifiably view events very differently from those who fly desks.

Former soldier Tim O'Brien makes this point clearly in his perceptive novel about the war in Vietnam, *Going After Cacciato*. But O'Brien is also clear about how limiting the soldier's view can be: "The common grunt doesn't give a damn about purposes and justice," he has Doc Peret say.

> "He doesn't even think about that shit. Not when he's out humping, getting his tail shot off. Purposes—bullshit! He's thinking about how to keep breathing. Or . . . or what it'll feel like when he hits that mine. Will he go nuts? Will he throw up all over himself, or will he cry, or pass out, or scream? What'll it look like—all bone and meat and pus? That's the stuff he thinks about, not purposes." [8]

According to Fussell, too many commentators on Hiroshima derive their sense of purpose from the war roles assigned to their social class: "The problem is one that touches on the matter of social class in America. Most of those with first-hand experience of the war at its worst were relatively inarticulate and have remained silent." In other words, those who did not *fight* do not have an appreciation for the events that concluded the war: "The degree to which Americans register shock and extraordinary shame about the Hiroshima bomb correlates closely with lack of information about the war," he argues. What follows this comment is a veritable explosion of resentment in which logic is abandoned and research is derided as the war records of selected American critics of the bombings are hauled out for derision.

"What did [John Kenneth Galbraith] do in the war?" Fussell asks. "He was in the Office of Price Administration in Washington, and then he was director of the United States Strategic Bombing Survey [which concluded that Japan would have surrendered without the atomic bombings and without being invaded]. He was 37 in 1945, and I don't demand that he experience having his ass shot off. I just note that he didn't."

The war record of David Joravsky, a distinguished historian of science at Northwestern University, is the next to be judged inadequate. "In an interesting exchange last year in the *New York Review of Books* [October 23, 1980]," Fussell writes, "Joseph Alsop and David Joravsky set forth the by now familiar arguments on both sides of the debate. You'll be able to guess which sides they chose once you know that Alsop experienced capture by the Japanese at Hong Kong in 1942 and that Joravsky made no mortal contact with the Japanese: a young soldier, he was on his way to the Pacific when the war ended."

And finally, there is the late professor of philosophy J. Glenn Gray, whose book *The Warriors* describes soldiers as "shocked and ashamed" when they heard about the atomic bombings, a reaction that Fussell explains by revealing that Gray spent the war at division headquarters, which "is miles behind the places where the soldiers experience terror and madness and relieve these pressures by sadism." That sentence and an additional paragraph or two discussing the Pacific War massacres from which, as Fussell says, "Hiroshima seems to follow in natural sequence," sound uncomfortably reminiscent of Vietnam War descriptions, and, indeed, it is the juxtaposition of the *bad war* with the *good war* that is bringing old soldiers like Fussell and Alsop out of the closet to defend Hiroshima. For in its current phase, the debate over Hiroshima and Nagasaki has little to do with how others see us; it has become strictly a matter of how we see ourselves.

A generation of warriors who considered their experience so virtuous that they can speak of massacres apparently without thinking of My Lai (Fussell says, "No Marine was fully persuaded of his manly adequacy who didn't have a well-washed Japanese skull to caress and who didn't have a go at treating surrendering Japs as rifle targets"), and who can speak of the savagery that existed on both sides as an adequate explanation for Hiroshima, do not want their history Vietnamized. If the war was just, then anything that contributed to victory was justified; and the atomic bombings, which appeared to bring the war to a conclusion, were, from a soldier's point of view, a gift from God.

But it was Truman, without Divine guidance to the best of our knowledge, who decided how that gift should be used. Aware of that, Fussell offers this extraordinary comment near the close of his essay: "Harry Truman was not a fascist, but a democrat. He was as close to a real egalitarian as we've seen in high office for a very long time. He is the only president in my lifetime who ever had the experience of commanding a small unit of ground troops obliged to kill people. He knew better than his subsequent critics [of Hiroshima and Nagasaki] what he was doing." Putting aside the suggestion that the experience of killing people in war is excellent preparation for Presidential decision-making in the nuclear age, let us move from combat experiences to historical research and inquire what *Truman was experiencing* and what he was thinking about as he sat behind his desk in the Oval Office in the spring and early summer of 1945.

Research in the President's Official File, and in the diaries, correspondence and records of his closest wartime advisers, reveals that while the war was an ever-present consideration, its conduct was not among Truman's primary tasks. The record of military successes, Roosevelt's deteriorating health, a growing concern with post-war problems and Truman's inexperience had shifted much of the daily management of the conflict away from the White House during 1945. The new President would officiate over victory, but he would not be credited with having led the nation to it. The problems of the post-war world loomed larger before Truman than they ever had before Roosevelt, and they occupied more of his time. His performance would be judged on what he accomplished *after* the war.

The Soviet Union was the primary post-war problem. Joseph Stalin was breaking the Yalta Agreement, the Secretary of State reported to the President at their first meeting on April 13, and soon after, Averell Harriman, Ambassador to

Moscow, characterized Soviet behavior as nothing less than a "barbarian invasion of Europe." [9]

Operating on the principle that toughness was next to godlessness in Stalin's eyes, Truman launched several initiatives during his early weeks in office. His first—subjecting Foreign Minister V. M. Molotov to a tongue-lashing—had disastrous results. His second—the precipitous termination of lend-lease aid to the Russians the day after Germany surrendered—produced an even worse reaction. Casting about for a more effective diplomatic strategy, Truman turned to the counsel of his Secretary of War, Stimson, whose experience as the overseer of the atomic bomb project inspired the policy of caution and reasonable accommodation he recommended. It seemed to Stimson "a terrible thing to gamble with such big stakes in diplomacy without having your master card [atomic bomb] in your hand." [10] He viewed the bomb as the key to the post-war world. It would be "the most terrible weapon ever known in human history," he told Truman, noting that "if the problem of the proper use of this weapon can be solved, we would have the opportunity to bring the world into a pattern in which the peace of the world and our civilization can be saved." [11]

By the late spring of 1945, the implications of this weapon which had been created to win the war had become more problematic than the war itself. As the bomb moved toward completion, a dangerous (though now familiar) illusion was nurtured in the White House: the idea that the bomb was a panacea for America's diplomatic as well as its military problems. As preparations for the Potsdam Conference got underway, assurances that the weapon would work became increasingly important to the President. On June 6, he told Stimson that he had even "postponed" the summit conference "until the 15th of July on purpose to give us more time." And then, Stimson and Truman agreed, in an early linkage of arms control and diplomacy, that after the first bomb had been successfully used against Japan, a fitting exchange for an American offer to the Russians for the international control of atomic energy would be "the settlement of the Polish, Rumanian, Yugoslavian, and Manchurian problems." [12] And even before this discussion, Secretary of State–designate James F. Byrnes had told Truman that the bomb "might well put us in a position to dictate our own terms at the end of the war." [13]

Truman inherited the basic policy that governed the atomic bomb, just as he inherited every other policy related to the war, a point that commentators on both sides of the debate often ignore. It was therefore *possible* to use the bomb only because Roosevelt had made preparations to do so. Truman was *inclined* to use the bomb because of those preparations. But he *decided* to use it because there seemed no good reason not to. On the contrary, the bombs were available and the Japanese fought on; the bombs were available and precedents of burned cities were numerous; the bombs were available and $2 billion had been spent to create them; the bombs were available and revenge had its claim; the bombs were available and the Soviet Union was claiming too much. "The bomb," to quote Stimson, was "a badly needed equalizer." [14] Its use held out not only the hope of shocking Tokyo into submission but also the possible dividend of jolting Moscow into cooperation. "No man, in our position and subject to our responsibilities, holding in his hands a weapon of such possibilities," Stimson wrote in "The Decision to Use the Atomic Bomb," "could have failed to use it and afterwards looked his countrymen in the face." [15]

But a critical question remains: Were the bombings of Hiroshima and Nagasaki, as Fussell and Alsop claim, the quickest way to end the war? A considerable body of evidence suggests that the decision to use the bomb, which involved a decision to reject another recommended initiative, *delayed* the end of the war. American cryptographers had broken the Japanese diplomatic code before the war, and senior members of the Administration were aware of a struggle between peace and war factions within the Japanese government. Based on this privileged information, (referred to as "Magic" intercepts) and on his knowledge of Japanese politics gained from long experience as Ambassador to Japan, Acting Secretary of State Joseph C. Grew urged Truman during the final days of May to clarify the unconditional-surrender policy. It was an insurmountable barrier for the peace faction, he explained, for no Japanese government would surrender without assurances that the Emperor would not be deposed or the dynasty eliminated.[16] But Truman decided to reject Grew's advice, and an important question is *why?*

One answer is that he would not accept the political consequences that were likely to result from a public retreat from a policy that had become a political shibboleth since Roosevelt introduced the idea in 1943. Another answer is that he preferred to use the atomic bomb. This is the view offered by the authors of *Hiroshima and Nagasaki*: "The A-bomb attacks were needed not so much against Japan—already on the brink of surrender and no longer capable of mounting an effective counteroffensive—as to establish clearly America's post-war international position and strategic supremacy in the anticipated Cold War setting." Although this interpretation is difficult to "prove," any serious effort to interpret Truman's motives must confront the significant evidence in Stimson's diaries, in the Manhattan Project files and in the President's papers that supports it. "The bomb as a merely probable weapon had seemed a weak reed on which to rely," Stimson wrote in his memoir, *On Active Service in Peace and War,* "but the bomb as a colossal reality was very different."[17] This expected difference, it must be recognized, may have made the difference when Truman chose between unconditional surrender and the atomic bomb.

But whatever the reasons that led to the President's decision, the point that is relevant here is that many more American soldiers and Japanese of all types might have had the opportunity to grow old if Truman had accepted Grew's advice, the perspicacity of which became even clearer on July 13 when an intercepted message from Foreign Minister Shigenori Togo to Ambassador Naotake Sato in Moscow noted that "unconditional surrender is the only obstacle to peace."[18]

And unconditional surrender remained an obstacle to peace *even after* atomic bombs destroyed Hiroshima and Nagasaki. The Japanese did not surrender until the government of the United States offered assurances that neither the Emperor nor the imperial dynasty would be endangered. In his *New York Review of Books* article, published under the title "Was the Hiroshima Bomb Necessary?", Alsop camouflages this point by referring to "President Truman's wise decision to agree to preserve the imperial house as part of a surrender otherwise unconditional." But the details that Alsop recounts of the military's resistance to surrender are relevant *only* against the background of the demand for unconditional surrender. That policy, initiated in America, bound together a fracturing war party in Japan. To focus solely on the position taken by the military hard-liners, as Alsop does, misses the point. As Eugene Dooman, a senior Japan specialist in the State Department during the war, long ago pointed out to Herbert Feis (author of *Japan Subdued* and *The*

Atomic Bomb and the End of World War II), "the Army, and I mean the diehards like [Generals] Umetzu and Anami, never did countenance surrender, but a fission had already developed among the generals, as witness the intervention of General Tanaka, commanding the Eastern Army, against the troops sent to seize the emperor." [19]

In the early morning hours of August 10, in the Emperor's bomb shelter adjoining the imperial library, Premier Kantaro Suzuki startled his divided colleagues on the Supreme Council with the announcement, "Your Imperial Majesty's decision is requested." That decision, "to accept the Allied proclamation on the basis outlined by the Foreign Minister," brought the war to its conclusion—*on the condition* that the United States not compromise the prerogatives of the Emperor as supreme ruler or the survival of the dynasty.

When he came to consider those final, dramatic months of the war and the momentous decisions he influenced so heavily, Stimson (whose introspection and honesty seem out of place next to the modern political memoir) wrote "that history might find that the United States, by its delay in stating its position [on the conditions of surrender], had prolonged the war." [20]

NOTES

1. Ralph Bard to George Harrison, June 27, 1945 and Harrison to Stimson, June 28, 1945 are reprinted in Martin J. Sherwin, *A World Destroyed: Hiroshima and the Origins of the Arms Race* (New York, 1987), pp. 307–8. For the dissenting opinions of other high officials see, Gar Alperovitz, *The Decision to Use the Atomic Bomb and the Architecture of an American Myth* (New York, 1995), pp. 321–71.

2. The complete minutes of the Interim Committee meeting on May 31, 1945 are in Sherwin, *A World Destroyed*, appendix L. The quotation is cited on p. 302.

3. Rabhabinod Pal quoted in Richard Falk, Gabriel Kolko, Robert Lifton eds., *Crimes of War* (New York, 1971), p. 136. Hiroshima and the Holocaust are incomparable in my opinion. The bombing of Hiroshima, whatever complex motivations are ascribed to it, was an act of war with at least one of its goals being to end the war. The Holocaust's goal was to murder an entire people.

4. For a thorough analysis of Truman's speech see, Robert Jay Lifton and Greg Mitchell, *Hiroshima in America: Fifty Years of Denial* (New York, 1995), chapters 1 and 2.

5. Truman to Bishop Oxnam and John Foster Dulles, August 11, 1945, quoted in Sherwin, *A World Destroyed*, pp. xvii–xviii.

6. Kurt Vonnegut, Jr., *Slaughterhouse Five* (New York, 1969), pp. 116–17.

7. Ibid., p. 10.

8. Tim O'Brien, *Going After Cacciato* (New York, 1980), p. 239.

9. Quoted in Sherwin, *A World Destroyed*, p. 187.

10. Henry L. Stimson Diary, Stimson Papers, May 15, 1945.

11. Ibid., For Stimson's "Memo Discussed with the President, April 25, 1945," see Sherwin, *A World Destroyed*, appendix I, pp. 291–92.

12. Ibid., June 6, 1945.

13. Harry S. Truman, Memoirs, Vol I: *Year of Decision* (New York, 1995), p. 87.

14. Henry L. Stimson and McGeorge Bundy, *On Active Service in Peace and War* (New York, 1948), p. 638.

15. Henry L. Stimson, "The Decision to Use the Bomb," *Harper's Magazine*, February 1947, p. 106.

16. Joseph C. Grew, *Turbulent Era: A Diplomatic Record of Forty Years, 1904–1945, Vol. 2* (Boston, 1952) pp. 1406–42.

17. Stimson and Bundy, *On Active Service*, p. 637.

18. Robert J. C. Butow, *Japan's Decision to Surrender* (Stanford, 1954), p. 130. The original intercept was declassified in 1995: Ultra, "Magic"—Diplomatic Summary, No. 1205–1213, July 1945, War Department Office of A.C. of S., G–2, National Archives, Washington, D.C.

19. Eugene Dooman to Herbert Feis, "Dooman" folder, Herbert Feis Papers, Library of Congress, Washington, D.C.

20. Stimson and Bundy, *On Active Service*, p. 629.

III

THE FIRST CRITICS

*American, English and French newspapers spread elegant dissertations on the future,
the past, the inventors, the peaceful vocation and military consequences, the political
consequences, and even the independent nature, of the atomic bomb. We can sum up in one
sentence: technological civilization has just reached its final degree of savagery. . . peace is
the only battle worth waging. It is no longer a prayer, but an order which must rise up from
peoples to their governments—the order to choose finally between hell and reason.*

Albert Camus
August 6, 1945

It has been quite obvious since August 6th, dies magna et amara vale, *a great and bitter
day, that few if any commentators have wished to stand in the path of the landslide of
approbation. . . . To relieve the pressure upon my conscience, I hear and now declare that
I think the use of the atomic bomb, in the circumstances, was atrocious and abominable;
and that civilized peoples should reprobate and anathematize the horrible deed. . . .[L]et
this opinion be recorded: the action taken by the United States Government was in defiance of every sentiment and every conviction upon which civilization is based.*

James Martin Gillis
Editor, *Catholic World*

*We might remember the prophetic warnings to the the nations of old, that nations which
become proud because they were divine instruments must in turn stand under the divine
judgment. . . . The same power which encompassed the defeat of tyranny may become
the foundation of a new injustice. If ever a nation needed to be reminded of the perils
of vainglory, we are that nation in the pride of our power and our victory. The Pauline
warning fits us exactly: "Be not therefore high-minded, but fear."*

Reinhold Niebuhr

THE HORROR

AND

THE SHAME

The Editors of *Commonweal*

T HE WAR, AS WE WRITE, IS VIRTUALLY OVER. This is a fact in itself so moving and compelling that any comment rings hollow, falls wholly short of what hundreds of millions of hearts are feeling, hundreds of millions of minds are thinking. And yet, in these matter, there is at least a certain liturgy to be observed, a certain ritual to be uttered.

The fighting, thanks be to God, is over, which means that the killing and maiming is over. Let us all be determined that the hating also is over, not only the hatred of us, over which we have no control, but whatever hatred is lodged within us, over which we *have* control, and for which we are, each of us, strictly answerable.

The war is done, and we have more than we know to be thankful for. Mothers and fathers, wives and sweethearts are freed of the ugly and gnawing burden of anxiety. That indefinable strain that has kept us all under its tension is relaxed. For these things not only Americans but our enemies and our allies are thankful without prompting. But here is something more than a liturgy: We, Americans, have something immeasurably greater than personal relief to claim our thankfulness, something carrying with it terrible responsibility. We emerge from the most devastating conflict the world has ever known very nearly unscathed. Our fields are furrowed only by the plough, our factories are intact. Compared to other nations, we have lost but a handful of our men. We are thus the most powerful people on earth. And for a brief time, at least, we alone possess the most awful weapon yet devised. In our joy and triumph, in our freedom from the burden of these years, we must remember this. We must look forward soberly, and we must examine our conscience.

Two months ago (June 22) we were writing about poison gas. We said: "To the Orient we are bringing the latest inventions of our civilization. There is only one we have not brought. It is gas. If we use that we will have brought them all. Gas is no worse than flame. It is only that it is one more weapon. The last one we have to use. Until we invent a new one." And then we said: "The time has come when nothing more can be added to the horror if we wish to keep our coming victory something we can use—or that humanity can use."

Well, it seems that we were ridiculous writing that sort of thing. We will not have to write that sort of thing any more. Certainly, like everyone else, we will have to write a great deal about the future of humanity and the atomic bomb. But we will not have to worry any more about keeping our victory clean. It is defiled.

There were names of places in Europe which from the early days of the war were associated with the German idea that by disregarding the right of civilians you could shorten the war. These names of places—Rotterdam, Coventry—were associated, and seemed likely to be associated in men's minds for a great number of years, with a judgment of German guilt and German shame. There was a port in the Pacific which sheltered American naval power. It was attacked by air without warning and the name Pearl Harbor was associated, and seemed likely to be associated for many years, with a Japanese idea that you could win a war by attacking the enemy before declaring war on the enemy. The name Pearl Harbor was a name for Japanese guilt and shame. The name Hiroshima, the name Nagasaki are names for American guilt and shame.

The war against Japan was nearly won. Our fleet and Britain's fleet stood off Japan's coast and shelled Japan's cities. There was no opposition. Our planes, the greatest bombers in the world, flew from hard won, gallantly won bases and bombed Japanese shipping, Japanese industry, and already, Japanese women and children. Each day they announced to the Japanese where the blows would fall, and the Japanese were unable to prevent anything they chose to do. Then, without warning, an American plane dropped the atomic bomb on Hiroshima.

Russia entered the war. There was no doubt before or after Russia entered the war that the war against Japan was won. An American plane dropped the second atomic bomb on Nagasaki.

We had to invent the bomb because the Germans were going to invent the bomb. It was a matter of avoiding our own possible destruction. We had to test the bomb and we tested it in a desert. If we were to threaten the use of it against the Japanese, we could have told them to pick a desert and then go look at the hole. Without warning we dropped it into the middle of a city and then without warning we dropped it into the middle of another city.

And then we said that this bomb could mean the end of civilization if we ever got into a war and everyone started to use it. So that we must keep it a secret. We must keep it a sole property of people who know how to use it. We must keep it the property of peace-loving nation. That is what we said about the atomic bomb—together with odds and ends about motors the size of pin points which would drive a ship three times round the world—that is what we said about it, after we had used it ourselves. To secure peace, of course. To save lives, of course. After we had brought indescribable death to a few hundred thousand men, women and children, we said that this bomb must remain always in the hand of peace-loving peoples. For our war, for our purposes, to save American lives we have reached the point where we say that anything goes. That is what the Germans said at the beginning of the war. Once we have won our war we say that there must be international law. Undoubtedly.

When it is created, Germans, Japanese and Americans will remember with horror the days of their shame.

August 24, 1945

"Victory for What?" —The Voice of the Minority

Paul Boyer

I T WAS A FEW DAYS AFTER THE WAR'S END, and the victory celebration that had surged through downtown Chicago was still a fresh memory. But Fred Eastman of the Chicago Theological Seminary was not in a celebratory mood. "King Herod's slaughter of the innocents—an atrocity committed in the name of defense—destroyed no more than a few hundred children," he wrote bitterly to *Christian Century*; "Today, a single atomic bomb slaughters tens of thousands of children and their mothers and fathers. Newspapers and radio acclaim it a great victory. Victory for what?" The poet Randall Jarrell, stationed at an air force base in Arizona, had a similar reaction: "I feel so rotten about the country's response to the bombings at Hiroshima and Nagasaki," he wrote a friend in September 1945, "that I wish I could become a naturalized cat or dog."[1]

Eastman and Jarrell were not alone. From the moment the news of Hiroshima flashed across the nation, isolated voices of protest, ranging from troubled uneasiness to anguished dismay, could be heard. One must not exaggerate this response, but neither may one ignore it. Though a minority viewpoint, it has survived tenaciously, becoming more pronounced as the nuclear arms race—the bitter fruit of decisions taken in 1945—has grown in magnitude and menace.

This protest was not coordinated or organized, nor did it reflect a distinct ideological coloration. It was simply a spontaneous, anguished cry which some Americans, even at the end of a ferocious war, felt compelled to utter. Many were obscure; a few were prominent. Socialist Norman Thomas deplored the "pious satisfaction" of most commentators—including those on the Left—at Truman's announcement. The atomic destruction of a second city, Thomas wrote, was "the greatest single atrocity of a very cruel war." Stuart Chase, even as he speculated on the atom's peacetime role, warned that the obliteration of Hiroshima and Nagasaki, "whatever the rationalization," could "handicap the moral leadership of the United States . . . for generations to come." Surely, Chase insisted, Washington could have found a way to achieve its objectives "without this appalling slaughter of school children."[2]

In the nation's newspapers, the general editorial approval for the atomic bombing of Japan was moderated by a few expressions of moral uneasiness. The

Hartford Courant credited the bomb for ending the war, but added: "We cannot disregard the voice of our own conscience, which tells us that the new bomb is just as bestial and inhuman as the Japanese say it is." The *New York Herald Tribune* found "no satisfaction in . . . the greatest simultaneous slaughter in the whole history of mankind, and [one that] in its numbers matches the more methodical mass butcheries of the Nazis." The *Omaha World Herald* criticized as "almost sacrilegious" the unctuous tone of Truman's announcement "in using the name of a merciful God in connection with so Satanic a device." Far from being a reason for "exultation," this editorial continued, the Hiroshima news only underscored "that war is a degrading, dirty business." [3]

A few columnists struck a similar note. Marquis Childs, writing in the *New York Post* on August 10, called it a "supreme tragedy . . . that the new discovery . . . had to be used first for the destruction of human life." "Surely we cannot be proud of what we have done," wrote David Lawrence in the *U.S. News and World Report*. "If we state our inner thoughts honestly, we are ashamed of it." Richard L. Strout of the *Christian Science Monitor* posed troubling questions: "How can the United States in the future appeal to the conscience of mankind not to use this new weapon? . . . Has not the moral ground for such an appeal been cut away from under our feet?" [4]

From the grass roots, too, came a faint but distinct cry of dismay. Newspapers all over the country, noted one observer a few days after Hiroshima, were receiving letters "protesting the killing of the non-combatant civilians in Japan, calling it inhuman, and protesting our disregard of moral values."

The letters of this dissident minority were often extremely bitter. One called the bombing "a stain upon our national life"; another said it was "simply mass murder, sheer terrorism." An appalled reader of *Time* wrote:

> The United States of America has this day become the new master of brutality, infamy, atrocity. Bataan, Buchenwald, Dachau, Coventry, Lidice were tea parties compared with the horror which we . . . have dumped on the world. . . . No peacetime applications of this Frankenstein monster can ever erase the crime we have committed. [5]

The letters on the atomic bomb written to H. V. Kaltenborn included several of moral protest. "Why . . . did we choose to drop our first bomb on a crowded city, where 90% of the casualties would *inevitably be civilian?*" asked a St. Paul listener. "True, there were war industries in Hiroshima, but there are war industries in most of our American cities, and what would we think of an enemy who would wipe out our fair cities, *hospitals and all*, on such a pretext?" The expressions of moral outrage from Kaltenborn's listeners ranged from the articulate and thoughtful to the barely literate:

> Phooey America. That blood will scream up to our dear God—What will come next? . . . Bury the bomb and all the papers, it is too shocking news what America did with that knowledge. If we destroy innocent civilians we will be destroyed in return—that was a devilish act against Japan. [6]

Isolated and weak in contrast to the overwhelming chorus of approval for the atomic bombing of Japan, such expressions were nevertheless an authentic part of the larger mosaic of response to the bomb. In a 1946 epic poem called *The Bomb That Fell on America*, a California writer named Hermann Hagedorn included a section called "The Conscience of America" in which he attempted to convey the ethical unease that at least some were feeling. "The dead lie across our hearts," he wrote, "and fall in a black rain upon our souls." [7]

OPPOSITION TO THE BOMBING of Hiroshima and Nagasaki surfaced, too, in the pages of the black press. This is not to say, however, that the black reaction was unambiguously hostile. By 1945, leading black newspapers like the *Washington Afro-American* and the *Chicago Defender* were celebrating the exploits of black combat troops against the "Japs" on Okinawa and elsewhere, and when the atomic-bomb story broke they reported with pride that seven thousand blacks had been employed at Oak Ridge and that black chemists and mathematicians had been part of the Manhattan Project at the University of Chicago. "Negro Scientists Help Produce 1st Atom Bomb," headlined the *Defender* on August 18. [8]

But the dominant response of black opinion-molders quickly turned to hostility and skepticism. The seven thousand black workers at Oak Ridge, the *Washington Afro-American* noted in a follow-up story, had lived in segregated, inferior housing; performed menial jobs only; and had not (unlike the white workers) had a school provided for their children. In a variation of a familiar proposal, the *Defender* suggested that another $2 billion be allocated to social-science research "to isolate and destroy the venom of racial hate." [9]

The top leadership of the National Association for the Advancement of Colored People was uniformly critical. Executive Secretary Walter White commenting on Winston Churchill's determination to keep the bomb in "Anglo-Saxon" hands, observed that Chinese, Russians, Indians, and others could learn nuclear physics as well, and speculated that some day "an atomic bomb might be launched against London from the remote fastness of some part of the British Empire." A few weeks after Hiroshima, W. E. B. DuBois, the NAACP's director of research (and America's leading black intellectual), described Japan as "the greatest colored nation which has risen to leadership in modern times" and predicted that the humiliation of her spectacular defeat would slow the advance of dark-skinned peoples everywhere. Roy Wilkins, editor of the NAACP magazine the *Crisis*, linked the atomic bomb to other wartime tactics such as roasting Japanese soldiers alive with flamethrowers and attributed such barbarities to racist attitudes that viewed the Japanese as subhuman. Asked Wilkins in a September 1945 editorial on the bomb: "Who is bad and who is good? Who is barbarian and who is civilized? Who is fit to lead the world to peace and security, and by what token?" [10]

Woven through this black commentary was the suspicion that the bomb had been deliberately reserved for use against Asians rather than Europeans. The Hiroshima news, said the *Washington Afro-American*, "revived the feeling in some quarters that maybe the Allies are fighting a racial war after all." American military planners may have spared the Germans, who, "after all, represent the white race," this editorial suggested, and "saved our most devastating weapon for the hated yellow men of the Pacific." [11]

The black poet Langston Hughes developed all these themes in a bitter *Chicago Defender* column on August 18, 1945, putting his harshest comments in the mouth of "Simple," the uneducated but shrewd black he used as a journalistic persona in these years. "Them atom bombs make me sick at the stomach," says

Simple. Why wasn't the bomb used against Germany? "They just did not want to use them on white folks. Germans is white. So they wait until the war is over in Europe to try them out on colored folks. Japs is colored." The $2 billion spent on the bomb, Simple concludes, would have been better spent on decent housing, playgrounds, and education for the nation's poor—including education for whites who persisted in electing racists to Congress.[12]

AND WHAT OF THE CHURCHES? The response of the religious press and church bodies to the dropping of the atomic bomb was far from uniform. Evangelicals who stressed individual conversion and downplayed engagement with social issues remained comparatively silent on the bomb, or viewed it simply as further evidence of the need for personal evangelism. This response is illustrated in the pages of *United Evangelical Action*, the magazine of the National Association of Evangelicals, an organization of conservative Protestant denominations. While denouncing the "wholesale excesses of drunkenness and lust" on V-J Day, the editors made no comment on the atomic bombing of Japan. When a reader questioned this silence, they responded with a classic statement of the evangelical position:

> Our concern is not so much about the atomic bomb as about the people who control it. If the people are saved Christians, it will do the world no harm. If they are pagan, beware. . . . Our business is to preach the gospel. . . . We are unwilling to take any blame for the shortcomings of our social order beyond our own personal conduct.[13]

Nor can one assume that the church leaders and editors who did condemn the atomic bombing of Japan spoke for the great mass of the laity. Indeed, the findings of the public-opinion polls suggest that they probably spoke for only a minority even of their own constituencies. When these caveats have been noted, however, the fact remains that the greatest concentration of critical comment on the Hiroshima and Nagasaki bombings came from the churches. Though a minority viewpoint, this response laid the groundwork for and added a sharp intensity to the debate over the general moral implications of nuclear weapons.

One of the first responses came from the Federal Council of Churches, an association of liberal Protestant denominations. On August 9 (before news of the Nagasaki bombing was released), the president of the FCC, Methodist bishop G. Bromley Oxnam, and John Foster Dulles, chairman of its Commission on a Just and Durable Peace, issued a joint statement urging that no further bombs be dropped. "If we, a professedly Christian nation, feel normally free to use atomic energy in that way," they said, "men elsewhere will accept that verdict. Atomic weapons will be looked upon as a normal art of the arsenal of war and the stage will be set for the sudden and final destruction of mankind." To refrain from dropping additional bombs, they went on, was "the way of Christian statesmanship" and would be viewed not as evidence of weakness, but of "moral and physical greatness."[14]

Two weeks after Hiroshima, thirty-four prominent Protestant clergymen, including several well-known pacifists, addressed a letter to President Truman condemning the decision. One of the signers, Harry Emerson Fosdick of New York's Riverside Church, was particularly outspoken. In an early post-war sermon broadcast nationally Fosdick declared: "When our self-justifications are all in, every one of us is nonetheless horrified at the implications of what we did. Saying that Japan was guilty and deserved it, gets us nowhere. The mothers and babies of Hiroshima and Nagasaki did not deserve it." To argue that the "mass murder of whole metropolitan populations is right if it is effective," Fosdick went on, was to abandon "every moral standard the best conscience of the race ever has set up." [15]

Another independent religious voice of protest was that of John Haynes Holmes of the nonsectarian Community Church of New York. The atomic bomb, wrote Holmes in the September 1945 issue of his magazine *Unity*, was "the supreme atrocity of the ages; . . . a crime which we would instantly have recognized as such had Germany and not our own country been guilty of the act." The claim that the decision had hastened the end of the war, he added, was simply the familiar "end-justifies-the-means" argument and "as great and dangerous a fallacy as ever." Even on practical grounds the utilitarian argument might prove fallacious: "The atomic bomb is not going to stop here. What if it 'Speeds the end' not only of this war, but also of civilization? . . . The long range view in this case is a thing to chill the soul." [16]

In the publications of the mainstream Protestant denominations, one finds, even in the flush of victory, expressions of moral unease. The Baptist *Watchman-Examiner* on August 16, 1945, condemned the "ghastly slaughter of women and children who have not the remotest connection with a military objective." The response of the Methodist *Christian Advocate*, initially tentative, grew stronger with time. In September 1945 the editor, Roy L. Smith, wrote that the bomb illustrated the need to find alternatives to war, but found no basis for condemning its use against Japan so long as one accepted other forms of terror bombing. By March 1946, however, Smith was expressing growing qualms: "The moral conscience of the American people continues restless in the memory of the awful effects of the explosion, and as more detailed and dependable information comes in, this sense of uneasiness deepens." Quoting a proposal by David Lawrence, Smith concluded: "Let's rebuild Hiroshima as a symbol of spiritual reawakening." [17]

Other Methodist periodicals were even more outspoken. "There is no religion, however primitive, or law that can sponsor the horrors of this war," declared the *Central Christian Advocate*, published in Chicago, on August 30, 1945. "Hate and kill, kill without hate; any method, anybody, or better still, every method and everybody. This was a wonderful war." *Motive*, the magazine of the Methodist Student Movement, expressed its "unmitigated condemnation" of the atomic-bomb "atrocity" in an editorial titled: "We Have Sinned." *Motive* also published a list of the Methodist churches, schools, and social-welfare agencies in Hiroshima and Nagasaki as well as a play involving a dialogue between Satan and the Angel Gabriel that was, in effect, a bitter attack on the dropping of the atomic bomb. It "was ruthless and needless," says Gabriel. "One side was already defeated and helpless. . . . Do the Americans boast of it? Soldiers save their own lives by taking the lives of children? What courage, what honor is that?" Gloats Satan: "Dr. Gallup indicates that 85 percent of the American people approved. . . which gives me the largest majority I've had since prohibition." [18]

The interdenominational liberal weekly *Christian Century* not only took a strong initial stand against the decision to drop the bomb, but published several pages of letters from readers who shared its view. The obliteration of two cities by atomic bombs, it said on August 15, had brought to "perfect flower" von Clausewitz's doctrine of war without limit or restraint. "Short of blowing up the planet, this is the ultimate in violence," this editorial declared. "Instead of congratulating ourselves . . . we should now be standing in penitence before the Creator of the power which the atom has hitherto kept inviolate." *Christian Century's* August 29 editorial, "America's Atomic Atrocity," was even more out-spoken in condemning the "brutal disregard of any principle of humanity" that had placed the United States in an "indefensible moral position" and "sadly crippled" its "influence for justice and humanity." Predicting a reaction against Christianity in Japan, *Christian Century* called on the churches to "disassociate themselves and their faith from this inhuman and reckless act of the American government." (Deluged by critical letters, *Christian Century* tempered its stand a few weeks later. While still describing the atomic-bomb decision as "impetuous" and "wanton," the magazine now insisted that it had not condemned the action categorically, but only pointed out that the government had not persuasively shown that its use was essential to Japan's defeat.[19])

The closest thing to an authoritative Protestant response to the atomic bomb-ing of Japan was "Atomic Warfare and the Christian Faith," the report of a blue-ribbon commission presented to the Federal Council of Churches in March 1946. Chaired by Robert L. Calhoun, professor of historical theology at Yale, this twenty-two-member commission included an impressive array of theologians, philosophers, and church historians drawn from prominent seminaries, universi-ties, and such colleges as Oberlin and Haverford. Among its well-known members were Roland H. Bainton and H. Richard Niebuhr of Yale and John C. Bennett, Reinhold Niebuhr, and Henry P. Van Dusen of Union Theological Seminary. Like the council itself, the membership was drawn almost exclusively from Protes-tantism's liberal, "modernist" wing. The commission divided over whether the use of atomic bombs could ever be morally acceptable, but on the use already made of them, it was unanimous and unequivocal:

> We would begin with an act of contrition. As American Christians, we are deeply penitent for the irresponsible use already made of the atomic bomb. We are agreed that, whatever . . . one's judgment of the ethics of war in principle, the surprise bombings of Hiroshima and Nagasaki are morally indefensible.

The commission gave reasons for this damning indictment: the atomic attacks on two cities involved "the indiscriminate slaughter of non-combatants" in a particularly "ghastly form"; the first bomb had been dropped without specific warning or advance demonstration, and the second before Tokyo had been given a reasonable opportunity to react to the first; the bombs were dropped despite Japan's "hopeless" strategic position and the virtual certainty that she herself did not possess such weapons. Even if the atomic bomb shortened the war, the com-mission concluded, "the moral cost was too high. . . . We have sinned grievously against the laws of God and the people of Japan." Aid by American Christians to "the survivors of those two murdered cities," the Calhoun Commission said, would be "a token of repentance . . . cherished as long as men remember the first atomic bomb."

This call for repentance was not well received, however. The main result, commented one well-placed observer in 1950, was to produce "a barrage of argu-ments trying to apologize for our use of the atomic bomb in such a way as to deny any need for contrition."[20]

The leading voices of American Roman Catholicism were even more uniformly critical of the atomic bombing of Japan. Indeed, concludes historian Robert C. Batchelder, Catholic theologians and journals of opinion were "nearly unanimous in condemning the bomb's use." "The name Hiroshima, the name Nagasaki, are names for American guilt and shame," declared *Commonweal* in August 1945. This editorial sarcastically dismissed the justifications being offered ("To secure peace, of course. To save lives, of course") and the peaceful avowals being made by leaders who had just brought "indescribable death to a few hundred thousand men, women and children." [21]

Catholic World, the voice of the Paulist Fathers, called the surprise use of the atomic bomb against civilians "atrocious and abominable" and "the most powerful blow ever delivered against Christian civilization and the moral law." All "civilized people," this September 1945 editorial continued, should "reprobate and anathematize" this "horrible deed." Of the argument that the two doomed cities had been given sufficient advance warning, *Catholic World* said: "Let us not combine cruelty with hypocrisy, and attempt to justify wholesale slaughter with a lie." [22]

The judgment of the influential Jesuit journal *America*, while longer in coming, was no less devastating. If the justifications being given for America's decision to drop the bomb were morally sound, wrote a Jesuit theologian in *America* in 1947, then *any* belligerent in *any* just war could use atomic weapons with impunity; but if they were not, "then the United States committed an enormous wrong at Hiroshima, and duplicated it at Nagasaki." This author left no doubt of his view. The argument that the bomb had shortened the war, he said, "collapses against a primary principle of sound morality: no end—however good, however necessary—can justify the use of an evil means." The evil deeds of August 1945 were "of the gravest concern," he declared, because they sanctioned the substitution of "national pragmatism" for "the transcendence of the moral order." This writer sharply criticized the "obfuscation" of those who had responded to the destruction of Hiroshima and Nagasaki with calls for the abolition of war. While this was "a consummation devoutly to be wished," he said, no one should suppose "that by turning to it we have resolved the question of our past performance and proved our conscience clear." [23]

WHILE THEOLOGIANS DEBATED, the moral discourse over the atomic bombing of Japan emerged in an unlikely quarter. Readers of the *New Yorker* had little reason to suspect that the August 31, 1946, issue would not offer the magazine's usual urbane mélange of cartoons, humorous pieces, cultural comment, and reviews. The cover was a lighthearted collage of summer fun and games: swimming, sunbathing, tennis, croquet. In fact, however, the entire issue was devoted to a single long journalistic account entitled simply "Hiroshima." The author, thirty-one-year-old John Hersey, was born in China in 1914 and spent his first ten years there. Graduating from Yale, he joined *Time-Life* publications and during World War II produced many stories and three books based on his reportorial experiences in Europe. The best-known of his war stories, *A Bell for Adano*, appeared in *Liberty Magazine* in 1944; by early 1945 the book version had gone through fifteen printings. Planning a journalistic trip to Japan late in 1945, Hersey discussed with *New Yorker* editor William Shawn a possible piece on the atomic bomb. "Hiroshima" was the result. [24]

Hersey's essay had an immediate and profound impact. The book version became a runaway best-seller. The Book-of-the-Month Club distributed free copies to many of its 848,000 members. A reading of the entire work, in four half-hour segments, over the ABC radio network won the Peabody Award for the outstanding educational broadcast of 1946.[25]

A seasoned reporter and successful popular writer, Hersey in *Hiroshima* adopted a tried-and-true journalistic technique, describing in minute detail the activities of six Hiroshima residents before, during, and after the bomb fell: a young secretary; a widowed seamstress; a German Jesuit missionary; a Japanese Methodist minister; a young physician affiliated with a large, modern hospital; and an older physician who operated a small private clinic. This was a form familiar to American readers. Photographers like Dorothea Lange, novelists like John Steinbeck, and journalists like James Agee had explored the impact of the Great Depression by focusing on individuals, and the genre had been transferred to the battlefront in the war dispatches of Ernie Pyle, the London broadcasts of Edward R. Murrow, and the cartoons of Bill Mauldin. In books like Richard Wright's *Native Son* or James Farrell's Studs Lonigan trilogy, this form of individualized social realism could be tough, hard-boiled, and even brutal. But in the hands of other writers—Erskine Caldwell, William Saroyan, Thornton Wilder—it took on a sentimental and picaresque quality.

Hersey was closer to the latter school. Indeed, his *Hiroshima* was modeled on Wilder's *The Bridge of San Luis Rey*, which offered biographical vignettes of several ordinary people randomly united in death by the collapse of a bridge in Peru, while *A Bell for Adano* sentimentally described a liberated Italian village and the efforts of an American occupation official, one Major Joppolo, to replace a church bell melted down by the Fascists. To be sure, occasional grim details give the story an authentic wartime flavor: "At the corner . . . the two men came on a dead Italian woman. She had been dressed in black. Her right leg was blown off and the flies for some reason preferred the dark sticky pool of blood and dust to her stump." But such passages are rare amid the descriptions of picturesque village life and encounters between simple local folk and friendly, well-meaning Americans. The publisher's promotional copy made clear how readers should approach *A Bell for Adano*, describing it as a story of "The Human Side Of War: . . . the wonderful, simple people of Adano—the fishermen, the officials, the pretty girls, the children who ran in the streets shouting to the American soldiers to throw them caramels, . . . the American who broke through red tape and discovered the heart of Italy."[26]

Given Hersey's journalistic background, and his weakness for the sentimental and melodramatic, the restraint with which *Hiroshima* unfolds is striking. The book is remarkably free of either sentimentality or sensationalism. It begins in a quiet, understated fashion: "At exactly fifteen minutes past eight in the morning, on August 6, 1945, Japanese time, at the moment when the atomic bomb flashed above Hiroshima, Miss Toshiko Sasaki, a clerk in the personnel department of the East Asia Tin Works, had just sat down at her place in the plant office and was turning her head to speak to the girl at the next desk." As in *A Bell for Adano*, there are scenes of horror that embed themselves in the memory, such as the description of a group of some twenty soldiers in a park some distance from the blast's epicenter: "Their faces were wholly burned, their eye sockets were hollow, the fluid from their melted eyes had run down their cheeks. (They must have had their faces upturned when the bomb went off; perhaps they were anti-aircraft personnel.) Their mouths were mere swollen, pus-covered wounds, which they could not bear to stretch enough to admit the spout of the teapot." [27] But such scenes were not heightened for dramatic effect. Indeed, they receive no more emphasis than the everyday details of uninjured persons coping with all-encompassing disaster. In a style so uninflected it struck some readers as heartless, Hersey gave the same weight to horror, heroism, and mundane banality.

In general, the reception of *Hiroshima* was overwhelmingly approving. Of hundreds of letters, postcards, and telegrams that poured into the *New Yorker* offices, the vast majority were favorable. Most reviews were enthusiastic. "Nothing that can be said about this book can equal what the book has to say," wrote Charles Poore in the *New York Times;* "It speaks for itself, and in an unforgettable way, for humanity." The *Christian Century* reviewer could hardly contain himself: "Once in a lifetime you read a magazine article that makes you want to bounce up out of your easychair and go running around to your neighbors, thrusting the magazine under their noses and saying: 'Read this! Read it now!'" [28]

To many reviewers, Hersey's unemotional prose was a distinct asset, heightening the impact of his account. "The calmness of the narrative," said anthropologist Ruth Benedict in the *Nation*, "throws into relief the nightmare magnitude of the [bomb's] destructive power." A few, however, were sharply critical. "Mr. Hersey's . . . excessively subdued effect . . . left the facts to speak for themselves, and they have not spoken loudly enough," wrote the anonymous reviewer in the (London) *Times Literary Supplement.* The living "occupy all the foreground, and the mounds of dead are only seen vaguely in the background." Dwight Macdonald, editor of the one-man journal of opinion *Politics*, attacked the book's "suave, toned-down, underplayed kind of naturalism"—a stylistic flaw he blamed on both the *New Yorker*'s influence and Hersey's defects as a writer: "no style, no ideas, no feelings of any intensity, and no eye for the one detail that imaginatively creates a whole." If only Hemingway could have written the account, he lamented! Ultimately, said Macdonald, *Hiroshima*'s stylistic shortcomings sprang from a "moral deficiency" in Hersey's vision: "The 'little people' of Hiroshima whose sufferings Hersey records in antiseptic *New Yorker* prose might just as well be white mice, for all the pity, horror, or indignation the reader—or at least this reader—is made to feel for them." Perhaps, Macdonald concluded, "naturalism is no longer adequate, either esthetically or morally, to cope with the modern horrors." [29]

No such tentativeness moderated the negative judgment of novelist Mary McCarthy. Far from being an indictment of atomic war, McCarthy wrote, Hersey's piece actually diminished the atomic bomb by treating it as one would a natural catastrophe—a fire, flood, or earthquake—solely for its "human interest" value. To recreate the Hiroshima bombing by interviewing survivors, she said, was "an insipid falsification of the truth of atomic warfare. To have done the atom bomb justice, Mr. Hersey would have had to interview the dead." Hersey, she charged, had filled his bombscape "with busy little Japanese Methodists; he has made it familiar and safe, and so, in the final sense, boring." Hersey had also failed, she went on, to confront "the question of intention and guilt" or even to identify the source of the disaster that overwhelms his subjects. Hersey's failure, she said, reflected the inevitable constraints of the elite magazine for which he was writing. "Since the *New Yorker* has not, so far as we know, had a rupture with the government . . . it can only assimilate the atomic bomb to itself, to Westchester County, to smoked turkey, and the Hotel Carlyle." [30]

These criticisms offer a mélange of insightful and highly questionable judgments. It is doubtful, for example, that Hersey's failure to dwell on the United States as the source of the catastrophe means that the book must be relegated to the genre of hurricane and earthquake stories. Readers were only too aware of the source of the cataclysm. The *Christian Century* reviewer found it "excruciating" to identify himself, "as every American must, with the hand that tripped the bomb release that sent compound tragedy hurtling into the unsuspecting city." [31] Nor does even a cursory reading sustain McCarthy's charge that the focus on a few individual survivors obscures the magnitude of the disaster. No one could finish *Hiroshima* without confronting a catastrophe of horrendous proportions. "A hundred thousand people were killed by the atomic bomb," says Hersey on page 4, and this stark fact reverberates through the numerous references to vast devastation, piles of bodies, throngs of dazed and wounded survivors, and hordes of victims inundating shattered hospitals. "Of a hundred and fifty doctors in the city," he writes, "sixty-five were already dead and most of the rest were wounded. Of 1,780 nurses, 1,654 were dead or too badly hurt to work." [32]

If Hersey's technique underplayed some facets of the truth of Hiroshima, it cast others in sharper relief. He gave careful attention to the lingering effects of radiation exposure—still in 1946 a little-understood phenomenon and one that most early accounts barely touched upon. And he sensitively explored the varied psychological responses of people finding themselves still alive in the midst of mass death: the man who deliberately turned back toward the burning city, never to be seen again; the young mother who crouched motionless for hours, cradling her dead baby; the lassitude and passivity of many survivors; the guilt of others like the Methodist minister Kiyoshi Tanimoto, murmuring apologies to the dead and dying; the mingled fear and excitement of the children. As we have seen, the book ends with a matter-of-fact account by a ten-year-old survivor: "I saw a light. I was knocked to my little sister's sleeping place. . . . The neighbors were walking around burned and bleeding. . . . My girl friends Kikuki and Murakami . . . were looking for their mothers." [33]

Hersey was not writing in a cultural vacuum, or bringing first news of some unknown event. For a year, the obliteration of Hiroshima and Nagasaki had been the subject of enormous public attention. What one might call the panoramic background of an atomic attack—the sheets of flame, the mushroom cloud, the mass destruction, the instantaneous death of thousands—was already vividly present in the consciousness of Hersey's readers. But that unearthly panorama had been largely devoid of human content. Of course, the human reality was always implicit in the casualty statistics and the photographs of endless rubble. And sometimes it was made explicit: a March 1946 *Collier's* article, "What the Atomic Bomb Really Did," included graphic details such as dress fabric imprints burned into the skin of women survivors; in May 1946 the *Saturday Review* published a survivor's account that in some respects anticipated Hersey's.[34] More typically, however, the statistics of devastation and death were simply recited as prefatory to a plea for international control, civil defense, or some other cause. On a canvas whose broad-brush background scenes were already familiar, Hersey etched several vividly realized foreground figures. In isolation, his account does seem limited and incomplete; in the context of his readers' experience, its great impact becomes more understandable.

As for McCarthy's (inaccurate) complaint that the book is dominated by "busy little Japanese Methodists," this contains its own unpleasant whiff of racial, religious, and class prejudice. Commenting in 1976 on the Macdonald-McCarthy reaction to *Hiroshima*, critic John Leonard offered a harsh judgment:

> The literary intellectual tries to cope by appropriating the abyss for himself. . . . Not even the survivors of the unimaginable will be allowed to possess it. It is too big, too important, for them; they are irrelevancies. This, of course, isn't really coping; it is striking an attitude. It is, moreover, greedy and elitist, a kind of critical imperialism: my categories are better than your categories, and what do ordinary people know anyway, unworthy as they are of their tragedy? [35]

Macdonald's suggestion that Hersey's brand of naturalism was inadequate to the "modern horrors" was undeniably true. But would any style have been "adequate"? Hersey himself gives perhaps unconscious hints in *Hiroshima* of his awareness of this inadequacy. Whenever *books* are mentioned, it is as an absurd irrelevancy. The secretary Toshiko Sasaki nearly dies when the blast topples a bookcase over on her. "There in the tin factory, in the first moment of the atomic age," observes Hersey, "a human being was crushed by books." Another survivor recalls: "I started to bring my books along, and then I thought, 'This is no time for books.'" [36] Perhaps Hersey was merely the hapless target of Macdonald's larger realization that the "modern horrors" had undermined not just a particular style, but the entire literary enterprise.

John Hersey himself always contended that he had deliberately chosen the understated, reportorial style of *Hiroshima* not to diminish but to heighten the emotional impact. "The flat style was deliberate, and I still think I was right to adopt it," Hersey wrote early in 1985. "A high literary manner, or a show of passion, would have brought *me* into the story as a mediator; I wanted to avoid such mediation, so the reader's experience would be as direct as possible." Without making inflated literary claims, one may still credit his considerable achievement in transforming the subhuman "Japs" of wartime propaganda back into Japanese: human beings who loved their children, bled when they were cut, and spent their time in life's ordinary routines. Hersey achieved this by a journalist's eye for telling detail: the hand-lettered signs in the rubble with such queries as "Sister, where are you?"; the school girls singing to keep up their spirits as they lay pinned under a fence; the small boat on the shore of the Ota River, its five-man crew sprawled dead around it in various positions of work.[37]

Hiroshima may have left Dwight Macdonald cold, but others found the book profoundly affecting. "I had never thought of the people in the bombed cities as individuals," one young reader wrote. A veteran of the Manhattan Project found himself weeping as he read the book, and "filled with shame to recall the whoopee spirit" with which he had welcomed the bombing of Hiroshima. The definitive response, perhaps, was that of the Catholic journal *America*:

> Despite the miles of print, and endless reels of photographs . . . it is this *New Yorker* report which most shudderingly brings home to the reader the utter horror of the atom bomb. . . . one curse of the modern world is that individuals are becoming . . . mere faceless ciphers. . . . We may escape the atom bomb because men with souls will realize that it dooms men with souls.

Hersey, in short, reminded Americans of what Rev. Tanimoto forced himself to repeat over and over as he aided hideously burned victims: "These are human beings." [38]

But what was the larger effect of this heightened awareness? Some have suggested, in the words of one historian, that Hersey "laid the groundwork" for a fundamental moral reassessment of the bomb decision and "contributed to a continuing dialogue over the justification for atomic warfare." Indeed, it is true that during the periods of intense engagement with the nuclear threat that have occurred at intervals since 1945, *Hiroshima* has always been rediscovered as a primary text. One must also acknowledge, however, that its immediate effect seems curiously ephemeral and elusive. Published just as a long cycle of diminished public engagement and activism on the nuclear front was beginning, it did little to reverse that trend. *Hiroshima* neither reenergized the international-control movement nor launched a vigorous public debate over the bombing of Hiroshima and Nagasaki. Of hundreds of letters in which readers reported how deeply Hersey's account had moved them, only a handful expressed feelings of guilt or a determination to work politically to prevent future atomic war.

For the minority already politically engaged or disturbed by the moral questions surrounding the atomic bomb, Hersey's book intensified their commitment or concern. For most readers, however, it seems to have had no such effect. Providing a deeper understanding of Hiroshima's human meaning, it did not lead further. Indeed, for many, the very act of reading seems to have provided release from stressful and complex emotions. Like the funeral rituals that provide a socially sanctioned outlet for grief and mourning, *Hiroshima* may have enabled Americans of 1946 both to confront emotionally what had happened to the people of Hiroshima and Nagasaki and, in a psychological as well as a literal sense, to close the book on that episode. Perhaps in this sense, it was less a stimulus to action and reflection than a cathartic end point.

This effect was intensified by Hersey's emphasis on the victims' patience and resignation. This was war, he reported survivors as saying, and such things must be expected. He described the eerie silence of Hiroshima's Asano Park where hundreds of the grievously injured quietly endured their suffering. (Describing *Hiroshima* as "a capsule of Japanese life" and "a source-book on Japanese behavior," anthropologist Ruth Benedict assured *Nation* readers that "patient fortitude" and a helpless passivity suggestive of "sheep without shepherds" was absolutely in character, reflecting behavior patterns "inculcated for centuries.") Here was implicit expiation for Americans. The Japanese themselves had accepted their fate. They did not rage against those who had dropped the bomb. One could empathize with their ordeal, even admire their stoic endurance, and still maintain one's personal moral distance. [39]

Hiroshima is sometimes linked with other American books that had a profound cultural impact—Thomas Paine's *Common Sense*, Harriet Beecher Stowe's *Uncle Tom's Cabin*, Upton Sinclair's *The Jungle*, Rachel Carson's *Silent Spring*. In fact, it is very different. These other works were energizing, spurring readers to engagement and activism. One can trace their social and political ramifications in a quite direct fashion. *Hiroshima* was not such a ringing call to action. Its closest psychological parallel in American literature, perhaps, is to a classic from another war, *The Red Badge of Courage*. Like *Hiroshima*, Stephen Crane's novel was praised for its realism, its freedom from cant, and its delineation of the experiences and feelings of individuals overwhelmed by death and destruction. But, again like *Hiroshima*, it induces an almost elegiac mood. The reader is not stirred to action, but left with the feeling that he has gained a deeper understanding of war's human meaning, and through understanding, emotional release. The ending of *The Red Badge of Courage* might almost stand as an epigraph to *Hiroshima*:

> The youth smiled. . . . He had rid himself of the red sickness of battle. The sultry nightmare was in the past. He had been an animal blistered and sweating in the heat and pain of war. He turned now with a lover's thrust to images of tranquil skies, fresh meadows, cool brooks—an existence of soft and eternal peace.
> Over the river, a golden ray of sun came through the hosts of leaden rain clouds.

In the intense but strictly circumscribed engagement with the Hiroshima reality offered by John Hersey, it was as though Americans were saying: "We have now faced what we did. We have been told. We have experienced its full human horror. But we must get on with our lives. We can now put all that behind us." It is perhaps not irrelevant to note that, for all its success, *Hiroshima* was not the number one bestseller of 1946. That honor went to *The Egg and I*, a lighthearted comedy about life on an Oregon chicken farm.

NOTES

1. Fred Eastman, Letter to the Editor, *Christian Century*, August 29, 1945, p. 983; Randall Jarrell to Margaret Marshall, September 1945, in *Randall Jarrell's Letters: An Autobiographical and Literary Selection*, edited by Mary Jarrell with Stuart Wright (Boston, 1985), p. 130.
2. "Stuart Chase Says," *Common Sense*, October 1945, p. 29, quoted in Paul F. Boller, Jr., "Hiroshima and the American Left: August 1945," *International Social Science Review* 57 (1982), 24; Norman Thomas, *The Call*, August 13, 1945, pp. 4, 5, quoted in ibid., p. 24; Norman Thomas, "When Cruelty Becomes Pleasurable," *Human Events*, September 26, 1945.
3. "We Are Not Proud of It," *Omaha Morning World Herald*, August 8, 1945; Donald Porter Geddes, ed., *The Atomic Age Opens* (New York, 1945), p. 44; "The Annihilation of Hiroshima," *New York Herald Tribune*, August 9, 1945, p. 22.
4. "A Moral Calamity," *Progressive*, August 20, 1945, p. 3; Marquis W. Childs, "The State of the Nation," *New York Post*, August 10, 1945; David Lawrence, "What Hath Man Wrought!" *U.S. News and World Report*, August 17, 1945, pp. 38-39.
5. Walter G. Taylor, New York City, to the editor, *Time*, August 27, 1945; "Doubts and Fears," *Time*, August 20, 1945, p. 36 (quoting *New York Times* letter); Geddes, *Atomic Age Opens*, p. 42; Maureen Fitzgerald, "'Sixteen Hours Ago . . .' America at the Threshold of the Atomic Age," unpublished seminar paper, University of Wisconsin, Spring 1984.
6. Letters to H. V. Kaltenborn from A. M. Hendrickson (August 13, 1945); K. F. Scallan (August 9, 1945); and Charles May (undated), Kaltenborn Papers, State Historical Society of Wisconsin, Madison, box 107.
7. Hermann Hagedorn, *The Bomb That Fell on America* (Santa Barbara, 1946), p. 33.
8. *Chicago Defender*, August 18, 1945, p. 1; *Washington Afro-American*, August 11, 1945; "Colored Scientists Aided Atom Study," *Washington Afro-American*, August 18, 1945, p. 1; "The Front Page," *Race Relations: A Monthly Summary of Events and Trends*, August–September, 1945, p. 53.
9. "Splitting the Atom of Race Hate," *Chicago Defender*, August 18, 1945, p. 12; *Washington Afro-American*, August 11, 1945.
10. "The Atomic Bomb," *The Crisis*, September 1945, p. 249; Walter White, "Atom Bomb and Lasting Peace," *Chicago Defender*, September 8, 1945; W. E. B. DuBois, "Negro's War Gains and Losses," *Chicago Defender*, September 15, 1945.

11. "Are we Prepared for Peace?" *Washington Afro-American*, August 18, 1945, p. 1.

12. Langston Hughes, "Simple and the Atom Bomb," *Chicago Defender*, August 18, 1945, p. 12.

13. "Roving Reporter," *United Evangelical Action*, September 1, 1945, p. 8; Editor's Note, *United Evangelical Action*, September 15, 1945, p. 2.

14. "Churchmen Speak on Atomic Bomb," *Federal Council Bulletin*, September 1945, p. 6. See also "Statement on Control of the Atomic Bomb," *Federal Council Bulletin*, October 1945, p. 6 (Statement of the Federal Council of Churches Executive Committee).

15. Harry Emerson Fosdick, *On Being Fit to Live With: Sermons on Post-war Christianity* (New York, 1946), pp. 20, 76, 77; "Godless Götterdämmerung," *Time*, October 15, 1945, p. 62.

16. John Haynes Holmes, "Editorial Comment," *Unity*, September 1945, pp. 99–100.

17. Roy L. Smith, "In My Opinion," *Christian Advocate*, September 27, 1945, p. 3; "Let's Rebuild Hiroshima," *Christian Advocate*, March 28, 1946, p. 4; *Watchman-Examiner*, August 16, 1945, quoted in Robert C. Batchelder, *The Irreversible Decision, 1939–1950* (Boston, 1962), p. 171.

18. Robert H. Hamill, "The Atom Explodes, or Those Blasted Japs," *Motive*, November 1945, pp. 44, 45; "The New Bomb," *Central Christian Advocate*, August 30, 1945, p. 3; "We Have Sinned," *Motive*, October 1945, p. 19; William Watkins Reid, "Hiroshima and Nagasaki Methodists," *Motive*, November 1945, p. 44.

19. *Christian Century* Editorial, August 15, 1945, p. 923; "America's Atomic Atrocity," August 29, 1945, pp. 974–75; "Atrocities and War," September 26, 1945, p. 1086; "On the Atomic Bomb," August 29, 1945, pp. 982–84 (letters).

20. Federal Council of the Churches of Christ in America, Commission on the Relation of the Church to the War in the Light of the Christian Faith, *Atomic Warfare and the Christian Faith* (New York, 1946), pp. 11, 12, 19; Edward L. Long, Jr., *The Christian Response to the Atomic Crisis* (Philadelphia, 1950), p. 16.

21. "Horror and Shame," *Commonweal*, August 24, 1945, pp. 443–44; Batchelder, *Irreversible Decision*, p. 170.

22. "The Atom Bomb," *Catholic World*, September 1945, pp. 449-51.

23. Edgar R. Smothers, S.J., "An Opinion on Hiroshima," *America*, July 5, 1947, pp. 379–80.

24. Michael J. Yavenditti, "John Hersey and the American Conscience: The Reception of 'Hiroshima,'" *Pacific Historical Review* 43 (1974): 32, 34.

25. Irving J. Gitlin, "Radio and Atomic-Energy Education," Journal of Educational Sociology 22 (1949): 327; Joseph C. Goulden, *The Best Years, 1945–1950* (New York, 1976), p. 181.

26. John Hersey, *A Bell for Adano* (New York, 1965), pp. 5–6; advertising copy on flyleaf; Yavenditti, "Hersey and the American Conscience," p. 34.

27. John Hersey, *Hiroshima* (New York, 1946), pp. 3, 68.

28. Russell S. Hutchinson, "Hiroshima," *Christian Century*, September 25, 1946, p. 1151; Charles Poore, *New York Times*, November 10, 1946, p. 7.

29. Dwight Macdonald, "Hersey's 'Hiroshima,'" *Politics*, October 1946, p. 308; (London) *Times Literary Supplement*, December 7, 1946, p. 605; Ruth Benedict, "The Past and the Future: *Hiroshima* by John Hersey," *Nation*, December 7, 1946, p. 656.

30. Mary McCarthy, "The Hiroshima *New Yorker*," *Politics*, October 1946, p. 367. For a more recent criticism in a similar vein see Kingsley Widmer, "American Apocalypse: Notes on the Bomb and the Failure of Imagination," in Warren French, ed., *The Forties: Fiction Poetry, Drama* (Deland, Fla., 1969), p. 143.

31. Hutchinson, "Hiroshima," p. 1151.

32. Hersey, *Hiroshima*, pp. 4, 33.

33. Ibid., pp. 37–38, 40, 50, 54, 76, 90, 118.

34. John A. Siemes, S.J., "Hiroshima: Eye-Witness," *Saturday Review of Literature*, May 11, 1946, pp. 24–25, 40–44; Robert DeVore, "What the Atomic Bomb Really Did," *Collier's*, March 2, 1946, pp. 19ff.

35. John Leonard, "Looking Back at Hiroshima Makes Uneasy Viewing," *New York Times*, August 1, 1976.

36. Hersey, *Hiroshima*, pp. 23, 48.

37. Ibid., pp. 49–50, 88, 116; John Hersey to author, January 24, 1985.

38. Hersey, *Hiroshima*, p. 61; Natalie Mochlmann to *New Yorker*, September 3, 1946, quoted in Yavenditti, "Hersey and the American Conscience," p. 38; Alice Kimball Smith, *A Peril and a Hope: The Scientists' Movement in America, 1945–1947* rev. ed. (Cambridge, Mass., 1971), p. 80; "*New Yorker* and the Soul," *America*, September 14, 1946, p. 569.

39. Ruth Benedict, "The Past and the Future," *Nation*, December 7, 1946, pp. 656–57.

LEAVING

THE BOMB

PROJECT

Joseph Rotblat

ORKING ON THE MANHATTAN PROJECT was a traumatic experience. It is not often given to one to participate in the birth of a new era. For some the effect has endured throughout their lives; I am one of those.

This essay is not an autobiography; it describes only my involvement in the genesis of the atomic bomb. All extraneous personal elements are left out, but their exclusion does not mean that they are unimportant. Our hopes and fears, our resolutions and actions, are influenced by an infinite number of small events interacting with each other all the time. Because of this, each of us may react differently to the same set of conditions. The experience of every Los Alamite is unique.

At the beginning of 1939, when the news reached me of the discovery of fission, I was working in the Radiological Laboratory in Warsaw. Its director was Ludwik Wertenstein, a pupil of Marie Curie and a pioneer in the science of radioactivity in Poland. Our source of radiation consisted of 30 milligrams of radium in solution; every few days we pumped the accumulated radon into a tube filled with beryllium powder. With this minute neutron source we managed to carry out much research, even competing with Enrico Fermi's prestigious team, then in Rome, in the discovery of radionuclides. Our main achievement was the direct evidence of the inelastic scattering of neutrons; my doctoral thesis was on that subject.

In the earlier experiments on inelastic scattering we used gold as the scatterer. By the end of 1938 I had begun to experiment with uranium, so when I heard of the fission of uranium, it did not take me long to set up an experiment to see whether neutrons are emitted at fission. I soon found that they are—indeed, that more neutrons are emitted than produce fission. From that discovery it was a fairly simple intellectual exercise to envisage a divergent chain reaction with a vast release of energy. The logical sequel was that if this energy were released in a very short time it would result in an explosion of unprecedented power. Many scientists in other countries, doing this type of research, went through a similar thought process, although not necessarily evoking the same reaction.

In my case, my first reflex was to put the whole thing out of my mind, like a person trying to ignore the first symptom of a fatal disease in the hope that it will go away. But the fear gnaws all the same, and my fear was that someone would put the idea into practice. The thought that I myself would do it did not cross my mind, because it was completely alien to me. I was brought up on humanitarian principles. At that time my life was centered on doing "pure" research work, but I always believed that science should be used in the service of mankind. The notion of utilizing my knowledge to produce an awesome weapon of destruction was abhorrent to me.

In my gnawing fear, the "someone" who might put it into practice was precisely defined: German scientists. I had no doubt that the Nazis would not hesitate to use any device, however inhumane, if it gave their doctrine world domination. If so, should one look into the problem to find out whether the fear had a realistic basis? Wrestling with this question was agonizing, and I was therefore glad that another pressing matter gave me an excuse to put it aside. This other matter was my move to England, where I was to spend a year with Professor James Chadwick in Liverpool, on a grant to work on the cyclotron which was then being completed there. This was my first trip abroad, and the upheaval kept me busy both before the journey in April 1939 and for some time afterward, because I spoke very little English, and it took me a long time to settle down.

Throughout the spring and summer the gnawing went on relentlessly. It intensified with the increasing signs that Germany was getting ready for war. And it became acute when I read an article by S. Flügge in *Naturwissenschaften* mentioning the possibility of nuclear explosives. Gradually I worked out a rationale for doing research on the feasibility of the bomb. I convinced myself that the only way to stop the Germans from using it against us would be if we too had the bomb and threatened to retaliate. My scenario never envisaged that we should use it, not even against the Germans. We needed the bomb for the sole purpose of making sure that it would not be used by them: the same argument that is now being used by proponents of the deterrence doctrine.

With the wisdom of hindsight, I can see the folly of the deterrent thesis, quite apart from a few other flaws in my rationalization. For one thing, it would not have worked with a psychopath like Hitler. If he had had the bomb, it is very likely that his last order from the bunker in Berlin would have been to destroy London, even if this were to bring terrible retribution to Germany. Indeed, he would have seen this as a heroic way of going down, in a *Götterdämmerung*.

My thinking at the time required that the feasibility of the atomic bomb be established, one way or the other, with the utmost urgency. Yet I could not overcome my scruples. I felt the need to talk it over with someone, but my English was too halting to discuss such a sensitive issue with my colleagues in Liverpool. In August 1939, having gone to Poland on a personal matter, I took the opportunity to visit Wertenstein and put my dilemma before him. The idea of a nuclear weapon had not occurred to him, but when I showed him my rough calculations he could not find anything scientifically wrong with them. On the moral issue, however, he was unwilling to advise me. He himself would never engage in this type of work, but he would not try to influence me. It had to be left to my own conscience.

The war broke out two days after I returned to Liverpool. Within a few weeks Poland was overrun. The stories that Hitler's military strength was all bluff, that his tanks were painted cardboard, turned out to be wishful thinking. The might of Germany stood revealed, and the whole of our civilization was in mortal peril. My scruples were finally overcome.

By November 1939 my English was good enough for me to give a course of lectures on nuclear physics to the Honors School at Liverpool University, but by then the department's senior research staff had disappeared: they had gone to work on radar and other war projects. I had, therefore, to approach Chadwick directly with an outline of my plan for research on the feasibility of the atom bomb. His response was typically Chadwickian: he just grunted, without letting on whether he had already thought of such a plan. Later I learned that other scientists in the United Kingdom did have the same idea, some of them with similar motivation.

A few days later Chadwick told me to go ahead and gave me two young assistants. One of them presented a problem. He was a Quaker and as such had refused to do war work. He was therefore sent to Liverpool University for academic duties—but was diverted to work with me on the atom bomb! I was not allowed to reveal to him the nature of our research, and I had qualms of conscience about using him in such an unethical way.

The main idea which I put to Chadwick was that for the atom bomb the chain reaction would have to be propagated by fast neutrons; otherwise it would not differ much from a chemical explosive. It was therefore important to measure the fission cross-section for fast neutrons, the energy distribution of fission neutrons, their inelastic scattering, and the proportion of those captured without producing fission. It was also relevant to find out whether stray neutrons might cause a premature start of the reaction, which meant determining the probability of spontaneous fission of uranium.

We built up a small team of young but devoted physicists and used the cyclotron to tackle some of these problems. Later we were joined by Otto Frisch, who measured the fast neutron fission cross-section for uranium-235. I had the idea of using plutonium, but we had no means of making it. As a result of these investigations, we were able to establish that the atom bomb was feasible from the scientific point of view. However, it also became clear that in order to make the bomb a vast technological effort would be required, far exceeding the manpower and industrial potential of wartime Britain. A top-level decision was reached to collaborate with the Americans. And so I found myself eventually in that "wondrous strange" place, Los Alamos.

In March 1944 I experienced a disagreeable shock. At that time I was living with the Chadwicks in their house on the Mesa, before moving later to the "Big House," the quarters for single scientists. General Leslie Groves, when visiting Los Alamos, frequently came to the Chadwicks for dinner and relaxed palaver. During one such conversation Groves said that, of course, the real purpose in making the bomb was to subdue the Soviets. (Whatever his exact words, his real meaning was clear.) Although I had no illusions about the Stalin regime—after all, it was his pact with Hitler that enabled the latter to invade Poland—I felt deeply the sense of betrayal of an ally. Remember, this was said at a time when thousands of Russians were dying every day on the Eastern Front, tying down the Germans and giving the Allies time to prepare for the landing on the continent of Europe. Until then I had thought that our work was to prevent a Nazi victory, and now I was told that the weapon we were preparing was intended for use against the people who were making extreme sacrifices for that very aim.

My concern about the purpose of our work gained substance from conversations with Niels Bohr. He used to come to my room at eight in the morning to listen to the BBC news bulletin. Like myself, he could not stand the U.S. bulletins which urged us every few seconds to purchase a certain laxative! I owned a special radio on which I could receive the BBC World Service. Sometimes Bohr stayed on and talked to me about the social and political implications of the discovery of nuclear energy and of his worry about the dire consequences of a nuclear arms race between East and West which he foresaw.

All this, and the growing evidence that the war in Europe would be over before the bomb project was completed, made my participation in it pointless. If it took the Americans such a long time, then my fear of the Germans being first was groundless. When it became evident, toward the end of 1944, that the Germans had abandoned their bomb project, the whole purpose of my being in Los Alamos ceased to be, and I asked for permission to leave and return to Britain.

Why did other scientists not make the same decision? Obviously, one would not expect General Groves to wind up the project as soon as Germany was defeated, but there were many scientists for whom the German factor was the main motivation. Why did they not quit when this factor ceased to be? I was not allowed to discuss this issue with anybody after I declared my intention to leave Los Alamos, but earlier conversations, as well as much later ones, elicited several reasons. The most frequent reason given was pure and simple scientific curiosity— the strong urge to find out whether the theoretical calculations and predictions would come true. These scientists felt that only after the test at Alamogordo should they enter into the debate about the use of the bomb.

Others were prepared to put the matter off even longer, persuaded by the argument that many American lives would be saved if the bomb brought a rapid end to the war with Japan. Only when peace was restored would they take a hand in efforts to ensure that the bomb would not be used again. Still others, while agreeing that the project should have been stopped when the German factor ceased to operate, were not willing to take an individual stand because they feared it would adversely affect their future careers.

The groups I have just described—scientists with a social conscience—were a minority in the scientific community. The majority were not bothered by moral scruples; they were quite content to leave it to others to decide how their work would be used. Much the same situation exists now in many countries in relation to work on military projects. But it is the morality issue at a time of war that perplexes and worries me most.

Recently I came across a document released under the Freedom of Information Act. It is a letter, dated May 25, 1943, from Robert Oppenheimer to Enrico Fermi, on the military use of radioactive materials, specifically, the poisoning of food with radioactive strontium. The Smyth Report mentions such use as a possible German threat, but Oppenheimer apparently thought the idea worthy of consideration, and asked Fermi whether he could produce the strontium without letting too many people into the secret. He went on: "I think we should not attempt a plan unless we can poison food sufficient to kill a half a million men." I am sure that in peacetime these same scientists would have viewed such a plan as barbaric; they would not have contemplated it even for a moment. Yet during the war it was considered quite seriously and, I presume, abandoned only because it was technically infeasible.

After I told Chadwick that I wished to leave the project, he came back to me with very disturbing news. When he conveyed my wish to the intelligence chief at Los Alamos, he was shown a thick dossier on me with highly incriminating evidence. It boiled down to my being a spy: I had arranged with a contact in

Santa Fe to return to England, and then to be flown to and parachuted onto the part of Poland held by the Soviets, in order to give them the secrets of the atom bomb. The trouble was that within this load of rubbish was a grain of truth. I did indeed meet and converse with a person during my trips to Santa Fe. It was for a purely altruistic purpose, nothing to do with the project, and I had Chadwick's permission for the visits. Nonetheless, it contravened a security regulation, and it made me vulnerable.

Fortunately for me, in their zeal the vigilant agents had included in their reports details of conversations with dates, which were quite easy to refute and to expose as complete fabrications. The chief of intelligence was rather embarrassed by all this and conceded that the dossier was worthless. Nevertheless, he insisted that I not talk to anybody about my reason for leaving the project. We agreed with Chadwick that the ostensible reason would be a purely personal one: that I was worried about my wife whom I had left in Poland.

And so, on Christmas Eve 1944, I sailed for the United Kingdom, but not without another incident. Before leaving Los Alamos, I packed all my documents—research notes as well as correspondence and other records—in a box made for me by my assistant. En route I stayed for a few days with the Chadwicks in Washington. Chadwick personally helped me to put the box on the train to New York. But when I arrived there a few hours later, the box was missing. Nor, despite valiant efforts, was it ever recovered.

The work on the Manhattan Project, as I said at the outset, has had an enduring effect on my life. Indeed, it radically changed my scientific career and the carrying out of my obligations to society. Work on the atom bomb convinced me that even pure research soon finds applications of one kind or another. If so, I wanted to decide myself how my work should be applied. I chose an aspect of nuclear physics which would definitely be beneficial to humanity: the applications to medicine. Thus I completely changed the direction of my research and spent the rest of my academic career working in a medical college and hospital.

While this gave me personal satisfaction, I was increasingly concerned about the political aspects of the development of nuclear weapons, particularly the hydrogen bomb, about which I knew from Los Alamos. Therefore, I devoted myself both to arousing the scientific community to the danger, and to educating the general public on these issues. I was instrumental in setting up the Atomic Scientists Association in the United Kingdom, and within its framework organized the Atom Train, a traveling exhibition which explained to the public the good and evil aspects of nuclear energy. Through these activities I came to collaborate with Bertrand Russell. This association led to the foundation of the Pugwash Conferences, where I met again with colleagues from the Manhattan Project, who were also concerned about the threat to mankind that has arisen partly from their work.

After 40 years one question keeps nagging me: have we learned enough not to repeat the mistakes we made then? I am not sure even about myself. Not being an absolute pacifist, I cannot guarantee that I would not behave in the same way, should a similar situation arise. Our concepts of morality seem to get thrown overboard once military action starts. It is, therefore, most important not to allow such a situation to develop. Our prime effort must concentrate on the prevention of nuclear war, because in such a war not only morality but the whole fabric of civilization would disappear. Eventually, however, we must aim at eliminating all kinds of war.

THE ATOM
BOMB &
AHIMSA

Mahatma Gandhi

Editors' Note: The Indian nationalist leader, Mahatma Gandhi, an advocate of nonviolent action, made a number of remarks following the atomic attacks on Hiroshima and Nagasaki. His most extensive comments were made during a speech in Poona, Gujarat, in July 1946, on the eve of the first anniversary of the bombings. Two months later, speaking in New Delhi he observed: "Nonviolence…is the only thing that the atom bomb cannot destroy. When I first heard that the atom bomb had wiped out Hiroshima, I did not move a muscle. I said to myself, 'Unless the world now adopts nonviolence, it will spell certain suicide for mankind'."

IT HAS BEEN SUGGESTED BY AMERICAN FRIENDS that the atomic bomb will bring *Ahimsa* (nonviolence) into being as nothing else could. If they mean that the bomb's destructive power will so disgust the world that it will turn away from violence for the time being, then perhaps it will. But I think this is very much like a man glutting himself on delicacies to the point of nausea. He turns away from them only to return with redoubled zeal after the effect of nausea is over. Precisely in the same way will the world return to violence with renewed zeal after the effect of its disgust has worn off.

Often good does come out of evil. But that is God's not man's plan. Man knows that only evil can come out of evil as good comes out of good. Although atomic energy has been harnessed by American scientists and army men for destructive purposes, it is undoubtedly within the realm of possibility that it may be utilized by other scientists for humanitarian purposes. However, this is not what was meant by my American friends. They are not so simple as to pose a question which implies such an obvious truth. An arsonist uses fire for a destructive and nefarious purpose. Yet, a mother makes daily use of fire to prepare nourishing food.

As far as I can see, the atomic bomb has deadened the finest feelings which have sustained mankind for ages. There used to be so-called laws of war which made it tolerable. Now we understand the naked truth. War knows no law except that of might. The atom bomb has brought an empty victory to the Allied armies.

It has resulted for the time being in the soul of Japan being destroyed. What has happened to the soul of the destroying nation is yet too early to see. The forces of nature act in a mysterious manner. We can only solve the mystery by deducing the unknown result from the known results of similar events. A slave holder cannot hold a slave without putting himself or his deputy in the cage holding the slave.

Let no one run away with the idea that I wish to raise a defense of Japanese misdeeds which occurred in the pursuit of Japan's own unworthy ambitions. The difference was only one of degree. I may assume that Japan's greed was more unworthy. But greater unworthiness confers no right on the less unworthy to destroy without mercy men, women and children in particular areas of Japan. The only moral which can be legitimately drawn from the supreme tragedy of the bomb is that it shall not be destroyed by counter-bombs. Violence cannot be destroyed by counter-violence.

Mankind will only emerge out of violence through nonviolence. Hatred can only be overcome by love. Counter–hatred only increases the surface expression as well as the depth of hatred. I am aware that I am repeating what I have stated many times before—and practiced to the best of my ability and capacity. What I originally said [about nonviolence] was nothing new. It is as old as the mountains. While I would not recite any copybook maxim, I did announce what I believed in with every fiber of my being. Sixty years of practice in various walks of life has only enriched this belief and it has been fortified by the experience of friends. It is the central truth by which one can stand alone without flinching. I believe in what Max Muller said years ago, namely, that truth needs to be repeated as long as there are men who do not believe it.

BETWEEN
HELL AND
REASON

Albert Camus

THE WORLD IS WHAT IT IS, that is, nothing much. Since yesterday, this is what everybody knows, thanks to the tremendous concert which the radio, newspaper, and information agencies have just started on the subject of the atomic bomb. We are informed, indeed, in the middle of piles of enthusiastic commentaries, that any city of average size can be totally razed by a bomb the size of a soccer ball.

American, English and French newspapers spread elegant dissertations on the future, the past, the inventors, the peaceful vocation and military consequences, the political consequences, and even the independent nature, of the atomic bomb. We can sum up in one sentence: technological civilization has just reached its final degree of savagery. We will have to choose, in a relatively near future, between collective suicide and the intelligent use of scientific conquests.

In the meantime, it is permissible to think that there is some indecency in celebrating in this manner a discovery which, first of all, places itself at the disposal of the most awful destructive rage which—over the centuries—humankind has ever displayed. Surely no once except an unrepentant idealist will be surprised [to learn] that in a world given over to the wrenches of violence, incapable of any control, indifferent to justice and the simple happiness of human beings, science devotes itself to organized murder.

These discoveries must be recorded, commented upon according to what they are, announced to the world, so that humankind can have an accurate idea of her destiny. But to surround these terrible revelations with a quaint or humorous literature is simply not tolerable. As it was, we were not breathing easily in a tormented world. Now we are confronted with a new agony, one that has every chance of being final. Humanity is probably being given its last chance. And this could be the pretext for a "special edition." But it should more surely be the subject of much reflection a good deal of silence.

Moreover, there are other reasons for being cautious about the science fiction which the newspapers are offering us. When we hear the diplomatic editor of Reuters agency announce that this invention voids treaties and makes even the decision of Potsdam outdated, and hear him comment that it doesn't matter that the Russians are at Königsberg or Turkey in the Dardanelles, we cannot help but assume that this fine concert has intentions which have little to do with scientific disinterestedness.

Let us be clear. If the Japanese capitulate after the destruction of Hiroshima and as a result of intimidation, we shall rejoice over it. But we decline to deduce from such a serious bit of news anything other than the decision to plead even more energetically in behalf of a true international society: a society where major powers will not have greater rights than the small or intermediate size nations, where war—a scourge that has become definitive solely as a result of human intelligence—will no longer depend on the appetites or specific doctrines of this or that state.

Faced with the terrifying perspectives which are opening up to humanity, we can perceive even better that peace is the only battle worth waging. It is no longer a prayer, but an order which must rise up from peoples to their governments—the order to choose finally between hell and reason.

Combat
August 6, 1945

COMMENTARY ON "BETWEEN HELL AND REASON"

Ronald E. Santoni
Translator

The editorial essay by Camus—which I entitled "After Hiroshima: Between Hell and Reason"—is likely the first published response by a philosopher to the first use of atomic weaponry against a major population center. That it has not—to the best of my knowledge—been reproduced earlier in an English language publication[1] may, in itself, be a commentary on the ideological near-sightedness and existential indifference of even philosophers to atomic destruction and the threat of nuclear extinction. Certainly post-World War II Anglo-American analytic philosophy has not been marked by an urgent concern with the problems of war and peace, destruction and survival, in an atomic or nuclear age.

Although the 12½ kiloton bomb dropped on Hiroshima pales in comparison to the devastational power of contemporary nuclear megatonnage, Camus has remarkable insights into the dehumanizing terrors and apocalyptic meanings of Hiroshima. He is hardly surprised that, in a world too often insensitive to issues of human decency and justice, and blind to the inhumanity of violence, science should "devote itself to organized murder." He understands that in this "most awful destructive rage" ("la plus formidable rage de destruction"), technological civilization "has reached its final degree of savagery" ("son dernier degré de sauvagerie"). He understands that Hiroshima is not an occasion for rejoicing, but a time for intense reflection, for making known these "terrible revelations," for informing humanity of its fragility, for alerting it to its possible destiny. In advance of his time, he warns that humanity is likely confronting "its last chance."

Yet doom and the final—humanly invented—scourge are not his final message. The genuinely human response to the plague must, in the end, be creative.

Man must be faithful to humanity, however inhuman the plague may be. We must plead and work ever so much harder in behalf of a "true international society"; a society of decency and justice, in which human beings care for one another as sisters and brothers, in which states subordinate their own wants and ideological preferences to global survival and well-being, in which the equal rights of all nations give way to the rights of humanity. The Nuremberg obligation must be translated into our global obligation. To use subsequent words of Camus: Hiroshima leaves us with the awesome but necessary human task "of keeping the world from destroying itself." [2]

As philosophers concerned with the meaning and destiny of human existence, we can hardly—in good faith—ignore the atomic and thermonuclear threat to human meaning and destiny. The Socratic tradition calls not simply for the analysis and clarification of concepts but for a radical examination and critical scrutiny of all presupposed or established doctrines. And, as Noam Chomsky has pointed out, no profession has a better claim than philosophy to be concerned with the moral and intellectual culture of civilization, or to have adequate tools for criticizing prevailing ideology and public policy.[3] And given current "official" thinking about the feasibililty of tactical nuclear war and the moral justifiability of resort to nuclear war for "just causes," philosophers have, I think, the moral obligation to contribute their work to a clarification and painstaking reevaulation of present nuclear policy and values. By doing this work—especially when the continuation of vested national self-interests or ideological practices may lead to holocaust or even extinction—philosophers will be contributing not solely to a reexamination and re-creation of values and meanings, but to the continuation of life on our planet.

In a world plagued by the human threat of nuclear incineration, the minimal social responsibililty of philosophers is surely to keep creation alive. Clearer concepts, more knowledgeable debate, more careful and more humane reasoning, greater global concern and sensivity, prepare us for more responsible and more moral action. In that creative action lies the choice of reason over hell, and our commitment to preventing the unthinkable from happening.[4]

NOTES

1. My sometimes collaborator, William Gay, shares in this judgment. I know of no philosopher who has greater familiarity with philosophical bibliography concerning issues pertaining to the arms race and nuclear war. See e.g., William Gay and Marysia Lemmond "On Philosophy and the Nuclear Debate" (*Journal of Social Philosophy*, 15, Summer 1987) and William Gay and Michael Pearson, *The Nuclear Arms Race* (Chicago: The American Library Association, 1987).

2. These words appeared in his acceptance speech for the Nobel Prize in Literature, which he presented in Stockholm, Sweden, December 10, 1957.

3. Noam Chomsky, "Philosophers and Public Policy" (*Ethics*, 79, October 1968), pp. 1-9, esp. p.5.

4. I have expressed themes similar to the ones here on other occasions, most recently in an article with William Gay, "Philosophy and Genocide", in *Genocide: A Critical Bibliographic Review* (London Publishing Limited, 1988). See also, e.g. Ronald E. Santoni, "Men First and 'Philosophers Afterward'" (*International Philosophical Quarterly*, Vol IX, December 1969), pp. 600-604, and Ronald E. Santoni, "The Arms Race, Genocidal Intent, and Individual Responsibility" (*Philosophy and Social Criticism*, Number 3 and 4, 1984, pp. 9-18).

THE

DECLINE

TO BARBARISM

Dwight Macdonald

WHAT FIRST APPALLED US WAS ITS BLAST. "TNT is barely twice as strong as black powder was six centuries ago. World War II developed explosives up to 60% more powerful than TNT. The atomic bomb is more than 12,000 times as strong as the best improvement on TNT. One hundred and twenty-three planes each bearing a single atomic bomb, would carry as much destructive power as all the bombs (2,453,595 tons) dropped by the Allies on Europe during the war." *

It has slowly become evident, however, that the real horror of The Bomb is not blast but radioactivity. Splitting the atom sets free all kinds of radioactive substances, whose power is suggested by the fact that at the Hanford bomb plant, the water used for cooling the "pile" (the structure of uranium and other substances whose atomic interaction produces the explosive) carried off enough radiation to "heat the Columbia River appreciably." *Time* added: "Even the wind blowing over the chemical plant picked up another load of peril, for the stacks gave off a radioactive gas." And Smyth notes: "The fission products produced in one day's run of a 100,000-kilowatt chain-reacting pile of uranium might be sufficient to make a large area uninhabitable."

There is thus no question as to the potential horror of The Bomb's radioactivity. The two bombs actually used were apparently designed as explosive and not gas bombs, perhaps from humanitarian considerations, perhaps to protect the American troops who will later have to occupy Japan. But intentions are one thing, results another. So feared was radioactivity at Hanford that the most elaborate precautions were taken in the way of shields, clothes, etc. No such precautions were taken, obviously, on behalf of the inhabitants of Hiroshima; the plane dropped its cargo of half-understood poisons and sped away. What happened? The very sensitivity of the Army and the scientists on the subject is ominous. When one of the lesser experts who had worked on the bomb, a Dr. Harold Jacobson of New York, stated publicly that Hiroshima would be "uninhabitable" for seventy years, he was at once questioned by FBI agents, after which, "ill and upset," he issued another

---

*Time, August 20, 1945.

statement emphasizing that this was merely his own personal opinion, and that his colleagues disagreed with him.

But recent news from Japan indicates that perhaps Dr. Jacobson was right and his eminent colleagues wrong. After stating that 70,000 persons were killed outright in the two explosions and 120,000 wounded, Radio Tokyo on August 22 continued: "Many persons are dying daily from burns sustained during the raids. Many of those who received burns cannot survive the wounds because of the uncanny effects which the atomic bomb produces on the human body. Even those who received minor burns, and looked quite healthy at first, weakened after a few days for some unknown reason." Howard W. Blakeslee, the Associated Press Science Editor, commented that these "probably were victims of a phenomenon that is well known in the great radiation laboratories of the United States." Two kinds of burns are produced by the rays from an atomic explosion: the gamma, or X-ray type, which is always delayed and which finally produces on the skin the same effect as an ordinary burn, and which also produces *internal* burns; and burns made by streams of released neutrons. The latter, in laboratory tests made on animals (in Japan, we used human beings), produced no apparent effect at first, but resulted in death a few days later because the neutron rays had destroyed so many white corpuscles. The first wave of neutrons released by the bomb may have struck the earth, releasing more neutrons, and so on; the poisonous effects may persist indefinitely.

Now all this may be mere propaganda (though it will be interesting to see if Hiroshima and Nagasaki are put out of bounds for American troops). But the point is that none of those who produced and employed this monstrosity really knew just how deadly or prolonged these radioactive poisons would be. Which did not prevent them from completing their assignment, nor the Army from dropping the bombs. Perhaps only among men like soldiers and scientists, trained to think "objectively"—i.e., in terms of means, not ends—could such irresponsibility and moral callousness be found. In any case, it was undoubtedly the most magnificent scientific experiment in history, with cities as the laboratories and people as the guinea pigs.

The official platitude about Atomic Fission is that it can be a Force for Good (production) or a Force for Evil (War), and that the problem is simply how to use its Good rather than its Bad potentialities. This is "just common sense." But, as Engels once remarked, Common Sense has some very strange adventures when it leaves its cozy bourgeois fireside and ventures out into the real world. For, given our present institutions—and the official apologists, from Max Lerner to President Conant of Harvard, envisage at most only a little face-lifting on these—how can The Bomb be "controlled," how can it be "internationalized?" Already the great imperialisms are jockeying for position in World War III. How can we expect them to give up the enormous advantage offered by The Bomb? May we hope that the destructive possibilities are so staggering that, for simple self-preservation, they will agree to "outlaw" The Bomb? Or that they will forswear war itself because an "Atomic" war would probably mean the mutual ruin of all contestants? The same reasons were advanced before World War I to demonstrate its "impossibility"; also before World War II. The devastation of these wars was as terrible as had been predicted—yet they took place. Like all the great advances in technology of the past century, Atomic Fission is something in which Good and Evil are so closely intertwined that it is hard to see how the Good can be extracted and the Evil thrown away. A century of effort has failed to separate the Good of capitalism (more production) from the Evil (exploitation, wars, cultural barbarism). *This* atom has never been split, and perhaps never will be. . . .

The Bomb produced two widespread and, from the standpoint of The Authorities, undesirable emotional reactions in this country: a feeling of guilt at "our" having done this to "them," and anxiety lest some future "they" do this to "us." Both feelings were heightened by the superhuman *scale* of The Bomb. The Authorities have therefore made valiant attempts to reduce the thing to a human context, where such concepts as Justice, Reason, Progress could be employed. Such moral defenses are offered as: the war was shortened and many lives, Japanese as well as American, saved; "we" had to invent and use The Bomb against "them" lest "they" invent and use it against "us"; the Japanese deserved it because they started the war, treated prisoners barbarously, etc., or because they refused to surrender. The flimsiness of these justifications is apparent: *any* atrocious action, absolutely *any* one, could be excused on such grounds. For there is really only one possible answer to the problem posed by Dostoyevsky's *Grand Inquisitor:* if all mankind could realize eternal and complete happiness by torturing to death a single child, would this act be morally justified?

Somewhat subtler is the strategy by which The Authorities—by which term I mean not only the political leaders but also the scientists, intellectuals, trade unionists and businessmen who function on the top levels of our society—tried to ease the deep fears aroused in every one by The Bomb. From President Truman down, they emphasized that The Bomb has been produced in the normal, orderly course of scientific experiment, that it is thus simply the latest step in man's long struggle to control the forces of nature, in a word that it is Progress. But this is a knife that cuts both ways: the effect on me, at least, was to intensify some growing doubts about the "Scientific Progress" which had whelped this monstrosity. Last April, I noted that in our movies "the white coat of the scientist is as blood-chilling a sight as Dracula's black cape. . . . If the scientist's laboratory has acquired in Popular Culture a ghastly atmosphere, is this not perhaps one of those deep intuitions of the masses? From Frankenstein's laboratory to Maidanek [or, now, to Hanford and Oak Ridge] is not a long journey. Was there a popular suspicion, perhaps only half conscious, that the 19th century trust in science was mistaken . . . ?"

These questions seem more and more relevant. I doubt if we shall get satisfactory answers from the scientists (who, indeed, seem professionally incapable even of asking, let alone answering, them). The greatest of them all, who in 1905 constructed the equation which provided the theoretical basis for Atomic Fission, could think of nothing better to tell us after the bombings than: "No one in the world should have any fear or apprehension about atomic energy being a supernatural product. In developing atomic energy, science merely imitated the reaction of the sun's rays. ["Merely" is good!—DM] Atomic power is no more unnatural than when I sail my boat on Saranac Lake." Thus, Albert Einstein. As though it were not precisely the natural, the perfectly rational and scientifically demonstrable that is now chilling our blood! How human, intimate, friendly by comparison are ghosts, witches, spells, werewolves and poltergeists! Indeed, all of us except a few specialists know as much about witches as we do about atomsplitting; and all of us with no exceptions are even less able to defend ourselves against The Bomb than against witchcraft. No silver bullet, no crossed sticks will help us there. As though to demonstrate this, Einstein himself, when asked about the unknown radioactive poisons which were beginning to alarm even editorial writers, replied "emphatically": "I will not discuss that." Such emphasis is not reassuring.

Nor was President Truman reassuring when he pointed out: "This development, which was carried forward by the many thousand participants with the utmost energy and the very highest sense of national duty . . . probably represents the greatest achievement of the combined efforts of science, industry, labor and the military in all history." Nor Professor Smyth: "The weapon has been created not by the devilish inspiration of some warped genius but by the arduous labor of thousands of normal men and women working for the safety of their country." Again, the effort to "humanize" The Bomb by showing how it fits into our normal, everyday life also cuts the other way: it reveals how inhuman our normal life has become.

The pulp writers could imagine things like the atom bomb; in fact, life is becoming more and more like a Science Fiction story, and the arrival on earth of a few six-legged Martians with Death Rays would hardly make the front page. But the pulp writers' imaginations were limited; *their* atom-bombs were created by "devilish" and "warped" geniuses, not by "thousands of normal men and women"—including some of the most eminent scientists of our time, the labor movement (the Army "warmly" thanked the AFL and the CIO for achieving "what at times seemed impossible provision of adequate manpower"), various great corporations (du Pont, Eastman, Union Carbon & Carbide), and the president of Harvard University.

Only a handful, of course, knew what they were creating. None of the 125,000 construction and factory workers knew. Only three of the plane crew that dropped the first bomb knew what they were letting loose. It hardly needs to be stressed that there is something askew with a society in which vast numbers of citizens can be organized to create a horror like The Bomb without even knowing they are doing it. What real content, in such a case, can be assigned to notions like "democracy" and "government of, by and for the people?" The good Professor Smyth expresses the opinion that "the people of this country" should decide for themselves about the future development of The Bomb. To be sure, no vote was taken on the creation and employment of the weapon. However, says the Professor reassuringly, these questions "have been seriously considered by all concerned [i.e., by the handful of citizens who were permitted to know what was going on] and vigorously debated among the scientists, and the conclusions reached have been passed along to the highest authorities." Smyth continues:

> These questions are not technical questions; they are political and social questions, and the answers given to them may affect all mankind for generations. In thinking about them, the men on the project have been thinking as citizens of the United States vitally interested in the welfare of the human race. It has been their duty and that of the responsible high Government officials who were informed to look beyond the limits of the present war and its weapons to the ultimate implications of these discoveries. This was a heavy responsibility. In a free country like ours, such questions should be debated by the people and decisions must be made by the people through their representatives. It would be unkind to subject

the above to critical analysis beyond noting that every statement of what-is contradicts every statement of what-should-be.

Atomic Fission makes me sympathize, for the first time, with the old Greek notion of *hubris*, that lack of restraint in success which invited the punishment of the gods. Some scientist remarked the other day that it was fortunate that the only atom we as yet know how to split is that of uranium, a rare substance; for if we should learn how to split the atom of iron or some other common ore the chain reaction might flash through vast areas and the molten interior of the globe come flooding out to put an end to us and our Progress. It is *hubris* when President Truman declares: "The force from which the sun draws its powers has been loosed against those who brought war to the Far East." Or when the *Times* editorialist echoes: "The American answer to Japan's contemptuous rejection of the Allied surrender ultimatum of July 26 has now been delivered upon Japanese soil in the shape of a new weapon which unleashes against it the forces of the universe." Invoking the Forces of the Universe to back up the ultimatum of July 26 is rather like getting in God to tidy up the living room. It seems fitting that The Bomb was not developed by any of the totalitarian powers, where the political atmosphere might at first glance seem to be more suited to it, but by the two "democracies," the last major powers to continue to pay at least ideological respect to the human-itarian-democratic tradition. It also seems fitting that the heads of these govern-ments, by the time The Bomb exploded, were not Roosevelt and Churchill, figures of a certain historical and personal stature, but Attlee and Truman, both colorless mediocrities, Average Men elevated to their positions by the mechanics of the sys-tem. All this emphasizes that perfect automatism, that absolute lack of human con-sciousness or aims which our society is rapidly achieving. As an uranium "pile," once the elements have been brought together, inexorably runs through a series of "chain reactions" until the final explosion takes place, so the elements of our soci-ety act and react, regardless of ideologies or personalities, until The Bomb explodes over Hiroshima. The more commonplace the personalities and senseless the institutions, the more grandiose the destruction. It is *Götterdämmerung* with-out the gods.

The scientists themselves whose brain-work produced The Bomb appear not as creators but as raw material, to be hauled about and exploited like uranium ore. Thus, Dr. Otto Hahn, the German scientist who in 1939 first split the uranium atom and who did his best to present Hitler with an atom bomb, has been brought over to this country to pool his knowledge with our own atomic "team" (which includes several Jewish refugees who were kicked out of Germany by Hitler). Thus Professor Kaputza, Russia's leading experimenter with uranium, was decoyed from Cambridge University in the thirties back to his native land, and, once there, refused permission to return. Thus a recent report from Yugoslavia tells of some eminent native atom-splitter being high-jacked by the Red Army (just like a valu-able machine tool) and rushed by plane to Moscow.

Insofar as there is any moral responsibility assignable for The Bomb, it rests with those scientists who developed it and those political and military leaders who employed it. Since the rest of us Americans did not even know what was being done in our name—let alone have the slightest possibility of stopping it—The Bomb becomes the most dramatic illustration to date of that fallacy of collective responsibility which I analyzed in "The Responsibility of Peoples."

Yet how can even those immediately concerned be held responsible? A general's function is to win wars, a president's or prime minister's to defend the interests of the ruling class he represents, a scientist's to extend the frontiers of knowledge; how can any of them, then, draw the line at the atom bomb, or indeed anywhere, regardless of their "personal feelings?" The dilemma is absolute, when posed in these terms. The social order is an impersonal mechanism, the war is an impersonal process, and they grind along automatically; if some of the human parts rebel at their function, they will be replaced by more amenable ones; and their rebellion will mean that they are simply thrust aside, without changing anything. The Marxists say this must be so until there is a revolutionary change; but such a change never seemed farther away. What, then, can a man do *now?* How can he escape playing his part in the ghastly process?

Quite simply by not playing it. Many eminent scientists, for example, worked on The Bomb: Fermi of Italy, Bohr of Denmark, Chadwick of England, Oppenheimer, Urey and Compton of U.S.A. It is fair to expect such men, of great knowledge and intelligence, to be aware of the consequences of their actions. And they seem to have been so. Dr. Smyth observes: "Initially, many scientists could and did hope that some principle would emerge which would prove that atomic bombs were inherently impossible. The hope has faded gradually. . . ." Yet they all accepted the "assignment," and produced The Bomb. Why? Because they thought of themselves as specialists, technicians, and not as complete men. Specialists in the sense that the process of scientific discovery is considered to be morally neutral, so that the scientist may deplore the uses to which his discoveries are put by the generals and politicians but may not refuse to make them for that reason; and specialists also in that they reacted to the war as partisans of one side, whose function was the narrow one of defeating the Axis governments even if it meant sacrificing their broader responsibilities as human beings.

But, fortunately for the honor of science, a number of scientists refused to take part in the project. I have heard of several individual cases over here, and Sir James Chadwick has revealed "that some of his colleagues refused to work on the atomic bomb for fear they might be creating a planet-destroying monster." These scientists reacted as whole men, not as specialists or partisans. Today the tendency is to think of peoples as responsible and individuals as irresponsible. The reversal of both these conceptions is the first condition of escaping the present decline to barbarism. The more each individual thinks and behaves as a whole Man (hence responsibly) rather than as a specialized part of some nation or profession (hence irresponsibly), the better hope for the future. To insist on acting as a responsible individual in a society which reduces the individual to [insignificance] may be foolish, reckless, and ineffectual; or it may be wise, prudent and effective. But whichever it is, only thus is there a chance of changing our present tragic destiny. All honor then to the as yet anonymous British and American scientists—Men I would rather say—who were so wisely foolish as to refuse their cooperation on The Bomb! This is "resistance," this is "negativism," and in it lies our best hope.

politics
September 1945

WHEN
CRUELTY
BECOMES
PLEASURABLE

Norman Thomas

EN YEARS AGO not a corporal's guard of Americans would have defended mass obliteration bombing in war. It was forbidden by what passed for international law. To be sure, the British and French had used it occasionally as a cheap way of dealing with refractory natives. But when, on a larger scale, Mussolini bombed the poor huts of the Ethiopians we were horrified; and when his aviator son gave lyric praise to the beauty of burning villages, disgust was added to horror. Five years ago the Nazi bombing of London so stirred American sympathy for its courageous victims as to make the barbarity a great factor in bringing us into the war.

One year ago our radio newscasters scarcely bothered to keep rejoicing out of their voices as they boasted that the tonnage of fire bombs and blockbusters dropped by Allied airmen in one night over Germany was greater than the Germans had used in their blitzkrieg over England. Six months ago the more complete destruction of inflammable Japanese cities brought joy and hope for speedy victory. We had come a long way in ten years. Then, on August 6, came the new age of the atomic bomb—of which America is very temporarily the monopolist—that bomb which Felix Morley well called "an encroachment on the innermost mystery of the universe." Two bombs wiped out two cities: the latest estimates are that 70,000 men, women and children were killed; 120,000 injured—they are still dying of mysterious hurts; and 290,000 made homeless.

Exultation in our new found power and joy in the victory and peace we think it brought are tempered by fear of the future and a sense of guilt. But the latter emotion most of us are fairly successful in suppressing. Press and radio help us by fixing our attention on the horrors of prison camps rather than on the infinitely greater horrors of Hiroshima and Nagasaki. A Detroit newspaper, in a fair summary of a speech of mine, put "guilt" in quotation marks when it recorded my reference to the guilt of the atomic bomb. A woman insisted that I and others who spoke of American guilt were outrageously championing the Japanese people against our own. She asserted that the Japanese—all of them—were responsible for the torture of American prisoners of war. She completely reversed Jesus' emendation of the ancient law of an eye for an eye and a tooth for a tooth, so as to exact for each maltreated American prisoner the lives of countless children guilty only of being born in Japan.

By coincidence the same paper which reported my speech also carried a story of the fantastic lies which the Japanese Government had fed its people. Among these lies were circumstantial reports of the excellent treatment accorded British and American prisoners of war! How far, then, are the Japanese people to be held responsible for that which they did not know? It is not merely isolated individuals who use atrocity stories to quiet their consciences over the fate of Hiroshima and Nagasaki. To headline the former is apparently a policy of our Government and is certainly the policy of our press. Concerning the reiterated emphasis on tales of cruelty the *Washington Post* editorially observes: "When cruelty becomes common-place, it ceases to horrify; it even becomes pleasurable to contemplate."

Meanwhile, the emphasis on prison atrocities has accomplished its purpose. It has diverted popular attention from the dangerous stupidities of our peace policy and has silenced our sense of guilt. Although Japanese cruelties to prisoners were less terrible than Nazi destruction of whole peoples, American racial feeling makes us bitter toward the Japanese. Earlier that feeling had made us sanction the greatest single blow ever dealt our own civil liberties: the evacuation of American citizens of Japanese blood from their homes into concentration camps, without hearing or trial.

Our bombs killed not people but "yellow monkeys"; in language attributed to Admiral Halsey, "bestial apes" whom it was equally "a pleasure to burn or to drown." After the formal surrender our chivalrous warrior was quoted as announcing that he would "like to have kicked each Japanese delegate in the face." From audience reaction at newsreels I fear such sentiments are more popular than General MacArthur's words of justice and tolerance. More rational than justification of atomic bombing by Japanese atrocities is Winston Churchill's argument that it saved a million American and a quarter as many British lives. But that lacks the merit of assured truth. We know now that MacArthur transmitted Japanese surrender proposals to President Roosevelt upon which the latter never acted. We know that more official overtures were sent through Stalin. But in our "democracy" we don't know just what they were—it isn't always wise that we should be told for what we fight and die.

Apparently these Japanese overtures were in line with the Cairo Declaration. Were the differences between them and the terms essential to lasting peace so great that they could not have been removed, if there had been any spiritual imagination or vigor of negotiation to match our scientific boldness? Was it really necessary that more of our sons should have been slain and Stalin brought into the war at a price great enough to make him the probable master of Asia almost as much as of Europe? In the words of Admiral Nimitz, it was a "well-known fact" that the Japanese were interested in peace "long before" the atomic bomb was dropped and before Russia's entry into the war.

Even if winning the war required some supreme demonstration of overmastering might, would not a nation fit for such awful power have found a way to demonstrate it without the destruction of thousands upon thousands of human guinea pigs? And what can possibly excuse the second bomb over Nagasaki before the physical and political effects of the first had been learned? This destruction of Nagasaki was the greatest single atrocity of a very cruel war. No condemnation of war criminals or assessment of reparations will be just, in the eyes of God or history, which ignores that fact. In this statement we have behind us the authority of Dr. Samuel Allison, head of the Institute of Nuclear Studies of the University of Chicago, and 17 of his colleagues in developing the bomb whose use over Japanese cities they pronounced "a great tragedy" which might have been avoided.

The dead are dead, and all our tears will not bring them back. But the future may yet be spared the destruction which new war, inevitably waged with these Satanic weapons, will bring upon us. The other day Chancellor Hutchins of the University of Chicago declared that atomic energy requires for its control a world state for which we had not thought us ready but which we must now accept in principle. I share his sentiments, but am compelled to add that there are few signs that the need for a world authority is making us ready for it. Fear of new and deadly weapons has never conquered war nor given men wisdom for new social institutions. It might be possible to achieve a world authority so cursed by hates, jealousies and injustices that war would not be conquered so much as made civil rather than foreign. But such civil war would also be waged with atomic explosives.

A world federation—less than a world state—which can cope with the atomic bomb must rest on a realization of human brotherhood of which post-war passions and lack of generosity and justice give little sign. America, temporarily mistress of power that has no parallel, might lead the way to that brotherhood. But only if our national conscience will do a thing unprecedented in human history: bring humility to conquerors and a willingness to practice that virtue of repentance which we so stridently demand of our enemies. It is only a brotherhood of the humble and contrite in heart, who seek reconciliation in mutual forgiveness, that can be trusted to employ atomic energy.

Human Events
September 26, 1945

THE
RETURN TO
NOTHINGNESS

Felix Morley

ACCORDING TO JAPANESE REPORTS, accepted in Washington as probable truth, some 30,000 human beings were blasted into eternity by the first atomic bomb, exploded over the city of Hiroshima on August 6. Of the 160,000 who were injured by this act of annihilation, directed at a community of a quarter of a million persons, additional thousands are said to have died in subsequent agony from the delayed cremation of the neutron rays. The same report on after-effects comes from Nagasaki, where on August 9 the second atomic bomb caused a somewhat smaller number of casualties. If December 7, 1941, is "a day that will live in infamy," what will impartial history say of August 6, 1945?

At Pearl Harbor the target was an isolated naval base; the material destruction was virtually limited to warships and military installations; the relatively small loss of life was for the most part confined to men who had voluntarily enlisted in the armed services. At Hiroshima the target was the heart of a teeming city. The great majority of those obliterated were civilians, including thousands of children trapped in the thirty-three schools that were destroyed. It was pure accident if a single person slain at Hiroshima had any personal responsibility for the Pearl Harbor outrage. These victims, like ourselves, were merely the helpless instruments of the ruthless Moloch of Totalitarian Government.

Pearl Harbor was an indefensible and infamous act of aggression. But Hiroshima was an equally infamous act of atrocious revenge. Because perpetuated by a nation that calls itself Christian, on a people with less lofty spiritual pretensions, eventual judgment may call our action ethically the more shameful, morally the more degrading, of the two. Unless we find some way of expiation, future missionaries to Japan will have difficulties in rationalizing the atomic bomb. Undoubtedly Hiroshima shortened the war. The atomic bomb may well have saved more lives than it has destroyed to date. But to say that is to excuse rather than to explain.

The price we have paid for victory is terribly high. And perhaps the cost of this last installment, at Hiroshima, is even heavier for us than for the Japanese. For its measurement is the loss of ideals which, far more than our moral strength, have made America great and distinctive in the long human story. The measurement of our loss may be seen, for instance, in the miserable farce put on by those who tried to reconcile mass murder of "enemy children" with lip service to the doctrine that God created all men in his image. We tend to forget, also, that under our system of government each of us must carry individual responsibility for the decisions of our rulers, civilian or military. The brilliant scientists who designed, the intrepid flyers who released, the atomic bomb are actually less responsible than the rest of us for its effects. They were our servants, paid by us to do what we wanted done.

The German people, we have decreed, have corporate responsibility for the acts of their National Socialist state. So, at Nazi concentration camps, we have paraded horrified German civilians before the piled bodies of tortured Nazi victims. We have drafted German women to bury these pitiful dead. We have forced German prisoners in this country to witness pictures of these abominable deeds. It would be equally salutary to send groups of representative Americans to blasted Hiroshima. There, as at Buchenwald, are many unburied dead. There are many towards whose bereavement we can scarcely feel vindictive. There is a spiritual desolation for which we cannot dodge responsibility. We can be proud that so many Americans would individually be glad to assume all risks in this stricken area—if our Government would permit exercise of the quality of mercy in which our people heretofore have never been deficient.

Atonement is not the least of the considerations raised by the atomic bomb. There is a weapon different in kind as well as in degree from all its predecessors in the long list of lethal instruments. It bears as little relationship to the now commonplace "blockbuster" as the latter has to the stone axe of Neanderthal man. Both the manner and the extent of this new release of uncontrollable energy are encroachments on the innermost mystery of the universe. Instinctively we know that such trespassing invites proportionate penalties.

The fear that has gripped men's hearts, since the blasting of Hiroshima, is not primarily due to anticipation that our cities will eventually meet the same fate, logical though such outcome would be. Our fear is much more akin to that which still accompanies the sense of personal and collective sin. Expectation of retribution is only a part of the fear which springs from consciousness of sin. The sense of shame and degradation is only a part of this fear. Most important in this unease is the loss of individual dignity and spiritual peace—the consciousness of being hopelessly adrift; of having lost contact with those standards by which men really live.

Long before our age of science there were men who foresaw its coming and who sought in advance of the necessity which now confronts us to lead human intelligence to the service of principle rather than that of passion. One such prophet was Thomas Aquinas, who in the thirteenth century worked out that universal Christian synthesis which the atomic bomb destroys. Few today will deny surpassing insight to that passage in the *Summa Theologica* where St. Thomas wrote, almost 700 years ago, "in all created things there is a stable element, even if this be only primary matter, and something belonging to movement, if under movement we include operation. New things need governing as to both, because even that which is stable, since it is created from nothing, would return to nothingness were it not sustained by a Governing Hand."

Great effort has been made to picture the atomic bomb as an eminently laudable achievement of American inventiveness, ingenuity and scientific skill. On the day of the destruction of Hiroshima the floodgates of official publicity were swung wide. Rivers of racy material prepared in our various agencies of Public Enlightenment poured out to the press and radio commentators whose well-

understood duty it is to "condition" public opinion. Puddles of ink confusedly outlined the techniques whereby we have successfully broken the Laws of God.

Never has any totalitarian propaganda effort fallen more flat. Instead of the
anticipated wave of nationalistic enthusiasm, the general reaction was one of
unconcealed horror. Even the immediate Japanese surrender, even the joy of
"going places" on unrationed gas, even the universal sense of relief over the ending of the war, has not concealed an apprehension which reflection does less than
nothing to diminish. Many who cannot voice their thoughts are nonetheless
conscious of the withdrawal of the Governing Hand, are well aware that at the
crossroads we have chosen the turning which leads back to Nothingness.

In London, last week, Parliament ratified the Charter of the United Nations.
Consideration was as perfunctory as that given the subject by our Senate. Emphasized was the futility of this elaborate mechanism in the light of announcement
that two major Allies intend to withhold the secret of the atomic bomb from the
third most powerful partner. So a country dedicated by its founders to individual
enlightenment now controls a secret which makes the individual look as does the
insect in respect to D.D.T. Quite naturally our new scale of values loses its moral
grandeur and shifts to insect values—"full employment" or "security" within the
meticulously organized anthill of the expanding State. We have won the war. Now
what is our purpose for the Power we control?

Human Events
August 29, 1945

OUR
RELATIONS
TO JAPAN

Reinhold Niebuhr

I T WAS INEVITABLE that the final surrender of Japan, ending the costliest war
of human history, should be greeted with a delirium of joy all over the world,
and in America particularly. It was the Japanese attack upon us which brought us
into the war; and for many portions of our population Japan was a more natural
enemy than Germany. Yet among the more sober and thoughtful sections of our
nation the victory over Japan leaves a strange disquiet and lack of satisfaction.

There are many reasons for this. The most obvious one is that the victory was
secured, or at least hastened, by the use of the atomic bomb. There is naturally a
very great apprehension about the introduction of this frightful instrument into the
science of warfare, and an uneasiness of conscience about its immediate use in this
war, in order to hasten its end. But the use of this bomb was only the climax of the
use of methods of warfare, including obliteration and incendiary bombing, which
exceeded anything we used against Germany. The difference was not by design,
but was caused by the fact that certain types of incendiary bombs were perfected
too late to be used against Germany, but not too late for Japan. Yet one is left
uneasy by the difference—because we used more terrible instruments against the
Japanese than they used against us—which would not have been the case in regard
to Germany.

But we must go even further in analyzing the sense of disquiet in our relation
to this fallen enemy. We not only used the most terrible weapons to encompass the
defeat but we also proceeded against Japan with political warfare, which had gained
its momentum from our conflict with Germany but which had little justification in
our relations to Japan. We demanded unconditional surrender. The slogan of
"unconditional surrender," falsely transferred from the realm of purely military
relations to that of political relations, was unwise enough in our approach to
Germany, and undoubtedly helped to arm our foe with the strength of a final
desperation. But in our dealings with Germany we could at least quiet our uneasiness about the use of this slogan by the thought that Germany was in the clutches
of a tyranny which had a slogan of its own, which matched our slogan. It was: "All
or nothing." The Nazis were determined to leave the nations in ruins, if they
should fail to gain victory. They probably had the power in any case to hold a

defeated and destroyed nation in the struggle until its cities were completely reduced to rubble; and the tyranny had operated with such efficiency that there was no possibility of establishing an alternate German government. We would have had to take over in Germany in any case, and try to rebuild the nation from the ground up.

The situation was different in Japan. Japanese militarists were probably as fanatic as the German Nazis. But many Americans have maintained (and subsequent events have proved their analysis to be correct) that Japan had various resources of sanity which Germany did not have. The imperial house could become a rallying point against the militarists. Furthermore, there were industrialists and capitalists in Japan who would have been called "liberal" in another day. We do not vouch for their perfect virtue; but they were quite obviously opposed to the adventures of the military crowd from the beginning, and they most certainly contributed something to the political situation which made final capitulation possible. No doubt they were prompted primarily by motives of survival as a class. Despite the fact that there are no completely pure motives in politics (and possibly not in life), American liberalism recently allowed itself an orgy of the most nauseous self-righteousness; for liberal journals were almost unanimous in warning against any possible peace which might emanate from Japanese capitalists. This type of liberalism would rather annihilate a foe completely than enlist the aid of any elements in an enemy country which are not absolutely "pure." The policy is usually accompanied by the foolish hope that if we can completely destroy we will also be able to build a more ideal social structure out of these complete ruins. There is no vainer hope in human history; and it is prompted by a peculiarly dangerous type of "liberalism" in which the imperial power impulse has become strangely mixed with moral idealism. We will destroy nations in order to make "democracies" out of them.

As it happened, Japan did finally sue for peace and proved thereby that it did have resources, which Germany lacked. It made only one condition. It desired to retain the imperial house. The motive behind this request was quite obviously that Japan wanted to avoid complete social chaos; for the imperial house is, of course, the apex of a whole hereditary and organic social structure, the destruction of which would mean decades of chaos and foreign intervention in its affairs. The governments of the world wisely decided to amend their "unconditional surrender" policy to allow for the condition. But not so all our liberal journalists and commentators. Almost with open voice they advised the government against this offer. Even Raymond Swing seemed certain that the Emperor must go. Americans United, an organization which includes almost all internationalist organizations of the nation, committed the absurdity of asking the President not only to reject the Japanese offer, but to hale the Emperor before a war criminals court. Mayor LaGuardia solemnly advised the Japanese people to murder the emperor and thus insure peace.

We can hardly be proud of the sentiments expressed by Americans in general, and by "liberals" in particular, in the fateful days during which the surrender was negotiated. The wine of success is a very heady wine. No nation has ever embarked upon the hazardous business of ruling the world, in company with two partners, with a more blithe ignorance of the meaning of customs and continuities, of sentiments and unique loyalties among the people to be "ruled" than we. We have arrived at an ignorant idealism according to which the world is divided into two classes: American democrats and all the other "lesser breed without the law" who do not share our democratic creed and must therefore be fascists. If a man, such as Undersecretary Grew, with his long experience in Japan, expresses the conviction that the Emperor ought not to be deposed of, there are liberal journalists who request his removal by the President on the ground that he is an appeaser of fascists. Thus the passions of war have introduced poison into the sentiments of liberalism; and the pride of a powerful nation has blinded the eyes of large elements in our populations, whose clear sight is necessary, if America power is to be used responsibly.

Instead of glorifying in the fact that now the Japanese Emperor will take orders "from an American General," a popular theme upon the radio in recent weeks, we might more profitably make a sober analysis of our assets and liabilities in the task which confronts us as we seek to govern an Asiatic people. If we make that analysis honestly we will have to admit that our racial pride contributed to the tension which finally resulted in war with Japan; and that there are great perils that the incidents of the occupation of Japan will increase the racial animosity between the East and the West.

We must admit moreover that if Japan had not been quite so stupid and fanatic in its militaristic ventures, it might well have become the spear point of an Asiatic revolt against the white man's dominance. It may be a good thing for the peace of the world that Japan was not creative enough to be the leader of such a venture. But this still does not prove that it is a good thing for the white man to seek to govern an Asiatic people from the ground up. We must destroy the war-making powers of Japan. Will we also have the wisdom to make our total occupation of the islands as brief as possible and be content with more remote and less obvious control of the life of an alien people? The pride of victors is always a great hazard to justice. When it is mixed with ethnic and color pride it may produce an intolerable arrogance.

All this does not mean that our cause against either Germany or Japan was not "just." We were indeed the executors of God's judgment yesterday. But we might remember the prophetic warnings to the nations of old, that nations which become proud because they were divine instruments must in turn stand under the divine judgment and be destroyed. The virtues of men have only a short-range efficacy. We may be virtuous in this context; and just in that relationship; and the instruments of divine judgment in performing such and such a peculiar responsibility. But this does not guarantee our virtue tomorrow. The same power which encompassed the defeat of tyranny may become the foundation of a new injustice. If ever a nation needed to be reminded of the perils of vainglory, we are that nation in the pride of our power and our victory. The Pauline warning fits us exactly: "Be not therefore high-minded, but fear."

Christianity & Crisis
September 17, 1945

NOTHING

BUT

NIHILISM

James Martin Gillis

FOR DAYS AND WEEKS AFTER THE DROPPING of the first atomic bomb on Japan, there was a landslide of comment, scientific, pseudo-scientific and fantastic, opinions, explanations, rejoicings, and even of thanksgiving to God. Somewhere in the enormous mass of matter dislodged, as it were, by the bomb, there may have been a moral judgment, apart from the Pope's. If so, I confess I did not find it though I searched diligently. What I hoped to discover was an expression of the conviction in my own mind that we, the people of the United States of America and perhaps with us the people of Britain, have struck the most powerful blow ever delivered against Christian civilization and the moral law. I would call it a crime were it not that the word "crime" implies sin and sin requires consciousness of guilt. Even more deplorable than the act itself is the fact that those who prepared the bombing, those who carried it out, and the whole nation—or two nations—which welcomed the news of it, seem to have had neither doubt nor scruple about its morality. It is pathetic and tragic to the last degree that whole peoples whose civilization is called Christian, that is to say whose beliefs and traditions, moral and religious, are presumably founded on the Gospel, had to all appearances no doubt that what was done was permissible and laudable.

It has been quite obvious since August 6th, *dies magna et amara valde*, a great and bitter day, that few if any commentators have wished to stand in the path of the landslide of approbation. I have no desire to be a martyr, sacrificed to public opinion; I do not delude myself with the fancy that my opinion is of even infinitesimal importance. But simply to relieve the pressure upon my conscience, I here and now declare that I think the use of the atomic bomb, in the circumstances, was atrocious and abominable; and that civilized peoples should reprobate and anathematize the horrible deed. It may turn out that in this opinion I shall be all alone: I write too early to know. I may also be wholly mistaken. But let this opinion be recorded: the action taken by the United States Government was in defiance of every sentiment and every conviction upon which civilization is based.

Some time ago in this magazine (May 1944, and August, 1944) we carried a discussion of the morality of indiscriminate or "saturation" bombing, the kind that is done for the primary purpose of destroying civilian morale without regard to what is known to the theologians as *Moderamen inculpatae tutelae*. It would require a dissertation to explain that principle adequately, but it may be expressed with sufficient accuracy in two sentences. First: it is morally permissible to bomb objects of military importance, railroads, bridges, munitions dumps, factories producing instruments of war, even if in doing so, one unintentionally kills innocent persons. Second: it is not morally permissible to bomb innocent people directly and purposely.

Readers of that discussion may remember that it centered about a pamphlet—say rather a brochure of some size—by Vera Brittain, *Massacre by Bombing*, published here in March 1944 (first printed in England in 1940 under the title *Seed of Chaos*). Also it may be recalled that my own opinion, formed many years ago from the study of Catholic moral theology, was—at least so I think—supported by both contestants in a learned debate in *The Clergy Review* (London, December 1940, and February 1941).

Suffice it now to say, without repeating the argument, that I see no reason to make a distinction in favor of an atomic bomb over any other kind of bomb. Rather the contrary. The more destructive the instrument the more grievous the crime. Nor will it do to say that the population of Hiroshima was warned by bulletins dropped from planes in advance. It is absurd to think—and as a matter of fact no honest person would say he thinks—that 350,000 people can vacate a city. And when a bomb, as we have seen in the diagrams, destroys all life within a circumference of 200 miles or more, it would be adding insult to injury to say that the inhabitants of that city should have got out of the way. Let us not combine cruelty with hypocrisy, and attempt to justify wholesale slaughter with a lie.

Japan complained that the bombing was a violation of international law, and in particular of Article 22 of the Hague Convention. One American apologist retorted—as if it made any difference—that Japan had not signed the Hague Convention! We signed it, and that suffices.

Furthermore, the point in question is not the Hague Convention, but the universal and everlasting moral law. And here we come upon the essential evil. The American people have for some years past been indoctrinated with the heresy that there is no such thing as a universal, everlasting moral law. Professors of ethics (whose ideas slowly seep down into the popular mind) say there is no Absolute, that is to say, no God; and that if there were, we have no means of knowing His mind, or even if He is a person and has a mind; that there is no such thing as Natural Law; that laws are temporary and arbitrary, made up, so to speak, as we go along; that the law which served our ancestors may be obsolete in our days; that morals are only *mores*, customs which come and go; that in consequence an action held immoral (as for example President Roosevelt and Prime Minster Churchill held obliteration bombing immoral in 1939), may become moral by 1945; and vice versa; that it is irrelevant therefore to quote ourselves of yesterday as a guide or a norm to ourselves of today; that to be specific, the atomic bomb might have been considered an immoral instrument before it was invented, but that once invented and used, it becomes ethically good; that it would be diabolical if used by our enemy before we had discovered it, but that it is something for which to thank God, as Mr. Churchill did, if we discover it and employ it first. Evidently this is ethical anarchy. But it is the ethics of the ordinary man in the street and of them usual professor in the university. If that kind of "ethics" prevails, our Christian civilization will dissolve in a gas like the bodies of the 100,000 or 300,000 victims of the first atomic bombing. Nothing remains but nihilism.

A professor of physics at the Sorbonne in Paris is said to have predicted the atomic bomb fifteen or twenty years ago, but to have warned the nations not to use it. Its destructive action, he said, might not stop but continue in every direction and to any distance. Cities, he declared, might crumble and dissolve into a gas. Of that professor's view I am, of course, no judge. I know little of physics and less of chemistry. But I can see in his dire warning a symbol and a metaphor. It may be that the annihilating force of the bomb released over Hiroshima will be repeated over all Japan, and in the next war over all the earth. Likewise the annihilating force not of a bomb but of an ethical theory may be released in every country and over the entire globe. The results in both cases will be similar. It will be horrible if we annihilate a civilization.

No discussion of this question however incomplete can neglect the argument that the atomic bombs were used to bring about a quicker surrender of the Japs and thereby in the end to save lives. The plea is specious but unethical. The end does not justify the means. It is not permissible to do evil that good may come. If obliteration bombing is evil—and such alone is the question—it cannot be made good by the supposition or even the certainty that it will in the long run be more merciful than a surely legitimate way of making war.

I have said above—or rather have supposed—that the use of the atomic bomb was approved by the people at large. It is gratifying to know, however, that they did not accept the news with jubilation. On August 9th, three days after the news broke, Phelps Adams in the New York *Sun* said:

> For forty-eight hours now, the new bomb had been virtually the only topic of conversation and discussion in Washington. For two days, it has been an unusual thing to see a smile among the throngs that crowd the streets. The entire city is pervaded by a kind of sense of oppression and among many persons there is a sense of fear that forces some to admit—a little shamefacedly—that they would be happier if this $2,000,000,000 gamble had failed and if the knowledge humanity had just gained in the laboratory could somehow be bundled up in a sack and lost in the river like an unwanted kitten.

Perhaps, after all, the people are wiser than their leaders. The professor and the philosophers forbid them to believe that the moral law is universal and everlasting. But that "sense of oppression" and that "shamefacedness" are an indication that the law of God is written in the fleshly tablets of the heart of man. May it never be erased.

Catholic World
September 1945

WHAT
HATH MAN
WROUGHT!

David Lawrence

MAN HAS AT LAST brought forth a weapon that reduces war to an absurdity. Man has discovered that a means of destroying whole nations is available out of the minerals of the earth and that no people can hope to remain secure against the atomic bombs of another people no matter how distant one country may be from the other. A single airplane riding high in the stratosphere, unobserved and undetected because of its great speed propelled by this new energy, can appear suddenly over London or Washington or Detroit or Pittsburgh or any city in a peaceful area and destroy human lives by the hundreds of thousands in just a few seconds. No longer are armies and navies or even air forces by themselves an adequate defense.

Peoples throughout the world feel an unprecedented urge to find ways and means of avoiding war. We have been brought face to face with stark reality—that wars cannot hereafter be tolerated and that peoples never again allow one-man governments to exploit them and drive them into war. Greater than the atomic bomb itself is the challenge to man to rise above this new means of world suicide and to implant throughout the human race an understanding of the futility of combat and the need for removal of the basic causes of international friction. God did not provide this new weapon of terror. Man made it himself with the God-given brains and skill of the scientist. Previously other weapons like the submarine and the airplane had been introduced. We were permitted to defy the laws of gravity and fly through the air and we were permitted to move men and supplies under water. But man turned those inventions into methods of carrying on warfare more intensive and more terrible than ever.

A few decades ago man did not think it fair or sportsmanlike to attack non-combatants. War was reserved for armies and navies. Civilians behind the line were immune. At the beginning of World War II we were horrified to see the German air forces murdering civilians in Warsaw and later at Rotterdam. Then came reprisals. The single action of a German maniac—who by skillful propaganda appealing to those in economic distress had seized possession of the minds and energies of a whole people and had directed them along the paths of revenge and brutality—caused other nations to follow suit and bomb cities.

We—the great, idealistic, humane democracies on the so-called civilized side—began bombing men, women and children in Germany. Last week we reached the climax—we destroyed hundreds of thousands of civilians in Japanese cities with the new atomic bomb. Perhaps these many thousands of Japanese men, women and children who were blown to bits by the atomic bombs may not have died in vain. Perhaps somewhere on this earth a scientific experiment of the magnitude we have just witnessed had to be invoked to impress everybody with the indescribable horror of man's latest achievement. Yet we had already been winning the war against Japan. Our highest officials have known for some time that Russia was planning to enter the war in the Far East as soon after V-E Day as she could deploy her troops and supplies over the long stretches of the Trans-Siberian Railroad.

The surrender of Japan has been for weeks inevitable. It has come now as anticipated. We can rejoice that hostilities are to cease at last. But we shall not soon purge ourselves of the feeling of guilt which prevails among us. Military necessity will be our constant cry in answer to criticism, but it will never erase from our minds the simple truth that we, of all civilized nations, though hesitating to use poison gas, did not hesitate to employ the most destructive weapon of all times indiscriminately against men, women and children. What a precedent for the future we have furnished to other nations even less concerned than we with scruples or ideals! Our guilt is also the guilt of all mankind which failed to find a way to prevent war. The dispatchers say Germany was working feverishly along the same scientific road and that Hitler would not have hesitated to use such a weapon against Britain. But Hitler has been killed and Germany has been beaten. Could an announcement of the test of the atomic bomb made in New Mexico recently have been used as a dramatic means of persuading the Japanese militarists to release their people and surrender?

Surely we cannot be proud of what we have done. If we state our inner thoughts honestly, we are ashamed of it. We can justify the bombing as a means of saving precious American lives and shortening the war. Yet we cannot suppress the wish that, since we lately had been warning the people of Japan against air attack on certain cities, we might have warned them against staying in the specific area where we first wished to demonstrate the destruction that could ensue from the continued use of the atomic bomb.

All the world knows that the secrets of the atomic bomb cannot long be withheld from the scientists of nations large and small. The tiniest nation with a laboratory and certain raw materials will have a weapon that can be used to destroy its neighbors. All nations thus will in time become equal in potential strength. The weak will stand alongside the strong demanding new respect and new consideration. The Charter of the United Nations furnishes now an even more timely means of collaboration by all nations, large and small. New responsibility has been imposed on the larger nations which at the moment can so readily manufacture atomic bombs. But we shall miss the entire significance of the new discoveries if we do not apply a spiritual interpretation. It is man and not God who must assume responsibility for this devilish weapon. Perhaps He is reminding all of us that man-made weapons can, if their use is unrestrained, destroy civilization, and that man still has the chance to choose between the destructive and constructive use of the findings of science.

What will man say to this? Will he foolishly toy with the new weapon, build huge factories and husband supplies of atomic energy against potential enemies?

Or will man see that at last there must be the greatest surrender that has been known from the beginning of time—a surrender to reason and the processes of tolerance and forbearance, a surrender to unselfishness and self-restraint, a surrender to conscience and the will of God as the only way to survive in this world? Will man see at last how he has been exploited by the seekers of so-called glory, the power-mad militarists and domineering egotists who get possession of the reins of government, sometimes by constitutional and sometimes by unconstitutional means, while craven, submissive persons sit by and follow a course of what they deem to be individual safety?

The challenge of the atomic bomb, therefore, is plain. Since individual security can vanish in an instant, peoples everywhere must organize their national life so that no ruler anywhere, by using specious pretexts, by suppressing or intimidating the press or the radio, can seize military control of a government. Peoples must be alert to maintain peace. Peoples must exercise the power that belongs inherently to them and must reason with each other through free governments and God-controlled statesmen.

The adjudication of all disputes and controversies must hereafter be submitted to tribunals and courts of justice. Man must see that only in the philosophy of Moses and Jesus, Mohammed and Confucius, who have sought in their time to teach billions of persons a universal goodness can there be an elevation of man from the nadir of his brutality to the lofty heights that so long have been the goal of a righteous civilization. The world of tomorrow must be a world of law and morals. Centuries of exhortation have in vain sought the same result. The world has intermittently listened. Now the world must listen incessantly or be destroyed. There must be peace on earth and good will between factions inside nations as well as between nations themselves. Conflicts between religious sects and races must end so that our spiritual energies can be concentrated on a common purpose—the achievement of a real brotherhood of man. For at last it has been demonstrated to all of us that only by following His guidance in our daily conduct as individuals and as nations can we hope to fulfill our true mission as the children of God on earth. It is the only road left now—the road of mutual forbearance. It is the way to survival and human happiness.

U.S. News & World Report
August 17, 1945

Gentlemen:

You Are Mad!

Lewis Mumford

We IN AMERICA ARE LIVING AMONG MADMEN. Madmen govern our affairs in the name of order and security. The chief madmen claim the titles of general, admiral, senator, scientist, administrator, Secretary of State, even President. And the fatal symptom of their madness is this: they have been carrying through a series of acts which will lead eventually to the destruction of mankind, under the solemn conviction that they are normal responsible people, living sane lives, and working for reasonable ends.

Soberly, day after day, the madmen continue to go through the undeviating motions of madness: motions so stereotyped, so commonplace, that they seem the normal motions of normal men, not the mass compulsions of people bent on total death. Without a public mandate of any kind, the madmen have taken it upon themselves to lead us by gradual stages to that final act of madness which will corrupt the face of the earth and blot out the nations of men, possibly put an end to all life on the planet itself.

These madmen have a comet by the tail, but they think to prove their sanity by treating it as if it were a child's skyrocket. They play with it; they experiment with it; they dream of swifter and brighter comets. Their teachers have handed them down no rules for controlling comets; so they take only the usual precautions of children permitted to set off firecrackers. Without asking for anyone's permission, they have decided to play a little further with this cosmic force, merely to see what will happen at sea in a war that must never come.

Why do we let the madmen go on with their game without raising our voices? Why do we keep our glassy calm in the face of this danger" There is a reason: we are madmen too. We view the madness of our leaders as if it expressed a traditional wisdom and a common sense: we view them placidly, as a doped policeman might view with a blank tolerant leer the robbery of a bank or the barehanded killing of a child or the setting of an infernal machine in a railroad station. Our failure to act is the measure of our madness. We look at the madmen and pass by.

Truly, those are infernal machines that our elected and appointed madmen are setting. When the machines go off, the cities will explode, one after another, like a string of firecrackers, burning and blasting every vestige of life to a crisp. We know that the madmen are still making these machines, and we do not even ask them for what reason, still less do we bring their work to a halt. So we, too, are madmen: madmen living among madmen: unmoved by the horror that moves swiftly toward us. We are thinking only of the next hour, the next day, the next week, and that is further proof that we are mad, for if we go on in this fashion, tomorrow will be more heavy with death than a mortuary.

Why has this madness seized us: Do not ask now; it is here. Have we then no sanity left that will give us strength to cry out against the madmen and contend with them: Have we not the power to stifle the infernal machines they have created and to baffle their preparations for the casual suicide of the human race? Has no one raised a hand to halt the madmen? Yes: here and there, in the gutters, on the rooftops, pushed through a grating, or slipped under a door by a silent hand, are the scrawls of a message, a frantic series of messages, addressed to all of us. These messages have been written by the greatest of the madmen, the men who invented the super-infernal machine itself; the men who, in the final throes of their dementia, were shocked back into sanity.

The shocked ones, the awakened ones, are the only people who show a normal awareness of danger, and the proof of this fact is that their frantic signals are dismissed as madness. The louder they shout to us, the more inaudible their voices become. The moment they awakened to the cosmic evil they had brought about, the awakened ones were bound over to silence by the watchful agents of the uniformed madmen. So they send us their messages in scattered fragments, or they whisper it to private ears in passing, since their keepers will not permit them to speak aloud in such a fashion that every man, woman, and child would understand their story and set for self-preservation.

The ruling madmen do not dare to let us read the whole message of the imprisoned ones, lest we be suddenly jolted into sanity. The President, the generals, the admirals, the administrators are afraid that their own madness might become more evident if the scattered words the awakened ones send us were to be put together and read as a single sentence. For the President, the generals, the admirals, and the administrators have lied to us about their infernal machine; they have lied by their statements and even more they have lied by their silences. They lie because it is no longer an infernal machine, but hundreds of infernal machines presently no longer hundreds but thousands these unrestrained madmen will soon have enough power to disembowel, with a push-button command, all the living spaces of mankind. Day by day the stockpiles of chaos grow larger.

The power that the madmen hold is power of an order that the sane alone know that they are not sane enough to use. But the madmen do not want us to know that this power is too absolute, too godlike, to be placed in any human hands: for the madmen dandle the infernal machine jauntily in their laps and their hands eagerly tremble to push the button. They smile at us, these madmen: they pose for fresh photographs, still smiling: they say, being madmen, "We are as optimistic as ever," and their insane grin is prophetic of the catastrophe that awaits us.

Lying to us about the secret that is no secret, the madmen also lie to themselves, to give their lie the further appearance of truth, and their madness the outward garb of sanity. Not knowing any other use for their machine but destruction, they multiply our capacities for destruction. Their every act is an act of madness; even now, in the middle of the Pacific Ocean, they plan a further madness, with a monkey-like curiosity to discover a new secret that is no secret. One mad act has led to second mad act, the second to a third; and the end will be a morbid compulsion to achieve the last irretrievable act of world madness–in the interests of security, peace, and truth.

The madmen act as if nothing were happening, as if nothing were going to happen: they are taking the madman's usual precautions with the madman's usual confidence. But the awakened ones, those who are still the madmen's prisoners, know better than this. The pleading words they have guardedly sent us have been lying around for months, and only our paralyzed bodies and our dead minds have kept us from picking the fragments up and piecing them together. Let us read their plain message: It is the only warning we will ever have.

Here is the message of the awakened ones:

"The madmen are planning the end of the world. What they call continued progress in atomic warfare means universal extermination, and what they call national security is organized suicide. There is only one duty for the moment: every other task is a dream and a mockery. Stop the atomic bomb. Stop making the bomb. Abandon the bomb completely. Dismantle every existing bomb. Cancel every plan for the bomb's use; for these clever plans are based on stark madness. Either dethrone the madmen immediately or raise such a shout of protest as will shock them into sanity. We have seen the infernal machine in action, and we hold that this action is not for man to invoke.

"We know there is no quick way out of this madness, for the cooperation of mankind cannot be purchased cheaply by terror; but the first step, the only effective preliminary step, it to put an end to the atomic bomb. You cannot talk like sane men around a peace table while the atomic bomb itself is ticking beneath it. Do not treat the atomic bomb as a weapon of offense; do not treat it as a weapon of retaliation; do not treat it as an instrument of the police. Treat the bomb for what it actually is: the visible insanity of a civilization that has ceased to worship life and obey the laws of life. Say that as men we are too proud to will the rest of mankind's destruction even if that madness could for a few meaningless extra moments save ourselves. Say that we are too wise to imagine that our life would have value or purpose, security or continuity, in a world blasted by terror or paralyzed by the threat of terror." So reads the message of the awakened ones.

While the whole world writhes in a spasm of madness, let us in America be mad with a method, mad with a purpose. Let us say No to the atomic bomb rather than say No to life itself. Let us awaken the sleeping sanity of the peoples of the world by calling them together and showing them our guilty hands, our hands already stained with a madman's blood, still clenched in a madman's purpose, and then let us say these plain words:

"We have awakened. We are men once more. You have nothing to fear from us. We will dismantle our atomic bombs and allow you to put a guard over our stockpiles: America's sanity today shall be the world's sanity tomorrow. Whoever seeks to be sure as to our good intentions, let him come into our country, go where he pleases and examine the most secret laboratories and factories. We have nothing to hide, except that which only madmen would continue to hide. With this act of faith, we have awakened from the nightmare of the infernal machine and our sleepwalking progress toward annihilation. Wake up! men and brothers on every continent. Let us all cease thinking that the cosmic power we hold is only a child's skyrocket. The atomic bomb is not for any of us to use—ever. Let us put it aside, as if it were unconceived and inconceivable. For we have nothing to fear from each other but our normal madness: the madness of those who would calmly bring the world to an end simply by dotting their i's and crossing their t's as they have always done. On any other terms but this common faith in our common cause, mankind is doomed."

Meanwhile, the clockwork in the infernal machine ticks and the final day draws near. The time has come for action: the compulsive automatic motions of the madmen must be sternly halted. Let the awakened ones be ungagged, and let one of them be placed at the elbow of every man holding high public office, as the priest was once at the elbow of the king, to whisper the words "Humanity" and "One World" in the leader's ear, when he slips into the dead language of tribal isolation. The secret that is no secret must be laid open; the security that is no security must be yielded up; the power that is annihilation must give way to the power that is birth.

The first move toward sanity lies with us. Abandon the Atomic Bomb! Give it up! Stop it now! That is the only order of the day. When we have performed this duty the next step will be visible, and the next duty will add a new safeguard against the smooth automation of the madmen. But we must be quick to overcome our own madness. Already the clockwork is ticking faster, and the end—unless we act with the awakened ones—is closer than anyone yet dares to think.

The Saturday Review of Literature
March 2, 1946

JOHN HERSEY
AND THE
AMERICAN
CONSCIENCE

Michael J. Yavenditti

O F ALL THE ACCOUNTS OF THE ATOMIC BOMBINGS, probably none has been more widely read and appreciated by Americans than John Hersey's *Hiroshima*.[1] Hersey's little book has provided a generation of students with their most moving—and often their only—representation of an atomic bombing from the point of view of those who survived it. If *Hiroshima* has enduring appeal, its precise impact on readers from 1946 to the present is difficult to gauge. We should guard, moreover, against the assumption that Hersey's account is "merely" a timeless literary classic. To understand its popularity and significance, the work should be examined in the context of the time in which it first appeared.

In 1945, Americans generally applauded the use of two atomic bombs on Japanese cities. According to the Gallup poll of August 16, 1945, 85 percent of those Americans surveyed approved the atomic bombings while only 10 percent disapproved and 5 percent had no opinion.[2] Although the *Fortune* survey of November 30, 1945, undertaken by Elmo Roper, superficially suggested more doubts, it nevertheless demonstrated that fully 76.2 percent of those surveyed either approved the atomic bombings without reservations or actually desired that more atomic bombs had been dropped on Japan.[3]

Some articulate Americans bitterly censured the atomic bombings. Most spokesmen for Roman Catholicism condemned the bombings because those responsible had ignored the distinction between combatants and non-combatants. Thirty-four eminent Protestant clergymen signed a petition to President Harry S. Truman denouncing the atomic "atrocity" and comparing it to the Japanese bombardment of defenseless civilian populations. One woman, echoing a frequently expressed complaint, suggested that the United States should have followed "the way the Lord conducted things at Sodom and Gomorrah" and given "ample notice to the civilians of Hiroshima."[4]

Yet most Americans praised the bomb for ending a bloody war. For Americans with bitter memories of such events as the Pearl Harbor attack and the Bataan Death March, Hiroshima and Nagasaki were appropriate vengeance for Japan's alleged deceptions and atrocities. Americans who had earlier condoned the destruction of enemy cities by conventional bombs and incendiaries saw the atomic bomb as a more efficient form of obliteration bombing. An understandable pride in the extraordinary cooperative achievement of American science, industry, and government also helped minimize objections to the atomic bombings.[5]

In the post-war period, Americans not only approved the atomic bombings, they also became increasingly apathetic about the controversy regarding the bomb's use. No single event created this apathy, but several mutually reinforcing developments, which dulled American sensitivities, diminished interest in the debate. One such development involved fear of the potentially dangerous after-effects of radiation. Japanese sources charged that the atomic bomb had contaminated the earth of Hiroshima with radioactivity, killing 30,000 to 60,000 Japanese in the two weeks after the bombing. Yet General Leslie R. Groves, wartime director of the Manhattan Project, convincingly refuted this claim.[6] Dr. Stafford L. Warren, who headed a team of American medical investigators in Japan, stated that less than eight percent of all Japanese fatalities from the bomb came from gamma radiation.[7] For those Americans who still had misgivings about radiation poisoning, Groves told them that doctors had assured him "it is a very pleasant way to die." Hampered by censorship restrictions, the mass media made little effort to challenge these statements or to arouse American sympathy over the radiation effects of the bomb.

To be sure, Americans were not universally apathetic about atomic energy and its potentially harmful as well as beneficial implications for their future. Many atomic scientists, the National Committee on Atomic Information (NCAI), the United World Federalists, and such journalists as Norman Cousins and Raymond Gram Swing alerted the American public to the horrors of atomic warfare and to the urgent need for international control of atomic energy. Furthermore, some evidence, notably that contained in reports of the United States Strategic Bombing Survey (USSBS), had emerged which questioned the military necessity of using the atomic bomb to defeat Japan.[8] Although few Americans read the USSBS reports (which, in any case, offered as much support to the defenders as to the critics of the atomic bombings), limited discussion of them in the mass media kept alive the waning controversy over the bomb's use.[9]

Nevertheless, one year after the atomic bombings of Hiroshima and Nagasaki, Americans had learned too little about the bomb to become aroused over its use against Japan. Since the United States still enjoyed a monopoly on the weapon, Americans had no immediate fear of atomic attack.

Even though popular wartime images of the Japanese were softening slowly, the lessening hostility produced little American soul-searching about the atomic bombings. On the contrary, in early and mid-1946 much of the writing about the bombed cities stressed several interrelated themes, none of which gave Americans cause to regret the bomb's use. First, Hiroshima and Nagasaki were universalized and rendered less disturbing to the American conscience by the alleged response of their survivors; citizens of the two cities eventually reacted just as victims of other wartime and natural calamities—by returning to their devastated cities and beginning the task of reconstruction.[10] At the same time, journalists increasingly portrayed Hiroshima and Nagasaki as symbols of the birth of a new Japan dedicated to rehabilitation, peace, progress and reconciliation. The American press depicted Hiroshima, in particular, as a microcosm of the Japanese nation which was progressing steadily under wise American tutelage and developing a pacifist outlook which would curb Japan's warlike tendencies in the future.[11]

Then, on August 31, 1946, the *New Yorker* devoted its entire issue to an account of the first atomic bombing that was written by a young but well-known journalist, John Hersey. Entitled simply "Hiroshima", the article was an immediate sensation. Newsstand copies quickly disappeared, and within a few days, original issues became collector's items.[12] An enthusiastic reader exclaimed that "no one is talking about anything else but the Hersey article for the last two days, either in trains, restaurants, or at home. . . ."[13] Praising it as "one of the great classics of the war," a *New Republic* editor declared that, "if it is eligible for a Pulitzer Prize and doesn't get it, the judges should go take a Rorschock [*sic*]."[14]

Although initially published in a magazine of limited circulation, "Hiroshima" quickly acquired a wider audience. *New Yorker* readers urged that it be reprinted "by the millions."[15] Scientists' organizations, the NCAI, the Army, and the Atomic Energy Commission clamored for thousands of copies, which these groups intended to distribute in order to impress Americans with the power of the new weapon.[16] Hersey and the *New Yorker* permitted newspapers to reprint it on two conditions: that all profits go to the Red Cross and that the article must not be abridged.[17] The entire text of the article was read in four special half-hour broadcasts, with all commercials cancelled, over the American Broadcasting Company and many of its affiliates from September 9 through September 12.[18] The article quickly reached international audiences through similar broadcasts or through pirated printed editions.[19] Published as a book in 1946, it became a best-seller and a Book-of-the-Month Club selection.[20]

The author of this remarkable article was born in China and educated at Yale University. Hersey had worked for *Time-Life* publications in the late 1930s, and then, after Pearl Harbor, had turned his attention to wartime reporting. Before the appearance of "Hiroshima" Hersey had written many articles for national magazines and three books with wartime settings.[21] He later declared:

> Looking back, I find that in most of my story telling, in both journalism and fiction, I have been obsessed, as any serious writer in violent times could not help being, by one overriding question, the existential question: What is it that, by a narrow margin, keeps us going, in the face of our crimes, our follies, our passions, our sorrow, our panics, our hideous drives to kill?[22]

What has interested Hersey is man's staying power, his "refusals to be destroyed by devilments devised by the foul side of the human mind."[23]

In writing "Hiroshima," however, Hersey was guided more by his concern for human interest than by an explicit philosophy of human nature. "Hiroshima" was popular, not because Hersey advanced theories about the will to survive, but because he did what no one had accomplished before: he recreated the entire experience of atomic bombing from the victims' point of view. The contrast between the apparently objective simplicity of his prose and the enormity of the phenomenon he describes makes "Hiroshima" all the more graphic and frightening for most readers.

Father John A. Siemes, a Jesuit priest in Hiroshima, had published an eyewitness account of the atomic bombing prior to the appearance of "Hiroshima."[24] But the Siemes article did not enjoy wide circulation, nor did it satisfy the longing of some informed Americans that the bombing should be rendered less abstract, static and impersonal. Despite the many post-bombing pictures and discussions of Hiroshima and Nagasaki, three scientists wrote:

> . . . the full horror of the destruction has not yet been shown in pictures or described in words. It is hard to portray the effects that heat and gamma rays . . . had on people. The fires that raged unchecked for days after the explosions were not photographed from the ground. The pictures of steel-frame buildings that still stand and appear to be only slightly harmed do not show the wrecked partitions and furniture or the remains of the people who were inside. Finally, it is hard to visualize the paralysis of nearly all fire-fighting and medical services. Many injured persons died in fires because there were no first-aid facilities left to help them.[25]

While Hersey did wish to make the experience of atomic bombing less abstract, he was not writing as a propagandist, polemicist, or spokesman for groups interested in atomic energy.[26] The article grew out of a trip Hersey made to China and Japan in October and November 1945 for *Life* and the *New Yorker*. Before he departed, he discussed with William Shawn, co-managing editor of the *New Yorker*, the possibility of an article on Hiroshima.[27] Although the *New Yorker* traditionally specialized in light, urbane articles, it had also carried many war stories, and its sponsorship of "Hiroshima" was not unusual.

As Hersey researched his story in Japan, he also searched for a method of presentation which would capture the human element. He re-read Thornton Wilder's *Bridge of San Luis Rey*, in which Wilder examined the significance of an event in terms of the past experience of several characters. Wilder's approach apparently reinforced Hersey's inclination to use this literary technique, which Hersey had employed previously in *Into the Valley* and *Men On Bataan*.

For technical details concerning the bomb's damage, he drew upon his own observations, those of Japanese and American scientists, preliminary USSBS data, and especially upon interviews with Japanese who experienced the blast. After interrogating approximately forty people, Hersey settled upon six individuals— five Japanese and one German Catholic priest—around whose experiences he constructed the article. Although the ordeal of these informants may have been representative of the Hiroshima survivors, the individuals in a sense were not. Several of them enjoyed greater status, higher income, or more education, than the average Hiroshima resident. Hersey chose these six largely because he could bridge the language barrier more easily with them than he could with many other survivors whom he interviewed.

In writing the article, Hersey deliberately—though indirectly—expressed his own feelings about the bomb by emphasizing the specific terrors of the characters he described. Instead of moralizing or preaching, he intended "to help readers to find their own deepest feelings about this new instrument of killing, rather than to require that they accept [mine]."[28] When Hersey first learned of the atomic bomb from a radio address by President Truman, he had a sense of despair—but less a feeling of guilt or compassion for the victims than a fear for the future of the world. Hersey felt at the same time greatly relieved, convinced that the bomb would end the war against fascism and militarism. Subsequently, as reports by other journalists about the damage appeared in the press, he experienced a growing sense of discomfort. When he arrived in Hiroshima he found that researching the story "was a kind of horror." [29] Hersey came to question the wisdom of dropping the bomb, but he remained unconvinced that a trial demonstration of it on an uninhabited island would have persuaded the Japanese to surrender.

Like most Americans in 1945, Hersey regarded the Japanese as a tenacious, even fanatical, enemy, and undoubtedly his own observations on Guadalcanal and elsewhere in the Pacific reinforced rather than weakened this impression.[30] Yet Hersey's wartime articles and books did not betray the irrational, racist, anti-Japanese feelings that characterized the writing of some American reporters. His objectivity was particularly remarkable because he had been exposed during his youth in China to the strong anti-Japanese prejudices of the Chinese. At the time he heard President Truman's announcement of the bomb, his views on Japanese wartime tenacity made him feel that the weapon might at least help to cut short the killing. The human devastation caused by explosive and incendiary raids on other Japanese (and German) cities seemed to him just as morally reprehensible as the killing done by the atomic bomb; to Hersey "what had been added was a terrifying factor of efficiency." [31] His first-hand observations in Japan gave him a sense of revulsion toward the weapon, a compassion for its victims, and a deliberately understated admiration for the survivors as fellow human beings.

After what Hersey recalls as a "close editing" of the manuscript by *New Yorker* editors, it was ready for publication.[32] He did not submit his material to the U.S. government for censorship clearance. He originally intended to write only one short article but, as the manuscript lengthened, he prepared four articles to run in successive issues. Concerned about maintaining reader interest over four issues, coeditor William Shawn suggested putting the entire manuscript in one issue. On August 31, 1946, this was done—for the first time in *New Yorker* experience. The decision to devote the entire issue to "Hiroshima" came too late to change the tranquil picnic-scene cover, but some advertisements which seemed grotesque or shocking juxtaposed with the article, were removed.[33]

The result was a minor literary bombshell. Entirely a factual account, "Hiroshima" described individuals with whom readers could identify. For perhaps the first time since Pearl Harbor, thousands of Americans confronted Japanese who were ordinary human beings and who manifested few of the stereotyped Japanese warrior traits of fanaticism and sadism. Moreover, Hersey allowed Americans to visualize the actual experience of the Japanese in Hiroshima—the initial surprise of the inhabitants, the terrible fire storm, the devastation of medical services, and the frightened, bleeding, confused survivors. The article also touched the sympathies of readers because Hiroshima, previously spared by American bombers, had been totally undamaged by conventional bombing. The appearance of several airplanes on the morning of August 6 alarmed few military personnel or civilians, who thought the planes were part of normal reconnaissance flights which regularly flew over the city. Many, therefore, did not seek shelter. Consequently, the atomic attack demonstrated the savage power of the new weapon in an almost laboratory-type experiment on human beings and seemingly confirmed a prior rumor among Hiroshima residents "that the Americans were saving something special for the city." [34]

Hersey wrote a story of suffering and tragedy which did not become maudlin. A few vivid images contrasted strikingly with his generally lean prose, indelibly fixing them in the minds of his readers. For example, Father Wilhelm Kleinsorge unexpectedly encountered a score of soldiers in Asano Park: "their faces were wholly burned, their eyesockets were hollow, the fluid from their melted eyes had run down their cheeks. . . . Their mouths were mere swollen, pus-covered wounds, which they could not bear to stretch enough to admit the spout of the teapot."[35] When the Reverend Mr. Kiyoshi Tanimoto attempted to lift an injured woman into a boat, "her skin slipped off in huge, glove-like pieces."[36] Hersey counterpoised a few graphic scenes like these with examples of heroism and endurance. The overall effect compelled readers to believe, with more assurance than some survivors felt, that the victims were human beings.

If debunkers seemed to minimize the power of the bomb, Hersey provided a powerful antidote.[37] The bomb used at Hiroshima, he observed, was a relatively "primitive" weapon, and scientists "knew that theoretically one ten times as powerful—or twenty—could be developed."[38] More vividly than all previous publications combined, "Hiroshima" suggested for Americans what a surprise atomic attack could do to an American city and its inhabitants. Although Hersey quoted the official estimate of 78,500 killed, he believed this was a conservative calculation, and he placed the death toll at 100,000. Indirectly, he refuted the claim that flimsy Japanese construction caused most of the destruction, for he noted that Japanese building regulations, since the 1923 earthquake, set much higher construction standards than normal American building codes. He made available to readers new findings that estimated Japanese fatalities from radiation at twenty percent of the total; and, perhaps more importantly, he graphically depicted death and suffering from radiation poisoning. Survivors of the blast and fire, including those with no visible wounds, often showed the symptoms of radiation sickness in the days and weeks after the bombing: nausea, headache, diarrhea, faintness, loss of strength, low white-blood-cell counts, anemia, hemorrhaging, fever, and loss of hair. While many recovered from radioactive poisoning, others died from it and attendant complications.

That the six survivors "were among the luckiest in Hiroshima" made the bombing even more terrible.[39] Hersey reported that most Japanese did not hate the Americans and that the survivors felt a strong sense of community spirit after the bombing. But he concluded by raising the ethical question of the bomb's use, leaving it unresolved and challenging readers to examine their own thoughts.

Americans were fascinated by Hersey's article. Some readers complained that "Hiroshima" was inconsistent with typical *New Yorker* fare, and they criticized the magazine for devoting an entire issue to the story. Most readers approved it enthusiastically, however. A study of a random sample of 339 letters, telegrams, and postcards to the *New Yorker* dated within two weeks of the article's appearance revealed that readers approved the story's publication by a ten to one margin.[40] Correspondents frequently agreed with one reader who declared: "God bless and keep the editors who showed such courage and cared so much for humanity and civilization."[41] Hersey's effort to characterize the bombing in human terms was, for many readers, an unqualified success. A university student wrote that, before reading "Hiroshima," "I had never thought of the people in the bombed cities as individuals."[42] According to others, the most pertinent implication of the article was its eloquent testimony to the need for effective international control of the bomb and for eliminating the conditions that breed war.[43]

By the very horror which it described, "Hiroshima" revived the moral question of whether the United States should have used the bomb. Some observers thought that the vast popularity of the story testified, in part, to the guilty consciences of many Americans.[44] Eleven percent of the *New Yorker* correspondents mentioned the shame or responsibility they felt for making this deed possible.[45] In some instances, this shame was merely expressed as a "vague feeling of being uncomfortably ill-at-ease." [46] For others the impact evidently provoked a drastic change in their earlier attitudes toward dropping the bomb. One young scientist, previously quite proud of his role in the Manhattan Project, reported he "wept as I read" the article and was "filled with shame to recall the whoopee spirit" with which he and others greeted the news of the Hiroshima bombing in 1945.[47] Another reader, who in 1945 approved dropping the bomb, wrote after reading the article: "I am bitterly humiliated that my country should have been the one to first (or at all) invoke this method of warfare." [48]

Most of these people who stated or implied that "Hiroshima" changed their thinking about America's use of the bomb did not offer specific alternatives to the destruction of Hiroshima and Nagasaki. Responding rather spontaneously and evidently still emotionally keyed-up by the story, they usually wrote only in general terms of their shame and horror.

Still other readers, who had previously deplored the use or manner of using the bomb, employed "Hiroshima" to reinforce and restate their earlier protests. A conscientious objector, who had spent twenty-eight months in prison because he opposed war, argued that Hersey's story "completely vindicates the stand of conscientious objectors in the United States." [49] Hersey's discussion of radioactivity inspired Norman Cousins, editor of *Saturday Review*, to an impassioned indictment of the atomic attacks. He asked rhetorically:

> Do we know that many thousands of human beings in Japan will die of cancer during the next few years because of radioactivity released by the bomb? Do we know that the atomic bomb is in reality a death ray, and that the damage by blast and fire may be secondary to the damage caused by the radiological assault upon human tissue? [50]

According to columnist Milton Mayer, who had bitterly censured both the atomic bombings and the scientists who had worked on the Manhattan Project, "Hiroshima" was more than the greatest reporting of our time: it was prophetic." [51] *The Messenger*, published by the Evangelical and Reformed Church, regarded the story as a graphic reminder of America's inexcusable atrocity.[52]

A few writers, who had been critical of the atomic bombings before the *New Yorker* article appeared, complained because Hersey had failed to condemn the bomb's use decisively enough. Dwight Macdonald, editor of *Politics*, and Mary McCarthy, a prominent writer, denounced the apparent moral objectivity which many readers praised. Macdonald "found it so dull that I stopped reading it half-way through." Criticizing the "moral deficiency" of its literary naturalism. Macdonald charged that the Hiroshima victims "might just as well be white mice, for all the pity, horror or indignation the reader—or at least this reader—is made to feel for them.[53] Mary McCarthy agreed with Macdonald that Hersey's non-polemical stance and his emphasis on the survivors' recovery and the continuity of life rendered the bomb safe and familiar. She insisted that "Hiroshima" minimized "the atom bomb by treating it as though it belonged to the familiar order of catastrophes—fire, flood, earthquake—which we have always had with us and which offer to the journalist . . . an unparalleled wealth of human interest stories, examples of the marvelous, and true-life narratives of incredible escapes."[54]

Confronted with the implied challenge posed by "Hiroshima," many Americans remained unshaken in their previous approval of the atomic bombings. Even readers who warmly admired the story and sympathized with the victims still insisted that the bombing was justified. Hersey only told us what we have long known, insisted a *New York Times* editorial—that war is terrible and that the atomic bomb heightens its terror by concentrating its destruction in time and space.[55] Many "Hiroshima" readers invoked the familiar arguments that despite its horror the bomb ended the war, making an invasion unnecessary; that the Japanese had committed many wartime atrocities; and that, in any case, the United States was fortunate to develop and use the bomb before the enemy did.[56]

What alarmed a few readers was the suspicion that Hersey, the *New Yorker,* and other unnamed sources deliberately sought to make Americans feel guilty about the atomic bombings. "The atomic bomb is nothing more or less than a super-powered explosive capable of lethal side effects," declared one irate reader, who went on to suggest that "propaganda" like "Hiroshima" was designed to confuse the American public. A university professor reported that "Hiroshima" made his friends lament America's past use of the bomb and oppose its future use. He wrote: "You and Hersey have, I fear, brought a large segment of high minded Americans to the mourners' bench where they are practically groveling in a welter of conviction of sin." The professor feared that "this Hersey-Atbomb [*sic*] stuff" might provoke the kind of disarmament movement which, he said, crippled America's defenses before the war.[57]

Hersey had not intended to write an exposé. But by inviting a sympathetic, vicarious identification with the atomic bomb victims, his article did inspire self-questioning and indignation. "Hiroshima" prompted some Americans to rethink their previous approval of the atomic bombings, while it intensified the anger of those who had initially condemned the bomb's use.

Yet in retrospect one of the most striking features of the American reception of "Hiroshima" is how little, rather than how much, protest it inspired against the atomic bombings. Hersey's study did not precipitate a wave of petitions to President Truman censuring the decision to drop the bomb. To express their sorrow and apprehension over the atomic bombings, some Americans engaged in ceremonial acts of contrition: they made monetary donations to relieve the suffering of survivors and held commemorations to mark the anniversary of the first atomic attack.[58] A "Hiroshima" reader suggested that the *New Yorker* inform readers how they could make contributions "to offset some of their guilt feelings over the whole miserable business."[59] A special commission of the Federal Council of the Churches of Christ in America valued efforts on behalf of the stricken cities and their survivors as at least "a token" of American repentance and as a wholesome gesture toward reconciliation.[60]

These symbolic acts of penitence and good will, however, were very sporadic during the immediate post-war period, and few can be tied directly to the publication of "Hiroshima." Early expressions of contrition never assumed the proportions of campaigns in the 1950s and 1960s when the bomb-scarred "Hiroshima Maidens" came to the United States for medical treatment and when American and foreign peace groups attempted to exploit the reputed guilt feelings of former Major Claude R. Eatherly, pilot of the weather plane over Hiroshima.[61]

Furthermore, soon after the appearance of Hersey's work, two accounts justifying the decision to build and use the atomic bomb appeared in prominent American magazines. Although not intended as rebuttals to Hersey, they did enter into the general public controversy which his article helped revive. Karl T. Compton published his article, "If the Atomic Bomb Had Not Been Used," in the December 1946 issue of the *Atlantic Monthly*. Compton provided little new information, but his study carried the stamp of authority; Compton was familiar with the development of the Manhattan Project, and, like Hersey, he drew upon his own observations and interviews in Japan. Claiming the bomb shortened the war by providing a face-saving excuse for Japan's leaders to surrender, Compton vigorously insisted that a costly invasion of the Japanese homeland was the alternative to the atomic bombings.[62] The Compton article, publicly applauded by President Truman,[63] was followed in February 1947 by former Secretary of War Henry L. Stimson's essay, "The Decision to Use the Atomic Bomb," published in *Harper's*.

This article, possibly written at Truman's request, was designed to reassure Americans who debated the wisdom and necessity of using the bomb.[64] Evidently suspicious of segments of the American intelligentsia, Stimson also hoped to shape the way future generations of Americans regarded the first atomic bombing. He explained to Truman:

> The criticisms which it [the article] has been intended to answer as far as possible were made mainly by Chicago scientists, some of whom had been connected with the development of the [atomic bomb] project. The article has also been intended to satisfy the doubts of that rather difficult class of the community which will have charge of the education of the next generation, namely educators and historians.[65]

Stimson stressed how carefully American decision-makers proceeded before they decided to drop the bomb. For the first time Americans learned concretely, though briefly, about the advisory role that certain high ranking scientists played in this decision. Stimson conveyed the impression that decision-makers reluctantly agreed to the surprise use of the bomb on urban targets only after rejecting alternative possibilities: an advance warning, a demonstration on an unpopulated area, or the exploration of Japanese peace feelers. Perhaps Stimson's most convincing argument was attributing to American decision-makers *before* the bomb was used an awareness of its likely psychological impact on Japanese leaders. Various government and military spokesmen, as well as the USSBS had underlined the face-saving value of the bomb. Now Stimson stated clearly that American decision-makers had anticipated precisely the course of events which transpired. "The bomb thus served *exactly the purpose we intended*," he wrote. "The peace party was able to take the path of surrender, and the whole weight of the Emperor's prestige was exerted in favor of peace."[66]

If troubled Americans or defenders of the atomic bombings still possessed doubts, in early 1947 they received comfort from an unexpected source. Metro-Goldwyn-Mayer studios prepared its full length feature film, "The Beginning or The End," in cooperation with the Federation of American Scientists, the War

Department, and the White House.[67] Perhaps because the film required government approval, it presented the decision to use the bomb in a manner favorable to American political leaders. In any case, the White House and the War Department approved the final script.[68]

Although the movie claimed to be "basically a true story," it was so only in the most general sense. It combined an essentially authentic survey of the Manhattan Project with two insipid, fictional love stories. More importantly, it exploited melodrama and distorted history to justify the bomb's use. The reservations that some Manhattan Project scientists had about the development and use of the bomb were not treated as seriously as the success of the Manhattan Project itself. In dealing with the actual decision to drop the bomb, the movie emphasized the great care with which the President proceeded by showing the actor playing President Truman suffering sleepless nights and holding numerous conferences on the subject with his advisors. Finally, the Truman character implied that leaflets would be dropped which would warn of an atomic attack and urge the Japanese to evacuate; this false implication was repeated later on the flight to Hiroshima when one crew member remarked: "We've been dropping warning leaflets on them for ten days now. That's ten days more warning than they gave us before Pearl Harbor."[69]

The Compton and Stimson articles, as well as "The Beginning or The End," should not be viewed as one-dimensional counterattacks on Hersey which were designed deliberately and exclusively to offset whatever guilt "Hiroshima" might have generated. Although they could have this effect, their importance is more subtle. The articles and movie are significant less for refuting Hersey than for reflecting what Americans wanted to believe about the Manhattan Project: that those who guided and worked on it were humane, resourceful, and responsible; and that American leaders had used the bomb only after a brief but appropriate period of doubt and secret debate. Americans could, with no apparent inconsistency, appreciate Hersey's work without also engaging in a collective *mea culpa* or demanding scientific and governmental scapegoats to salve their own consciences. The bomb apparently *had* ended the war, and in the absence of persuasive evidence to the contrary, few Americans were disposed to reverse their initial approval.

The remarkable response to "Hiroshima," therefore, should be understood in the context of the controversy over Hiroshima and Nagasaki in mid-1946. "Hiroshima" appeared when apathy over the atomic bombings and even the bomb itself was intensifying and spreading. American sensibilities had been dulled not only by the reports of Groves, but also by the way the mass media had portrayed the static remains of the atomic-bombed cities. The numerous post-bombing photographs and newsreels of Hiroshima and Nagasaki made them look like any other war-devastated city. Americans could comprehend that one bomb had caused the damage, but the media did not fully demonstrate that Hiroshima and Nagasaki were qualitatively different from other kinds of wartime catastrophes. Dwight Macdonald and Mary McCarthy thought that Hersey also failed to make the distinction, but Hersey's readers often did see the difference.[70]

Hersey restored for a time the awe and anxiety that Americans felt when they first learned of the new weapon. But he did more. By building his story around six survivors whose experiences he sketched compassionately in vivid detail, Hersey encouraged readers to empathize with the Japanese victims rather than to view them with detachment, indifference, or hatred.

Of equal importance, "Hiroshima" transferred the experience of atomic attack from the traditional categories of war horrors to a more unique level. The article seemingly persuaded many readers that atomic bombing was qualitatively different from other kinds of bombings. Raids on population centers with conventional bombs and incendiaries could wreak terrible havoc, but inhabitants ordinarily had some advance warning and could seek shelter. In addition to the element of surprise, the atomic bomb seemed to transform the nature of air warfare by investing enormous potential destruction in a few aircraft. Because the devastation was disproportionate to the size of the weapon and the few planes needed for delivery, atomic bombing acquired a different character from the familiar, massive air raids of World War II. Finally, "Hiroshima" suggested that atomic bombing protracted the agony and uncertainty of its victims by introducing a new phenomenon in warfare, radiation sickness. Hersey implied that radioactivity, temporarily at least, affected the reproductive processes, and he demonstrated three terrible aspects of radioactive poisoning: it destroyed organic life rather than material objects; it could later strike unexpectedly the survivors of the initial blast and fire; and, contrary to General Grove's assertion, it definitely was not "a very pleasant way to die."

"Hiroshima" undoubtedly was, as Lawrence Wittner suggests, "the real source of long-term guilt reactions" for some Americans concerning the atomic bomb. Wittner adds: "It is surely one of the curiosities of twentieth-century American life that this recurrent theme of America's collective guilt, so deeply moving and compelling for some, in fact touched so few." [71] This is particularly true for the immediate post-war period, for the guilt produced by the bomb and especially by "Hiroshima" can easily be exaggerated. Hersey's work aroused many readers but incited few of them. It enabled American readers to reaffirm their humane sentiments and to examine their consciences, but "Hiroshima" did not require Americans to question the legitimacy of the bomb's use. Hersey did not write a call to action or a polemic against American decision-makers. Had he done so, his appeal might well have been reduced.[72] Hersey struck precisely the right note by inviting readers to view the bomb victims as objectively and sympathetically as he had. Since his principal informants were all civilians, Hersey, probably unintentionally, encouraged Americans to sharpen the distinction between ordinary "decent" Japanese citizens on the one hand and Japan's supposedly ruthless and fanatical rulers and soldiers on the other. Making this distinction was an important step if some Americans were to suffer "long-term guilt reactions."

The failure of "Hiroshima" in the post-war period to arouse many Americans to public protest came not from alleged weaknesses of the story but from the endurance of popular wartime attitudes and the temporary monopoly on the atomic bomb which the United States enjoyed. Any major reversal of public opinion regarding the atomic attacks required a more drastic change in attitudes toward the Japanese than even "Hiroshima" could achieve in 1946 and 1947. The war, moreover, conditioned Americans to condone virtually any weapon or method of warfare employed by the United States that might end the conflict quickly. Changes in attitudes toward the bomb's use, therefore, had to grow in part from the realization that criteria other than military necessity might have equal or greater validity in the conduct of war. Furthermore, Americans would have to share the ominous dread that they might, at any moment, experience the fate of Hiroshima and Nagasaki, a dread which could only occur when a potential enemy actually possessed nuclear weapons. Finally, a thorough reevaluation of the morality and wisdom of the bomb's use required more information than Hersey could supply. Americans needed additional knowledge concerning the military situation in the Pacific in August 1945, the circumstances that culminated in the decision to drop the bomb, and the efforts before August 6 by some scientists and officials to prevent the surprise use of the bomb on urban areas. "Hiroshima" did not analyze these and other specific diplomatic, political, and military considerations. Nor did Hersey speculate on the implications for the United States if a rival power acquired atomic bombs.

Yet if the American conscience grew more rather than less troubled in later years over the atomic attacks on Japan, Hersey was as responsible as any other person. Subsequent writers confronted directly the necessity of the bomb's use on Japan and analyzed the meaning of Hiroshima as the prelude to a spiraling nuclear arms race. But Hersey laid the groundwork for later assessments by posing the issue of atomic bombing from the standpoint of the human victims. By raising certain moral questions, rather than resolving them, Hersey heightened American sensitivities and contributed to a continuing dialogue over the justification for atomic warfare.

NOTES

1. John Hersey, *Hiroshima* (New York, 1946). Subsequent citations are from the Bantam Book edition, 1959.

2. American Institute of Public Opinions (AIPO) poll, Aug. 26, 1945. *Public Opinion Quarterly*, (Fall 1945), 385.

3. "Fortune Survey: Use of Atomic Bomb," *Fortune*, Dec. 1945, p. 305. See also *Fortune* poll, Nov. 30, 1945, *Public Opinion Quarterly*, (Fall 1945), 530. More specifically, the *Fortune* poll discovered that 53.5 percent endorsed the atomic bombings without qualifications; 22.7 percent advocated "using many more of them before Japan had a chance to surrender"; 13.8 percent favored a demonstration of the bomb on an "unpopulated region," followed by its use on a Japanese city if Japan still refused to surrender; and 4.5 percent opposed using the bomb under any circumstances.

4. *New York Times*, Aug. 20, 1945; "News of the Christian World: Clergymen Urge Truman to Bar Atomic Bomb," *Christian Century*, Sept. 12, 1945, p. 1040; Mrs. J. L. Weisman to Editor, *Minneapolis Star-Journal*, Sept. 3, 1945; see also *New York Herald Tribune*, Sept. 17, 1945; "A Woman to Editor," ibid., Aug. 14, 1945; David Lawrence, "What Hath Man Wrought!" *U.S. News*, Aug. 17, 1945, p. 39; Ernest L. Meyer, in *Progressive*, Oct. 15, 1945.

5. Michael John Yavenditti, "American Reactions to the Use of Atomic Bombs on Japan, 1945–1947" (Ph.D. dissertation, University of California, Berkeley, 1970) pp. 211–285.

6. The War Department brought thirty-one reporters to Alamogordo, New Mexico, where they walked over the site of the first atomic explosion. Groves and his aides informed the reporters that surface radiation at Alamogordo was nearly eliminated and pointed out that at Hiroshima and Nagasaki the bombs exploded far above ground, reducing to practically zero the amount of residual radio-activity. See Leslie Nakashima, in *New York Times*, Aug. 31, 1945; "The Winning Punch," *Newsweek*, Sept. 3, 1945, p. 22; *New York Times*, Aug. 23 and 25, 1945; William L. Laurence, in ibid., Sept. 12, 1945; "Atomic Footprint," *Time*, Sept. 17, 1945, p. 68; "New Mexico's Atomic Bomb Crater," *Life*, Sept. 24, 1945, pp. 27–31; William L. Laurence, *Dawn Over Zero* (New York, 1945), pp. 244–245.

7. Senate Special Committee on Atomic Energy, "Hearings: Atomic Energy Act of 1945," 79 Cong., 1 and 2 sess. (1945–1946), pp. 508–513. By early 1946, however, American officials were gradually revising upward the estimated casualties from gamma radiation. *New York Times*, March 12, 1946; "Bomb's Aftereffects," *Time*, Feb. 4, 1946, p. 66; "Death by Gamma Ray," ibid., March 24, 1946, p. 77.

8. United States Strategic Bombing Survey, *Japan's Struggle to End the War* (Washington, 1946), *passim;* United States Strategic Bombing Survey, *Summary Report (Pacific War)* (Washington, D.C., 1946) p. 26, *passim.*

9. See especially Raymond G. Swing, MS radio broadcasts for the American Broadcasting Company, April 5 and 26, May 17, June 7 and 12, 1946, Swing Papers.

10. Lindesay Parrott, in *New York Times*, Feb. 26, 1946; *Stars and Stripes* (Pacific Edition), April 17, 1946.

11. Lindesay Parrott, in *New York Times*, Aug. 7, 1946; "A Time to Dance," *Time*, Aug. 19, 1946, p. 86; "Progress Report," ibid., April 22, 1946, p. 18; "How U.S. Runs Defeated Japan: Emphasis on National Reform," *U.S. News*, Jan. 25, 1946, pp. 24–25; Harry Paxton Howard, in *Progressive*, June 17, 1946.

12. A second-hand copy brought eighteen dollars at one auction. *New Yorker* to John W. Haigh, Sept. 13, 1946, *Hiroshima* Papers, in possession of John Hersey, New Haven, Connecticut; Mike Goldgar to *New Yorker*, Sept. 10, 1946, ibid.

13. Marjorie S. Coleman to *New Yorker*, Aug. 30, 1946, ibid.

14. Bruce Bliven, *Hiroshima*, review of *Hiroshima*, by John Hersey, *New Republic*, Sept. 9, 1946, p. 300.

15. Mrs. Edward Roth to *New Yorker*, dated Thursday, *Hiroshima* Papers; see also A.M. Weinberg to *New Yorker*, Sept. 1, 1946, ibid.; Julie d'Estournelles to *New Yorker*, Aug. 30, 1946, ibid.; Richard B. Hovey to *New Yorker*, Sept. 3, 1946, ibid.

16. Albert Einstein to Friend, Sept. 6, 1946 (mimeographed letter), Emergency Committee of Atomic Scientists Papers, University of Chicago; Livingston Hartly to *New Yorker*, Aug. 30, 1946, National Committee on Atomic Information (NCAI) Papers, Manuscript Division, Library of Congress; R. Hawley Truax to Hartly, Oct. 22, 1946, ibid.; A. E. Casgrain to Hazel L. Rice, Jan. 8, 1947, ibid.; Charles Poore, "The Most Spectacular Explosion in the Time of Man," review of *Hiroshima*, by John Hersey, *New York Times Book Review*, Nov. 10, 1946, p. 7

17. Poore, "The Most Spectacular Explosion in the Time of Man," p. 7.

18. *New York Times*, Sept. 9, 1946. This broadcast subsequently won the Peabody Award for 1946 as an outstanding educational program; a *Billboard* magazine poll of radio editors judged it the best public service program of 1946. To mark the second anniversary of the attack on Hiroshima, ABC, in August 1947, carried interviews with five of the six survivors who were leading characters in Hersey's story. *Chicago Daily Tribune*, Aug. 5, 1947.

19. Poore, "The Most Spectacular Explosion in the Time of Man," p. 7.

20. The Book-of-the-Month Club distributed hundreds of thousands of copies of *Hiroshima* free to its subscribers, with the comment that "we find it hard to conceive of anything being written that could be of more importance at this moment to the human race." Quoted in ibid., p. 7.

21. The books were *Men on Bataan* (New York, 1942); *Into the Valley: A Skirmish of the Marines* (New York, 1943); *A Bell for Adano* (New York, 1944).

22. John Hersey, *Here to Stay* (New York, 1964), p. vii.

23. Ibid., p. viii.

24. John A. Siemes, S. J., "The Atomic Age: Hiroshima: Eye-Witness," *Saturday Review of Literature*, May 11, 1946, pp. 24–25, 40–44; "From Hiroshima: A Report and a Question," *Time*, Feb. 11, 1946, pp. 26–27.

25. R. E. Marshak, E. C. Nelson, L. I. Schiff, "Atomic Bomb Damage—Japan and USA," *Bulletin of the Atomic Scientists* (May 1, 1946), p. 6. See also Robert E. Marshak, E. C. Nelson, and L. I. Schiff, *Our Atomic World* (Albuquerque, N. M., 1946), p. 18; H[enry] S[eidel] C[anby], "Mass Death in Miniature" (editorial), *Saturday Review of Literature*, Sept. 8, 1945, p. 18; J. Russell Smith to Committee [*sic*] on Atomic Information, Aug. 5, 1946, NCAI Papers.

26. Unless otherwise indicated, the paragraphs on the preparation of *Hiroshima* draw upon my interview with John Hersey, at New Haven, Conn., Sept. 19, 1967.

27. Hersey does not recall who originated the idea for a story on Hiroshima. He remembers that it was one of about ten ideas for articles that came up in an editorial conference.

28. Hersey to author, July 30, 1971.

29. Interview with Hersey, Sept. 19, 1967.

30. See John Hersey, "Kamikazi" [*sic*], *Life*, July 30, 1945, pp. 68–75; Hersey, *Into the Valley*, especially pp. 55–56, 82.

31. Hersey to author, July 30, 1971.

32. According to a *Time* magazine article, Harold Ross, the *New Yorker* editor, "was a little afraid that Hersey's sympathetic piece on the Hiroshima Japanese might sound a little anti-American—so he got Hersey to explain why the U.S. dropped the bomb." "Without Laughter," *Time*, Sept. 9, 1946, p. 50.

33. See also ibid. Despite these last minute modifications, several readers still commented on the incongruity of the article and the advertisements.

34. Hersey, *Hiroshima*, p. 3.

35. Ibid., p. 67.

36. Ibid., p. 59.

37. George Probst to *New Yorker*, Sept. 9, 1946. *Hiroshima* Papers; Poore, "The Most Spectacular Explosion in the Time of Man," p. 7.

38. Hersey, *Hiroshima*, p. 105.

39. Ibid., p. 111.

40. Joseph Luft and W. M. Wheeler, "Reaction to John Hersey's *Hiroshima*," *Journal of Social Psychology* (Aug. 1948), 138.

41. Judith English to *New Yorker*, n.d., *Hiroshima* Papers.

42. Natalie Moehlmann to *New Yorker*, Sept. 3, 1946; ibid., see also "Comment on the Week: *New Yorker* and the Soul," *America*, Sept. 14, 1946, p. 569; Alan Stoltman, "When the Bomb Fell," review of *Hiroshima*, by John Hersey, *New Masses*, Dec. 24, 1946, p. 27.

43. John A. Ullman and Eleanor G. Ullman to *New Yorker*, Aug. 30, 1946, *Hiroshima* Papers; Muriel Frodin English to *New Yorker*, Sept. 8, 1946, ibid.; Raymond G. Swing, MS radio broadcast for the American Broadcasting Company, Aug. 30, 1946, Swing Papers; Mrs. Hazel L. Rice to NCAI, Dec. 23, 1946; NCAI Papers.

44. Kiyoshi Kawakami, "America and Hiroshima," *Human Events*, Dec. 4, 1946, n.p.; Ruth Benedict, "The Past and the Future," review of *Hiroshima*, by John Hersey, *Nation*, Dec. 7, 1946, p. 656; T. R. B., "Washington Wire—A Nice Holiday," *New Republic*, Sept. 9, 1946, p. 280.

45. Luft and Wheeler, "Reactions to John Hersey's *Hiroshima*" p. 137. Some readers, however, distinguished between certain levels of responsibility and attributed the primary blame for the atomic bombing to those government leaders who decided to use the bomb. See, for example, Luella Whitworth Jackson to *New Yorker*, Sept. 8, 1946, *Hiroshima* Papers.

46. Natalie Moehlmann to *New Yorker*, Sept. 3, 1946, ibid.; see also Barbara Bettman to *New Yorker*, Sept. 4, 1946, ibid.

47. A. Squires to J. Balderstone, Sept. 7, 1946, quoted in Smith, *A Peril and a Hope*, p. 80.

48. Mary Cuenod to *New Yorker*, Sept. 7, 1946, *Hiroshima* Papers; see also G. A. Ausband, Jr., to *New Yorker*, Sept. 2, 1946, ibid.; Marcia Mitchell to *New Yorker*, Sept. 20, 1946, ibid.; Catherine Curtis to *New Yorker*, Sept. 10, 1946, ibid.

49. Albon Man to *New Yorker*, Sept. 2, 1946, ibid.; see also "Sub Heads: Monatons," *Fellowship*, Oct. 1946, p. 159.

50. N[orman] C[ousins], "The Survival of Literacy" (editorial), *Saturday Review of Literature*, Sept. 14, 1946, p. 14.

51. Milton Mayer, in *Progressive*, May 19, 1947.

52. *Hiroshima* (editorial), *The Messenger*, Sept. 17, 1946, p. 6; "Nuremberg" (editorial), ibid., Oct. 15, 1946, pp. 4–5; "Morally Indefensible" (editorial), ibid., Dec. 24, 1946, pp. 8–9.

53. [Dwight Macdonald,] "Hersey's *Hiroshima*," *Politics*, Oct. 1946, p. 308.

54. Mary McCarthy to Editor, ibid., Nov. 1946, p. 367.

55. Editorial, *New York Times*, Sept. 9, 1946.

56. W. H. M'Nair to Editor, *New York Herald Tribune*, Sept. 20, 1946, E. S. H. to Editor, ibid., Sept. 16, 1946; Eleanor H. Ziegler to *New Yorker*, Sept. 13, 1946, *Hiroshima* Papers; Constance Manss to *New Yorker*, Aug. 31, 1946, ibid.; Robert T. Bean to *New Yorker*, Sept. 8, 1946, ibid.; Paul J. Bilbert to *New Yorker*, Sept. 15, 1946, ibid.

57. Loren C. MacKinney to *New Yorker*, n.d., *Hiroshima* Papers.

58. Carl Heath Kopf, "News of the Christian World: Bonds Will Aid Bombed Colleges," *Christian Century*, Jan. 30, 1946, p. 156; "News of the Church: To Aid Atom Bomb Sufferers," *Southern Churchman*, Jan. 26, 1946, p. 12; *Chicago Daily Tribune*, Nov. 15, 1946; David Lawrence, "Let's Rebuild Hiroshima" (editorial), *U. S. News*, March 1, 1946, pp. 26–27; Park J. White, Jr. to Editor, *Fellowship*, Feb. 1946, p. 31; *New York Times*, July 26 and Aug. 5, 1947; Walter Sullivan, in ibid., Aug. 7, 1947.

59. Catherine Curtis to *New Yorker*, Sept. 10, 1946, *Hiroshima* Papers.

60. Report of the Commission on the Relation of the Church to the War in the Light of the Christian Faith, *Atomic Warfare and the Christian Church* (New York, March 1946), p. 19; see also "A Letter to Kagawa" (editorial), *Christian Century*, July 30, 1947, pp. 918–919; *Report of Buckstep Conference of Episcopal Pacifist Fellowship*, June 25–28, 1946, in *Hiroshima* Papers; Walter D. Calvert, "Universalists Condemn Atomic Bomb," *Christian Century*, Nov. 13, 1946, p. 1380; Louis Fisher, in *Progressive*, Aug. 11, 1947.

61. Lifton, *Death in Life*, p. 341; William Bradford Huie, *The Hiroshima Pilot* (New York, 1965); Claude Eatherly, *Burning Conscience: The Case of the Hiroshima Pilot Claude Eatherly told in his letters to Gunther Anders* (New York, 1962).

62. Karl T. Compton, "If the Atomic Bomb Had Not Been Used," *Atlantic Monthly*, Dec. 1946, pp. 54–56. Compton was president of Massachusetts Institute of Technology. During the war, he served as chief of the Office of Scientific Research and Development field office and as a member of the Interim Committee, a secret *ad hoc* body which advised President Truman on the wartime use of the atomic bomb and the future international control of atomic energy.

63. Harry S. Truman to Karl T. Compton, Dec. 16, 1946, Harry S. Truman Papers, Harry S. Truman Library, Independence, Mo. (microfilm used and cited through the courtesy of Martin Sherwin, Ithaca, N.Y.). The first two paragraphs of Truman's letter were reprinted in the *New York Times*, Jan. 28, 1947; *Atlantic Monthly*, Feb. 1947, p. 27; and *Bulletin of the Atomic Scientists*, Feb. 1947, p. 40. According to *Time*, Truman "rebuked" Compton for not emphasizing that the President carried the ultimate responsibility for dropping the bomb. "Least Abhorrent Choice," *Time*, Feb. 3, 1947, p. 20.

64. Truman to Compton, Dec. 16, 1946. Truman Papers; Truman to Henry L. Stimson, Dec. 31, 1946, Henry L. Stimson Papers, Yale University Library; Henry L. Stimson, "The Decision to Use the Atomic Bomb," *Harper's*, Feb. 1947, pp. 97–107.

65. Stimson to Truman, Jan. 7, 1947, Stimson Papers.

66. Ibid., p. 106 (italics added). It would be interesting to know for certain whether American leaders really did anticipate the psychological shock value of the bomb on Japanese leaders, or whether, subtly influenced by the *ex post facto* findings of the USSBS studies, Stimson attributed in 1947 more foresight to American decision-makers in mid-1945 than in fact they possessed. There is, in any event, no doubt that Stimson had read one of the most important Strategic Bombing Survey reports, *Japan's Struggle to End the War.* (See Stimson, "The Decision to Use the Atomic Bomb," p. 105, n.) In writing his article Stimson also had at his disposal a classified document, "Strategic Plans For The Defeat of Japan." According to a War Department historian, this document was "a summary of the strategic concepts which formed the basis for all the [wartime] planning papers submitted to you" by the War Department. (Rudolph A. Winnacker to Stimson, Nov. 12, 1946, Stimson Papers.) This summary indicated that wartime planners thought "psychological pressure ought to be brought to bear against Japan's will to resist in order to bring about, if possible, an early surrender and a corresponding economy of lives and resources." ("Strategic Plans For The Defeat of Japan," Enclosure IV, attached to ibid.) The summary, however, made no specific mention of the atomic bomb as part of any psychological campaign against Japan's people or leaders.

67. For a more extensive discussion of the making, characteristics, and impact of "The Beginning or The End," see Yavenditti, "American Reactions to the Use of Atomic Bombs on Japan," pp. 384–395. See also Smith, *A Peril and a Hope*, pp. 314–318.

68. Smith, *A Peril and a Hope*, p. 317; M-G-M Announcement, "Facts about the making of M-G-M's remarkable motion picture 'THE BEGINNING OR THE END'" p. 5, NCAI Papers.

69. Although there is some question as to whether warning leaflets of any kind were dropped on Hiroshima before August 6, 1945, certainly they did not warn of atomic attack. Robert Jay Lifton asserts that warning leaflets, which did not mention the atomic bomb or any new weapon, "were dropped on Hiroshima from American planes on July 27." But when he visited Hiroshima in 1962, he found only one person who remembered picking up a warning leaflet. (Lifton, *Death in Life*, p.17). The scene with Truman deliberately falsified the historical record and represented an obvious effort to justify the bomb's use. It is not clear who originated the idea for this scene, but the White House obviously approved it, and the scientists who served as technical advisors for the film apparently did not complain about it. Harrison Brown was the only reviewer at the time to note what he called the "most horrible falsification of history"—the idea "that Hiroshima had been warned of the approaching attack." Harrison Brown, "The Beginning or the End: A Review," *Bulletin of the Atomic Scientists*, March 1947, p. 99.

70. See especially Rev. Alan Jenkins, "Hersey's *Hiroshima*—Challenge to Christians," sermon, Oct. 27, 1946, in *Hiroshima* Papers.

71. Lawrence S. Wittner, *Rebels Against War: The American Peace Movement, 1941–1960* (New York, 1969), pp. 130, 131.

72. "A quarter of a century has gone by since *Hiroshima* was published, and generations of school children have read it, and the letters I still get in considerable numbers suggest that the book *has* had a moral impact. . . . I believed, and I still believe that the tension that came from the deliberate suppression of horror. . . gave an effect far more morally disturbing [than] would have been achieved had I shouted or screamed my outrage." John Hersey to author. July 30, 1971.

THE

"HIROSHIMA"

NEW YORKER

Mary McCarthy

MAY I ADD SOMETHING TO YOUR COMMENT on the "Hiroshima" *New Yorker?** The editors of that magazine imagined, and you yourself in your comment take for granted, that the Hersey piece was an indictment of atomic warfare. Its real effect, however, was quite the opposite. What it did was to minimize the atom bomb by treating it as though it belonged to the familiar order of catastrophes—fires, flood, earthquakes—which we have always had with us and which offer to the journalist, from Pliny down to Mr. Hersey, an unparalleled wealth of human interest stories, examples of the marvelous, and true-life narratives of incredible escapes. The grandness of the disaster and the smallness of the victims are ideally suited to the methods of journalism, which exaggerates and foreshortens simultaneously. The interview with the survivors, *(Mrs. Margaret O'Reilly, of 1810 Oak Street, housewife, speaking to reporters, said: "When I first smelled smoke, I threw an old coat on and woke the baby," etc.)* is the classic technique for reporting such events— it serves well enough to give some sense, slightly absurd but nonetheless correct, of the continuity of life. But with Hiroshima, where the continuity of life was, for the first time, put into question, and by man, the existence of any survivors is an irrelevancy, and the interview with the survivors is an insipid falsification of the truth of atomic warfare. To have done the atom bomb justice, Mr. Hersey would have had to interview the dead.

But of this Mr. Hersey is, both literally and temperamentally, incapable. He is the *New Yorker's* reporter-at-large, not Virgil or Dante—hell is not his sphere. Yet it is precisely in this sphere—that is, in the moral world—that the atom bomb exploded. To treat it journalistically, in terms of measurable destruction, is, in a sense, to deny its existence, and this is what Mr. Hersey has accomplished for the *New Yorker* readers. Up to August 31 of this year, no one dared think of Hiroshima—it appeared to us all as a kind of hole in human history. Mr. Hersey has filled that hole with busy little Japanese Methodists; he has made it familiar and safe, and so, in the final sense, boring. As for the origin of the trouble, the ques-

---

*Editors' Note: Mary McCarthy is referrring to Dwight Macdonald's essay "The Decline to Barbarism." See *Hiroshima's Shadow*, p. 263.

tion of intention and guilt—which is what made Hiroshima more horrifying, to say the least, than the Chicago Fire—the bombers, the scientists, the government, appear in this article to be as inadvertent as Mrs. O'Leary's cow.

There is no question that the *New Yorker's* editors did not deliberately plan the August 31 issue as an anniversary celebration of the atom bomb (though one wonders whether they were not competing just a little with it in this journalistic coup that allowed a single article to obliterate the contents of the magazine). The point is that the *New Yorker* cannot be against the atom bomb, no matter how hard it tries, just as it could not, even in this moral "emergency," eliminate the cigarette and perfume advertising that accompanied Mr. Hersey's text. Since the *New Yorker* has not, so far as we know, had a rupture with the government, the scientists, and the boys in the bomber, it can only assimilate the atom bomb to itself, to Westchester County, to smoked turkey, and the Hotel Carlyle. ("Whenever I stay at the Carlyle, I feel like sending it a thank-you note," says a middle-aged lady in an advertisement.) It is all one world.

Politics
November 1946

THE

LITERACY

OF SURVIVAL

Norman Cousins

OUR COLLEAGUE, the wry, dry *New Yorker* magazine, has declared a one-week moratorium in regular publishing in order to present in full John Hersey's report on Hiroshima. All the crisp ingredients that go into the regular weekly *New Yorker* package—the cartoons, departments, articles, stories, even the finger-in-the-eye short fillers and comment—all these have been set aside to accommodate a book-sized article on the victims and near-victims of the first city in history to be killed by an atomic weapon.

Ever since it began publishing almost twenty-five years ago, the *New Yorker* has stayed pretty close to its beat, displaying a cool, dry-eyed attitude about Manhattan, and, for that matter, about life in general. If it should be wondered why such a periodical should suddenly travel 12,000 miles away from its self-assigned theater of editorial operations to publish an intimate, unsophisticated, from-the-heart account of what happened to a Japanese city more than a year ago, the answer is to be found not only in the importance of Mr. Hersey's article, which is in the best tradition of Defoe writing about the destruction of St. Vincent Island, or Pliny about the eruption of Vesuvius, but in the fact that most Americans have not as yet recognized the implications of the precedent set by us in unleashing atomic warfare.

Do we know, for example, that many thousands of human beings in Japan will die of cancer during the next few years because of radioactivity released by the bomb? Do we know that the atomic bomb is in reality a death ray, and that the damage by blast and fire may be secondary to the damage caused by radiological assault upon human tissue? Have we as a people any sense of responsibility for the crime of Hiroshima and Nagasaki? Have we attempted to press our leaders for an answer concerning their refusal to heed the pleas of the scientists against the use of the bomb without a demonstration, on the basis of which an ultimatum would have been issued to Japan, which would thus have had the responsibility for making the decision as to whether atomic bombs would be used on human beings? And now that we have learned from a Navy spokesman that Japan was ready to quit even before Hiroshima, what happens to the argument that numberless thousands of American lives were saved?

Do we know, finally, that the atomic bomb is the perfect weapon against America, and that by our use of it—at a time when no other nation had it—we have almost guaranteed its general use in the next war? We used it when it served our purpose to do so—and other peoples are not so dense that they cannot see that our present anxiety stems not from any deep moral convictions but from the knowledge that our concentrated population and centralized industry make the most vulnerable major nation.

These questions are implicit rather than explicit in Mr. Hersey's article; they are not academic, they are not marginal, they are not to be separated from the problem of building a workable peace. And through its treatment of the Hersey article, the *New Yorker* may have hit upon a device that could be tremendously effective if applied on a national scale. What the country needs today is a moratorium on its normal activity, habits, and general routine; which is to say, a moratorium on trivia in order to acquire a basic literacy on the questions of our time. Let us have a National Concentration Week, during which we can ponder not only the implications of Hiroshima and Nagasaki, moral and political, but the problem of competitive national sovereignty in an atomic age. Let all our communication and educational resources be mobilized for the articulation of a set national values on which a platform for leadership might be built. If it did nothing else, it might at least enable the American people to recognize a crisis when they see one and are in one.

The Saturday Review
September 14, 1946

AN
OPINION
ON HIROSHIMA

Edgar R. Smothers, S.J.

ACTIONS AND REACTIONS IN WORLD WAR II went far toward numbing the conscience of Americans to the evil of indiscriminate attack upon the people of enemy nations. In destruction of non-military life and non-military wealth by aerial bombing, we were surpassed by none. The moral indignation which we officially professed at recourse to such measures by our enemies gave place to pleas for the defense when it was our turn to face the charge of cruelty, and our argument was the same as theirs: such methods would shorten the war and eventually save more lives than they destroyed.

This argument collapses against a primary principle of sound morality: no end—however good, however necessary—can justify the use of an evil means. Until the apologists of Hiroshima meet that issue, their contention that the war was shortened, that lives were saved, that it was the less abhorrent alternative, remains inconclusive; as does the argument that our acts were justified by the antecedent and surpassing guilt of the enemy. If the measure taken at Hiroshima was licit, then any belligerent in a just war may lawfully use it. If it was not licit, then the United States committed an enormous wrong at Hiroshima, and duplicated it at Nagasaki.

It is true that those twin blows of unique effectiveness had their moral precedent in the long series of indiscriminate bombings of Cologne, of Hamburg, of Berlin, of Tokyo. But if it was wrong to use the atom bomb, that merely completes the tale of wrong. It is begging the essential question to assume that because we obtained certain desired results—whether with block-busters, with incendiaries or with atomic bombs—our action was therefore right.

The atom bomb is a weapon of war vastly superior in physical power to those that have gone before. It could be licitly used, provided it were used under the requisite conditions of all just wars. One of those conditions is that the means employed in any given instance must be apt and necessary to a just defense, to the exclusion of means which of their nature exceed the limit of a just defense.

The attack upon Hiroshima was deliberately aimed, as former Secretary of War Henry L. Stimson properly acknowledges, against a dual target: "that is, a military installation or war plant surrounded by or adjacent to houses and other buildings most susceptible to damage." In other word, the whole complex of a great city was the object of attack. Upon it the blow fell without warning. Does such a measure lie within the valid conception of a just defense? If so, no government, in a war deemed just, can hesitate to adopt it whenever it promises to hasten victory and to save the lives of combatants. Does such a measure exceed the conditions of a just defense? Then the United States committed a wrong of unusual magnitude at Hiroshima and at Nagasaki.

No apologist entitled (like Mr. Stimson or President Truman) to speak for our national leadership has, to my knowledge, met the issue squarely. Heretofore, after a pragmatic defense of our act, the apologists have led off into an appeal for the universal abolition of war—a consummation devoutly to be wished. Let it not be supposed, however, that by turning to it we have resolved the question of our past performance and proved our conscience clear. That would be to connive at our own obfuscation.

To take by direct, deliberate act, the life of an unarmed human being who is justly chargeable with no capital crime is a serious matter. That was the action, multiplied many thousand times, of our national leadership in ordering the atomic attack upon two Japanese cities. How is it possible to justify it?

If the lives of the men in our armed services were an absolutely sovereign good—as the logic of the usual argument might imply—the question would rise as to whether we should not have followed other policies before we got into war, and whether we should not have explored all possibilities of peace before we had won our unconditional surrender. It is a grievous wrong to sacrifice the life of a single human being, combatant or not, without just necessity. But no human life is so sacred that it ought to be spared at the cost of destroying by positive, deliberate act another human being who is not culpably accountable as unjust aggressor or as sentenced criminal.

The wrong committed at Hiroshima, so long as it is defended, remains a matter of the gravest concern, because it sanctions the denial, on the most imposing scale, of the transcendence of the moral order and the intrusion of national pragmatism in its place. If the temporal advantage of the United States were the ultimate norm of morality, one could see no decisive objection to our use of the atom bomb upon the ordinary population of an enemy country—expediency alone would be norm enough. If, however, the ultimate norm of morality is of a higher order, if it has to do with the rightness of man's acts in relation to God, then temporal expediency must accept the subordinate role that belongs to it.

Just and necessary war, fought with all just and necessary weapons of war, must be allowed, in common with the main tradition of Christianity. Promiscuous attack upon armed and unarmed alike—upon men, women and children, upon great concentrations of ordinary human beings who in overwhelming majority are objectively convictable of no belligerent status—is, with that same tradition, to be rejected, whatever may be the alternative.

America
July 5, 1946

HAS IT COME TO THIS?

A. J. Muste

THE WAR AND THE ATOMIC BOMB have given us a demonstration of the logic of material power and military might: raise them to the nth degree and what you have is weakness, defenselessness, man reduced to impotence and threatened with extinction by the creature of his own brain. But with the emergence of the atomic bomb we were also given a demonstration of what might be called the logic of atrocity.

We set out to defend and extend democracy and peace by means of war—reluctantly, because we knew that modern war is an atrocious thing. We were stirred by the atrocities against the Jews, and the Chinese, and others. Surely, these things must be stopped, if not avenged. And how could you stop mad dogs and hyenas and monkey-men except by the means of modern scientific warfare, atrocious as that admittedly was?

Now where are we? We who preached day in and day out against atrocities turned thousands upon thousands of Japanese soldiers into blackened corpses with flame-throwers. A veteran addressing other veterans writes: "You have watched a man regulate his flame-thrower so that he could set a soldier afire rather than killing him outright. . . . From your own experience you know that Americans shot prisoners in cold blood, strafed life-rafts, mutilated the bodies of enemy dead. . . . You have seen that many such 'crimes' are military necessities." But we did not stop with the use of flame-throwers on combatants.

It was we and our allies, who according to the president of the International Red Cross, killed two hundred and fifty thousand people, mostly civilians, in one night in Dresden. It was we—United States bombers—who destroyed all but one or two Japanese cities of any size, who burned a hundred thousand people to death in one night in Tokyo. But we did not stop there. We dropped the atomic bomb on Hiroshima. And that was not enough. A few days later we dropped a bigger and better one—though it is said not to have been so well aimed—on Nagasaki.

There was no clear "military necessity" to "justify" these crowning atrocities. There is good reason to think that peace with Japan might have been made months before, but it did not suit Russian designs or our own. However that may be, at the time the bombs were dropped negotiations were under way, Japanese power had

309

been crushed. According to such authorities as General LeMay, the Secretary of War and the Secretary of State, the war would have been over in a week or so anyway. Louis Fischer in the *Progressive*, October 22, 1945, refers to a speech made shortly before by Admiral Chester W. Nimitz at a celebration in his honor at Washington, D.C. Admiral Nimitz said, "The atomic bomb did not win the war against Japan. The Japanese had, in fact, already sued for peace before the atomic age was announced to the world with the destruction of Hiroshima and before the Russian entry into the war. In saying that the atomic bomb played no decisive part, from a purely military standpoint, in the defeat of Japan, this is no effort to minimize the awful power of this new weapon."

The public has generally been led to believe that a land invasion of Japan was imminent in August and thus the launching of the atomic bombs saved the lives of thousands of American troops who would have perished in that operation. But a land invasion was in any case still many weeks away. The United States Strategic Bombing Survey, supplementing Admiral Nimitz's statement and supporting it with evidence, has effectively disposed of all such "justifications" for the use of the atomic bombs on Japanese cities. In its report, as summarized in the *New York Times* of July 14, 1946, the following passages occur:

> It seems clear, however, that air supremacy and its exploitation over Japan proper was the major factor which determined the timing of Japan's surrender and obviated any need for invasion. Based on a detailed investigation of all the facts and supported by the testimony of the surviving Japanese leaders involved, it is the Survey's opinion that certainly prior to Dec. 31, 1945, and in all probability prior to Nov. 1, 1945, Japan would have surrendered even if the atomic bombs had not been dropped, even if Russia had not entered the war and even if no invasion had been planned or contemplated. . . . The Hiroshima and Nagasaki atomic bombs did not defeat Japan, nor by the testimony of the enemy leaders who ended the war did they persuade Japan to accept unconditional surrender. The Emperor, the Lord Privy Seal, the Prime Minister, the Foreign Minister and the Navy Minister had decided as early as May of 1945 that the war should be ended even if it meant acceptance of defeat on allied terms.

Discount every one of these considerations, assume for the sake of the argument and for the sake of our sensibilities that they do not exist and still there is no scintilla of justification for the refusal of the plea of the scientists who had made the diabolical instrument that it should be demonstrated on some uninhabited Japanese island before being unloosed on hundreds of thousands of babies, women and helpless old people. Mr. Henry L. Stimson, Secretary of War during World War II, suggests in an article in the February 1947 issues of *Harper's Magazine* that the United States had only two atomic bombs ready in August 1945. If Japanese leaders had been summoned to observe an experimental detonation and the bomb proved a dud, Japanese war morale would have been stimulated and this would have resulted in the loss of more American lives. The obvious question occurs: Could representative Japanese not have been summoned to witness the effects of a bomb after its explosion? In that case the invitation could have simply been withheld if the experiment had fizzled. Elsewhere we shall show that on quite practical and non-idealistic grounds many atomic scientists believed at the time that some such course would have been far wiser.

It must be noted also that the war with Germany was over and that by this time it had long been known to our military and political leaders that the Germans had not been able to develop the atomic bomb and share their discovery with the Japanese. No one believed that the Japanese had the bomb or would shortly have it. Even the contention that some American lives were saved—and it was the claim that undoubtedly large numbers had been saved which reconciled Americans to the use of the atomic bombs or caused them to rejoice in it—rests on the slenderest foundation.

If we in such circumstances could launch this apocalyptic horror upon the world, what can we say to any nation which may launch atomic bombs, or biological warfare, against us under the conditions of frightful, unbearable tension which will presently exist in the world unless the threat of atomic war is extinguished? But not only have we left ourselves no moral ground on which to protest against whatever atrocities may be perpetrated against us. How can we possibly persuade anyone else or ourselves that if we have atomic bombs at all we shall not use them if we deem it expedient? There is not the slightest guarantee even that we shall not launch bombs first, take the offensive, if a sharp international crisis develops. The military will have an overpowering argument for doing so: "Who but an insane man or an agent of the enemy would wait until some enemy"—or one of General Arnold's "ostensibly friendly nations"—"first destroys forty million Americans?" After what has happened, who can imagine a President standing in Roosevelt's or Truman's place refusing in such an hour to sign the order to shoot?

Thus it has fallen upon this "Christian" nation, incessantly declaiming against the perpetrators of atrocities, and still doing so, to perpetrate the ultimate, atomic atrocity—needlessly—and so to remove all restraint upon atrocity. That is the logic of the atrocious means. With fatal precision the means in war become more destructive, both of physical life and of moral standards and spiritual values. Has it come to this? Yes, it has come to this.

Not By Might, 1947

IV

CENSORING HISTORY AT THE SMITHSONIAN

The President, the generals, the admirals and the administrators have lied to us about their infernal machine: they have lied by their statements and even more they have lied by their silences.

Lewis Mumford

For whatever it costs to buy influence, you can now have your own version of our nation's history displayed and opposing views suppressed at the Smithsonian Institution. Since the Smithsonian has close to thirty million visitors a year, three quarters of them American citizens, this tampering threatens widespread misapprehension about our nation's history, with potentially disastrous consequences. In a democratic society a national museum has a particularly heavy responsibility to research the nation's history and to recount it faithfully. Our form of government is predicated on an informed citizenry; and our best guide to the future is our understanding of the past.

Martin Harwit
Former Director of the
Smithsonian Air & Space Museum

We are concerned about the profoundly dangerous precedent of censoring a museum exhibition in response to political pressures from special interest groups. . . . [I]t will send a chilling. . .message that certain aspects of our own history are "too hot to handle," so susceptible to contested points of view that they must be excluded from the public mind.

Eric Foner, Gary Nash, Michael Kammen
Organization of American Historians

THE BATTLE

OF THE

ENOLA GAY

Mike Wallace

W HEN THE *ENOLA GAY* WENT ON DISPLAY in June 1995, visitors to the Smithsonian's National Air and Space Museum (NASM) found a truncated airplane: Only fifty-six feet of fuselage could be squeezed into the building. But more than wings were missing. So was the exhibition that got sheared away after a campaign of vilification arguably without precedent in the annals of American museology.

In the summer of 1994, reports flaming through the mass media had denounced the impending show as a monstrous attempt to recast the history of World War II. A typical description, by the *Washington Post*'s Eugene Meyer, called it "an anti-nuke morality play in which Americans were portrayed as ruthless racists hell-bent on revenge for Pearl Harbor, with the Japanese as innocent, even noble victims fighting to defend their unique culture from 'Western imperialism.' " Editorials blasted "anti-American" curators and warned that "revisionists" had hijacked the museum to promulgate politically correct (PC) history. Air Force veterans responded angrily. Here they were, amidst the festivities marking the fiftieth anniversary of the Normandy landings, ready to take their turn in the sequence of celebrations. Instead, said the media, youthful visitors to the Smithsonian would soon find their grandparents reviled as racists and war criminals.

These assertions were based on a misconstruction of NASM intentions, and a profound misrepresentation of what the curators actually wrote. Few of the angry vets ever read the proposed scripts—not unreasonably, given that each of the eventual five was over five hundred pages long and none was easily available. Neither had many of the pundits, most of whom cribbed their analysis from a series of articles by John T. Correll, editor of *Air Force Magazine*. My review of the scripts and their fate suggests that most of Correll's charges were unwarranted, some outrageously so. I do not claim that NASM officials were fault free. There were indeed problems with their first draft—though mostly these were errors of omission rather than commission—and their handling of the crisis once it blew up left much to be desired. But by no means did they deserve the abuse heaped upon them. More than individual reputations are at stake here. The scrapping of the *Enola Gay* exhibition raises troubling questions about the future of public historical discourse in the United States. The successful campaign to muzzle the Smithsonian was a battle fought on the history front of America's ongoing culture war. This essay seeks to understand the event and to set it in its larger context.

The initial script of "Crossroads: The End of World War II, The Atomic Bomb, and The Origins of the Cold War" (January 12, 1994) had five parts, one per gallery, each consisting of proposed label copy and suggested artifacts. The first section ("A Fight to the Finish") dealt primarily with the final year of the war. The introductory segment asserted Japan's culpability for the sequence of events that led to the bomb. Recapitulating Japan's 1930s expansionism ("marked by naked aggression and extreme brutality"), it sketched the course of the war from Pearl Harbor on, mentioning Japanese atrocities, use of slave labor, racist attitudes, and maltreatment of prisoners of war ("often starved, beaten, and tortured.") It then—in a space dominated by a kamikaze aircraft looming overhead—zeroed in on the fierce Japanese resistance at Iwo Jima and Okinawa, finding in it "a terrible warning of what could be expected in the future."

The section did include two shortly to be infamous sentences: "For most Americans, this war was fundamentally different than the one waged against Germany and Italy—it was a war of vengeance. For most Japanese, it was a war to defend their unique culture against Western imperialism." These were not great sentences—not wrong, in context, but easily misrepresented. Americans were in a fury in 1945—and why *shouldn't* they have been, given Pearl Harbor, four years of ferocious war, and recently declassified accounts of the Bataan Death March? Many were calling for revenge, some even for extermination. But this is not to say—nor did the script—that the war, or the bomb, was only motivated by vengeance. Nor was it wrong to observe that the Japanese believed unconditional surrender would mean the end of the emperor system and the collapse of their culture. Or that many Japanese—then and to this day—represented their racist exploitation of other Asians as a shield against western imperialism. The script did not ratify this self-perception, it demonstrated it, as crucial to understanding the tenacity of Japanese resistance.

But opponents wrenched the sentences out of context and used them to stoke outrage. Even after they were swiftly dropped, and the Smithsonian had explicitly and indignantly denied the construction put upon them, critics trotted them out again and again, in the absence of any other sentence that would so well serve their purpose. Correll also argued that this section did not represent the history of Japanese aggression graphically enough to offset the emotional impact of later material on the effects of the bombing. Counting the number of photographs of suffering Americans and finding it lower than the number depicting suffering Japanese, he charged that a victimology thesis lay embedded in the structure of the exhibition. He was partly right about the effect, totally wrong about the intention. There was no plot to delete evidence of Japanese wickedness in order to manipulate visitors into finding Americans immoral. Any exhibition focused on the *Enola Gay* and its bombing run would, almost by definition, depict more Japanese than American casualties.

But curators did face a museological conundrum. Ground Zero artifacts and images, no matter how few their number, pack a wallop. So does the *Enola Gay*. Together they could overshadow almost anything in a merely introductory section. Designers at first resisted a "balance of corpses" approach—giving, for example, equal space to the slaughter at Nanking, where more died than at Hiroshima and

Nagasaki—in part because they rejected the vengeance thesis that they were accused of promulgating. It was the critics, after all, who insisted that Hiroshima was justified not because of prior Japanese outrages—although they had to be fed into the moral equation—but as a military action taken to expeditiously end the war Japan had started.

The curators, moreover, were assuming that most visitors already knew something about Pearl Harbor and the war in the Pacific—subjects treated extensively in an adjacent NASM gallery. This was a mistake. For most young Americans, those events are as distant as the Punic Wars. The museum admitted its mistake. In succeeding drafts the curators would expand the initial section, adding dramatic material on Japanese outrages (though none would tackle the history of American expansionism in Asia, nor would any critic remark on this oversight). Finally the staff would design a four-thousand-square-foot prefatory exhibition on the war in the Pacific. Tellingly, the addition of this contextual material would fail to assuage the critics.

Correll's passion for context stopped short when it came to the second section, an analysis, housed in one of the smaller galleries, of "The Decision to Drop the Bomb." Here the objection was to problematizing something deemed utterly unproblematic. Truman dropped the bomb to shorten the war and save lives, period. Raising questions about that decision, from the vantage point of "hindsight" was infuriating and illegitimate. But questions were raised at the time, and by the nation's preeminent civilian and military leaders. The endgame of World War II raised tactical and strategic issues of great political, moral, and military complexity. The script reviewed some debates that arose among participants at the time, and later between historians, explicitly labeling them as "Controversies." Why did these explorations create such an uproar?

One firestorm erupted over a hypothetical question: if the United States had to invade Japan to end the war, how many Americans would have died? The conventional popular wisdom on this subject is that perhaps half a million would have fallen. But this was a post-war judgment. In 1947, former Secretary of War Henry Stimson, intent on rebutting Hiroshima critics like John Hersey, claimed there would have been over one million American *casualties*. Truman later claimed a half million *lives* were at risk, a figure that Churchill doubled.

The exhibit draft, for all that it was accused of employing hindsight, relied instead on wartime estimates by MacArthur, Marshall, and various joint chiefs of staff planning committees, rather than using after-the-fact figures that even the American Legion admitted were "incredibly high." It concluded that it "appears likely that post-war estimates of a half million American deaths were too high, but many tens of thousands of dead were a real possibility." This enraged the critics. They claimed NASM had pruned the figure to render the bomb-drop immoral, as if only a gigantic quantity of saved lives could offset the enormous number of civilians actually killed. There is, one would hope, some statistic that might generate moral misgivings. Would saving one–thousand American soldiers or one hundred justify killing one–hundred-thousand civilians? But the script never raised such a question, never challenged the position that if an invasion had been the only alternative, the savings in lives would have justified the bombings.

The tougher question—which the script did ask—is whether or not an invasion was necessary in the first place. Huge numbers of veterans believed that it was inevitable, and that dropping the bomb therefore saved their lives, and the lives of many Japanese as well. But were they right? The exhibit script offended some by recalling that powerful wartime figures believed it was possible to end the war with neither nuclear bombings nor an invasion. Leading military men insisted that the combination of blockade and conventional bombing had brought Japan to its knees. Top navy admirals "believed that its blockade could force Japan to quit the war, while many army air forces' generals thought firebombing could force surrender by itself or in conjunction with the blockade." The script also cited the U.S. Strategic Bombing Survey, conducted after the surrender, which said the war would "certainly" have ended before the end of 1945, probably before November 1.

Label copy also took note of direct military opposition to nuclear weapons. The show quoted a statement made in 1950 by Admiral William D. Leahy, Truman's chief of staff, in which he denounced the bombing as adopting "ethical standards common to barbarians in the dark ages," but added cautiously that "1945 documents only suggest that he was skeptical that the atomic bomb would ever work." It mentioned General Eisenhower's claims in 1948 (and later) that he had opposed its use in conversations with Truman at Potsdam in 1945, but suggested that "corroborating evidence for these assertions is weak." [1] The script did not, however, engage the contemporary and post-war reservations of American airmen such as Henry H. ["Hap"] Arnold, the commanding general of the U.S. Army Air Forces, or Generals Carl Spaatz and Curtis LeMay. [2]

One "Historical Controversy" panel asked: "Would the War Have Ended Sooner if the United States Had Guaranteed the Emperor's Position?" The text noted some scholars believe this. More to the point, Acting Secretary of State (and former ambassador to Japan) Joseph Grew, Navy Secretary James Forrestal, Assistant Secretary for War John McCloy, General Douglas MacArthur, Admiral Leahy, Winston Churchill, and Herbert Hoover were among the many who thought that modifying the unconditional surrender formula to allow retention of the Emperor would strengthen the peace faction, aid in winning and effectuating an early surrender, and facilitate the post-war occupation. Truman rejected this advice—though in the end, after the bombs were dropped, Hirohito was allowed to retain his throne.

Some historians say Truman (counseled by Secretary of State James Byrnes) feared that modification would provoke vehement popular and congressional protest. Some even argue that by waiting until the A-bombs were ready in August, the U.S. high command may have muffed an opportunity to end the war in June, thus costing American lives. The script, however, said no such thing. It stated instead that while "it is possible that there was a lost opportunity to end the war without either atomic bombings or an invasion of Japan," these alternatives were "more obvious in hindsight than they were at the time." Citing the counter-argument—that it took the shock of the bombs (and Russian intervention) to "give Hirohito a face-saving way to force a surrender on his hard-liners"—and noting the impossibility of proving either case, the text concluded that this particular debate "will remain forever controversial."

Another question was asked: Did Truman drop the bombs primarily to forestall Soviet creation of the Asian sphere of influence, and gain diplomatic leverage in the already emerging Cold War? There are historians who argue this. The show did not. It said explicitly that "most scholars have rejected this argument, because they believe that Truman and his advisers saw the bomb first and foremost as a way to shorten the war." Concern about the Russians only "provided one more reason for Truman not to halt the dropping of the bomb."

Was dropping atom bombs on cities a violation of rules of war? There were strictures against attacking civilian populations; democracies had denounced fascists for violating these rules in Barcelona, Guernica, London, and China; and reservations about bombing civilians were raised by Eisenhower, Leahy and Marshall. But the show argued that for most Americans, the earlier moral constraints against killing civilians had already crumbled in the course of a savage war, and that most key decision-makers "did not see [nuclear attacks] as being drastically different than conventional strategic bombing. . . ."

Was dropping the bomb racist? In Europe, the U.S. Army Air Forces stuck to precision attacks on military targets—or at least professed to—as late as the Dresden firebombing, when Marshall and Stimson publicly disavowed any policy of "terror bombing on civilian populations." Days later General LeMay napalmed Tokyo, launching an incendiary campaign that killed more civilians in five months than the Allies had in five years of bombing Germany. Some historians have argued that anti-Asian racism helps explain the difference in approach.

The script, however, did not even raise the issue. It did note that most Americans considered their European enemies to be good people misled by evil leaders, while viewing Japanese as "treacherous and inhuman." The text traced this disparity in attitude to contemporary horror at Japanese atrocities and to long-standing anti-Asian racism. (The script also underscored *Japanese* racism, observing that "Allied people and leaders were pictured as inhuman demons, lice, insects, and vermin," and that "propaganda made frequent reference to the 'Jewish' nature of the Allied cause.") Nevertheless, the proposed label copy insisted that nuclear weapons would have been used against Germans had they been ready in time, thereby denying the charge of racial motivation.

Should there have been warning or a demonstration? The script mentioned the objections raised by scientists and officials like McCloy and Undersecretary of the Navy Ralph Bard. (It did not, oddly, mention the reservations expressed by General Marshall. In May 1945 Marshall said the bomb should be dropped only on a "straight military objective such as a large military installation," and then, if necessary, on a manufacturing center, but only after civilians had been warned so they could flee.) The text also laid out the "valid concerns that a warning could endanger Allied servicemen and that a demonstration might be ineffective or a failure"—objections on which Truman relied. And it emphasized that Hiroshima at that time was still a military target—all too readily, in the opinion of some historians.

The important thing to note about this part of the exhibition is that, overall, it adequately and appropriately provided visitors with a sense of the complexities of the bombing decision and the controversies surrounding it. It is possible to quarrel with this or that formulation. The information could have been presented in greater depth, and more dramatically, perhaps by using videotapes of historians and participants. Some of the label copy could have been, and almost certainly would have been, formulated more cogently. It was, after all, a first draft; few writers would want their initial efforts subjected to such fierce and public scrutiny. But given those attacks, what is striking is the text's conformity with the findings of responsible scholarship, its moderate and balanced stance on the issues, and the fact that, in essence, it supported Truman's decision.

The third section, "The World's First Atomic Strike Force," was planned for the cavernous arena where the giant plane was to be housed. Here the exhibition script presented the pilots' story "extensively and with respect," as Correll admitted on one occasion. Indeed the show emphasized the bravery and sacrifices of those who fought. But neither Correll nor anyone else ever again remarked on this vast mass of material, which so starkly contradicted claims that the NASM dishonored veterans. Nor was there ever any discussion of the fifteen-minute videotape the museum put together with crew members from the two bombers, a commemorative component that veterans who saw it loved.

Critics seized instead on the fourth section, "Cities at War," which looked at Hiroshima and Nagasaki's role in the Japanese military effort, and then depicted the nuclear devastation wrought upon them. Here visitors were to have moved into a somber space of giant blowups, powerful objects, and taped reminiscences of survivors. Correll decried not only the number but the nature of the artifacts included—a lunchbox containing "carbonized remains of sweet green peas and polished rice," a fused rosary. But the stubborn facts are that high school girls were out in force on August 6, clearing rubble at what became Ground Zero, and that Nagasaki was the center of the Catholic community in Japan. It is possible that a more understated display may have been more effective, and aroused less ire, though opponents disliked even its later, toned-down version.

Was the museum, as charged, angling for America to "apologize for its use of the atomic bomb to end World War II?" asked NASM's then-director Dr. Martin Harwit? "Of course not! Should we show compassion for those who perished on the ground? As humans beings, I believe we must." The analysis of bomb damage, moreover, was intended to educate, not manipulate. Information about the split-second annihilation caused by the blast, the way the seventy-two-hundred-degree Fahrenheit heat vaporized people, and the short and long-term effects of radiation, made clear the error of contemporary assumptions that nuclear bombs were merely bigger versions of conventional ones. Some critics argued there was no need for NASM to rehearse such gruesome information as it was already widely known. Alas, the latest Gallup Poll found that one in four Americans do not even know an atomic bomb was dropped on Japan, much less what impact it had when it exploded.

In the last gallery, a code on "The Legacy of Hiroshima and Nagasaki" spoke to this educational vacuum. It treated the bombings as not simply the end of World War II but as "symbols of the arrival of the nuclear age and as a glimpse of the realities of nuclear war." Although the exhibit could hardly do more than gesture at the complex history of the Cold War in the space allotted, it did at least raise some important issues. It offered an all-too-brief survey of the post-war nuclear arms race. It noted the invention of hydrogen bombs, a thousand times more powerful than their atomic predecessors. It mentioned the buildup of world stockpiles to seventy thousand warheads by the mid-1980s. It sketched the emergence of anti-nuclear movements concerned about atomic-test fallout and radioactive wastes. It discussed the end of the Cold War and the signing of arms control agreements. And it referred to the continuing dangers of nuclear proliferation and atomic terrorism. Its concluding panel stated: "Some feel that the only solution is to ban all nuclear weapons. Others think that this idea is unrealistic and that nuclear deterrence—at a much lower level—is the only way that major wars can be prevented."

THE DRAFT COMPOSED ON JANUARY 12 was discussed by a group of scholarly advisers on February 7, 1994.[3] Most had suggestions for improvement but almost everyone was basically laudatory. Dr. Richard Hallion, the Air Force Historian, called it "a great script." He joined with his military historian colleague Herman Wolk in pronouncing it "a most impressive piece of work, comprehensive and dramatic, obviously based upon a great deal of sound research, primary and secondary," in need only of a "bit of 'tweaking'."

The Air Force Association (AFA) thought differently. During the previous summer and fall, Harwit, with admirable if incautious openness, had actively solicited the group's involvement. Though he received a strongly negative response to a July 1993 concept treatment, Harwit nevertheless sent along the January 1994 draft script for review. The AFA, breaching confidentiality, leaked it to media and veterans groups, accompanied by a slashing Correll critique in the April 1994 issue of *Air Force Magazine*—a sneak attack that set the terms and tone of the ensuing debate. (Hallion now also became a vigorous critic, the "great script" of February becoming "an outright failure" by April.)

Over the following months inaccurate and malicious accusations tumbled forth in a variety of forums. The *Washington Times* said Truman's reasoning for using the bomb "was dismissed by the curators in favor of a theory that he ordered the bomb dropped to impress Soviet leader Josef Stalin." The *Wall Street Journal* said scriptwriters "disdain any belief that the decision to drop the bomb could have been inspired by something other than racism or blood-lust." Picking up on Correll's claim that kamikaze pilots were treated "with near-mystical reverence," the *Journal* decried the "oozing romanticism with which the *Enola* show's writers describe the kamikaze pilots." The curators had supposedly called them "youths, their bodies overflowing with life," a charge reporter Ken Ringle repeated the next day in the *Washington Post*. But the quoted text was in fact an excerpt from a pilot's journal, included to give viewers "insight into [the kamikaze's] suicidal fanaticism, which many Americans would otherwise find incomprehensible."

Washington Times columnist R. Emmett Tyrrell, Jr. called the museum staff a bunch of "politically correct pinheads." Had one million Americans died invading Japan, Tyrrell added, "surely that would have left some of the present pinheads... fatherless or even, oh bliss, unborn." Lance Morrow, writing in *Time*, found the script "way left of the mark." It managed to "portray the Japanese as more or less innocent victims of American beastliness and lust for revenge." "A revisionist travesty," the text "seemed an act of something worse than ignorance, it had the ring of a perverse generational upsidedownspeak and Oedipal *lese majeste* worthy of a fraud like Oliver Stone."

Increasingly, critics charged anti-Americanism. When Harwit asked if veterans really suspected the National Air and Space Museum was "an unpatriotic institution," Correll replied: "The blunt answer is yes." The AFA editor began probing the Smithsonian staff's backgrounds. Director Harwit had a suspicious resumé. He had been born in Czechoslovakia and raised in Istanbul, Correll noted, before coming to the United States in 1946. Harwit had, to be sure, joined the U.S. Army in 1955–57, but he had been "influenced" by his work on nuclear weapons tests at Eniwetok and Bikini. This experience had led him to assert that "I think anybody who has ever seen a hydrogen bomb go off at fairly close range knows that you don't ever want to see that used on people." As for the curators, Correll pointed out that "none of them [were] veterans of military service," that one (Tom Crouch) planned a lecture at the "Japanese Cultural and Community Center of Northern California," and that another (Michael Neufeld) was of Canadian origin.

Ringle of the *Washington Post* observed that the said Canadian had spent his undergraduate years at the University of Calgary from 1970–74, "when Americans were fleeing to Canada to escape the Vietnam War." Ringle contrasted Neufeld with an elderly American prisoner-of-war (POW), who during an interview came "close to tears" wondering if the curator was not suggesting "that the thousands of Japanese killed by those bombs were somehow worth more than the thousands of American prisoners in Japan?"

Pundits hammered at the curators' deficient patriotism. Jeff Jacoby of the *Boston Globe* claimed the script was "anti-American." Jonathan Yardley in the *Washington Post* called it as "a philippic not merely against war but against the United States," a piece of "anti-American propaganda." The American Legion, too, said the script inferred "that America was somehow in the wrong and her loyal airmen somehow criminal. . . ." One disgruntled veteran, noting that the Japanese "have bought most of Hawaii and lots of the United States," added: "Let's hope they have not bought the Smithsonian."

Congressmen picked up the un-American refrain. Sam Johnson (R–Texas), an Air Force fighter pilot for twenty-seven years and a POW in Vietnam for seven, denounced the scripts as "a blatant betrayal of American history." Peter Blute (R–Massachusetts) fired off a letter to Smithsonian Secretary Robert McCormick Adams, co-signed by twenty-three colleagues, condemning the proposed exhibit as "biased" and "anti-American."

Unprepared for such a barrage, Smithsonian officials scrambled to placate their opponents. Distancing himself somewhat from his curators, Harwit told his staff that "a second reading shows that we do have a lack of balance and that much of the criticism that has been levied against us is understandable." He called for revisions to accommodate legitimate concerns. The staff of NASM issued a second version of May 31—now renamed "The Last Act: The Atomic Bomb and the End of World War II"—and then a third on August 31. Each expanded the treatment of earlier Japanese aggression. Each cut out some of the objects and language deemed objectionable. Each was greeted by renewed demands for additional changes.

Congresspeople escalated their involvement. Senator Nancy Kassebaum (R–Kansas) was already on record as insisting that "we should not interpret the dropping of the bomb as we look at it today," but rather "put it in the context of the time" (as if the script had not run into trouble for doing precisely that). On September 19, she introduced a Sense of the Senate Resolution. It declared that even with the latest changes the script was "revisionist and offensive." The Senate enjoined the NASM to avoid "impugning the memory of those who gave their lives for freedom" (though even Correll had admitted it treated the veterans "with respect"). Senator Slade Gorton (R–Washington) laid out even more explicitly the kind of historical interpretation the government might deem acceptable. He attached to the Interior Department's appropriation bill a provision that Congress "expects" the *Enola Gay* exhibit to "properly and respectfully recognize the significant contribution to the early termination of World War II and the saving of both American and Japanese lives."

On September 21, the day Gorton's injunction was adopted, Smithsonian officials sat down for their first marathon negotiating session with the American Legion. The Institution had turned to the nation's premiere veterans' group, using the good offices of Smithsonian Undersecretary Constance Newman, thinking perhaps that if it could be persuaded to sign off on a script, further assaults might be forestalled. For a time the strategy seemed to be working. "This exhibit is taking a more balanced direction," said a Legion spokesman. "It's not a propaganda piece by any means." But to obtain this support museum representatives had to submit to a line-by-line script review—"they drafted pages while we talked," boasted a Legion spokesman—and to accept extensive transformations. High-ranking Smithsonian officials believed they were responding to valid concerns raised by an important focus group, addressing issues of style not substance, and grouping caveats (but not eliminating them) in order to emphasize the main line. But the scripts that emerged from this process—a fourth on October 3, and a fifth and final one on October 26—had been shorn of nuance and controversy.

The last version evoked Japanese *Bushido* ideals ("Die but never surrender") to justify asserting that invasion "casualties conceivably could have risen to as many as a million (including up to a quarter of a million deaths)." This estimate, museum spokesmen conceded, was not based on any new evidence but was an "extrapolation" from Okinawa casualties. The treatment of alternatives to invasion, debates over unconditional surrender, questions about Nagasaki, the reservations of high ranking military and civilian figures like Leahy, Eisenhower and even Truman himself—all were now drastically reduced, or deleted altogether. Further Ground Zero images and artifacts—especially those depicting women, children and religious objects—were jettisoned; only a single picture of a corpse remained. The last section dealing with nuclear proliferation was scrapped.

The exhibition, originally an effort to understand the *Enola Gay's* mission, had become an effort to justify it. As the script now summarized the story: "Japan, although weakened, was not willing to surrender. The atomic bomb offered a way to change that. A bloody invasion loomed if atomic bombs did not force Japan to surrender. . . . For Truman, even the lowest of the estimates was abhorrent. To prevent an invasion he feared would become 'an Okinawa from one end of Japan to the other' and to try and save as many American lives as possible, Truman chose to use the atomic bomb."

The last words were given to six veterans who had written NASM during the controversy. Four of the six cited letters endorsed the script's thesis. "I honestly feel," wrote one, "that millions of lives, both American and Japanese, were saved by that one crew on that one airplane!" "Americans, in my estimation, should make no apologies for strategic firebombing or dropping the atomic bomb," said another. "It took that to win the war!" So thoroughgoing and one-sided were the changes that they amounted to a recantation. As the outgoing national commander of the Legion reported to his troops: "We went face to face with the Smithsonian officials, and they blinked."

Now it was the scholarly community's turn to protest. The Organization of American Historians' (OAH) executive committee wrote the Smithsonian's board of regents on September 19, urging them "to support the National Air and Space Museum staff." On October 22, it condemned "threats by members of Congress to penalize the Smithsonian Institution." The OAH also deplored "the removal of historical documents and revisions of interpretations of history for reasons outside the professional procedures and criteria by which museum exhibitions are created." On November 16, a group of forty-eight "historians and scholars" charged a "transparent attempt at historical cleansing." They protested the excision of documents, the removal of artifacts, the whiting out of contemporary and historical debates, and the alteration of interpretations in the absence of new evidence. Though "we yield to no one in our desire to honor the American soldiers who risked their lives during World War II to defeat Japanese militarism," the historians said, the deletion of so many "irrevocable facts" had reduced the exhibit "to mere propaganda, thus becoming an affront to those who gave their lives for freedom."

Peace groups, too, objected. The Fellowship of Reconciliation, Physicians for Social Responsibility, Pax Christi USA and others declared that pressure from military and veterans groups had "compromised the integrity of the exhibit." Activists met with NASM officials on December 15, 1994 to decry "political censorship." They demanded the exhibit state that why the bomb was dropped and whether it had been necessary to end the war "are matters of vigorous scholarly and public debate on which Americans do legitimately disagree." Amid all this uproar, the organized museum community remained noticeably silent.

THE FOCAL POINT OF THESE CHARGES and countercharges was the newly arrived Smithsonian secretary, I. Michael Heyman. Before his official installation on September 19, 1994, the former chancellor of the University of California at Berkeley had opposed AFA-inspired pressure on NASM. Writing in August for the October issue of *Smithsonian Magazine*, the incoming secretary urged resisting those who "want the exhibition to be devoted solely to the justifications for dropping the bomb (with omissions of its effects)." Curators, he insisted, were educators not propagandists.

After his installation, Heyman tried to use the outcry from the scholars and peace groups to carve out a middle ground position. "The Institution is now being criticized from both ends of the spectrum—from those who consider the exhibition as a 'revisionist' product critical of the United States to those who accuse us of staging an exhibition which glorifies the decision of the United States to use atomic weapons. . . . This indicates to me that we are probably squarely in the middle, which, as a national institution, is not a bad place to be."

But the AFA was not interested in compromise; it wanted unconditional surrender. The revision of October 26, Correll admitted, had corrected many of "the worst offenses," removed most "anti-American speculation," and attained "parity" in casualty photos. No matter: it was still not "an acceptable salvage job." It continued to ask questions, "to doubt, probe and hint." "I don't think there should be doubts about whether that policy [of unconditional surrender] is right," Correll declared, in effect setting himself above most of the nation's wartime leaders. It was, he concluded, "no longer enough to clean up this exhibition script." Now it was "imperative" that Smithsonian officials go after the curators who had "produced such a biased, unbalanced, anti-American script in the first place."

The American Legion, however, remained a stumbling block. In October, Director of Internal Affairs Hubert R. Dagley II had rejected narrow views of the controversy that denounced the show only as "an unflattering portrayal of one branch of the armed forces" or "an indictment of strategic bombing." The Legion expressed what it considered more high-minded concerns—the exhibit's "potential to undermine not only our people's faith in their forefathers, but also their confidence in a referred and respected American institution"—the Smithsonian. Although it rejected an outright endorsement, it did not condemn the script it had helped produce.

But the Legion came under attack from media-inflamed veterans for being "more liberal" and "not as combative" as the AFA. By January, the group was backing away from neutrality, claiming the fifth script had not gone far enough, and hinting that without additional changes it would shift over to opposition. Indeed, on January 4, National Commander William M. Detweiler made an in-house recommendation to call for cancellation. Changes were forthcoming, but not ones the Legion was looking for. In mid-November, a delegation of historians led by advisory committee member Barton Bernstein had met with Harwit. They presented him with documentary evidence falsifying the October 26, draft's claim that, in the crucial meeting on June 18, 1945, Truman had been given an estimate of 250,000 casualties for the invasion of Kyushu. They cited Admiral Leahy's diary entry, written that evening, which stated that "General Marshall is of the opinion that such an effort will not cost us in casualties more than 63,000 of the 190,000 combatant troops."

On January 9, 1995, Harwit—his scholarly integrity on the line—proposed to the Legion a change in this volatile subject. He submitted two pages of new label copy. They did not, as was widely reported, accept 63,000 as an "official" figure; the historians all agreed such numbers were speculative. But the new text did drop the 250,000 figure, along with equally ungrounded claims that American casualties "conceivable could have risen to as many as one million (including up to a quarter of a million deaths)." The revised text continued, however, to underscore Truman's awareness that Japan had "some two million troops defending the home islands"; his fear of "an Okinawa from one end of Japan to the other"; the likelihood that many additional Allied and Asian lives would have been lost; and the fact that for Truman, "even the lowest of the casualty estimates was unacceptable." It concluded, as before, that "to save as many lives as possible, he chose to use the atomic bomb."

This may have been more accurate but it made the Legion leadership's already shaky position completely untenable. On January 19, seizing the opportunity Harwit had naively handed them, they called for the show's cancellation. In a public letter to President Clinton, they charged the Smithsonian with including "highly debatable information which calls into question the morality and motives of President Truman's decision to end World War II quickly and decisively by using the atomic bomb."

Five days later, on January 24, eighty-one congresspeople sent a letter to Secretary Heyman demanding Harwit's ouster for his "continuing defiance and disregard for needed improvements to the exhibit." Opposition opinion now crystallized around a suggestion of General Paul Tibbets, the man who had named the *Enola Gay* (after his mother) and piloted it over Hiroshima. Early in the debate, Tibbets, unhappy that many were "second-guessing the decision to use the atomic weapons," had issued a soldierly injunction: "To them, I would say, 'Stop!'" The plane, Tibbets declared, needed only an eleven word label. "'This airplane was the first one to drop an atomic bomb.' You don't need any other explanation." Tibbets wanted no questions, no controversies, no account of bombs bursting in air.

Facing special hearings in the House and Senate, threats to the Smithsonian's budget (77 percent of which came from the federal government), and a loss of confidence among corporate contributors on whom he was counting to fund a planned 150th anniversary celebration in 1996, Secretary Heyman called it quits. On January 30, 1995, adopting Tibbet's position, he scrapped the exhibition in favor of "a display, permitting the *Enola Gay* and its crew to speak for themselves." Heyman argued this was the wrong show in the wrong place at the wrong time.

The NASM had "made a basic error in attempting to couple an historical treatment of the use of atomic weapons with the fiftieth anniversary commemoration of the end of the war." The veterans "were not looking for analysis," he said, "and, frankly, we did not give enough thought to the intense feelings such an analysis would evoke." The implication was that curators should have waited a few years or even a decade, until the old soldiers had faded away.

JOHN CORRELL INTRODUCED NASM curators to his constituency; let me introduce his constituency to the wider world. The Air Force Association has been presented throughout this affair as a veterans organization. Even Harwit described it as "a nonprofit organization for current and former members of the U.S. Air Force." But a perusal of the ads in Correll's *Air Force Magazine (AFM)* makes instantly clear that it is a good deal more than that. In marked contrast to the American Legion's journal, where the wares on sale include hearing aids, power mowers, Florida retirement homes, and talking memo-minders, *AFM*'s pages are festooned with glossy advertisements for sleek warplanes produced by various of the Air Force Association's 199 Industrial Associates (whose ranks include Boeing, du Pont, Martin Marietta, Northrop Grumman, Rockwell, and Lockheed, which hawks its F–16 to Correll's readers for only "a $20 million price tag.")

The AFA, in fact, is the air wing of what Dwight Eisenhower called the military-industrial complex. It was founded in 1946 at the instigation of Hap Arnold (with Jimmy Doolittle as first president). Arnold, hyperattentive to public relations, set up the AFA to lobby for creation of an independent air force, to fight post-war budget cutbacks, and to "keep our country vigorously aroused to the urgent importance of air power." It has been the semiofficial lobbying arm of the United States Air Force ever since. In succeeding decades the AFA institutionalized relations with the defense industry by sponsoring mammoth expositions of military hardware (known to critics as the "arms bazaar"); opposed Kennedy's test-ban treaty; denounced Johnson's refusal to unleash air power in Vietnam (a Correll predecessor deplored America's renunciation "of the use of even the smallest of nuclear weapons"); battled the peace movement; railed against the "anti-military, anti-industry" atmosphere of the 1970s; and warned about the dangers associated with a "relaxation of tensions, and an end to the Cold War."

But the Cold War ended, as did the glory days of the Reagan buildup, and the AFA turned to fighting the cutbacks in military budgets "demanded by the liberal community." During the period Correll was assaulting the Air and Space Museum, his magazine featured articles like "Another Year, Another Cut," "Boom and Bust in Fighter Procurement," "This Isn't the Bottom Yet," "More Base Closures Coming Up," and "The Case for Air Power Modernization." When not urging Congress "to shift the burden of the cuts to entitlement spending—and thus spare defense," *AFM* writers were warding off attacks from the Army ("They need money," said Correll, "and they are ready to take a bite out of the Air Force to get it") or making preemptive strikes on the Navy.

In an era of imperiled budgets and reduced political clout—a function, Correll believed, of the diminishing percentage of veterans in the country and Congress—the AFA was more than ever concerned with image. "Attitude surveys show waning desire among young people to join the military," Correll noted, a decline he attributed in part to negative portrayals by the news media and entertainment industry. Whether one thinks well or ill of the AFA's positions, it should come as no surprise to find it paying meticulous attention to how the premiere achievement of American air power—arguably the one instance in which strategic bombing, not an army invasion or a navy blockade, triumphantly ended a major war—would be treated at the most popular museum in the world.

The AFA's relationship with the NASM moreover, was consanguineous. Hap Arnold, who fathered the AFA in 1946, begat the NASM the very same year. Arnold wanted to give aviation a history and extend the wartime interest in aeronautics into the next generation. The general saved large numbers of his war birds from being converted to scrap metal, and he lobbied Congress for a museum. To bolster his case, Arnold sought and received supporting petitions from 267 museum boosters, many of them representatives of such aviation firms as Northrop, Lockheed, Douglas, McDonnell, Sperry, Sikorsky and Republic, the same constituency from which AFA would draw its Industrial Associates. One witness stressed that a museum could win thousands of future voters to the cause of aviation, voters who in turn would influence their congressman "to develop aviation, both civil and military, in the years to come."

In the decades after Congress established the National Air Museum (expanded to embrace Space in 1966), relations with the AFA were cordial and fraternal. In 1949, for instance, the National Air Museum cooperated with the Air Force Association in putting on the National Air Fair, the country's largest air show to date. It was at this event that the *Enola Gay*, flown in by Colonel Tibbets from storage in Arizona, was officially presented to the Smithsonian. When the museum's drive for a building on the mall got stalled during the Vietnam War, it was reignited by Senator Barry Goldwater, board chairman of the AFA's Aerospace Education Foundation and soon-to-be recipient of its highest honor, the H. H. Arnold Award, Goldwater declared the NASM "a cause that is right" and "a cause that deserves a fight." A properly housed museum that presented a "patriot's history" would, he argued, inspire the nation's "air and space minded" young people. Interestingly, Goldwater did not think the *Enola Gay* should be included in that story. "What we are interested in here are the truly historic aircraft," he explained to a congressional committee. "I wouldn't consider the one that dropped the bomb on Japan as belonging to that category."

After the new building opened in 1976, the NASM blossomed. Its world-class collection of airplanes (like Lindbergh's *Spirit of St. Louis*) accumulated over decades by the indefatigable Paul Garber, along with the awesome lunar landers, moon rocks, and missiles assembled during the triumphal era of space flight, helped attract enormous crowds. The NASM became the most massively visited museum in the world, welcoming in recent years over eight million people a year. But NASM went beyond simply amassing aircraft. It was one of the first museums anywhere to seriously examine the evolution of aviation and astronautic technology. Like most museums of science and industry, however, NASM kept its focus on the hardware, adopting an evolutionary approach that assumed technological development was inherently progressive. It was, as former director (and former astronaut) Michael Collins said, "a cheery and friendly place," marked by a "spirit of optimism." Another former director, Walter Boyne, a career Air Force officer, prolific historian, and AFA member, kept the institution on the same path.

Relatively little attention was paid to the social consequences of flight, particularly military flight. The WW I and WW II galleries remained little more than cabinets of aero-curiosities. The collections of planes and mementos, the heroic murals, the mini-shrines (fashioned from personal effects and reminiscences) to AFA deities Hap Arnold and Jimmy Doolittle—none of these grappled with the fundamental purpose of war, the infliction of damage on the enemy. This did not trouble the museum's corporate sponsors or military donors or the Air Force Association. The institution was largely run by ex–military personnel; it featured gleaming civilian and military aircraft (most of them emblazoned with corporate logos and/or service insignia); it trumpeted aviation's very real technological accomplishments while ensuring that seldom was heard a discouraging word. The NASM promoted just the kind of public image that Arnold, Goldwater and the AFA had always intended to foster.

NASM did not lack for critics, however. A 1979 *White Paper on Science Museums* suggested that its decontextualization of artifacts and its cozy compliance with the promotional demands of corporate donors made it "basically a temple to the glories of aviation and the inventiveness of the aerospace industry." Later commentators concurred in calling it "a giant advertisement for air and space technology." And by the late 1980s the Smithsonian Council agreed that it was no longer "intellectually or morally acceptable to present science simply as an ennobling exploration of the unknown," or technology merely as "problem solving beneficial to the human race."

In 1987 Cornell astrophysicist Martin Harwit was chosen over an air force general to be the new NASM director. Harwit set out to demonstrate the social impact of aviation and space technology—the ways it transformed daily life "both for the good and the bad." This applied to the military sphere, too. "No longer is it sufficient to display sleek fighters," he said, while making no mention of the "misery of war." The NASM continued to do traditional kinds of AFA-friendly programming. It put on a commemorative program for the fiftieth anniversary of Jimmy Doolittle's raid over Tokyo. It mounted an exhibit (curated by Neufeld, the suspect Canadian) that honored the P–47 Thunderbolt, delighting the two-thousand-member association of its former pilots. Harwit also supported Richard Hallion (later a vigorous critic of the *Enola Gay* scripts) in creating a laudatory show on air power in the Gulf War.

But Harwit also authorized new departures. NASM treatment of military hardware had heretofore invariably skirted its lethal purposes, even in the case of Nazi weaponry. Label copy for the museum's V-2 rocket emphasized its progressive role in the history of technology. In 1990, however, the V-2 was given new panels which recounted its use as an indiscriminate instrument of murder (they included the NASM's first-ever image of a corpse); noted it was built by concentration camp prisoners, thousands of whom perished in the process; demonstrated how scientists like Wernher Von Braun avoided grappling with the ethical implications of their work; and provided superior technical detail about rocketry. Press reaction was startled but positive. One reviewer hailed the new "truth in labeling" as "striking in comparison to the fairy tale it has replaced. . . ."

Another novel exhibition deployed an American Pershing II missile side-by-side with a Soviet SS-20 as the twin foci of an examination of arms control agreements. This, too, garnered only positive reports. Next, in 1991, the institution replaced its old World War I gallery—whose artifacts had fallen prey to insect infestation—with a rich and imaginative show. It began with popular culture images depicting the war as a series of romantic duels between "knights of the air"—pulp magazine accounts, a compilation of clips from Hollywood films, and

Snoopy and his flying doghouse ("Curse you, Red Baron"). The origin of these images—which resonate to this day—was traced to wartime newspapers, businesspersons, and government propagandists who seized on the courage and daring of individual aces to portray aerial combat as a chivalric adventure. But the careful analyses that followed made clear the grim and unglamorous realities of fighter pilot life and death. Powerful dioramas of trench warfare and discussions of particular battles also demonstrated the important but secondary role of wartime air power, and dramatic displays on Germany's air attacks on London illustrated the birth of civilian bombing.

Again, reaction in the mainstream press was overwhelmingly favorable. Hank Burchard of the *Washington Post* was astonished to find such "rank heresy" in an institution "that has from the beginning served as the central shrine of the military-industrial complex." Though he complained that the exhibition still soft-pedaled the realities of aerial combat, which was "more akin to assassination than to jousting," he concluded: "But hey, a museum largely run by pilots can hardly be expected to badmouth them, and anyway this is a quibble compared with the quantum leap forward into historicity that this exhibition represents."

Finally, a direct precursor of the *Enola Gay* show—a five-minute videotape on the restoration process, which included powerful images of bomb damage—attracted considerable visitor attention and no negative commentary whatever. To key NASM staff it seemed that these plaudits and silences had cleared the way for the *Enola Gay*. Despite the continuing trepidation of some within the institution, they swept ahead with plans for the exhibition.

From the perspective of the AFA these new initiatives must have seemed like serpents wriggling their way into the Garden of Eden. Certainly Correll's April 1994 *AFM* critique of the *Enola Gay* exhibit included a retroactive blast at the World War I exhibition—that "strident attack on air power"—as having been a harbinger of what followed. Everything about it appalled him. The curators' notion that "dangerous myths have been foisted on the world by zealots and romantics." The criticism of the "cult of air power," with the sainted Billy Mitchell among the designated offenders. The "theories" quoted in the exhibit's companion book about military air power having the potential for "scientific murder" (Correll apparently forgetting for the moment that the offending phrase was actually Eddie Rickenbacker's, the most famous of all U.S. aces, who reminded Americans that "fighting in the air is not a sport. It is scientific murder.") The way the show emphasized "the horrors of World War I" (as opposed to its upbeat dimensions?) And above all, the fact that it "takes a hostile view of air power in that conflict," to the point where "the military airplane is characterized as an instrument of death."

To his credit, Correll published in the June 1994 *AFM* a strong rejoinder from Richard H. Kohn, former chief of air force history for the U.S. Air Force. The NASM, Kohn argued, had in recent years succeeded "in broadening the scope and value of its exhibits by presenting thoughtful, balanced history rather than mere celebration of flight and space travel." The World War I exhibit, he said, was "not at all hostile to air power. It presents the war realistically and explains aviation's role in it." It was Correll, not the curators, who favored a "political use of the museum: to downplay war's reality and to glorify military aviation." Such a bias, Kohn insisted, "would not be in keeping with the museum's or the Smithsonian's mission and would embarrass the Air Force community, which, having experienced the history, would want it presented truthfully—with strength, balance, sensitivity and integrity."

Correll was having none of it. He believed, borrowing the words of a fellow editor, that "a new order is perverting the museum's original purpose from restoring and displaying aviation and space artifacts to presenting gratuitous social commentary on the uses to which they have been put." People come to NASM to see old aircraft, Correll claimed. "They are not interested in counterculture morality pageants put on by academic activists." It was precisely because curatorial "interests and attitudes have shifted" that the *Enola Gay* exhibit had gone wrong. It was imperative that the Smithsonian's "keepers and overseers take a strong hand and stop this slide" and get the museum back on track.

Here, I think, one can see the structural faultlines that underlay the surface struggle over texts. How the *Enola Gay* was to be interpreted was important in its own right. How to interpret the meaning of Hiroshima was of vital significance both to the AFA and to NASM; indeed the plane itself had been entwined in the institutional lives of both organizations since their inception. But the curators' exhibition plans for the *Enola Gay* were also seen as the latest in a series of museological departures that taken together signaled AFA leaders that "their" institution was being taken away from them. They were determined to get it back. The wrestling match over control of the interpretation was emblematic of the struggle for control of the institution. The AFA, less interested in improving the scripts than in axing their opponents, adopted a policy of taking no prisoners. Convinced the curators were subverting the museum, it was but a short step to accusing them of subverting the Republic.

In the supercharged atmosphere surrounding the fiftieth anniversary of Hiroshima, Correll's charges easily touched off a museological conflagration. But to understand why it developed into a national incident we need to examine the larger context. For the battle of the *Enola Gay* was only one of several engagements that broke out that summer, all along the "History Front" of a wider Culture War.

ON OCTOBER 20, JUST AS THE FIFTH and final *Enola Gay* script was emerging from the latest round of revisions, the history wars escalated once again. Lynne Cheney, former head of the National Endowment for the Humanities (NEH), launched a preemptive strike in the *Wall Street Journal* against the *National Standards for United States History*, due to be issued five days later. Several years in the making, and funded in 1992 by the NEH while Cheney was still director, the document was intended as a voluntary guide for teachers. Astonishingly ambitious, it offered broad analytical themes, over twenty-six hundred specific classroom exercises, and suggestions for encouraging historical thinking. Over six thousand teachers, administrators, scholars, parents, and business leaders were involved in the drafting process, which was marked by wide-ranging open debates, and the involvement of thirty-five advisory organizations, including the Organization of American Historians, the Organization of History Teachers, the American Historical Association, the National Education Association, and the American Association of School Librarians.

No matter. In her *Wall Street Journal* piece, and in subsequent articles and interviews, Cheney chanted the standard mantra: An inner core group—gripped by a "great hatred for traditional history," and intent on "pursuing the revisionist agenda"—had "in the name of political correctness," made sure that a "whole lot of basic history" did not appear. She proved this to her satisfaction by adopting Correll's pseudostatistical method. "Counting how many times different subjects are mentioned in the document yields telling results," she wrote ominously. Traditional heroes were underrepresented, women and minorities mentioned too often; references to (black female) Harriet Tubman cropped up more often than to (white male) Ulysses S. Grant. In addition, the *Standards* lacked "a tone of affirmation," directed attention to social conflict, and invited debate not celebration. Predictably, she concluded her initial blast with a call for battle against the all-powerful "academic establishment."

Cheney's analysis bordered on the disinformational. The *Standards* were not a textbook, a dictionary of biography, or a compendium of important facts, much less a pantheon or catechism. Counting white faces and listing a few famous absentees was therefore disingenuous: The issues and events that the document urged exploring patently required reference to the supposedly spurned generals and presidents. In addition, bean counters more scrupulous than Cheney discovered not only that the vast majority of cited individuals were in fact white males, but that the two most-often-mentioned of the genus were Richard Nixon and Ronald Reagan.

Cheney's real objections—assuming they were motivated by more than mere personal ambition and political calculation—seemed to be to the paradigmatic shift the *Standards* represented. In its pages the American past was not a simple saga of remarkable men doing remarkable deeds. Those deeds were included—despite Cheney's charges, for example, the Constitution was treated extensively—but so, too, were less laudatory dimensions of the historical record. Slavery was examined, not to denigrate the American past, but to understand it. And the *Standards*, like much contemporary scholarship, embraced the experience of ordinary people—as heroes of their own lives and as collective actors on the world-historical stage.

Some fellow conservatives—notably Diane Ravitch—were also critical of the *Standards* but balked at Cheney's demand that they be scrapped. Especially given the *Standards* drafters expressed willingness to respond to substantive objections, such as complaints that monetarist theories explaining the Great Depression were slighted, or that a few dozen (out of twenty-six hundred) classroom exercises could arguably be described as shepherding students to preselected conclusions.

But most of the crew that copied Correll now echoed Cheney. Though few in numbers—far fewer than the multitudes that had fashioned the *Standards* —their command of media megaphones allowed them to manufacture another uproar. Rush Limbaugh weighed in four days after Cheney's initial intervention. With his usual insouciant disregard for facts, he informed his radio audience that the "insidious document" had been "worked on in secret." In truth, the drafts had been hammered into shape in countless sessions of democratic discussions embracing enormous numbers of participants, including twenty-three days of formal (tape recorded) meetings, and hundreds of copies had been dispatched to all who requested them. Limbaugh pronounced it "an intellectually dishonest, politically correct version of American history" that ought to be "flushed down the toilet." With yawning predictability, columnist Charles Krauthammer called it "a classic of political correctness." *The Wall Street Journal* bundled letters on the subject under the headline: History Thieves. And John Leo o'er-hastily objected to the elevation of one Ebenezer McIntosh, a "brawling street lout of the 1760s," to the heroic stature of a Sam Adams; unfortunately for Leo, McIntosh turned out to be an important leader of the Stamp Act Demonstrations in Boston. Not for three weeks did a major national news story—in the *New York Times*—do much more than parrot Cheney's charges, and by then, the election was over.

Victory in November 1994 did not stem the Republican assault on revisionists. Indeed, their accession to political power shaped the *Enola Gay* endgame. On January 24, sixty-eight Republicans (including House Majority Leader and Gingrich ally Dick Armey) and thirteen Democrats demanded Martin Harwit's ouster. Representative Blute elaborated: "We think there are some very troubling questions in regard to the Smithsonian, not just with this *Enola Gay* exhibit but over the past ten years or so, getting into areas of revisionist history and political correctness. There are a lot of questions that need to be answered."

January 26, critics began tying the two issues together. Columnist George Will claimed "the Smithsonian Institution, like the history standards" was "besotted with the cranky anti-Americanism of the campuses. . . ." Lynne Cheney, in guileful congressional testimony, seized on one of the twenty-six hundred teaching examples to argue that fifth or sixth graders who learned about the end of World War II from the proposed history standards would know only that the United States had devastated Hiroshima, but nothing of Japanese aggression. In fact the standards called explicitly for analysis of the "German, Italian and Japanese drives for empire in the 1930s"; and a suggested teaching activity for seventh and eighth graders was to construct a time line that included the "Japanese seizure of Manchuria in 1931." Also on January 26, Speaker Gingrich named Representative Sam Johnson—the ardent *Enola Gay* show critic who had alerted him to the issue—to the Smithsonian's board of regents. The following day Gingrich announced he had found "a certain political correctness seeping in and distorting and prejudicing the Smithsonian's exhibits," and declared the museum should not be "a plaything for left-wing ideologies." [4]

Four days later Heyman scuttled the *Enola Gay* exhibit.[5] Now in full retreat, he also announced "postponement" for at least five years of a planned exhibit on air power in Vietnam; suggested that critics of "political correctness" in recent interpretive exhibits had a point; and promised the regents he would review and, where necessary, rectify current exhibits that board members believed reflected "revisionist history." Heyman refused to fire Harwit, but then long-time Smithsonian critic Senator Ted Stevens (R–Alaska) announced he would go ahead in mid-May 1995 with previously threatened hearings on the philosophical underpinnings of the exhibit. On May 2, Harwit resigned. The continuing controversy, he said, had convinced him "that nothing less than my stepping down from the directorship will satisfy the Museum's critics." Regent Sam Johnson immediately made clear that Harwit's departure was not enough, that only a full scale purge of "revisionists" would do.

The actual exhibition opened on June 28, 1995. It proved even more of a retreat than had been anticipated. Heyman claimed it simply reported "the facts" but it was heavily larded with AFA-style interpretation. The label copy declared that "the use of the bombs led to the immediate surrender of Japan and made unnecessary the planned invasion of the Japanese home islands. Such an invasion, especially if undertaken for both main islands, would have led to very heavy casualties among American and Allied troops and Japanese civilians and military. It was thought highly unlikely that Japan, while in a very weakened military condition, would have surrendered unconditionally without such an invasion." This, of course, finessed a host of issues, among them the role of the Soviet declaration of war (utterly unmentioned here), the question of whether a *conditional* surrender might not have ended the war with neither invasion *nor* bombing, and the considered judgment of many wartime leaders that the Japanese might well have surrendered before the earliest possible invasion.

Nor, apart from a twenty-second video snippet showing bomb effects (which may or may not have included an almost subliminal image of a corpse), and label copy saying that the two bombs "caused tens of thousands of deaths" (by most accounts, a gross understatement), was there any confrontation with the destruction of Hiroshima and Nagasaki. "I really decided to leave it more to the imagination," Heyman said at a June 27, news conference.

The "aircraft speaks for itself in this exhibit" the secretary added, and indeed NASM scattered additional pieces of the giant plane throughout the embarrassingly bare galleries, trying to fill them up with mammoth chunks of metal. But, in fact, it is the *Enola Gay's* pilot and crew who speak on its behalf, in a sixteen-minute concluding video presentation. It is certainly appropriate to include the crew's reminiscences as part of the story. But why should their ringing retroactive justification of their mission (and that of their colleagues over Nagasaki) be privileged, and the troubled post-war reflections of men like Eisenhower, Leahy and even Truman himself be proscribed? It is as if the plane that dropped the atomic bomb were an artifact akin to a kettle or a wedding dress, which required only some donor-provided information about its original usage.[6]

FOR ALL THE NEW ELITE'S LIBERTARIAN PROFESSIONS about reducing the power of big government, they seem drawn to authoritarian solutions. In the case of the Air and Space Museum, congresspeople laid down an official historical "line" and demanded the firing of curators who did not toe it. Gingrich himself believes our ailing culture can be cured through state intervention, "first of all by the people appointed to the Smithsonian board." Regent Sam Johnson—Newt's first cultural commissar—agrees completely that "this Congress has an opportunity to change the face of America," and makes clear that his goal is "to get patriotism back into the Smithsonian."

In the case of the *Enola Gay*, Japan served as an acceptable substitute for the Evil Empire. Attacks on the exhibition gained strength and plausibility from Japan's egregious approach to its past. Americans (and Asians) had been rightfully indignant at the cabinet ministers, educators, and curators who for decades downplayed or denied Japan's record of aggression, in sharp contrast to Germany's willingness to apologize for the criminal activities of its fascist state. The Hiroshima Peace Memorial Museum presented its city and country solely as martyrs and victims, as if the war had begun the day the bomb was dropped. This allowed critics to charge that National Air and Space—which was to have borrowed artifacts from the Hiroshima Museum—shared (or had been ensnared by) its lenders' politics.[7]

But those politics had begun to change. Under pressure from internal critics, particularly socialist and pacifist groups, Japan had taken significant steps toward accepting responsibility for launching the war and committing atrocities. Historians like Professor Yoshiaki Yoshimi, by irrefutably proving that Korean "comfort women" had been forced to service the Imperial Army, prodded the government into reversing its denial of responsibility. Leading intellectuals and politicians (including the Socialist Prime Minister Tomiichi Murayama) called for a Parliamentary apology to the Asian countries Japan invaded. Although this met with vehement opposition from a coalition of conservative parties, bureaucrats and business leaders, a 1994 poll found the Japanese people believed 4 to 1 that their country had not adequately compensated the citizens of conquered nations.[8]

In Hiroshima itself, recently elected Mayor Takashi Hiraoka argued "that when we think about the bomb, we should think about the war, too." Overcoming opposition from groups like the Great Japan Patriots Party, he won installation of new exhibitry in June 1994, just as the *Enola Gay* affair was heating up, which described in detail the city's role in the war effort.[9]

This makes the Smithsonian's cancellation particularly ironic, with the Americans (under pressure from the right) refusing to reflect on the past just as the Japanese (under pressure from the left) were beginning to confront it. Ironic and unfortunate, in that closing down a public historical enterprise that transcended narrow nationalist interpretations muffed an opportunity to bind up old war wounds and reconcile former enemies. Still, if Japan continues along this "revisionist" path, it will be harder for American xenophobes to replicate a triumph which, in any event, was rooted in singular circumstances. And while Japan may be a tough competitor, it is a capitalist competitor, and an ally to boot: It will not be as easy to (as it were) "yellow-bait" intellectuals as it once was to "red-bait" them.

NOTES

1. Leahy's judgment in 1950 was: "It is my opinion that the use of this barbarous weapon at Hiroshima and Nagasaki was of no material success in our war against Japan," as "the Japanese were already defeated and ready to surrender because of the effective sea blockade and the successful bombing with conventional weapons." Eisenhower asserted in 1963 that Japan "was seeking some way to surrender with a minimum loss of 'face'" and that "it wasn't necessary to hit them with that awful thing."

2. Arnold, Spaatz, and LeMay opposed dropping the atomic bomb except as part of an invasion. Arnold pressed these views as late as the Potsdam Conference in late July 1945, but in the end deferred to General Marshall. After the war, Arnold said that "atomic bomb or no atomic bomb, the Japanese were already on the verge of collapse," and LeMay believed that "even without the atomic bomb and the Russian entry into the war, Japan would have surrendered in two weeks." Some think these judgments stemmed from fear that superbombs would torpedo the generals' dreams of a postwar independent air force with seventy wings and thousands of fliers.

3. The group included: Barton J. Bernstein of Stanford, a student of nuclear policy; Stanley Goldberg, a scholar studying General Groves and his Manhattan Project; Akira Iriye of Harvard, a historian of Japanese American relations; Richard Rhodes, author of *The Making of the Atomic Bomb*; Martin Sherwin, Dartmouth historian and author of *A World Destroyed: The Atomic Bomb and the Grand Alliance*; Victor Bond, a medical doctor at Brookhaven National Laboratory; Edward T. Linenthal, student of American attitudes to war memorials; Dr. Richard Hallion, Air Force Historian; and, contrary to claims that curators consulted no one with actual wartime experience, Edwin Bearss, chief historian of National Park Service, a decorated Marine veteran, present at Pearl Harbor, wounded at Guadalcanal, and a strong supporter of the script. This group met only once, although they were also consulted, over succeeding months, on a seriatim basis.

4. It is hard to imagine that if Newt had ever actually set foot in the National Air and Space Museum he would not have been pleased with the WW I exhibition his allies so detested. Gingrich claims as a transformational defining moment his visit, at age 15, to the Verdun battlefield. There he peered through the windows of an ossuary containing the bones of one-hundred-thousand unidentified bodies. "I can still feel the sense of horror and reality which overcame me then," he wrote in his 1984 book *Window of Opportunity*. "It is the driving force which pushed me into history and politics and molded my life." The WW I exhibition features a giant photograph of the Verdun Ossuary. Pity he is intent on denying others even an echo of the experience he founded so moving and instructive.

5. President Clinton, whose past and present relations with the military left him in no position to challenge the decision, observed with his usual caution that while "academic freedom" was an issue

here, he "nonetheless felt that some of the concerns expressed by veterans groups and others had merit."

6. Not surprisingly, after previewing the exhibition on June 21, Tibbets wrote Heyman he was "pleased and proud" of it. It simply presented the "basic facts," he argued preposterously, without any "attempts to persuade anyone about anything." This happy outcome, Tibbets added, "demonstrates the merits and the positive influence of management"—whose firm hand was again in evidence on opening day, when twenty-one demonstrators with the *Enola Gay* Action Coalition were hauled away by a U.S. Park Police SWAT team.

7. "They are bending over backwards it looks like to accommodate the Japanese," said Sam Johnson. Ironically, curator Tom Crouch was on record as being "really bothered, angered, by the way that the Japanese find it so difficult to put wartime issues in real context. Their view is to portray themselves as victims." Crouch, however, saw parallels in this country. "As I listen to the folks who criticize this [exhibit], I hear something similar to that. There's real discomfort about looking at destruction on the ground. . . . I hear critics saying, 'Don't tell part of the story.' They want to stop the story when the bomb leaves the bomb bay."

8. A "Japan Committee to Appeal for World Peace '95," composed of scholars and cultural workers, called for an "apology and compensation for damages to the Asian peoples whom we victimized," and urged the Japanese government and Diet to "clearly articulate the government's self-reflection on Japan's responsibility for past colonial rule as well as the Asia–Pacific War. . . ." The political establishment teetered back and forth on this issue. Prime Minister Murayama went to Beijing in spring 1995 and said: "I recognize anew that Japan's actions, including aggression and colonial rule, at one time in our history caused unbearable suffering and sorrow for many people in your country and other Asian neighbors." He also wrote a scroll: "I face up to history."

The Japanese nationalist right did not. Shigeto Nagano, justice minister and former chief of staff of the army, insisted in May 1995 that the massacre of hundreds of thousands of Chinese at Nanking in 1937 was a "fabrication," and he reaffirmed that Japan, in invading Asian countries, had been "liberating" them from Western colonial powers. On May 12, 1995, however, a Tokyo High Court ruling of the previous October was affirmed, thus sanctioning Japanese historian Sabuto Ienaga's thirty-one-year struggle against the Education Ministry for whitewashing schoolbook accounts of the massacre. The court also revoked the Ministry's theretofore accepted right to determine historical "truth."

On June 6, 1995, the right-wing Liberal Democratic Party forced a compromise on the Parliamentary apology front. A resolution carried the lower house expressing remorse for causing "unbearable pain to people abroad, particularly in Asian countries." But the wording was ambiguous enough to allow for varying interpretations (thus "Hansei" could mean "remorse," or merely "reflection"). The upper house refused even to consider such a resolution. A week later, on June 14, the government responded by establishing a fund to provide medical and social welfare assistance to former comfort women. Although it fell short of what some of the women had demanded, it was accompanied by a statement of remorse and apology.

Finally, Prime Minister Murayama, on August 15, during fiftieth anniversary commemorations of the war's end, made the most explicit declaration yet. Noting the damage and suffering caused by Japan he said: "I regard, in a spirit of humility, these irrefutable facts of history, and express here once again my feelings of deep remorse and state my heartfelt apology." "Our task," he added, "is to convey to the younger generations the horrors of war, so that we never repeat the errors in our history."

9. Similarly, Tokyo's Metropolitan Edo–Tokyo Museum mounted a major exhibition for the March 1995 fiftieth anniversary of the city's being firebombed. Though retaining a focus on domestic suffering, it included information on 1930s and 1940s militarism. (Video clips showed Japanese bombers attacking Chongquing.)

UNCONDITIONAL SURRENDER AT THE SMITHSONIAN

John W. Dower

FIFTIETH ANNIVERSARIES OF HISTORICAL EVENTS—particularly wars—breed controversy. The emotion-laden memories of survivors from the events of a half-century ago collide with the skepticism and detachment of younger generations. Historians with access to previously inaccessible (or ignored) material offer new perspectives. Politicians milk the still palpable human connection between past and present for every possible drop of ideological elixir.

The fiftieth anniversary of the end of World War II in Asia has become especially contentious. Why is this so, when presumably we are commemorating victory over an enemy generally regarded as aggressive, atrocious, and fanatical? The answer, of course, is that defeating Japan ultimately entailed incinerating and irradiating tens of thousands of men, women, and children with a weapon more terrible than any previously known or imagined.

Unfortunately, Americans have been denied a rare opportunity to use the fiftieth anniversary of Hiroshima and Nagasaki to reflect more deeply about these world-changing developments. This opportunity was lost early this year when the Smithsonian Institution, bowing to political pressure, agreed to drastically scale back a proposed exhibit at the National Air and Space Museum in Washington depicting the development of the atomic bombs and their use against Japan.

As initially envisioned by the Smithsonian's curators, the exhibition would have taken viewers through a succession of rooms that introduced, in turn, the ferocity of the last year of the war in Asia, the development of the bomb, the unfolding imperatives behind the U.S. decision to use the weapon against Japan, preparation for the *Enola Gay* mission that dropped the first bomb on Hiroshima (with the fuselage of the *Enola Gay* itself being the centerpiece of the exhibition), the human consequences of the bombs in the two target cities, and the nuclear legacy to the post-war world. Occasional placards were to have summarized controversies that have emerged in scholarship and public discourse on these matters over the past decades.

This ambitious proposed exhibit proved to be politically unacceptable. The Senate unanimously denounced the original draft script as being "revisionist and offensive to many World War II veterans." It was grossly misleading and morally obtuse, the critics declared, to focus the exhibit so intensely on questions about the bombs, and on the Japanese suffering in Hiroshima and Nagasaki, without comparable portrayal of Japanese atrocities that extended from Nanking to Pearl Harbor to Bataan to Manila. The chief historian of the Air Force (who had privately praised the original draft) asked publicly how the Smithsonian had managed to make a hash of such a "morally unambiguous" subject as the use of the bombs.

Confronted by such criticism, the Smithsonian—like Japan 50 years earlier—surrendered unconditionally. Visitors to the Air and Space Museum will encounter a small exhibition featuring the fuselage of the *Enola Gay* and a brief commentary explaining that this was the plane that dropped the first atomic bomb, following which, nine days later, Japan surrendered. The artifact, it is now argued, speaks for itself.

Artifacts do not speak for themselves, and the decision to scrap original plans for an ambitious and nuanced exhibition represents the triumph of patriotic orthodoxy over serious historical reflection and reconstruction. No one denies that the Smithsonian's original script had problems and needed revisions (the curators themselves readily circulated their first draft for critical comments). The benign and minimalist exhibit we have ended up with, however, is a travesty—an appallingly simplistic and nationalistic way of representing one of the most momentous and destructive developments of the twentieth century. Instead of using the fiftieth anniversary of Hiroshima and Nagasaki to reflect on the confluence of triumph and tragedy that occurred in August 1945, we have turned this into another occasion to perpetuate a heroic national myth.

The orthodox account argues that the war in Asia was a brutal struggle against a fanatical, expansionist foe (which is true, albeit cavalier about European and American colonial control in Asia up to 1941). This righteous war against Japanese aggression was ended, the heroic narrative continues, by the dropping of the atomic bombs, which saved enormous numbers of American lives that otherwise would have been sacrificed in the invasion of Japan that was deemed necessary to force a surrender. As the Senate's condemnation of the Smithsonian's plans put it, the atomic bombs brought the war to a "merciful" end.

President Truman and his advisers clearly did consider the bombs as a way of hastening the war's end and saving American lives. Few historians, however, now regard this as the only motivation behind the decision. Facts that complicate the orthodox narrative, for example, include the Soviet entry into the war against Japan on August 8, 1945, two days after Hiroshima. Most Japanese accounts then and since weigh the Soviet declaration of war as being at least as shocking as the Hiroshima bombing to the Japanese leadership. The United States had long solicited Soviet entry into the war against Japan, and knew it was imminent. Why the haste to drop the bomb before the effect of the Soviet declaration of war could be measured?

The heroic narrative similarly fails to question the need for the atomic bombing of Nagasaki on August 9, which occurred before Japan's high command had a chance to assess Hiroshima and the Soviet entry. Indeed, even many Japanese who now accept that Hiroshima may have been necessary to crack the no-surrender policy of the Japanese militarists maintain that Nagasaki was plainly and simply a war crime.

Also generally neglected in the heroic narrative is that the United States was not on the brink of invading Japan in August of 1945. The preliminary assault, aimed at the southern island of Kyushu, was slated for no earlier than November 1, and the invasion of Tokyo and the Kanto area on the main island of Honshu would not have commenced until March 1946. There was time to consider options. Other information suggests that an invasion may not have been necessary at all. A famous report by the U.S. Strategic Bombing Survey, published in 1946, concluded that Japan was so materially and psychologically weakened by August 1945 that it would have been forced to surrender by year's end, and probably by November 1—without the atomic bombs, without the Soviet entry, and without an invasion.

Alternatives to using the atomic bombs on civilian targets also became known after Japan's surrender. Navy planners, for example, believed that intensified economic strangulation would bring Japan to its knees; the country's merchant marine had been sunk by 1945. Within the Manhattan Project, the possibility of dropping the bomb on a "demonstration" target, with Japanese observers present, had been broached but rejected—partly for fear that the demonstration bomb might be a dud and would lead the Japanese to fight even more ferociously. Conservative officials such as Undersecretary of State Joseph Grew, the former ambassador to Japan, argued that the Japanese could be persuaded to surrender if the United States abandoned its policy of demanding unconditional surrender and guaranteed that the emperor would be allowed to keep his throne. Through their code-breaking operations, the Americans also were aware that, beginning in mid-June, the Japanese had made vague overtures to the Soviet Union concerning negotiating an end to the war.

While it was fear of a Nazi bomb that originally propelled the Manhattan Project, it now is known that U.S. planners had identified Japan as the prime target for the atomic bomb as early as 1943—a year or more before it became clear that Germany was not attempting to build such a weapon. One reason for this shift of target was the fear that if the bomb didn't work, sophisticated German scientists and engineers might be able to disassemble it and figure out how to build their own. (No one worried that the Japanese had this capability.)

The development and deployment of the bombs also became driven by almost irresistible technological and scientific imperatives—what some scientists later referred to as the "technically sweet" challenge of the Manhattan Project. J. Robert Oppenheimer later confided that after Germany's surrender on May 8, 1945, he and his fellow scientists intensified their efforts out of concern that the war might end before they could finish. Secretary of War Henry Stimson, the elder statesman who took deep pride in his moralism, observed at one point that it was essential to try the new weapon out on a real target. The original justification for moving to a new order of destructive weaponry had evaporated, and the weaponry itself had begun to create its own rationale.

Sheer visceral hatred abetted the targeting of Japan for nuclear destruction. Although many critics of the Smithsonian's original plans took umbrage at a statement calling attention to the element of vengeance in the American war against Japan, few historians (or honest participants) would discount that this was a factor. Japan had, after all, attacked the United States. "Remember Pearl Harbor—Keep 'em Dying" was a popular military slogan from the outset of the war, and among commentators and war correspondents at the time it was a commonplace that the racially and culturally alien Japanese were vastly more despised than their German allies.

U.S. leaders also had post-war politics on their minds—both global and domestic. Documents declassified since the 1960s make unmistakably clear that from the spring of 1945, top-level policy-makers hoped that the bomb would dissuade Stalin from pursuing Soviet expansion into Eastern Europe and elsewhere. Some individuals closely involved with the development of the bomb (such as Arthur Compton, Edward Teller, and James Conant) further argued that the new weapon's very horrendousness compelled its use against a real city, so that the post-war world would understand the need to cooperate on arms control. At the same time, shrewd readers of the domestic political winds in the United States warned that if the Manhattan Project ended with nothing dramatic to show for its efforts, the post-war Congress surely would launch a hostile investigation into the huge disbursal of secret funds.

The Japanese now estimate that within months of the attacks, around 140,000 people probably died in Hiroshima and 70,000 in Nagasaki. That is about double the figures typically reported in Western accounts, which are based on U.S. calculations made shortly after the bombs were dropped.

Such figures fail to take into account the peculiar long-term legacies of nuclear devastation. Because of the uncertain genetic effects of radiation poisoning, for example, *hibakusha*, as the atomic bomb survivors are known, became undesirable marriage prospects. And although no genetic harm to succeeding generations has been identified, irradiated survivors and their progeny have lived with gnawing fear that the curse of the bombs may be transgenerational. In the Japanese idiom, many survivors suffer "keloids of the heart" and "leukemia of the spirit."

More concretely, Japanese continue to die of atomic-bomb related diseases. Survivors suffer higher-than-normal rates of leukemia and cancers of the thyroid, breast, lung, stomach, and salivary glands. Moreover, infants exposed to radiation *in utero* before the eighteenth week who were born mentally retarded now are 50-year-old retarded adults, many with elderly parents who agonize over what will become of these microcephalic "pika babies" after the parents die.

Another fact commonly neglected in the orthodox American treatment of the bomb is that thousands of the victims were not Japanese. According to Japanese estimates, between, 6,500 and 10,000 Koreans were killed in Hiroshima and Nagasaki; Koreans themselves put the number even higher. (Most of these Koreans were colonial subjects of Japan who had been conscripted for heavy labor.) The bomb also killed more than 1,000 second-generation Japanese-Americans who had been temporarily living in Hiroshima when the Japanese attacked Pearl Harbor in 1941 and whom the war had prevented from returning to the United States. Scores of Chinese likely died in the nuclear blasts as well, along with small numbers of Southeast Asian students, British and Dutch POWs, and European priests. About two dozen Caucasian-American POWs survived the atomic bombing of Hiroshima, only to be beaten to death by Japanese *hibakusha*.

In Japan, as might be expected, popular memory of the atomic bombs tends to begin where the conventional American narrative leaves off—with what took place beneath the mushroom clouds of Hiroshima and Nagasaki. The Japanese dwell on the extraordinary human misery the bombs caused, providing intimate stories about the shattering of individual lives. Kenzaburo Oé, the 1994 Nobel laureate in literature, called attention to this in a series of influential essays written in the early 1960s. In Oé's rendering, the *hibakusha* were "moralists," for they had experienced "the cruelest days in human history" and never lost "the vision of a nation that will do its best to materialize a world without any nuclear weapons."

This perception of the significance of Hiroshima and Nagasaki—starkly different from that conveyed in the triumphal American narrative—clearly has the potential to become myopic and nationalistic. Japan risks turning the attacks on Hiroshima and Nagasaki into a "victimization" narrative, in which the bombs fell from heaven without context—as if war began on August 6, 1945 and ended on August 9, and innocent Japan bore the cross of witnessing the horror of the new nuclear age. But Oé's account, like most other popular Japanese discourse on these matters, is more subtle than this. Since the early 1970s, the Japanese media have devoted much attention to the thesis that "victims" can simultaneously be the victimizers of other—as the *hibakusha* in Hiroshima demonstrated when they beat to death American POWs.

It is virtually a cliché in the U.S. media that the Japanese suffer from historical amnesia and are incapable of honestly confronting their World War II past. There is much truth to this. For many years, Japanese textbooks presented a sanitized version of the conflict. Schoolchildren were taught that Japan "advanced" into China, rather than "invaded" its neighbor. Doubt was cast on the reality of the Rape of Nanking. Japan's colonial repression of other Asians was barely mentioned. To the present day, conservative politicians have refused to support a clear and unequivocal official statement acknowledging Japan's acts of aggression and atrocity and forthrightly apologizing for them.

At the same time, however, domestic debate on these matters has been far more intense than the foreign media usually acknowledges. In recent years—especially since the death of Emperor Hirohito in 1989—the textbooks have become more forthright, while the Japanese national media have carried detailed commentary on virtually all aspects of Japan's war behavior. In this context, certainly in light of the fiasco at the Smithsonian, it is anomalous for Americans to be accusing others of sanitizing the past and suffering from historical amnesia.

In the end, one of the greatest legacies of World War II was the redefinition of the legitimate targets of war to include non-combatant women, children, and men. Japan itself was one of the first countries to act out this new view of war; its bombing of Chinese cities in 1937 was passionately condemned by the League of Nations and the United States as behavior beyond the pale of civilized people. Picasso's great mural of the bombing of Guernica in the same year by the fascists during the Spanish Civil War evoked the shock that similar barbarity aroused.

By the end of World War II, however, even the democratic nations had accepted the targeting of civilian populations as proper and inevitable. Earlier in 1945, British and U.S. air forces obliterated much of Dresden after previously fire-bombing other German cities. In Japan, U.S. saturation bombing devastated Tokyo and 63 other cities, killing around 100,000 civilians in Tokyo alone. The atomic bombs were simply a more efficient way of terrorizing enemies and destroying a newly legitimized target: civilian morale.

In the fires of Hiroshima and Nagasaki, triumph and tragedy became inseparable. At the same time, America's victory became fused with a future of inescapable insecurity. The bombs marked both an end and a beginning. They marked the end of an appalling global conflagration that killed more than 55 million people and the beginning of the nuclear arms race—and a world in which security was forever a step away.

MEMORY,
MYTH AND
HISTORY

Martin J. Sherwin

C ENTRAL TO EVERY PUBLIC DEBATE ABOUT HISTORY is a question, seldom discussed, but one that must be investigated and answered before any intelligent discussion can proceed: How did the public acquire its information about the topic under discussion? Or, more generally and colloquially: How do we know what we know? This article addresses that question with respect to the atomic bombings of Hiroshima and Nagasaki and, by implication, suggests that answering it is the first order of business for historians engaged in public debates involving issues of historical accuracy.

The fiftieth anniversary of the end of World War II, with its attendant controversy at the Smithsonian's National Air and Space Museum (NASM) over the historical exhibit that was to accompany the display of the *Enola Gay*, the B-29 that dropped an atomic bomb on Hiroshima, produced a turning point in the public debate about the end of the war against Japan. It is one of the ironies of that controversy that the politically motivated censorship of the *Enola Gay* exhibit drew national attention to the historical research that veterans' organizations and their Congressional allies found objectionable. In writing about this research most of the mainstream press in the United States continued to support the atomic bombings as necessary and justified, while simultaneously acknowledging that the American public had been told a distorted version of the truth.

Thus, as visitors to the Air and Space museum viewed the *Enola Gay* surrounded by nostalgia, myth and trivia, readers of the weekly, *Newsweek*, learned more about the so-called revisionist case than they would have learned if the first, and much maligned, script, "The Crossroads: The End of World War II, the Atomic Bomb and the Origins of the Cold War," had become the basis for the *Enola Gay* exhibit.[1] No doubt the lessons of all this are as debatable as the issues, but one thing seems certain: in 1995 the history of 1945 remained a hostage to the politics of memory, and how that history was written played an important role in the politics of national security policy during the Cold War.

The *Enola Gay* debate is not only a poignant example of a clash between memory and history. It is also about the politics of history, and the political uses of history. Though fifty years in the past, Americans continue to live in the shadow of World War II, which is to say that personal memories of the war remain a part of the current debate over the history of the war. In this environment memory and history inevitably conflict, for memory, the living voice of the past, is personal and particular, while history, the scholarly reconstruction of the past, is universal and critical.[2] Memories may contribute to the construction of history, but history does not necessarily validate memory.

In the United States, the "collective memory" of World War II sees the war as "our finest hour." In Europe, we defeated a nation of fascist maniacs who were infected with racial madness and hell-bent on dominating the continent. In Asia, we destroyed a power-crazed military machine that had bombed, raped and plundered Koreans, Chinese and Southeast Asians, in addition to attacking, without a declaration of war, the U.S. Pacific Fleet at Pearl Harbor. And after we had defeated them, we fed them, put them back on their economic feet, and tutored them in democracy. In the American collective memory it was not simply the "Good War." It was the most just of wars, the model war, the most righteous of wars, and a war—as leaflets dropped on Japanese cities in July 1945 stated—in which America "[stood] for humanity."[3]

America without that image is unimaginable to the generation that fought the war, and to those in subsequent generations who have defined their lives by this image. If we did some terrible things, they had to be done; the Germans and Japanese brought the punishment they received—their well-deserved punishment many members of the war generation would say—on themselves. These attitudes are not the ravings of a reactionary fringe; they are the deeply felt beliefs of a broad spectrum of Americans. Readers of this essay may be familiar with Paul Fussell's ahistorical and mean-spirited article, "Thank God for the Atomic Bomb," in which critics of the atomic bombings are dismissed derisively as effete and ignorant.[4] But listen to a less contentious memory, the voice of Alvin Kernan, distinguished professor emeritus of English at Princeton University, a Navy enlisted man during World War II, who writes that, "The [atomic] bomb[s] gave [life] to me in my way of reckoning, and while others may feel otherwise, I was grateful and unashamed. In after years, on the faculty of liberal universities where it was an article of faith that dropping the bombs was a crime against mankind and another instance of American racism, I had to bite my tongue to keep silent, for to have said how grateful I was to *the* bomb would have marked me a fascist, the kind of fascist I had spent nearly five years fighting!"[5] Before such deeply held beliefs—the beliefs of warriors based on *their* memories of *their* war—historical research and rational argumentation is powerless to persuade.

Reinforcing the power of the warriors' individual and collective memories to resist the construction of critical histories of Hiroshima, Nagasaki, and of strategic bombing in general, were the demands and politics of the emerging Cold War. The image of American moral superiority was promoted even more than usual during the Cold War, and our increasing reliance on nuclear deterrence created powerful resistance to criticism of the wartime use of nuclear weapons. Early questions about the necessity of destroying Hiroshima and Nagasaki were replaced with answers, and the answers given left no room for ambiguity.

American society has an especially strong intolerance for ambiguity. Perhaps it results from our system of government which, in contrast to a parliamentary system, severely limits the spectrum of views we debate. Our public dialogues are driven towards over-simplification and clarity. More than in other democratic societies our problems are discussed in either/or terms: good or bad, right or wrong. Ambiguity and complexity are unwelcome, even viewed with suspicion in our political culture.

Unlike any other American war, World War II was an *un*ambiguous war, a war with clarity of purpose and an unprecedented shared sense of national unity. But victory left an ambiguous legacy—our relationship to our erstwhile Soviet ally. In 1947 George Kennan's containment policy suggested one way of dealing with our Soviet problem; but it too was ambiguous: as a political strategy it was too complex, and as an analysis it was too subtle.

The Berlin Blockade of 1948 transformed the American foreign policy environment. It not only recast the former German enemy into heroic victim of Soviet communism, but it led to the resolution of containment's ambiguities. As an American airlift kept west Berlin supplied, B-29 bombers capable of delivering nuclear weapons were moved ostentatiously to England. Our air power and our monopoly of nuclear weapons offered a direct way to deal with the Soviet threat—strategic nuclear bombing.[6]

With nuclear weapons and strategic bombing at the center of the United States' emerging Cold War defense strategy, the ambiguities inherent in the containment policy disappeared. The Cold War may have been a poor substitute for World War II, but World War II was an ideal model for the Cold War. The demand for clarity drove our politics, and our politics eliminated ambiguity. Stalin substituted for Hitler, Communism replaced National Socialism, and Soviet cities were targeted as so many Hiroshimas and Nagasakis. Memories of World War II coexisted comfortably with the perceived requirements of the Cold War, stifling any serious critical discussion of strategic bombing that had begun in the spring of 1945 in journals such as *The Christian Century, Christianity and Crisis, The Saturday Evening Post*, and that had continued after the war with criticisms of Hiroshima and Nagasaki.[7]

No one who looks closely at the arguments surrounding the atomic bombings will fail to recognize that there is more than a matter of history at stake. Hiroshima not only introduced the nuclear age to the world, but it also served as the symbolic coronation of American global power. The atomic bomb, as contemporary cartoonists depicted it, was our scepter, and its use contributed to the image of our international authority. But power was not the only foundation for that authority. "The position of the United States as a great humanitarian nation" was also important, Ralph Bard had written to Stimson in June, 1945 urging that the Japanese be warned several days prior to the attack.[8]

Bard's advice went unheeded and, perhaps, it should be no surprise that the initial irony of Hiroshima was that the very act symbolizing our wartime victory was quickly turned against our peacetime purposes. At the 1946–48 Tokyo War Crimes Trials, which, like the Nuremberg trials, were a symbolic expression of our moral authority, Justice Rabhabinod Pal of India cited the atomic bombings of Hiroshima and Nagasaki as evidence against our claim to rule in Asia by right of superior virtue. Those bombings, he wrote in a dissenting opinion, were "the only near approach [in the Pacific War] to the directive . . . of the Nazi leaders during the Second World War." [9]

Anticipating the issues of just cause and morality that Pal raised, the earliest public explanations for the bombings sought to assure the world that our actions had been morally justified. "We have used [the atomic bomb]," President Truman announced, "in order to shorten the agony of war, in order to save the lives of thousand and thousands of young Americans." [10]

However, Truman's private explanation, written on August 11, 1945, in response to criticism of the atomic bombings from none other than John Foster Dulles, was more revealing: "Nobody is more disturbed over the use of Atomic bombs than I am but I was greatly disturbed over the unwarranted attack by the Japanese on Pearl Harbor and their murder of our prisoners of war. The only language they seem to understand is the one we have been using to bombard them. When you have to deal with a beast you have to treat him as a beast. It is most regrettable but nonetheless true." [11]

But in the aftermath of Hiroshima, as the incredible destructive force of nuclear weapons became better known, the weapons themselves began to appear increasingly bestial and, therefore, to some at least, ideal as the instruments for a new national security policy—nuclear deterrence. Yet even here, the debate over the atomic bombings of Hiroshima and Nagasaki was relevant, for it was of paramount importance to those who wished to rely on nuclear weapons for national security, that they not be tarnished with a sense of guilt that could inhibit their use as instruments of diplomacy and, if necessary, war.

Henry L. Stimson, Secretary of War from 1940 to 1945, was the most important formulator of the history of the atomic bombings of Hiroshima and Nagasaki; in modern political parlance, he was its chief "spin doctor." Writing in 1947 to President Harry S. Truman, to explain why he wrote his seminal article, "The Decision to Use the Atomic Bomb," Stimson noted that his "article has also been intended to satisfy the doubts of that rather difficult class of the community which will have charge of the education of the next generation, namely educators and historians."[12]

To satisfy those potential doubters, Stimson explained that the Truman administration faced the choice of either using atomic bombs or invading Japan. The sole motivation for the atomic attacks, he wrote, was to save American lives by ending the war as quickly as possible.[13] Missing were references to the idea, frequently discussed in his diary, that a dramatic demonstration of the bomb during the war would help to control Stalin's ambitions afterwards. Nor did he discuss the Japanese messages intercepted by United States military intelligence indicating that the Japan had been trying to surrender "conditionally" since June 1945.[14] Assisted by the chilling effect that the Cold War had on debate, and the long delay before the relevant documents became available to historians, Stimson achieved his goal.[15] Most Americans—and for a very long time perhaps most educators and historians as well—accepted his explanation of "the decision to use the atomic bomb."

As I have written elsewhere, ending the war quickly was certainly *one* of the motivations for using the atomic bombs. But there were others that promoted, reinforced, and perhaps even overtook the one put forward by Stimson. These included: (1) the impact that the bomb(s) were expected to have in curbing Stalin's ambitions in Eastern Europe and the Far East; (2) the pressure that senior Manhattan Project administrators felt to validate the tremendous cost in money, materials, and talent spent to build atomic bombs; (3) the momentum to use these new weapons created by the strategy of urban bombing; (4) revenge for Pearl Harbor, and the ghastly treatment of American prisoners of war.[16]

Reinforcing the political motivations behind the Stimson article is another letter, this one from the man who first urged Stimson to write it. James B. Conant, President of Harvard, and former chief science administrator of the Manhattan

Project, had written to Stimson in the autumn of 1946—in the aftermath of the publication and radio broadcast of John Hersey's *Hiroshima*—that the growing criticism of the atomic bombings was undermining the credibility of the United States' nuclear monopoly. As he later explained to Stimson, after carefully editing an early version of the article: ". . . if the propaganda against the use of the atomic bomb had been allowed to grow unchecked, the strength of our military position by virtue of having the bomb would have been correspondingly weakened, and with this weakening would have come a decrease in the probabilities of an international agreement for the control of atomic energy. I am firmly convinced," Conant went on to note, "that the Russians will eventually agree to the American proposals for the establishment of an atomic energy authority of worldwide scope, *provided* they are convinced that we would have the bomb in quantity and would be prepared to use it without hesitation in another war." [17]

So the international politics of atomic diplomacy as well as domestic political considerations were introduced from the first into the discussion of why atomic bombs were used at the end of World War II, and these same considerations have continued to undermine and circumscribe the effort to bring to public attention the research that has been done on this subject over the past thirty-five years.

I WAS A MEMBER OF THE ADVISORY COMMITTEE OF HISTORIANS to the ill-fated *Enola Gay* exhibit. When first recruited, I told the museum staff member who phoned that I opposed calling celebratory attention to the *Enola Gay* on the fiftieth anniversary of its historic mission. Even if one believed that it had played a critical role in ending a terrible war, I was opposed to an exhibit that might be interpreted as celebrating the deaths of 150,000 to 200,000 Japanese civilians, mostly old men, women and children.

My view was not a comment on the courage or morality of the men who manned the B-29s. It was based on my belief that killing—even in war—is something that as a nation we should publicly regret rather than celebrate. Furthermore, this fiftieth anniversary presented a unique opportunity for Americans and Japanese to heal the wounds of war by jointly celebrating its most positive result, the birth of Japanese democracy. Mourning together for those who died on both sides of the war is a necessary step toward healing the wounds of war. (Just such a healing event was held in Dresden, Germany, on February 13, 1995, when "General John M. Shalikashvili, Chairman of the Joint Chiefs of Staff," the *New York Times* reported, "joined his German and British military counterparts and the Duke of Kent, representing Queen Elizabeth II, to lay wreaths at a vast cemetery called Heidefriedhof, where many of the dead from 50 years ago are buried.") [18]

The counter argument was that the historical exhibits that were being planned to accompany the *Enola Gay* would make it clear that this was not a celebration of nuclear destruction, but an educational exhibit about the origins of the nuclear age. Even the Hiroshima and Nagasaki peace museums had agreed to lend National Air and Space Museum (NASM) several artifacts. Although skeptical that an exhibit that adequately reflected critical historical research could be mounted at NASM, I accepted a position on the advisory committee with the understanding that I came to it with deep reservations.

On February 7, 1994 the advisors, having received a draft of the exhibit script several weeks earlier, met at NASM for their first, and only, meeting. I was critical of the script. My complaints can be summarized under two headings: First, the historical section was not attractively designed. The history of the decision-making process was told through documents that were to hang passively on the museum's walls. I urged the curators to create an interactive exhibit that challenged visitors to assume the roles of Truman, Stimson, James Byrnes, or others involved in the decision-making process, and discover what influenced their views in the spring of 1945.

Second, and more seriously, many important documents that revealed what the decision-makers thought were missing from the exhibit. No one who read the selected documents would understand why so many historians have come to believe that the President and Secretary of War had been less than candid in their explanations of why atomic bombs had been used. The documents I was referring to included excerpts from Stimson's diary that repeatedly referred to the important post-war advantages the United States would gain in dealing with the Soviet Union if atomic bombs were used successfully against Japan.[19]

I also wanted to include Undersecretary of the Navy Ralph Bard's memorandum to Stimson of June 27, 1945 recommending that atomic bombs not be used without giving the Japanese at least 2 or 3 days warning, and the Joint Planning Staff estimates of the number of Americans likely to be killed if an invasion was necessary. The estimate, based on an analysis of other Pacific theater operations such as Iwo Jima and Okinawa, were considerably lower than the figure of 500,000 killed that both Stimson and Truman published.[20] Finally, while the artifacts from Hiroshima and Nagasaki were powerful reminders that atomic bombs do horrible things to people, they would not help visitors understand *why* the bombs were dropped on cities. In summary, I judged the commemorative character of the exhibit dominant and ubiquitous, and the historical portion marginalized and unappealing.

My view was contradicted by the reactions of the other advisors, most especially the historians from the Air Force, Dr. Richard Hallion and Dr. Herman Wolk, who staunchly defended the script. "Overall this is a most impressive piece of work," Hallion wrote to one of the curators after the meeting, "[it is] comprehensive and dramatic, obviously based upon a great deal of sound research, primary and secondary."[21]

The script *was* based on sound research. The curators had studied the literature thoroughly. They had a sophisticated understanding of the evidence and the arguments. But under the circumstances, their approach to the exhibit had been extremely cautious, for political reasons. It was this caution that Hallion and Wolk supported, and that led another advisor, Edwin Bearss Chief Historian of the National Parks Service, to endorse the Air Force view with a letter of his own. "As a World War II combat veteran," Bearss wrote to a curator, "I commend you and your colleagues who have dared to go that extra mile to address an emotionally charged and internationally significant event in an exhibit that, besides enlightening, will challenge its viewers."[22]

John Correll, the editor of *Air Force Magazine*, had a decidedly different opinion of the exhibit. In his view, it not only suffered from too much of the PC he disliked, but even worse, it was insufficiently endowed with the PC he exploited for his living, *Patriotic Correctness*. Correll considered the exhibit biased against the Air Force, pro-Japanese, and anti-American. His article condemning the exhibit script, "War Stories at Air and Space," which served as a clarion call to veterans groups, was a deceptive critique that took quotations out of context, and used McCarthyite innuendo to impugn the patriotism of Martin Harwit, the director of NASM. "For most Americans," Correll quoted the script as stating, "this war was fundamentally different than the one waged against Germany and Italy—it was a war of vengeance. For most Japanese, it was a war to defend their unique culture against Western imperialism." What Correll failed to note, and what journalists who repeated this inflammatory quotation without reading the original script failed to discover, was that this sentence came near the end of a section that frankly and clearly summarized the brutality of Japanese militarism: "Japanese expansionism was marked by naked aggression and extreme brutality. The slaughter of tens of thousands of Chinese in Nanking in 1937 shocked the world. Atrocities by Japanese troops included brutal mistreatment of civilians, forced laborers and prisoners of war, and biological experiments on human victims," the section reads in part.[23]

Correll's article reflected his long-standing disaffection with the curators and historians at NASM who, under Harwit's administration, had been mounting exhibits that included critical discussions of the consequences of air and space technology. The Air and Space Museum, he insisted, was ignoring its "basic job. . . the restoration and preservation of aircraft." Yet in the past decade, other Smithsonian museum directors had successfully sponsored challenging exhibits, and previous critical exhibits at the NASM had received some excellent reviews.[24]

But the *Enola Gay* exhibit was different for several reasons. First, the public criticism of the exhibit began in the planning stages and just six months before a congressional election in which conservative forces were in the ascendancy. Second, the event being commemorated was the 50th anniversary of the end of World War II, the "Good War," and the museum's administration failed to publicly respond (until it was too late) to charges that it was denigrating the memory of the men who had fought in that crusade. And, finally, the curators had created an exhibit that probed how the Japanese thought about the war, a virtue that critics distorted by interpreting any recognition of the humanity of Japan's soldiers as an anti-American bias.

Within a month of the publication of "War Stories," and a companion article, "The Decision that Launched the *Enola Gay*," that ignored thirty years of critical historical research on the subject, a broad spectrum of veterans groups, led by the 3.1 million member American Legion, had enlisted congressional allies in support of their criticisms of the script.[25] Senators and Congressmen eagerly rushed to condemn the exhibit.[26] Senator Nancy Kassebaum offered a resolution in the Senate, and dozens of Congressmen signed letters that threatened retribution against the staff and the museum if the script was not modified to the satisfaction of its critics. Behind these letters and resolutions (in addition to politics as usual), was an astonishingly self-righteous view of the atomic bombings. "There is no excuse," Congressman Sam Johnson and six of his colleagues wrote to I. Michael Heyman, Secretary of the Smithsonian, "for an exhibit which addresses *one of the most morally unambiguous events of the 20th century* to need five revisions," [emphasis added].[27]

What had begun as a debate over interpreting and balancing the public presentation of an historical event of transcendent importance, was quickly turned by congressional intervention into a "political cleansing" operation against both the exhibit and NASM's staff.[28] The political agendas of those who joined in this assault varied: the veterans sought to control the public presentation of the Hiroshima narrative; the Air Force Association wanted NASM's administration returned to more accommodating hands; and conservative politicians saw another issue they could use in their culture wars crusade.

The exhibit's critics called for two very different sorts of fundamental changes to the script. In the first instance, they demanded that the exhibit be expanded to include a history of Japanese aggression and atrocities that began with Japan's invasion of China in the 1930s, an arguably reasonable alternative framework for the exhibit.[29] But, they also insisted upon something that was objectionable and unconscionable: the removal of all documents critical of the use of the atomic bombs. This blatant demand for *censorship* eliminated passages from the memoirs of Dwight D. Eisenhower and Admiral William D. Leahy among other texts. The American Legion also insisted on the removal of the statement (generally recognized as a fact) that, "to this day, controversy has raged about whether dropping this weapon on Japan was necessary to end the war quickly."[30]

Heyman, who had inherited this unenviable situation in the fall of 1994, chose the path that Japan had resisted—unconditional surrender. Without ever saying a word against censorship, on January 30, 1995 he canceled the exhibits that were to accompany the *Enola Gay.* "I have concluded," he stated in his announcement of the cancellation, "that we made a basic error in attempting to couple a historical treatment of the use of atomic weapons with the 50th anniversary commemoration of the end of the war."[31]

His actions and explanation have led me to revise Santayana's famous aphorism, "Those who cannot remember the past are condemned to repeat it." I am now more inclined to worry that, "Those who insist only on their memories of the past condemn others to remain ignorant of it." The *Enola Gay* debacle at the National Air and Space Museum is a reminder of how completely the politics of the Cold War—in its reinforcement of America's collective memory of the Good War—circumscribed all discussions of the war's ambiguities. This special protection accorded the history of Hiroshima for so many decades, unites the task of "unspinning" Stimson's history of Hiroshima with the more considerable challenge of disentangling U.S. politics from its Cold War culture.

For fifty years the public debate over the atomic bombings of Hiroshima and Nagasaki has been framed—and distorted—by a non-event: the invasion of Japan. To frankly confront the legacy of Hiroshima and Nagasaki, it is necessary to consider another alternative future. What if atomic bombs had *not* been used against Japanese cities? When that the question is asked, it is generally raised rhetorically in support of the assumption that the atomic destruction of those cities acted as a deterrent to the future use of nuclear weapons: in Korea, Berlin, Cuba, or Vietnam.[32]

This strikes me as more rationalization than logical deduction. Consider what might have occurred if Stimson had followed the logic of his own assessments of the dangers associated with nuclear weapons, and had convinced Truman that the United States should do everything possible (other than invading Japan) to end the war without using them. What would have been the consequences of this decision? As all senior administrators of the Manhattan Project feared, a congressional committee would have conducted an investigation into why the Truman administration had failed to use an extraordinarily expensive new bomb that had been ready before the end of the war.

Stimson, a Republican, who served two Democratic administrations that had led the country to victory, would have been called to defend his recommendation.

In his defense, he would have said to Congress—and the American public, and the world—what he had said to Harry Truman on April 25, 1945: "The world in its present state of moral advancement compared with its technical development would be eventually at the mercy of such a weapon. In other words, modern civilization might be completely destroyed." It is our nation's responsibility, he would have gone on to argue, to avoid such destruction, and "if the proper use of this weapon can be solved, we would have the opportunity to bring the world into a pattern in which the peace of the world and our civilization can be saved." [33] In support of his decision he might have quoted the Franck Report that was sent to him in June 1945 from the atomic scientists at the University of Chicago. "We urge that the use of nuclear bombs in this war be considered as a problem of long-range national policy rather than military expediency," they had written arguing against dropping atomic bombs on Japanese cities. [34]

Stimson would have gone on to say that our nation is too moral to set a precedent to use such a weapon. He would have insisted that the American people would not want their government to behave like the German government that had initiated gas warfare in World War I, or like the Japanese government, which had initiated the urban bombing of civilians in China. Once a precedent is set, he would have said, its repetition follows inevitably. Perhaps he would have borrowed some language from Undersecretary of the Navy Ralph Bard's memorandum of June 27, 1945 that urged reconsideration of the decision to use atomic bombs in order to preserve "The position of the United States as a great humanitarian nation." [35]

He would have explained that the United States had built atomic bombs in self-defense, having reason to believe that the Germans were working along the same lines. But to have initiated nuclear war when there were alternatives available (other than invasion), would have made the American government vulnerable to charges that it had engaged in barbaric acts on a par with its enemies. We have our own values, our own standards, he would have said. They are the standards that must guide our behavior. These weapons not only burn and blast, but they kill by radiation. They have the characteristics of poison gas and biological weapons. Americans would not want their government to be the first to use them, he would have concluded.

Congress and the American people would have agreed that President Truman had done the right thing in avoiding the use of nuclear weapons. The press would have written editorials affirming that we are morally superior, as we have always insisted. To save the lives of American soldiers we had reluctantly accepted the Nazi–Japanese precedent of strategic bombing, but to save civilization we had resisted the temptation to use nuclear weapons. Such a hearing would have had exactly the opposite effect that Hiroshima and Nagasaki had on American (and Soviet) attitudes toward nuclear weapons. Rather than validating them as weapons of war, our refusal to use them would have relegated them to the category of chemical and biological weapons—weapons beyond the moral pale.

Perhaps the international control of atomic energy would have been achieved. But even if not, is it likely that Stalin, faced with the challenge of rebuilding a devastated nation, would have initiated a costly, *crash* program to build a weapon that the United States had refused to use in war? [36] It is also doubtful that the United States government would have been in a position to so completely embrace nuclear weapons as the cornerstone of U.S. national security policy if relations with the Soviets had deteriorated into a Cold War. Such a reversal of policy would have been extraordinarily difficult after Stimson's testimony and the policies of marginalizing nuclear weapons that would have followed in its wake.

A principled stand against nuclear weapons at the outset of the nuclear age, by the nation that possessed a nuclear monopoly, might very well have changed world history. The lesson of Hiroshima is not that atomic war is too horrible to contemplate, again. As we have relearned from Robert McNamara's memoir, the Joint Chiefs of Staff did not hesitate to recommended the use of nuclear weapons in Vietnam when they ran out of conventional solutions. What Hiroshima appears to have taught those who plan and fight wars is that nuclear weapons are useful, if you can get away with using them.[37]

The atomic bombings of Hiroshima and Nagasaki did not contribute to preventing the next nuclear war—they made it more likely.

NOTES

1. "Why We Did It," *Newsweek*, July 24, 1995, pp. 22–30. The article acknowledges previously controversial points such as, (1) "Groves was determined to demonstrated the power of what he called 'the gadget,'" p. 23, (2) Stimson saw the bomb as a "'mastercard' in the great game of diplomacy," p. 25, (3) that the Japanese were trying to surrender on condition that the Emperor's safety was guaranteed, p. 26, (4) "from a military perspective, there was no particular urgency to end the war right away," p. 26, (5) that Truman engaged himself in "some comforting psychological denial" by claiming that a military base rather than women and children had been the target, p. 27, (6) "Hirohito had decided to surrender before Nagasaki," p. 28, (7) "After some semantic dithering over the meaning of unconditional surrender, the Allies agreed to allow Hirohito to keep his throne after all, in order to get the war over with," pp. 22–30. See also, letter from the Historians Committee for Open Debate on Hiroshima to Michael Heyman, Secretary of the Smithsonian, July 31, 1995. The letter details the distortions and factual errors in the *Enola Gay* exhibit and calls for appropriate alterations. In author's possession.

2. Henry Rousso, *The Vichy Syndrome: History and Memory in France Since 1944* (Cambridge MA, 1991), p.2.

3. Mark Selden, "Before the Bomb: The 'Good War', Air Power and the Logic of Mass Destruction," *Contention*, (Fall 1995), 113–32 .

4. Paul Fussell, "Hiroshima: A Soldier's View: 'Thank God for the Atom Bomb'," *The New Republic*, August 22–29, 1981, pp. 26–30. [See Section II]

5. Alvin Kernan, *Crossing the Line: A Bluejacket's World War II Odyssey* (Annapolis, 1994), p. 155.

6. On this issue see Carolyn Eisenberg, "The Berlin Blockade and the Militarizing of American Foreign Policy, 1948–49," and Gar Alperovitz and Kai Bird, "A Theory of the Cold War: U.S. Policy, Germany and the Bomb" (papers presented at the Organization of American Historians, Washington, D.C., March 31, 1995). The most important new study of U.S.–German policy is Eisenberg, *Drawing the Line: The American Decision to Divide Germany, 1944–1949* (Cambridge, 1996).

7. Uday Mohan and Sanho Tree, "The Ending of World War II: Media Perspectives in the 1940s–1960s and Early 1990s" (paper presented at the American Historical Association, Chicago, January 6, 1995). The United States Strategic Bombing Survey's analysis of the Pacific War concluded that Japan would have surrendered before the planned November invasion even if atomic bombs had not been used.

8. Ralph Bard to George Harrison, June 27, 1945 and George Harrison to Henry L. Stimson, June 28, 1945 are reprinted in Martin J. Sherwin, *A World Destroyed: Hiroshima and the Origins of the Arms Race* (New York, 1987), pp. 307–08. For other dissenting opinions of military leaders see, Gar Alperovitz, *The Decision to Use the Atomic Bomb and the Architecture of An American Myth* (New York, 1995), pp. 321–71.

9. Rabhabinod Pal quoted in, Richard Falk, Gabriel Kolko, Robert Lifton eds., *Crimes of War* (New York, 1971), p. 136. Pal's analogy overlooks a critical distinction: The goal of the Nazi holocaust was genocide, but genocide was clearly not a goal of U.S. policy.

10. Robert J. Lifton and Greg Mitchell, *Hiroshima in America: Fifty Years of Denial* (New York, 1995), p. 27. See also chapters 1 and 2 for a detailed account of the development of President Truman's announcements about the bombings of Hiroshima and Nagasaki.

11. Harry S. Truman to Bishop Oxnam and John Foster Dulles, August 11, 1945, quoted in Martin J. Sherwin, *A World Destroyed: Hiroshima and the Origins of the Arms Race* (New York, 1987), pp. xvii–xviii.

12. Henry L. Stimson, "The Decision to Use the Atomic Bomb," *Harper's Magazine*, February 1947, pp. 97–107.

13. Stimson, "Decision to Use the Atomic Bomb," p. 106. See also, Stimson to Truman, January 7, 1947, Harry S. Truman folder, The papers of Henry L. Stimson, Sterling Memorial Library, Yale University, New Haven, CT.

14. A significant number of the most interesting "Magic" intercepts were declassified early in 1995. A July 13, 1945 message states that "His Majesty . . . desires from his heart that [the war] may be quickly terminated." Foreign Minister Togo to Ambassador Sato in Moscow. Ultra intercepts, War Department, Office of A.C. of S., G–2, National Archives, Washington, D.C. The two most important publications in English on the surrender of Japan are, Herbert Bix, "Japan's Delayed Surrender: A Reinterpretation," *Diplomatic History* (Spring 1995) and Robert J. C. Butow, *Japan's Decision to Surrender* (Palo Alto, 1954).

15. Henry L. Stimson's diaries, the first major source for revising Stimson's own explanation for the atomic bombings of Hiroshima and Nagasaki, first became available to researchers in 1959. They may be seen at Sterling Memorial Library, Yale University, New Haven, CT, or purchased from the library on microfilm.

16. Sherwin, *A World Destroyed*, p. 198. For impact on Soviets see Stimson's diary, December 31, 1944, February 15, May 10, 13, 14, 15, and June 6, 1945; for pressure on administrators see Sherwin, *A World Destroyed*, p. 199; for strategic bombing, see Michael Sherry, *The Rise of American Air Power* (New Haven, 1987); for revenge see Truman's response to John Foster Dulles' protest against the atomic bombings: "When you have to deal with a beast, you have to treat him [Japanese] like a beast." August 11, 1945, quoted in Sherwin, *A World Destroyed*, pp. xvii–xviii.

17. Conant to Stimson, January 22, 1947, Conant folder, Stimson Papers. For a thorough discussion of the role that Conant played in initiating and shaping Stimson's article, see, James Hershberg, *James B. Conant: From Harvard to Hiroshima and the Making of the Nuclear Age* (New York, 1993), chap. 16.

18. *New York Times*, February 14, 1995, p. A6.

19. Stimson diaries, December 31, 1944, May 10, 13, 14, 15, June 6, 1945.

20. Both documents are reprinted in full in the appendices of Sherwin, *A World Destroyed* (1987 edition): Bard, pp. 307–08; casualty estimates, pp. 335–63.

21. NASM "News." A press release, no date, with the title: "Favorable Comments about the Exhibition 'The Last Act: The Atomic Bomb and the End of World War II.'" The subtitle reads: "Advisory Board Comments on the January and April Scripts." p.1.

22. Edwin Bearrs to Tom Crouch, February 24, 1994. Ibid.

23. John T. Correll, "War Stories at Air and Space," *Air Force Magazine*, April 1994, pp. 24–29. "The Crossroads: The End of World War II, the Atomic Bomb and the Origins of the Cold War" [script no. 1, January 12, 1994], p. 5.

24. Correll, "War Stories," pp. 26–27, 29. In response to the controversial exhibit at the National Museum of American Art, "The West As America," a *Washington Post* editorial had praised the "move away from the traditional heroes, politicians, and objects in glass cases and toward a wide, fluid, social-history approach." Quoted in Correll, "War Stories," p. 27.

25. John T. Correll, "The Decision That Launched the *Enola Gay*," *AFM*, April 1994, pp. 30–34.

26. The Air Force Association has compiled for distribution a bound volume, *The Enola Gay Debate, August 1993 – May 1995.* Hereafter *AFA, EGD.* It is a broad ranging collection that contains, among much other information, numerous letters from Congressmen to senior Smithsonian Institution administrators.

27. Senate Resolution 257, 103rd Congress, 2nd Session, submitted by Senator Nancy Kassebaum, "A resolution to express the sense of the Senate regarding the appropriate portrayal of men and women of the armed forces in the upcoming National Air and Space Museum's exhibit on the *Enola Gay*"; agreed to by unanimous consent, September 24, 1994. Sam Johnson, et al. to Heyman, December 13, 1994, *AFA, EGD.*

28. On November 16, 1994 approximately 50 historians (which expanded to over 100 during the following week) signed a letter to Heyman urging him to resist censorship ("historical cleansing") of the exhibit. The secretary's failure to respond led to the formation of "The Historians' Committee for Open Debate on Hiroshima."

29. The original exhibit, as its subtitle noted, was planned as an introduction to the nuclear age: "The End of World War II, the Atomic Bomb and the Origins of the Cold War." The alternative framework demanded by the exhibit's critics was a history of the Pacific War.

30. Ralph Bard's memorandum of June 27, 1945 urging advanced notice to the Japanese and noting that the Japanese are looking for a way to surrender, had been inserted into the second (April 1994) script at my suggestion, but later was eliminated during negotiations with the American Legion. The "to this day" quotation was in the first script, "The Crossroads: The End of World War II, The Atomic Bomb and the Origins of the Cold War," [first draft of the *Enola Gay* script] January 12, 1994, p. 2.

31. "Smithsonian Scuttles Exhibit," *Washington Post*, January 31, 1995, p. A1.

32. Not surprisingly, the *Newsweek* article concludes on this point: "[The atomic bombings] also allowed the world to see how truly awful the bomb was—one reason, perhaps, that it has not been used since." p. 30.

33. "Memo discussed with the President, April 25, 1945" reprinted in Sherwin, *A World Destroyed*, p. 291–92.

34. Sections of the Franck Report are reproduced in *A World Destroyed* (1987 edition), pp. 323–33.

35. Ralph Bard to George Harrison (Stimson's Assistant), June 27, 1945, Harrison passed Bard's memorandum to Stimson with a cover note on June 28, reprinted in Sherwin, *A World Destroyed*, p. 307.

36. David Holloway writes that "Hiroshima had demonstrated the power of the bomb and American willingness to use it. Stalin wanted to restore the balance by acquiring a Soviet bomb as quickly as possible." *Stalin and the Bomb* (New Haven, 1994), p. 132.

37. Robert McNamara, *In Retrospect: The Tragedy and Lessons of Vietnam* (New York, 1995), pp. 160, 234, 275, 343–44.

SMITHSONIAN

SUFFERS

LEGIONNAIRES'

DISEASE

Stanley Goldberg

IN AUGUST 1945, I was an eleven-year-old paperboy for the afternoon *Cleveland Press*. On the afternoon of August 6, the bundled papers waiting for me had a banner headline saying: "Atom Bomb Hits Japan." The second line said: "Blast Force Equals 2,000 Blockbusters." Amazing. Although the news was momentous, the readers of the *Cleveland Press*—at least the readers on my route—had to wait for it. I read every word of the several articles on this new thing called an atomic bomb before delivering the papers. In the coming years, I continued to read everything I could on the atomic bomb—as well as on the promise of nuclear energy and the field of nuclear physics. In a way, that was the start of my professional career as a historian of science. And that interest—an obsession, really—eventually led me to play a role in the recent *Enola Gay*–Smithsonian Institution fiasco—a long-running and ultimately dispiriting morality play in three acts.

In the fall of 1984, Roger Kennedy, the director of the Smithsonian's National Museum of American History, asked me to meet with him and some of the museum's curators to discuss the fact that nowhere in the museum was there a mention of two of the defining moments of the twentieth century: the obliteration of Hiroshima and Nagasaki by atomic bombs. There was enthusiasm around the table that day for mounting such an exhibit in time for the fortieth anniversary of the bombing. Kennedy asked me to identify artifacts, produce a "script," and oversee the installation. In museum-speak, a script is the blueprint that specifies how an exhibition will be laid out, and what artifacts, photos, and documents it will present. The script also contains the language that will be in the "labels."

The 1985 exhibit—composed of Hiroshima and Nagasaki-type bomb casings as well as photos and artifacts in two display cases—sketchily described both the Manhattan Project and the destructive power of the bombs. Because I was worried about the emotional impact the exhibit might have on unprepared visitors, I drained the emotion from the labels. Nevertheless, the guiding principle of the exhibit was simple, even simple-minded. I wanted to make it clear that nuclear devastation was not merely an abstract topic discussed by Cold War theorists. Nuclear weapons—and their effects—were real. Among the artifacts were roof tiles that had bubbled from the heat. One of the photos showed a man whose head was badly flash-burned, except where his hat had offered some protection.

The exhibit was well received. Scheduled to be on the floor only during the month of August, it was retained through November. Kennedy asked me to undertake a yearlong study as to how a large and permanent exhibit could be handled. I plunged in, but a year later, the museum's administration had lost its enthusiasm. Although the Smithsonian gets public money, many of its activities must be funded privately, and private funding for an atomic bomb exhibit had not been forthcoming. That was no great surprise. When it came to fundraising for not-very-popular projects, curators at the museum sometimes spoke of the museum administration as having "a whim of iron."

To this day, the Smithsonian's National Museum of American History has no separate display on the Manhattan Project or the use of atomic bombs in war. It does, however, have a small and spare atomic display tucked into a larger exhibit on "Science and American Life." Given the failure of the American History Museum to pursue the project, I was surprised and pleased in 1991 when I learned that the Smithsonian's National Air and Space Museum would install a major exhibit on the end of World War II, which would be in place by May 1995.

The exhibit—called "The Last Act: The Atomic Bomb and the End of World War II"—would feature the front portion of the *Enola Gay* fuselage, and it would explore the role played by the atomic bomb in bringing the war to an end. I was asked, along with nine others, to serve on the Exhibit Advisory Board. The first draft of the exhibit script, put together by the museum's curators and distributed to the advisory board in January 1994, was a heavyweight—upwards of 750 pages of text and illustrative material. The board met with the curators in February to go over the script. Our role was to review and suggest. The content of the final exhibit, we believed then, would be in the hands of the curators.

Rather than retelling the whole story of the Pacific war, which would not have been possible in the space allotted, the curators linked the atomic bombings to the evolution of the strategic bombing campaign of the XXI Bombing Command of the 20th Air Force, General Curtis LeMay's outfit that was systematically incinerating one Japanese city after another. Rather than having to use hundreds of planes in a raid, the Air Force could now achieve the same effect with one plane. The theme did not originate with the curators; it had been explored widely and thoroughly over the years. See, for instance, Michael S. Sherry's definitive *The Rise of American Air Power,* pubiished in 1987.

The flow of the script was logical. After some unremarkable references to the start of the war and the attack on Pearl Harbor, the exhibit began with V-E Day and concentrated on the battles for Iwo Jima and Okinawa. Together, these two campaigns were almost as costly in American casualties as the first three years of the Pacific war. The decision to use the bomb—and how to use it—was a complicated one, but the curators had done a fine job of making the subject accessible to a general audience. That was no easy task. The story line then moved to an exploration of the "miracle" of the design and production of the B-29. This was followed by a section on the training of the crews chosen to deliver the bombs—the 509th Composite Group—and the construction of the 509th facilities on the island of Tinian in the Marianas. After describing—in words, photos, and artifacts—the scene at and near ground zero in Hiroshima and Nagasaki, the exhibit ended with a section on the legacy of the atomic bomb: an abrupt halt to the war, and a fierce and competitive nuclear arms race between the United States and the Soviet Union.

The advisory committee represented a wide range of disciplines and professional expertise. But there was unanimous agreement at the advisory board meeting that the initial approach of the curators was sound. Although the curators' plan was not the only one they could have used, they had done a careful and professional job. The task now at hand was one of fine tuning. This is not to say that members of the advisory board had no criticisms. Some of us believed the script overemphasized the role that international politics played in the decision to use the bomb—the argument that the bombs represented the first shots in the coming Cold War. In fact, there were at least several other overarching reasons for using the bomb—all important, but some of which had gotten short shrift in the script. First, there was the momentum of the Manhattan Project itself, the biggest single scientific and industrial enterprise of the war. There were also considerations of domestic politics, which guaranteed that the Truman administration would pay a fearful price if the American people ever learned that a superweapon had been developed but not used. Personal ambition also played a part, particularly General Leslie Groves's conviction that he was playing *the* pivotal role in ending the war, and J. Robert Oppenheimer's obsessive concern with the kind of immortality the bomb would bring him. Finally, humanitarian concerns that the war should be ended quickly, not only for the sake of Americans but for the Japanese. Although peace factions within the Japanese government were exploring ways to end the war and they might have prevailed, Japanese militarists were still running the show in the summer of 1945. Meanwhile, the fire-bomb raids continued. General LeMay believed that his men would be able to burn down every Japanese city of consequence by October. Had the war continued that long, the continued firebombing would almost surely have produced hundreds of thousands of civilian casualties.

All of these concerns were a matter of emphasis. They could have been addressed by a little refining. There was nothing odd or unexpected or sinister about that. One would never expect that a first-draft script of a complex topic would not raise questions in a peer-review process. Some labels had to be reworded, expanded, shortened. But the consensus of the advisory board was clear: The exhibit would inform, challenge, and commemorate. As Air Force Historian Richard Hallion, a member of the board, put it in his written remarks: "Overall, this is a most impressive piece of work, comprehensive and dramatic, obviously based upon a great deal of sound research, primary and secondary."

Shortly after the advisory board meeting, the script was leaked to the Air Force Association. When I heard through the grapevine that the association was unhappy with it because of its alleged pro-Japanese and anti-American and anti-nuclear bias, I was neither surprised nor alarmed. The curators had presented a solid script rooted in the latest historical scholarship. Besides, it was common knowledge that the Air Force Association believed that the Air and Space Museum should be devoted exclusively to celebrating the accomplishments of U.S. air power and space ventures. But when the budding controversy was picked up by the news media, and when the American Legion joined in, I began to realize that the exhibit was in for a tough go.

For starters, there was simply no agreement on the meaning of "history." In writing history, professional historians follow a process analogous to the methods identified with science. They develop ideas about how and why something happened and then they test those ideas against whatever documentary evidence they can locate. Finally, they make their data and conclusions available to other historians to be confirmed and refined—or ripped and shredded.

But journalists sometimes follow a different process. The arcana of scholarly methodology would not only bore readers and viewers, it would drive them away. Readers and viewers love controversy and conflict, and journalists devote great energy and talent to reporting it. Once the Air Force Association and the American Legion got into the act, the ingredients for a fine drama were in place. On one side were some of the vets who actually fought the war, or their spiritual descendants. On the other side were academic curators and historians, often described as "revisionist," and sometimes seen as picky and pedantic.

In late September, Ken Ringle, a *Washington Post* reporter, summed up the controversy admirably, without quite realizing it. In an article in the *Post*, he contrasted the documentary evidence used by historians with the memories of veterans who served in the Pacific. Documentary evidence was "old history, a scholarly abstraction composed of archival records, argumentative books, and . . . fading images on black and white film." Living history came from veterans.

One of the vets Ringle quoted was Grayford C. Payne, who had been a prisoner of war in Japan from 1942 to 1945. With tears in his eyes, Payne said he was sure that the atomic bombs had saved his life. If an invasion of the home islands had taken place, he and his buddies would have been executed. Powerful flesh-and-blood stuff; documents compete poorly with human interest. Ringle's piece seemed to imply that the opinions of the veterans he interviewed were a more accurate guide to what happened in the war than histories of the war based on archival materials. Subsequent editorials in the *Post* gave explicit support to that view.

In an August 7 op-ed piece in the *Post*, Martin Harwit, director of the Air and Space Museum, defended the original script as well as his efforts to placate critics. Nevertheless, he wrote, "We have found no way to exhibit the *Enola Gay* and satisfy everyone." A week later, the *Post* responded editorially, suggesting that Harwit and the curators assumed their critics had less "intellectual sophistication." This, said the *Post*, "naturally rankles with veterans and other groups that offered detailed and substantive criticisms of the initial plan which they said was emotionally rigged to create an anti-nuclear perspective and to present Japan overwhelmingly as a victim country fighting only to preserve its 'culture'."

The *Post* charged that the curatorial failings reflected an "inability to perceive that political opinions are embedded in the exhibit or to identify them as such—opinions—rather than as universal, 'objective' assumptions all thinking people must necessarily share. This confusion is increasingly common in academia and owes much to the fashionable and wrong academic notion that objectivity is unattainable anyway and that all presentations of complex issues must be politically tendentious." The editorial made me wonder if any member of the *Post* staff had actually read the script. The personal experiences of individuals *are* important to historians. But they are just some of the pieces in a puzzle that has many different kinds of pieces. That's a basic point, but one that seemed to elude most journalistic observers.

By August 1994, it was clear that the Air Force Association and the American Legion didn't have a better hand than Harwit and the curators—but they had the upper hand. They were adept at working with the press and putting their particular flag-waving, human-interest spin on the story. As early as May, the Air and Space Museum curators had begun negotiating the content of the exhibit and the wording of the labels directly with representatives of the Air Force Association and the American Legion. The advisory board, which had met just once—in February—was simply out of the picture.

From the start, the Air Force Association and the American Legion exploited early lapses in judgment by the curators. These were lapses that the advisory board had noted at its February meeting, and which surely would have been fixed in the normal course of events without much hassle. For example, the board objected to a first-draft label that ended with the following passage:

> For Americans this [Pacific] war was fundamentally different than the one waged against Germany and Italy—it was a war of vengeance. For most Japanese, it was a war to defend their unique culture against Western imperialism.

To critics of the proposed exhibit, that passage was the smoking gun, and it was widely disseminated to the press. The *Post* editorial I quoted a moment ago referred to it, as did countless newspapers. But the passage had been ripped from its context. The full label said:

> In 1931 the Japanese Army occupied Manchuria; six years later it invaded the rest of China. From 1937 to 1945, the Japanese Empire would be constantly at war.
>
> Japanese expansionism was marked by naked aggression and extreme brutality. The slaughter of tens of thousands of Chinese in Nanking in 1937 shocked the world. Atrocities by Japanese troops included brutal mistreatment of civilians, forced laborers and prisoners of war, and biological experiments on human victims.
>
> In December 1941, Japan attacked U.S. bases at Pearl Harbor, Hawaii, and launched other surprise assaults against Allied territories in the Pacific. Thus began a wider conflict marked by extreme bitterness. For most Americans, this war was fundamentally different than the one waged against Germany and Italy—it was a war of vengeance. For most Japanese, it was a war to defend their unique culture against Western imperialism. As the war approached its end in 1945, it appeared to both sides that it was a fight to the finish.

That is solid history, not an absurdity. The label wasn't wrong; it just needed fine tuning. The contempt that both countries had toward each other during the war has been well documented, for example by John Dower in *War Without Mercy*. That contempt was fully explored in the original script. Nevertheless, the advisory board suggested that the "imperialism" paragraph be recast to emphasize the role of Japanese militarism.

The meaning of many other labels was badly distorted by the critics. Air Force Historian Hallion, who had found the first-draft script so praiseworthy at the advisory board meeting, decided later, after the initial attacks by the Air Force Association, that the curators had "resisted addressing basic deficiencies of the exhibit even during subsequent 'grudging' revisions." He told *Post* reporter Ringle that

Harwit and the curators insisted on focusing on the devastation of Hiroshima and Nagasaki and resisted portraying Japanese aggression and atrocities. Hallion also told a *Washington Times* reporter, Josh Young, that "the information [in the exhibit] is biased. It doesn't permit the visitor to reach an informed conclusion. The visitor comes away with the impression that the bomb should not have been dropped. It doesn't take into account the severity of the war or the complexities of the decision."

Some of the artifacts that were to be displayed in the exhibit also unhinged critics. The exhibit that I helped put together for the Smithsonian's National Museum of American History in 1985 went to great lengths to avoid shocking the viewers, but the proposed 1995 Air and Space Museum exhibit was confrontational in its choice of photos and artifacts. Among the more unsettling artifacts, loaned to the Smithsonian by the Hiroshima Peace Memorial Exhibit, were items belonging to a group of schoolmates: a student's lunch box containing the carbonized remains of sweet peas and polished rice; a water bottle; and a wooden clog revealing, by blast-induced darkening, the outline of a foot. Photos depicted the devastation of the city and badly burned people.

Critics charged that such displays were designed to evoke sympathy for the Japanese. The exhibit, they said, should contain artifacts and photos depicting Japanese atrocities. In fact, the curators were simply trying to show the effects of an atomic bomb. Those effects were real, and they are hard to face up to. The Hiroshima bomb detonated over a hospital, not a tank factory or an ordnance works. Nearby schools were in session, filled not with soldiers but with children. Two bombs killed upwards of 200,000 people immediately and over the following weeks and months. Most were civilians. That is history; that is context.

Many of the critics believed that the contents of the labels should be limited to artifact identification. Paul Tibbets, the pilot of the *Enola Gay*, said that history would be best served by that approach. Many museum curators around the nation would agree with him. There is a long-standing debate among museum curators over the context issue. Some curators say that artifacts should speak for themselves, and they cite the traditional role of bare-bones labels in art museums, which usually identify the artist, the year the work was completed, and the title of the work, if it has one. But works of art are not the same as museum artifacts. The essence of art is that it is a subjective expression of an artist. That is why it is "art" instead of a mailbox or a screwdriver or a paper clip. A work of art has as many subjective meanings as it has viewers. But in this context, the fuselage of the *Enola Gay* and the carbonized remains of a child's lunch are not *objets d'art*. They are *evidence*—surviving fragments of past events.

By the end of 1994, on orders from Harwit, the curators had done four revisions of the script, the last two in close consultation with American Legion critics. In the first revision, a "pre-exhibit" display occupying some 4,000 square feet was added, containing fifty photos, some of which depicted Japanese atrocities early in the war. The pre-exhibit also would have displayed a U.S. carrier-based fighter plane. The final two revisions involved line-by-line consultations between representatives of the American Legion and the curators. Among the changes: the removal of archival documents showing that some government officials and military leaders did not believe the bomb should be used, and that some highly placed U.S. officials thought the target city should at least be warned. The curators were also forced to eliminate some artifacts and photos. The lunch box, for instance, had to go.

The most difficult issue was the question of American casualties. The Air Force Association and the American Legion argued that the bombs were used to end the war quickly, thus avoiding the need for an invasion of the Japanese home islands, which would have produced perhaps a million or more U.S. casualties. Few historians who have looked closely at the documentary record believe that any high-level military planner actually thought that in 1945. Harwit and the American Legion representatives eventually *negotiated* a figure—229,000—for the expected number of U.S. casualties, if Project Olympic, the invasion of Kyushu planned for November, had taken place. Then—in mid-September—the American Legion pronounced the exhibit flawed, but passable. The Air Force Association was still unhappy.

Agreeing to a figure of 229,000 was a mistake. Those of us on the advisory board who were familiar with the documentary evidence knew the casualty figure was still high. The generals and admirals who were actually planning the invasion were projecting lower numbers for the invasion of Kyushu. Barton Bernstein, a Stanford historian who has looked at the question for years, persuaded Harwit that, in light of the available evidence, 63,000 casualties was a better figure. And on January 9, Harwit informed Legion officials that the script was being changed accordingly.

That was the final insult, insofar as the American Legion was concerned. From the perspective of the Legion, Harwit had broken his word. The Legion—backed by several members of Congress—called on Smithsonian Secretary I. Michael Heyman and President Clinton to take the exhibit out of the hands of Harwit and his curators, at the very least. But what they really hoped for, they said, was that the Smithsonian would cancel the exhibit altogether. As William M. Detweiler, the commander of the American Legion said, the museum leadership had managed to antagonize everyone on all sides of the issue.

On January 30, 1995, Smithsonian Secretary Heyman announced the cancellation of the original *Enola Gay* exhibit. In its place, he said, would be a simple display of the front portion of the *Enola Gay*'s fuselage and perhaps some videotaped interviews with surviving crew members. "I have taken this action, for one overriding reason," Heyman said. "I have concluded that we made a basic error in attempting to couple an historical treatment of the use of atomic weapons with the fiftieth anniversary commemoration of the end of the war. But we need to know which of many goals is paramount, and not confuse them. In this important anniversary year, veterans and their families were expecting, and rightly so, that the nation would honor and commemorate their valor and sacrifice. They were not looking for analysis, and frankly, we did not give enough thought to the intense feelings such an analysis would evoke."

The scaled-down exhibit opened in June instead of the middle of May, as originally planned. Many historians said they were relieved by the cancellation of the full-scale exhibit, arguing that it had been so eviscerated that it was better not to mount it at all. I don't share that view. Yes, each new draft of the script bore the scars of censorship. But even in its damaged state, the exhibit would have challenged viewers to rethink their comfortable notions about Hiroshima and Nagasaki, the end of the war, and the origins of the Cold War. In recent months, I have privately discussed the stillborn exhibit with some members of the American Legion. And it is clear that the motives and concerns of the Legion and the Air Force Association were, in some respects, fundamentally different.

Air Force Association press releases as well as the remarks of individual members of the association suggest that their campaign to discredit the *Enola Gay* exhibit was designed, in part, to embarrass the Smithsonian and force the resignation of Harwit. Under that scenario, he would have been replaced with someone whose idea of a good museum was strictly celebratory—and therefore congenial with the Air Force Association's views. For the American Legion, the issue was much different. From a Legion perspective, the exhibit appeared to slight the contributions that veterans of the Pacific war made to victory over Japan. When *Post* reporter Ringle interviewed Grayford C. Payne, the prisoner of war quoted a moment ago, Ringle noted that the curators had said the question of whether it was necessary and right to drop the bombs still "continues to perplex" the nation.

To Payne, the curators sounded as if they were saying "that the thousands of Japanese killed by those bombs were somehow worth more than the thousands of American prisoners in Japan. . . . After all we'd been through? . . . What about the women and children I saw bayoneted and buried alive . . . by the Japanese in the Philippines? What about the hundreds of thousands of Chinese hacked to pieces in the Rape of Nanking?" Perhaps it is no overstatement to say that for the American Legion, the issue was sentiment. But for the Air Force Association, the issue was power. It wanted "its" museum back.

Some say that the big loser in the *Enola Gay* flap was the public, not the Smithsonian. There's some truth to that. Ordinary men, women and children have been denied the opportunity to assess different interpretations—supported by artifacts and documents—regarding the end of World War II, which have emerged from an intense study of the documented views and actions of the major actors who shaped the events in the Pacific in the summer of 1945.

In this fiftieth anniversary year of the end of the war, there is no dearth of information about the bombings. There has been an explosion of articles, books, and television specials about the first and only uses of atomic weapons in warfare, each presenting a distinctive and sometimes unique interpretation of the evidence concerning the motives behind the decisions of our leaders. Unfortunately, if someone wants to see an interpretation accompanied by actual artifacts that bear on the story, he or she will have to visit Hiroshima or Nagasaki.

The public *was* a big loser. But so was the Smithsonian. Last year, the administration of the Air and Space Museum forced the curators of the exhibit to negotiate directly with representatives of lobbying groups like the Air Force Association and the American Legion. Meanwhile, twenty-eight members of Congress signed a letter to the secretary of the Smithsonian denouncing the exhibit and urging him to intercede. Director Harwit was confronted by twenty-one members of Congress, some of whom wanted to know why the curators were being so un-American. Sen. Christopher "Kit" Bond, a Republican from Missouri, wrote a letter to one of the curators, accusing the curator of being un-American. Bond said he would keep his eye on the curator.

As the controversy unfolded, I suggested to Harwit and the curators that the advisory board could play a useful role as a buffer between the curators and the critics. That idea got nowhere. In September, I resigned from the advisory board, as a protest. I was outraged that the museum administration had exposed the curators to the direct pressure of organizations such as the Air Force Association and the American Legion. And I was thunderstruck when members of Congress became actively involved.

The fact that a significant portion of the funds for the Air and Space Museum comes from public sources no more entitles members of Congress—or anyone else—to censor the conclusions of sound historical scholarship than does the fact that public monies support other kinds of research and writing projects. That kind of thought control should have no place in a government committed to democracy. I believed that that issue had been settled in the 1950s, when McCarthyism was laid to rest. Apparently, I was wrong.

How the
U.S. Press
Missed the
Target

Tony Capaccio and Uday Mohan

FIFTY YEARS AFTER THE U.S. BOMBING MISSIONS over Hiroshima and Nagasaki, ideological fallout from the atomic bomb has settled over Smithsonian Institution's National Air and Space Museum. Following months of text changes, charges of anti-Americanism, and the resignation of the museum's director, an exhibit originally scheduled to open in May 1995 has finally opened in July 1995, as a pared down version of what was supposed to be a complex retelling of President Harry S. Truman's decision to use the atomic bomb. Instead, the exhibit is not much more than the 60-foot fuselage of the B-29 Superfortress *Enola Gay*, the plane that dropped the bomb on Hiroshima on August 6, 1945, instantly killing at least 70,000 Japanese. Air Force historian Richard P. Hallion, a former science and technology curator at the Air and Space Museum and an exhibit adviser, ruefully calls the exhibit "a beer can with a label."

The dispute that brought about this truncated exhibit was over which version of atom bomb history would be highlighted. The controversy was largely fueled by media accounts that uncritically accepted the conventional rationale for the bomb, ignored contrary historical evidence, and reinforced the charge that the planned exhibit was a pro-Japanese, anti-American tract. The conventional view reflects the sober accounts of Truman and his secretary of war, Henry Stimson: The A-bombs saved as many as one million American soldiers who would have been killed or wounded in an invasion of the Japanese mainland—"Our Boys or the Bomb?" as one *Washington Post* op-ed headline put it. This position was defended by veterans groups, most prominently the American Legion and the Air Force Association, which campaigned vigorously against the initial plans for the exhibit.

The other version comes from historians who, since the mid-1960s, have been reassessing Truman's decision in light of documents and memoirs. They have found that President Truman did not face the stark choice of either an invasion or the bomb. He had other alternatives. Scholars argue that no documents back up claims made by Truman and others that an invasion of Japan would have cost as many as one million American casualties. Archival evidence reveals that a number of factors contributed to Truman's decision to drop the bomb, including bureaucratic momentum, political imperatives, psychological factors and the desire to

contain an expansionist Soviet Union. Many historians have concluded the administration saw deterrence of the Soviets as a secondary benefit; they generally agree
that ending the war quickly was the dominant reason.

Several prominent scholars maintain that some combination of the Soviet
Union's August 8 entry into the Pacific war, modification of unconditional surrender terms, a blockade, and conventional bombing most likely would have forced
the Japanese to surrender—without the use of the A-bomb—before the planned
allied invasion of November 1, 1945. These elements in fact contributed significantly to Japan's surrender on August 15. In their view, the dropping of a second
atomic bomb on August 9 on Nagasaki, which instantly killed at least 40,000,
cannot be justified on any political, military or moral grounds.

As journalists prepared for the inevitable flurry of fiftieth anniversary stories
in August 1995, they had a chance to test such assessments and evaluate how well
they would stand up against the conventional explanation for Truman's decision.
The resources, both documentary and human, are readily available. However, a
survey of the coverage of the *Enola Gay* exhibit flap, as well as earlier anniversary
coverage, indicates there has been little willingness by major media organizations
to reassess the A-bomb decision with the same energy applied to other great historical controversies, such as the Kennedy assassination or the Cuban missile
crisis. The overall coverage of the exhibit controversy "wasn't very thorough," says
George Washington University history professor Ronald Spector, author of the
widely acclaimed World War II Pacific theater history book, *Eagle Against the Sun.*
"I don't think there was much of an attempt to really understand the issues that
were involved."

A July 1993 Air and Space Museum planning document clearly describes what
the Smithsonian initially intended for the exhibit scheduled to open this summer:
"The primary goal of this exhibition will be to encourage visitors to undertake a
thoughtful and balanced re-examination of these events in the light of political and
military factors leading to the decision to drop the bomb, the human suffering
experienced by the people of Hiroshima and Nagasaki and the long term implications. . . . This exhibit can provide a crucial public service by re-examining these
issues in the light of the most recent scholarship." The museum's plan, however,
was derailed by a sophisticated public relations campaign launched by the Air
Force Association (AFA), a 180,000-member nonprofit organization headquartered
in Arlington, Virginia.

The AFA first heard about the exhibit in August 1993 after the museum disseminated planning documents. The group believed the plans were flawed, so it
contacted the museum and began what it once called a "constructive dialogue."
During the next seven months AFA officials quietly lobbied the museum to change
the tone of the exhibit. Frustrated by what they felt to be only "cosmetic changes,"
AFA officials decided to go public in March 1994. They issued a press release, titled
"Politically Correct Curating at the Air and Space Museum," stressing what they
saw to be an imbalance in the script between the depictions of Japanese suffering
at ground zero in Hiroshima and Nagasaki and the dearth of images depicting years
of Japan's unspeakable brutality against other Asians and allied prisoners of war.

The AFA's release introduced the now infamous "war of vengeance" quote that
reverberated throughout the debate: "For most Americans, it was a war of
vengeance. For most Japanese, it was a war to defend their unique culture against
Western imperialism." It was those two sentences, endlessly repeated by the media

outside of their original context, that did the most damage to the museum's credibility. The AFA had other serious problems with the first draft of the exhibit script. "A recurring undertone in the plans and scripts has been suspicion about why the United States used the atomic bomb," stated one association analysis. "Museum officials have seemed reluctant to accept the explanation that it was a military action, taken to end the war and save lives."

Another AFA document suggested that the exhibit section titled "The Decision to Drop the Bomb" should be renamed "The Decision that Ended the War" and "revised to reflect widely accepted scholarship—that President Truman analyzed the . . . estimates of potential casualties, and made the decision to use the awesome military weapon in order to save lives. . . . All revisionist speculation should be eliminated." Curators did not expect the attacks. "We believed in rational discussion. We didn't want to get into a knife fight," says one shell-shocked Air and Space Museum official. But Thomas Crouch, chairman of the Air and Space Museum's aeronautics department and chief exhibit curator, concedes that "what went wrong was we didn't give enough thought to the emotional link that's still in the minds of obviously a great many Americans that binds the idea of the bomb, the memory of the bomb. . . to the euphoria at the end of World War II."

The controversy ignited in the summer of 1994 after the release of the first of four eventual script revisions. First, in a widely publicized statement, *Enola Gay* pilot Paul Tibbets called the planned exhibit a "package of insults" in a speech to a military group. Then, in mid-July the AFA released internal Air and Space Museum documents, including an April 16, 1994, memo from museum director Martin Harwit acknowledging the exhibit lacked balance. But the key story— based partly on the internal museum documents the AFA released—was a July 21 *Washington Post* Style section piece by Eugene L. Meyer that elevated the controversy to national status when it caught the eye of Republican Rep. Peter Blute of Massachusetts. "The critics accuse the Smithsonian of choosing political correctness over historical accuracy in the presentation," Meyer wrote. "They charge that the exhibit as planned will portray the Japanese largely as suffering, even noble victims and the Americans as racist and ruthless fighters hell-bent on revenge for Pearl Harbor."

So alerted, Blute issued a letter on August 10, co-signed by twenty-three other legislators, condemning the museum for proposing an "anti-American" and "biased" exhibit. The lawmakers wanted "an objective account of the *Enola Gay* and her mission rather than the historically narrow, revisionist view contained in the revised script." Stanford University professor Barton Bernstein, a well-known atomic bomb historian, is amazed at how little press scrutiny the AFA received. "Any reporter who gave it four seconds of thought would conclude that the Air Force Association is a not a mainline, impartial group on this," he says. "It's a service lobby." The AFA would keep up its media campaign for eleven months. By the group's own account, it was cited in more than 400 print and broadcast stories during the height of the controversy—from August 1994 through the end of January. Combined with the efforts of the American Legion, which began highly publicized, line by line negotiations with curators in September 1994, the AFA campaign forced the museum to kill its original exhibit concept on January 30.

After members of Congress intervened, the story, as covered by the media, degenerated into a shouting match, with the veterans' groups doing most of the shouting. But instead of covering the veterans' charges *and* the historical debate, the media focused narrowly on the allegations of imbalance and anti-Americanism. By most accounts, the media coverage of the museum controversy itself was scrupulously fair, at least within the standard news formula of reporting charges and countercharges. Even Air and Space Museum spokesman Michael Fetters is satisfied with the way the museum was treated by the press. "All I can ask is that before they go with a story that will really provoke a reaction is give us a call and give us an opportunity to respond," says Fetters. "Most of the reporters of the major dailies did that and I'm satisfied. They definitely made a good effort to get a response."

Fetters acknowledged a common observation made by reporters interviewed for this story: "Our own office didn't respond as strongly as we could have so we bear a lot of the responsibility" for the way the coverage turned out. Some of the earliest accounts, which appeared in May 1994, were the most evenhanded, especially a May 9 story by *Wichita Eagle* reporter Tom Webb. It ran on the Knight-Ridder wire and was published by at least seventeen newspapers, including the *Philadelphia Inquirer, Omaha World-Herald, San Diego Union-Tribune, Orlando Sentinel, Arizona Republic,* Portland's *Oregonian,* and the *Orange County Register.* Webb gave equal weight to the veterans' charges and the Smithsonian's response. He also included the curators' views, which debunked the large casualty figures predicted in the event of an invasion of Japan that have been used to justify the bomb. Unfortunately those passages were often cut in the versions that ran.

The *Washington Post* first covered the debate as a federal bureaucracy story on May 31 in a "Capital Notebook" column on its Federal Page. In contrast with the paper's later critical coverage, it concluded somewhat sympathetically: "There is something to be said for an exhibit that suggests that warplanes are not simply expensive sporting devices to be used for movie props or flyovers at presidential funerals." But the overall tone of coverage became more strident following Rep. Blute's letter. Reporters, columnists and editorial writers often used criticism by the AFA, the American Legion and other veterans groups as a club to beat on the museum. Former Air and Space Museum Director Harwit, who resigned in May 1995, due to the negative publicity, is more critical of the news coverage than Fetters. He believes many reporters weren't open to the curators' perspective. "I did have the feeling the stories [reporters] had in mind when they came in to see us were the stories they wrote when they left," he says. "It had nothing to do with what we were going to say because what we said would have made their stories differ so much from those that were already in the press."

But Harwit reserved his sharpest criticism for editorial writers. "Columnists took this over and these allegations were in hundreds of newspapers," he says. "One editorialist would write something and then in a day or two you'd see exactly the same wording or the same quotes" in other stories or columns.

Editorial writers in particular did land some hard punches. Perhaps the most damaging piece was written by *Washington Post* Editorial Page Editor Meg Greenfield in an August 14 op-ed column titled "Context and the *Enola Gay.*" Blute spokesman Bob Gray says it was instrumental in neutralizing political support for the museum. "What the tenor of the debate suggests," she wrote, "is a curatorial inability to perceive that political opinions are embedded in the exhibit or to identify them as such—opinions—rather than as universal objective assumptions all thinking people must necessary share."

Meanwhile, the *Tulsa World* concluded that "a distance of fifty years makes it easy to make half-baked judgments on history." Syndicated columnist Charley Reese of the *Orlando Sentinel* repeated a favorite AFA sound bite, stating that the problem was "the intellectual arrogance of the museum director." A *Providence Journal Bulletin* editorial lamented: "Unfortunately, this latest example is all too characteristic of the way left-wing politics have smothered the Smithsonian's historical presentations." Similarly, the *Indianapolis Star*, published in the same city as the American Legion, opined that "a revisionist faction has tried to turn the planned display. . . into an American-bashing enterprise." And syndicated columnist Jeff Jacoby of the *Boston Globe* called the exhibit script "tendentious and manipulative. . . . It portrays the United States and the Allies as militaristic and racist."

Given the emotions stirred by the controversy, one would expect strong editorial opinions. But often these columns—and many of the news stories—contained factual errors and script passages taken out of context that exacerbated an already polarized debate. Perhaps the most glaring gap in the coverage was the failure to challenge the standard "our boys or the bomb" assumption—that the Allied forces would have had to invade Japan if the atomic bombs hadn't been dropped. "If you look at the weight of the historians who have written about this, and I'm not a historian of the era, but I've read some of the histories, it seems the evidence is very, very strong," says syndicated columnist Charles Krauthammer of the *Washington Post*. Jacoby agrees. "My best judgment is that this is by and large a settled historical conclusion," he says. "There were major preparations underway for an invasion and it was the use of the bomb that made that invasion unnecessary."

A number of historians say that the AFA, Krauthammer, Jacoby and the other journalists who accepted this "conclusion" are mistaken. "It wasn't that way," says J. Samuel Walker, the historian at the Nuclear Regulatory Commission. "Number one, there were alternatives. Number two, it wasn't at all clear that an invasion was necessary. Clearly, many high officials within the Truman White House and advisers thought the war was practically over. It's less clear Truman felt that way." University of Southern Mississippi military history professor John Ray Skates, who has written a critical assessment of the planned invasion, says, "It's always couched in this false dichotomy of either the bomb or the invasion. The connections between the use of the bomb and the decision to invade Japan are neither direct nor close."

The view offered by historian Martin Sherwin in the 1987 edition of his book, *A World Destroyed*, was incorporated by the curators in the ill-fated exhibit. He wrote, "The choice in the summer of 1945 was not between a conventional invasion or a nuclear war. It was a choice between various forms of diplomacy and warfare. While the decision that Truman made is understandable, it was not inevitable. It was even avoidable." University of Nebraska professor Peter Maslowski, in the Spring 1995 issue of *The Quarterly Journal of Military History* (*MHQ*), noted how out of the four primary options Truman faced, the bomb or invasion "remain so vivid in the national consciousness that it is as if they were always the only possibilities." At the time, however, none of the options—bomb, invasion, blockade or a negotiated settlement that modified the demands for Japan's unconditional surrender—"was self-evidently better than the others." He concluded that "strictly speaking, the bombs were not necessary . . . but . . . represented a way to avoid the difficulties inherent in the other three" options.

Newsweek also botched the bomb versus invasion issue. A December 12 story quoted Walker's assessment out of context to reinforce the premise that the exhibit script failed to give due consideration to the "bomb or invasion" dilemma Truman faced. "Did the bomb prevent an invasion of Japan that would have made Normandy look like a training exercise or not?" wrote former Tokyo bureau chief Bill Powell, now based in Berlin. "The subject is of fierce dispute among historians. But as J. Samuel Walker . . . wrote recently, 'the historical consensus . . . which held that the bomb was used primarily for military reasons [i.e. to avoid a bloody invasion of Japan] . . . continues to prevail.'" But in the same Winter 1990 issue of *Diplomatic History*, Walker also wrote: "The consensus among scholars is that the bomb was not needed to avoid an invasion of Japan and to end the war within a relatively short time. It is clear that alternatives to the bomb existed and that Truman and his advisers knew it. . . . [I]t bears repeating that an invasion was a remote possibility." Powell concedes he had not seen the entire Walker article and based his story on files from other *Newsweek* reporters. "Perhaps I misinterpreted his quote," he says.

One of the most unfair and unfortunate aspects of the coverage was the consistently poor way reporters and columnists handled the infamous two-sentence "war of vengeance" quote. Although the museum removed the lines in a May 31, 1994 draft, they were repeated for more than a year by the press as representative of the museum's mindset in organizing the exhibit. They were picked up and hammered home in stories and editorials in newspapers ranging from the *Washington Times* to the *Tulsa World, Rocky Mountain News* and Portland's *Oregonian*. They were uttered on the radio by Rush Limbaugh and National Public Radio newscasters, and they were turned into a graphic for the *MacNeil/Lehrer News Hour.*

"That quote always, always came up," says museum spokesman Fetters. Despite a summer full of script changes "all the veterans groups had to do was talk about 'that *Enola Gay* exhibit that portrayed the Japanese as victims and Americans the aggressors,' and then they would use the 'war of vengeance' quote and all of the sudden we would be fighting that January 1994 script again." Krauthammer recalled the quote in a August 19 piece with special indignation, noting that although it had been cleaned up "you can imagine the prejudices of those who would write such a thing and the kind of exhibit they would put on." A fair comment, perhaps. Read in isolation, the quotes are inflammatory. But published in the context of what preceded it—something virtually no journalist, including Krauthammer, saw fit to do—the sentences, while clumsy and open to misinterpretation, are less offensive. Here is the full passage:

> In 1931 the Japanese Army occupied Manchuria; six years later it invaded the rest of China. From 1937 to 1945, the Japanese Empire would be constantly at war. Japanese expansionism was marked by naked aggression and extreme brutality. The slaughter of tens of thousands of Chinese in Nanking in 1937 shocked the world. Atrocities by Japanese troops included brutal mistreatment of civilians, forced laborers and prisoners of war, and biological experiments on human victims. In December 1941, Japan attacked U.S. bases in Pearl Harbor, Hawaii, and launched other surprise assaults against allied territories in the Pacific. Thus began a wider conflict marked by extreme bitterness. For most Americans, this war was fundamentally different than the one waged against Germany and Italy—it was a war of vengeance.

> For most Japanese, it was a war to defend their unique culture
> against Western imperialism. As the war approached its end in 1945,
> it appeared to both sides that it was a fight to the finish."

MHQ Editor Robert Cowley, agrees the quote was portrayed inaccurately. "If you give the full thing it's not nearly so bad. But what was quoted was that last sentence," he says. "If you take that out of context it's much worse and in that sense, Krauthammer was not being entirely honest. But what we got was that last sentence. Once that was out of the bag, it was hard to stop the conflagration." Krauthammer stands by his use of the quote. "Anybody who could write that clearly is seeing the Japanese defending their culture against Western 'imperialism.' That certainly cast them as victims."

The *Washington Times* also attacked the museum for the quote. "I couldn't believe that [passage]," says *Times* Editor in Chief Wesley Pruden. "I thought, 'My God. If that's the quality of historian they've got at the Smithsonian we ought to look into it.' . . . It was almost as if they were talking about something that happened on another planet." Pruden, like many journalists, had not seen the entire page, relying instead on previously published accounts. When he was shown the page during an interview, he conceded that "perhaps" his paper ran the quote out of context. "Maybe we should have put that text in a sidebar or graphic of some kind, it probably would have been a good idea," he said. "But I think it pretty much expresses what they had in mind."

As for what the quote intended, curator Michael Neufeld offers this explanation: the media "misread our mindset or misinterpreted our mindset. It was an attempt to interpret what was in the minds of each side at the time. It's not what we thought the Japanese were all about. We were trying to explain what they thought they were all about." AFA Chief of Media Relations Jack Giese defends the association's repeated references. The passage, he says, was only one of three in the initial 500-page script of text and photos to clearly acknowledge Japanese aggression—a point conceded by the curators and subsequently corrected.

The other most common mistakes in the coverage involved the projected number of casualties from an invasion of Japan and the presumption that the exhibit called U. S. motives racist. In his July 21, 1994 story, "Dropping the Bomb: Smithsonian Exhibit Plan Detonates Controversy," the *Washington Post's* Meyer wrote that "military planners estimated upwards of 800,000 American casualties would result from a planned two-stage invasion." In an interview, Meyer conceded that the casualty figure was an extrapolation made by Air Force historian Richard Hallion in 1994, not a wartime planning estimate. After another historian questioned the figure, Meyer did not use it in subsequent stories.

Meyer also mischaracterized key themes in the scripts. For example, in a September 30 story, Meyer wrote that early scripts "suggested that American war planners, including President Harry S. Truman, were motivated less by concern over American casualties than by a desire to impress the Soviet Union with the new weapon, and to justify the expenditure of $2 billion in the production of the bomb." The scripts, however, clearly stated that "most scholars have rejected this argument." Meyer says, "my article did not say that the early scripts made such claims. It said the scripts 'suggested' conclusions. They did so through sheer repetition of the 'impress-the-Soviets' and price-tag factors, and by understating Truman's concern with lives lost in a possible invasion."

An August 1 piece by *USA Today* columnist Tony Snow was typical of the way the racism issue played. Snow wrote: "A later piece of text raises a racism charge: 'Some have argued that the atomic bomb would never have been dropped on Germans because it was much easier for Americans to bomb Asians than white people.' No serious historian takes this view, but the Smithsonian curators included it." In fact, the issue was raised by the curators as a "historical controversy" and answered in the script: "The consensus of most, if not all, historians is that President Roosevelt would have used the bomb on Germany if such an attack would have been useful in the European war."

When asked if he unfairly pulled the quote out of context, Snow replied, "If I had to go back and look twice, I probably would have stuck in a parenthetical to say that they make note of the fact that no historian [agrees]." But the fact that the curators raised the issue, he added "implicitly gave some sense of credence" to it.

On August 29, the *Wall Street Journal* printed one of the most damaging errors just as congressional and editorial pressure was building against the museum. In an editorial titled "War and the Smithsonian," the *Journal* stated that "it is especially curious to note the oozing romanticism with which the *Enola* show's writers describe the *kamikaze* pilots. . . . These were, the script elegiacally relates, 'youths, their bodies overflowing with life.' Of the youth and life of the Americans who fought and bled in the Pacific there is no mention." The *Journal's* observation was picked up the next day by *Washington Post* reporter Ken Ringle, who wrote that "just yesterday, for example, an editorial in the *Wall Street Journal* found it 'especially curious to note. . . .'" He then repeated the statement. The quote the *Journal* attributed to elegiac curatorial prose was actually written after the war by a surviving *kamikaze* pilot, Ensign Yukiteru Sugiyama. This was clearly spelled out in the script text. *Journal* spokesman Roger May and Ringle refuse to discuss the mistake. "We don't do postmortems on editorials," May says.

On September 26, Ringle contributed "At Ground Zero: Two Views of History Collide Over Smithsonian A-Bomb Exhibit," a 3,780-word piece that pitted a Bataan Death March survivor's perspective against the museum's. The former POW, Grayford C. Payne, told Ringle that "all of us who were prisoners in Japan—or were headed for it to probably die in the invasion—revere the *Enola Gay*. It saved our lives." In a recent interview, Ringle argued that the Smithsonian's "perceptions are vastly different from the population at large. I can only say if the academic historians were right and all the curators were right, there would be no political pressures the other way."

A traditionally disorganized group, historians entered the debate in the fall of 1994—much too late to influence public opinion. And they found getting much more than a sound bite was difficult, says a *New York Times* editorial assistant, Timothy McNulty, who wrote a Week In Review piece on February 5, 1995 summarizing the controversy. "It was harder for them to get their points across as easily as it was for the veterans," says McNulty. The veterans' side "was a lot more understandable because everyone was used to it. When you see people criticize or question Truman's decision, he's a legend. You knew how the vets would react." Some reporters did attempt to weave the historical debate in with the exhibit controversy, but they were exceptions. *USA Today* reporter Andrea Stone, for one, consistently incorporated the views of historians in her pieces. And while the public was continually informed about the veterans groups' take on the exhibit plans, news organizations failed to report that a number of historians had actually praised the museum for its efforts.

Edwin Bearss, special assistant to the director of the National Park Service and a member of the exhibit's advisory board, wrote in February 1994, "As a World War II Pacific combat veteran, I commend you and your colleagues who have dared to go that extra mile to address an emotionally charged and internationally significant event in an exhibit that, besides enlightening, will challenge its viewers." Even Hallion, one of the critics' favorite sources, had some kind words about the original script. "Overall, this is a most impressive piece of work, comprehensive and dramatic, obviously based upon a great deal of sound research, primary and secondary," he wrote in a February 1994 note. Nor did reporters get their hands on mid-July assessments from the Joint Chiefs of Staff or the Pentagon's chief historian, Alfred Goldberg. Both judged the museum to be making progress in rewriting a flawed first script. In a July 15 memo to museum curator Michael Neufeld on the second script, Goldberg noted, "My overall impression of the *Enola Gay* script is favorable. It shows evidence of careful research and an effort to realize a balanced presentation."

By focusing exclusively on the veterans' charges the news media failed to convey the bigger story: Whose version of the historical record is closer to explaining why the atomic bombs were dropped, the veterans groups or the Air and Space Museum curators? The AFA and other veterans groups wanted "all revisionist speculation" removed. Many of the arguments on the other side—the view of the decision based on archival research—were ably represented by a cover story in the January/February 1995 issue of *Civilization*, a bimonthly magazine published by the Library of Congress. The article, "Why We Dropped the Bomb," was written by William Lanouette, the author of a 1993 book on Leo Szilard, one of the creators of the A-bomb. Although Lanouette's story was available in mid-December— several weeks before the Smithsonian abandoned its original concept for the exhibit—no reporter referred to his carefully edited findings. "[I]t still seems fair to conclude that the predominant reason for dropping the bomb was the belief that it would end the war quickly and spare American soldiers," he wrote. "But other factors clearly influenced that decision." Those factors included bureaucratic momentum, political justification, psychological factors and post-war diplomacy.

Lanouette endorsed J. Samuel Walker's conclusion that an invasion was an "unlikely possibility." Moreover, he noted that the United States' insistence on unconditional surrender when the Japanese wanted to retain their emperor "may have foreordained the use of the bomb." The piece also pointed out that "Truman's new secretary of state, James F. Byrnes and a number of military leaders saw the awesome weapons as a way to make the Soviets 'more manageable'. . . ." Indeed, Byrnes told *U.S. News & World Report* in 1960 that "of course" the bomb was dropped to finish the war before the Soviet Union entered on August 8. "We were anxious to get the war over with as soon as possible," he said. "In the days immediately preceding the dropping of that bomb his [Truman's] views were the same as mine—we wanted to get through the Japanese phase of the war before the Russians came in."

A database search found only two stories that addressed the latest historical evidence in any depth. One, a January 31 *New York Times* piece written by reporter John Kifner, wove in the views of atomic bomb historian Gar Alperovitz—who said it could be documented that "the bomb was not only unnecessary, but known in advance not to be necessary"—with the less critical positions of Stanford's Bernstein and *MHQ's* Cowley. Kifner also discussed the problem of inflated casualty estimates for a proposed invasion of the Japanese mainland. Kifner's piece was nearly matched by reporter Rod Dreher of the *Washington Times*, who wrote a January 20 round-up of historians' views debunking the high pre-invasion casualty estimates used by exhibit critics. Dreher's editors, however, apparently forgot about his story when they ran a piece a week later that included a chart listing estimates of between 500,000 and 1 million troops killed or wounded in an invasion. "We blew it," admits *Times* Editor in Chief Pruden.

Of all the historical issues mishandled by the press during the exhibit debate, the question of estimated casualties in an invasion of Japan looms largest. The casualty projections became a contested point because much of the coverage erroneously implied or assumed that President Truman only had two choices: use the atomic bomb or invade. According to an article in the Winter 1993 issue of *Diplomatic History* by Stanford University history professor Barton Bernstein, in the summer of 1945 the Joint Chiefs of Staff "had estimated American fatalities between about 25,000 and about 46,000" if a two-phased invasion was necessary. "Before Hiroshima, those estimates had been translated into about 132,500 to 220,000 casualties (fatalities, wounded and missing)."

The one million casualty figure cited by reporters stems from Truman and his secretary of war, Henry Stimson. In a February 1947 *Harper's Magazine* article, Stimson wrote: "[S]uch operations might have been expected to cost over a million casualties to American forces alone." In a January 1953 letter to Army Air Force historian James Cate, Truman wrote that General George Marshall told him "that such an invasion would cost at a minimum one quarter of a million casualties and might cost as much as a million, on the American side alone." Two years later Truman wrote in his memoir, "General Marshall told me that it might cost half a million American lives to force the enemy's surrender."

Besides Stimson and Truman, sources used by reporters included William Manchester's 1978 book on General Douglas MacArthur, *American Caesar*, and David McCullough's 1992 biography, *Truman*. Manchester wrote that MacArthur "told Stimson that Downfall [the invasion's code name] would 'cost over a million casualties to American forces.'" Manchester, however, cannot verify the number. It was not footnoted, which, he said in a recent interview, "was an oversight." He says, "I among others, found this figure. Its reliability can be questioned. I think it's largely irrelevant. In an invasion there would have been an enormous loss of life." McCullough cited what he said was an assessment written by a member of Marshall's staff that not invading "would save no less than 500,000 to one million lives." McCullough admitted in *Defense Week* last October that he had misread a document in which Marshall's staff was *debunking* the claim that an invasion would cause that many casualties.

There is no doubt that Stimson's figure is suspect. Instead of one million casualties, Stimson's outline of the *Harper's* article initially read, "If [the] atomic bomb works [it] might save hundred [sic] thousands of American lives."

McGeorge Bundy, who helped write Stimson's *Harper's* article and went on to become national security advisor for the Kennedy and Johnson administrations, also questioned the number. In his 1988 book, "Danger and Survival," he wrote, "Defenders of the use of the bomb, Stimson among them, were not always careful about the number of casualties expected. Revisionist scholars are on solid ground when they question flat assertions that the bomb saved a million lives." The Truman figures are problematic as well. Truman's draft letter to Cate said Marshall told him 250,000 casualties would be the minimum price of an invasion. But David Lloyd, a White House aide, noted this recollection conflicted with Stimson's claims and changed the wording, with Truman's permission, to include the one million casualty estimate. Even after seventeen years on the job, diplomatic historian Larry Bland, editor of George Marshall's papers, has not found any documentation supporting the casualty claims attributed to the general. "I've looked and looked to find something specific to back up Truman's claim that Marshall said something about a million or a half-million casualties," says Bland. "I never saw any figure like that."

A number of journalists covering the *Enola Gay* exhibit debate suggested the "politically correct," "revisionist" critique of President Truman's decision resulted from a generational and ideological gap. And at least two of them, *Washington Post* reporter Ken Ringle and columnist Edwin Yoder, specifically cited divisions over the Vietnam War as a major reason for questioning the decision to drop the bomb. Such observations, however, ignore history. From the mid-1940's through the mid-1960's a number of prominent military officers and civilians questioned the necessity of the bomb. Military critics included General Dwight Eisenhower, Admiral William Leahy, Truman's chief of staff, and General "Hap" Arnold, commander of the Army Air Force. Among the civilian critics were *Time* magazine founder Henry Luce; David Lawrence, the staunchly conservative editor of *United States News*, now *U.S. News & World Report*; and Hanson Baldwin, the *New York Times'* leading military affairs analyst.

For example, in a 1948 speech Luce stated, "If, instead of our doctrine of 'unconditional surrender,' we had all along made our conditions clear, I have little doubt that the war with Japan would have ended no later than it did—without the bomb explosion which so jarred the Christian conscience." In his 1950 book, *Great Mistakes of the War*, Baldwin also suggested the bomb had been unnecessary. In 1958, William F. Buckley Jr.'s *National Review* twice questioned Truman's decision. In 1965, *Life* magazine ran a highly positive review of historian Gar Alperovitz's *Atomic Diplomacy*. The book, which has been called the first serious challenge to the idea that the only reason for dropping the atomic bomb was to quickly end the war, suggested that concern about post-war relations with the Soviet Union was the key factor.

Ten years later *U.S. News & World Report* ran one of the last examples of a critique by the news media. The magazine reprinted portions of interviews from 1960 with five World War II insiders, including Truman's secretary of state, James F. Byrnes; Edward Teller, a physicist who built the bomb; and Lewis Strauss, assistant to the secretary of the Navy during the war and later the head of the Atomic Energy Commission. Only Byrnes unequivocally supported Truman's decision.

The occasional questioning by the media began to fade just as scholars, picking through the archival material that slowly became available, began to seriously question why Truman had used the bomb. Journalists did not keep up with advances in scholarship. By 1985, the fortieth anniversary of Hiroshima, news organizations raised fewer critical questions even while offering the most extensive coverage to date. *The Chicago Tribune, New York Times, Washington Post*, and *Los Angeles Times* published more than 100 items in the summer of 1985. *Newsweek* and *Time* ran special sections that together totaled more than forty pages. *Life* devoted an entire issue to World War II, including a section titled "Top Secret: A Great Invasion the A-Bomb Canceled." ABC's *Nightline* "re-created" the invasion of Japan that never took place, leaving the historical issues to a brief and un-illuminating exposition.

Apart from some of the opinion pieces in the four newspapers reviewed, an essay in *Time*, and a news story in the *New York Times*, the media barely mentioned the serious nature of the historical controversy. The majority of the opinion pieces supported the use of the bomb. The last time the issue came up before the Smithsonian controversy was in December 1991, the fiftieth anniversary of Pearl Harbor, when President Bush asserted that Truman's decision was "right because it spared the lives of millions of American citizens." A database search found that in the ensuing coverage, the approximately 130 print and television news and opinion stories that mentioned Hiroshima failed to seriously challenge Bush's statement. Reflecting on the dearth of historical analysis that typified the *Enola Gay* exhibit coverage, Mark Johnson of Media General News Service summed up the problem in the following way. "What would have been nice to do for a lot of people was to sit down in a research library and read everything they could about how the atomic bomb was created and what happened when it went off," he says. "I would have liked to have gotten more space and have written a history lesson, which you can't do."

No one expects reporters on deadline to be budding Barton Bernsteins. But the realities of time and space do not mean that the conventional wisdom on the A-bomb has to be uncritically passed along to the public. There was ample opportunity and time as the issue unfolded for reporters to incorporate the latest research into their stories. In this case the media's shortcomings are all too obvious. Journalists did not do enough research and failed to hold the veterans' version of history to the same exacting standard they used in judging the curators' version. The initial exhibit had flaws of context and historical perspective—but not as serious and certainly not as ill-informed as the media coverage led the public to believe.

THE WAR

OF THE

OP-ED

PAGES

HOW A GENUINE DEMOCRACY SHOULD CELEBRATE ITS PAST

John W. Dower

I HAD AN UNUSUAL EXPERIENCE shortly after the Smithsonian Institution surrendered unconditionally to critics in late January and abandoned its plans for a major exhibition at the National Air and Space Museum on the use of the atomic bomb to end World War II. I was, to coin a phrase, "disinvited" from giving two public, off-campus talks, both of which had been roughly framed in terms of "thinking about the bomb." The disinvitations were conveyed in a genteel manner, of course. I remained welcome, my erstwhile sponsors explained. I should just come prepared to focus on a different aspect of American-Japanese relations. The bombs that the United States dropped on Japan simply had become "too controversial" a topic.

Thus, in ways that have gone virtually unreported by the mass media, the dispute over the Smithsonian's exhibit has emerged as a case study of the many levels at which censorship can operate in an ostensibly democratic society—ranging from overt political repression (epitomized by Congressional pressure to change the Smithsonian exhibit and cut the institution's appropriations) to subtle forms of self-censorship. Confounded by a vitriolic campaign against "revisionist" interpretations of a "good war" by conservative forces both inside and outside government, the nation's premier institution of public history did more than just jettison its plans for a serious retrospective look at the use and consequences of the atomic bomb. The Smithsonian also indefinitely postponed plans for an exhibition on an even more controversial moment in recent American history: the Vietnam War. In addition, it announced that the current exhibition on "Science in American Life" (at its National Museum of American History) would be revised, in yet unspecified ways, to modify critical mention of negative byproducts and consequences of twentieth-century science. In the latter instance, the Smithsonian is responding to criticism by professional scientific societies.

Not content with these victories, the Smithsonian's critics have demanded that heads roll. Curators have been placed under intense political scrutiny. Congress has held hostile hearings on the planning for the original *Enola Gay* exhibit. The director of the National Air and Space Museum recently resigned under pressure, and it is an open secret that morale among members of the Smithsonian's professional staff has been shattered. In this new McCarthyism, the catchall indictment is no longer "Communism" but rather "political correctness" or even just plain "revisionism." Few people in the media or among the general public seem to find the enforcement of a purely celebratory national history alarming. We praise other countries, especially those in the former Communist camp, for engaging in critical reappraisal of the past. We castigate the Japanese when they sanitize the war years and succumb to "historical amnesia." Yet at the same time, we skewer our own public historians for deviating from Fourth of July historiography. We are so besieged by polemics and sound bites that almost no one has time to dwell on the irony of demanding a pristine, heroic, official version of a war that presumably was fought to protect principled contention and the free play of ideas.

It is in this milieu that the chill of self-censorship has appeared. My "disinvitations" do not appear to be isolated events. After the Smithsonian was brought to its knees, a fellow historian similarly was disinvited by the newsletter of a major archive from contributing a critical essay on President Harry S. Truman's decision to use the bomb. A television program to mark the anniversary of the devastating Tokyo air raids of March 9 and 10, 1945—in which the United States inaugurated the policy of targeting Japanese civilians—was canceled by the network. A scholarly symposium on the use of the atomic bomb, scheduled to be held at one of the service academies, was abruptly moved at the last moment, to the campus of a private college (and the military officers who participated appeared in civilian dress).

In this climate of political pressure and self-censorship, academics should attempt at the very least to do four things. First, we must convey to the public how we go about historical scholarship. Second, we must make more broadly known what we have learned or concluded from our specialized studies. Third, we must try to define what "celebrating" the American experience ideally should mean. Finally, in light of the Smithsonian's sad capitulation to the purveyors of an official historical orthodoxy, academics—social scientists and humanists in particular—must give serious attention to the appropriate mission of "public history." What, in brief, do these tasks entail?

As the Smithsonian controversy and the larger "culture wars" have revealed, "revisionism" has become a mark of political incorrectness, according to conservatives. There have been miserable excesses on all sides of this debate, and, in our present age of invective and unreason, it is a daunting task to try to convey to the public the idea that critical inquiry and responsible revision remain the lifeblood of every serious intellectual enterprise. Serious historians, like serious intellectuals generally, draw on new perspectives and data to reconsider and rethink received wisdom. The challenge of this task is difficult to convey to people who believe in fixed, inviolable historical truths. It is doubly difficult where patriotic gore and a "good war" are concerned. The same people who speak of inviolable truths, however, also generally are receptive to language that evokes "the perspective of time" or the "judgment of history." Popular wisdom thus holds open a door through which historians can enter to try to explain—judiciously and painstakingly—how the passage of time, the discovery of new information, the posing of new questions all may lead to revised understanding and reconstruction of past events. (The Smithsonian's own spokesmen, caught in the whirlwind, never vigorously tried publicly to explain and defend the serious historical considerations on which their original plans rested.)

In the case of the fiftieth anniversary of the end of World War II, what we scholars *know* in our specialized areas of expertise is certainly conspicuously different from what viewers will encounter at the stripped-down display at the Air and Space Museum, which consists of little more than a section of the fuselage of the *Enola Gay*, the B-29 Superfortress that dropped the atomic bomb on Hiroshima, and the taped reminiscences of the bomber's crew. We now know, for example, that many imperatives, in addition to saving American lives, propelled the decision to drop the bombs on Hiroshima and Nagasaki in August 1945. We also know that the American military had not planned to invade Japan until several months after the bombs were dropped, that Japan was on the verge of collapse before the atomic bomb was used, and that alternatives to the bomb were considered and rejected.

We know, too, that the dead in Hiroshima and Nagasaki included not only Japanese but also many thousands of Koreans, who had been conscripted for hard labor by their Japanese overlords; more than 1,000 Nisei who were trapped in Japan after Pearl Harbor; a small number of white American prisoners of war, most of them beaten to death by Japanese survivors of the bombing of Hiroshima; and smaller numbers of Chinese, Southeast Asians, and Europeans. We now also know that the total number of people killed in Hiroshima and Nagasaki, most of them civilians, was considerably greater than initial estimates—more than 200,000 by the most persuasive current estimates (and thus more than twice the total number of U.S. fighting men killed in the entire course of the Pacific War).

Through film, photographs, and personal accounts, we gradually have become better able to visualize the peculiar grotesqueries of death from nuclear radiation. Much of the documentary record of the human consequences of the bombing was initially censored by U.S. authorities. (Atomic-bomb survivors in occupied Japan were not allowed to publish accounts of their experience until late 1948, for example, and film footage from Hiroshima and Nagasaki remained classified for two decades.) Moreover, years passed before many survivors found it psychologically possible to articulate their traumatic experiences in words or drawings—some of which have become accessible to Americans only in recent decades. The horror of the early deaths from radiation poisoning was initially concealed from the world and is still little known outside Japan. Similarly, the long-term medical consequences of exposure to radiation from the bombs remain known mainly to specialists. These legacies range from mental retardation among infants *in utero* at the time to a higher-than-normal incidence of various cancers, especially leukemia, among survivors.

"Lack of context" is an argument hitherto monopolized by the Smithsonian's critics, who charged that the institution's original plans for its exhibition failed to convey adequately the nature of the war before 1945 and the aggressive, atrocious, fanatical behavior of the Japanese military machine. Such criticism was reasonable. Instead of leading to a fuller exhibition, however, it has resulted in a "commemorative" display, in which basic knowledge about the use and consequences of the bomb itself has been completely excised. Thus it has become the responsibility of academics and ordinary citizens to publicly convey the knowledge, perspectives, and controversies deemed unpatriotic and improper in official circles. And, indeed, in recent months, many academics and universities have taken up the challenge, through lectures and symposia on the war and the bombs. In the most politically visible and courageous example of such assumption of responsibility, American University in Washington, D.C. is sponsoring an exhibition on the human consequences of a nuclear strike, based in major part on materials from Hiroshima that were to be included in the Smithsonian's exhibition.

Such activities are crucial to countering the chill of self-censorship. At the same time, they also should be understood as an attempt to promote a true celebration of what America ideally stands for—namely, tolerance of dissenting voices and the capacity to confront and transcend past evils. This may be a dream, but it is a dream worth struggling for. The alternative is to accept the current public definition of celebration: the parroting of nationalistic myths and honking of patriotic horns. If this more radical notion of celebration is to be honored, however, we must turn serious attention to what we mean by "public history." The argument that has temporarily won the day is clear and explicit. Tax supported institutions such as the Smithsonian (or the National Endowment for the Humanities or the National Endowment for the Arts) have no business endorsing criticism of our national experience. Their mission is to praise, exalt, beautify, and glorify all that America has been and has done.

This is precisely what we criticize and ridicule when espoused by other nations and other cultures, and we should practice what we preach. America has much to be proud of and a great deal to think critically about. Sometimes, as in the case of the last "good war" and the almost nonchalant incineration of hundreds of thousands of enemy civilians that accompanied it, it seems excruciatingly difficult to separate our truly heroic from our horrendous deeds. Yet we must face these terrible ambiguities squarely—and do so at our public, as well as our private, institutions—or else stop pretending to be an honest and open society. That is the kind of "public history" worth struggling for in a genuine democracy.

The Chronicle of Higher Education
June 16, 1995

THE ENOLA GAY: A NATION'S, AND A MUSEUM'S, DILEMMA

Martin Harwit

FORTY-NINE YEARS AGO THIS WEEKEND, the United States dropped an atomic bomb on Hiroshima and then another on Nagasaki. A year from now, on the fiftieth anniversary, Americans will commemorate these pivotal events. But we lack a national consensus on what to say. Two divergent but widely held views define the dilemma. One view sprang up as soon as the bombs exploded and the war ended. Its proponents are united on the many details that need to be included in their story. Properly told, it appeals to our national self-image. The other point of view, slower in coming to the fore, is more analytical, critical in its acceptance of facts and concerned with historical context. It is complex and, in the eyes of some, discomfiting.

The first view recalls the morning of Aug. 6, 1945, when three B-29 Superfortresses arrived over Japan's Inland Sea. One of the aircraft, the *Enola Gay*, named for the pilot's mother, approached its Hiroshima target, released its heavy payload, then veered to distance itself from the bomb. Seconds later, at 8:15 A.M. the atomic bomb exploded over Hiroshima. The crew was stunned by the sight. The blast rocked the aircraft. The twenty-nine-year-old pilot, Colonel Paul W. Tibbets, commander of the 509th Composite Group, which was trained and tasked to deliver the bomb, was awed by the sight of the burning, devastated city below. To his copilot he remarked, "I think this is the end of the war." Five days and another atomic bomb later, Japan surrendered.

Our troops were ecstatic. They would not have to die by the many tens of thousands in a bloody invasion of Japan. They'd go home instead, settle down with their sweethearts, have children and lead normal lives. They had been asked to save the world for democracy, had accepted the challenge at great personal risk, and had come through victorious.

Approaching the fiftieth anniversary of Hiroshima next year, these same men, now in their seventies, have asked the National Air and Space Museum, into whose care the *Enola Gay* was entrusted after the war, to put their aircraft on exhibition. They want the museum to tell their story the way they have always told and retold it—a story of fighting a ruthless enemy, perpetrator of barbaric massacres in China, the infamous attack at Pearl Harbor, the death march at Bataan, torture and executions in prison camps, kamikaze raids on our warships and deaths by the thousands for every Pacific island wrested away; a story of the world's top physicists working in secrecy to perfect a mighty weapon; a story of a powerful new aircraft, designed, built and first flown in just 24 months; a story of ordinary citizens, men and women, working together to defeat a ferocious enemy. These are the themes emphasized by those who fought so hard to secure freedom for their children and grandchildren.

Those children and grandchildren by now are mature citizens. For them the atomic bomb has added associations: ICBMs, megaton warheads, the DEW line, 45-minute warnings, first strike, Mutually Assured Destruction, nuclear winter . . . Theirs was not a world of two small atomic bombs but of 50,000, many of which are 1,000 times more powerful than those that destroyed Hiroshima and Nagasaki. Next year these younger people will not only commemorate a bomb that ended the most terrible war, but also they will have reason to celebrate the restraint that has prevailed for half a century in which no man, woman or child has been killed by an atomic bomb. They want to extend that record to all time. The *Enola Gay* symbolizes the end of one era and the beginning of another. For an older generation, the aircraft meant the end of World War II; for younger people, it ushered in the nuclear age. The postwar generations respect their fathers for the sacrifices they made, but they also realize that the nuclear bombs that saved their fathers' lives continue to threaten their own and their childrens'.

These conflicting views pose the dilemma the National Air and Space Museum faces as we prepare an exhibition of the *Enola Gay* for 1995. We want to honor the veterans who risked their lives and those who made the ultimate sacrifice. They served their country with distinction. But we must also address the broader questions that concern subsequent generations—not with a view to criticizing or apologizing or displaying undue compassion for those on the ground that day, as some may fear, but to deliver an accurate portrayal that conveys the reality of atomic war and its consequences. To that end, the museum proposes to tell the full story surrounding the atomic bomb and the end of World War II; to recall the options facing a newly installed President Truman, who had never heard of the bomb until the day he was sworn in; to examine the estimates of the casualties Truman anticipated if U.S. troops had to invade Japan; to consider the extent to which his wish to impress a threatening Soviet Union influenced his decision to drop the bomb; to exhibit the destruction and suffering on the ground at Hiroshima and Nagasaki; and to recall the escalating numbers of weapons in the superpowers' nuclear arsenals during the Cold War, and their current decline.

Faced with a number of alternatives, the museum has chosen to provide not an opinion piece but rather the basic information that visitors will need to draw their own conclusions. This is our responsibility, as a national museum in a democracy predicated on an informed citizenry. We have found no way to exhibit the *Enola Gay* and satisfy everyone. But a comprehensive and thoughtful discussion can help us learn from history. And that is what we aim to offer our visitors.

The Washington Post
August 7, 1994

THE CURATORS CAVE IN

Kai Bird

IT WAS A HUMILIATING SPECTACLE, scholars being forced to recant the truth. Curators at the Smithsonian's Air and Space Museum in Washington have been compelled by veterans' groups to rewrite the text for an exhibit on the bombing of Hiroshima. The show, which will feature the forward fuselage of the *Enola Gay*, the plane that dropped the bomb, is scheduled to open next year to commemorate the 50th anniversary of the event. All summer the museum's curators faced mounting pressure from the American Legion, the Air Force Association and dozens of politicians. A hostile press portrayed the curators as anti-American, leftist and motivated by their anti-Vietnam War generation instincts rather than scholarship and archival evidence. So late last month the curators bowed to political reality. During two closed-door sessions with representatives of the American Legion, they agreed to censor their own historical knowledge. Worse, the Smithsonian officials agreed to introduce new language in the text that most historians will regard as flat-out falsehoods. This is not to defend everything in the original Smithsonian text: it was hardly judicious to describe the Pacific war as a "war of vengeance" for most Americans. But such criticisms are minor compared to what has been done by way of promoting pure mythology.

At the heart of the dispute is the inaccurate but understandable belief of the veterans that the atomic bomb saved their lives from being sacrificed in an invasion of Japan. At the veterans' groups insistence, the text will now state that 1945 casualty estimates went up to "conceivably as many as one million," and that "to try and save as many American lives as possible, Truman chose to use the atomic bomb." Many well-known scholars—including Barton J. Bernstein, Martin J. Sherwin, Robert Messer, James Hershberg, Gar Alperovitz, Melvyn P. Leffler and Stanley Goldberg—have noted that there is compelling evidence that diplomatic overtures, coupled with assurances on the post-war status of the Emperor and the impending entry of the Soviet Union into the war, probably would have led the Japanese to surrender long before an American invasion could be mounted. Unfortunately this evidence didn't begin emerging until the 1960s, long after the public had been convinced that dropping the bomb had saved many American lives.

The million-casualty figure was first used by Secretary of War Henry Stimson in a 1947 *Harper's* article but without any supporting evidence. According to the historian James Hershberg, the figure "instantly became the orthodox defense for bombing Hiroshima and Nagasaki." No scholar of the war has ever found archival evidence to substantiate claims that Truman expected anything close to one million casualties or even that such huge casualties were conceivable. Mr. Bernstein, a Stanford historian who has pored over declassified military planning documents, could not find a worst-case estimate of higher than 46,000 deaths. J. Samuel Walker, the chief historian for the U.S. Nuclear Regulatory Commission, has written that "the consensus is that the bomb was not needed to avoid an invasion of Japan." He said, "It is clear that alternatives to the bomb existed and that Truman and his advisers new it. The hoary claim that the bomb prevented 500,000 American combat deaths is unsupportable."

Truman's diary, released in 1979, shows that he knew from decoded Japanese cables that the enemy was about to surrender unconditionally. The only barrier was Tokyo's request for an assurance that the monarchy be retained. In the diary, Truman referred to this intercepted intelligence as the cable from the "Jap Emperor asking for peace." He wrote on July 17, 1945 that he believed Stalin would "be in the Jap war by August 15. Fini Japs when that comes about." It would seem then that Truman realized the war would end long before the U.S. could mount an invasion of the Japanese home islands, the first phase of which was not scheduled until November 1. Similarly, General Dwight D. Eisenhower, Assistant Secretary of War John J. McCloy and many other top advisors to the President all believed that even without the bomb, the war would end without an invasion.

According to Stephen E. Ambrose, author of a much-lauded Eisenhower biography, the Allied commander told Secretary Stimson of his "belief that Japan was already defeated and that dropping the bomb was completely unnecessary." (This anecdote was removed from the Smithsonian text at the behest of the veterans' groups.) After the war, the U.S. Strategic Bombing Survey examined the intelligence evidence that had been available to the White House at the time. It concluded in a 1946 report that "certainly prior to December 31, 1945 and in all probability prior to November 1, 1945, Japan would have surrendered even if the atomic bombs had not been dropped, even if Russia had not entered the war, and even if no invasion had been planned or contemplated."

Historians continue to proffer a wide range of suggestions about why Truman nevertheless approved the atomic bombing: the Manhattan Project's bureaucratic momentum, a fear of domestic political consequences if the public perceived we were negotiating an end to the war on any terms other than unconditional surrender, the assumption that as Secretary of State James F. Byrnes told the physicist

Leo Szilard, "rattling the bomb might make Russia more manageable." None of this disparages the patriotism of World War II veterans, who were willing to lay down their lives to defeat Japanese militarism. But neither should we question the integrity of scholars who labor in the archives at the difficult task of peeling away layers of historical truth. The Smithsonian should display history with all its uncomfortable complications and not feel-good national myths.

The New York Times
October 9, 1994

THE SMITHSONIAN AND THE BOMB

ONE TROUBLING LEGACY of the Reagan and Bush Administrations was the so-called "culture wars," in which members of Congress tried to throttle scholarly and artistic expression by politicizing government support for the arts and humanities. The National Endowment for the Arts and the National Endowment for the Humanities were both severely damaged by the partisan tampering. A hangover from this period is the presumption that Congress should decide what art is hung on gallery walls and what versions of history are depicted in government-funded films and museum exhibitions. Some Congressmen threaten to withdraw government funding for cultural activity that becomes controversial or offends a given constituency's point of view.

The Smithsonian Institution finds itself at just such a juncture owing to protests about a proposed exhibition marking the fiftieth anniversary of the bombing of Hiroshima and Nagasaki. Set to open next summer, it is entitled "The Last Act: the Atomic Bomb and the End of World War II." Veterans groups have found fault with it, and two dozen members of Congress complained to Robert McCormick Adams, the Smithsonian's secretary, that it depicts the Americans as aggressors and the Japanese as victims because it does not give adequate justification for the bombing. That was not the exhibition's original purpose; initially it focused on what happened when the bombs struck the Japanese cities. But after the protests, it was expanded to include the bloody fighting in the Pacific, which preceded the decision to bomb.

That was a good idea. Any treatment of the war that includes only the last six months, and the nuclear bombing itself, is by its very nature far too narrow. Martin Harwitt, the director of the National Air and Space Museum, acknowledges as much. But Representative Peter Blute, Republican of Massachusetts, is still not satisfied. He demands that the exhibition "undergo a massive revision or rewrite." The Smithsonian is the premier cultural institution in the country; surely it can find a way to incorporate various criticisms without line-by-line supervision from members of Congress who are neither historians nor curators. The problem with endless tampering by Congress is that some critics will not be satisfied with anything short of complete vilification of the Japanese and uncritical glorification of the American war effort.

What is needed is a balanced accounting of the political and military considerations that went into President Truman's decision. There has been an unresolved half-century debate about the morality of that decision. The bombing and the debate are historical facts. Any fair exhibition should reflect both the content of the debate and its unresolved nature. To reflect on the brutality of war in general and this bombing in particular does not detract from the heroism of American troops nor the historic importance of winning an atomic arms race the U.S. and its allies had no choice but to join and win. The Smithsonian would probably have worked its way to a more balanced exhibition without pressure from Congress. In fact, months before Congress intervened, Mr. Harwit wrote to his curators telling them that the exhibition was one-sided. That is how the process ought to work: curators propose, review committees advise, the exhibition gradually comes into focus. That process was short-circuited by the protests, but it is not too late to get it back on track.

Editorial
The New York Times
September 5, 1994

WORLD WAR II, REVISED
OR, HOW WE BOMBED JAPAN OUT OF RACISM AND SPITE

Charles Krauthammer

AUGUST IS THE TRADITIONAL MONTH for reflecting on the atomic bomb. Next August, the fiftieth anniversary of the bombing of Hiroshima and Nagasaki, will be the occasion for even more reflection. In commemoration, the National Air and Space Museum in Washington is preparing an exhibit. On display will be more than the *Enola Gay*, the B-29 that delivered the bomb. The walls of text and choice of exhibits will display also the degree to which elite American museums, like the universities, have fallen to the forces of political correctness and historical revisionism. Three years ago the National Museum of American Art disgraced itself with a crudely anti-American exhibit of frontier Western art that former librarian of Congress Daniel Boorstin described as "perverse, historically inaccurate, destructive." Now from Air and Space comes the Pacific War revised.

The original script for "The Last Act: The Atomic Bomb and the End of World War II" elicited such fierce criticism from veterans that Air and Space appointed an internal review team. Its report was highly, if politely, critical of the exhibit's tone and content. Some of the review team's recommended changes have been made, but the original script betrays the ideology and intentions of the curators. It said of the Pacific War endgame, for example, that "for most Americans . . . it was a war of vengeance. For most Japanese, it was a war to defend their unique culture against Western imperialism." The quote was later cleaned up, but you can imagine the prejudices of those who would write such a thing and the kind of exhibit they would put on.

It is an exhibit that underplays Japanese savagery in the conduct of World War II (and against the rest of Asia in the decade of depredation that preceded

Pearl Harbor) and devotes much attention to American racism. It quotes Hitler declaring, "I want no war against women and children. I have been given the Luftwaffe instructions to attack only military objectives," then two script pages later quotes General George Marshall saying, "There won't be any hesitation about bombing civilians—it will be all-out." It is an exhibit with dozens of wrenching photos and touching artifacts from Hiroshima heavily weighted toward those from women and children. "Missing from this exhibit," noted the review team, "are other representative artifacts belonging to soldiers, factory workers, government officials etc." This in a museum that sports a German V-2 rocket display accompanied by 13 photographs, exactly one of which shows any victims. It is an exhibit, in short, that subtly and not so subtly casts the Japanese as victims, the kamikaze pilots as heroes and the Americans as the vengeful heavy.

Under the heading "Historical Controversies," the exhibit asks: "Would the bomb have been dropped on the Germans?" It begins its answer thus: "Some have argued that the United States would never have dropped the bomb on the Germans, because Americans were more reluctant to bomb 'white people' than Asians." Allied reluctance to bomb "white people" will certainly come as news to the survivors of Dresden (POW Kurt Vonnegut among them). The fact is that the A-bomb was built to be used against Germany. "Some have argued?" Some have argued that the earth is flat. Some have argued that the Holocaust never happened. We don't give wall space in our national museums to such "controversies." The exhibit finally resolves the "controversy" with "historians have concluded that President Roosevelt would have used the bomb on Germany." No kidding. (After my inquiries about this section, which appears in the very latest script, a museum official informed me that he thought it is now dropped, though he could not yet confirm. Welcome news, if true. But how could such prejudicial rubbish have been penned in the first place?)

The essential if undeclared judgment of the authors of this commemoration is that we should never have dropped the bomb. Not just because of the amply displayed horror but because other measures—"some combination of blockade, firebombing, an Emperor guarantee, and a Soviet declaration of war"—"would probably have forced a Japanese surrender." ("Would probably" is now changed to "might.") These kinds of cozy, easy judgments made at the safe distance of fifty years and 7,000 miles have earned the deserved contempt of those like Paul Fussell, author of classic critical studies of World War I and World War II, who were there. Writing on the thirty-sixth anniversary of Hiroshima, in a piece subtitled (quoting William Manchester) "Thank God for the Atomic Bomb," he pointed out the horror and cost of the alternative to the bomb, the planned invasion of Japan. "On Okinawa, only weeks before Hiroshima, 123,000 Japanese and Americans killed each other." Moreover, "invasion was not just a hypothetical threat. . . . It was genuinely in train, as I know because I was to be in it." Fussell was a second lieutenant leading a rifle platoon in Europe, preparing to be shipped to the Pacific for the invasion of Honshu. The bomb meant "we were going to live, we were going to grow up to adulthood after all"—and so would hundreds of thousands of others, American and Japanese.

The Air and Space commemoration of Hiroshima promises to be an embarrassing amalgam of revisionist hand-wringing and guilt. What to do? General Paul Tibbets, the man who commanded the *Enola Gay*, has the right idea: Hang the plane in the museum without commentary or slanted context. Display it like

Lindbergh's plane, with silent reverence and a few lines explaining what it did and when. Or forget the whole enterprise and let the Japanese commemorate the catastrophe they brought on themselves.

The Washington Post
August 19, 1994

BEYOND THE SMITHSONIAN FLAP: HISTORIANS' NEW CONSENSUS

Gar Alperovitz

THE EMOTIONAL FLAP over the Smithsonian Institution's plan to exhibit the *Enola Gay*, the B-29 that dropped the first atomic bomb on Hiroshima, reminds us that the nuclear age is now a half-century old and that we have not yet sorted out the basic facts about how it all began. Unfortunately, both sides in the Smithsonian debate mixed and muddled important questions. The initial exhibit plans, for instance, minimized American casualties prior to Hiroshima and paid scant attention to Japanese brutality or to the war before 1945 in general. Martin Harwit, the director of the National Air and Space Museum, added insult to injury by gratuitously characterizing the debate as a fight between the new generation and old veterans "now in their seventies."

Nothing is gained by downplaying the long history which led to the events of 1945 or by side-stepping Japan's responsibility for the Rape of Nanking, the Bataan death march and the brutal horror of slave labor in its prison camps. On the other hand, the Air Force Association and other critics have exaggerated the number of lives "saved" by the atomic bomb and have themselves ignored a good deal of well-known historical research—especially concerning the alternatives available to U.S. policymakers in 1945. Unfair aspersions have also been cast on the motives of the Smithsonian staff as they struggled to develop a "balanced" display. A petition sent to Smithsonian Secretary Robert McCormick Adams by twenty-four congressmen uses the term "anti-American" to describe the exhibit.

While it is impossible to defuse all the emotions around the *Enola Gay* exhibition, research findings of the last two decades can help clarify several basic questions: *In retrospect, was the bombing of Hiroshima and Nagasaki necessary?* There is far less disagreement among knowledgeable experts about this than many think. As early as 1946, for instance, the official U.S. Strategic Bombing Survey concluded on the basis of a massive investigation that Japan, in all probability, would have surrendered prior to November 1, 1945 and would certainly have surrendered before December 31, 1945—even if the atomic bomb had not been dropped, Russia had not entered the war in the Pacific or even if no Allied invasion had been contemplated.

Similarly, a 1946 War Department Operations Division study, discovered only in 1989, concluded that "the Japanese leaders had decided to surrender and were merely looking for sufficient pretext to convince the die-hard Army Group that Japan had lost the war and must capitulate to the Allies." It judged that the entry of Russia into the war in early August would almost certainly have furnished this pretext and would have convinced all responsible leaders that surrender was unavoidable. This official study concluded that well before the bombings, even an initial November 1945 landing on the island of Kyushu was only a "remote" possibility and that a full invasion of Japan proper in 1946 would not have been necessary.

Did U.S. policymakers nonetheless believe that using the atomic bomb was the only way to end the war? The most recent full-scale review of modern expert studies was conducted by J. Samuel Walker, currently chief historian of the U.S. Nuclear Regulatory Commission, and an analyst not associated with any of the contending camps. His study concluded: "Careful scholarly treatment of the records and manuscripts opened over the past few years has greatly enhanced our understanding of why the Truman administration used atomic weapons against Japan. . . . The consensus among scholars is that the bomb was not needed to avoid an invasion of Japan. . . . It is clear that alternatives to the bomb existed and that Truman and his advisors knew it."

Especially important to the new scholarly understanding was the 1978 appearance of President Truman's "lost" diary. Although some writers still disagree with what Walker terms "the consensus," the diary suggests that Truman understood well before August 1945 the same point made subsequently by the War Department study: that the powerful "jolt" of the expected Red Army attack on Japan in early August would so shock the already teetering Japanese that the fighting would likely end. U.S. intelligence experts had made the same point as early as April 1945. In mid-June 1945, General George Marshall told Truman personally that the shock of a Russian declaration of war might well "lever" Japan into surrendering almost immediately. In fact, securing Russian help in case the "atomic" bomb test should fail was one of Truman's primary reasons for going to Potsdam to meet Stalin in July 1945. After the Soviet leader confirmed Russia would declare war on Japan by mid-August, the President's diary states: *"Fini* Japs when that comes about." The next day, Truman wrote a confident letter to his wife saying that with the Russian declaration of war "we'll end the war a year sooner now, and think of the kids who won't be killed!"

It also seems clear to many scholars that U.S. political and military leaders understood that a minor modification of the "unconditional surrender" formula—allowing Japan to keep its Emperor-god—would likely have ended the fighting. This was done in the end, of course—Japan still has an Emperor—but virtually everyone at the highest level of the U.S. government (except Secretary of State James F. Byrnes) urged that it be done before, not after, using the atomic bomb. Particularly significant in this debate are coded messages intercepted in mid-July 1945 showing that the Japanese Emperor had personally intervened to try to bring the war to an end. (Truman's diary refers to the "telegram from Jap[anese] Emperor asking for peace.")

Did the U.S. military feel strongly that the bomb had to be used? Early in 1945, U.S. military leaders thought that an invasion of Japan was quite likely but things changed a great deal over the summer. After mid-July 1945 there is little contemporaneous evidence that top World War II military leaders believed the atomic bomb was the only way to avoid an invasion. When General Dwight D. Eisenhower, for example, was told about the decision to drop the bomb, he told Secretary of War Henry L. Stimson that the news gave him "a feeling of depression." Eisenhower later recalled in his memoirs telling Stimson of "my belief that Japan was already defeated and that dropping the bomb was completely unnecessary, and . . . that our country should avoid shocking world opinion by the use of a weapon whose employment was, I thought, no longer mandatory as a measure to save American lives."

William D. Leahy, the conservative admiral who in 1945 held a position similar to today's chairman of the Joint Chiefs of Staff, was even more outspoken: "The use of this barbarous weapon at Hiroshima and Nagasaki was of no material assistance in our war against Japan. . . . [I]n being the first to use it, we . . . adopted an ethical standard common to the barbarians of the Dark Ages. I was not taught to make war in that fashion, and wars cannot be won by destroying women and children." Nor did leaders of the Air Force demand that the atomic bomb be used. General Henry H. "Hap" Arnold, the Army Air Forces commander, later said that "it always appeared to us that atomic bomb or no atomic bomb the Japanese were already on the verge of collapse." Servicemen at lower levels obviously were not privy to top secret information in mid-July 1945. In fact, they were repeatedly told—partly to keep morale high, partly to keep pressure on the Japanese—that they were going to invade. It is no reflection on these men who were ready and willing to risk their lives to point out the modern research findings. August 1945 was neither the first nor the last time when soldiers in the field were not fully informed of what their leaders at the very top were thinking.

What about the expected casualties of a U.S. invasion of Japan? Obviously, if the judgment expressed by Eisenhower, Leahy, Arnold and others is correct—if the war could have been ended by the combination of the Russian declaration of war and assurance to Japan that its Emperor would not be harmed—then no deaths would have occurred in an invasion. At most there might have been some small number of additional casualties as the details of the surrender were worked out.

What if Eisenhower and the others were wrong and an invasion was necessary? Scholars as diverse in political orientation as the liberal Barton Bernstein and military historian John Ray Skates have studied the actual 1945 planning documents and agree on what they show. A November 1, 1945 landing on Kyushu might have resulted in 20,000-25,000 U.S. deaths in a worst-case scenario. An invasion in the spring of 1946 would have resulted, according to U.S. military planners at the time, in 46,000 deaths. Occasionally, writers on the Hiroshima controversy quote Leahy's comment of June 18, 1945 in which he suggested there would be a 35 percent casualty rate during an invasion. This 35 percent figure is then applied to a total possible assault force which might have been involved in a Kyushu landing to suggest a huge number of U.S. deaths. During this same discussion, however, George Marshall presented far lower planning estimates. Moreover, Leahy's percentage was quickly challenged by the Chief of Naval Operations, Admiral Ernest J. King and Leahy did not mention it again. That very same day, Leahy wrote in his private diary that he believed the war could easily be ended long before an invasion.

It is sometimes also held that more Japanese would have been killed if the conventional bombing of cities had been continued. But this, in fact, had been made a low priority by August 1945 on the basis of Air Force experience in Europe. Why then were the atomic bombs used? Here there is far more debate among scholars. Some historians hold that Truman feared he would be criticized as "soft" on the Japanese if he told them they could keep the Emperor before using the bomb. Some writers also suggest that because huge sums were spent developing the new weapon, the American political leadership found it impossible not to use it. Yet another group has probed the intricacies of decision-making through an analysis of bureaucratic dynamics.

Most relevant to the Smithsonian flap is substantial scholarly acceptance, of the once controversial idea that diplomatic issues—especially the hope of strengthening the West's hand against the Soviet Union—played a significant role in the decision. In his memoirs, Truman reported that Byrnes told him in April 1945 that "the atomic bomb might well put us in a position to dictate our own terms at the end of the war. . . ." In May 1945 atomic scientist Leo Szilard conferred with Byrnes and came away saying, "Mr. Byrnes did not argue that it was necessary to use the bomb against the cities of Japan in order to win the war. . . . Mr. Byrnes's view [was] that our possessing and demonstrating the bomb would make Russia more manageable in Europe." Although writers still debate precisely how much weight to accord such Cold War factors, respected Yale historian Gaddis Smith speaks for many experts when he says, "It has been demonstrated that the decision to bomb Japan was centrally connected to Truman's confrontational approach to the Soviet Union."

The Washington Post
October 16, 1994

ENOLA GAY: A NEW CONSENSUS . . .

Gar Alperovitz

THE SMITHSONIAN'S RADICAL SCALING BACK of the planned *Enola Gay* exhibit seems to have done little to calm the furor over America's use of the atomic bomb to end World War II. Congressional hearings on the subject are planned, and more than eighty members of Congress have called for the resignation of Martin Harwit, director of the Air and Space Museum. The charge against him is rank "revisionism." Robert Newman's op-ed article awhile back ["What New Consensus?", November 30] showed in dramatic detail ways in which the arguments of both modern and traditional critics have often been misrepresented in the debate over the bombing of Hiroshima—and it demonstrates how an excessive concern with quite secondary points can be used to avoid the central questions in the historical debate.

At issue is the nature of the consensus of modern studies on the use of the atomic bomb. The most recent "literature review" of expert research (published in the respected journal Diplomatic History) was written by J. Samuel Walker, chief historian of the U.S. Nuclear Regulatory Commission. Newman attacks my essay, "Beyond the Smithsonian Flap: Historians' New Consensus" [Outlook, October 16], for quoting Walker "as approving [my] thesis about atomic diplomacy." But this is a false accusation. What I quoted was Walker's extremely important conclusion that the "consensus among scholars is that the bomb was not needed to avoid an invasion of Japan"—and further: "that alternatives to the bomb existed and that Truman and his advisors knew it." Not only did I make no claim that Walker approved what Newman calls the "atomic diplomacy" thesis, I explicitly stressed that "writers still debate precisely how much weight" to attach to the now widely accepted fact that impressing the Soviet Union was a significant factor in the atomic bomb decision. I also pointed out that "many experts" agree, however, with such scholars as Yale's Gaddis

Smith (not Walker) that the Hiroshima decision "was centrally connected with Truman's confrontational approach to the Soviet Union."

Much of Newman's article is devoted to attacking two government studies I mentioned in my essay: the 1946 official U.S. Strategic Bombing Survey (USBSS) and a top-secret intelligence study done for the War Department the same year. USBSS concluded that : "Certainly prior to 31 December 1945, and in all probability prior to 1 November 1945, Japan would have surrendered even if the atomic bombs had not been dropped, even if Russia had not entered the war, and even if no invasion had been planned or contemplated." The second study concluded that the "Japanese leaders had decided to surrender and were merely looking for sufficient pretext to convince the die-hard Army group that Japan had lost the war and must capitulate to the Allies"—and further, that the shock of the early August Russian declaration on its own would almost certainly have furnished this pretext.

My article on the modern consensus did not, in fact, rely on the 1946 studies with which Mr. Newman quarrels. I preferred to use most of the available space for more important matters. Among the numerous post-1946 research findings that were the basis of my article were documents that advised that the war would likely end when the Russians attacked Japan and a very great deal of evidence showing President Truman was advised that assurances to the Japanese that they could keep their Emperor would also likely do the trick. Critical too, were intercepted cables showing the personal intervention of the Emperor to attempt to stop the fighting. I also cited Gen. Marshall's presentation to President Truman on June 18, 1945, on the Russian option. However, even earlier—on April 24, 1945—the Joint Intelligence Committee advised the Joint Chiefs of Staff that the air-sea blockade, the strategic bombing and the collapse of Germany were having such enormous effect that "the entry of the U.S.S.R. into the war would together with the foregoing factors, convince most Japanese at once of the inevitability of complete defeat." What was needed to turn this realization into surrender, it went on, was to offer assurances for the Emperor.

Most significant of all was the 1978 discovery of President Truman's personal journal and, in 1982, the release of private letters to his wife, Bess. In his journal of July 17 the President states: "He'll [Stalin] be in the Jap War on August 15th. . . ." and then goes on to comment: "Fini Japs when that comes about." The next day he characterizes one of the intercepted messages as the "telegram from Jap Emperor asking for peace." In letters to his wife the President writes: "I've gotten what I came for—Stalin goes to war August 15 with no strings on it. . . . We'll end the war a year sooner now, and think of the kids who won't be killed!" Moreover, there was plenty of time to test whether the Red Army attack plus a clarification of the terms would work: The invasion of Japan was not planned to take place until the spring of 1946; even an initial landing on the island of Kyushu could not have occurred for another three months.

All of this also bears on what Japanese officials told the U.S. Strategic Bombing Survey and other official investigators in late 1945 and 1946. No one disputes that in the conditions they actually faced—especially threats to the Emperor—the Japanese were prepared to fight to the death. But that was exactly the point: Changing these conditions—and in particular offering assurances for the Emperor—was what the whole debate was about. Newman writes as if he were the only person to have studied the USBSS materials. Unfortunately, he fails to mention that the somewhat rambling interviews did not ask the Japanese directly if they would have surrendered without the bomb if assurances had been given or when the Red Army attacked. He also does not mention that other Japanese leaders implicitly or explicitly volunteered similar opinions. Indeed, one of those Newman cites—Baron Hiranauma, president of the Privy Council—made it quite clear in a part of the interview Newman does not mention that the only condition he had felt it worth fighting for was a guarantee for the Emperor.

Newman also quotes three-time Prime Minister Prince Konoye to the effect that the "army had dug themselves in the mountains and their idea . . . was fighting from every little hole or rock in the mountains." But he ignores the very next question put to Konoye, and his answer: "Would the Emperor have permitted them to do that?" "I don't think the Emperor would have let them go that far. He would have done something to stop them." Many contemporaneous Japanese records as well as other interviews have since documented the June 1945 decision of the Imperial Conference to attempt to end the war. The modern research findings also provide perspective on the debate over casualty estimates. Although it was entirely reasonable for medical support personnel to plan for the worst-case scenarios that Newman cites, it is also true that lower-level officials were unaware of developments at the highest reaches of White House decision-making. Self-evidently, if the war could have ended through assurances for the Emperor plus the Russian shock, there would have been no invasion casualties.

Additionally, as many experts have observed, the estimates actually used by General Marshall for his presentation to President Truman were in the range of 25,000 to 46,000 deaths *if*—and only if—an invasion actually went forward. Newman's contention that MacArthur wished to play down casualties does not extend to Marshall, who has rarely been accused of deceiving the President. I also quoted President Eisenhower's statement that at Potsdam he advised Secretary of War Stimson that "Japan was already defeated and that dropping the bomb was completely unnecessary." Wondrously, Newman seems to know better what went on in private between the two men. Boldly contradicting Eisenhower he states: "Ike did not tell Stimson it was a mistake to drop the bomb." There is no evidence whatsoever to back this claim.

Even the speculative essay by Barton Bernstein that Newman cites merely raised unanswerable questions about Eisenhower's oft-repeated recollection of this discussion. I prefer the work of the man who by all accounts knows most about Eisenhower, his respected biographer, Steven Ambrose: Eisenhower, Ambrose testifies, consistently stated not only that he advised Stimson the bomb was not needed but that he personally urged President Truman not to use it.

The Washington Post
February 4, 1995

WHAT NEW CONSENSUS?

Robert P. Newman

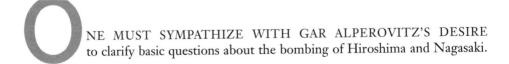

ONE MUST SYMPATHIZE WITH GAR ALPEROVITZ'S DESIRE to clarify basic questions about the bombing of Hiroshima and Nagasaki.

No doubt, as he says, research findings of the past two decades should help. But where are they? Alperovitz's first two citations in his article "Beyond the Smithsonian Flap: Historians' New Consensus" [Outlook, October 16] are of 1946 publications and a manuscript declassified in 1977. Begin with issue number one, as cited by Alperovitz: Was the bombing necessary? Alperovitz leads off with the 1946 report of the U.S. Strategic Bombing Survey (USSBS). This group, authorized by Franklin Roosevelt at the request of the Army Air Forces, went first to Germany then to Japan seeking to find out whether strategic bombing was effective. After a little less than two months of research in Japan, the survey concluded that Japan would probably have surrendered by November 1, certainly by December 31, 1945, with no atomic bombs, no Russian entry into the Pacific war and no invasion.

This USSBS conclusion was very congenial to Alperovitz and to his mentor, P. M. S. Blackett, the British physicist and Nobelist who first said in 1948 that Truman had dropped the bomb not to end the war but to intimidate the Russians. One would think that Alperovitz would check this conclusion out carefully (Blackett couldn't; the materials were all classified when he wrote), evaluate its credibility and explain to his readers why he accepted it. He does none of this. Instead, he applies impressive-sounding adjectives to USSBS. It was a "massive" investigation, says Alperovitz. It was, in a sense; USSBS had a thousand employees in Japan for almost two months. But were they qualified to collect and evaluate evidence on as disputed a subject as when Japan would have surrendered? He also notes that it was an "official" study—as if its being done by the government certifies its authority.

The surviving records of USSBS are available at the National Archives on 514 rolls of microfilm. They give us a pretty good idea of what this startling report was built on. USSBS, in the publication Alperovitz cites, "Japan's Struggle to End the War," tells us that the evidence on Japan's surrender "is chiefly in the testimony obtained by Survey interrogation" of the Japanese leaders who were involved. Digging out all the relevant interviews requires much sitting and staring at a screen, but it is worth it. USSBS tells us that there were twenty-four Japanese leaders in the "influential" category. More reliable "unofficial" studies identify closer to sixty in that category, but the survey was there only two months, and the people doing it had no first-class Japanologists to guide them, so we can forgive them for missing a few. However, they interviewed only fourteen of the twenty-four they did classify as important.

And what did these fourteen say? One of them said something supporting Alperovitz's contention. This was Marquis Kido, the lord privy seal. And he ought to know. But as one reads the transcript, it is obvious that his American inquisitor is leaning on him, cross-examining for at least fifteen minutes before Kido changes his tone and says, "I personally think that the war would have ended before November 1." The rest of the Japanese leaders interviewed said something else entirely, even though it put them at risk of a war crimes trial.

Admiral Nomura, Japan's prewar negotiator with Secretary of State Cordell Hull and in 1945 a member of the Privy Council, said that "it was the destiny of our country to continue this very unwise war to the very end." Prince Konoye, three-time prime minister, told his USSBS interrogators in response to a specific question about whether the war would have ended before November 1, "Probably [it] would have lasted beyond that. . . . The army had dug themselves caves in the mountains, and their idea . . . was fighting from every little hole or rock in the mountain." Field Marshal Hata, commander of the 2nd General Army (Hiroshima) in 1945, told USSBS, "We intended to stand and fight on the beaches. . . . However, when the atom bomb was dropped on Hiroshima, I believed there is nothing more we can do, we might as well give up." Baron Hiranuma, president of the Privy Council, was asked about causes of surrender. He noted that Japan had been devastated by conventional bombing, but "then there came the atomic bomb, so that the country was faced with terrible destructive powers, and Japan's ability to wage war was really at an end."

The other principals of the Japanese state say similar things: General Kwabe, Admiral Nagano, Chief Cabinet Secretary Sakomizu, Premier Baron Suzuki, General Takashima, Admiral Takata, Admiral Tomioka, General Wakamatsu—not one of them offers any warrant whatsoever for the early surrender hypothesis. And Marquis Kido? He was obviously yielding to the demands of his captors when he finally agreed to the November 1 date. Two years later, he told the Tokyo War Crimes Trial court that the Nagasaki bomb and Soviet entry had tipped the balance for surrender and that he, as privy seal and a peace activist, had saved "another 20 million of my innocent compatriots from war ravages and also the Americans tens of thousands of casualties which would have been caused had Japan gone on fighting to the bitter end." So even the one thin reed on which USSBS might have justified its case disappeared.

But why did USSBS so corrupt its conclusions? USSBS was the brainchild of the Army Air Forces. General Hap Arnold, commanding, wanted to show that air power could win wars that it had defeated Japan before Hiroshima and that the United States should create an independent air force after the war with a strength of seventy wings. But atomic bombs would not require many planes, nor a big air force—or so the thinking went at the time. Thus Army Air Forces enthusiasts were not enamored of super bombs, which would make their thousands of fliers obsolete. USSBS wrote their bias into its conclusions: The atom bomb was not necessary; conventional bombing would win wars.

Admiral Ralph Ofstie, ranking Navy officer on the survey, said of one of the air forces' reports, "The volume presents a completely inaccurate and entirely biased account of our war against Japan which is of absolutely no historical value, consistently misrepresents facts, and indeed, often ignores facts and employs falsehood." There are several more paragraphs of purple prose. But Ofstie did not control what USSBS published. Alperovitz goes on to tell us that a War Department Operations Division study, "discovered only in 1989," agrees with USSBS conclusions. But this document, a puff piece by one Colonel R. F. Ennis, was never lost, and when it was declassified by an archivist in 1977, it was available to anyone who wanted it. And while it is a "study" of sorts, it is not an investigation of Japan's decision to surrender.

On January 29, 1946, Col. Ennis's superior told him to study how the October 1945 typhoon that struck Japan would have affected the American invasion of Kyushu (Operation OLYMPIC), scheduled for November 1, had it gone forward. Two of Ennis's six pages discuss how the typhoon might have affected the American forces (not much). The third discusses how it would have affected the Japanese defenders (also not much). Then three pages deal with "Growth of Surrender Psychology" and "Development in Event Operation OLYMPIC Proved Necessary." Here Ennis is in fantasy land. One wonders what tea leaves he was consulting.

Ennis alleges that the Emperor told a cabinet meeting on June 20 that Japan should have a plan to close the war at once, and "As a result of this statement by the Emperor, Premier Suzuki decided to stop the war." But in fact there was no cabinet meeting that day. Suzuki did not see the Emperor; Togo and Kido did. Kido persuaded the Emperor to call a meeting of the Supreme Council for Direction of the War in two days. The Ennis study also says, "Investigation shows that there was little mention of the use of the atomic bomb by the United States in the [Japanese] discussions leading up to the August 9 decision." Of course there wasn't before August 6, when we dropped the first one. After August 7 when reports from Hiroshima began coming in, the subject was on every lip. Ennis says Soviet entry into the war alone would have "almost certainly" terminated the war; he cites no warrant for this. There is none. The Ennis discovery is worthless.

Alperovitz in his research should have discovered some of the detailed reports of Kyushu defenses by investigators on the spot, such as the sixteen-page report of Edmund J. Winslett. Winslett had been officer in charge of photographic intelligence for the U.S. Sixth Army. He toured the scheduled landing areas immediately after the war to see how good his intelligence had been. Winslett's conclusion is rather different from that of Colonel Ennis in the Pentagon: "After a personal survey of the areas in which our invasion landings were scheduled to take place, I am convinced that the greatest battle the American Armies have ever won was the one which was never fought—the invasion of Kyushu."

By the spring of 1945, though, American political and military leaders were so casualty-shy that they could not be candid about the ferocious Japanese resistance expected on the home islands. Iwo Jima and Okinawa had horrified all of them. MacArthur especially was motivated to play down anticipated casualties. As military historian Edward Drea notes: "The notion of leading the greatest amphibious assault in history—fifteen divisions versus nine at Normandy—held overwhelming appeal to MacArthur's vanity." If the expected casualties were too high, Truman might have canceled the invasion and waited for Japan to starve. The medical services were not ego-involved in casualty estimates, however. One of the documents Alperovitz apparently did not locate is the lengthy report "Medical Services in the Asiatic and Pacific Theaters," Chapter 15 of which gives a table of "Estimated Casualties and Calculated Whole Blood Requirements, OLYMPIC." Total casualties, D-Day plus 120—394,859. Whose figures are more nearly correct—the casualty-shy commanders Alperovitz cites, or the medics who had to prepare? We can't know, but if we had to rely on only what Alperovitz presents, we couldn't even raise the question.

Alperovitz invokes the opinions of Barton Bernstein, the scholar who knows the most about the decision to drop the bomb, when he agrees with Bernstein. But Alperovitz ignores Bernstein's compelling study of Eisenhower's attitude in July 1945. Ike did not tell Henry Stimson it was a mistake to drop the bomb, despite what Ike says in his memoirs. Alperovitz quotes Ike's self-serving claim, but ignores Bernstein's careful analysis. J. Samuel Walker's writings are misrepresented by Alperovitz. He quotes Walker as approving his thesis about atomic diplomacy. But Walker had trouble making himself clear on this matter. He also writes: "No scholar of the subject accepts in unadulterated form Alperovitz's argument that political considerations dictated the decision. . . . The consensus of the mid-1970s, which held that the bomb was used primarily for military reasons and secondarily for diplomatic ones, continues to prevail." Alas, the Smithsonian will gain no guidance from the "New Consensus" supposedly described in Alperovitz's articles. It is neither new nor a consensus.

The Washington Post
November 30, 1994

DROPPING A BOMB OF AN IDEA

Jonathan Yardley

THE NATIONAL AIR AND SPACE MUSEUM has done the right thing, but for the wrong reason. Its decision to tone down or expunge much of the anti-American commentary that had been written for next year's display of the *Enola Gay*, the plane that dropped the atomic bomb on Hiroshima, is self-evidently welcome. It is most unfortunate, though, that the museum reached it in response not to the facts but to pressure from special-interest groups. The most outspoken and influential of these is the American Legion. It has lost much of the political clout that it enjoyed before Vietnam, when its leverage was roughly comparable to that now wielded by the National Rifle Association, but it is still the most prominent veterans organization and it still commands attention in Washington. Attention is precisely what the Air and Space Museum granted it, during two remarkable closed-door meetings—one lasting twelve hours, the second ten—in which the *Enola Gay* exhibition's text and displays were discussed in exceedingly fine detail.

As a result of these discussions, the exhibition will be considerably less inflammatory than had been planned by those curators who conceived and shaped it. Their stated intention had been not simply to present as much of the bomber as can be fit into the museum but to "address the significance, necessity and morality of the atomic bombings of Hiroshima and Nagasaki . . . [because] the question of whether it was necessary and right to drop the bombs . . . continues to perplex us." Among other things, they intended to tell visitors to the exhibition—many of them young Americans whose ignorance of history is infinite—that "for most Americans, this . . . was a war of vengeance. For most Japanese it was a war to defend their unique culture against Western imperialism." In other words, the Air and Space Museum meant to turn an exhibition of a weapon of war into a philippic not merely against war but against the United States. Lining itself up with the zealots of academe who prowl the liberal arts departments muttering against "American imperialism," the Air and Space Museum was prepared to use an exhibition of the technology of warfare as a springboard to leap into generalizations of the most sweeping and insupportable nature.

There are, obviously, a great many things to be said about all of this, many of which already have been said. There is no need for another homily on the transparent evils of political correctness, so one will not be delivered in this space. Still, there are other matters worth raising. The first is that the Air and Space Museum seems to have lost its way. Since when did it become not merely a museum of technology but also a forum for the enlightenment and conversion of the politically and morally obtuse? The Air and Space Museum is a quasi-official agency of the U.S. government. Under precisely what authority is it seeking to engage in what can fairly be called anti-American propaganda?

A second point, as suggested earlier, is that the museum has decided to revamp its exhibition not because it has seen the error of its ways but because it is engaged in damage control. There is not the slightest evidence that any of those who put together the original design of the exhibition have been convinced that the Pacific war was something other than U.S. aggression against a Japan determined to protect its cultural heritage. To see the war in those terms falls somewhere between self-delusion and insanity, but that is not merely how certain people at the Air and Space Museum see it, but also how they meant to persuade the rest of us to see it, especially—in the words of Martin Harwit, director of the museum—"those generations of Americans too young to remember how the war ended." There can be no doubt that, if only they had their druthers, the museum's curators would prefer to offer the exhibition in these terms, even after their twenty-two hours of face-to-face negotiation with veterans of the war and their representatives.

Which leads to the third and most important point. A common if unspoken assumption at this late hour of the twentieth century is that we are so fully in command of information that it is no longer possible for us to get the facts wrong. The insertion of time capsules in the cornerstones of new buildings, not so long ago a cherished custom, is no longer widely practiced because it is assumed that they are no longer necessary. Just as we have preserved all the information accumulated during World War II, so too we are preserving for future generations all the information about our own time. Capsules containing today's newspaper and copies of Top 40 recordings are no longer necessary because everything is saved, whether in its original form or on CD-ROM or some other form. But the business at the Air and Space Museum reminds us that even in the age of information overload, historical truth is as mysterious and evasive as it ever was. You can preserve everything imaginable about the war in the Pacific, down to the most detailed and conservative projections of U.S. casualties in an invasion of Japan, but that will not prevent someone so inclined from interpreting the mission of the *Enola Gay* as (a) a racist attack on the Japanese, (b) a way of proving the cost-effectiveness of the Manhattan Project and/or (c) a placating gesture to Harry Truman's political opposition.

You can assemble all the facts on earth, but you can't make people interpret them for what they are. Especially now, when the rank odor of deconstruction hangs over the scholarly community, it is easy for people to fabricate intellectual arguments for the triviality of facts and then to find whatever "meaning" they choose in such facts, or non-facts, as they are willing to "deconstruct" for their ideological convenience.

History changes because people change. Sometimes it changes for the better. Four decades ago it was commonly accepted among educators in the South and elsewhere that slavery, though "peculiar," was paternalistic and benign; we know better now, and have revised history accordingly. By the same token, it is entirely possible that eventually historians will reach an understanding of the *Enola Gay's* mission that is more subtle than the one commonly held by those of us old enough to remember the day its ghastly load was dropped. But such a judgment must be the fruit of careful, dispassionate research and debate, not of ideology and moral smugness. The latter produce only bad history which is precisely what the Air and Space Museum wanted to feed us.

The Washington Post
October 10, 1994

HIROSHIMA, REWRITTEN

Barton J. Bernstein

"NEITHER THE ATOMIC BOMBING nor the entry of the Soviet Union into the war forced Japan's unconditional surrender. She was defeated before either of these events took place." That kind of "revisionist" statement—implying that the atomic bombing of Japan was unnecessary—has so angered veterans' organizations that they have forced the Smithsonian Institution to announce yesterday that it was gutting its controversial exhibit of the B-29 that dropped the bomb on Hiroshima in August 1945. Yet the words were written not by some revisionist historian, nor by someone who knew little about the brutality of World War II in the Pacific. They were written shortly after V-J Day by Brigadier General Bonnie Fellers for use by General Douglas MacArthur, the Army's triumphant commander in the Pacific.

Other high-ranking military men expressed similar sentiments. "It is my opinion that the use of this barbarous weapon at Hiroshima and Nagasaki was of no material success in our war against Japan," wrote Admiral William Leahy, the wartime Chairman of the Joint Chiefs of Staff in 1950. "The Japanese were already defeated and ready to surrender because of the effective sea blockade and the successful bombing with conventional weapons. . . . My own feeling was that in being the first to use it, we had adopted an ethical standard common to the barbarians of the Dark Ages."

After his White House years, President Dwight D. Eisenhower, looking back on his earlier service as a five-star general, also said he considered the bombing both unnecessary and morally dubious. In 1963, he said: "The Japanese were ready to surrender and it wasn't necessary to hit them with that awful thing. . . . I hated to see our country be the first to use such a weapon." (Ike's objections, like Leahy's, were purged from the Smithsonian script even before the exhibition was cut back.) In May 1945, 10 weeks before Hiroshima, General George C. Marshall, the Army's Chief of Staff, said an atomic bomb should be dropped only on a "straight military objective such as a large military installation," and then, if necessary, on a manufacturing center—but only after civilians were adequately warned so they could flee. He did not want to break the old moral code against killing noncombatants. This counsel was, of course, rejected.

The point is not whether Fellers and MacArthur and Leahy and Eisenhower were correct or incorrect about whether the bombing was necessary, and under what circumstances. Nor is it, as some have too easily contended, that these men had such thoughts before Hiroshima. The point is that after the war, a number of

America's top military leaders chose to express their doubts, and sometimes even their objections. If they could do so then without having their patriotism challenged, it is dismaying that their judgments have now been deemed too harsh for American eyes and ears.

The New York Times
January 31, 1995

THE TREND OF HISTORY

THE SMITHSONIAN INSTITUTION ANNOUNCED yesterday that it will cancel the controversial *Enola Gay* exhibit. This show, covering 10,000 square feet of museum space, was the curatorial staff's effort to re-examine the premises behind the decision to drop the atomic bomb on Hiroshima and Nagasaki. Instead of all this, the museum now says it'll simply display the plane's fuselage and maybe a video of the crew's memories. This decision arrives in the midst of similar controversies over public television, the arts and humanities endowments and the national standards for U.S. and world history. With the *Enola Gay* exhibit thrown over the side, it's inevitable that we'll be hearing and reading a lot now about the dark, descending night of Republican intolerance and philistinism. About the right's "refusal" to address "uncomfortable truths" or allow for "alternative views" of history and America's culture.

We take it as one of the great benefits of the November 8 election that it has brought subjects like this bursting to the surface. Or as the president of the Federation of State Humanities Councils put it recently: "Historians need to come to terms with the fact that the public's nose is in the tent." This remark comes from a recent article in the *Chronicle of Higher Education* titled "Who Owns History?" Exploring the disputes over the *Enola Gay* and the history standards, the *Chronicle* collected views from leading figures in the U.S. history profession. Insofar as the *Enola Gay* effort was supposed to be about challenging the general public's assumptions, these *Chronicle* statements are worth noting for what they reveal about the history profession's *shared* premises. UCLA's Gary Nash, who headed up the national standards project, says: "None of us realized we were walking into a political buzzsaw." Then Anita Jones, the executive secretary of the Organization of American Historians offers that: "There's a growing sense that history doesn't belong to academics. People are asserting their own version."

No doubt this disconcerts the historians because as Peter Stearns, dean of humanities and social sciences at Carnegie-Mellon, notes: "Much of the so-called new history—social history, the history of minorities and ordinary Americans, of non-Western groups—has widespread support." But despite "widespread support," something clearly has gone wrong for the historians. Professor John Diggens, Graduate Center of the City University of New York explains: "The electorate has indicated that it is conservative, but there are almost no conservatives in the historical profession."

We are fully prepared to believe that both the *Enola Gay* curators and the standards project's architects are genuinely surprised at the controversy they've stirred.

After all, they've been revising history strictly inside the parameters of "new history" for years with virtually no opposition outside the profession. Tenure decisions are based on one's contributions to the new history; their journals are filled with it. There's been no opposition from school presidents, trustees, the media or the Smithsonian's regents. So when the Smithsonian's curators create an exhibit that says the winning of the American West was an act of capitalist pillage, they do so in the secure knowledge that no one they know is going to object. And when the historians who earned their degrees from 1965 onward conclude that Western Civilization is properly viewed as simply an "alternative" to other "viable" civilizations, they must be right—because no one they know objects. What a wonderful world it must be. One can almost hear the cheerful certitude behind the *Enola Gay* planning, or the composition of the manual of exercises accompanying the history standards.

The screaming coming now from these quarters convinces us of one thing: After the election of November 8, the United States suddenly got a lot bigger. The public, as the remarks above suggest, has indeed stuck its snoot inside the sanctums tended to these many years by the historians and the arts community. The letters that this page has published on these subjects also make it clear to us that the critical opposition is not some up-from-the-swamps booboisie of popular caricature. It's smart—and angry. How the history profession pushed its "new history" this far without challenge is another story. But the challenge to the *Enola Gay* show and the history standards proves we are going to have a long debate now over the assumptions that have guided these efforts. We also understand the historians' and artists' fear that one set of assumptions is simply going to be imposed by fiat in place of their own. That would be unfortunate, we guess. But we don't plan to feel very sorry for these academics and arts activists. They wrote the book on driving one's opponents out of the departments and institutions.

Editorial
The Wall Street Journal
January 31, 1995

THE SMITHSONIAN CHANGES COURSE

IN ANNOUNCING A SHARPLY SCALED-BACK VERSION, essentially a cancellation, of its planned anniversary exhibit about the *Enola Gay*, the Smithsonian Institution has ended up in about the only place it could have. Secretary I. Michael Heyman says the National Air and Space Museum will forget all the interpretive material about the war's end, the bomb's effect, the decision to drop it and the dawn of the nuclear age; instead, it will put on display the *Enola Gay*'s fuselage, a label explaining what it is and some footage about the mission and the crew. While this is an intellectual abdication, a visitor shown the plane that dropped the atomic bomb on Hiroshima and ended World War II is unlikely to go away without some reflecting on war and history.

It is important to be clear about what happened at the Smithsonian. It is not, as some have it, that benighted advocates of a special-interest or right-wing point of view brought political power to bear to crush and distort the historical truth. Quite the contrary. Narrow-minded representatives of a special-interest and revisionist point of view attempted to use their inside track to appropriate and hollow out a historical event that large numbers of Americans alive at that time and engaged in the war had witnessed and understood in a very different—and authentic—way.

The incident inflicts severe damage not just on its immediate perpetrators but on the Smithsonian. Mr. Heyman said Monday he will launch reviews of Air and Space Museum management and of the way the Smithsonian handles potentially inflammatory topics; the regents who backed him up include several who have called most loudly for oversight. Mr. Heyman says, moreover, that he has "some problems with the idea that our exhibits can be advocacy pieces"; he notes that curators, especially at a national museum such as the Smithsonian, have broader public obligations than academic scholars in departments. These are the right questions to ask. They ought to get a full airing at the series of symposia Mr. Heyman also proposes to run this spring with the University of Michigan on the question of how museums handle controversial topics.

Over the longer term, this confidence-undermining episode constitutes a threat to the Smithsonian's stature and independence. But the museum brought this danger on itself by the fecklessness with which it left itself open to legitimate attack on a fiercely contested topic whose delicacy and complexity it ought to have appreciated without all the fuss.

Editorial
The Washington Post
February 1, 1995

. . . OR HIROSHIMA 'CULT'?

Edwin M. Yoder Jr.

THE SMITHSONIAN'S DECISION, after months of controversy, to let the *Enola Gay* speak for itself on the fiftieth anniversary of the bombing of Hiroshima isn't bad as far as it goes. But the display of the plane's fuselage, unadorned by speculative texts, will go no further than the fatuities of the initial exhibit design to explain to visitors what all the shouting is about. The decision leaves the unfortunate impression that the American Legion and other veterans' groups, backed by congressional bullying, have vanquished a horde of muddled curators who sought to turn the exhibit into a revisionist assault on American pride and values. But in any quest for historical understanding—surely the primary function of a museum—neither celebration nor assault is appropriate, though having neither is better than having either.

The exhibit of the B-29 that dropped the bomb got entangled in a quarrel that began a quarter-century ago over the decision to use the bomb. That quarrel is in turn a byproduct of the great quarrel over Vietnam—far more a product of the furies of the 1960s than of the war planning of the 1940s, when President Truman and his advisors made the decision. That connection is persuasively established in Robert Newman's forthcoming book, "Truman and the Hiroshima Cult." Newman, a professor of journalism at the University of Pittsburgh, documents the way in which revisionist views of Harry Truman and the atomic bomb sprang from the tragic national division over Vietnam—as did so many other twisted perspectives on the generation that won World War II and designed America's strategy in the Cold War.

The 1960s were the seedbed of the view that the chief U.S. motive for using atomic weapons against Japan was not to jolt Japan into surrender and save scores of thousands of lives but to discourage Soviet adventurism in Europe by means of "atomic diplomacy"—nuclear intimidation. This thesis as Newman shows, required the tendentious rearrangement of all sorts of collateral history—the "discovery" that anticipated U.S. and Allied casualty figures in an invasion of the Japanese home islands were greatly exaggerated; that the Japanese leaders were war-weary rather than narrowly divided between a peace party and still powerful and impenitent military fanatics; that Harry Truman cold-bloodedly ignored Japanese peace overtures; that he refused to qualify the unconditional surrender demand in a timely way to accommodate Japanese determination to keep their emperor; and that the United States used a "barbaric" weapon against Japan which it would never have used against Germany—reflecting the "racism" of U.S. war policy. The range of such revised views is from half-truths to outrageous falsehoods.

Writing in the *New York Times* on the "gutting" of the *Enola Gay* exhibit, Barton Bernstein of Stanford finds it deplorable that such exalted military figures as Dwight D. Eisenhower and Admiral William Leahy could freely express misgivings about the use of the bomb, but that such reservations are now deemed ineligible for inclusion in the *Enola Gay* exhibit. He has a point. But these second thoughts came years later and were not uncolored by service rivalries; and Eisenhower, whose experience was in the European theater, may have known less than we know now of the fanaticism of the still-ascendant Japanese militarists in 1945. Bernstein quotes General Marshall as directing the use of the bomb against "military installations," as if to say that Hiroshima was not such an installation. Hiroshima was a place of troop concentration. It was also the headquarters of the Japanese command planning the defense of Kyushu, the island that was to be the target of the first Allied assault in November 1945. The revisionists seldom acknowledge how formidably the Japanese were fortifying Kyushu, preparing a defense that might well have made Okinawa (where more than 12,000 Americans died) look like a picnic. Nor do they mention 7,000 kamikaze planes remaining in the Japanese inventory, after they had done such hideous damage to U.S. ships in the Okinawa campaign that the War Department kept its extent secret.

There is much to know about the context in which the decision to drop the atomic bomb was made. The "Hiroshima cult," as Newman calls it, is just that. It isn't history. Those who are content with cults, whether celebratory or derogatory, will worship as they like. Those who want history will read Newman.

The Washington Post
February 4, 1995

TRUMAN WAS RIGHT IN 1945

Albert R. Hunt

L
AST YEAR, America universally celebrated the fiftieth anniversary of the
World War II Normandy invasion. This month, there is considerably less
celebration as we commemorate the fiftieth anniversary of the end of the war in
the Pacific. Instead, there is a renewed attack by revisionist historians on Harry
Truman's decision to drop the atomic bomb on Japan. The late president is being
assailed in new books, articles and television documentaries. These critics argue
that the Japanese could have been coaxed into surrendering without the devastating destruction of the two bombs dropped on Hiroshima and Nagasaki. The
choice between using the A-bomb or invading Japan, with perhaps hundreds of
thousands of casualties, is a myth, they charge. Instead, more skillful statecraft,
coupled with Russian entry into the war would have caused Japan to succumb a
little bit later. The more diabolical revisionists contend this wasn't about saving
American lives; rather, it was to intimidate the Soviet Union. The villain was Secretary of State James Byrnes, who manipulated a weak and naive Harry Truman.

The case is unpersuasive, starting with the distorted picture it paints of
Truman and some of his top advisers like Army Chief of Staff George Marshall,
one of the most honorable men to ever serve this country. The critics view the
situation through the prism of today and side-step both how the situation looked
to the decision-makers in 1945 and the political realities facing them. "The issues
that concerned Truman and his advisers at the time, and the debate within the
administration, point to motives and judgments that are very different from some
ascribed by subsequent critics," writes *Washington Post* reporter Walter Pincus,
who exhaustively examined the available documents and convincingly knocks
down the revisionists' case.

If the real purpose was to put the fear into the Russians, why drop the second
atomic bomb, or, as President Truman did, give the go-ahead for subsequent
bombs until the Japanese surrendered? The Hiroshima bomb would have achieved
that purpose. Moreover, the vast majority of Truman experts ascribe less influence
in this decision to Mr. Byrnes than to Secretary of War Henry Stimson and
General Marshall. "The three most important people were Truman, Stimson
and Marshall," says David McCullough, the acclaimed historian and Truman biographer. The Byrnes-as-Svengali argument is "utter poppycock," says George
Elsey, who as a young Naval Intelligence officer assigned to the White House was
in constant proximity to President Truman during the critical deliberations.

What America faced in mid-1945 was a clearly defeated but intransigent Japan.
Plans were set for an invasion of Japan commencing November 1 with a force,
eventually, of more than a million. Almost all the behavior that summer belies the
contention that Japan was ready to capitulate if only America would soften the
demand for unconditional surrender and explicitly state the Emperor could
remain. While U.S. intelligence revealed there were Japanese civilian leaders, and
even some military men, who wanted to sue for peace, documents clearly suggest
the hard-liners held the upper hand before Hiroshima. Even after Nagasaki,
Defense Minister Anami argued the fight-to-the-end case.

Moreover, for Harry Truman to start negotiating over surrender terms that July—reversing his revered predecessor Franklin Roosevelt's position—would have been disastrous. It likely would have entailed prolonged negotiations while as many as 1,000 Americans a week were being killed. American public opinion was in no mood to accommodate an enemy that had attacked Pearl Harbor, engaged in the infamous Bataan death march and whose kamikaze pilots were killing Americans at that very moment. "Suppose Truman held back," conjectures George Elsey. "What would Congress and the public have done if they later learned that we had a weapon in our hands and hadn't used it while many Americans died? I think the answer is impeachment."

The most dramatic backdrop was the bloody and brutal eighty-two-day battle to take Okinawa, which cost almost 13,000 American lives and three times as many casualties. "If you want one explanation as to why Truman dropped the bomb: 'Okinawa!'" says David McCullough. "It was done to stop the killing." There are dozens of contemporaneous Truman quotes and writings proving that point. Okinawa was considered merely a warm-up to the big invasion starting on Kyushu Island, where the Japanese had deployed over a half-million soldiers to defend the homeland. President Truman was told the casualties could be as high as 500,000; the revisionists charge that was exaggerated. But even if it would have been only 46,000, as some critics claim, that would have increased American WW II deaths in the Pacific by 50 percent!

Thus in July of 1945, here is what President Truman faced: The most reliable intelligence reports declared that even if the Soviets entered the war, the Japanese wouldn't surrender, as General Marshall said, short of a U.S. invasion, which would be the deadliest battle of the war. The alternative was to drop this dreadful weapon which, if it worked—a real uncertainty—would kill an estimated 20,000 Japanese, according to the government's top scientist, Robert Oppenheimer. There was considerable feeling that the A-bomb might stun the Japanese into surrendering or at least strengthen the hands of the minority peace faction in Tokyo. It is impossible to imagine any strong leader coming to any other conclusion.

Of course there were terrible consequences, starting with tragic civilian casualties. And the whole secretive process of the Manhattan Project engendered a general penchant for secrecy after the war that proved detrimental. Was the use of the A-bomb immoral? Of course it was. The war was immoral. But would an invasion have been more moral with the loss of tens of thousands of Americans and hundreds of thousands of Japanese, more than were killed at Hiroshima and Nagasaki? Of course not.

Finally, like many Americans I bring a parochial perspective. In early August 1945, a young naval officer, who'd spent most of the war in the Pacific, was stationed in Manila, with a wife and a two-year-old son he'd barely met back in the states. If the bomb hadn't been dropped and the invasion started in November, he probably would have been involved. As it was, the war ended August 15, and four months later Lt. Cmdr. Albert R. Hunt came home. My mother and I, and later two brothers and a sister, were able to share many happy years with my Dad. For that, I'm grateful for the courage and leadership of Harry S. Truman.

The Wall Street Journal
August 3, 1995

NAGASAKI

Stanley Goldberg*

THE SECOND ATOMIC BOMB used against the Japanese in World War II exploded over Nagasaki at 11:00 a.m., August 9, local time. A day later in Washington, D.C., according to an entry in Secretary of Commerce Henry Wallace's diary, President Truman said at a cabinet meeting that "he had given orders to stop atomic bombing. He said the thought of wiping out another 100,000 people was too horrible. He didn't like the idea of killing, as he said, 'all those kids'." In fact, the record of the sequence of events between the day the specific order to use the atomic bomb was issued, July 25, and August 10, strongly suggest that President Truman did not know about the attack on Nagasaki until after it happened.

This is what we do know: On June 6, Truman approved the recommendation of a committee chaired by Secretary of War Henry Stimson, The Interim Committee, that once it was tested, the bomb be used against Japan without warning. Then on July 5, his diary recorded that he had given Stimson his "final order of the bomb's use," in which he told Stimson that he wanted it used on military targets and not women and children. On July 23, 1945, when Truman was already in Berlin for the Potsdam conference, his diary recorded that the bomb would be used sometime between August 1 and August 10.

The orders for dispatching the bombs to Japan were issued on July 25 by General Thomas Handy, head of the Army Operations Department and acting Army Chief of Staff in General George C. Marshall's absence. (General Marshall was also in Potsdam.) There is no evidence that President Truman ever saw them. The orders were formally addressed to General Carl Spaatz, commander of Strategic Air Forces. But though Handy signed the orders, they had actually been drafted, on orders of General Marshall, the day before, by Major General Leslie R. Groves, the hard driving commanding officer of the Manhattan Engineer District. Those orders were so carefully worded that they left considerable discretion to the field commander for the date, time of attack, and choice of target. That would seem to have given General Carl Spaatz a free hand. The particulars would depend on local conditions. However, General Spaatz was not really in command of this operation. General Groves was. In a separate, Groves-drafted memo, approved by Marshall, but not seen by Truman, the chain of command for authorizing the dropping of each atomic bomb began with General Groves. The orders which Groves had drafted and which Marshall had approved called for the first bomb to be dropped "after about 3 August" and the second and subsequent bombs to be "delivered on the above targets as soon as made ready by the project staff. . . ."

Hiroshima was bombed on August 6. But as early as July 24, Groves began pressing, by cablegram, for the Los Alamos team on Tinian to speed up the delivery to Japan of the second bomb, originally scheduled for 11 August. Against their

---

* Editors' Note: This article was unpublished at the time of Stanley Goldberg's death in 1996. An advisor to the Smithsonian Institution, Goldberg was at work on a biography of General Leslie Groves.

own better judgment, Manhattan Project scientists and engineers on Tinian suspended some of the tests originally planned, and sent off the second bomb in the early morning hours of August 9. The record shows no evidence of President Truman's involvement at any level.

But there are things the record does show. On the morning of August 10, the head of the Experimental Physics Division at Los Alamos, Robert F. Bacher, was supervising the loading of a completed plutonium core into a truck. The core was scheduled to be flown to San Francisco and then on to Tinian that day. The scheduled target was Kokura, on about August 20. As the loading process proceeded, Bacher saw, off in the distance, Laboratory director J. Robert Oppenheimer running toward him, calling Bacher's name. Bacher responded immediately, informing Oppenheimer that he would be with him as soon as the core was on its way. That, Oppenheimer responded, was what he had to talk to Bacher about. He then told Bacher to stop loading the core. Oppenheimer had received an urgent phone call from Manhattan Engineer District headquarters in Washington, telling him that, on order of the President, under no circumstances were any more plutonium cores to be shipped to Tinian unless Oppenheimer received explicit orders to do so from President Truman. Since Truman could have given such an order at any time between July 24 and August 9, it strongly suggests that the bombing of Nagasaki came as a surprise to him. After July 24, the loop between Tinian and Washington included only General Groves and his representatives on the island.

There are two obvious interpretations to explain the pressure Groves exerted on his Tinian-based minions. The first is that he wanted to make sure that both types of atomic bombs were used before the end of the war so as to justify the expense. He may have been fearful that after the uranium bomb destroyed Hiroshima, the Japanese might surrender before the second, plutonium bomb could be used. On the other hand, Leslie Groves was a patriot. He might have speeded up the second bomb in the belief that the sooner it was used, the sooner the war would be over. My own conclusion is that both motivations are likely to have been operative.

Groves had not been a member of the Interim Committee, but as an invited guest he sat in on every meeting, including those in which the question of using the bomb on the Japanese had been debated. As Groves wrote to a close colleague shortly after the end of the war: "I had to do some good hard talking at times. One thing is certain—we will never have the greatest congressional investigation of all times."

He was absolutely right.

THE REVISIONISTS' AGENDA

Stephen S. Rosenfeld

ON THE FIFTIETH ANNIVERSARY OF—not to pretty it up—the American nuclear obliteration of Hiroshima, I can report having taken a second look and come out pretty much where I was thirty to thirty-five years ago. President Harry Truman did the right thing in dropping the first and only atomic bombs on Japan. The revisionist critics have much of interest to add but also much that is diversionary and in any event not mind-changing. They have made the argument, for instance, that additional deadly conventional bombing of Japanese cities or the Soviet Union's entry into the Pacific war or a continuing naval blockade or an offer to let Japan keep the Emperor could have brought about a Japanese surrender and mooted a casualty-costly American invasion. Hence the conclusion that there was no military need to drop the bomb.

But this seems to me to skip past the quite rational and widespread contemporary American apprehension that the Japanese were still capable of a ferocious homeland defense. Not to speak of the quite understandable and widespread contemporary American feeling that no quarter could be given to such a duplicitous and bloody foe and that no weapon or tactic that promised to spare further American casualties (whatever the estimate of their number) could be ruled out. As to the notion that emerging high strategy dictated dropping the bomb to intimidate the Soviet Union, a wartime ally already turning likely postwar rival, it brings to mind Jimmy Carter's famous confession to "lust in my heart." No doubt such a strategic impulse was pumping in various Washington hearts—although its presence in Truman's remains poorly documented. But it was not guiding Truman's policy. Anyway, events were soon to confirm that the bomb was of no value in keeping the Kremlin from swallowing Eastern Europe.

Like many others, I find myself finally guided by a particular view of Truman the man. He was ruled in these matters much less by strategic globe-twirling than by a basic instinct to do his duty by American fighting men. That is who he was. The wartime use of the new weaponry was not an ignominious act in which an unprepared and manipulated president gratuitously killed masses of Japanese and let loose a nuclear genie that permanently coarsened human life. It was a courageous and characteristic moment when, as Thomas Powers puts it in the July *Atlantic*, Truman used "the weapon he had. He did what he thought was right, and the war ended, the killing stopped. . . . The bombing [conventional as well as nuclear] was cruel, but it ended a greater, longer cruelty." It also ushered in a demilitarized, democratic Japan in a world where the nuclear powers were able to stay at peace with each other for a half-century. Not a small harvest.

The critics have an agenda—not an ignoble agenda but one that goes well beyond instructing us to face up to our true history. It is to repudiate the moral basis of nuclear weapons. If their use in the one situation where they were actually employed can be shown to be unnecessary, illegitimate and even depraved, then a powerful change will have been wrought in the political culture in which strategic decisions and historical judgments are made. Some of the critics have a further agenda: to put on Truman and the United States the responsibility for inaugurating the Cold War.

Nuclear weapons are different, but not just because a single one could devastate a Japanese city more "efficiently" than could many squadrons of conventional bombers. It's because, as everyone knows now, they could devastate not only our country but the planet. A wise policy will reduce the uses and possessors of nuclear weapons to a minimum. But the weapons, now that we and others have them, cannot be undone. This is a difficult conclusion for people who believe that nuclear weapons, being so attractive to the wielders of power, inherently resist sane control. It is anathema to those who believe that Americans, among nuclear others, cannot be counted on to use power well. But both of those propositions can be proven wrong by wise policy.

As for blaming Truman for ginning up the Cold War, the charge arises from a long and bitter political as well as scholarly debate. For most people the debate ended when Soviet power relented and then collapsed. This freed Eastern Europe and opened up Moscow's archives; the two developments made it utterly clear where the true responsibility lay. Truman made his mistakes, but he got the big things straight, including dropping the bomb on Japan.

The Washington Post
August 4, 1995

ENOLA GAY: 'PATRIOTICALLY CORRECT'

Kai Bird

TESTIFYING BEFORE A HOUSE SUBCOMMITTEE on March 10, I. Michael Heyman, the secretary of the Smithsonian, promised that when he finally unveiled the *Enola Gay* exhibit, "I am just going to report the facts." But when the exhibit was opened on June 28, it contained a text that presents an unqualified orthodox defense of the bomb: that it saved lives, ended the war and obviated the need for a costly invasion. The critical label at the heart of the exhibit makes the following assertions: The atomic bombings of Hiroshima and Nagasaki "destroyed much of the two cities and caused many tens of thousands of deaths." This grossly understates the known fact that at least 200,000 men, women and children died at Hiroshima and Nagasaki. (Official Japanese records calculate a figure of more than 300,000 deaths—nearly triple the number of U.S. soldiers killed during the course of the entire Pacific war.)

"However," claims the Smithsonian, "the use of the bombs led to the immediate surrender of Japan and made unnecessary the planned invasion of the Japanese home islands." Presented as fact, this sentence is actually a highly contentious interpretation. Many historians believe the Soviet entry into the war—which is not even mentioned in the exhibit—provided the final "shock" that persuaded the Japanese to surrender. And it is a fact that even after Hiroshima and Nagasaki were bombed, the Japanese still insisted upon a condition to the surrender—namely, that the Emperor would be allowed to remain on the throne. This was precisely the clarification of surrender terms that many of Truman's own advisors had urged on him prior to Hiroshima.

Worse, the Smithsonian's label takes the highly partisan view that it was "thought highly unlikely that Japan, while in a very weakened military condition, would have surrendered unconditionally without such an invasion." Nowhere in the exhibit is this interpretation balanced by other views. Visitors to the exhibit will not learn that many U.S. leaders—including General Dwight D. Eisenhower, Admiral William D. Leahy, War Secretary Henry L. Stimson and Assistant Secretary of War John J. McCloy—thought it highly probable that the Japanese would surrender well before the earliest possible invasion, scheduled for November 1945. It is spurious to assert as fact that obliterating Hiroshima in August obviated the need for an invasion in November. This is merely an interpretation—the very thing Secretary Heyman said he would ban from his exhibit.

In yet another label, the Smithsonian asserts: "Special leaflets were then dropped on Japanese cities three days before a bombing raid to warn civilians to evacuate." The very next sentence refers to the bombing of Hiroshima on Aug. 6, 1945, directly suggesting that the civilian inhabitants of Hiroshima were given a warning. This is incorrect. No evidence has ever been uncovered that leaflets—issuing a warning of either conventional or atomic attack—were dropped on Hiroshima.

In a sixteen-minute video film in which the crew of the *Enola Gay* are allowed to speak at length about why they believe atomic bombings were justified, Colonel Paul Tibbets flatly asserts that Hiroshima was a "definite military target." Nowhere in the exhibit is this false assertion balanced by contrary information. Hiroshima was chosen as a target precisely because it had been very low on the previous spring's campaign of conventional bombing, and therefore was a pristine target on which to demonstrate the atomic bomb. James Conant, a member of the Interim Committee that advised President Truman, defined the target for the bomb as a "vital war plant employing a large number of workers and closely surrounded by workers' houses." There were indeed military factories in Hiroshima, but they lay on the outskirts of the city. The *Enola Gay* bombardier's instructions, however, were to target the bomb on the center of this civilian city.

For most historians, the few words in the exhibit that attempt to provide some historical context for viewing the atomic bomber amount to more than propaganda for a patriotically correct, yet largely discredited orthodox justification of the atomic bombings. The exhibit dishonors the very principles of free speech and free inquiry for which more than 100,000 Americans sacrificed their lives in the struggle to defeat Japanese fascism fifty years ago. At a moment when Americans are asking our erstwhile World War II enemies—and the Russians—to confront their own history honestly and openly, this exhibit stands as a monument to official history and censorship.

The Washington Post
July 7, 1995

SHADOWS

We appeal, as human beings, to human beings: Remember your humanity and forget the rest.
Albert Einstein and Bertrand Russell

THE DAY

HIROSHIMA

DISAPPEARED

Dr. Shuntaro Hida

I
N 1944, WHEN I ARRIVED at my new post as a medical officer at the Hiroshima Military Hospital, the attitude of Japan's population toward the war effort was still one of relative support. It was a year prior to the atomic bombing. The authority of the Japanese Army was still recognized and accepted. However, by early 1945 many Japanese began to feel uneasy about the outcome of the war despite the daily government reports of battlefield victories. These reports, of course, were nothing but complete fabrications. By this stage many large cities in Japan had been subjected to heavy air raids by the American Air Force and had suffered terrible destruction from fire bombings.

It was strange to us that Hiroshima had never been bombed despite the fact that the B-29 bombers flew over the city every day. Only after the war did I come to know that Hiroshima, according to American archives, had been kept untouched in order to preserve it as a target for the use of nuclear weapons. In early 1945 we carried patients into the shelters at every air raid alarm because we did not know which alarm might signify an actual bombing. The atmosphere of the city was free and easy among both troops and citizens because they had never experienced an actual air raid. For example, until the summer of 1945, the Chief of Staff of the District Headquarters (DHQ) had still not heeded those who advised him to move the military hospital to the countryside for the sake of safety.

Most of the patients we treated had been wounded or taken ill on the battlefield. They were witnesses to each battle and could give eyewitness accounts of the damage sustained by our forces: which of our units had been completely destroyed, how many warships had been sunk or planes shot down. Although the government carefully concealed this information from the public, it had become the general view inside the hospital, based on common sense, that we had no chance of winning the war. Once the Japanese Army was defeated in the Philippines and at Okinawa, the country quickly recognized that the struggle would soon reach our own mainland. At this stage the army in Hiroshima finally began to evacuate all their non-combatant forces to the nearby countryside. Since a number of detachments tried to move at the same time, it became very difficult to find a suitable place for the large number of medical workers and patients in the military hospital. As a consequence, we were required to divide the patients and hospital personnel into several groups. These were moved to several schoolhouses and to a number of Buddhist temples and shrines in nearby areas.

Unexpectedly, I was ordered by DHQ to construct an underground shelter for the central hospital by digging a tunnel through the mountainside in the village of Hesaka about 1.5 miles north of the city. In the early part of May, I left Hiroshima with about three hundred soldiers and proceeded to my new post as commander of the "shelter digging brigade." Despite the lack of many materials that we needed, it was by chance that on the 5th of August we finished constructing the new shelter for the hospital. It was just one day before the first atomic bomb, *Little Boy*, was dropped upon the population of Hiroshima. Regrettably, it was dropped too hastily. After the success of the first atomic bomb explosion, code-named "Trinity," in Alamogordo, New Mexico, no animal experiments related to the great danger of radioactivity on human beings had been done despite the grave dangers predicted by many scientists. Perhaps, if the American administration and its military authorities had paid sufficient regard to the terrible nature of the fiery demon which mankind had discovered and yet knew so little about its consequences, the American authorities might never have used such a weapon against the 750,000 Japanese who ultimately became its victims.

On August 5, I called DHQ in Hiroshima and reported that we had completed our task. I expected a sympathetic order directing us to stay one more night at the village in order to recover from our labor. Instead, I was told, "Come back at once with all your soldiers." It was an order and I could not willfully disregard it. Therefore, I directed my company to prepare at once to depart for Hiroshima. After expressing our thanks to the leading personalities of the village, we began our journey leaving a small number of personnel to complete the remaining tasks and prepare for the opening of the new underground hospital. Since that day, I have been tortured with a terrible regret. A single question has lingered in my mind: Why did I not manage to find some excuse for DHQ and stay in the village at least one more night? If I had done so, the lives of three hundred soldiers would not have been lost.

We entered Hiroshima about eight o'clock in the evening of the fifth as the long summer day was drawing to a close. Both the Director and the Chief of General Affairs at the hospital were away on official business in Osaka, so I was unable either to submit my report or to receive new orders. While I killed time wandering about the hospital area, I received an unusual request from the duty officer. I was asked to wait upon a group of senior medical officers who had come to stay at the hospital that evening. In those days, it had been a bad practice among those who came and went between the front and Tokyo on official business to stay at the military hospital in Hiroshima instead of a hotel. The city's hotels did not serve meals at this stage of the war.

I arranged the dinners in the X-ray room. Since all the windows were covered with black curtains, I did not switch off the lights each time an air raid alarm sounded. Having to perform an unpleasant duty, I eventually ended up getting drunk on *sake* with the medical officers who were passing through. Once I saw with my own eyes that the last of our visitors was dead drunk, I lay down on the bed which had been arranged for all of us in the room. If I had slept there through the night, I would have been killed the next morning. However, in the middle of the night, I was woken by an old farmer who had been guided to me by one of the hospital's guards. The farmer's granddaughter had heart disease and had become ill during the night. When I was stationed in the village of Hesaka, I had treated her. It was an urgent call and I had to go at once. Although I was still drunk and it was difficult for me to move, the farmer loaded me on the back of his bicycle and bound me to his waist.

My memory of the trip is vague. I only recall with certainty that I saw the beautiful stream of the River Ohta reflecting the twinkling of dust particles in the night's light. As the bicycle moved along, I held onto the farmer's belt to prevent myself from falling. I woke in the morning with the sun shining in my face. The day was breaking: the sixth of August. It was ten past eight and too late for me to reach the hospital in time for the opening hour. I jumped out of bed. The farmer who had slept beside me had begun his daily work. A clattering sound of a well bucket drawing water reached my ears from the back yard. Drawing near the patient, I observed her. Her attack had abated and she had fallen into a deep sleep. Yet, in order to assure her well-being, I took a syringe from my bag and began to cut the neck of an ampoule.

The sky was a clear blue. At an extraordinary height, a B-29 bomber came into view, shining silver in the light. It moved very slowly and appeared as if it had stopped in mid-air. It was approaching Hiroshima. "It must be the usual scouting," I thought. I pushed the air out of the syringe without paying any more attention to the plane and was preparing to place the needle into the young woman's arm. At that very moment a tremendous flash struck my face and a penetrating light entered my eyes. All of a sudden my face and arms were engulfed by an intense heat. Instinctively, I covered my face with both my hands. I still remember uttering the word "Ah!," but I do not remember, even now, whether I ever gave the injection. Within an instant I was crawling on mats which lay on the floor and tried to flee outside by creeping along the surface. I expected to hear shouts of "Fire!" but I saw only the blue sky between my fingers. The tips of the leaves on the porch had not moved an inch. It was extraordinarily quiet. "Might it only be a dream?" I thought. And then I looked toward the city of Hiroshima.

MY WHOLE HEART TREMBLED AT WHAT I SAW. There was a great fire ring floating over the city. Within a moment, a massive deep white cloud grew out of the center of the ring. It grew quickly upward, extending itself further and further from the ring's center. At the same time I could see a long black cloud as it spread over the entire width of the city. It spread along the side of the hill in our direction and began to surge over Ohta Valley toward Hesaka village, enveloping in its path all the woods, groves, rice fields, farms and houses. What I saw was the beginning of an enormous storm created by the blast as it gathered up the mud and sand of the city and rolled it into a huge wave. The delay of several seconds after the monumental flash and the heat-rays permitted me to observe, in its entirety, the black tidal wave as it approached us.

Suddenly I saw the roof of the primary school below the farmer's house easily stripped away by the cloud of dust. Before I could think about taking cover my whole body flew up in the air. The shutters and screens flew about me as if they were scraps of paper. The thatched roof of the farmer's house was blown away with the ceiling still attached. A moment later I could see the blue sky above me where the roof had been. Then I was lifted by the wave, carried ten meters across two rooms, and thrown against a large Buddhist altar. The huge roof and a large quantity of mud fell upon me with a crashing sound. I felt some pain, but there was no time to think. I crept outside groping to find my way. My eyes, ears, nose, and even my mouth were filled with mud. Fortunately, because the big pillars or walls were strong, the farmer's granddaughter was only pressed under the straw bed. In this way, she was saved from being crushed. With all my strength I pulled her out of the house onto the verandah. Opening her clothes, I put my ear to her breast directly. I had no stethoscope, but I made sure that her heart was beating normally. I was greatly relieved to hear her heart and turned to look once more over the city of Hiroshima.

"Look! A blazing column is shooting up," I said to myself. A scarlet column of fire disguising its head as a huge cloud was climbing higher and higher into the sky as if it intended to break through to the heavens. All at once, a chill ran down my spine, and an inexplicable fear crawled up my belly. "What is this? What am I looking at now?" I thought. Although I was only twenty-eight years old, the experience of any age would have been inadequate to grasp this completely unknown world which burned before me.

The giant cloud rose above the city and trampled the whole of Hiroshima under its blazing column. I was kneeling on the ground and responding instinctively to the sight before me. Before I was barely aware of it, an ominous wind began to disturb the leaves, and the cry of villagers reached my ears as they called out to one another. Everything was obscured with a sand-like dust as if we were in a fog. Above the hazy scene the bright sky of August still shone. The giant cloud or *kinoko gumo* (Japanese for "mushroom-shaped cloud") was expanding upwards and outwards into the heavens above, changing its appearance into a range of five colors, as if it intended to totally blot out the clear brightness of the sky.

The farmer, who had brought me from the city on his bicycle, appeared from the back of what had been his house. He was clearly filled with fear and doubt. He could not understand why or how his house had been suddenly destroyed. Since he had been working on the other side of the house behind the main wall, he had been protected from the flash and thermal rays. When I pointed up to the monster cloud, he lost the strength in his legs and suddenly sat on the ground. As quickly as I could, I explained to him that his granddaughter was well and asked him to lend me his bicycle. I decided that I had to return to Hiroshima as soon as possible.

I hurried along the Ohta River on the bicycle. The dry white country road led straight to the foot of the *kinoko gumo*. Not a dog was there, not a man. "What happened under that fire, that cloud?" I was filled with awe. But I was a medical officer and my overwhelming sense of duty was driving me forward. Only this self-conceit compelled me to push forward on the bicycle and to overcome the fear. There was an *ishijizo* (a Buddhist stone statue) by the road halfway to the city. From there the road ran straight down and then turned sharply to the left where the foot of the mountain jutted into the river. I sped down at top speed toward the curve when suddenly something came into my view. I quickly braked. The bicycle was thrown into the air and I fell face forward into a bush. Ignoring the pain I stood up and was surprised to see a figure which appeared from around the corner.

It was anything but "a man." The strange figure came up to me little by little, unsteady on its feet. It surely seemed like the form of a man but it was completely naked, bloody and covered with mud. The body was completely swollen. Rags hung from its bare breast and waist. The hands were held before the breasts with palms turned down. Water dripped from the tips of the rags. Indeed, what I took to be rags were in fact pieces of human skin and the water drops were human blood. I could not distinguish between male and female, soldier or citizen. It had a curiously large head, swollen eyelids and big projected lips grew as if they formed half of its face. There was no hair on its burned head. I stepped backwards in spite of myself. Surely this strange thing was a "man." But it was a man of burnt flesh hanging like rawhide, and it was covered with blood and mud.

He appeared to be able to see. He found me with his burnt eyes and hastily tried to reach me. It must have been his last exertion for he took his final step and fell. Immediately, I came to his side and tried to feel his pulse. But his skin was completely burnt and there was no place where I could touch him in order to feel the beat of an artery. His body convulsed and I could not find any sign of life. I was in need of someone to help me but could find no house close by. I had to hurry to the hospital and intended to leave the spot immediately, but I could not make myself move another step. I looked at the road before me. Denuded, burnt and bloody, numberless survivors stood in my path. They were massed together, some crawling on their knees or on all fours, some stood with difficulty or leaned on another's shoulder. Not one showed any sign which forced me to recognize him or her as a human being. I was at a loss as to what to do because I carried no medicine or medical instruments with me. It was impossible to push my way through those miserable victims. I jumped into the river with no hesitation.

I waded down to the river cutting through the luxuriant summer overgrowth of grass along the bank. Volumes of dark smoke blown by a harsh wind began to eddy along the surface of the water. The burning wind blew against my face and hot smoke choked my lungs. I realized that the furious wind was coming from the fire in the city. Soon, I noticed that the rock of the river bed had changed to sand under my feet, and I knew that I had reached Choju-En, one of the famous parks on the outskirts of the city. I was already caught in a storm of blazing wind with deep red flames. Whenever the intensity of the heat became too great, I dove under the water and held my breath. The bright sky of high summer could not be seen above the smoke. The water itself turned deep red, reflecting the blazing flames. A black driving wind blew against my cheeks.

The river divided into two branches at that point. One of them led straight into Hiroshima Bay, and the other one, the Kanda River, turned to the left. The Hesaka road crossed over the Kanda River by a suspension bridge and ran into the city, passing the site of an Engineering Corps on the opposite bank. Suddenly, as I tried to make out a familiar landmark the wind changed its direction. The dark smoke which obscured my vision moved downstream. Unexpectedly, the blue sky appeared with the brightness of high noon. I saw that the long bank of the river at Choju-En was filled with a large number of burned human beings. They occupied the bank as far as the eye could see. The greatest number lay in the water rolling slowly at the mercy of the waves. Most of them must have been corpses. Countless survivors crept toward the river one after another, some crawling over others. The suspension bridge was in flames with black smoke billowing from the structure. Despite this, many flesh-like creatures moved slowly across the bridge at a snail's pace. Many fell into the water as their strength ebbed out of them.

The Engineering Corps on the opposite bank was exploding and dark smoke filled the sky above the flames. Sparks colored the dark cloud accompanied by thunderous sounds, as if a fireworks display had been set off. A number of survivors fell into the water, driven forward by the heavy fire in the city. Others, finding their way barred by the river, also fell into the water. Intending to enter the city, I simply could not take one step forward and would have gone on standing there blankly. I confronted a great many survivors without human faces or a capacity for speech. They walked past me, as best they could, as they tried to flee Hiroshima. Some of the corpses in the river came to the surface while others stayed suspended beneath the surface. As they floated and swirled down the river, they knocked against my body. Whenever I saw a little innocent baby among them, I looked up to the sky and bit my lip hoping to control myself from crying. Above me rose the enormous mushroom-shaped cloud with its five colors. It seemed to rise to an infinite height where it could touch the blue sky above and leave below the whirling black smoke of our world.

At that time, two metal boats of the Engineering Corps filled with soldiers rowed down the river under command of a young officer. I knew him quite well because he had been engaged under my command in the tunnel work above Hesaka during the previous month. When the boat he was in arrived at the spot where I stood in the river, he jumped into the water and, holding the boats, said loudly, "Go back to Hesaka at once. It is filled with wounded. They are waiting for you, doctor." I understood the state of affairs at once. He shook my hand and disappeared in the smoke with his soldiers, promising to look into the fate of the military hospital. To my sorrow, it was the last time I saw him.

My return to Hesaka was a terribly difficult and long journey because this time I had to go upstream. As I struggled against the current passing under bushes which stood along the bank, I encountered many victims who were taking their final breaths. They fell into the river from the road in a desperate desire for water. I did not know what time it was; my watch had become useless once it had been immersed in the river. Finally, I arrived at the familiar levee of Hesaka. As I climbed out of the river and onto the bank, I looked over the village. In spite of myself I collapsed and sat on the ground. In fact, I was so exhausted that I could not keep standing. However, I believe what really caused my legs to give way was the extraordinary scene before my eyes.

Two important roads met at a "T" junction in the village. One of them passed through Hesaka going north along the river from Hiroshima; the other road ran perpendicular to the first, going over the pass along the Geibi railway from Kaidaichi town. I now stood exactly at the junction. What a fearful sight it was! As far as the eye could see, victims filled the road, the school grounds and all the other open places in the village. The primary school that I had used as the base for construction work until the preceding day had lost its entire roof. Nearly all the buildings in the school complex had been destroyed, leaving only one structure that faced a hill at the back of the school grounds. The area was filled with debris. Yet, the cruelest sight was the number of raw bodies that lay one upon the other. Although the road was already packed with victims, the terribly wounded, bloody and burnt, kept crawling in one after another. They had become a pile of flesh at the entrance to the school. The lower layers must have been corpses because they emanated a peculiarly nasty smell characteristic of the dead that mingled now with burnt, bloody flesh.

The tent for medical treatment had been set up temporarily on the corner of the grounds, and Captain Atsushi Fujimoto, the president of the branch hospital who had arrived at his post only the previous day, was fully involved in first aid treatment along with his aides. In a room of the school that had narrowly escaped collapse, the village headman, the schoolmaster and other staff people were conferring but were bewildered by the enormity of the situation they faced. As soon as I entered, the village headman stood up and pointed out of the window. He mumbled something. As if they were sparrows perched on an electric wire, the villagers with folded arms stood in lines on the narrow footpaths which crossed the rice fields. They had left their houses in fear with nowhere to go as the burnt and disfigured victims of the bombing had one after another silently entered their homes.

I immediately pointed out emergency measures which had to be taken by the village authorities: an alarm had to be sounded in order to gather all the villagers together; an emergency kitchen had to be organized to prepare rice supplied by the army; a large quantity of seed oil, soybean oil and rags had to be gathered to treat burns; and finally an emergency crematorium had to be set up. Someone murmured after my last suggestion, "We do not cremate but inter only." I said, "Good. Bury all you want. I can see more than five hundred corpses at one glance. Will you attempt to dig up all your paddy fields and turn them into graveyards?" After this brief argument, and in response to my request, the village headman and his assistant were compelled to offer their own forest lands to set up the crematorium.

The villagers gathered at the village office and began to prepare the emergency kitchen and burn treatment center. There were only women and older men available to assist. All the young people were fighting at the front. Some of the very aged set about gathering the corpses under the command of a sergeant. The temporary stretchers were made with bamboo and straw rope, and hundreds of terrible-looking corpses were carried to the crematorium one after another. They were barely recognizable as human bodies, but appeared more like masses of burnt flesh. No tears or sentimentality could be indulged toward those who were no longer alive. Our most urgent and important responsibility remained with the victims who were still breathing. Even if many of those we attended were to die, our duty was to the living. As we worked, countless survivors continued the trek toward Hesaka to seek refuge from the fiery foot of the *kinoko gumo*.

When the rice gruel was boiled and the victims who lay all over the ground had been given some aid, they were covered with straw mats to shield them from the strong sunlight. But many of them died quickly under the mats and were carried out of the emergency encampments on bamboo stretchers. As soon as one disappeared, a new one filled the vacant space. A great number of our patients suffered from injuries as well as burns. The nurses, sanitary soldiers, and village women applied rags immersed in soybean oil on the burns of the victims. They carried the oil dressings in their hands and applied the oil directly to the burns. Some sprinkled the wounds with wet leaves. Although this treatment had been neglected as a mere popular remedy, as far as I know the victims who were treated in this way were all helped.

On this first day I was one of only three doctors at Hesaka who were engaged in giving first aid treatment. At that stage no medicines or medical instruments had yet arrived at the new hospital in Hesaka and key personnel had arrived only the day prior to the bombing. We used all the instruments and materials that we could find in the village. Despite their small quantity, most of these precious items were generously donated by a local doctor's family. The doctor was at the front. I stopped some bleeding, put sutures in some wounds and pulled out pieces of glass.

At one point a small boy, four or five years old, was brought to me. His cries were piercing. However, his pain was not due to an unusual burn. A large piece of broken glass had plunged into his belly and had cut the peritoneum. His large intestines had broken through the wound like a hydrangea. I bound its root and burned it with red-hot tongs after making sure that the intestine had not severed. The boy finally lost consciousness. After the surgery he was brought to an old village woman who was fond of children. On the same day an old woman was brought to us who had been trapped under a concrete wall which had collapsed. One of her arms had been crushed by the wall. Fortunately, she was freed and brought to Hesaka with her arm discolored and hanging by her side. There was simply no way to save her except to cut off her dead arm. The preparation for amputation was put in order at once. She was bound firmly on a door. The operation had to be done under local anesthesia. Her arm was separated from her shoulder with the utmost skill by a surgeon who had refined his skills at the front. The old woman fainted from the fearful pain. Her daughter, who had held her mother's arm during the operation, dropped it on the ground because of its unexpected weight. The bloody arm rolled quite a distance as if it were a living thing and settled at the edge of the road. To my shock as the arm came to rest, one of the white fingers on the hand pointed to the Giant Cloud which had risen over Hiroshima. Although it was only reflecting the evening glow from the western sky, the cloud stood like a column of fire enveloped by a scarlet blaze.

I remember there was a young girl whose body was cruelly burnt on the upper half of her torso. She had no clothing or even rags to cover her. She had no wounds below her waist and her clear skin had caught people's eyes. Someone who could not tolerate her nudity had wound a cloth around her waist. Yet, the girl had already been driven mad. As often as a cloth was placed on her, she ripped it off and tore it to pieces. She walked amidst the crowded encampments filled with dead and wounded, her burnt and contorted face frozen in a terrible grimace. There were some moments when she stumbled over the dead and other times she fell on the wounded. Whenever she moved, her exposed white thighs seemed in some way to threaten others as if they were strange living things. Someone lost patience with her and pushed her harshly. The girl fell and began to cry loudly. She clung to an unknown corpse while she wept. The sun set in the dark sky. We could see how the *kinoko gumo* was beginning to change its shape. It hovered over us like an ominous and distant presence. Without any lights we continued to treat the wounded throughout that dark night.

As night descended, I prepared to extract a broken yet large piece of plate glass that had plunged deep into the burnt breast of a young girl. A careful technique and the utmost concentration of spirit were necessary to extract it. Furthermore, a sharp edge was pointing toward other vulnerable organs. While I completed the necessary preparations, I was distracted by a young mother who carried her baby on her back and had for some hours tearfully pleaded with me to help her. Her appearance was frightful. Her face had been brutally burned. She repeated the same request so often that I remembered every detail she gave that day. Her house had been enveloped in flames in a split second. Giving up her other three children who were burned to death, she ran away with the youngest baby, carrying it on her back. Of course, the baby was a substitute for all the others. "Doctor, please help my baby. Please," she repeated incessantly. The baby seemed to be one or two years old. He was already dead and exuded a putrid smell. There was a large wound on the back of his thigh and clearly there was nothing which could be done for the child.

I was about to pull out the broken glass from the breast of my patient. I grabbed the point with a Kocher clamp and concentrated my whole spirit into my fingertips so that I would not break the glass. At that precise moment the young mother grabbed hold of me. I was compelled to shake off her arm. Nevertheless, the glass plate broke into pieces and the remainder descended deeper into the patient's breast. The people around us gasped. "I will help your child," one said. I turned to her and said, "Let us take the baby down from your back." I held her arm, untied the rope and took the baby in my arms. There was no burn anywhere on his cold skin. One of the nurses applied antiseptic solution thoroughly to his large gaping wound and bandaged it firmly. I said, "It's okay. Do not awaken him tonight. You must sleep so that your milk will flow well tomorrow morning." The young mother joined her hands together toward me again and went away holding her dead baby on her bloody breast to where no one knew. At this sight people wept aloud all at once. I felt human feeling coming to life again for the first time since the bombing. My eyes were ready to overflow with tears. I spoke to myself and bit my lip so that I would not cry. If I had cried, I would have lost my courage to keep standing and working.

A NIGHTMARISH EVENING DESCENDED UPON US as the whole village was turned into a field hospital. As we worked through the night, the mysterious form of the *kinoko gumo* spread out over the starlit sky. It was even more frightening and strange than it had been in the daytime. A variety of human voices filled the fields surrounding our medical station with a terrible medley of groans, sobs and shouts. A heartless wind blew through the twigs in the trees on the hills behind us. The Ohta River went on alone flowing toward the south as if to show us that time is forever. We went on during the night treating the wounded by candlelight. The number of wounded increased throughout the hours of darkness as blast victims found their way into the village by the two roads which met at Hesaka. Stretcher groups worked all night carrying the dead to the grove in the forest which had been set aside for the crematorium. Yet, despite how hard the stretcher bearers labored, the number of victims grew all around us.

Sergeant Nario Sugiyama came to report. He had deep-set eyes. He said that they had carried off more than two hundred bodies but still there were countless more on the road. He wanted my permission to leave the bodies until the next day because the teams were so exhausted. Of course, I nodded my permission. When he was about to go after bowing to me, I suddenly heard a loud voice, "Bomber! Enemy!" Someone blew out the candle immediately. The familiar roar of a B-29 bomber reached my ears from the sky above. A deep and terrified silence fell upon the whole school. A cold fear crept into everyone's heart. There was one common thought: "Could it happen again? Would there be another flash?" The memory of that shocking moment that very morning stilled every heart. Sometimes near, sometimes far, the metallic sound of the B-29 came in waves. Little by little the roar faded. It seemed to take an eternity, as if to prolong the fear. Someone cried out with a sorrowful voice from the darkness, "Why us? We are only innocent women, children, and the old!" A child's cry cut into our hearts, "Mother! Oh, Mother!" Suddenly, people broke into tears all at once and the night air over the ruins of Hesaka's primary school shook with sobs.

I stepped away in silence and searched for a place where I could be alone. Picking out a cigarette from my breast pocket, I struck a match. The yellow ring lit a tear on my cheek.

"Please! Somebody!" A shrill voice suddenly called out in alarm near the entrance to the school, "Please! Somebody!" As I looked through the darkness, I could see several army paramedics surrounding a crouched figure. Weaving my way through the wounded, I ran toward them and saw a face as white as a sheet with long, disordered hair. She held a baby in her left arm and pressed her left breast with her right hand. Between her fingers a large quantity of blood was spurting out of her chest.

"Take heart. Don't give up," we encouraged her. The surgeon ran up. "Where are you from?" we asked.

"Hakushima cho."

"Where is your husband?"

"If he were alive, he would be here to help," she answered.

The sterilized Kocher was thrust quickly into the wound and roughly clamped the broken blood vessel. I bound the thread firmly in the flesh of her breast, concentrating with all my might on the tip of my finger which was slippery with clammy blood. When the surgery was finished, I stood up with great relief, having succeeding in stopping the bleeding. The woman held her child gently to her breast and began to comfort the infant.

The weather on the morning of August 7 was clear like it had been a day earlier. The small village of Hesaka was filled with visitors who came in search of their relatives and friends. This added to the great number of wounded who had already found their way to the village. The branch hospital was simply over-whelmed with the burned victims and corpses. As soon as day broke, the stretcher groups resumed their grim task and carried bodies out of the village one by one. A fire was going in the makeshift crematorium which had been set up in a grove at the end of the village. The sun rose over the peak which stood above the valley. The smoke which drifted up from the crematorium appeared pink in the morning mist.

Everyone on our team had managed to get some sleep during the night. At dawn I threw myself once again into the varied tasks of emergency medical treatment. We also handed out food and water to a long line of survivors. I no longer cared about the bloody smell on my fingers as I distributed food. About 10 A.M., an emergency call from District Headquarters was transmitted to our unit. No one knew where or how the transmission had reached us. However, it was decided to send me as a liaison. We were fortunate that at that moment our team suddenly increased in number as a relief corps arrived with a full load of material and medicine. They had carried the supplies on the backs of horses from several distant branch hospitals.

I left Hesaka and walked down the road beside the river that on the preceding day I had traveled by bicycle. The *kinoko gumo* which had spread across the city of Hiroshima was changing from a mushroom shape into a common dark cloud. Corpses were everywhere along the route. The wounded followed me with only their eyes, having no energy to speak. Only the river flowing beside the road moved with a semblance of life.

It was not long before I arrived at Choju-En. The suspension bridge had not burnt down. However, several black bodies still lay upon it. I crossed the river in waist-deep water. White smoke rose in thick clouds over the grounds of the Engineering Corps. It had been completely burned away. A breeze blew through the site, stoking small flames in the piles of burned charcoal and rubble that remained. The road ran into the city from there passed under the Sanyo railroad

line. I climbed up on the levee and stood on the track. Although I could not understand how it could happen, the surface of all the railroad ties were burnt in exactly
the same manner. And then looking up I saw what had once been Hiroshima.
There was no city but only a burnt field. The entire town had been reduced to
ashes in a single day. I could see the water in Hiroshima Bay shining against the
light of a summer day. The only obstruction to my view of the sea were a few ruins
of buildings. The familiar tower of Hiroshima Castle was nowhere to be found.

Some people were walking in a line through the city searching for their friends
and family here amidst the smoking ruins. Of course, at that time no one knew that
many of those who came to the city that day in search of others would themselves
be killed by residual radiation. I ran down the levee toward the stone wall, which
showed the location of the District Headquarters. All roads had disappeared under
the ruins of the city's houses and only tangled electrical wires revealed a road's
direction. I began to walk toward the Castle's stone wall, guided by electrical wires
in the debris. Ashes were still smoldering and small fires burned here and there.
Flesh and bone that had been nearly incinerated could be seen under foot and
sometimes I thought I could hear a groan.

Finally, I reached the burned fields where the military hospital had stood. In
front of the main office lay three corpses. Their flesh had been burnt black beyond
all recognition. In the debris of the smoldering kitchen two dead horses lay under
the rubble. My eyes were drawn to the remaining portions of their shiny black skin
and I wondered about their deaths in the fire. I saw the ruins of the wards with broken iron beds lined up side by side. To my surprise, all their legs were similarly
bent. It showed clearly the enormous strength of the bomb blast. Despite the distance between the hospital and the center of the blast, all the iron frames regardless of their strength had been crushed at one stroke. "What kind of power was
this?" I wondered. It was only at that moment that I grasped the dreadful truth
about the force of the weapon I had seen and heard only the day before. As
I walked among the ruins, I saw human skeletons covered with ash lying on the
melted wire mesh of the broken beds. The crushed frames stood side by side.
There were many bodies whose intestines had been forced out of their rectums.
I thought they had probably died instantly before the fire affected them.

I crossed the lawn and entered the grounds of the army corps that had stood
next to the hospital grounds. At regular intervals there were lines of dead soldiers
in orderly rows. They had clearly been struck down during their morning training
period. The left sides of their faces and left arms were all similarly burned. It was
clear they had died having been hit by the monumental force of the bomb blast.
I quickened my pace and reached the moat above which Hiroshima Castle had
once stood. Lotus leaves had risen to the water's surface and large fish floated with
their bellies up. A number of smaller fish were still alive but their backs had all
been burned a uniform white. The old stone wall of the Castle still stood and its
reflection was visible in the moat. A pine tree with a beautiful spread of branches,
which had been torn apart at its trunk, had fallen into the moat and lay in
a grotesque posture half in, half out of the water. The great tower gate of this
historic castle had vanished. It had completely burned down. A pile of charcoal
flared up here and there at the place where it had stood. Of course, there was no
guard at a gate that no longer existed.

On my way to the ruins of the Castle's tower I saw a man sitting against the
trunk of a big zelcova tree which had stood beside a small pond. He had no clothes

on except for a pair of short pants. His bare skin was strangely white. I realized immediately that he was a foreign prisoner. He must have been a crew member of a plane which had been shot down during the past several months. His hands were tied behind his back. He had also been tied to the trunk of the tree. Upon hearing me approach he turned his boyish face toward me and appealed to me in English. Although I could not understand what he said, I knew from his gestures that he clearly wanted water. I saw the pond. Although covered with slime, its surface dazzled in the noonday light. Momentarily, I felt uneasy. The young man was one of the enemy who had burned and killed so many ordinary people. My hesitation soon faded away. Standing silently behind him I cut the rope with my sword. He could not understand why he had suddenly become free. He crept backward looking at me. Without speaking I pointed at the pond and quickly walked off toward the Castle. In Hiroshima the will to continue the war after that day had simply disappeared. Elsewhere in Japan the fight had somehow kept on. I had impulsively set the prisoner free and when I later reflected upon what I had done it made my heart beat rapidly.

The District Headquarters of the Japanese Army was located in front of the wreckage that had been the Castle's tower. Although it was called DHQ, nothing remained except for the terribly wounded men who had survived. Lying on the ground was a senior officer who was completely swathed in bandages except for his eyes. There were a few other officers, also heavily bandaged, who sat on the ground around him. The unit flag was raised but given the condition of the group it hardly expressed a sense of authority. When I approached the group, a man stood up and reported the actual condition of his corps. He was so badly burned that he could only stand with the greatest difficulty. After he ended his report, the next officer followed. While I listened, I began to realize that no unit contained more than a hundred soldiers. The army of the Hiroshima Division had virtually disappeared. Although I was covered with mud and dust, my relatively normal appearance must have seemed strange because the others were in a dreadful condition with burns and blood. If I remember correctly, the full complement of staff and patients at the Hiroshima Hospital prior to the attack had been approximately 1,500. When I arrived, there were only seventeen who were confirmed to be alive.

It was my turn. As concisely as I could, I reported on the state of affairs at the Hesaka branch hospital. On the pretext of my duty as a doctor, I left the Castle in haste after giving my report. Although I had no intention of feeling guilty, it still pricked my conscience that I had freed the prisoner without permission. After leaving DHQ, I walked straight toward Hiroshima's railroad station. As I walked, I could only see the rubble of tiles and stones that had been the city. At the time of the bombing a group of soldiers who were ill had been at the station. They were among a group of patients who were being transferred from the city. They had arrived much earlier in Hiroshima, where they had moved into the hospital and made it their home. It is sad to think about them, for they were all lepers. Men like these already lived lonely lives in the isolation ward, which was itself still more isolated within the inner part of the infection ward. As a volunteer I had been in charge of their treatment and had been struck by the severity of their lives. Now I found myself walking along a rail line near the station. The sun was blazing. I could see into one of the streetcars where I could recall each face one by one. They had been my patients. I saw a few corpses standing as they hung from the straps in the tram car.

The railroad station had been reduced to burnt embers. The first repairs had begun on the main line. There were many people who had gathered at the station. They had come long distances on foot to search for their relatives. There were many corpses in a large area in front of the station and they gave off the peculiar smell of burnt flesh. I tried to speak to some of the people around me, but no one had any information. I picked up a few grains of sand and put them in my palm. A blast of wind blew them off, one by one, as if each was a symbol of my dear lost people to whom I could not say good-bye.

I BELIEVE IT WAS ABOUT A WEEK AFTER THE BOMBING that an unexpected event happened. Unusual symptoms began to appear in the survivors at Hesaka. The unusual development might have actually started earlier. We thought that perhaps we had failed to notice the unusual changes in the conditions of many patients because so many victims were dying every day from severe burns and other fatal wounds.

Within a week of the bombing most of those patients we had expected to die were all dead. Signs of recovery began to appear little by little in patients who had survived their severe burns. Although the appearance of many of those who recovered was appalling due to their burns, the depth of the burns was comparatively shallow. Therefore, despite outward appearances which might have caused an observer to be pessimistic, we actually began to expect many of the survivors to recover quite rapidly from the worst of their physical trauma.

During this period a field hospital was set up. The main structure consisted of mesh screening supported by poles. The ground inside was covered with straw mats. Medical groups made up of personnel sent from military hospitals in every district took charge of all the patients, including those in the various farmers' houses that we had used as wards. The Director of the Hiroshima Hospital, who had been away at the time of the attack, had returned and the hospital was beginning to recover its various functions. However, the number of medical technicians was still inadequate for the mass of patients. Therefore, the walking wounded helped as did the women's club. The doctor's wife whose breast wound had been sutured was now fully active. Her infant was being cared for by an older woman while she worked among the wounded.

Our principal task was to treat patients mainly for burns and blast wounds. We experienced few serious infections in spite of insufficient treatment and imperfect sterilization. A large number of flies flocked to the wounds of severely injured victims who were unable to move. Large white maggots crowded into their eyes, ears, and noses. It was strange but we were actually helped by the maggots, which ate all the necrotic tissue and thus cleaned the wounds.

It was just at the point when we thought we were beginning to make some headway that the unusual development occurred. A report from a nurse suddenly raised the curtain on a serious affair which started us upon a restless search for a solution to a problem which we had never before seen. The nurse described how some patients had experienced sudden attacks of high fever which had risen above forty degrees Celsius. We ran to her unit in a hurry. The patients were sweating profusely. Their tonsils had also become necrotic. We were confused by the severity, the suddenness and the violence of their symptoms. And, then they began to bleed from their mucous membranes and soon spat up quantities of blood.

The bleeding was sudden and violent. Although emergency transfusions and infusions of Riger's solution were given, the number of seriously afflicted patients continued to increase. All at once the new symptoms took hold of entire groups of survivors. In fact, we initially thought that this was a form of typhoid or dysentery. Of course, clotting agents and homeostatic medicines were used, but they had no real effect except to ease our own minds and give us a sense that we were doing everything we possibly could. It was also at this time that an uncanny form of depilation, or hair loss, began among the survivors. When patients raised their hands to their heads while struggling with pain, their hair would fall out with a mere touch of the fingers. Quite soon their heads appeared as if they had been shaven. Experiencing severe symptoms of fever, throat pain, bleeding and depilation, the survivors fell into a dangerous condition within an hour of the onset. Very few patients who came down with these sudden symptoms escaped death despite all our efforts with Riger's solution and even blood transfusions.

The survivors seemed to fall ill in groups of seven or eight. These same groups appeared to die together. As I look back on it now, those who were irradiated with the same dose of radiation at the same distance from the epicenter fell ill simultaneously and died together. They did nothing except obey the laws of nuclear physics, just like irradiated experimental animals. At the time as physicians we could not know that our patients were dying because of an atomic bomb, which could kill them long after the blast. General Headquarters of the Japanese Army had announced that a new and powerful bomb had been used, but we still knew nothing about its radioactive element. We earnestly thought at the time that it must be a form of dysentery that was killing the survivors because intestinal bleeding was so common in the majority of cases.

Under the command of the Director, autopsies were performed in the dead of the night. They were kept secret from the patients and the villagers. It was a rainy and dark night when I laid one of the corpses on a sheet of metal and cut the abdominal skin with a sharp knife. The dead had been piled up in the field waiting for cremation. The Director held an umbrella over me. The purpose of the autopsy was to determine whether or not inflammation had caused the bleeding in the intestines. Under the candlelight I examined the mucous membranes, carefully flushing them with water from a bucket, but no signs of dysentery were found.

Finally, the situation took a new turn when we heard the rumor that the Navy's radio station in Kure had monitored an American radio broadcast stating that an atomic bomb had been used in Hiroshima. We now understood the peculiar syndrome which we had been unable to explain. Our patients were suffering acute radioactive sickness, which was causing a disorder in the organs that made blood for the human body. If we had known these facts earlier, we could not have provided an effective treatment. Some began to say that vitamin-rich persimmon leaves could effectively counter this syndrome. The leaves were instantly gathered and used with great conviction by many survivors. In general, the doctors dismissed this remedy as no more than superstition. However, the treatment actually proved to be effective for many people.

There were some strange cases which could not be explained. Masao Tamura's house was at the corner of an old street in Hakushi-macho which was surrounded by white walls. He led a frugal, lonely life with his wife after his three sons had been sent to the front. On the morning of August 6, while he was having breakfast, his precious teacup was accidentally broken to pieces. He was fond of the cup, which was so unique that he could not bring himself to drink without it. Wearing no clothes except a pair of short pants, he went to the air raid shelter in the garden to take a similar cup from storage. The moment he entered the shelter and closed the thick cover over his head, the bomb exploded. His house collapsed on his wife with a thunderous sound, covering her with glass and blood. Fire broke out here and there and, when he put his head out of the shelter, he saw the flames in clouds of smoke.

He jumped out of the shelter, shouting, "Fire!" He found his wife unconscious and bathed in her own blood. She soon regained consciousness and they ran to make their escape from the fires which were consuming Hakushi-macho. They arrived at the Kanda River. As flames from the burning city were mirrored on its surface, the waters of the river seemed as if they were about to catch fire. They passed a sleepless night as they took refuge half submerged in the river. The next morning, Masao Tamura crossed over the pass toward Hesaka with his wife on his back. She had lost her capacity to go any further. They established themselves in the shed of a farmer's house. By chance, I had lodged at this couple's house after I had returned from my foray into Hiroshima. While I pulled out pieces of glass penetrating his wife's body, I listened to the man's report.

On the fourth day after the bombing, Mr. Tamura borrowed a hoe and a cycle trailer and went back into the city under the burning sun. He was wearing only a pair of short pants. He managed to find his house with great difficulty. Amidst the ruins of his home he uncovered the entrance to the air raid shelter and he returned carrying the family's clothing, bedding, and other belongings on the trailer. Washing off the dust and sweat beside a well in Hesaka, he became aware of several blisters as big as a thumb on both of his kneecaps. Yet, he could not remember anything unusual on his knees when he was sitting on a tree stump that morning having a pipe. Moreover, he had no recollection of having burned himself that day. He felt no pain or itching. And, because he was dead tired, he slept that night ignoring the blisters that had appeared.

The next morning, to his surprise, the bubbles spread out from his ankle to his knee as if he had put a rubber balloon on his legs. An army paramedic who had come to treat Mrs. Tamura removed the secretion in the blister with a syringe remarking that it was strange for sunburn. The edema recurred in short time. Masao Tamura extracted the fluid with a needle by himself. The swelling and removal of fluid continued for four or five days; as often as he removed the fluid, the urticaria recurred like a living thing. The victims who were dying with strange symptoms began to increase in number, and he began to feel uneasy so he asked me to examine him soon. I could not respond to his request because I was hard pressed with dangerously ill patients. One evening, I found some free time and hurried to see him.

When I entered the shed, I saw his wife holding her husband. She was sobbing. Masao Tamura had breathed his last, lying in a pool of blood. At noon that same day I had seen his smile. As he waved I heard him say, "Please drop in on your way home. I will make good tea." After my brief encounter with him, Masao Tamura had returned to the farmer's house and fallen seriously ill. His entire body was covered in sweat and he scratched his neck complaining of pain in his throat. Soon he began to bleed from the nose and passed bloody excrement. "I was in the shelter so I never met with *pika don*," he told his wife. "Yet, even so, my hair!

It's not possible!" (*Pika don* was the name people had given to the atomic bomb.) Beneath his palm, hair fell out as if it had been swept away. Why had Masao Tamura, who did not receive direct radiation in the air raid shelter, still die with the same symptoms as those victims who had been directly irradiated? It would be a long time before we could solve this riddle.

At this juncture, I wish to describe a couple that my uncle knew because their deaths also seemed to be connected to this phenomenon. Yoshio Yamamoto was a businessman. He was forty years old and healthy. On that day, August 6, he had gone fishing in the Ohbatake Channel but had left at midnight. Just before noon on the sixth, he heard that Hiroshima had been attacked and was in flames. The train could not take him as far as Hiroshima. He walked from Hatsukaichi-cho seeing the burning sky of Hiroshima from about ten miles away. When he reached the Hatsukaichi-cho area of Hiroshima where his house had been, the entire area was ablaze. As he struggled to search for his family amidst the flames, someone told him that they had seen a woman resembling his wife at the nearby Nigitsu Shrine. At midnight he found her in the riverbed beneath the shrine. They were glad to be in each other's arms again. The next morning they left Hiroshima to see if they had any surviving relatives in the town of Itsukaidi.

They never reached there and their happiness was soon shattered. First, his wife died on the tenth day after the bombing. Next, to my surprise, Yoshio Yamamoto breathed his last as he followed her to death, apparently due to his overwhelming grief. Yet, much later I heard the actual details of their final hours. It was described to me by the doctor who attended them and felt their last pulse. According to his account, they suffered from high fever, bleeding, necrosis of the tonsils and depilation similar to those who had received direct radiation. Strangely, Mrs. Teruko Yamamoto had neither been burned nor hurt. At the time of the blast she was in an inner room and had not received direct radiation. The doctor was unable to assign a cause to Mr. Yamamoto's death because he had been on a fishing boat in the Ohbatake Channel about forty miles from Hiroshima at the time of the blast.

In speaking of strange deaths, I should tell the story of the young mother who made me pretend to treat her dead baby. About two weeks after that night I found her in the village. She had managed somehow to partially recover and was even helping in the care of other patients. It seemed as if she had overcome her tremendous sorrow. Yet, on her face ugly keloids began to erupt. She thanked me for the kindness I had shown to her lost baby. She did not complain about her loss. I was pleased that she had regained her strength and with her healthy spirit had overcome her grief. But alas, a few days later to my surprise, I heard of her death. Suddenly, she bled from her mouth, nose and rectum. Also, her hair suddenly dropped off and within fifteen minutes of the other symptoms appearing she began running a high fever.

Although the survivors escaped an early death, the approach of death from atomic illness was not slowed. The fire which burned in the crematorium day and night could not keep pace with the number of bodies, which steadily increased. They were laid on the footpath in the rice field and lay silently side-by-side waiting their turn. Earlier we had feared the rapid and seemingly endless increase in survivors arriving at Hesaka. Now there was a rapid decrease. A few were able to seek refuge with their relatives. The number of newly arrived survivors declined within a fortnight, but the dead who could not be numbered still grew. They were changed into an uncanny light smoke and disappeared over the sky of Hesaka.

Toward the end of August it became possible to take patients from Hesaka to hospitals in the San-In District because the Geibi Line was reopened for traffic. The line had been cut off since the bombing. This event cast the whole village into a frenzy of activity. Patients who could walk were able to go home if they went to Matsui City and transferred to another line. Although the Sanyo Line had been reopened two days after the bombing, it was difficult for the wounded to find a seat on the train. The war had now ended and the trains were already filled with soldiers who had been demobilized in every district.

One morning at seven o'clock a group of survivors was gathered at the local railway station to await the train. I went to the station to bid them good-bye. Some were leaning on their staffs and others were holding onto the shoulders of friends they had made while lying on the footpaths in the rice fields. They all felt relieved to be alive and were anticipating the joy of seeing their families. Among them was a couple I knew. He was a sergeant-major and was one of my friends. He had brought his fiancee to Hiroshima from his native village and they were happily married three days before the bombing. On that morning they were both seriously wounded. The sergeant was on his way to DHQ while his wife had been at home in her kitchen. Fortunately, they did not die and escaped to Hesaka separately where they lay on the ground of the primary school.

Without knowledge of each other they were brought together when the patients who lay between them died and were carried out of the school. Initially, they were not aware of one another because their faces had been cruelly burned. However, it was not long before they recognized each other's voices. They were overjoyed at their chance meeting and cried in each other's arms. This heart-warming episode was known to all the patients and villagers at once. It was a topic which gave joy and the hope of living to people who were tortured with hellish pain. Having been encouraged by all the well-wishers and fellow sufferers in the village, it appeared that their physical strength was recovering day by day except for the ugly keloid scars. Eventually, they were able to help us treat other patients.

The sergeant came to me with his wife and expressed thanks for my treatment. His wife was neatly dressed. The clothing was a parting gift from a villager. He lowered his head to me many times saying, "I am going to work to grow rice with all my might and mind." As he was about to go out through the door, he stumbled against the threshold. Suddenly, he knelt down holding his mouth with his hand. Blood flowed between his fingers. This incident occurred in the wink of an eye. I was filled with pity as I saw his wife holding onto her husband as he was carried out on a bloody stretcher. He collapsed on the bed where he was placed and began to run a fever. Whenever he tore at his hair, it fell out. His wife, astounded and stricken, was crying and clinging to her husband. A few minutes later, her tears were replaced by blood, too, and the same fate befell her hair. Despite our efforts to nurse the couple through the night, the sergeant took his last breath the next morning and his wife soon followed in the steps of her husband.

It was not the only tragedy which happened that morning at the station. The train came into the station slowly, trailing white smoke behind it. The people who were waiting patiently began to board the train with a great joy. Suddenly, a shrill voice cried out from behind the crowd. A middle-aged woman, who said she was going back home to Toyana, fell down on the platform. As if it were a signal, others among those who had already entered the train began to experience pain and high fever. The whole platform became a place of utter confusion. Since the schedule had to be maintained, the unfortunate patients were left in the care of a rescue party as the train started for the north, making the mountainside echo with its piercing whistle. In all, six patients, including the sergeant and his bride, died among those who on that day had been happily looking forward to their return home.

Most of the survivors left Hesaka with the next three trains. Some went to the hospital in the San-In District, some went home, and some had to go to distant places to find relatives in spite of the fact that they had been born in Hiroshima. But their homes and families in Hiroshima had disappeared in a single moment. We do not know what happened to those who departed without incident.

Translated and Edited by Fumiko Nishizaki and Lawrence Lifschultz

THE
UNSURRENDERED
PEOPLE

Kenzaburo Oé

EW PEOPLE TODAY VIEW THE WORLD in terms of a dualism of good and evil. Certainly it is no longer fashionable to do so. But, all of a sudden one summer, an absolute evil intruded into the lives and consciousness of the A-bomb victims. To counter that absolute evil, it became necessary to have an absolute good in order to recover a human balance in the world and to persevere in resisting that evil. From the instant the atomic bomb exploded, it became the symbol of all human evil; it was a savagely primitive demon and a most modern curse. The attempt to accord it positive value as a means of ending the war quickly did not, however, bring peace even to the minds of all the airmen who carried out the atomic attack. The atomic bomb embodied the absolute evil of war, transcending lesser distinctions such as Japanese or Allies, attacker or attacked.

Even while the smoke still rose from the wasteland of total destruction, human goodwill began to go into action as people made their first moves toward recovery and restoration. This action was seen both in the injured victims' will to live and in the efforts of doctors who worked, in a virtual vacuum of supplies and support systems, to treat the victims. Initiated soon that summer morning by the people in Hiroshima, the acts of goodwill were essential to resisting that ultimate thrust of accumulated science which produced the atomic bomb. If one believes that there is some kind of human harmony or order in this world, then he must also believe that the efforts of the Hiroshima doctors were somehow sufficient to cope with the demonic aftermath of the atomic disaster.

For my part, I have a kind of nightmare about trusting in human strength, or in humanism; it is a nightmare about a particular kind of trust in human capability. Toward this kind of humanism (and it is nothing more than a kind of humanism), I have a strong antipathy; so much so that I cannot help thinking about it from time to time. My nightmare stems from a suspicion that a certain "trust in human strength," or "humanism," flashed across the minds of the American intellectuals who decided upon the project that concluded with the dropping of the atomic bomb on Hiroshima. That "humanism" ran as follows: If this absolutely lethal bomb is dropped on Hiroshima, a scientifically predictable hell will result. But the hell will not be so thoroughly disastrous as to wipe out, once and for all, all that is good in human society. That hell will not be so completely beyond the possibility of human recovery that all mankind will despise their humanity merely at the thought of it. It will not be an unrelieved hell with no exit, or so devastatingly evil that President Truman will, throughout his life, be unable to sleep for thinking of it. There are, after all, people in Hiroshima who will make the hell as humane as they possibly can. . . . I suspect that the A-bomb planners thought in such a way; that in making the final decision they trusted too much in the enemy's own human strength to cope with the hell that would follow the dropping of the atomic bomb. If so, theirs was a most paradoxical humanism.

Suppose that the atomic bomb had been dropped, say, on Leopoldville in the Congo, instead of on Hiroshima. Initially, a huge number of people would have died instantly; then wounded survivors, forced to accept total surrender, would have continued to die for many months to come. Epidemics would have spread, and pests would have proliferated in the desolate ruins. The city would have become a wasteland where human beings perished without cease or succor. There would have been no one to dispose of the dead. And when the victor would come in to investigate the damage—after the threat of residual radiation had passed—they would have experienced the worst nausea ever. Some of them would never be sane, normal persons again. One whole city would have been rendered as deadly as a huge death chamber in a Nazi concentration camp. All the people would have been doomed in death, with no sign of hope to be found. . . . Such a scenario is shocking to even the toughest mind. Unless some slave driver's descendant had been available to make the decision, the dropping of an atomic bomb on Leopoldville would have been postponed without setting a future date.

What actually happened in Hiroshima when the atomic bomb was in fact dropped was not quite as horrible as the preceding scenario. For one thing, the people who survived in Hiroshima made no particular effort to impress on those who dropped the bomb what a dreadful thing they had done. Even though the city was utterly devastated and had become a vast, ugly death chamber, the Hiroshima survivors first began struggling to recover and rebuild. They did so, of course, for their own sakes; but doing so served also to lessen the burden on the consciences of those who had dropped the atomic bomb.

The recovery effort has continued for two decades, and continues even now. The fact that a girl with leukemia goes on suffering all her life, not committing suicide, surely lessens—by just one person's portion—the A-bomb droppers' burden of conscience.

It is quite abnormal that people in one city should decide to drop an atomic bomb on people in another city. The scientists involved cannot possibly have lacked the ability to imagine the hell that would issue from the explosion. The decision, nevertheless, was made. I presume that it was done on the basis of some calculation of a built-in harmony by virtue of which, if the incredibly destructive bomb were dropped, the greatest effort in history would be made to counterbalance the totality of the enormous evil to follow. The inhumane damage caused by this demonic weapon would be mitigated by the humane efforts of those struggling to find what hope they could in the desperate situation.

The notion of "balancing" also reflects a "confidence in human strength," itself a reflection of confidence in the strength of humanism. But it is the attacking wolf's confidence in the scapegoat's ability to set things straight after the pitiless damage is done. This is the gruesome nightmare I have about humanism. Perhaps it is no more than an overanxious delusion of mine.

I think of the patience of the A-bomb victims quietly awaiting their turns in the waiting room of the Atomic Bomb Casualty Commission on the top of Hijiyama hill. At least it is true that their stoicism greatly reduces the emotional burden of the American doctors working there.

I have little knowledge of the Bible. It seems to me, though, that when God made the rain fall for forty days and nights, he fully trusted that Noah would rebuild human society after the Great Flood ended. If Noah had been a lazy man, or a hysterical man given to despair, then there would have been great consternation in God's heaven. Fortunately, Noah had the needed will and ability, so the deluge played its part within God's plan for man, without playing the tyrant beyond God's expectations. Did God, too, count on a built-in harmony of "balancing out?" (And if so, does God not seem rather vicious?)

The atomic destruction of Hiroshima was the worst "deluge" of the twentieth century. The people of Hiroshima went to work at once to restore human society in the aftermath of this great atomic "flood." They were concerned to salvage their own lives, but in the process they also salvaged the souls of the people who had brought the atomic bomb. This Great Flood of the present age is a kind of Universal Deluge which, instead of receding, has become frozen; and we cannot foretell when it will thaw and flow away. To change the metaphor, t he twentieth century has become afflicted with a cancer—the possession of nuclear weapons by various nations—for which there is no known cure. And the souls salvaged by the people of Hiroshima are the souls of all human beings alive today.

The immediate action taken by the doctors of Hiroshima soon after the great disaster was a brilliant and impressive performance, though one hindered by enormous difficulties. One of the research projects that they conducted, however, involved some fearsome implications. I regard the questionnaire used in this project as the most morally ominous to appear so far in post-war Japan. The questions were put in a casual, modest, and even business-like manner; even so, the questions involved, by implication, a harsh accusation.

The questionnaire (only half a sheet of paper) was distributed in 1958 by the Hiroshima City Medical Association (HCMA) to its members who were surviving A-bomb victims. The replies were compiled with the following prefatory remark: "We respectfully express our condolences to the families of those who unfortunately died after having answered the questions." The compiled results were printed and inserted in the "Hiroshima A-bomb Medical Care History." [1] The print however, is very unclear (the editors apparently did not recognize the terrible implications of the questions). So far as I could make out (using a magnifying lens), the questions were as follows:

1. Where were you at the time of the atomic bombing (8:15 A.M., August 6, 1945)?
   In military service.
   At an evacuation site [i.e. outside Hiroshima]
   In Hiroshima City
2. Did you participate in relief activity following the bombing? If so, please give the place and period of time of your participation.
   Place:
   Period:

3. Did you receive any injury caused by the atomic bomb (e.g. external wound, burn, serious symptoms, etc.)? If so, please specify.
4. Please give the name(s) of any other doctor(s) who participated in post-bombing relief activity.

No doubt the HCMA members receiving the questionnaire felt compelled to indicate frankly whether they fulfilled their responsibilities at that time of extensive, urgent need. If there were any doctors who, though exposed to the bomb, were not directly hurt yet fled Hiroshima and did not take an active part in relief of the victims, they must have felt, when they received this questionnaire, as if they had been stabbed by a sharp knife. If the awesome impact of the bombing had robbed any Hiroshima doctor of all desire to engage in rescue work, it would not have been, humanly speaking, particularly abnormal. But after receiving the questionnaire, such a doctor could hardly have slept soundly.

In any case, the questionnaire was distributed, and the doctors responded frankly. Let me quote some sample answers (the parenthetical note gives the respondent's address and distance from the hypocenter at bombing time.)

> *Nobuo Satake*, deceased. (Fujimicho 2-chome; 1.1 km) Was at Fujimicho 2-chome at bombing time. Received an external wound on the head. Because he had practiced part-time for years, he continued to give medical treatment from that day as necessary for the relief of personnel in the clothing depot. But, on September 7, his wife died with radiation symptoms; and from about September 10, he also developed multiple radiation symptoms (e.g. loss of hair, subcutaneous hemorrhage, fever), and was compelled to cease giving emergency aid. His radiation symptoms continued for about three weeks afterward.
>
> *Takeharu Tsuchiya*, deceased. (Sendamachi 1-chome; 1.5 km) Was at home at bombing time. Suffered slight head lacerations. As there were injured persons in his family, he went with his family to a private house near the armory; but he was forced to go to the armory and engage in aid there, with the late Hideo Yuki and others, until the end of the war. He was then sent to Hesaka village and till October served in a first-aid station set up there by Hiroshima City.
>
> *Sadaji Yonezawa* (Funairi Honmachi; 1.4 km) Was at Funairi Honmachi at bombing time. Suffered cuts on the back of both hands, on the chest, and on the legs. From August 6 to August 8 he took charge of first aid in Funairi Public School, along with another doctor, Hideo Furusawa. (Ten days after joining the first-aid unit, he died with radiation symptoms.)
>
> *Kunitami Kunitomo*, deceased. (Hakushima-kukencho; 1.7 km) Was at home at bombing time. Was buried under his house (the entire house and all furnishings were burned) but crawled out and escaped to the riverside behind his home, where he spent the night. From the following day (August 7), still wearing a bloody shirt, he engaged in aid to injured victims in the first-aid station at Kanda Bridge. About four months later, he moved to Etajima

[an island in Hiroshima Bay]. Besides his initial injuries, other
symptoms subsequently appeared: general fatigue, loss of appetite,
loss of hair and intense itching all over the body. From spring in
1948, reddish-purple eczema and skin ulcers appeared all over his
body; these symptoms were treated variously. He finally died with
radiation symptoms in March 1949. (Information supplied by
his family.)

As is clear from these examples, the doctors in Hiroshima joined in medical
relief at once, despite their own injuries. The doctors themselves, like the patients
who suffered in their arms, did not know the true cause of the shocking symptoms
and the terrible pain; they shared the same strong anxiety with their patients. What
it was like at the relief sites can be imagined from the following excerpt from the
memoirs of Dr. Yoshimasa Matsusaka, then a senior member of the Hiroshima
Prefecture Medical Association.

I had barely escaped death but thought that I must try to take care of
the helplessly injured citizens. As I could not walk, I had my son
(a medical student at the time) carry me on his back to the East
Police Station and bring out a chair from the station for me to sit on.
Then he fixed the rising-sun flag to a pole at our impromptu relief
site. We then began activity with the cooperation of my three
nurses and of those in the neighborhood capable of helping. (When
taking refuge from the bombed area, my family had packed a suitcase
with a volunteer guard uniform, a fire helmet, a watch, two thousand
yen, a par of *tabi* [split-toe Japanese socks], and a rising-sun flag;
these items were immediately useful.)

Although it was called medical aid, all of the stored medical supplies had been burned. In the police station there was only a little oil
and mercurochrome, so of necessity I could only apply the oil to the
burns and the mercurochrome to the open wounds of the many
injured people who gathered there. To help revive the unconscious,
we used some whiskey which I got from the police chief, Mr. Tanabe.
I realized that the main thing I could do was to encourage the injured
patients, and having a doctor on hand was surely a psychological
stimulant for the casualties. While eagerly awaiting the coming of a
relief team, I used up all the oil from the police station on the many
burns and wounds.

According to the "Hiroshima A-bomb Medical Care History," there were 298
doctors in the city of Hiroshima at the time of the bombing. All doctors were forbidden by the Air Defense Rescue Ordinance (1943) to evacuate to places outside
the city. This ordinance applied to dentists, pharmacists, nurses, midwives, and
public health nurses as well. That is, they were forced to stay in the city; but after
the bombing, they willingly devoted themselves to relief activity. Could it be that
those who sent the questionnaire to surviving doctors did not need to worry about
whether the questions were too blunt or insensitive because the senders, too, had
taken an active part in relief work and knew about—because they had personally
witnessed—the devoted relief activities of their fellow doctors?

437

Sixty of the Hiroshima doctors were killed instantly by the atomic bomb. Among surviving medical personnel, 28 doctors, 20 dentists, 28 pharmacists, and 130 nurses were able to undertake relief work in a healthy condition; and as indicated by the questionnaire samples, many doctors engaged in emergency efforts despite their own serious injuries. The numbers needing treatment, however, soon swelled to more than one hundred thousand in the city alone [and over a hundred thousand more had taken refuge outside the city]. If medical personnel ever had reason to become exhausted and fall completely into despair, the handful of doctors and their colleagues trying to cope with massive need in desolated Hiroshima were such a group. In fact, one young dentist did commit suicide in despair. He had joined in the rescue work even though he had suffered fractures in both hands and burns on half his body. After overworking himself, he suffered a "nervous break-down." Was this not a quite normal condition, given his experience and exhaustion? He had asked an older doctor why the people of Hiroshima still had to suffer so much even after the war had ended—and, of course, there was no adequate reply to such a question. Thirty minutes after the discussion ended, the young dentist strung a rope from a bolt jutting out from a broken wall and hanged himself. He realized that not only were people suffering now that the war had ended but also that they would continue to suffer for many years to come. A different kind of tragic battle was just beginning and would go on affecting later generations for decades. It was too much; in despair he killed himself. This young man's imagination was extremely human; but the strain of what he foresaw was more than he could bear. Only when we appreciate the tragic but by no means unnatural fate of this young dentist can we fully appreciate the remarkable efforts of the Hiroshima doctors "who did not commit suicide in spite of everything." A handful of doctors, some of them injured and all surrounded by a city full of casualties, had the brute courage to care for over a hundred thousand injured people with only oil and mercurochrome. The very recklessness of the doctors' courage was the first sign of hope in Hiroshima follow- ing the Great Flood of atomic destruction.

TWENTIETH-CENTURY LITERATURE has dealt with a variety of extreme situations, most of which are concerned with the evil found in man or in the universe. If the word "evil" sounds too moralistic, it may be replaced with "absur- dity." But in the various extreme situations—wars, storms, floods, pestilence— there is usually some sign of hope and recovery. These signs are found not in the fearful crisis dimensions of extremity but, rather, in the human goodwill and in the order and meaning that appear implicitly in the faint light of everyday life. A plague that ravages a city in North Africa, for example, appears as an abnormal phenomenon; but the doctors and citizens who struggle against it rely on their normal everyday human traits such as mechanical repetition, routine habits, and even patient endurance of tedium.

If a person is so clear-eyed as to see a crisis in its totality, he cannot avoid falling into despair. Only the person with duller vision, who sees a crisis as part of ongoing life, can possibly cope with it. It is precisely the "dullness," the restricted vision, that permits one to act with reckless human courage in the face of crisis, without succumbing to despair. The lesser vision is backed by patience and, in fact, is capable of penetrating insight into the nature of a crisis.

Immediately after the atomic bombing in Hiroshima, it is recorded, a certain prophetic voice said that no grass would grow in Hiroshima's soil for seventy-five years. Was it the voice of a foolish prophet who made a hasty mistake? Hardly. It was the voice of one making a forthright observation of a crisis situation. The prophecy soon proved false when late summer rains washed the wasted land and urged it to new growth. But was not the true damage done at a deeper level? I remember the strong, physical nausea I felt when, through a microscope, I saw the magnified leaf cells of a specimen of *Veronica persica Poir*,[2] the cells were slightly crooked in an unspeakably ugly way. I wonder whether all plants that now grow green in Hiroshima may not have received the same fatal damage.

There is no way of keeping one's balance in daily life and not be overwhelmed by crises except to believe in the green grass if it sprouts from the scorched earth before our very eyes, and thus not indulge in desperate imaginings so long as nothing abnormal happens. This is the only truly human way of living in Hiroshima. No one would continue indefinitely to make one effort after another if there were absolutely no hope for several decades that the grass would grow green again; but human beings cannot help hoping, at least for a while, that the grass will grow.

It takes a person of great care and insight to watch for any abnormality in the green grass even while it grows abundantly and healthily. A person, that is, who is humanist in the truest sense—neither too wildly desperate nor too vainly hopeful. Such genuine humanists were definitely needed in Hiroshima in the summer of 1945. Fortunately, there were such people in Hiroshima at the time; and they were the first cause for hope of survival in the midst of the most desolate wasteland of human experience.

When the young dentist agonized, "Why must the Hiroshima people suffer even after the war's end?" (and thereby marked the onset of another cruel battle), the older doctor remained silent. Even if the young man had shouted his question loud enough to be heard around the world, none of us could have answered him. His query merely voiced an absurdity for which no one has the answer. So, the old doctor kept quiet. He was busy with relief work and, naturally, overworked. Thirty minutes later the young man hanged himself, perhaps because he realized that the old doctor's silence was not just that of one individual, but of all human beings. No one could have prevented so desperate a man, with so absurd a question, from committing suicide. Hence, he hanged himself. The old doctor survived and continued his relief work, and he became known as the doctor with dull but daring eyes, a man who never succumbed to despair.

That is not to say that the old doctor never uttered a word of despair in his heart. He may well have been seized with a sense of despair heavier than the young man's; but he did not surrender to it. Indeed, he had neither the freedom to surrender nor the time for suicide. With what a bitter, grief-stricken heart he took down the lifeless body of the young dentist from the broken wall—the corpse of his young co-worker whose fatal affliction was mental, not physical, despite his fractured hands and half-burnt body. Each evening the bodies of the dead were piled up in the hospital yard and burned. Perhaps the old man himself had to put the young man's body on the great heap of corpses. Surely an absurd question still lingered in his bitter, heavy heart: "Why did the Hiroshima people still suffer so, even after the war had ended?" Yet, for twenty years he never surrendered; he simply could not.

The old doctor, Fumio Shigeto, could have been overwhelmed by a despair far heavier than that of the young dentist, for he came to know concretely and increasingly what the young man had felt and vaguely feared.

Dr. Shigeto had arrived at the Hiroshima Red Cross Hospital just a week before the atomic disaster occurred. But that unprecedented event linked him to Hiroshima for life and made him a genuine Hiroshima man. Following the explosion, the first thing the doctor did, after getting back on his feet with a bloody head at the east entrance of Hiroshima Railroad Station, was to run through the utterly destroyed and still flaming streets to the Red Cross Hospital, closer than the railroad station to the central bombed area. At first, complete silence hovered over everything there. Then, suddenly, fierce cries filled the city, and these cries never ceased during the rescue activity of the doctor and his colleagues at the Red Cross Hospital. Soon the dead bodies piled up in the hospital yard began to emit a relentless foul odor.

Give Me Water
Give me water!
Oh! Give me water to drink!
Let me have some!
I want rather to die—
To die!
Oh!
Help me, oh, help me!
Water!
A bit of water!
I beg you!
Won't anyone?
Oh–Oh–Oh–Oh!
Oh–Oh–Oh–Oh!
The heaven split;
The streets are gone;
The river,
The river flowing on!
Oh–Oh–Oh–Oh!
Oh–Oh–Oh–Oh!
Night!
Night coming on
To these eyes parched and sore;
To these lips inflamed.
Ah! The moaning of a man,
Of a man
Reeling,
Whose face is
Scorched, smarting;
The ruined face of man!
　　　　　　　—TAMIKI HARA

Source: *Give Me Water—Testimonies of Hiroshima and Nagasaki,* edited by A Citizens' Group to Convey Testimonies of Hiroshima and Nagasaki, 1972.

While persevering in rescue work, Dr. Shigeto approached the moment of awesome reality when the nature of the overwhelming, grotesque explosion would be revealed to him. Many others in Hiroshima were on the threshold of the same critical moment. A medical scholar who from his days as an unpaid junior assistant in Kyushu Imperial University's department of internal medicine had been interested in radiology, he discovered that hermetically sealed X-ray film stored in the Red Cross Hospital had been exposed [by radiation] and that camera film with which he had tried to photograph the A-bomb victims' injuries had likewise been rendered useless. When investigating the city streets, he picked up tiles on which the outline of a shepherd's purse [herb] had been imprinted. In his mind, the horrifying truth about the bomb's radioactivity began to take shape clearly. Three weeks later atomic scientists from Tokyo confirmed the nature of the bomb—an atomic bomb made with uranium (U-235).[3]

Confirmation of the bomb's nature, however, by no means resolved the immense difficulty facing the doctors: how to treat the various radiation injuries. The atomic scientists merely confirmed for Dr. Shigeto and others that the "enemy" they struggled with was the worst and strongest ever encountered. And all they had to treat the massive, complex injuries with were surgical instruments and injections of camphor and vitamins.

How did the doctors cope with what they increasingly recognized as acute radiation symptoms? Dr. Tsurayuki Asakawa, chief of internal medicine in Hiroshima Red Cross Hospital at the time, speaks very frankly about this predicament, as recorded in the "Hiroshima A-bomb Medical Care History":

> People with no discernible injuries came and said that they felt listless, though they did not know why. In time, they developed nosebleeds, bloody stools, and subcutaneous hemorrhages; then they would die. At first, we did not know the cause of death. As it was common sense when an illness is not clearly diagnosed to check the patient's blood, I went to the hospital basement to fetch blood analysis equipment; and when I examined the blood cells, I was astonished. It was, I realized, only natural that the patients had died, for their white cell counts were extremely low. They could not possibly have lived.

I am impressed by this physician's "common sense," by his perseverance in a crisis situation. There was however, no medicine available to treat what he discovered. For nosebleeds, he could not insert a pressure tampon into the nose; the doctor did not know clearly the cause of the nosebleeds. By the time the bleeding began, the A-bomb victims were already on the verge of death.

By the winter following the atomic bombing, most of the patients with acute radiation symptoms had died; and, at least outwardly, the critical stage of radiation illness had passed. In the struggle against the worst-ever attack on human life, mankind was defeated before the battle had hardly begun. The doctors faced such severe handicaps that they were in a losing position from the outset. Even so, Dr. Shigeto and his colleagues never surrendered. They simply could not, for leukemia—the most dreadful aspect of the enemy—was beginning to rear its ugly head.

Although the enemy's overwhelming power became unmistakably clearer, the doctors did not surrender. More precisely, they simply refused to surrender. There was nothing whatsoever in the situation that encouraged them not to give up; they simply refused to do so.

If they had surrendered, the "Hiroshima A-bomb Medical Care History" would have concluded with an account of defeat after the first few pages. Neither did the occupation forces that came into Hiroshima soon after the bombing know how to cope with the enormous monster they themselves had released. They sought clues by setting up the Atomic Bomb Casualty Commission atop Hijiyama hill and by undertaking medical examinations. But treatment of the stricken people depended entirely upon the human efforts of the surviving doctors in the A-bomb–assaulted city. And the doctors never surrendered, even though enveloped by darkness more real and urgent than that which drove the young dentist to suicide. For two decades they could not, they simply would not, give up. The atomic monster increasingly exhibited its painful, ominous powers—always superior to the strength of the doctors. But Dr. Shigeto and his colleagues stood fast.

Even now there is no evidence that the human goodness which served the hapless victims has gained the upper hand over the human evil which produced the atomic bombs. People who believe, however, that in this world human order and harmony eventually recover from extremity, will perhaps take courage from the twenty-year struggle of the Hiroshima doctors—even though it cannot yet be said that they have won their battle.

NOTES

1. *Hiroshima Genbaku Iryoshi* 1961. Published by Hiroshima Genbaku Shogai Taisaku Kyogikai [Hiroshima A-bomb Casualty Council], Hiroshima.

2. Malformed flowers of *Veronica persica Poir* are shown in figure 5.5 of *Hiroshima and Nagasaki: The Physical, Medical, and Social Effects of the Atomic Bombings* (Tokyo/New York, 1981), p.85.

3. Scientists from the Technology Agency, the Imperial Headquarters, the army and navy, Kyoto and Osaka imperial universities, and the Institute for Physical and Chemical Research in Tokyo entered Hiroshima soon after the atomic bombings. At a joint army–navy meeting held August 10 under the auspices of the Imperial Headquarters, it was first confirmed that the bombs were atomic bombs. Various random measurements for radioactivity, however, indicated the need for systematic measurement, which was not begun until September 1945. *Hiroshima and Nagasaki*, pp. 503-504.

SUMMER

FLOWER

Tamiki Hara

I WENT DOWNTOWN AND BOUGHT SOME FLOWERS, thinking I would visit the grave of my wife. In my pocket I had a bundle of incense sticks that I had taken from the Buddhist altar in my home. August 15 would be the first anniversary for the soul of my wife, but it was doubtful whether my native town would survive until then. Although most factories were closed that day due to electric power rationing, there was no one to be seen except myself—walking along the street with flowers, in the early morning. I did not know the name of the flowers, but they looked like a summer variety with the rustic beauty of their tiny yellow petals.

As I sprayed water over the gravestone exposed to the scorching heat of the sun, divided the flowers into two bunches and put them in the vases on either side, the grave appeared rather refreshed, and I gazed at the flowers and the stone for a while. Underneath the grave were buried not only the ashes of my wife but also those of my parents. After burning the incense sticks that I had brought and making a bow, I drank out of the well beside the grave. Then I went home by way of Nigitsu Park. The scent of the incense remained in my pocket throughout that day and the next. It was on the third day after my visit to the grave that the bomb was dropped.

My life was saved because I was in the bathroom. On the morning of August 6, I had gotten up around eight o'clock. The air-raid alarm had sounded twice the night before and nothing had happened, so that before dawn I had taken off my clothes and slept in my night robe, which I had not put on for a long time. Such being the case, I had on only my shorts when I got up. My younger sister, when she saw me, complained of my rising late, but I went into the bathroom without replying.

I do not remember how many seconds passed after that. All of a sudden, a powerful blow struck me and darkness fell before my eyes. Involuntarily I shouted and held my hands over my head. Aside from the sound of something like the crashing of a storm, I could not tell what it was in the complete darkness. I groped for the door, opened it, and found the veranda. Until then, I had been hearing my own voice exclaiming "Wah!" amid the rushing sounds, agonized at not being able to see. But after I came out to the veranda, the scene of destruction gradually loomed in the dusk before my eyes and I became clearly conscious.

It looked like an episode from a loathsome dream. At first, when the blow struck my head, and I lost my sight, I knew that I had not been killed. Then I became angry, thinking that things had become very troublesome. And my own shouts sounded almost like the voice of somebody else. But when I could see, vaguely as it was, the things around me, I felt as if I were standing stage center in a tragic play. Certainly I had beheld such a scene in a movie. Beyond the clouds of dust, patches of blue sky began to come into view. Light came in through holes in the walls and from other unexpected directions. As I walked gingerly on the boards where the tatami flooring had been blown off, my sister came rushing toward me. "You weren't hurt? You weren't hurt? Are you all right? Your eyes are bleeding. Go wash right away." She told me that there was still water running in the kitchen scullery.

Finding myself completely naked, I turned to my sister and asked her, "Can you at least get me something to put on?" She was able to pull out a pair of shorts from the closet that had been saved from destruction. Someone rushed in with a bewildered gesture. His face was smeared in blood. He wore only a shirt. This man was an employee of a nearby factory. Seeing me, he said, "It's lucky you were saved." Then he bustled away, muttering, "Telephone . . . I have to make a telephone call."

There were crevices everywhere, and the doors, screens, and tatami mats were scattered about. The pillars and doorsills were clearly exposed, and the whole building was filled with a strange silence. Later I was told that most houses were completely destroyed in that area, but my second floor did not give way; even the floorboards remained firm. My father, a painstaking builder, had built our house about forty years before and it had been solidly constructed.

Tramping about over the littered mats and screens, I looked among scattered articles for something to wear. The book which I had left half-read the night before was there on the floor with its pages turned up. The picture frame which had fallen from the beam overhead stood tinged with death in front of the *tokonoma*. I found my canteen quite unexpectedly, and then my hat. Still unable to find my pants, I started looking for something else to cover myself.

K of the factory office appeared on the veranda of the drawing room. Seeing me, he cried in a sad voice, "I'm hurt! Help me!" and dropped down in a heap where he stood. Blood was oozing from his forehead, and his eyes were glistening with tears.

"Where is it?" I asked, and he distorted his pale wrinkled face, saying, "My knees," as he held them with his hand. I gave him a strip of cloth, and I drew over my own legs two pairs of socks, one over the other.

"It's started to smoke. Let's get out of here. Help me get away." K, who was considerably older than I but usually much more vigorous, seemed to be highly disturbed.

Looking out from the veranda, I could see nothing recognizable except the clusters of flattened houses and a ferro-concrete building a little farther away. Beside the toppled-over mud wall there was a tall maple tree whose trunk was torn off halfway up; the twigs had been thrown into the wash basin. Suddenly K stopped by the air–raid shelter, and said, "Why don't we stay here? There's a water tank, besides . . ." When I said, "No, let's go to the river," he asked me wonderingly, "The river? Which direction is the river?"

I took a night robe out of the closet, handed it to him, and tore the shelter curtain. I picked up a cushion, too. When I turned the mat on the veranda, I found my emergency bag. I felt relieved and put the bag on my shoulder. Small red flames rose from the warehouse of the chemical factory next door. We went out over the completely twisted maple.

That tall tree had stood in the corner of the garden for a long time, and had been an object of dreamy imagination in my childhood. Recently I had come back and started living at my own home after a long time, and now I thought it odd that even this tree did not evoke the same old sweet memory. What was strange was that my home town itself had lost its soft natural atmosphere, and I felt it to be something like a composition of cruel, inorganic matter. Every time I went into the drawing room facing the garden, the title, *The Fall of the House of Usher*, spontaneously sprang to my mind.

K and I climbed over the crumbling houses, clearing obstacles from our path, and walked slowly at first. We came to level ground, and knew that we were on the road, where we walked faster down the middle. Suddenly there called a voice from behind a crushed building, crying, "Please!" Turning back, I found that the voice belonged to a woman with a bloodstained face walking toward us. "Help me!" she cried, following us desperately. We had walked on for some time when we passed an old woman who stood in the middle of the path with her legs wide apart. She was crying like a child, "The house is catching fire! The house is catching fire!" Smoke rose here and there from the crumbling houses, and suddenly we came upon a spot where breaths of flame belched furiously.

We passed it running. The road became level again, and we found ourselves at the foot of Sakae Bridge. Here the refugees gathered one after another. Someone who had stationed himself on the bridge cried out: "Those who are strong enough, put out the fire!" I walked toward the grove of Asano Park, and there became separated from K.

The bamboo grove had been mowed down, and a path made through the grove under the tramping feet of refugees. Most of the trees overhead had been torn apart in midair, and this famous old garden on the river was now disfigured with pockmarks and gashes. Beside a hedge was a middle-aged woman, her ample body slumped over limply. Even as I looked, something infectious seemed to emanate from her lifeless face. It was the first such face I had seen. But I was to see many, many more that were more grotesque.

In the grove facing the riverbank I came across a group of students. These girls had escaped from a factory, and all had been injured slightly, but now, trembling from the freshness of the thing that had happened before their very eyes, they chattered excitedly. At that moment my eldest brother appeared. He wore only a shirt, but looked unhurt. He had a beer bottle in one hand. The houses on the other bank of the river had collapsed and were on fire, but the electric poles still stood. Sitting on the narrow road by the riverbank, I felt I was all right now. What had been threatening me, what had been destined to happen, had taken place at last. I could consider myself as one who survived. I have to keep a record of this, I said to myself. But I scarcely knew the truth about the air raid then.

The fire on the opposite bank of the river raged more furiously. The scorching heat reached this side of the river, so that we had to dip the cushion in the rising water and put it over our heads. Then someone shouted, "Air raid! People with white clothing should hide under the trees!" All the people crowded into the heart of the grove.

The sun sent forth its bright rays, and the other side of the grove seemed to be on fire. A hot wind blew overhead, and black smoke was fanned up toward the middle of the river. Then the sky suddenly grew dark, and large drops came down in torrents. The rain reduced the heat momentarily, but soon the sky cleared up again. The fire on the other bank was still burning. Over on this side, my eldest brother, my younger sister, and a couple of people from our neighborhood whose faces I recognized had appeared. We got together and talked about what had happened that morning.

My brother had been seated at a table in his office when a flash of light raced through the garden. The next instant, he was blown some distance from his seat and for a while found himself squirming around under the wreckage of the house. At last he discovered an opening and succeeded in crawling out. From the direction of the factory he could hear the student workers screaming for help, and he went off to do what he could to rescue them.

My sister had seen the flash of light from the entrance hall and had rushed as fast as she could to hide under the stairs. As a result, she had suffered little injury.

Everyone had at first thought that just his own house had been hit by a bomb. But then when they went outside and saw that it was the same everywhere, they were dumb founded. They were also greatly puzzled by the fact that, although the houses and other buildings had all been damaged or destroyed, there didn't seem to be any holes where the bombs had fallen. The air raid warning had been lifted, and shortly after that there had been a big flash of light and a soft hissing sound like magnesium burning. The next they knew everything was turned upside down. It was all like some kind of magical trick, my sister said, trembling with terror.

The fire on the opposite bank had no sooner begun to die down when someone said that the trees in the garden on this side of the river had caught fire. We could see wisps of smoke rising in the sky behind the grove. The water in the river remained at high tide and did not recede.

I walked along a stone embankment down to the water's edge and discovered a large wooden box floating along at my feet, and around it bobbed onions that had spilled out. Pulling the box to me, I took out the onions and handed them to people on the bank. The box had been thrown out of a freight train which had been overturned on the bridge upstream. While I was picking up the onions, there came a voice crying, "Help!" Clinging to a piece of wood, a young girl drifted in the middle of the river, floating at one time and sinking at another. I took a large timber and swam toward her pushing it. Although I had not swum for a long time, I managed to help her more easily than I had expected.

The fire on the opposite bank, which had slackened for a while, had started raging again. This time, murky smoke mingled with the red flames, and as the roiling mass expanded, the heat of the flames seemed to grow more intense with each second. When the fire finally burned itself out, there remained only an empty carcass. It was then that I sensed a wall of air undulating toward us over the water. Tornado! Even as the thought struck me, a blast of wind passed over our heads. The grass and trees around me trembled, and whole trees were plucked out and snatched high into the air. I don't remember exactly what color the air around us was at that time. I think it must have been wrapped in a kind of weird greenish glow, the kind you see in pictures of Hell.

446

When the tornado had passed, the sky showed that evening was near. My second elder brother appeared quite unexpectedly. His shirt was torn in back, and there was a brushing trace the color of thin India ink on his face which later became a suppurating burn. Coming home on business, he had sighted a small airplane in the sky and then three strange flashes. After being thrown on the ground, he had run to rescue his wife and the maid-servant, who were struggling under the collapsed house. He entrusted his two children to the maid and let them escape before him, and then spent much time in saving the old man who lived next door. His wife had been worrying about the children who had gone off with the maid when she heard the maid shouting to her from the opposite bank. The maid said her arms hurt so much she couldn't carry the children any longer and she wanted someone to come and help her right away.

The grove of Asano Park was little by little catching fire. If night came on and the fire reached the part of the grove where we were, we would be in trouble, so we thought we had better cross over to the other bank while it was still light. But where we were there was no boat to ferry us across. My eldest brother and his group decided to go around by way of the bridge, but my second elder brother and I walked upstream, still hoping to find a ferryboat. The sinking sun made everything around us look pale, and both on and beneath the bank there were pale people who cast their sinister shadows on the water. Their faces were so puffy and swollen you could hardly tell whether they were men or women, with eyes that were mere slits and horribly blistered lips. They lay on their sides, their painful limbs exposed, barely breathing. When we passed before them, these strange people spoke to us in faint, gentle voices, "Give us some water."

Someone called me in a sharp, pitiful voice. Below I saw a naked young boy whose lifeless body was completely sunk in the water, and two women squatting on the stone steps less than four feet from the corpse. Their faces were swollen twice their natural size, distorted in an ugly way, and only their scorched rumpled hair showed that they were women. Looking at them, I shuddered rather than felt pity. But the women had noticed me. "That mattress over by those trees is ours. Would you be good enough to bring it over here?" they pleaded.

Looking over at the trees, I saw that there was in fact a mattress there. But a man who looked like he was mortally wounded was lying on it, so there was nothing I could do.

My brother and I found a little raft, untied the rope, and rowed toward the opposite bank of the river. Daylight had already turned dusky when the raft reached the sand beach on the other side, and the area was scattered with wounded townsmen. A soldier who was squatting by the river said to me, "Let me drink some hot water." I had him lean against my shoulder and we walked together. As he staggered on the sand, the soldier muttered, "It's much better to be killed." I made him wait beside the path.

Nearing a water supply station I beheld the large burned head of a human being slowly drinking hot water out of a cup; the enormous face seemed to be made up of black soybeans, and the hair above the ears was burned off in a straight line where the man's cap had not protected it. I filled a cup and took it to the soldier. As I did so, I saw another soldier, badly wounded, down on his knees in the river, bending over and intently lapping up the river water.

People were starting to cook their supper, burning pieces of wood on the sandy beach. For some time now, I had been aware of a girl with a terribly swollen face lying close by my side and begging for water. After a while, it dawned on me that it was the maid from my second elder brother's house, the one who had gone off with the children and had earlier been calling for help. She had just been going out the kitchen door with the baby strapped on her back when the blinding flash had come and her face and hands and breast had been burned. My brother had sent her off ahead of him with the baby and the older girl, but when she got to the bridge, she somehow lost the older girl. Still carrying the baby, she had made her way down here to the riverbed. When the flash came, she had held up her hand to shield her face, and now the hand hurt her so much she felt like tearing it off, she said.

As the tide began to rise, we all moved up the bank. Night had fallen, and a breeze sprang up. It was too cool for us to sleep, and we kept hearing voices here and there crying desperately for water. Nigitsu Park was nearby but it was now wrapped in darkness, and we could see only faintly the broken trees. My brothers lay in a hollow in the ground and I placed myself in another shallow place. Close to me lay three or four wounded schoolgirls. "The grove over there has started burning," someone said. "Don't you think we'd better move away from here?" Getting out of the hollow, I saw flames glaring over the top of the trees ahead of us, but there was no sign of the fire spreading up to our spot.

"Does it look as though the fire is going to come over this way?" a wounded girl asked in a frightened voice. When I assured her it was all right, she said, "I wonder what time it is now. Do you think it's twelve o'clock yet?"

There must still have been an undamaged siren somewhere, for we heard its warning faint in the distance.

"I wish morning would come!" one of the schoolgirls complained.

A chorus of soft voices could be heard calling, "Mother! Father!"

"Does it look as though the fire is coming over this way?" the wounded girl asked again.

From the direction of the riverbed came death cries, in a young voice still strong. "Water! Water! Please! . . . Mother . . . Sister . . . Mitchan! . . ." The agonized words, interspersed with moans and weak gasps of pain, seemed to wrench his whole body. One time when I was little I walked along the embankment here and came to the riverbed to catch fish. The memory of that hot summer day remains strangely vivid in my mind. There was a big billboard stuck up in the sand advertising Lion toothpaste, and every now and then from the direction of the railway bridge came the rumble of a passing train. It was a peaceful scene that now seemed like a dream.

By the time morning came, the voices from the night before had ceased, though the piercing death cries that had wrung my heart still rang in my ears. As the scene gradually brightened, a morning breeze began to blow. My eldest brother and my sister went off in the direction where our house had stood, saying they would make their way from there to the East Parade Ground, having heard that a dispensary had been set up there. My second elder brother and his family started off for the East Parade Ground, too. I was about to set out for the parade ground myself, when a soldier nearby asked if I would take him with me. He was a big man, and he must have been badly wounded, because he hung on my shoulder and dragged his feet gingerly along the ground as though they were broken things. We had to pick our way among formidable obstacles, shattered glass here, corpses there, objects that were still hot and smoldering. By the time we got to

Tokiwa Bridge, the soldier said he was too exhausted to go another step and asked me to leave him there. I did as he told me and went off alone in the direction of Nigitsu Park.

Here and there were houses that had collapsed but had escaped the fire, and everywhere were the scars of that flash of light that had raked over the scene. In an empty lot a crowd of people had gathered. A trickle of water was leaking from the water main. It was there that I chanced to learn that my niece—my second elder brother's child who had gotten separated from the maid yesterday—was safe at the refugee area in the *Tōshōgū* Shrine.

I hurried off to the garden of the shrine, and came on my little niece just as she and her mother had found each other. The day before, after becoming separated from the maid at the bridge, she had gone off with some other people and made her way here. Now, when she caught sight of her mother, the strain was suddenly too much for her and she burst out wailing. Her head was black and painful looking from burns.

A dispensary had been established near the entrance to the *Tōshōgū* Shrine. With each case a policeman formally asked the patient his permanent address and age; and the patient, even after receiving a slip of paper identifying him, still had to wait about an hour in a long row, under the scorching sun. Patients who were able to join that row were more fortunate than the rest. Now someone cried furiously, "Soldier! Soldier! Help me! Soldier!" A horribly burned young girl rolled in anguish on the roadside. And near her was a man in the uniform of an air defense guard, who complained in feeble voice, "Please help me, ah, Nurse, Doctor!" as he laid his head, swollen and bloated with burns, on a stone, and opened his blackened mouth. No one gave heed to him. Policemen, doctors, and nurses came from other towns to help, but they were rather few in number.

The maid from my elder brother's family had come to the dispensary with my brother, and I helped her to join the row of persons awaiting treatment. Her face and hands were getting more and more swollen and she seemed to want to squat on the ground. When her turn finally came and she had finished being treated, we had to look around for some place to rest. Everywhere we looked in the grounds of the shrine there were wounded people, but there was nothing like a tent or a thicket of trees where we could take shelter. Finally we propped some thin pieces of lumber up against the stone fence surrounding the shrine to make a kind of roof and crawled in under them. For the next twenty-four hours, this cramped space was home for the six of us, my second elder brother and his wife, their two girls, the maid and myself.

Right next to us someone had set up a similar kind of shelter where a man moved around briskly on a piece of matting. Presently he struck up a conversation with us. He had no shirt or undershirt, and all that was left of his trousers was a piece around his waist and part of one leg. His arms, his legs and his face were burned. He said he had been on the seventh floor of the Chūgoku Building when the explosion came, and we could see he had been injured in the blast. He must have had great presence of mind, however, as he had asked people to help him and had somehow managed to flee all the way here.

About that time, a young man with a military cadet's belt, his body smeared all over with blood, pushed his way into the man's shelter. The man was incensed. "Here, here! Get out of here! As sore as I am, I'm not going to have you bumping into me! There're any number of other places you can go—why do you want to squeeze in here! Come on now, get out!" he spluttered in a voice like a bark. The blood-smeared youth got to his feet with a dazed look.

A few yards away from us, two schoolgirls lay groaning for water under a cherry tree, faces burned black, their thin shoulders exposed to the scorching sun. They were students of the girls' commercial school who had met the disaster while potato digging in the vicinity. A woman in work trousers whose face had been smoke-dried joined them. Placing her handbag on the ground, she stretched out her legs listlessly, oblivious to the dying girls. The day was drawing to a close. When I thought of spending another night in a place like this, I became strangely uneasy. The second night dragged by. Before dawn some unknown voice took up a Buddhist invocation, a sound suggesting that people were dying all the time. The two commercial students died when the morning sun was high. A policeman, when he had finished examining the girls' bodies lying face down in the ditch, approached the dead woman in work trousers nearby. He opened her handbag and found a savings passbook and public loan bonds in it. She still wore the traveling suit in which she had been struck.

About noon, the air-raid warning sounded again and the roar of planes was heard. Although I had become used to the ugliness and misery around me, my fatigue and hunger became more and more intense. My second elder brother's two sons were off at school in the city when the disaster occurred and we still did not know what had happened to them. People died one after another, and their bodies were left as they were. Men walked restlessly, without hope of assistance.

The desperate clarion call of the bugle came from the parade ground. Meanwhile, my brother's little girls sobbed miserably from their burns and the maid kept constantly begging for water. And then, just as I thought we were coming to the end of our endurance, my eldest brother appeared. He had stopped the previous day at Hatsukaichi, to which his sister-in-law had evacuated, and had hired a wagon. He was here with the wagon now, ready to take us away.

My second elder brother, his family, my sister, who had meanwhile joined us, and I all got in the wagon and we left the *Tōshōgū* Shrine and went toward Nigitsu. As we were going from Shirashima past the entrance of Asano Garden, my second elder brother caught sight of a body in the vacant lot toward the West Parade Ground. It was clothed in yellow pants that were familiar to him. It was Fumihiko, his son. Fluid flowed from a swelling on the boy's breast the size of a fist. His white teeth were dimly visible in his blackened face, and the fingers of both hands were bent inward with the nails boring into the skin. Beside him sprawled the body of a schoolboy and that of a young woman. They lay slightly apart. Both had become rigid in their last positions. My second older brother stripped off Fumihiko's nails and his belt for a keepsake. Placing a name card on him, we left the spot. It was an encounter too sad for tears.

The wagon then passed Kokutaiji Temple and Sumiyoshi Bridge, and came to Koi, giving me an almost full view of the burned sites of the busiest quarters. Amid the vast, silvery expanse of nothingness that lay under the glaring sun, there were the roads, the river, the bridges, and the stark naked, swollen bodies. The limbs of these corpses, which seemed to have become rigid after struggling in their last agony, had a kind of haunting rhythm. In the scattered electric wires and countless wrecks there was embodied a spasmodic design in nothingness. The burnt and toppled streetcar and the horse with its huge belly on the ground gave me the impression of a world described by a Dali surrealist painting. The tall camphor tree in the precincts of Kokutaiji Temple had been felled completely, and the gravestones too were scattered. The Asano Library, with only its outer block left, had been turned into a morgue. The roads were still smoky here and there and were permeated with a cadaverous smell. Somehow it seems that impressions of the scene are more aptly put in *katakana*:*

> *The strange rhythm of the human bodies,*
>   *inflamed and red,*
> *That mingle with the glaring wrecks*
>   *and the cinders of grayish white*
> *In the vast panorama—*
> *Is this all that has happened, or is it*
>   *what could have happened?*
> *Oh, the world stripped of all in an*
>   *instant.*
> *How the swollen belly of the horse*
>   *glares beside the toppled streetcar.*
> *And the stench of the smoldering wires!*

The wagon proceeded along the endless road through the debris. Even on the outskirts of the city, the houses all had collapsed, and it was only after we had passed Kusatsu that we were at last liberated from the shadow of disaster and were greeted by the sight of living green. The appearance of the dragonflies that flitted so swiftly above the emerald rice paddies was touchingly refreshing to my eyes. From here stretched a long, monotonous road to Yawata Village. Night had fallen by the time we reached there, and all was dismally quiet.

The next day, our miserable life—of the aftermath—truly began. The wounded did not recover satisfactorily, and even those who at first had been strong gradually grew weak from lack of food. Our maid's arm suppurated badly, and flies gathered around the burned part, which finally became infested with maggots. No matter how often we sterilized the area, the maggots never ceased to infest the wound. She died a little more than a month later.

Four or five days after we had moved to the village, my nephew, who had been last seen on his way to school, suddenly reappeared. On the morning that he had gone to his school—his building later was to be evacuated—he had seen the flash from inside his classroom. In an instant he hid himself under the desk, and was buried under the falling ceiling, but crawled out through a crevice. There were only four or five boys who had escaped—the rest were killed by the first blow. The survivors ran toward Hiji Hill, and he vomited white fluid on the way. Then he went to the home of one of his friends with whom he had escaped, and there he was sheltered. About a week after his return, my nephew's hair began to fall out, and his nose bled. His doctor declared that his condition was already critical, but my nephew gradually gained his strength again.

My friend N suffered a different experience. He was on his way to visit an evacuated factory, and his train had just entered a tunnel. As the train came out, he

---

Katakana characters are much simpler and starker in appearance than the other forms used in writing Japanese.

saw three parachutes floating down through the air over Hiroshima several miles behind. Arriving at the next station, he was surprised to find that the window glasses were broken. By the time he reached his destination, detailed information already had been circulated. He took the first train back to Hiroshima. Every train that passed was filled with people grotesquely wounded. When he arrived at the town, he could not wait until the fire was quenched, and so he proceeded along the still hot asphalt road.

He went first to the girls' high school where his wife was teaching. On the site of the classrooms lay the bones of the pupils, and on the site of the principal's office lay bones that seemed to have belonged to the principal. Nothing could he identify as the remains of his wife. He hurried back to his own home. Being near Ujina, the house had crumbled without burning. Yet he could not find his wife there either. Then he examined all the bodies lying on the road that led from his home to the girls' school. Most of the bodies were lying on their faces, so that he had to turn them over with his hands in order to examine them. Every woman had been changed miserably, but his wife's body was not there. Finally he wandered around without direction. He saw some ten bodies heaped in a pile in a cistern.

Then there were three bodies that had become rigid as they held a ladder set against the riverbank, and others stood waiting in a row for the bus, the nails of each fastening against the shoulders of the one ahead. The terrible scene of the West Parade Ground was beyond description. There were piles of soldier corpses all around—but the body of his wife was not to be found anywhere.

My friend N visited all the barracks, and looked into the faces of the severely wounded people. Every face was miserable beyond words, but none of the faces was his wife's. After looking for three days and nights at so many charred bodies, dead and living, N at last went back to the burned site of his wife's school.

Translated by George Saito

HIROSHIMA

MEMORIES

Hideko Tamura Snider

TODAY I LIVE IN THE UNITED STATES, where I'm a social worker in the Radiation Oncology Department at the University of Chicago Hospitals. The work is rewarding. Over the decades, the diagnostic and therapeutic uses of ionizing radiation have probably helped millions of people around the world.

But just a few blocks away is a monumental bronze sculpture by Henry Moore. It is called *Nuclear Energy*, and it marks the spot where Enrico Fermi's talented team of Manhattan Project physicists achieved the first self-sustaining chain reaction in December 1942. To me, *Nuclear Energy* terrifyingly resembles a mushroom cloud, and I avoid going near it.

Perhaps that is because I recall a warm sunny day in another city, when I was a child of ten. On that day, August 6 in Hiroshima, the sun and the earth melted together. On that day, many of my relatives and classmates simply disappeared. I would never again see my young cousin Hideyuki, who had been like a brother to me, or Miyoshi, my best friend. And on that day of two suns, my Mama would not come home for lunch.

Tokyo was my home until Japan invaded China. During the war, Papa was drafted into the Imperial Army in 1938. He first served as a private in Northern China; after Pearl Harbor, he became a high-ranking logistics officer based in Hiroshima, his home city. During most of the war, Mama and I lived with Papa's family, the Tamuras, one of the most respected families of the city. Their home—actually, a large and elegant estate on the Ota River, just over a mile from the center of Hiroshima—would be a wartime refuge. The Tamuras would make sure Mama and I were well cared for.

Papa, Jiro Tamura, was the second son of Hidetaro Tamura, the founder of the Tamura cartel, a combine that produced sewing needles and rubber goods. It had branches in China and Manchuria, and employed about 3,000 people. Grandpa Tamura was a kindly man, even in business. Among his workers were handicapped men and women only he would hire. He made sure the job was fitted to their abilities. I especially remember "Ben-san," who had severe curvature of the spine. He had light duties at the factory, and he used to help in the gardens at the Tamura estate. I also remember the time a man who had become unhappy at work climbed to the top of a sixty-foot chimney. Grandfather shut down the factory so the man would not be harmed by heat and smoke, and he waited for the man to tire and come down. Grandfather died of a heart attack before the end of the war. Perhaps that was not such a sad thing.

My Papa had thick, dark brown, curly hair, quite like the painter he had always wanted to be. He was of average height, but wiry and powerful. His sturdy shoulders carried me as we strolled among the *Yomise* vendors after supper. During the week, he worked for Nissan Motors in Tokyo as a salesman. On weekends, he painted. In earlier years, he had wanted to attend the Tokyo Art Institute rather than law school. But his parents did not permit him to do that. "Art" was not a substantial profession for a Tamura man.

My mother, Kimiko Kamiya, was "Mama" to me, never *oka-san* (mother). She was slender and tall. Her large, expressive eyes, long thick eyelashes, and well-defined eyebrows were not typical Japanese features. She was striking when she dressed up; heads turned when she walked down the street. Like other Japanese mothers, she was always busy cooking, sewing, knitting, and cleaning house. She made all my clothes, and she was a speedy knitter. Everything seemed effortless to her, whether making dolls or teaching me how to fold an origami "ghost" on a rainy day. Step by step, she took me through the intricate folding process with the simple square papers. It was like magic.

Years later, I saw *The King and I*, and I was reminded of Mama. Like Anna, she shared her open spirit with others by singing. Her voice was soft, humming tunes new and old—Scottish, Irish, German, French, Italian, Russian, and, of course, Japanese. Mama was not "traditional." She had great affection for Western culture and clothing. So did Papa. The story books they bought me included *Aesop's Fables* and Andersen's fairy tales. *Snow White, Sleeping Beauty, Cinderella*, and *Hansel and Gretel* were part of my life, as were *Robinson Crusoe, Tom Sawyer, Huck Finn*, and *Robin Hood of Sherwood Forest*.

After moving to the Tamura estate in Hiroshima, my cousin Hideyuki became my brother-in-residence. He knew little about life in Tokyo. But he was a master climber, a catcher of insects, and an excellent player of marbles and paper pachinko. I learned and practiced his crafts so we could play together. He loved having a playmate.

When Hideyuki was occupied, the vast garden of the estate was at my disposal. There were beautifully shaped pine trees, giant rocks, and stone lanterns. Azalea bushes, flowering trees, evergreens, and maples were laid out so that one was awed by beauty from any vantage point. In the winter, the camellias bloomed in bright red, pink and white, next to shiny green holly leaves with red berries. Early spring brought azaleas of every color, as well as aromatic golden and silver lilacs. Condiment plants grew in shady spots, and a small orchard produced figs and persimmons. Besides birds and insects, there was a variety of stunningly colored lizards and large ground frogs covered with unsightly warts.

Shortly after our arrival in Hiroshima, Papa reported for duty. After basic training, he was assigned to the transport division because of his driving experience from his Nissan days. Despite the patriotic fervor of the time, we were secretly delighted that he had not been assigned to the infantry.

On the morning of father's departure to the China front, the Tamura clan gathered at Ujina harbor with festive foods and *sake*. Decanters were filled and emptied quickly. Men sang send-off songs; women filled plates for the men. I was very sad; my Papa was leaving, but no one seemed to grieve. The family congratulated him for having the good fortune to serve his country and his emperor. Afterward, Mama tried to comfort me. But she, too, wept.

NEWS OF THE DECLARATION OF the Greater East Asian war reached our family on December 8, 1941, in the sixteenth year of the Showa Emperor. I was only six years old when the war expanded to include the United States and Britain, and I could understand very little of what was happening. But I sensed that something terribly wrong was taking place, and I knew that I could no longer see American movies, which I loved. "Hush," I was told. I mustn't even speak of American movies to others. Papa, who had just come home after serving a tour in China, was called back to the army. He would soon become an officer supervising transportation on the Inland Sea. His headquarters would be in Hiroshima, and he would be able to come home at night.

My school in Hiroshima was the elite Seibi Military Academy, which my father and his brother, Uncle Hisao, had attended. Seibi Academy, run by the Imperial Army in the ancient Samurai tradition, was far more rigorous than public school. It was like an austere military compound, with tall, green poplar trees bordering spacious school yards. The teachers were firm and demanding, but well liked. Inside the school gate was a stone structure like a mausoleum, in which were the *goshinei*, the sacred pictures of the Emperor and the Empress. One was not permitted to walk past it without offering some expression of deepest respect and humility. We were taught to offer our deepest and most reverent bow, the *saikeirei*.

That made me think of a day at my school in Tokyo, when the Emperor and Empress were to pass by. Although we were marched down to the street to greet them, our heads were to remain in the *saikeirei* position so that the imperial couple would not see our faces and we could not see theirs. But I looked up anyway and saw the sweet face of our Empress. No one else saw her. I had been told that anyone who looked would be blinded. My eyes, however, were not affected.

At the Seibi Academy, both girls and boys rehearsed the military code of honor and the marching routine daily. We paid respect to war heroes and the heroic war dead in every formal activity. On the eighth day of every month, the anniversary of the declaration of war, all of us marched to the Gokoku Shrine. The children whose fathers had died in action lined up in front. As the months and years passed, more and more children joined the line.

Those who had sacrificed their lives with special courage were called *gunshin*—military saints. We were taught that the seven men chosen to act as undersea human torpedoes in the attack on Pearl Harbor were *gunshins*. No one disputed their dedication, but I wondered why there had been only seven. The men had been allowed to bid farewell to their families; their mothers were said to have been proud to give their sons to their country. We heard self-sacrifice in the war praised again and again until it made us all feel that dying for our country was most desirable. Although we were children, it gave us a sense of purpose to think that we might die for a cause, the most glorious of which was to die for the Emperor. Nevertheless, I could never quite imagine becoming a human torpedo.

Our school days usually began with an assembly. The principal, who stood on a wooden platform a few feet off the ground, issued instructions and announcements. This was followed by rigorous calisthenics performed to lively music from a speaker. As the war progressed, building stamina became ever more important. The drill began to include long-distance running; carrying a partner on our back while marching was also added. At midday, there was additional stamina building in which we stripped to our underpants so that we could give our bodies wet or dry washcloth rubs for twenty to thirty minutes. Winter and summer, we rubbed our bodies furiously outdoors. The teachers praised us when our skin glowed pink, proof of a job well done. For the older girls, it was embarrassing to stand unclothed on the same lawn with boys of the same age and male teachers. But this was wartime.

Competitive sports were no less important. We had to reach certain goals in gymnastics, short- and long-distance running, hurdles, jumps, vaulting, turning bars, rope climbing, and throwing. Failure was not acceptable. One worked at it until the effort was adequate. The performances were closely timed, recorded, and rewarded. A red badge marked the greatest achievement, whereas blue and brown badges indicated less merit. I earned my red badge after performing fifty front wheels on the bar and nearly fainting from exhaustion. Homework, of course, was compulsory—during school holidays, over the new year, and throughout the spring and summer.

By the winter and spring of my fourth-grade year, the mood of the country began to change drastically. The war losses were slowly coming to light. Japan might not win. My first real sense of grief came when the principal announced at our morning assembly that the troops stationed on Attu Island had committed ritual suicide rather than surrender. We sang for the fallen heroes:

> To the sea
> A willing corpse in water.
> To the mountain
> A willing corpse in the thickets.
> Never turning back,
> As we serve our Supreme Master.

THE TAMURA CHILDREN ATTENDING THE SEIBI ACADEMY walked to school together every day. Cousin Hideyuki and Cousin Kiyotsune were beginning to notice pretty girls in school, and I was starting to notice some of their athletic friends. I also admired Kiyotsune's gymnastic ability. He and I often waited for one another to walk home together, chatting about this and that. Once he began asking whom I really liked, calling out names and asking "yes" or "no." He saved his name for last. How sweet he was. I never got to tell him how much I admired him.

By 1945, B-29s flew all over Hiroshima prefecture on bombing missions. Tokyo was firebombed, and my Aunt Kimie was burned to death. In Hiroshima, shelters had been dug everywhere, and hurriedly built cement cisterns held water. We were drilled time and again on how to put out fires caused by incendiaries. Air raid sirens went off day and night. All of our clothes had labels sewn in with our names and addresses.

Kamikaze missions were being flown and hailed, but fuel for planes was running low. The draft age was lowered to seventeen, and children in high school were mobilized to do public labor. Finally, school-age children, in the sixth grade and under, were ordered out of the cities in a mass evacuation. The departure date for the children of the Seibi Academy was April 10. We would go to Kimita, a village in the mountains. That was frightening, but at least I would be with my best friend, Miyoshi.

For weeks, Mama worked at her sewing machine, whipping up my clothes, *zabuton* cushion, and futon. There was a weight limit for how much could be taken, so Mama kept checking the weight of the bundle she was preparing. We went over its contents in detail, but she saved a little pouch for last, which she placed in my hand. "This is part of us," she said. "Papa's nail clippings and my hair."

The Kimita elementary school was a spacious, two-story building. There wasn't much playground equipment—no factory-built jungle gym, but there was a wooden one, held together by ropes. The forty Seibi Academy children formed their own groups in the school, but schooling itself became less and less important. In the end, we went to school only on rainy days. Otherwise, we worked outdoors. The work was beyond our abilities, even after the stamina training at the academy. We dug up giant pine roots, built hearths, and tried to extract pine oil for airplane fuel. Some children wielded shovels; others carried rocks on their backs. Soon, food became scarce, and we were sent out in small groups to collect edible plants. We quickly learned which grasses were edible and tasty, and what mountainside had more curly fern buds.

Bathing was difficult at first. We would work all day and often go to bed dirty. Soon, everyone had lice. We became like a tribe of monkeys, constantly bending over to pick lice eggs out of a friend's hair. We were ashamed. Eventually, the Seibi group was divided up, and three or four would go to neighboring farmhouses for bathing, once or twice a week. The farmhouses lacked plumbing, and their wells seldom had pumps. We drew the water and built the fires to heat it. But we loved our bathing day, sitting with friends, checking the fire, and talking idly while waiting for a nice warm bath. It was almost like being back in Hiroshima.

Our letters home were censored by the teachers, who refused to mail anything that even hinted that we were unhappy. But we were. We were always hungry, and health-related problems, especially bed-wetting, grew worse among the children. Miyoshi and I almost got into a fight one morning when I woke up in a drenched futon after she had slept in my bedroll with me. My underwear was dry, but hers wasn't.

Miyoshi and I became convinced that our lives were more endangered by staying in the mountains and being hungry and lice-infested. I was having stomach problems and frequent toothaches. We secretly mailed an uncensored letter from the village post office saying that we wanted to come home. On the afternoon of August 4, our mothers came to get us. Miyoshi and I were like a pair of kittens, snuggling up to our liberators. Our mothers suggested we remain another day, just to rest, before going home. But Miyoshi and I were desperate to leave that place, so we all returned to Hiroshima August 5. As we went to our separate homes, Miyoshi and I promised to play together again soon.

The sun was shining in the garden on the morning of August 6, a Monday. A sense of gratitude welled up in me. I had escaped the countryside. No more mad dashes to the cold stream to wash up at dawn. No more heavy rocks to carry on my back. No more lice. No more going to bed amid the muffled sounds of weeping after the lights went out. No more gnawing hunger. I was a child again, held within the protective embrace of my mother and father.

Papa was already working at the harbor when I awakened. Hideyuki was at school. Mama soon went off to join her obligatory work detail, which was tearing down abandoned houses in the town center so they would not provide fuel in the event of an incendiary attack. If possible, she would try to slip away by lunchtime so she could spend some time with me.

I lay back on my futon to read a paperback story about a Samurai duel that Hideyuki had loaned me. It was warm and the breeze was gentle. I wore nothing but underpants. When the air raid warning siren went off at about 7:15, I turned on the radio. The voice seemed casual. Three enemy planes were heading toward the city. It hardly seemed worth worrying about. Hundreds, yes. But three? I remembered the first time planes had flown over in the middle of the night on their way to another city. Paralyzed with fear, I had clutched Mama, asking her, "Are we going to be hit?" She didn't know. But whatever happened, she had said, we would be together.

About 7:30, the radio announcer said the air raid warning had been canceled. The enemy planes had turned around. It was safe to go outside. I turned off the radio and went back to reading the Samurai story. About forty-five minutes later, an intense duel between rival swordsmen was about to take place in my book when a blinding flash swept across my eyes. In a fraction of a second, I looked out the window toward the garden as a huge band of white light fell from the sky down to the trees. Almost simultaneously, a thunderous explosion gripped the earth and shook it. I jumped up and braced myself next to a large pillar, as Mama had told me to do if a bomb hit nearby. Pieces of the heavy clay-tile roof fell about me. It was dark, as if the sun had disappeared in the thick black air and swirling wind. My mother had taught me to "live" if an air raid came—to flee fire, to seek the river. But now, there seemed to be no alternative to death as the earth heaved.

Suddenly, the wind and the motion stopped. The thick air began to clear. I was covered with soot and debris, but alive. The pillar had held, protecting me, giving me a breathing space. I tried to clear a larger space, but the tangled pieces were more than I could handle. I cried out, and Aunt Fumiko's faint voice answered. "Where are you, Hideko?" She helped me get out. Although she was battered and scratched, her baby daughter was unhurt. After the flash, she had shielded the baby with her body.

After several loud yells, we found Grandmother Tamano and Aunt Kiyoko. They were bleeding and bruised and moving about aimlessly, as if in shock. Suddenly, we heard Fumiko's husband, Uncle Hisao, calling for help. He was sitting just outside the rear gate. His torn and blackened shirt was stained with blood and his eyes seemed hollow. He had been cut with flying glass and blood streamed from his throat, where a nail had been driven. He repeated over and over, "*Mo Dame da* . . . this is the end, this is the end." Aunt Fumiko sobbed as she picked out pieces of glass stuck in his skin.

My injuries were minor, a few cuts and bruises and a gashed right foot. I threw some clothes on and then tried to get everyone to leave as quickly as possible. Mama had told me, again and again, that in a bomb attack, fire would follow. But my grandmother and aunts and uncle lay under a tree in the garden and seemed not to hear me as they nursed their wounds. I wanted to cry. Mother had told me not to wait, to escape before the fire came. Across the street, a medium-sized factory burst into flame and I knew that a wind shift could bring it to the remains of our house. I screamed, "Fire, fire, you've got to leave, you've got to get away!" No one responded. I could not wait. My mother must be obeyed. As I ran from the garden, I kept shouting, "Please leave!"

Running and walking away, I passed neighbors, disheveled and confused. They paid little attention to passers-by; no one recognized me. Their attention was fixed on getting out and looking for members of their own families. Houses had fallen in or were barely standing. Small flames were starting to spread like torches and the wind fanned them into fireballs. I heard cries of people asking for help. But I could respond only to my inner voice, my Mama saying, "Go to the water, child, stay close to the river, save yourself from fire."

As I headed toward the Ota River, limping and dragging my right foot, more injured people began moving the same way, in the general direction of the city's outer limits. Their clothes were torn and burned; some were naked or nearly so. I tried to look for someone I might know. There were no familiar faces. Reaching the river, I saw a small group of adults and children, their hands clasped in prayer. An older man, perhaps the head of a family, directed them to pray for the safety of others left behind. Explosions from the direction of the army base across the river rent the air every half minute or so. "They got the arsenals," someone said.

Suddenly, someone called my name. It was Noriko, a girl who lived next door. Her face and arms were very red. She had run from the school yard of her elementary school and now she was escaping the city with her family.

"Nori-chan, what happened to you?" I said.

"There was a flash and it burned me," Noriko answered.

"Yes, I saw the flash," I said. "It was like a white waterfall. Did your school get a direct hit?"

"It must have," she said.

As we talked, large blisters formed on Noriko's face and it became so swollen that I could scarcely recognize her any more. She said some of the children were in much worse shape than she, and the teachers were so injured that they could offer no help. She didn't know what happened to the other children or the teachers. I was grateful that there was a family I could walk with, even though Noriko was in such pain that she had to stop talking.

At the river, we saw a young schoolgirl slowly walking along, with pieces of skin hanging from her arms. Someone said she was trying to cool her burned skin, but as she rubbed water on it, it came off. She cried in pain. The girl who could not assuage the pain with river water, Noriko's swollen face, the growing stream of burned and lacerated people, were but grains of sand on a vast beach. The horror was too great for comprehension.

THANKS TO A KINDLY DRIVER who piled refugees into his truck, I made it to the countryside, where I was taken in by a farm family. The next morning, the farmer offered to bicycle into Hiroshima to seek out my family. He knew the Tamura home, one of the grandest in the city. When he returned at day's end, he said he had found my father at the burned-down house, but not my mother. He learned that Uncle Hisao had been patched up by a surgeon friend. Grandma Tamano and Aunt Kiyoko and Aunt Fumiko were bruised, but otherwise unhurt. Baby Kumiko was fine. We survivors of the Tamura household would meet at the home of a family friend in Kabe township.

The reunion in Kabe was not joyous. My mother was missing as was Hideyuki, Uncle Hisao and Aunt Fumiko's only son. Although I was an only child, Hideyuki had been like a brother. I adored him. But like a brother, he had terrified me at times. The Tamuras had a bomb shelter deep in the garden, behind the trees and rocks. Hideyuki was obsessed with B-29s, which were systematically burning Japan's cities. To Hideyuki, the B-29 was a marvelous work of engineering. When the bombers flew over Hiroshima on their raids elsewhere, he would slip out of the shelter and go up to the roof of the house, where he would stare at them with binoculars. The rest of us would scream for him to come down, but his fascination with B-29s remained undampened. But now he was missing, and we had learned that a single B-29 with one bomb had caused the damage.

After the fires had burned out, we returned to Hiroshima to search for Hideyuki and my mother. Because the injured had fled in all directions and because the center of the city had disintegrated, there were no clues as to where to start. We began by checking out the "rescue" stations—schools, police yards, and temples—where the dying awaited medical care that did not exist.

In the police yard, my eyes were caught by a naked young woman, scantily covered by a thin blue cloth. Her petite body was curled up and she was breathing with great difficulty. A tag pinned to the cloth gave her name. She was a kindergarten teacher from my neighborhood. I tried to ask if she was all right. She whispered, "It is so hard. It is so hard." Her body began to shake and convulse and then she died. There were no marks on her, no cuts or blood or burns. I could not understand, and I was terrified.

At the next rescue station—a temple—the singed and blackened bodies lay on the floor unattended. The stench of rotting flesh filled the air. Soft moans were the only signs of life. I called out Mama's name. It was difficult to think of her lying there, one of those disfigured, helpless people. But I could not bear thinking of Mama dying alone. Calling her name caused people to stir. They asked for water, but I had none. No one did.

At the third rescue station, I decided to sing Mama's favorite lullabies and melodies, which we used to sing together. I prayed, "Please God, let the wind carry the tune to my Mama." As I let the wind carry the melody of my soft humming, tears began to roll down my cheeks. But I wept quietly. I did not want the wind to carry the sound of my sobs to Mama, who I was sure was very hurt and dying. Otherwise, she would have returned to us by then.

I did not find Mama at the rescue stations. Uncle Hisao and Aunt Fumiko failed to find Hideyuki. We were told that my friend Miyoshi had died. However, Cousin Kiyotsune was found alive in the front yard of the Red Cross Hospital by his parents. He died a few days later. We learned that most of Hideyuki's friends from the Hiroshima First Middle School were either dead or missing. Many had been crushed under the collapsed classrooms while others had been scorched in the melting heat. Kiyotsune's mother told Aunt Fumiko, "You may be lucky. You didn't have to watch your son's end. You won't keep on seeing how he had to die." Tomoko, another of my second cousins and a playmate, never came home from school. She was never found. Her mother went into seclusion for the rest of her life.

One day, one of Hideyuki's classmates found Uncle Hisao and Aunt Fumiko. The classmate—Hara—had been among the few who escaped the collapsed school. He had fled the fires and joined a crowd moving toward Mt. Hijiyama when he saw Hideyuki. Hideyuki was badly burned, naked to his calf girdle and army boots. He walked awkwardly, ghost-like, with his hands raised before him. He told Hara to go on although he could not. Hara took Hisao and Fumiko to the spot where he last saw Hideyuki lying on the ground. The bodies had been removed. My aunt and uncle asked around if anyone had noticed their son lying there. People said there had been many bodies and the soldiers had hauled them away. No one knew where the bodies had been cremated.

In early September, we learned about Mama. A neighbor had been with her at the moment the bomb exploded. She and Mama were inside a concrete building near the center of the city. Because the neighbor had her two small children with her, and Mama had had a miscarriage in July, they had been excused from having to do the laborious outside work. They were just inside the entranceway when the bomb exploded. Mama pulled her straw hat down over her ears and ran inside, just as the building fell in on her. The neighbor stayed in the entranceway and covered her children. She escaped before fire consumed the building.

My father went to the ruins of the building. There were several remains, so he could not tell which had been his wife. Then he stumbled upon an army canteen he had loaned her. Next to it were half-burnt, half-weathered remains. He brought Mama's ashes home in his army handkerchief. I begged him to take me back to the place where he had found her. He refused. It was not a sight for me to remember, he said. To this day, I ask myself, "Was she crushed instantly?" I pray that she was.

MORE THAN TWENTY-THREE YEARS after the bombing, Papa traveled to Chicago to be at my wedding. Over the years, we had seldom spoken of the unspeakable past. But on that trip, he shared something with me that I had never heard before.

He had been at his post at the harbor, more than two miles away, and he had been well shielded by a sturdy building when the bomb burst. A few hours afterward, he had encountered a young American prisoner of war wandering in a daze. The young man looked no older than seventeen, with blond hair and blue eyes, and was naked except for his boxer shorts. He was surrounded by a crowd of injured civilians, mostly old men and women, carrying stones which they were about to use against him. My father, speaking as an army officer, reproached the otherwise ordinary and peaceful citizens. The young American, he said, was a prisoner under the protection of the military. He was not armed and he was obviously not about to harm anyone. They must not become killers themselves.

Later, Papa said, he learned that the bomb had killed forty to fifty American prisoners of war who were located near the epicenter. As the officer in charge of the clearing task force, he was asked if the bodies of the prisoners should be cremated along with the Japanese. He told the workers that the American soldiers should be granted their own country's custom, which was to be buried. By the banks of the Ota River, the Americans who perished in Hiroshima were buried. My father said he often wondered long after the war about the handsome young man with the fearful eyes, and about his parents. They must have grieved for their son, who almost surely never came home. As he spoke, there were tears in his eyes.

BEYOND THE ASHES

A DIALOGUE

BETWEEN

TAKASHI HIRAOKA &

HITOSHI MOTOSHIMA

Editors' Note: The following is an excerpt of an exchange between the Mayor of Hiroshima, Takashi Hiraoka and the Mayor of Nagasaki, Hitoshi Motoshima. The dialogue was published by the Japanese monthly journal Sekai *in February 1995.*

ekai: This year marks fifty years since Japan lost the war and atomic bombs were used. The Japanese people are trying to understand how to cope in the present with problems of the past and how to link an understanding of those problems with their future. Fifty years are not simply a convenient place to leave the past behind us. How should we commemorate this anniversary year?

Hitoshi Motoshima: A half-century after the atomic bomb we are still faced with the moral question of how to aid and assist those who survived the attacks. Among several groups of bomb victims there is a view that it was our country that started the war and it was our country that brought about the suffering and sacrifice which the victims have had to endure. Therefore, they argue that it is this country's responsibility to provide aid to all victims of the war. In my view, the first step is to provide relief for the atomic bomb victims. They are a special case. What is special about them is that they managed to survive the atomic bomb, which was a weapon designed to kill indiscriminately. It was a weapon which people could never have imagined and which should never have been used. Many of those who initially survived died later as a consequence of their exposure to radiation. They physically deteriorated in the years after the attack. Victims of the atomic bomb have lived with loneliness, illness, and discrimination. Those who are still alive should be the first to receive reparations from the relief legislation. It can serve as an entry point for providing aid to all the others who were sacrificed in the war. . . .

By offering national reparations to the surviving atomic bomb victims we can begin once again to reflect on what the war means to us. It causes us to reflect historically on why this war happened, which inflicted indescribable suffering on people, and on where the responsibility for the war should be placed. We need to pledge as a nation never to participate in nuclear war. I had hoped that the relief legislation could serve as a starting point from which to begin paying damages to many people. For example, the victims of the war in Okinawa and those who survived the Tokyo air raids need to be considered. I thought Japan was learning how to approach this issue from the way Germany had developed its relief legislation. However, it is extremely disappointing that the final legislation has obscured all these matters.

Takashi Hiraoka: While we ask the country to take responsibility for the consequences of having started the war, we must continue to assert that nuclear weapons are exceptionally inhumane weapons and that they are a violation of international law. We need also to recognize that by emphasizing the atomic bomb as a special case, we risk losing the connection to the issue of war victims in general. How would you approach this problem?

Hitoshi Motoshima: Those killed by the atomic bomb are the same as those killed by the Tokyo air raids in the degree of pain they suffered. However, the atom bomb killed indiscriminately, on a large scale, in an act unforgivable from a human perspective. The wounds of survivors from conventional weapons usually heal over time, but as the years pass the effects of radiation emerge slowly in those who survived the atom bomb. They have lived with a unique physical and emotional pain stretching over many years and I believe it is appropriate to give them special compensation. Still, whether people died after one year, after ten years, or at the moment of the bombing, they are united in that they are victims of war.

Takashi Hiraoka: How do you think we can avoid making a special case of the atom bomb and sustain the link between atomic bomb survivors and victims of war in general?

Hitoshi Motoshima: I think the way to so is by pledging absolutely never to wage war again.

Takashi Hiraoka: I agree.

Hitoshi Motoshima: If we fully comprehend the damage caused by this special weapon, we will pledge never to wage war a second time. This is how we should approach the issue.

Sekai: The [Japanese] government has refused demands for forty years to adopt any legislation to provide special assistance to atomic bomb survivors. What could they have been afraid of for so long?

Hitoshi Motoshima: The leaders of this country have refused to confront head-on issues raised by the war and the question of war responsibility. It is an extremely difficult issue. The Nanking Massacre and the activities of the 73RD Regiment were acts of cruelty carried out by military units. However, the issue we are considering is the rejection of war itself. Looked at from a historical perspective, it was the Europeans who first invaded Asia. Japan then joined in and also invaded others. In short, successive governments adopted an attitude which says,

"Everyone was doing the same; the war the Japanese fought was not the only war of aggression or the only bad war." By adopting such an attitude our national leaders have avoided recognizing the suffering of Japanese citizens caused by the war.

Takashi Hiraoka: Japan is a country to which capitalism came rather late. It copied the methods of the Western powers in order to enter into international society and through this process ended up in the Pacific War. Of course, there is a debate about whether we should call it "The Pacific War," "World War II," or "The Fifteen-Year War." It is hard to know how to settle this argument. As I think about it, the acceptance of responsibility consists of the country that carried out a war compensating the citizens who suffered as a result of it. However, in terms of legal theory, war is a high-level political act, an act of state, and it is very difficult to solve the question of legal responsibility. Still, I feel that we must not take this to mean that the government alone causes acts of war and that the citizens of a country do not have any responsibility.

Hitoshi Motoshima: In a time of war, there is always some glimmering cause which everyone follows, saying, "of course."

Takashi Hiraoka: It is because the banner of "justice" is always raised for people to fight under. Isn't it? In Japan's case, we first said that it was not a war, but a series of "incidents"— the "Manchurian Incident," the "Sino–Japanese Incident." These were explosive, localized events and so battles occurred, but we said it was not war. After some time, we came to call it the Great Asian War and raised the banners of universal brotherhood and "freeing the colonized Asian peoples from Europe and America." But since we kept Korea and Taiwan as colonies, our slogans did not have much force.

Hitoshi Motoshima: Nevertheless, public opinion was remarkably unified. Terms like "Holy War," the "Imperial Army," and the "Asian Co-Prosperity Sphere" were commonly used.

Takashi Hiraoka: Yes, we were really convinced that it was a just war.

Hitoshi Motoshima: I think it is a mistake when we speak about Pearl Harbor to claim that attacking first is wrong in all possible cases. Frankly, I do not think that America was 100 percent correct and Japan was 100 percent wrong. After all, America too has invaded places. After the passage of fifty years, we look at the most obvious and glaring reasons for the conflict and they turn out not to be always the right ones. Is this not the case?

Takashi Hiraoka: However, in order to move forward from where we are and learn from history, Japan needs to think about whether war was truly the only option and whether there were other paths which could have been chosen. At that time, people became convinced that war was the only choice. It was an idea which continued through to our entry into the war. Various attempts to apply the brakes had no effect. The front in China quickly expanded and we were in the thick of it. The Pacific War began in the same sort of way. With no clear end in sight we just kept on doing what we were doing. It strikes me that this way of proceeding with things as they are is something we still see in today's Japan.

You would expect that there would have constantly been moves at various stages to reach a resolution. At the time, there were all sorts of possible alternatives. When we entered the Pacific War, we were told by America to withdraw from China and return Manchuria. If we had been able to make such a decision, I wonder how different history might have been.

Sekai: Yet, clearly as time passed the range of choices narrowed.

Takashi Hiraoka: I also think we need to consider whether or not information was communicated properly to the people. It was not a situation where the citizens were participating in politics. Now it is possible for choices to be presented to people and for their judgment to be respected, but in that social system it was impossible. This is a perspective from which we can question whether it is correct to place full responsibility on the people of a country whose leadership carried out the war. In a democratic society, one can say, "You cast your vote and gave your support, didn't you?"

Sekai: In your view, did the problems that developed under the Imperial system end after the war with the transition to democracy?

Takashi Hiraoka: [Laughs] Well, that is a difficult question. We are moving toward a sort of "Japanology." The Japanese people are not very logical and get carried away by emotion. Ours is a society that emphasizes harmony. Consensus-building in itself is not a bad thing in Japan.

Hitoshi Motoshima: "Blindly following the crowd." In practice everyone tends to just follow without an opinion of their own.

Takashi Hiraoka: Have the Japanese changed substantially? Have they changed in these fifty years?

Hitoshi Motoshima: The Japanese can get carried away by things and the war was one of those times. It would have been good if at some point there had been a strong force saying, "This is wrong."

Takashi Hiraoka: Yes, that is true. Since the Japanese entered into the world arena after the Meiji Restoration, Japan has basically been aflame with nationalism and national consciousness. Countries that were late to modernize are all quite similar in this respect. Japan used nationalism in its efforts to modernize. It sought an objective by which to unify the people's spirit. In Japan's case it was an Imperial ideology; in America, perhaps, it was freedom and democracy. Nations create a symbol of popular unity and try to define public consciousness with it. In the future, that problem will appear in Third World nations as well.

Sekai: The thinking of the American Legion and other similar groups in the United States is that the war occurred between two nations, each believing they were fighting for justice. Now it is all water under the bridge. We fought the enemy and they fought us. However, they believe that in order to prevent their own loss of additional troops to fight the final battle they had no other choice than to drop the bomb.

Takashi Hiraoka: Truman said on August 9, 1945 that he dropped the bomb in order to end the war quickly. He claimed it saved 250,000 to 500,000 lives. It is a figure which has steadily grown: President Reagan said 1,000,000; President Bush said it saved all of several million! They emphasize how justified an act dropping the A-bomb was. Truman's official opinion was that it was right, but it seems that privately he was very troubled about it. I think the veteran groups' approach to this is similar.

Certainly it was an act of war, but it came from a weapon of slaughter that even now is exceptionally and fundamentally different from all others—a nuclear weapon. The main issue is what actually happened as a result of the bombing—the number of lives saved by the bombs will always be a matter of supposition. The narrative should not be that 300,000 people died and 1,000,000 were saved. It should be that an atrocity that should not have ever been committed by human beings occurred and the threat of similar acts continue to this very day. If you say that the act itself was correct, without questioning the effects, then you end up calling war by any means justifiable.

Hitoshi Motoshima: Still, it is a significant problem that public opinion around the world generally tends to follow the American explanation for what happened. Whether it is the question that dropping of the bomb hastened the conclusion of the war and thus saved certain people, or whether Japan deserved what happened, we must recognize what people believe.

Takashi Hiraoka: In terms of historical reality, Japan was just moments from giving up. Japan frequently approached the Allied nations during the spring of 1945. Nevertheless, America dropped not only one bomb, but two of them.

Hitoshi Motoshima: Since the Japanese authorities were still calling for a final battle on the Japanese mainland, a rapid conclusion of the war was not a simple matter.

Takashi Hiraoka: There is also a theory that America dropped the A-bombs as a show of strength to the Soviet Union. I don't know what the truth is, but however you look at it, it is a fact that they dropped the bombs onto what was already a hopeless situation. If they wanted to carry out an attack to annihilate Hiroshima and Nagasaki's military power, bombing and fire-bombing would have sufficed. International law has traditionally recognized acts of war that destroy military forces, but attacks on civilians are not allowed.

Hitoshi Motoshima: In international law there is the precept that when you destroy military facilities, and civilians there are injured, it is considered incidental and unavoidable.

Takashi Hiraoka: However, they did not need to drop any atomic bombs. In my view, the U.S. simply wanted to show the world that they had invented this terrible weapon.

Sekai: The two atomic bombs of August 1945 marked an historic turning point concerning war and nations that engage in war. The world entered a totally different realm of thinking. Up to that point the losing side after a war would typically set out to improve its weaponry. Thus, it would not have been surprising if Japan had decided to acquire an atomic bomb. As you both know, the question of acquiring atomic weapons was actually considered. However, the movement initiated by the atomic bomb victims and the efforts by Japanese throughout the country prevented us from going in that direction. I see in that something wonderful and valuable about the post-war era. What do you think?

Takashi Hiraoka: Three months after the surrender, the American Strategic Bombing Survey interviewed 5,000 people in Hiroshima, Nagasaki, and the surrounding areas. They say that fewer than 20 percent expressed anger about the atomic bomb at that time. Gradually anger did appear, but I don't know if the cause of that initial acceptance was a kind of despondency or whether because the post-war view symbolized in the phrase "ten million repentant people" was forced on them.

However, we may also think of it another way. People in the face of the extreme, large-scale destruction that occurred recognized that if this weapon were ever used again, it could lead to the eradication of human life. They were able to adopt such a perspective from an extremely heightened and very human point of view. They understood directly that the meaning of the atomic bomb was very different from that of previous weapons.

Hitoshi Motoshima: Some time after the end of the war, a Nagasaki liquor store owner discovered an unexploded shell buried under his building. They evacuated everyone within five hundred square meters and were able finally to dig it out. When they did, the owner of the store said, "Oh good, with this the post-war era comes to an end for me." I said, "That's not really true. There are even more destructive nuclear weapons. The earth is weighed down by them." He said, "Well, it's fine with me." [Laughs] I think this man reflected the sense that things outside your own experience are so enormous and terrifying that to try to help or even to think about them would not do any good.

However, atomic bomb victims are now talking about eradicating nuclear weapons. They did not do so at first. Initially, they were mourning the deaths of their mothers and fathers. They were suffering through illness. When a father loses a child in an auto accident and he says the person responsible for the road, or the other driver, was at fault, he initially turns his anger directly towards the perpetrator. But as years pass, the anger steadily becomes prayer that what happened to that child will not happen again—perhaps he puts up a little shrine, decorates it with flowers. In the same way, the bomb victims suffered for a very long time. Some of them suffered for a month, some for ten years, others for twenty. Only after a period of mourning and suffering were they able to think about disarmament.

Takashi Hiraoka: Their ideas were tempered through many years of hardship. I think a lot of things happened before they converged on the idea of nuclear disarmament. Really, the aims of the movement have changed a great deal. Of course, it has developed in good and fruitful directions. Even the expression we are now using—"national reparations"—was only arrived at after quite a bit of debate. It was an idea that just did not exist from the beginning. On this fiftieth year, we must articulate the direction that Japan as a nation should take. Concretely speaking, I think that means coming out against nuclear weapons. We need to hammer out these aims to the world: anti-war, pro-peace, anti-nuclear. This should also involve resolving post-war matters with those who suffered from Japan's actions during the war. The legislation should be a comprehensive approach and each issue should be addressed.

Hitoshi Motoshima: This is exactly right. I think a law precisely like the one Mayor Hiraoka described would have new meaning in the present day. Everyone knows that Japan currently has the power to develop nuclear weapons and also to maintain them. It has amassed a great deal of plutonium. Since Japan does not make its future position absolutely clear, foreigners are genuinely concerned that Japan might end up possessing nuclear weapons. Therefore, it is necessary to make our position clear by adopting publicly the three anti-nuclear guidelines: do not manufacture, keep, or provide nuclear weapons. The Japanese people accept these three anti-nuclear guidelines and I think that they should be put into law.

Sekai: I would like to ask each of you to recall your personal history. You have both said that it was not just leaders who made the war possible but also the enthusiastic support of the people in the country. What did each of you do during the war? How were you able to develop your humanistic viewpoints and your views on Asia after the war?

Hitoshi Motoshima: After my second year in high school I went into the army. Like everyone I declared publicly at the time that it was necessary to give my life for my homeland. I accepted the war as logical. I thought I should die for Japan. When I look back on it now, it was a very simplistic way of thinking.

Sekai: Were you sent to the front?

Hitoshi Motoshima: I did not go. It was a year too late to be sent. Kurume in Fukuoka Prefecture on Kyushu was a military town. Therefore, I had friends who were sent to the war zones. We were often awakened in the middle of the night. Hundreds of people would line up on both sides of the road carrying paper lanterns, and the groups that had been training until the day before marched through wearing their best clothes and shoes. They shouldered guns and carried backpacks. They were sent to the front. They were not able to see their siblings or families and most did not come back. These were indescribable scenes. They got on transport ships and when they looked back they sang songs about parting from their homeland. Near the end of the war most of their ships were sunk before they ever reached the war zones.

Sekai: Did you have any doubts about the war?

Hitoshi Motoshima: Frankly, at the time I did not. I thought it was perfectly natural. My body and soul were girded up and marshaled for war. Wasn't there a song at the time called "Wheat and Soldiers?" It went something like "slowly, slowly, the men and horses advance." It went on to say, "far, far away from the land of my home, now at last I know the true love for my land." However, to trample the soil of another country that did not invite you and call this a love of one's homeland is quite a mistake. [Laughs] It is not loving one's own land at all. I got used to all of it. In Westerns, sometimes, there are scenes where one or two people riding on horses give them a little switch on the back to turn them, and hundreds of cows come running after them. I think we were a great deal like a herd of cows.

Sekai: You became famous for your statement at the Nagasaki City Assembly when you said that the Emperor—and you, yourself, as well—were responsible for the war. What is your own war responsibility?

Hitoshi Motoshima: I became a cadet in the education unit of the Western unit of the army in Kumamoto. I was really quite good at it. [Laughs] It makes sense that I was good. I was a science major in high school and was therefore an expert on trigonometry and logarithms, and since our job was to teach surveillance, platoon leader training, and that sort of thing, I was better at it than the teacher. Due to this skill I was kept on domestic soil. If I had gone to the front, I might not still be alive, or I might have committed horrible acts. After all, it was our friends, fathers, and grandfathers who participated in the Nanking Massacre and other similar incidents. When they came home, however, they became the gentle people we know, which makes me think the military and war itself transforms people.

In the education unit classroom, I taught that the Emperor was God and Japan was the country of the gods and that in the end a divine wind ["kamikaze"] would blow—so we could not lose. I said with Japan as the leader of the world and the leader of Asia, the world would be happy. As one who made such statements, I certainly have war responsibility. Still, reparations for war responsibility at this point must be left to the government. If there are to be some sort of reparations to China or the Philippines, then it will be accomplished through the government. If the government acts, it shall be the will of the citizens as a whole. I do not know whether you can say that the children, old men, and old women during the war were responsible for it. However, I do think today all citizens need to bear that responsibility.

Takashi Hiraoka: I was in Korea during the war. I was in my second year at Ke Jo Middle School [Ke Jo is the Japanese colonial name for Seoul], preparing to enter Ke Jo Imperial University when Japan's surrender came. Around that time I was sent away as part of the mobilization of students for the war. There was a big Japanese nitrogen chemical plant in present day Hung Nam, North Korea. I had been working there from April 1945. As soon as the war was lost, I returned to Seoul where my parents were living.

At that time I simply did not think much about the issue of war responsibility. I was a second-year student at a high school under the old system. There may have been many people who thought about it, but I did not really think about this question. When the war ended, my Korean classmates with whom I thought I had gotten along well suddenly seemed distant. They went to town and cheered in the streets. I was not able to properly understand the situation. I understood that we had lost the war, but did not foresee what would happen because of losing. I even had friends who asked, "Will you still be staying as a settler?" It was not until the loss of the war and our evacuation that I realized that I had been living by using people as stepping-stones.

We retreated to Hiroshima because my parents were from there. When I saw the aftermath of the bomb, it was a terrible shock. After that, I began to study all sorts of things, and through that I learned the meaning of colonialism. Looking back, I realize that until then I was utterly oblivious. While I was in Hung Nam, the Soviet Union entered the war and I saw refugees come pouring in from the north. I did not properly grasp the gravity of these events. I just thought, "Oh, they are escaping to here, aren't they?" And then I went off to the beach or something. [Laughs]

Among my friends we would say to each other how we would all die sooner or later. We would say nonsensical things. I remember how once we cooked up all the canned goods and rice that we had stored up and had a party. Perhaps, this is what youth is like even in war. But I also remember from the same period that when the war was lost the Japanese in Korea were stunned. While I was trudging through the mountains on the way home from the factory, the Korean farmers were silently cultivating their fields. When I think of that image now, I am deeply moved. But this is only in retrospect. At the time I felt, "Japan lost, so what are they cultivating for? This is no time for farming, is it?" I cannot forget the image of the farmers plowing to survive, indifferent to the rise and fall of nations.

I was raised on the Korean peninsula and so I lived with a sense of nostalgia for Korea after the war. I would hear names of places that I knew during the Korean War. There were reports that today such-and-such a city had fallen or been attacked. The scenery of that place would come to my mind. And yet, I never went so far as to think about the truth, that Koreans living in Hiroshima and Nagasaki had been victims of the bomb. I realized that when I was a newspaper reporter in about 1963. I received a letter from a Korean atomic bomb survivor saying, "I was bombed in Hiroshima and am sick now. I want something to be done for me." It was only then that I began to take notice. I discovered that there were bomb victims who had been ignored in Korea. I wrote about it in the newspapers and also in this magazine, *Sekai*. Now I recognize that having supported colonialism is part of one's war responsibility.

Sekai: How did you feel when you came back to Hiroshima after the bombing?

Takashi Hiraoka: I came back to my hometown during winter vacation in 1945 and had a reunion with friends from elementary school. Eight months later, I got off the train in Hiroshima station to find burnt fields as far as the eye could see. The devastation was visible all the way to Ninoshima. It made a deep impression upon me. Most of my friends, who I had just visited, were dead. There were places with nothing but stepping-stones left where stores had probably been. There were burnt remains of some banks here and there.

Hitoshi Motoshima: Were there fire hydrants?

Takashi Hiraoka: I do not remember, but there were scorched bathtubs here and there. When I returned, the main roads had been rebuilt and the trains were running, but I remember coming across a skull at the approach to a bridge. I went to a traditional high school in Hiroshima. Of course, there were people who had relatives who died, but I did not fully take in the reality of the atomic bomb damage. Perhaps, I was stupid. I do not think I was even eighteen. Children are like that and I certainly was not very astute.

Hitoshi Motoshima: At the time, no one was able to absorb it all.

Takashi Hiraoka: Do you think so?

Hitoshi Motoshima: You were one of the better ones. After the war I vacillated back and forth. I did things such as honoring the Japanese imperial flag. But that's all right, is it not? I struggled, and finally reached my current state of mind. When you are young, you are not able to think very deeply unless something exceptional happens to you. At the time the war ended, I had taken my pupils up into the mountains to make a horse barn. Those days were quite something. We boldly climbed someone else's mountains to build a horse barn. [Laughs] At about eleven o'clock the students went to the foot of the mountain to get lunch, and when they came back five or six of them were gathered together, whispering. I asked them what they were doing, and they said, "The unit leader says the war is over. The Emperor said something." I asked if it was true and they said it was, so I announced it to everybody in the area. It was an interesting moment. There were people who jumped up and cheered and some who burst into tears. There were also a few who collapsed. I had the sense that a new era had begun for me.

Sekai: What do you have to say to the generations that have known neither war nor atom bombs or to the generations of the twenty-first century?

Takashi Hiraoka: We often speak of handing down experiences to the next generation, but in actuality it is a very difficult thing to do. All one can do is to learn it as history. It is a mistake to think it is easy to pass along an experience. No matter how you communicate a tragedy in words, the listener cannot experience it directly. Even among Hiroshima's children, the number who do not know what August 6 means has grown. I would like this [fiftieth anniversary] to be a year for us to think about what it might mean to be human. We are all looking for happiness. We would like to live a happy life. There are many who are aware that peace is crucial to protecting that happiness. Those who are protesting war or thinking about environmental problems have increased in numbers. As someone with an administrator's responsibility for seeking that basic happiness, I want to consider what can be done administratively.

Amid the destruction just after the loss of the war, many Hiroshima citizens gathered up a surprising amount of passion to begin discussing the future. They depicted a vision of what kind of city they would like to build. After the Peace City Construction Resolution was instituted, the enthusiasm waned. Now people are working as hard as they can to speak about the past. I get the sense that they are talking less about the future. Using the fiftieth anniversary as an opportunity, we should continue to discuss the past, but also talk more about what kind of society and what kind of world we will build from here on . . . I want to continue to have Hiroshima be the kind of city people of Asia and the world look at and say, "It represents my hopes."

Hitoshi Motoshima: I want a movement to urge the government to conclude definitively an overall treaty banning nuclear weapons. I believe that stressing the need to eliminate nuclear arms should not just be a Japanese issue, or even worse, just a symbol of Hiroshima and Nagasaki. At the Hiroshima Arms Reduction

Conference, Mayor Hiraoka was the only one who spoke of the necessity to entirely eliminate nuclear weapons. Everyone else stopped at arms reduction.

Takashi Hiraoka: Yes, that's true.

Hitoshi Motoshima: I said that I would like the Secretary General of the United Nations to take up the subject of nuclear arms.

Takashi Hiraoka: The officials will not use the words "nuclear arms elimination." They prefer to only say "arms reduction." So, it is up to us to speak out with greater force about the necessity of eliminating nuclear arms.

Hitoshi Motoshima: The concept of nuclear deterrence is essentially a belief that by keeping nuclear weapons you protect your own country's safety. It seems to me to be a notion of simply not wanting to give up what you think is your last round of ammunition.

Takashi Hiraoka: After the passage of fifty years, it should be clear that this philosophy and the structures which underlie it are bankrupt. The role of nuclear strength in world politics is at an end. Isn't this so in this fiftieth year after the bombing of Hiroshima and Nagasaki? There are few developing countries that still want to acquire nuclear weapons, but the idea that nuclear weapons can lead world politics by the ear and that they can be used for military power is out of date. They could not even use them in the Gulf War. This is because they have the lesson of Hiroshima and Nagasaki. Nuclear arms have become unusable weapons.

Hitoshi Motoshima: No! Can you really say that? I think leaders exist now who are no different from the American leaders who once gave the orders to drop the bomb. On the anniversary of August 9 last year, Prime Minister Murayama used the phrase "nuclear arms reduction and eventual nuclear arms elimination" twice. At the United Nations, Foreign Minister Kôno referred to "nuclear arms reduction and eventual nuclear arms elimination." I get the sense that some understanding is emerging, particularly in the Foreign Ministry. When I met Prime Minister Murayama, I asked him, "What do you mean by 'eventual'—does that mean that when the world comes to an end, nuclear arms will finally be eliminated?" First of all, the word "eventually" sounds strange in Japanese. Really it should be "as early as possible." If they cannot bring themselves to say this, then at least they should say that they stand for "nuclear arms reduction and then nuclear arms elimination." On the fiftieth year, I would like the government to adopt a diplomatic policy that supports "nuclear arms reduction and the swift elimination of nuclear weapons." We should join together with Hiroshima to work to make this a reality.

Second, rather than working for big goals, people should think about what is right in front of them. I wish to invite as many young people as I can to come to Nagasaki on field trips. There is no substitute for experience. This is why the atomic bomb exhibit at the International Culture Hall has been rebuilt three times, and now each year 1,100,000 visitors come to our city to view it. My five-year plan is to reach the goal of 2,000,000 visitors a year. I also want to try to urge more Asians to come in the future.

Hiroshima has become quite organized and this is very good in some respects. I would like to establish a university in Nagasaki like the Hiroshima City University to engage in peace studies and to sponsor international exchanges. We must communicate our view to the world. I would also like a local newspaper like the *Chugoku Shimbun* [a Hiroshima newspaper] to continue its pursuit of atomic issues. From now on we need an elite that works for peace. Since skilled storytellers who actually experienced the bomb are disappearing, we need people who will use logic to lead us towards peace. We need to train those leaders.

Takashi Hiraoka: Europe has reacted with great sensitivity to nuclear issues, but Asians are not as conscious about these issues as they need to be. Our appeals to them have been extremely weak. We need to organize conferences which will develop a greater sensitivity to nuclear questions among Asians.

Hitoshi Motoshima: In January and February of 1994, a Pacific Asia Regional Arms Reduction Conference met in Katmandu, Nepal. In Europe, nuclear and conventional arms reduction have progressed, but in Asia the main issues were Pakistani–India relations, problems in China and the surrounding countries, and— in northern Asia—the future of the Korean peninsula. Military matters are not the only serious problems for Asia; we have to think about famine, poverty, refugees, infringements on human rights, matters of a global scope such as the destruction of the environment and the squandering of resources, AIDS, and drugs. In other words, Asian nations have to think together about what life in the future should be.

First, I want to make a plea to India and China. China has nuclear weapons and India probably will have them soon. Even though the nuclear non-proliferation treaty will be renewed in 1995, India says they will not participate. Behind this assertion by India, there may exist a viewpoint, that under the right circumstances, may still be prepared to call for the elimination of nuclear weapons. This is also true in China. Perhaps, I am overstretching myself. I call upon both India and China, the two largest nations in the world, to advocate the total elimination of nuclear weapons on earth.

Translated by Sarah Frederick and Bruno Navasky

FIFTY YEARS

AFTER

HIROSHIMA

John Rawls

THE FIFTIETH YEAR SINCE THE BOMBING of Hiroshima is a time to reflect about what one should think of it. Is it really a great wrong, as many now think, and many also thought then, or is it perhaps justified after all? I believe that both the fire-bombing of Japanese cities beginning in the spring of 1945 and the later atomic bombing of Hiroshima on August 6 were very great wrongs, and rightly seen as such. In order to support this opinion, I set out what I think to be the principles governing the conduct of war—*jus in bello*—of democratic peoples. These peoples have different ends of war than non-democratic, especially totalitarian, states, such as Germany and Japan, which sought the domination and exploitation of subjected peoples, and in Germany's case, their enslavement if not extermination.[1]

Although I cannot properly justify them here, I begin by setting out six principles and assumptions in support of these judgments. I hope they seem not unreasonable, and certainly they are familiar, as they are closely related to much traditional thought on this subject.

(1) The aim of a just war waged by a decent democratic society is a just and lasting peace between peoples, especially with its present enemy.

(2) A decent democratic society is fighting against a state that is not democratic. This follows from the fact that democratic peoples do not wage war against each other, and since we are concerned with the rules of war as they apply to such peoples, we assume the society fought against is non-democratic and that its expansionist aims threatened the security and free institutions of democratic regimes and caused the war.[2]

(3) In the conduct of war, a democratic society must carefully distinguish three groups: the state's leaders and officials, its soldiers, and its civilian population. The reason for these distinctions rests on the principle of responsibility: since the state fought against is not democratic, the civilian members of the society cannot be those who organized and brought on the war. This was done by its leaders and officials assisted by other elites who control and staff the state apparatus. They are responsible, they willed the war, and for doing that, they are criminals. But civilians, often kept in ignorance and swayed by state propaganda, are not.[3]

And this is so even if some civilians knew better and were enthusiastic for the war. In a nation's conduct of war many such marginal cases may exist, but they are irrelevant. As for soldiers, they, just as civilians, and leaving aside the upper ranks of an officer class, are not responsible for the war, but are conscripted or in other ways forced into it, their patriotism often cruelly and cynically exploited. The grounds on which they may be attacked directly are not that they are responsible for the war but that a democratic people cannot defend itself in any other way, and defend itself it must do. About this there is no choice.

(4) A decent democratic society must respect the human rights of the members of the other side, both civilians and soldiers, for two reasons. One is because they simply have these rights by the law of peoples. The other reason is to teach enemy soldiers and civilians the content of those rights by the example of how they hold in their own case. In this way their significance is best brought home to them. They are assigned a certain status, the status of the members of some human society who possess rights as human persons.[4] In the case of human rights in war the aspect of status as applied to civilians is given a strict interpretation. This means, as I understand it here, that they can never be attacked directly except in times of extreme crisis, the nature of which I discuss below.

(5) Continuing with the thought of teaching the content of human rights, the next principle is that just peoples by their actions and proclamations are to foreshadow during war the kind of peace they aim for and the kind of relations they seek between nations. By doing so, they show in an open and public way the nature of their aims and the kind of people they are. These last duties fall largely on the leaders and officials of the governments of democratic peoples, since they are in the best position to speak for the whole people and to act as the principle applies. Although all the preceding principles also specify duties of statesmanship, this is especially true of (4) and (5). The way a war is fought and the actions ending it endure in the historical memory of peoples and may set the stage for future war. This duty of statesmanship must always be held in view.

(6) Finally, we note the place of practical means-end reasoning in judging the appropriateness of an action or policy for achieving the aim of war or for not causing more harm than good. This mode of thought—whether carried on by (classical) utilitarian reasoning or by cost-benefit analysis, or by weighing national interests, or in other ways—must always be framed within and strictly limited by the preceding principles. The norms of the conduct of war set up certain lines that bound just action. War plans and strategies and the conduct of battles, must lie within their limits. (The only exception, I repeat, is in times of extreme crisis.)

In connection with the fourth and fifth principles of the conduct of war, I have said that they are binding especially on the leaders of nations. They are in the most effective position to represent their people's aims and obligations, and sometimes they become statesmen. But who is a statesman? There is no office of statesman, as there is of president, or chancellor, or prime minister. The statesman is an ideal, like the ideal of the truthful or virtuous individual. Statesmen are presidents or prime ministers who become statesmen through their exemplary performance and leadership in their office in difficult and trying times and manifest strength, wisdom, and courage. They guide their people through turbulent and dangerous periods for which they are esteemed always, as one of their great statesmen.

The ideal of the statesman is suggested by the saying: the politician looks to the next election, the statesman to the next generation. It is the task of the student of philosophy to look to the permanent conditions and the real interests of a just and good democratic society. It is the task of the statesman, however, to discern these conditions and interests in practice; the statesman sees deeper and further than most others and grasps what needs to be done. The statesman must get it right, or nearly so, and hold fast to it. Washington and Lincoln were statesmen. Bismarck was not. He did not see Germany's real interests far enough into the future and his judgment and motives were often distorted by his class interests and his wanting himself alone to be chancellor of Germany. Statesmen need not be selfless and may have their own interests when they hold office, yet they must be selfless in their judgments and assessments of society's interests and not be swayed, especially in war and crisis, by passions of revenge and retaliation against the enemy.

Above all, they are to hold fast to the aim of gaining a just peace, and avoid the things that make achieving such a peace more difficult. Here the proclamation of a nation should make clear (the statesman must see to this) that the enemy people are to be granted an autonomous regime of their own and a decent and full life once peace is securely reestablished. Whatever they may be told by their leaders, whatever reprisals they may reasonably fear, they are not to be held as slaves or serfs after surrender, or denied in due course their full liberties; and they may well achieve freedoms they did not enjoy before, as the Germans and the Japanese eventually did.[5] The statesman knows, if others do not, that all descriptions of the enemy people (not their rulers) inconsistent with this are impulsive and false.

Turning now to Hiroshima and the fire-bombing of Tokyo, we find that neither falls under the exemption of extreme crisis. One aspect of this is that since (let's suppose) there are no absolute rights—rights that must be respected in all circumstances—there are occasions when civilians can be attacked directly by aerial bombing. Were there times during the war when Britain could properly have bombed Hamburg and Berlin? Yes, when Britain was alone and desperately facing Germany's superior might; moreover, this period would extend until Russia had clearly beat off the first German assault in the summer and fall of 1941, and would be able to fight Germany until the end. Here the cutoff point might be placed differently, say the summer of 1942, and certainly by Stalingrad.[6] I shan't dwell on this, as the crucial matter is that under no conditions could Germany be allowed to win the war, and this for two basic reasons: first, the nature and history of constitutional democracy and its place in European culture; and second, the peculiar evil of Nazism and the enormous and incalculable moral and political evil it represented for civilized society.

The peculiar evil of Nazism needs to be understood, since in some circumstances a democratic people might better accept defeat if the terms of peace offered by the adversary were reasonable and moderate, did not subject them to humiliation and looked forward to a workable and decent political relationship. Yet characteristic of Hitler was that he accepted no possibility at all of a political relationship with his enemies. They were always to be cowed by terror and brutality, and ruled by force. From the beginning the campaign against Russia, for example, was a war of destruction against Slavic peoples, with the original inhabitants remaining, if at all, only as serfs. When Goebbels and others protested that the war could not be won that way, Hitler refused to listen.[7]

Yet it is clear that while the extreme crisis exemption held for Britain in the early stages of the war, it never held at any time for the United States in its war with Japan. The principles of the conduct of war were always applicable to it. Indeed, in the case of Hiroshima many involved in higher reaches of the government recognized the questionable character of the bombing and that limits were being crossed. Yet during the discussions among allied leaders in June and July 1945, the weight of the practical means-end reasoning carried the day. Under the continuing pressure of war, such moral doubts as there were failed to gain an express and articulated view. As the war progressed, the heavy fire-bombing of civilians in the capitals of Berlin and Tokyo and elsewhere was increasingly accepted on the allied side. Although after the outbreak of war Roosevelt had urged both sides not to commit the inhuman barbarism of bombing civilians, by 1945 allied leaders came to assume that Roosevelt would have used the bomb on Hiroshima.[8] The bombing grew out of what had happened before.

The practical means–end reasons to justify using the atomic bomb on Hiroshima were the following. The bomb was dropped to hasten the end of the war. It is clear that Truman and most other allied leaders thought it would do that. Another reason was that it would save lives where the lives counted are the lives of American soldiers. The lives of Japanese, military or civilian, presumably counted for less. Here the calculations of least time and most lives saved were mutually supporting. Moreover, dropping the bomb would give the Emperor and the Japanese leaders a way to save face, an important matter given Japanese samurai culture. Indeed, at the end a few top Japanese leaders wanted to make a last sacrificial stand but were overruled by others supported by the Emperor, who ordered surrender on August 12, having received word from Washington that the Emperor could stay provided it was understood that he had to comply with the orders of the American military commander. The last reason I mention is that the bomb was dropped to impress the Russians with American power and make them more agreeable with our demands. This reason is highly disputed but urged by some critics and scholars as important. The failure of these reasons to reflect the limits on the conduct of war is evident, so I focus on a different matter: the failure of statesmanship on the part of allied leaders and why it might have occurred. Truman once described the Japanese as beasts and to be treated as such; yet how foolish it sounds now to call the Germans or the Japanese barbarians and beasts![9] Of the Nazis and Tojo militarists, yes, but they are not the German and the Japanese people. Churchill later granted that he carried the bombing too far, led by passion and the intensity of the conflict.[10] A duty of statesmanship is not to allow such feelings, natural and inevitable as they may be, to alter the course a democratic people should best follow in striving for peace. The statesman understands that relations with the present enemy have special importance: for as I have said, war must be openly and publicly conducted in ways that make a lasting and amicable peace possible with a defeated enemy, and prepares its people for how they may be expected to be treated. Their present fears of being subjected to acts of revenge and retaliation must be put to rest; present enemies must be seen as associates in a shared and just future peace.

These remarks make it clear that, in my judgment, both Hiroshima and the fire-bombing of Japanese cities were great evils that the duties of statesmanship require political leaders to avoid in the absence of the crisis exemption. I also believe this could have been done at little cost in further casualties. An invasion was unnecessary at that date, as the war was effectively over. However, whether that is true or not makes no difference. Without the crisis exemption, those bombings are great evils. Yet it is clear that an articulate expression of the principles of just war introduced at that time would not have altered the outcome. It was simply too late. A president or prime minister must have carefully considered these questions, preferably long before, or at least when they had the time and leisure to think things out. Reflections on just war cannot be heard in the daily round of the pressure of events near the end of the hostilities; too many are anxious and impatient, and simply worn out.

Similarly, the justification of constitutional democracy and the basis of the rights and duties it must respect should be part of the public political culture and discussed in the many associations of civic society as part of one's education. It is not clearly heard in day-to-day ordinary politics, but must be presupposed as the background, not the daily subject of politics, except in special circumstances. In the same way, there was not sufficient prior grasp of the fundamental importance of the principles of just war for the expression of them to have blocked the appeal of practical means–end reasoning in terms of a calculus of lives, or of the least time to end the war, or of some other balancing of costs and benefits. This practical reasoning justifies too much, too easily, and provides a way for a dominant power to quiet any moral worries that may arise. If the principles of war are put forward at that time, they easily become so many more considerations to be balanced in the scales.

Another failure of statesmanship was not to try to enter negotiations with the Japanese before any drastic steps such as the fire-bombing of cities or the bombing of Hiroshima were taken. A conscientious attempt to do so was morally necessary. As a democratic people, we owed that to the Japanese people—whether to their government is another matter. There had been discussions in Japan for some time about finding a way to end the war, and on June 26 the government had been instructed by the Emperor to do so.[11] It must surely have realized that with the navy destroyed and the outer islands taken, the war was lost. True, the Japanese were deluded by the hope that the Russians might prove to be their allies, but negotiations are precisely to disabuse the other side of delusions of that kind.[12] A statesman is not free to consider that such negotiations may lessen the desired shock value of subsequent attacks.

Truman was in many ways a good, at times a very good president. But the way he ended the war showed he failed as a statesman. For him it was an opportunity missed, and a loss to the country and its armed forces as well. It is sometimes said that questioning the bombing of Hiroshima is an insult to the American troops who fought the war. This is hard to understand. We should be able to look back and consider our faults after fifty years. We expect the Germans and the Japanese to do that—"*Vergangenheitsverarbeitung*"—as the Germans say. Why shouldn't we? It can't be that we think we waged the war without moral error?

None of this alters Germany's and Japan's responsibility for the war nor their behavior in conducting it. Emphatically to be repudiated are two nihilist doctrines. One is expressed by Sherman's remark, "War is hell," so anything goes to get it over with as soon as one can. The other says that we are all guilty so we stand on a level and no one can blame anyone else. These are both superficial and deny all reasonable distinctions; they are invoked falsely to try to excuse our misconduct or to plead that we cannot be condemned.

The moral emptiness of these nihilisms is manifest in the fact that just and decent civilized societies—their institutions and laws, their civil life and background culture and mores—all depend absolutely on making significant moral and political distinctions in all situations. Certainly war is a kind of hell, but why should that mean that all moral distinctions cease to hold? And granted also that sometimes all or nearly all may be to some degree guilty, that does not mean that all are equally so. There is never a time when we are free from all moral and political principles and restraints. These nihilisms are pretenses to be free of those principles and restraints that always apply to us fully.

NOTES

1. I sometimes use the term "peoples" to mean much the same as nations, especially when I want to contrast peoples with states and a state's apparatus.

2. I assume that democratic peoples do not go to war against each other. There is considerable evidence of this important idea. See Michael Doyle's two part article, "Kant, Liberal Legacies, and Foreign Affairs," *Philosophy and Public Affairs* (Summer and Fall 1983). See his summary of the evidence in the first part, pp. 206–232. Responsibility for war rarely falls on only one side and this must be granted. Yet some dirty hands are dirtier than others, and sometimes even with dirty hands a democratic people would still have the right and even the duty to defend itself from the other side. This is clear in World War II.

3. Here I follow Michael Walzer's *Just and Unjust Wars* (New York, 1977).

4. For the idea of status, I am indebted to discussions of Frances Kamm and Thomas Nagel.

5. See Churchill's remarks explaining the meaning of "unconditional surrender" in *The Hinge of Fate* (Boston, 1950), pp. 685–688.

6. I might add here that a balancing of interests is not involved. Rather, we have a matter of judgment as to whether certain objective circumstances are present which constitute the extreme crisis exemption. As with any other complex concept, that of such an exemption is to some degree vague. Whether or not the concept applies rests on judgment.

7. On Goebbel's and others' protests, see Alan Bullock, *Hitler: A Study in Tyranny* (London, 1952), pp. 633–644.

8. For an account of events, see David M. McCullough, *Truman* (New York, 1992), pp. 390–464; and Barton Bernstein, "The Atomic Bombings Reconsidered," *Foreign Affairs* (January–February 1995).

9. See McCullough's *Truman*, p. 458, the exchange between Truman and Senator Russell of Georgia in August 1945.

10. See Martin Gilbert, *Winston Churchill: Never Despair, Vol. VIII* (New York, 1988), reflecting later on Dresden, p. 259.

11. See Gerhard Weinberg, *A World at Arms* (Cambridge, 1994), pp. 886–889.

12. See Weinberg, p. 886.

VI

Documents

The way a war is fought and the actions ending it endure in the historical memory of peoples and may set the stage for future war. . . . Just and decent civilized societies—their institutions and laws, their civil life and background culture and mores—all depend absolutely on making significant moral and political distinctions in all situations. Certainly war is a kind of hell, but why should that mean that all moral distinctions cease to hold?

John Rawls

THE
PERIL OF
UNIVERSAL
DEATH

Albert Einstein and Bertrand Russell

JULY 9, 1955
LONDON

IN THE TRAGIC SITUATION WHICH CONFRONTS HUMANITY, we feel that scientists should assemble in conference to appraise the perils that have arisen as a result of the development of weapons of mass destruction, and to discuss a resolution in the spirit of the appended draft.

We are speaking on this occasion, not as members of this or that nation, continent, or creed, but as human beings, members of the species Man, whose continued existence is in doubt. The world is full of conflicts; and, overshadowing all minor conflicts, is the titanic struggle between Communism and anti-Communism.

Almost everybody who is politically conscious has strong feelings about one or more of these issues; but we want you, if you can, to set aside such feelings and consider yourselves only as members of a biological species which has had a remarkable history, and whose disappearance none of us can desire.

We shall try to say no single word which should appeal to one group rather than to another. All, equally, are in peril, and, if the peril is understood, there is hope that they may collectively avert it.

We have to learn to think in a new way. We have to learn to ask ourselves not what steps can be taken to give military victory to whatever group we prefer; for there no longer are such steps; the question we have to ask ourselves is: what steps can be taken to prevent a military contest of which the issue must be disastrous to all parties?

The general public, and even many men in positions of authority, have not realized what would be involved in a war with nuclear bombs. The general public still thinks in terms of the obliteration of cities. It is understood that the new bombs are more powerful than the old, and that, while one A-bomb could obliterate Hiroshima, one H-bomb could obliterate the largest cities, such as London, New York, and Moscow.

No doubt in an H-bomb war great cities would be obliterated. But this is one of the minor disasters that would have to be faced. If everybody in London, New York, and Moscow, were exterminated, the world might, in the course of a few centuries, recover from the blow. But we now know, especially since the Bikini test, that nuclear bombs can gradually spread destruction over a very much wider area than had been supposed.

It is stated on very good authority that a bomb can now be manufactured which will be 2,500 times as powerful as that which destroyed Hiroshima. Such a bomb, if exploded near the ground or under water, sends radioactive particles into the upper air. They sink gradually and reach the surface of the earth in the form of a deadly dust or rain. It was this dust which infected Japanese fishermen and their catch of fish.

No one knows how widely such lethal radioactive particles might be diffused, but the best authorities are unanimous in saying that a war with H-bombs might possibly put an end to the human race. It is feared that if many H-bombs are used there will be universal death—sudden only for a minority, but for the majority a slow torture of disease and disintegration.

Many warnings have been uttered by eminent men of science and by authorities in military strategy. None of them will say that the worst results are certain. What they do say is that these results are possible, and no one can be sure that they will not be realized. We have not yet found that the views of experts on this question depend in any degree upon their politics or prejudices. They depend only, so far as our researches have revealed, upon the extent of the particular expert's knowledge. We have found that the men who know most are the most gloomy.

Here, then, is the problem which we present to you, stark and dreadful, and inescapable: Shall we put an end to the human race; or shall mankind renounce war? People will not face the alternative because it is so difficult to abolish war.

The abolition of war will demand distasteful limitations of national sovereignty. But what perhaps impedes understanding of the situation more than anything else is that the term "mankind" feels vague and abstract. People scarcely realize in imagination that the danger is to themselves and their children and their grandchildren, and not only to a dimly apprehended humanity. They can scarcely bring themselves to grasp that they, individually, and those whom they love are in imminent danger of perishing agonizingly. And so they hope that perhaps war may be allowed to continue provided modern weapons are prohibited.

This hope is illusory. Whatever agreements not to use H-bombs had been reached in time of peace, they would no longer be considered binding in time of war, and both sides would set to work to manufacture H-bombs as soon as war broke out, for, if one side manufactured the bombs and the other did not, the side that manufactured them would inevitably be victorious.

Although an agreement to renounce nuclear weapons as part of a general reduction of armaments would not afford an ultimate solution, it would serve certain important purposes. First: any agreement between East and West is to the good in so far as it tends to diminish tension. Second: the abolition of thermonuclear weapons, if each side believed that the other had carried it out sincerely, would lessen the fear of a sudden attack in the style of Pearl Harbor, which at present keeps both sides in a state of nervous apprehension. We should, therefore, welcome such an agreement, though only as a first step.

Most of us are not neutral in feeling, but, as human beings, we have to remember that, if the issues between East and West are to be decided in any manner that can give any possible satisfaction to anybody, whether Communist or anti-Communist, whether Asian or European or American, whether White or Black, then these issues must not be decided by war. We should wish this to be understood, both in the East and in the West.

There lies before us, if we choose, continual progress in happiness, knowledge, and wisdom. Shall we, instead, choose death, because we cannot forget our quarrels? We appeal, as human beings, to human beings: Remember your humanity, and forget the rest. If you can do so, the way lies open to a new Paradise; if you cannot, there lies before you the risk of universal death.

RESOLUTION

WE INVITE THIS CONGRESS, and through it the scientists of the world and the general public, to subscribe to the following resolution:

"In view of the fact that in any future world war nuclear weapons will certainly be employed, and that such weapons threaten the continued existence of mankind, we urge the Governments of the world to realize, and to acknowledge publicly, that their purpose cannot be furthered by a world war, and we urge them, consequently, to find peaceful means for the settlement of all matters of dispute between them."

Max Born
Percy W. Bridgman
Albert Einstein
Leopold Infeld
Frederic Joliot-Curie
Herman J. Muller

Linus Pauling
Cecil F. Powell
Joseph Rotblat
Bertrand Russell
Hideki Yukawa

ATOMIC
WARFARE
AND THE
CHRISTIAN
FAITH

A Report by a Special Commission
of the Federal Council of Churches

THE ATOMIC BOMB gives new and fearful meaning to the age-old plight of man. His proudest powers have always been his most dangerous sources of peril, and his earthly life has been lived always under the threat of eventual extinction. Christians of earlier times have felt these truths more keenly than modern men, whose growing control over physical forces has led many of them to believe that science and technology would in time assure human safety and well-being. This hope has been dashed. Our latest epochal triumph of science and technology may prove to be our last. The scientists who know most about the nature of atomic energy have been the first to declare themselves frightened men. With admirable restraint, but with impressive urgency, they have sought to awaken both military leaders and civilians to the alarming realities which as scientists they see more clearly than laymen who lack their special knowledge. The new weapon has destroyed at one blow the familiar conceptions of national security, changed the scale of destructive conflict among peoples, and opened before us all the prospect of swift ruin for civilization and even the possibility of a speedy end to man's life on earth.

There is little doubt that as knowledge of the new weapon becomes more widespread, and the earlier talk of some technical defense against it is clearly seen to be unrealistic clutching at straws, fear of these possibilities will be shared by more and more citizens and statesmen. Whether universal fear, one of the most powerful of all human motives, will help to save us or to push us the more quickly to destruction depends on how it is directed. The fear of God and His laws can indeed be a source of saving wisdom, but the fear of fellowmen or life or death or any created thing can be disastrous. In particular, blind panic is premature surrender to the evil that is feared. It may result either in mental and moral paralysis, or in acts of suicidal desperation. Death is the outcome, in either case.

By contrast, a more clear-sighted fear not of dangerous forces but of unrighteous use of them or capitulation to them, and of the consequences of such violation of God's will, can lead toward a sustaining faith which misdirected panic is sure to lose. In the face of atomic bombs and radioactive gases, no less truly than in the presence of smaller perils, the rule is: Seek first the Kingdom of God, and

His righteousness, as the only sure ground of ultimate security. In a continuously perilous world, as on the battlefield, brave men who refuse to make personal safety their primary goal have a safety that cowards never know. A major task of the Church in the anxious months ahead will be to demonstrate a courageous fear of God and faith in His invincible goodness, in place of either complacency or panic before the awful energies now accessible for human use. Men have found new strength and wisdom to face repeated crises in the past. It seems right to reject despair and earnestly seek such needed strength once more.

It is a fundamental Christian conviction that amid all the perils of earthly life, the Lordship of God will prevail and His purpose of judgment and mercy will not be frustrated. Moreover, it has always been in moments of supreme despair, when men have turned to God in an agony of trust, that spiritual redemptive power has been released which has changed the shadow of night into a morning of new hope. Today also the prospects of man's life on earth are intimately bound up with the measure in which, through the gospel of Jesus Christ, the worldwide expansion and integrity of the Christian Church, and the diverse workings of the Holy Spirit, the lives of men become centered in God. The reality of God-centered thought and action, which it is the supreme task of the Church to cherish, is the one hope of securing a world order in which man's release of atomic energy would be employed for human welfare and not for world suicide. To develop such world order is a task of fearful urgency for both Church and State, for Christians and non-Christians alike—a task in which we must engage with mind, heart and strength as servants of God.

To that end, there is need first to face squarely the changes that the great discovery has made in our situation. The release of atomic energy brings new resources and a new kind of threat to civilized living. A new pattern of warfare has suddenly taken shape that may invalidate many traditional judgments about war. Certain theological problems have been set, almost overnight, in a new perspective. These changes must be examined briefly.

IT IS TOO EARLY TO WEIGH THE POSSIBLE BENEFITS that may come to mankind from suitably controlled atomic energy; and a detailed appraisal would, in any event, be largely a task for physical scientists and engineers. Perhaps it is within proper bounds to notice that the chief benefits now regarded as immediately accessible are the opening of new avenues for research in the physical and biological sciences, and the provision of new tools for medical practice. Beyond these immediate benefits, it seems conceivable that constructive use of atomic energy could bring a more equitable distribution around the globe of labor-saving power, and the consequent freeing of additional millions of people from drudgery, with the chance for spiritual growth that is now denied to multitudes of human burden-bearers. This result would be the more likely (at the price of greatly increased peril) if ways should be found to release atomic energy from elements more plentiful and widespread than uranium. At all events, for the present it seems to be agreed that although power plants designed to utilize the heat liberated by atomic fission are not far away, the industrial benefits to be expected in the near future are pale beside the deadly threat to our tenure of life on earth.

The present fact is that neither the possible range of benefit from atomic energy nor the possible range of destruction to which we are henceforth exposed is accurately calculable. Even the physicists, chemists, and engineers who have developed the atomic bomb do not know how far the effects of a massive attack with such bombs, or with radioactive gases, might go toward making the earth uninhabitable. Some hold it theoretically possible, though highly improbable, that the entire atmosphere might be destroyed by atomic chain reactions. Somewhat greater, it would seem, is the chance that the atmosphere might be vitiated by radioactive gases, so that neither plants nor animals could live. Short of such total obliteration, we are quite certain at least that the industrial basis of civilized life is now largely at the mercy of weapons already in existence. Moreover, this threat is apparently permanent, beyond the reach of any technological defense now conceivable. As far as our best minds can see, the only promising defenses against atomic warfare are moral and political, not physical defenses. This momentous fact is fundamental in our present situation. The basis of any hope for the redemption of mankind simply through progress in the sciences and technology, always an unsound hope, has been permanently wrecked by the latest achievement in that very progress.

This judgment is underscored by the changes in the pattern of warfare as it can now be envisioned. The march toward total war, which this commission and other theologians have judged irreconcilable with Christian principles, has been advanced a giant step further.[1] For the new weapons are especially well suited to indiscriminate destruction. In purely tactical bombing of such targets as fighting ships, beachheads, or fortifications, isolated from civilian areas, destruction might indeed be restricted to combatant units and equipment. But in the strategic bombing that has already become so large a factor in modern war, atomic weapons clearly belong with the tools for obliteration, not precision attack. A blast that incinerates four square miles of buildings at a time cannot be used to destroy a munitions plant or a railway yard and spare the city around it. Moreover, there is strong reason to expect that if another major war is fought, strategic bombing of key cities will have a still larger place from the very outset, and that rockets with atomic warheads, not piloted planes, will be the chief weapons for such attack. Since rockets and robots have even less precision than piloted bombers, whole cities and not simply factories or freight yards must be the targets, and all pretense of discrimination between military objectives and civilian homes would disappear. Even more all-inclusive would be attack with radioactive poison gases that were already known in 1940 as by-products of the work with uranium.[2] The logical end would be total war in grim truth.

Further, the new weapons alter in two morally fateful ways the balance between aggressive and defensive war. If two nations are armed with atomic weapons, both the incentive to strike a crippling blow first and the possibility of doing so are incalculably increased. The first phase of a future *Blitzkrieg* would require not days but minutes, and the destruction possible in the first blow is of a different order of magnitude from anything previously known. A premium is therefore placed on swift, ruthless aggression by any power that may believe itself in danger. Moreover, wholly new advantages can now be won through successful treachery. The planting of bombs by trained saboteurs in the key cities of a non-belligerent country can lay an effective basis for blackmailing or assassinating a neighbor so reduced to helplessness before a shot is fired. Thus, practices most revolting to ordinary human beings may well become accepted tactics of the new warfare, and conscientious statesmen may feel called upon to adopt them to forestall such action by a possible enemy. Finally, the uses of atomic weapons that can now be foreseen would make war not only more destructive and treacherous, but more irresponsible than ever. On the one hand, an aggressor who first employs such weapons in massive volume will be taking action the total result of which, as already noticed, is not now foreseeable, and certainly not controllable within predetermined limits. The immediate effects of single atomic bomb explosions are indeed localized within a few square miles. But the lethal effect of radioactive poisons would be vastly wider, and total destruction or vitiation of the earth's atmosphere, however unlikely, is believed to be not impossible.[3] Where the destructive effects of a massive concentration of atomic discharges might end is, therefore, in essential respects unpredictable. On the other hand, if a country were attacked with atomic bombs carried by rockets or planted by saboteurs, and attempted prompt retaliation, the reprisals might easily be directed against an offending third party, suspected but not guilty of the attack. In an atmosphere of general suspicion, atomic war would have, more than any previous form of combat, the characteristics of universal madness.

In this new perspective, both moral and theological problems raised by war assume new proportions and a new urgency. Hence, all men and Christians in particular are required to search their hearts and minds, to re-examine their principles and practices, and to seek with the greatest diligence for effective ways to abolish this diabolical horror. We can speak here only of some of the moral and social problems posed for the Church by atomic warfare: problems arising from the past and possible future uses of the new weapons, the need for international controls, and the distinctive moral and social role of the Church. We shall speak also of what seem necessary restatements of our convictions about man's part in history, God's justice and mercy, and the hope of eternal life.

WE WOULD BEGIN WITH AN ACT OF CONTRITION. As American Christians, we are deeply penitent for the irresponsible use already made of the atomic bomb. We are agreed that, whatever be one's judgment of the ethics of war in principle, the surprise bombings of Hiroshima and Nagasaki are morally indefensible. They repeated in a ghastly form the indiscriminate slaughter of non-combatants that has become familiar during World War II. They were loosed without specific warning, under conditions which virtually assured the deaths of 100,000 civilians. No word of the existence of atomic bombs was published before the actual blasting of Hiroshima. A prior demonstration on enemy soil (either in vacant territory or on a fortification) would have been quite possible and was actually suggested by a group of the scientists concerned. The proposed use of the atomic bomb was sure to affect gravely the future of mankind. Yet the peoples whose governments controlled the bomb were given no chance to weigh beforehand the moral and political consequences of its use. Nagasaki was bombed also without specific warning, after the power of the bomb had been proved but before the Japanese government and high command had been given reasonable time to reach a decision to surrender. Both bombings, moreover, must be judged to have been unnecessary for winning the war. Japan's strategic position was already hopeless, and it was virtually certain that she had not developed atomic weapons of her own.[4] Even though use of the new weapon last August may well have shortened the war, the moral cost was too high. As the power that first used the atomic bomb under these circumstances, we have sinned grievously against the laws of God and against the people of Japan. Without seeking to apportion blame among individuals, we are compelled to judge our chosen course inexcusable.

At the same time, we are agreed that these two specific bombing sorties cannot properly be treated in isolation from the whole system of obliteration attacks with explosives and fire-bombs, of which the atomic raids were the stunning climax. We are mindful of the horrors of incendiary raids on Tokyo, and of the saturation bombings of Hamburg, Dresden, and Berlin. We are mindful also that protests against these earlier obliterative methods were met chiefly by appeals to military necessity, whereas the eventual report of the Air Force's investigators has now admitted the military ineffectiveness of much of this planned destruction. All things considered, it seems necessary to include in any condemnation of indiscriminate, excessive violence not only the use of atomic bombs in August, 1945, but the policy of wholesale obliteration bombing as practiced at first by the Axis powers and then on a far greater scale by the Allies. We recognize the grievous provocation to which the Allied leaders were subjected before they adopted the policy, and the persuasiveness of wartime appeals by military leaders to the superior competence of soldiers to decide military policy. But we have never agreed that a policy affecting the present well-being of millions of non-combatants and the future relationships of whole peoples should be decided finally on military grounds, and we believe the right to criticize military policies on ethical grounds is freshly justified by the proved fallibility of competent professional soldiers in dealing with such problems in this war.[5] In the light of present knowledge, we are prepared to affirm that the policy of obliteration bombing as actually practiced in World War II, culminating in the use of atomic bombs against Japan, is not defensible on Christian premises.*

WE ARE AGREED, FURTHER, ON FOUR MAJOR THESES respecting future policy with regard to atomic warfare and other new methods for effecting mass destruction. First, these methods, more than the simpler combatant techniques of the past, lend themselves to belligerent practices that are intolerable to Christian conscience. They make it harder than ever before to give real effect to the traditional distinctions between combatants and non-combatants among the enemy, and between proportionate and excessive violence in conduct of the war. They tend to unlimited, indiscriminate destruction. They increase appallingly the problems of the aftermath of war, because indiscriminate destruction wrecks not only the military potential of the enemy but also his civil institutions, on which depend the re-establishment and maintenance of social order. Hence, it is more than ever

---

*Some who concur in the foregoing judgment find their grounds primarily in the circumstances under which particular raids were carried out rather than in the practice of obliteration bombing or in the nature of the weapons employed. They agree that what has been done is wrong, and that it would be wrong for any nation in the future to take the initiative in using such measures for its own advantage; but they believe the way should be left open to regard the use of atomic weapons under some circumstances as right. For they believe that in the present state of human relations, if plans for international control of aggression should fail, the only effective restraint upon would-be aggressors might be fear of reprisals, and that this possible restraint should not be removed in advance. Others hold that even if belligerent action be regarded as, in extreme circumstances, unavoidable and justifiable, obliteration bombing and the atomic bomb as utilized for that purpose cannot be justified. Still others hold that the atomic bomb has revealed the impossibility of a just war, and has shown the necessity for repudiation of all support of war by the Church. They judge that since in fact belligerent powers are virtually certain to use any means that seems needed to insure victory, condemnation of obliterative bombing or of surprise attack with atomic weapons entails condemnation of all war.

incumbent upon Christians to resist the development of situations in which these methods are likely to be employed.

Secondly, the only mode of control that holds much promise is control directed to the prevention of war. We recognize the probable futility, in practice, of measures to outlaw atomic weapons while war itself continues. Use of the newer weapons might indeed be temporarily restrained, on the part of some belligerents by concern for humanity, on the part of others by fear of retaliation. But experience indicates that in a struggle for survival one side or the other will resort to whatever weapons promise victory, and its opponent will feel constrained to adopt counter-measures in kind. War itself must go.

Thirdly, in pursuit of this aim, we believe the Churches should call upon the government of the United States, as present holder of existing atomic bombs and plants for producing them, to move more swiftly toward allaying distrust respecting their possible use. Such distrust on the part of former enemies, neutrals, and even allies of this country seems to us understandable under present conditions. At the same time its existence is a barrier to international goodwill, and a possible cause of future conflict. We therefore call upon the Churches to urge, first, that all manufacture of atomic bombs be stopped, pending the development of effective international controls. We urge, secondly, that the Churches call upon the government of the United States to affirm publicly, with suitable guarantees, that it will under no circumstances be the first to use atomic weapons in any possible future war. Such measures are to be thought of not as adequate means of control but as aids to the development of a better state of international confidence, in which effective measures for the prevention of war may the more readily be worked out.

For we believe, fourthly, that the only conceivable road toward effective control of atomic warfare and other forms of mass destruction is the road of international comity and joint effort. Whatever be one's judgment respecting the pattern of future world society, it is clear that the war-making powers of national states must be given up, and the maintenance of justice and peace among nations become an international responsibility. In the present situation, we are agreed that progress toward this end may best follow two lines: the adoption of such political measures as may strengthen and improve the existing United Nations Organization, and unceasing effort to further the growth of spiritual world community.

As to the former line of action, we are not competent to prescribe a political structure for international dealing with these problems. We are agreed, however, on two major propositions. First, exclusive trust in a political structure of any sort to solve the problems posed by atomic warfare would be a dangerous illusion. In particular, the hope for world government, useful as a guiding principle, cannot be turned into a program for immediate action without very serious confusion of aim. Although improvement of the United Nations Organization is imperative, world government in any literal sense of the term is not yet attainable, and rigid insistence on full world government now is in effect a vote for continued international anarchy. It might even tend to widen, not lessen, the distances among the Great Powers. Moreover, if world government could be imposed now, it would have to be by the overwhelming force wielded by a few powers in concert, and such forced rule would gravely imperil essential human liberty and growth. It is better to start with the imperfect accomplishments and promises of the provisional forms of cooperation that have actually begun to take shape, and earnestly to seek their improvement. For such improvement, the ideal of world government may indeed provide valuable guidance, to the end that as rapidly as possible reliance on force shall give place to reliance on common agreement and a growing body of law.

Secondly, international provision for the control of atomic research and its application to the problems of peace and war should fulfill certain elementary conditions. Ultimate control should be assigned to civilian, not military agencies. The development and use of atomic energies should be steadily held in the perspective of concern for the enhancement of human welfare, and both promotion and restrictions should be directed to that end. A major concern of the supervising agencies must be to assure a wide and equitable distribution of whatever economic benefits may result from the use of atomic energy, and to prevent monopolistic exploitation by cartels or other minority groups. The policies of supervision and control, moreover, should be calculated to safeguard intellectual freedom, both among responsible scientists of all nations and, as far as technical difficulties permit, among the peoples whose welfare is at stake. We can see only harm in a policy of attempted monopoly of either scientific research or political information by either national or international agencies. The only atmosphere in which growing rivalry and suspicion cannot thrive is an atmosphere of free and cooperative enterprise.

These demands for attention to the general welfare suggest the need that political and technical measures be sustained, directed and inspired by the development of spiritual world community. We know how vague and empty this term may seem, to many readers, without detailed elaboration for which there is no room here.[6] We recognize also that the essential nature and basis of community call for much more profound study. Here we may note four requirements for such a spiritual common life as the welfare of the peoples urgently demands. There must be established, in the midst of hostility and suspicion, a basis for mutual confidence. There must be evoked in every people a deep humility before God and men, a genuine readiness to acknowledge present faults and to learn better ways, a habit of self-criticism and of self-restraint toward others. There must be encouraged and increasingly satisfied a hunger and thirst after truth: the truth about men, their needs, shortcomings, common hopes, the truth about the world in which and with which they must live, the truth about God as the Beginning and the End of all human life. There must be made known, by word and deed, the sure ground of hope that Christians find in the God and Father of our Lord Jesus Christ. Only when the profound kinship of common need, quest, achievement, failure, and hope becomes a living groundwork of men's efforts to achieve a world order can such efforts endure the strain of repeated disappointment. The more fully we recognize that other men have the same needs, the same fears, the same weaknesses as we, the better we shall understand our common failures and the more patiently we shall seek to help one another rise above them.

THE MORAL AND SOCIAL ROLE OF THE CHURCH in world affairs clearly is to help this spirit grow. This is not a political task. In essence it is a work of reconciliation among men, carried on in the spirit of Jesus Christ, in dependence on the power of God—a work that no political agency, partisan by its very nature, can perform as well. Precisely because the Church is ecumenical and supranational in its being, worldwide in its membership and mission, it can speak directly to men and women of any nation in the name of one divine Father and one universal humanity.

Its first word in our present situation must be a call to active penitence, addressed to friends and former enemies alike. There is no useful place among us for sentimental self-accusation. But there is acute need for such humility as not many among victors or vanquished have yet shown: the humility of clear-headed, honest men who see how grievously they have squandered resources inherited from a long, laborious past and jeopardized what should have been a more enlightened future. We shall not rehearse here the sorry record of sin and misery of the years just ended.[7] But we must note with urgent concern the continuing abuses of power by the victorious great nations and the demonstrations of irresponsibility among both conquerors and conquered. That such faults are natural after an exhausting war is obvious. That they are excusable, not to say negligible, on that account is untrue. They call for genuine, effective repentance, in which Christians ought to take the lead.

The most appropriate and convincing expression of such repentance must be determined resistance to public policies of the victors that seek to cripple former enemy powers.[8] Military disarmament, as competent critics have insisted, is not the same as economic dismemberment. Destruction of the industrial basis of German and Japanese livelihood, already far advanced by strategic bombing and other military action, cannot now be completed on political grounds without adding heavily to the injustice already committed in the name of the Allied peoples. Against such compounding of injustice the Church must steadily protest, in the name of God and of the common sonship of all men.

Within the setting of Christian resistance to unjust public policies, there is need also for continual urging of more active provision for relief and rebuilding of devastated lands. Plainly the largest part of this load must be carried by governments, but the Christian Churches have a special duty to urge upon their members, their neighbors, and all appropriate public agencies the honoring of our obligations as victors. This is not optional generosity but plain justice. If it is right that aggressors be held to account for reparations, then it is only right that we make some specific amends for damage that has resulted from our wanton acts of destruction. We are well aware that to some of our fellow Americans, the matter appears very differently, and that any curtailment of the plenty to which we are accustomed is looked upon with resentment, even if it be for the benefit of needy or starving allies. Such callousness we are bound to view with shame. It is unwelcome further evidence of our corporate failure in human understanding or decency, and of our deep need for repentance.

We are well aware also of the inadequacy and the dangers of proposing specific acts of restitution: the inadequacy of singling out a few victims from among millions, the dangers of displaying in that way complacency, hypocrisy, or misunderstanding. To rebuild Hiroshima and Nagasaki, the victims of our most spectacular offenses, would be to restore only a small fraction of what our strategic bombings needlessly destroyed. To provide special aid for the survivors of those two murdered cities would be hardly more than a token of repentance. Yet we believe either would have lasting value for future human relations. The former task would require public funds or a large popular subscription. The latter could be undertaken by the Churches of the United States, and we hope that at least so much may be done. We do not forget that the fire-bombing of Tokyo and the area bombing in Germany entailed a greater mass of suffering, and we have no thought of suggesting that token reparations now can overbalance the harm done by excessive violence in wartime.

Whatever we can do will be at best a belated effort to make some amends for past failure. All of us are too deeply in debt to appear as simple benefactors. A more realistic view of our role is essential to the growth of healthy community life. But even a small effort to right injustice, if the effort be sincere, can have reconciling value far beyond its intrinsic weight. Our refusal to accept a share of the Boxer indemnity has had that effect. Relief or remembrance for the first victims of atomic warfare might be misunderstood, or might be cherished as long as men remember the first atomic bomb.

One other task the Church has been performing throughout the war. It has maintained fellowship among Christians on both sides of the fighting lines, and around the globe. Now that the shooting has stopped, the evidence of persisting unbroken relationships within the Church is accumulating steadily. There have been, of course, large and painful losses, and these must as far as possible be made good through patient knitting up of broken threads, re-establishment of understanding and confidence, shared worship, and initiation of new common tasks. It is too early to judge how well the Church's ecumenical fellowship has come through the storm. It may prove to be in better case than anyone dared hope. And if that be so, Christians will give thanks first to God, who is not helpless in the presence of human strife.

TO SPEAK THUS OF GOD is to raise the final group of questions we have had to reconsider in relation to the new warfare: questions of Christian faith, which is the Church's ultimate recourse in times of extreme pressure. First, we have had to recognize important new light on man's part in history.[9] The release and utilization of atomic energy has given a quite fresh view of the scope of the effects that may result from his freedom. For on the one hand it would appear that by suitable directing of this new resource, man may be able to prolong the period during which the earth will sustain human life. If this be so, if man can actually extend earthly history beyond its natural term, then he can, in principle, transcend natural limits more fundamental and significant than any physical barrier he has hitherto surmounted. On the other hand, it seems at least as likely that by misdirection of atomic energy, man can bring earthly history to a premature close. His freedom, then, is more decisive and dangerous than we had suspected. In making man a little lower than the angels, God seemingly has laid on him a weight of responsibility that has not only personal but cosmic import.

This startling disclosure of the true dimensions of man's freedom raises again, in new perspective, the question of God's power, justice and mercy. We have held steadily that all these aspects of God's sovereignty are discernible in war as well as in peace.[10] We reaffirm that view here, with a somewhat wider frame of reference to match the wider scope that now seems ascribable to human freedom. We believe in God still as Creator and Sovereign of heaven and earth. We believe also that His judgment and His mercy are present inseparably in every moment of history. But our conceptions of divine judgment and mercy in history need to be carried a step further. Divine justice and judgment, we still believe, are to be seen in the steady maintenance of a natural and moral order such that men can live and thrive in it only on condition that they yield to it an adequate measure of voluntary obedience, as well as a great hidden body of unconscious adaptations. This order, with the obligations it entails for man, stands fast in peace and in war. If man should violate its demands so grievously as to destroy civilization or even to extinguish all earthly life, the inexorable justice of God would thus be vindicated, not impugned.

For divine justice is not the "distributive" or "retributive" justice of a human law-court, balancing claims and counter-claims, but primarily the unswerving maintenance of natural and moral law for mankind and the world as a whole. This, we believe, is the necessary basis of human learning and moral betterment. As such, it is intended as a manifestation also of divine mercy, which we believe is not to be separated, in the purpose of God, from divine judgment. Suppose then that in a sudden tempest of atomic warfare human civilization or even all earthly human life were extinguished, by the acts of some men. The fatal decisions would be human decisions, not divine fiats. In as far as divine justice contributed to the outcome, it would be through the active preservation of dependable order. Nothing else than this could be regarded as consistent with the dependability of God. But the persons thus suddenly ending their lives on earth would come to the end in very different roles, some as active aggressors, and others as relatively innocent victims. This contrast is always present in massive man-made disasters, and poses in itself no new problem. But the inclusiveness and finality of a possible global annihilation puts the old problem with fresh urgency. How, in the face of such a cataclysm, is the mercy of God—nay, even the justice of God, in any personal sense—to be seen?

First of all, it must be remembered that the possible cataclysm is foreseeable, and such foresight can help to prevent the end from coming to pass. Such annihilation is possible only because of extraordinary gifts granted to man. Even if these gifts should be perverted, it is still right to recognize divine bounty in the grant itself, and in the opportunity to turn the gifts to good account rather than ill. Secondly, the saving power of God is such that from otherwise desperate situations in the past—the crucifixion of Jesus Christ and the scattering of his disciples, the persecution of the early Church, the submergence of the Roman Empire in a flood of barbarism—new life has been called forth. It is essential to remember that the new peril we confront today is not the impersonal closing down of an Age of Ice but a possible man-made disaster that will come, if at all, because of specific human decisions. These fateful decisions in turn will be made, if at all, because of underlying attitudes of fear, vengefulness, pride, or rashness. We know that the one good ground for hope that such human attitudes may be profoundly changed is the redemptive activity of God, and we are confident that as long as human life on earth goes on, there will be clear signs that His providence is steadily at work to change men's hearts and win them back from the edge of impending ruin. Finally, men of faith will find, even as time grows short, that strength is given them to live without panic—nay more, with quickened force and earnestness. In a word, until the possible disaster actually occurs, there is no great difficulty in seeing divine favor as well as divine rigor in our new situation.

If, in spite of all, through human malice or blundering a worldwide disaster should come, there is at least a fair chance that not all human life on earth would be destroyed. Urban civilization, dependent on heavy industry and on complex networks of communication and transport, would almost certainly be ended for a long time. The greater part of any survivors would most probably be agricultural or nomadic people in out-of-the-way places, who might not even know that a catastrophe had occurred. They could not, without straining terms, be regarded as a "faithful remnant," saved by reason of obedience to God, even though civilization were thought of as destroyed because of fatal disobedience. They would be ignorant rather than obedient. Yet there is no reason to doubt that God could make them also become great peoples, and bring to realization through them new stretches of history, perhaps new levels of spiritual community.

At any rate, there is no need to question whether, as long as man's life on earth continues, the justice and mercy of God surround him and can sustain him. We confidently affirm again that they do. But if a premature end of history should come, then plainly the nature of the problem posed is different. The problem then is whether beyond the end of history God's justice and mercy are still a ground for hope, or whether the stultification of human life by a premature end is to be feared.

To this final question we can answer partly in terms of experience, partly in terms of our Christian faith and hope. First of all, even while earthly life lasts, men by God's grace rise above it in many ways: in devotion to truth and honor, in love for God and neighbor, in self-sacrifice, in martyrdom, even in Christ-like life. Thus they achieve a dimension of living that is different in kind from sensation, natural impulse, and prudential self-interest. Such living is not stultified even if—as in martyrdom—it comes prematurely to a close. The quality of life so attained has become, we believe, a permanent gain, not subject to destruction by passage of time. This is true, secondly, because God lives and holds in eternal presence the life of His children in time. His creating and redeeming work will not end even if the earth be destroyed, and whatever men have done, whatever of human existence has been good, He will cherish forever. Finally, it is a part of our Christian faith that not only the high moments of men's lives but their very existence and fellowship as personal selves is safe in God's hands; that death is swallowed up in the victory we call resurrection, so that death has not the last word. How such triumph over death is best to be conceived, we do not know. No more than we can define or picture the being of God are we able to picture what He has in store for us. But we are confident that in it lies the answer to the final question concerning His justice and mercy. We trust in God, and look toward the future with sure hope.

This Report was prepared at the request of the Federal Council of the Churches of Christ in America. It was not intended to be adopted by the Council and was therefore not considered for adoption. Its publication is authorized as an expression of the opinion of the signers. The following members of the Commission on the Relation of the Church to the War in the Light of the Christian Faith have affixed their signatures to the report:

Robert L. Calhoun, *Chairman*
  Professor of Historical Theology,
  Yale University

John C. Bennett, *Secretary*
  Professor of Christian Theology
  and Ethics, Union Theological
  Seminary

Edwin E. Aubrey
  President, Crozer Theological
  Seminary

Roland H. Bainton
  Professor of Ecclesiastical History,
  Yale University Divinity School

Conrad J. I. Bergendoff
  President, Augustana College
  and Theological Seminary

B. Harvie Branscomb
  Dean of the School of Religion
  and Professor of New Testament,
  Duke University

Frank H. Caldwell
  President, Louisville Presbyterian
  Seminary

Angus Dun
  Bishop of the Washington Diocese
  of the Protestant Episcopal Church

Nels F. S. Ferre
  Professor of Christian Theology,
  Andover-Newton Theological
  Institution

Theodore M. Greene
  McCosh Professor of Philosophy,
  Princeton University

Georgia E. Harkness
  Professor of Applied Theology,
  Garrett Biblical Institute

Walter M. Horton
  Professor of Systematic Theology,
  Oberlin Graduate School of
  Theology

John Knox
  Professor of New Testament,
  Union Theological Seminary

Benjamin E. Mays
  President, Morehouse College

John T. McNeill
  Professor of Church History,
  Union Theological Seminary

Reinhold Niebuhr
  Professor of Applied Christianity,
  Union Theological Seminary

H. Richard Niebuhr
  Professor of Christian Ethics,
  Yale University Divinity School

Wilhelm Pauck
  Professor of Historical Theology,
  Chicago Theological Seminary

Douglas V. Steere
  Professor of Philosophy,
  Haverford College

Ernest Fremont Tittle
  Minister of First Methodist
  Church, Evanston, Ill.

Henry P. Van Dusen
  President, Union Theological
  Seminary

Theodore O. Wedel
  Warden of the College of
  Preachers, Washington Cathedral

NOTES

1. Federal Council of the Churches of Christ in America, Commission on the Relation of the Church to the War in the Light of the Christian Faith, *Atomic Warfare and the Christian Faith* (New York, 1946), pp. 67–69; Cf. John C. Ford, S. J., "The Morality of Obliteration Bombing," *Theological Studies*, pp. 261–309.

2. H. D. Smyth, *Atomic Energy for Military Purposes* (1945), 2.32, 4.26–4.28, 4.48; Cf. *Science News Letter*, August 25, 1945, p. 121.

3. Professor M. L. E. Oliphant, leader of the British physicists in the joint research program, is represented as declaring that a single gas attack with these poisons would destroy life over an area 1000 miles in radius. See *The Christian Century*, December 5, 1945, p. 1341.

4. Smyth, 13.3.

5. *The Relation of the Church to the War*, pp. 67–69.

6. Cf. *The Relation of the Church to the War*, pp. 14–19, 54–60, 75–79.

7. Ibid., pp. 10–21, 47–53.

8. Cf. ibid., pp. 67, 69.

9. For an account of our understanding of man, which in general we still believe to be valid, see ibid., pp. 30–32, 43–54.

10. Ibid., pp. 29–43, esp. 33–39.

JAPAN'S
STRUGGLE
TO END
THE WAR

United States Strategic Bombing Survey

... a telegram received on 6 May in the German embassy at Tokyo revealed that Hitler was dead, the promised new weapon had failed to materialize and that Germany would surrender within a matter of hours. Kido believed, presumably on Japanese Army representations, that the Army would not countenance peace moves so long as Germany continued to fight. It is not clear whether this was a face-saving position, designed to avoid a prior Japanese surrender. In any case on 9 May 1945, immediately after the Nazi capitulation, General Anami, the War Minister, asked the cabinet for an Imperial conference to reconsider the war situation. The significant fact, however, is that Japan was pursuing peace before the Nazis collapsed, and the impoverishment and fragmentation of the German people had already afforded a portent of similar consequences for an intransigent Japan.

6. The Hiroshima and Nagasaki atomic bombs did not defeat Japan, nor by the testimony of the enemy leaders who ended the war did they persuade Japan to accept unconditional surrender. The Emperor, the lord privy seal, the prime minister, the foreign minister and the navy minister had decided as early as May of 1945 that the war should be ended even if it meant acceptance of defeat on allied terms.

The war minister and the two chiefs of staff opposed unconditional surrender. The impact of the Hiroshima attack was to bring further urgency and lubrication to the machinery of achieving peace, primarily by contributing to a situation which permitted the prime minister to bring the Emperor overtly and directly into a position where his decision for immediate acceptance of the Potsdam declaration could be used to override the remaining objectors. Thus, although the atomic bombs changed no votes of the Supreme War Direction Council concerning the Potsdam terms, they did foreshorten the war and expedite the peace.

Events and testimony which support these conclusions are blue-printed from the chronology established in the first section of this report.

(a) The mission of the Suzuki government, appointed 7 April 1945, was to make peace. The position of negotiating for terms less onerous than unconditional surrender was maintained in order to contain the military and bureaucratic elements still determined on a final Bushido defense, and perhaps even more importantly to obtain freedom to create peace with a minimum of personal danger and internal obstruction. It seems clear however that *in extremis* the peacemakers would have peace, and peace on any terms. This was the gist of advice given to Hirohito by the Jushin in February, the declared conclusion of Kido in April, the underlying reason for Koiso's fall in April, the specific injunction of the Emperor to Suzuki on becoming premier which was known to all members of his cabinet.

(b) A series of conferences of the Supreme War Direction Council before Hirohito on the subject of continuing or terminating the war began on 8 June and continued through 14 August. At the 8 June meeting the war situation was reviewed. On 20 June the Emperor, supported by the premier, foreign minister and Navy minister, declared for peace; the army minister and the two chiefs of staff did not concur. On 10 July the Emperor again urged haste in the moves to mediate through Russia, but Potsdam intervened. While the government still awaited a Russian answer, the Hiroshima bomb was dropped on 6 August.

(c) Consideration of the Potsdam terms within the Supreme War Direction Council revealed the same three-to-three cleavage which first appeared at the Imperial conference on 20 June. On the morning of 9 August Premier Suzuki and Hirohito decided at once to accept the Potsdam terms; meetings and moves thereafter were designed to legalize the decision and prepare the Imperial rescript. At the conclusive Imperial conference, on the night of 9–10 August, the Supreme War Direction Council still split three-to-three. It was necessary for the Emperor finally to repeat his desire for acceptance of the Potsdam terms.

(d) Indubitably the Hiroshima bomb and the rumor derived from interrogation of an American prisoner (B-29 pilot) who stated that an atom bomb attack on Tokyo was scheduled for 12 August introduced urgency in the minds of the government and magnified the pressure behind its move to end the war.

7. The sequence of events just recited also defines the effect of Russia's entry into the Pacific war on 8 August 1945. Coming two days after the Hiroshima bomb, the move neither defeated Japan nor materially hastened the acceptance of surrender nor changed the votes of the Supreme War Direction Council. Negotiation for Russia to intercede began the forepart of May 1945 in both Tokyo and Moscow. Konoye, the intended emissary to the Soviets, stated to the Survey that while ostensibly he was to negotiate, he received direct and secret instructions from the Emperor to secure peace at any price, notwithstanding its severity. Sakomizu, the chief cabinet secretary, alleged that while awaiting the Russian answer on mediation, Suzuki and Togo decided that were it negative direct overtures would be made to the United States. Efforts toward peace through the Russians, forestalled by the imminent departure of Stalin and Molotov for Potsdam, were answered by the Red Army's advance into Manchuria. The Kwantung army, already weakened by diversion of its units and logistics to bolster island defenses in the South and written off for the defense of Japan proper, faced inescapable defeat.

There is little point in attempting more precisely to impute Japan's unconditional surrender to any one of the numerous causes which jointly and cumulatively were responsible for Japan's disaster. Concerning the absoluteness of her defeat there can be no doubt. The time lapse between military impotence and political acceptance of the inevitable might have been shorter had the political structure of Japan permitted a more rapid and decisive determination of national policies. It seems clear, however, that air supremacy and its exploitation over Japan proper was the major factor which determined the timing of Japan's surrender and obviated any need for invasion.

Based on a detailed investigation of all the facts and supported by the testimony of the surviving Japanese leaders involved, it is the Survey's opinion that certainly prior to 31 December 1945, and in all probability prior to 1 November 1945, Japan would have surrendered even if the atomic bombs had not been dropped, even if Russia had not entered the war, and even if no invasion had been planned or contemplated.

Source: Papers of Harry S. Truman, Files of Raymond R. Zimmerman, Harry S. Truman Library, Independence, Missouri.

THE GREW MEMO: EMPEROR AS POST-WAR CONSTITUTIONAL MONARCH

DEPARTMENT OF STATE

Memorandum of Conversation

Date: May 28, 1945

Subject: Appointment with the President, 12:35 p.m.

Participants: The President
                Judge Samuel Rosenman
                Acting Secretary, Mr. Grew.

After a conference this morning with Judge Rosenman I went with the Judge to see the President and set forth the purpose of our visit as follows:

In waging our war against Japan it is an elementary and fundamental concept that nothing must be sacrificed, now or in future, to the attainment and maintenance of our main objective, namely to render it impossible for Japan again to threaten world peace. This will mean the destruction of Japan's tools for war and of the capacity of the Japanese again to make those tools. Their military machine must be totally destroyed and, so far as possible, their cult of militarism must be blotted out.

With the foregoing fundamental concepts as a premise it should be our aim to accomplish our purpose with the least possible loss of American lives. We should, therefore, give most careful consideration to any step which, without sacrificing in any degree our principles or objectives, might render it easier for the Japanese to surrender unconditionally now.

While I have never undertaken to predict with certainty anything that the Japanese may do, we must remember that the Japanese are a fanatical people and are capable, if not likely, of fighting to the last ditch and the last man. If they do this, the cost in American lives will be unpredictable.

The greatest obstacle to unconditional surrender by the Japanese is their belief that this would entail the destruction or permanent removal of the Emperor and the institution of the Throne. If some indication can now be given the Japanese that they themselves, when once thoroughly defeated and rendered impotent to wage war in future will be permitted to determine their own future political structure, they will be afforded a method of saving face without which surrender will be highly unlikely.

It is believed that such a statement would have maximum effect if issued immediately following the great devastation of Tokyo which occurred two days ago. The psychological impact of such a statement at this particular moment would be very great.

In a public message to his troops sometime ago Chiang Kai-shek, whose country has suffered more from the Japanese than any other country, said that in his opinion a defeated and penitent Japan should be permitted to determine its own future political structure.

The idea of depriving the Japanese of their Emperor and Emperorship is unsound for the reason that the moment our backs are turned (and we cannot afford to occupy Japan permanently) the Japanese would undoubtedly put the

Emperor and Emperorship back again. From the long range point of view the best that we can hope for in Japan is the development of a constitutional monarchy, experience having shown that democracy in Japan would never work.

Those who hold that the Emperor and the institution of the throne in Japan are the roots of their aggressive militarism can hardly be familiar with the facts of history. For approximately 300 years the Japanese Emperors were deprived of their throne in practice and were obliged to eke out a precarious existence in Kyoto while the Shoguns who had ejected them ruled in Tokyo and it was the Shogun Hideyoshi who in the sixteenth century waged war against China and Korea and boasted that he would conquer the world.

The Emperor Meiji who brought about the restoration of the throne in 1868 was a strong man who overcame the militaristic Shoguns and started Japan on a moderate and peaceful course. The Emperors who followed Meiji were not strong men and it became relatively easy for the military extremists to take control and to exert their influence on the Emperors. If Hirohito had refused to support the military and approve the declaration of war in 1941, he would in all probability have suffered the fate of his predecessors. In any case whether he was or was not war minded he would have been powerless to stem the tidal wave of military ambition.

The foregoing facts indicate clearly that Japan does not need an Emperor to be militaristic nor are the Japanese militaristic because they have an Emperor. In other words, their militarism springs from the military clique and cult in the country which succeeded in gaining control even of the Emperor himself and rendered powerless the Emperor's advisers, who in the years before Pearl Harbor were doing their best to restrain the hotheads. The assassinations in February 1936 were undertaken by the military extremists for the specific purpose of purging the peace-minded advisers around the throne. General Tojo and his group who perpetrated the attack on Pearl Harbor were just as much military dictators as were the Shogun in the old days and the Emperor was utterly powerless to restrain them regardless of his own volition.

The foregoing facts do not in any way clear Hirohito from responsibility for the war for, having signed the declaration of war, the responsibility was squarely on his shoulders. The point at issue is that the extremist group would have had their way whether the Emperor signed or not. Once the military extremists have been discredited through defeat the Emperor, purely a symbol, can and possibly will be used by new leaders who will be expected to emerge once the Japanese people are convinced that their military leaders have let them down. The institution of the throne can, therefore, become a cornerstone for building a peaceful future for the country once the militarists have learned in the hard way that they have nothing to hope for in the future.

I then submitted to the President a rough draft of a statement which we might wish to consider including in his proposed address on May 31. The President said that he was interested in what I said because his own thoughts have been following the same line. He thereupon asked me to arrange for a meeting to discuss this question in the first instance with the secretaries of War and Navy, General Marshall and Admiral King and that after we had exchanged views he would like to have the same group come to the White House for a conference with him. I said that I would arrange such a meeting at once for tomorrow morning and I asked Judge Rosenman to join us, which he said he would do. (The meeting was arranged in Mr. Stimson's office in the Pentagon Building for 11:00 a.m. tomorrow.)

Judge Rosenman [Special Counsel to the President] thought that our draft statement could be somewhat tightened up and suggested three or four points which we shall endeavor to include in the statement.

Joseph C. Grew

Memorandum of Conversation with President Truman and Judge Samuel Rosenman by Acting Secretary of State Joseph C. Grew. Source: Joseph C. Grew Papers, Houghton Library, Harvard University, Cambridge, Massachusetts.

THE MARSHALL MEMO: CHANGE THE TERMS OF UNCONDITIONAL SURRENDER

TOP SECRET

WAR DEPARTMENT
OFFICE OF THE CHIEF OF STAFF

Washington

June 9, 1945

MEMORANDUM FOR THE SECRETARY OF WAR

Subject: Basic Objective in the Pacific War

With reference to your suggestion that we change the Combined Chiefs statement of our objective in the war against Japan from "unconditional surrender" to "complete defeat and permanent destruction of the war making power of Japan," this seems acceptable from the strictly military viewpoint with one possible exception. That is the necessity for having in the statement a formal provision that the objective must be pressed to limit the duration of the Pacific war as much as possible. The expression "at the earliest possible date" should therefore be included.

Viewing any proposed change from the political and psychological standpoint and remembering that we have held to the "unconditional surrender" wording for so long, it appears probable that a deviation at this time would occasion an undesirable amount of questioning and doubt as to the nature of our changed intentions. Our military difficulties arising from the problems of holding not only our own people but particularly our Allies, the British, to the task of achieving our objective in the Japanese war at the earliest possible date might thereby be increased.

Instead of trying to change the wording of this *top secret* paper which eventually, as a Combined Chiefs paper, must involve British agreement, but which *will never come to the eyes of the Japanese*, it would seem better that we take action to discourage public use of the term "unconditional surrender," which we all agree is difficult to define, and encourage instead more definitive public statements concerning our policy and war aims. We should cease talking about unconditional surrender of Japan and begin to define our true objective in terms of defeat and disarmament. We should, however, diligently avoid giving any impression that we are growing soft. It is believed that this course would answer the objections raised by Mr. McCloy.

The nature of the objective, whether phrased as "complete defeat" or "unconditional surrender," is going to be determined by the detailed instructions, and the suppression of the statement "unconditional surrender" will have little practical effect on the final result.

G. C. Marshall

Chief of Staff

Memorandum for Henry L. Stimson, Secretary of War from General George C. Marshall, Army Chief of Staff. Source "Japan (After Dec. 7/41)," Stimson Safe File, Entry 74A, Record Group 107, National Archives.

THE MCCLOY DIARY:
GENERAL MARSHALL
ARGUES RESTRICT
FIRST USE TO
MILITARY TARGET

MEMORANDUM OF CONVERSATION
WITH GENERAL MARSHALL AND THE SECRETARY OF WAR

May 29, 1945

Objectives toward Japan and methods of concluding war with minimum casualties.

The Secretary of War referred to the earlier meeting with the Acting Secretary of State and Mr. Forrestal on the matter of the President's speech and the reference to Japan. He felt the decision to postpone action now was a sound one. This only postponed consideration of the matter for a time, however, for we should have to consider it again preparatory, to the employment of S-1.* The Secretary referred to the burning of Tokyo and the possible ways and means of employing the larger bombs. The Secretary referred to the letter from Dr. Bush and Dr. Conant on the matter of disclosing the nature of the process to other nations as well as to Dr. Bush's memorandum on the same general subject. General Marshall took their letters and stated he would read them and give his views on their recommendations as soon as possible.

General Marshall said he thought these weapons might first be used against straight military objectives such as a large naval installation and then if no complete result was derived from the effect of that, he thought we ought to designate a number of large manufacturing areas from which the people would be warned to leave—telling the Japanese that we intended to destroy such centers. There would be no individual designations so that the Japs would not know exactly where we were to hit—a number should be named and the hit should follow shortly after. Every effort should be made to keep our record of warning clear. We must offset by such warning methods the opprobrium which might follow from an ill considered employment of such force.

The General then spoke of his stimulation of the new weapons and operations people to the development of new weapons and tactics to cope with the care and last ditch defense tactics of the suicidal Japanese. He sought to avoid the attrition we were now suffering from such fanatical but hopeless defense methods—it requires new tactics. He also spoke of gas and the possibility of using it in a limited degree, say on the outlying islands where operations were now going on or were about to take place. He spoke of the type of gas that might be employed. It did not need to be our newest and most potent—just drench them and sicken them so that the fight would be taken out of them—saturate an area, possibly with mustard, and just stand off. He said he had asked the operations people to find out what we could do quickly—where the dumps were and how much time and effort would be required to bring the gas to bear. There would be the matter of public opinion which we had to consider, but that was something which might also be dealt with. The character of the weapon was no less humane than phosphorous and flame throwers and need not be used against dense populations or civilians—merely against these last pockets of resistance which had to be wiped out but had no other military significance. The General stated that he

---

* Editors' Note: The coded notation "S-1" was the reference used to identify the atomic bomb project.

was having these studies made and in due course would have some recommendations to make.

The Secretary stated that he was meeting with scientists and industrialists this week on S-1 and that he would talk with the Chief of Staff again after these meetings and the General repeated that he would shortly give the Secretary his views on the suggestions contained in the latter above referred to.

Memorandum of Conversation between Gen. Marshall, Secretary Stimson, and Assistant Secretary of War John J. McCloy. Source: McCloy Diary, John J. McCloy Papers, Amherst College Archives, Amherst, Massachusetts.

THE LEAHY DIARY:
PROSPECT OF
A NEGOTIATED
SURRENDER

June 18, 1945

General of the Army, D. D. Eisenhower, arrived in Washington from Europe and led a parade from Army Headquarters to the Capitol Building. The streets were crowded by a larger number of spectators than has been seen before by anybody now in Washington.

In the Chamber of the House of Representatives, before a joint session of the House and Senate, General Eisenhower made a very well prepared address which was not delivered with particular skill. The galleries were crowded with visitors and on the floor of the Chamber seats were provided for the Supreme Court, Cabinet Officers, Ministers, and Ambassadors from foreign countries, and the American Chiefs of Staff.

Immediately following General Eisenhower's address we proceeded to the Statler Hotel and participated in a luncheon for 1,000 guests given by the City of Washington in honor of the General. . . .

From 3:30 to 5:00 P.M. the President conferred with the Joint Chiefs of Staff, the Secretary of War, the Secretary of the Navy, and Assistant Secretary of War McCloy, in regard to the necessity and the practicability of an invasion of Japan. General Marshall and Admiral King both strongly advocated an invasion of Kyushu at the earliest practicable date.

General Marshall is of the opinion that such an effort will not cost us in casualties more than 63,000 of the 190,000 combatant troops estimated as necessary for the operation.

The President approved the Kyushu operation and withheld for later consideration the general occupation of Japan. The Army seems determined to occupy and govern Japan by military government as is being done in Germany. I am unable to see any justification from a national defense point of view for a prolonged occupation of Japan. The cost of such an occupation will be enormous in both lives and treasure.

It is my opinion at the present time that a surrender of Japan can be arranged with terms that can be accepted by Japan and that will make fully satisfactory provision for America's defense against future trans-Pacific aggression.

Dined with the President at a dinner given in honor of General Eisenhower to a large number of military and political officers.

For the first time in my experience cocktails were served to the guests in the East Room of the White House. A number of enlisted man, brought by General Eisenhower from Europe, attended the dinner which was served on small tables filling the State Dining Room.

My place was at a center table which seated the President, General Eisenhower, Secretary of War Stimson, General Marshall, Field Marshal Maitland Wilson, the President of the Senate, the Speaker of the House, General Eaker, and a British Air Marshal.

Diary of Fleet Admiral William D. Leahy, Chief of Staff to the President and Member of the Joint Chiefs of Staff. Source: Leahy Diary microfilm, William D. Leahy Papers, Library of Congress, Manuscript Division.

The Forrestal Diary:
Japanese
Peace Feelers

TOP SECRET

STATE-WAR-NAVY MEETING

19 June 1945

Memorandum of the Meeting at the War Department, at which were present:
 Hon. Henry L. Stimson, Secretary of War;
 Hon. Joseph C. Grew, Acting Secretary of State;
 Hon. A. L. Gates, Assistant Secretary of the Navy for Air;
 Hon. John J. McCloy, Assistant Secretary of War;
 Maj. M. F. Correa, USMCR, Special Assistant to Secretary of Navy.

Three topics were discussed.

1. *Surrender Terms.*—Grew's proposal, in which Stimson most vigorously agrees, that something be done in the very near future to indicate to the Japanese what kind of surrender terms would be imposed upon them and particularly to indicate to them that they would be allowed to retain their own form of government and religious institutions while at the same time making it clear that we propose to eradicate completely all traces of Japanese militarism. Both Stimson and Grew most emphatically asserted that this move ought to be done, and that if it were to be effective at all must be done before any attack was made upon the homeland of Japan. Grew stated that he had addressed a letter to Judge Rosenman on Saturday last embodying his views and that Judge Rosenman had said he would take it up with the President on Sunday last. (Copy of above letter in "Top Secret" File). Mr. Grew was of the impression that the President had indicated that he was not in accord with this point of View. Mr. Stimson said that that was not his understanding but rather he felt that the President did not want to proceed with such a plan at this moment and in particular did not want the Departments to abate in any way their preparations for the ultimate attack because of the existence of such a plan. With this latter point he indicated he was heartily in accord. Mr. Gates stated that while he could not speak for Mr. Forrestal, he felt that in general Mr. Forrestal favored such an approach to the Japanese. Stimson and Grew further pointed out that Leahy, King and Nimitz were all in favor of some such approach being made to the Japanese.

2. *The Agenda for the Meeting of the Big Three in Berlin.*—As to this Mr. McCloy said that he felt a number of the matters which it was now proposed to discuss at Berlin relating to the occupation of Germany properly belonged in the Allied Control Council and were not important enough for such high-level discussion. He said however that the discussion of the Agenda for the meeting of the Big Three would take place at a later time and there was no further discussion of the point.

3. *Repatriation of Italian Prisoners of War.*—Mr. Grew raised this point again and it was pointed out that a memorandum on the subject by Mr. Grew had gone

directly from the President of the Joint Chiefs of Staff and Mr. Stimson said that he felt strongly that it would have been preferable to have the memorandum go to the Joint Chiefs of Staff through the Secretaries of War and Navy. The Joint Chiefs of Staff apparently have turned down any repatriation at the present time on the ground that the labor of these prisoners of war in this country is needed at least until the fall.

(Secret Diary)

JAPANESE PEACE FEELER   13 July 1945

The first real evidence of a Japanese desire to get out of the war came today through intercepted messages from Togo, Foreign Minister, to Sato, Jap Ambassador in Moscow, instructing the latter to see Molotov if possible before his departure for the Big Three meeting and if not then immediately afterward to lay before him the Emperor's strong desire to secure a termination of the war. This he said arose not only out of the Emperor's interest in the welfare of his own subjects but out of his interest toward mankind in general. He was anxious he said to see cessation of bloodshed on both sides. Togo said to convey to the Russians the fact that they wanted to remain at peace with Russia, that the Japanese did not desire permanent annexation of any of the territories they had conquered in Manchuria. Togo said further that the unconditional surrender terms of the Allies was about the only thing in the way of termination of the war and he said that if this were insisted upon of course the Japanese would have to continue to fight.

Sato's response to the above messages was to protest that the proposals were quite unrealistic; looked at objectively it was clear that there was no chance now of dividing Russia from the other Allies, that the Agreement on Poland, on Chapultepec, and the Conference at San Francisco showed that England, Russia and the United States were determined to act in concert. Togo's response was that regardless of Sato's views, he still desired him to carry out his instructions.

JAPANESE PEACE FEELER   15 July 1945

Messages today on Japanese-Russian conversations. Togo, Foreign Minister, insisted that Sato present to Molotov the request of the Emperor himself. Sato's replies insistently pointed out the lack of reality in Togo's apparent belief that there is a chance of persuading Russia to take independent action on the Eastern war. He stated very bluntly and without any coating how fantastic is the hope that Russia would be impressed by Japanese willingness to give up territory which she had already lost. He kept repeating that the Russians were completely realistic themselves and would be impressed by no gestures of this character. He said the only hope for Molotov's receiving a special envoy to Russia was if he presented the suggestion on the basis that the envoy would have a message to present from the Emperor of a totally different character than what had been contemplated in the Japanese similar proposal of a year ago to send a special envoy. He finally in his latest message said that he had made such

without further checking with his home office
)arture of Molotov and Stalin for Berlin. He had to
Molotov's deputy, who apparently was quite non-
Throughout Sato's message ran a note of cold and
s position; and he said that the situation was rapid-
of Japan's and Russia's cooperating in the security of
e would be any Manchukuo or even Japan itself left
inal messages was that it was clear that Japan was
defeated and that the only course open was quick
ing such fact. One gathered from the context that
hope of reliance on Russia was completely without
Russia could not afford any appearance of desertion
es, and, second, that it was clear from Soong's cur-
otov that Japan was practically facing the stark real-
in the world.
e conversations began before there could have been
ind-plane raids of the Third Fleet and several days
ent of Kamaishi.

R   ,   24 July 1945

was Japanese Ambassador at Moscow, began send-
response to direction from the Japanese Foreign
bilities of using the Russians as intermediaries for
n effect that such an attempt would be quite naive,
vis-à-vis England and the United States where she
en to imply a separation of viewpoint or objective.
Minister, kept returning to the point and insisting
that Sato tell Molotov of the Japanese desire to send Prince Konoye as a special
envoy. Sato asked to see Molotov but was put off with Lusofsky, who was non-
committal. He finally did see Molotov who was equally non-committal and said
that all Russia could do would be to listen to any message which Japan wished
to send.

Finally, on the first of July, Sato sent a long message outlining what he conceived to be Japan's position, which was in brief that she was now entirely alone
and friendless and could look for succor from no one, that she was being exposed
to continuous attack which might result in her practical extinction as a nation.
He strongly advised accepting any terms, including unconditional surrender, on
the basis that this was the only way of preserving the entity of the Emperor and
the State itself.

He finally concluded by implying that he realized what he was saying might
not be welcomed by the Government at home but that his conscience still forced
him to send the message. The response to his message was that the Cabinet in
council had weighed all the considerations which he had raised and that their
final judgment and decision was that the war must be fought with all the vigor
and bitterness of which the nation was capable so long as the only alternative was
the unconditional surrender.

SURRENDER   26 July 1945

In the past days Sato in Moscow has been sending in the strongest language to the Foreign Office at Tokyo his urgent advice for Japan to surrender unconditionally. Each time the Foreign Minister, Togo, responds by saying that they want Sato to arrange for the Russians to receive Prince Konoye as a special representative of the Emperor to Moscow. Sato's persistent reply to these messages was that this is a futile hope, that there is no possibility of splitting the concert of action now existing between Great Britain, the United States and Russia. He constantly uses the most deferential language, such as "I stand in respectful awe of his Imperial Highness, but"—we must face the hard fact that Japan is thoroughly beaten and that unless we act in consonance with that fact the state may disappear as a political entity in the modern world.

Diary of James V. Forrestal, Secretary of the Navy. Source: Forrestal Papers, Mudd Library, Princeton University, Princeton, New Jersey.

Japanese Peace Feelers

THE MAGIC INTERCEPTS: JAPANESE TERMS FOR CONDITIONAL SURRENDER

WAR DEPARTMENT

OFFICE OF A.C. OF S., G-2

No. 1205–13 July 1945

"MAGIC"—DIPLOMATIC SUMMARY*

MILITARY

I. Follow-up message on Japanese peace move: On 12 July—the day after advising Ambassador Sato of Japan's desire to "make use of Russia in ending the war"—Foreign Minister Togo dispatched the following additional message on the subject, labeled—"very urgent".

"I have no yet received a wire about your interview with Molotov. Accordingly, although it may smack a little of attacking without sufficient reconnaissance, we think it would be appropriate to go a step further on this occasion and, before the opening of the Three Power Conference, inform the Russians of the Imperial will concerning the ending of the war. We should, therefore, like you to present this matter to Molotov in the following terms.

'His Majesty the Emperor, mindful of the fact that the present war daily brings greater evil and sacrifice upon the peoples of all belligerent powers, desires from his heart that it may be quickly terminated. But so long as England and the United States insist upon unconditional surrender the Japanese Empire has no alternative but to fight on with all its strength for the honor and the existence of the Motherland. His Majesty is deeply reluctant to have any further blood lost among the people on both sides, and it is his desire for the welfare of humanity to restore peace with all possible speed.'"

"The Emperor's will, as expressed above, arises not only from his benevolence toward his own subjects but from his concern for the welfare of humanity in general. It is the Emperor's private intention to send Prince Konoye to Moscow as a Special Envoy with a letter from him containing the statements given above. Please inform Molotov of this and get the Russians' consent to having the party enter the country. (I shall telegraph the names of the members of the party later.)"

"Although it will be impossible for this delegation to get there before the big men in Moscow leave for the Three Power Conference, we must arrange for a meeting immediately after their return. Accordingly, I should like to have the trip made by plane, if possible. Please try to arrange for a Russian plane to go as far as Manchouli or Tsitsihar in northwest and north central Manchukuo respectively."

---

*Editors' Note: The Magic summaries were deciphered intercepts of high-level foreign messages. Formerly classified Top Secret Ultra, these intercepts of Japanese communications were read daily by Truman and his top advisors.

WAR DEPARTMENT

OFFICE OF A.C. OF S., G-2

No. 121S–13 July 1945

"MAGIC"—DIPLOMATIC SUMMARY

I. Tokyo considers surrender on basis of Atlantic Charter: In a message of 25 July (of which the last part is missing) Foreign Minister Togo instructed Ambassador Sato as follows:

"1. The question of the Special Envoy is naturally related very closely to the course of the Big Three Conference. Since Churchill and Attlee are scheduled to return to England, it is said that the Conference will be adjourned for a short while. I would therefore like you to take advantage of this opportunity and, if necessary, to travel to a place of the Russians' choosing in order to obtain an interview with Molotov and explain to him the intentions of the Japanese Government. Even if it proves impossible for Molotov to arrange such a meeting, your request for an interview will at least go a long way in impressing upon him our determination in this matter."

"2. In the interview, please try to get the Russians to adopt a positive attitude with respect to our proposal. Stress the fact that Japan has approached the Russians in the first instance with her request for mediation. Make clear that the sending of the Special Envoy would permit Stalin to acquire the reputation of an advocate of world peace and, further, that we are prepared to meet fully the Russian demands in the Far East (see the end of part 1 of my second message of 21 July*). Finally, inform them that, in the event that the Soviet Government remains indifferent to our request, we will have no choice but to consider other courses of action."

"3. Furthermore, as you are aware, various discussions are now taking place in England and especially in the United States with respect to the meaning of the demand for Japan's unconditional surrender. Judging from the speech [or "speeches"] of American 'spokesman' [word in English; plural was apparently intended] it would appear that although they are formally insisting to the end upon unconditional surrender they are actually prepared to mitigate the conditions if Japan surrenders quickly. For example, on the 19th, Navy Captain Zacharias (he is on the staff of the Office of War Information but he broadcast to Japan as a 'spokesman' of the United States Government) said that Japan has two alternatives: (1) to submit to a dictated peace after being destroyed; or (2) to surrender unconditionally and receive the attendant benefits stipulated in the Atlantic Charter. We believe that these statements should not be considered as purely strategic propaganda but that they are calculated to lead us on."

"The fact that the Americans alluded to the Atlantic Charter is particularly worthy of attention at this time. It is impossible for us to accept unconditional surrender, no matter in what guise, but it is our idea to inform them by some appropriate means that there is no objection to the restoration of peace on the basis of the Atlantic Charter."

"In all likelihood, the difficult point is the enemy's attitude of insisting on the form of an unconditional surrender. If America and England stick to this, the whole thing will inevitably break down over this one point. On the other hand, although the governments of Russia, England, and America may be cool toward our proposal of a Special Envoy on the ground that it may be a peace stratagem on our part, this—as I have stated repeatedly—is not merely a 'peace feeler' [words in English]."

2. Sato–Lozovsky meeting: Also on 25 July—but almost certainly before receiving the message noted above—Ambassador Sato sent to Tokyo two messages on the subject of an interview he had had that day with Vice Commissioner Lozovsky. Only parts of the two items are available; the last part of the first message reads as follows:

"Lozovsky said: 'As soon as I receive the document [presumably described in the earlier portion of the message] from you, I shall report to my Government and inform you promptly of any instructions I may receive.'"

*Togo was apparently referring to the following passage in his 21 July message: "We hope to deal with the British and Americans after first (a) having Prince Konoye transmit to the Russians our concrete intentions as expressed by the Imperial Will and (b) holding conversations with the Russians in the light of their demands in regard to East Asia." (DS 22 Jul 45).

Source: Magic Diplomatic Summaries, Record Group 457, National Archives.

THE STIMSON MEMO:
PRIOR WARNING WITH
"AMPLE TIME"

Washington

July 2, 1945

Dear Mr. President:

I am enclosing herewith a memorandum to you on the matter of the proposed warning to Japan, a subject which I have heretofore discussed with you. I have tried to state as succinctly as possible how the matter lies in my mind, and in the course of preparing the memorandum, I have consulted with the Secretary of Navy and the Acting Secretary of State, each of whom has approved the tenor of the memorandum and has subscribed to the recommendations contained in it.

I have also had prepared a proposed form of proclamation which has been discussed with representatives of the State Department and the Navy Department, as well as with officers of the General Staff but which has not been placed in final form or in any sense approved as a final document by the Secretary of State or the Secretary of Navy or the Joint Chiefs of Staff. It has been drafted merely to put on paper something which would give us some idea of how a warning of the character we have in mind might appear. You will note that it is written without specific relation to the employment of any new weapon. Of course it would have to be revamped to conform to the efficacy of such a weapon if the warning were to be delivered, as would almost certainly be the case, in conjunction with its use.

As these papers were primarily prepared as a possible background for some of your discussions at the forthcoming conference, this added element was not included, but a suitable provision could be readily added at the appropriate time.

I shall continue to discuss this matter with the Secretary of State, and the Secretary of Navy, as well as with the representatives of the Joint Chiefs of Staff, and will of course keep you currently informed of any further suggestions we may have.

Faithfully yours,

Henry L Stimson

Secretary of War

The President
The White House

Editors' Note: Henry Stimson reproduced his July 2 memorandum to President Truman in his 1947 *Harper's* article. However, Stimson at the time did not publish his cover letter to Truman which contradicted a key element of his *Harper's* argument regarding whether a specific warning of a nuclear attack ought to have been provided to the Japanese. The July 2 memorandum and Stimson's cover letter are reprinted in their entirety in this section. The *Harper's* article can be found on p. 197 of this volume.

WAR DEPARTMENT

Washington

MEMORANDUM FOR THE PRESIDENT

Proposed Program for Japan

1. The plans of operation up to and including the first landing have been autho-rized and the preparations for the operation are now actually going on. This situa-tion was accepted by all members of your conference on Monday, June 18th.

2. There is reason to believe that the operation for the occupation of Japan following the landing may be a very long, costly and arduous struggle on our part. The terrain, much of which I have visited several times, has left the impression on my memory of being one which would be susceptible to a last ditch defense such as has been made on Iwo Jima and Okinawa and which of course is very much larger than either of those two areas. According to my recollection it will be much more unfa-vorable with regard to tank maneuvering than either the Philippines or Germany.

3. If we once land on one of the main islands and begin a forceful occupation of Japan, we shall probably have cast the die of last ditch resistance. The Japanese are highly patriotic and certainly susceptible to calls for fanatical resistance to repel an invasion. Once started in actual invasion, we shall in my opinion have to go through with an even more bitter finish fight than in Germany. We shall incur the losses incident to such a war and we shall have to leave the Japanese islands even more thoroughly destroyed than was the case with Germany. This would be due both to the difference in the Japanese and German personal character and the differences in the size and character of the terrain through which the operations will take place.

4. A question then comes: Is there any alternative to such a forceful occupation of Japan which will secure for us the equivalent of an unconditional surrender of her forces and a permanent destruction of her power again to strike an aggressive blow at the "peace of the Pacific"? I am inclined to think that there is enough such chance to make it well worthwhile our giving them a warning of what is to come and a definite opportunity to capitulate. As above suggested, it should be tried before the actual forceful occupation of the homeland islands is begun and further-more the warning should be given in ample time to permit a national reaction to set in.

We have the following enormously favorable factors on our side—factors much weightier than those we had against Germany.

- Japan has no allies.
- Her navy is nearly destroyed and she is vulnerable to a surface and under-water blockade which can deprive her of sufficient food and supplies for her population.
- She is terribly vulnerable to our concentrated air attack upon her crowded cities, industrial and food resources.
- She has against her not only the Anglo–American forces but the rising forces of China and the ominous threat of Russia.

- We have inexhaustible and untouched industrial resources to bring to bear against her diminishing potential.
- We have great moral superiority through being the victim of her first sneak attack.

The problem is to translate these advantages into prompt and economical achievement of our objectives. I believe Japan is susceptible to reason in such a crisis to a much greater extent than is indicated by our current press and other current comment. Japan is not a nation composed wholly of mad fanatics of an entirely different mentality from ours. On the contrary, she has within the past century shown herself to possess extremely intelligent people, capable in an unprecedentedly short time of adopting not only the complicated technique of Occidental civilization but to a substantial extent their culture and their political and social ideas. Her advance in all these respects during the short period of sixty or seventy years has been one of the most astounding feats of national progress in history—a leap from the isolated feudalism of centuries into the position of one of the six or seven great powers of the world. She has not only built up powerful armies and navies. She has maintained an honest and effective national finance and respected position in many of the sciences in which we pride ourselves. Prior to the forcible seizure of power over her government by the fanatical military group in 1931, she had for ten years lived a reasonably responsible and respectable international life. My own opinion is in her favor on the two points involved in this question.

a. I think the Japanese nation has the mental intelligence and versatile capacity in such a crisis to recognize the folly of a fight to the finish and to accept the proffer of what will amount to an unconditional surrender; and
b. I think she has within her population enough liberal leaders (although now submerged by the terrorists) to be depended upon for her reconstruction as a responsible member of the family of nations. I think she is better in this last respect than Germany was. Her liberals yielded only at the point of the pistol and, so far as I am aware, their liberal attitude has not been personally subverted in the way which was so general in Germany.

On the other hand, I think that the attempt to exterminate her armies and her population by gunfire or other means will tend to produce a fusion of race solidity and antipathy which had no analogy in the case of Germany. We have a national interest in creating, if possible, a condition wherein the Japanese nation may live as a peaceful and useful member of the future Pacific community.

5. It is therefore my conclusion that a carefully timed warning be given to Japan by the chief representatives of the United States, Great Britain, China and, if then a belligerent, Russia, calling upon Japan to surrender and permit the occupation of her country in order to insure its complete demilitarization for the sake of the future peace. This warning should contain the following elements:

- The varied and overwhelming character of the force we are about to bring to bear on the islands.
- The inevitability and completeness of the destruction which the full application of this force will entail.

529

- The determination of the allies to destroy permanently all authority and influence of those who have deceived and misled the country into embarking on world conquest.
- The determination of the allies to limit Japanese sovereignty to her main islands and to render them powerless to mount and support another war.
- The disavowal of any attempt to extirpate the Japanese as a race or to destroy them as a nation.

A statement of our readiness, once her economy is purged of its militaristic influences, to permit the Japanese to maintain such industries particularly of a light consumer character, as offer no threat of aggression against their neighbors, but which can produce a sustaining economy, and provide a reasonable standard of living. The statement should indicate our willingness, for this purpose, to give Japan trade access to external raw materials, but no longer any control over, the sources of supply outside her main islands. It should also indicate our willingness, in accordance with our now established foreign trade policy, in due course to enter into mutually advantageous trade relations with her.

The withdrawal from their country as soon as the above objectives of the allies are accomplished, and as soon as there has been established a peacefully inclined government, of a character representative of the masses of the Japanese people. I personally think that if in saying this we should add that we do not exclude a constitutional monarchy under her present dynasty, it would substantially add to the chances of acceptance.

6. Success of course will depend on the potency of the warning which we give her. She has an extremely sensitive national pride and, as we are now seeing every day, when actually locked with the enemy will fight to the very death. For that reason the warning must be tendered before the actual invasion has occurred and while the impending destruction, though clear beyond peradventure, has not yet reduced her to fanatical despair. If Russia is a part of the threat, the Russian attack, if actual, must not have progressed too far. Our own bombing should be confined to military objectives as far as possible.

Henry L. Stimson

Source: Papers of Naval Aide, Harry S. Truman Library, Independence, Missouri.

The Bissell Memo: Prospects for Japan's Surrender

MILITARY INTELLIGENCE DIVISION G-2

Washington, D.C.

Estimate of the Enemy Situation

7 July 1945

Major General Clayton Bissell
Assistant Chief of Staff, G-2

POLITICAL SITUATION

1. *General Situation.* The political situation in Japan is dominated by the progressive deterioration of the military situation. Japan's political isolation following the collapse of Germany, the loss of Okinawa, and the great and growing destruction in Japan proper by American air raids, have convinced the Japanese that victory for them is impossible. As a consequence the present government's foreign and domestic policies are dominated by a strategy of defense. Meanwhile, the internal political structure has been strengthened to meet the threat of invasion.

2. *Internal Political Situation.* Increasing numbers of Japanese realize that eventual defeat is inevitable and cleavages are deepening between political groups that differ regarding the best way to meet the present national emergency. The prestige of the nationalist extremist elements continues to decline, and the political center of gravity in Japan in shifting toward more moderate elements. The present Suzuki Cabinet typifies this realignment. In order that the government may not without fear of interferences arising from the increasing public depression or from divisions within Japan's ruling groups, the government is taking extraordinary measures to insure rigid control. The central government and the governments of the eight administrative regions of Japan Proper have been empowered to govern by decree; steps have been taken to coordinate the military and civilian administrations; the Japanese people are being organized in a national defense corps which will facilitate strict control; the government has been granted practically unlimited freedom to expropriate property, regulate residence and mobilize manpower. These strengthened controls will aid the government either in coping with possible invasion or in seeking a negotiated peace.

While the government appears to be ready to use its new powers to prepare the Japanese people for a last ditch fight, this fact does not in itself lessen the probability that the government is anxious for a negotiated peace. Although recent information indicates that an increasing number of Japanese feel that Japan's only hope is to end the war by political means, it is apparent that the Japanese leaders feel that they may get better terms from the Allies if they give the impression that the people are determined to fight to the last man rather than accept unconditional surrender.

3. *Relations with Subject Peoples.* With the continued decline of Japan's military position, the Japanese will find it increasingly difficult to keep their puppet regimes under control and to secure the cooperation of subject peoples. Japanese proclamations, promises and political concessions are having diminishing influence, and mounting unrest among non-Japanese in all Japanese-controlled areas will probably oblige the Japanese to increase their repressive measures. Maintenance of peace and order, even in such long occupied territories as Korea and Manchuria, is becoming more and more difficult. Anti-Japanese activities among the Koreans are increasing, and nationalist elements in Korea are preparing for collaboration with the Allies. The state of mind of Manchuria's population, which is predominantly Chinese but also includes Korean, Mongol, and White Russian minorities, is giving the Japanese increasing concern. In Occupied China the Japanese have found it increasingly necessary to exercise direct control over civil administration and economic organization, relying less and less on the Chinese puppet administration. In Burma, the puppet troops came over to the Allied side as soon as Allied military advances made such action feasible. In Thailand, the government is already working in the Allied cause and is preparing for the day when Allied operations will render the use of Thai forces against the Japanese most useful. In French Indo–China, the Japanese have found it necessary to set aside the Vichy-appointed French colonial administration. Although in so doing, they have gained the friendship of some nationalist elements, other native groups who regard a Japanese-dominated government as a poor substitute for French colonialism would be willing to support any allied invader in whom they had trust for post-war independence.

4. *Foreign Policy.* Since defense by force of arms is proving less and less effective, and unconditional surrender is still unacceptable, many Japanese appear to believe that they must choose one of two solutions: (1) a deal with the Soviet Union whereby they can keep that country out of the war and possibly prolong hostilities until the Allies have grown weary of fighting; or (2) a negotiated peace. In an evident attempt to lay the groundwork for the first solution, the Japanese Government, as well as Japan's press and radio, have been exhibiting an extremely friendly attitude toward the Soviets and have been attempting to exploit every opportunity to cause dissension among the Allies, especially between the Anglo–Americans and the Russians. The Kuomintang–Chinese Communist impasse is a source of potential Allied friction and conflict which the Japanese will make every effort to utilize for their own ends. However, the Japanese leaders recognize the relative weakness of their diplomatic position vis-à-vis the Soviet Union, and it is estimated that they now realize that they will be unable to reach a fundamental political agreement with the Soviets.

The second alternative, a negotiated peace with the Allies, is favored by an influential and probably growing group. The Japanese are showing increasing sensitivity to Allied psychological warfare. They are proclaiming their determination to fight to the death, rather than accept unconditional surrender, but at the same time they are indicating their receptivity to more "honorable" terms. If the Japanese become convinced that the Soviets are planning to enter the Pacific War, they may be expected to indicate their extreme anxiety for peace prior to that time, possibly making the overtures through the U.S.S.R. The Japanese will probably continue their efforts to make a separate peace with China, with negative results. If the Japanese become convinced that the only terms they can expect are unconditional surrender, it is quite possible that they will continue the hopeless struggle until their power of resistance is completely destroyed.

5. *Possibility of Surrender.* It is believed that many Japanese now consider defeat to be probable. The increasing effects of sea blockade and the cumulative devastation wrought by strategic bombing should make this realization increasingly general. The entry of the Soviet Union into the war would finally convince the Japanese of the inevitability of complete defeat. Although individual Japanese willingly sacrifice themselves in the service of the nation, it is believed that the nation as a whole is not pre-disposed toward national suicide. Rather, the Japanese have a strong concept of national survival, regardless of the fate of individuals. They would prefer national survival, even through surrender, to virtual extinction.

The Japanese believe, however, that unconditional surrender would be the equivalent of national extinction, and there are as yet no indications that they are ready to accept such terms. The ideas of foreign occupation of the Japanese homeland and foreign custody of the person of the Emperor are most revolting to the Japanese. To avoid these two conditions and to insure national survival of their institutions the Japanese may soon be willing to withdraw from all the territory they have seized on the Asiatic Continent and in southern Pacific, and probably even to agree to the independence of Korea and to the practical disarmament of their military forces. The surrender of the Japanese government might occur at any time from now until the time of the complete destruction of all Japanese power of resistance, depending upon the conditions of surrender which the Allies might accept.

Source: ID # 926728, box 74, Assistant Chief of Staff for Intelligence Papers, Record Group 319, The National Archives, Washington, D.C.

THE FORRESTAL DIARY:
MCCLOY'S DISSENT
ON THE
EMPEROR AND
PRIOR WARNING

The White House
Washington

8 March 1947

MEETING WITH McCLOY

On another subject: McCloy recalled the meeting with President Truman at the White House at which the decision was taken to proceed with the invasion of Kyushu. He said this for him illustrated most vividly the necessity for the civilian voice in military decisions even in time of war. He said what he had to say was pertinent not merely to the question of the invasion of the Japanese mainland but also to the question of whether we needed to get Russia in to help us defeat Japan. At this particular meeting, which occurred in the summer of 1945, before the President went to Potsdam, where, under the pressure of Secretary Byrnes, he stated his principal mission would be to get the Russians into the war against the Japs, the President made the rounds of his military advisors and asked them to tell him whether the Japanese mainland invasion was necessary. They all agreed it was. He finally left it that they would proceed with the plannings for the invasion of Kyushu but that they were to raise the question with him again before its execution and he would reserve decision on whether or not the attack should be carried into the Tokyo plan.

As the meeting broke up, McCloy said he had not been asked but he wanted to state his views. (Neither Stimson nor I were at this meeting). He said that he thought before the final decision to invade Japan was taken or it was decided to use the atomic bomb political measures should be taken; the Japanese should be told of what had happened to Germany particularly in view of the fact that some of their people who had been in Germany were back in Japan and would be able to report on the destruction and devastation which they had witnessed; that the Japs should be told, furthermore, that we had another and terrifyingly destructive weapon which we would have to use if they did not surrender; that they would be permitted to retain the Emperor and a form of government of their own choosing. He said the military leaders were somewhat annoyed at this interference but that the President welcomed it and at the conclusion of McCloy's observations ordered such a political offensive to be set in motion.

Reminiscence of John J. McCloy recorded in the diary of James V. Forrestal, Secretary of the Navy. Source: President's Secretary's Files, Harry S. Truman Library, Independence, Missouri.

THE TRUMAN DIARY: SOVIET ENTRY MEANS THE JAPANESE ARE "FINI"

DIARY

Potsdam   July 17, 1945

Just spend a couple of hours with Stalin. Joe Davies called Maisky and made the date last night for noon today. Promptly a few minutes before twelve I looked up from the desk and there stood Stalin in the doorway. I got to my feet and advanced to meet him. He put out his hand and smiled. I did the same, we shook, I greeted Molotov and the interpreter, and we sat down. After the usual polite remarks we got down to business. I told Stalin that I am no diplomat but usually said yes & no to questions after hearing all the argument. It pleased him. I asked him if he had the agenda for the meeting. He said he had and that he had some more questions to present. I told him to fire away. He did and it is dynamite—but I have some dynamite too which I'm not exploding now. He wants to fire Franco, to which I wouldn't object, and divide up the Italian colonies and other mandates, some no doubt that the British have. Then he got on the Chinese situation, told us what agreements had been reached and what was in abeyance. Most of the big points are settled. He'll be in the Jap War on August 15th. Fini Japs when that comes about. We had lunch, talked socially, put on a real show drinking toasts to everyone then had pictures made in the back yard. I can deal with Stalin. He is honest—but smart as hell.

Potsdam   July 18, 1945

Ate breakfast with nephew Harry, a sergeant in the Field Artillery. He is a good soldier and nice boy. They took him off *Queen Elizabeth* at Glasgow and flew him here. Sending him home Friday. Went to lunch with P. M. at 1:30. Walked around to British Hqtrs. Met at the gate by Mr. Churchill. Guard of honor drawn up. Fine body of men, Scottish Guards. Band played Star Spangled Banner. Inspected Guard and went in for lunch. P. M. & I ate alone. Discussed Manhattan (it is a success). Decided to tell Stalin about it. Stalin had told P. M. of telegram from Jap Emperor asking for peace. Stalin also read his answer to me. It was satisfactory. Believe the Japs will fold up before Russia comes in. I am sure they will when Manhattan appears over their homeland. I shall inform about it at an opportune time.

Stalin's luncheon was a most satisfactory meeting. I invited him to come to the U.S. Told him I'd send the Battleship *Missouri* for him if he'd come. He said he wanted to cooperate with U.S. in peace as we had cooperated in war but it would be harder. Said he was grossly misunderstood in U.S. and I was misunderstood in Russia. I told him that we each could help to remedy that situation in our home countries and that I intended to try with all I had to do my part at home. He gave me a most cordial smile and said he would do as much in Russia.

We then went to the conference and it was my job to present the Ministers' proposed agenda. There were three proposals and I banged them through in short order, much to the surprise of Mr. Churchill. Stalin was very much pleased. Churchill was too, after he had recovered. I'm not going to stay around this terrible place all summer just to listen to speeches. I'll go home to the Senate for that.

Source: Robert H. Ferrell, Ed., Off the Record: The Private Papers of Harry S. Truman *Middlesex, 1982.*

THE McCLOY DIARY:
WARNING,
SURRENDER &
TRUMAN'S
"BIG RED APPLE"

Potsdam Conference

July 1945
Tuesday, July 17

Conferred with the Secretary of War, and with Harvey Bundy immediately after breakfast, preparatory to the visit of the Secretary of War to the Secretary of State. More in this morning re the Japanese approaches to Russia. The delivery of a warning now would hit them at *the* moment. It would probably bring what we are after—the successful termination of the war *and* at least put them in a great dither before it was turned down...

The Secretary went off to the President's for dinner, but I gather that it was rather difficult for him to find a satisfactory opportunity to talk with the President. That was unfortunate as the Japanese matter is so pressing. There are so many things to do if the Japanese collapse should come suddenly—there is the question of occupation of Shanghai, Korea, etc. Political guidance is very much needed if the soldiers are to be in a position to act effectively. The whole situation with Russia will be up sharply then, and we shall be having settlements with her in the Far East at the same time we are trying to work out our relations with her in the Middle East section—extremely important that is, too, for though it is all very well to write off the area as an operational area in war, it is there that the future oil reserves of the world repose. . . .

Monday, July 23 and Tuesday, July 24

Throughout it all the "big bomb" is playing its part—it has stiffened both the Prime Minister and the President. After getting Groves' report they went to the next meeting like little boys with a big red apple secreted on their persons.

The play, as I see it, is to show some indifference to what the Russians feel is their great card—participation in the Japanese war—I never felt that this was much of a trading point as I always felt they were coming in anyway.

They could not fail to come in and I still think they will no matter how indifferent we show ourselves to be. Certainly to show our indifference would be a good thing. There is no use foregoing any of our natural interests or traditions for Russian participation, particularly considering the state of the war and the nearness of Japanese collapse.

I hope the Secretary gets to see Stalin before he leaves. It does not now appear that he will leave as soon as we thought.

Diary of Assistant Secretary of War, John J. McCloy. Source: McCloy Diary, John J. McCloy Papers, Amherst, College Archives, Amherst, Massachusetts.

THE BROWN DIARY:
AUGUST 3RD
BYRNES
ACKNOWLEDGES
JAPAN
"LOOKING
FOR PEACE"

July 3, 1945

July 3 was a big day in Washington. So many friends turned out to the Byrnes' swearing-in ceremony that the president moved it outside in the Rose Garden. Dick Whaley administered the oath; the President held the commission. Mrs. Byrnes' bible (1902 M. B. Aiken) was used. When the oath was completed, the President said, "Jimmy kiss the Bible." He did and then handed it over to the President and told him to kiss it too. The President did so as the crowd laughed.

July 6

JFB talks to Hull for 20 minutes over the telephone. Asks his opinion on Japanese surrender terms and whether Emperor should be permitted to retain throne.

July 16

. . . Stalin arrives. Apparently already he is playing his cards for all be can get out of them. President and Byrnes want to tell Stalin about new explosive (atomic bomb) but Churchill says delay telling him.

July 17

Byrnes decided not to bring up Ben Cohen's plan to carve Ruhr out of Germany. See my memo to JFB opposing this plan. Told (JFB) of his conversation with Stalin and Molotov about Soong's conversations. Russia wants to control Dairen and Manchurian railroad. Says they want to make it free port, but oppose joint control.

July 18

JFB and Truman conferred with Stalin this morning. Stalin revealed that Japan had asked to send mission to Moscow to talk peace. Said Emperor did not want to continue bloodshed, but no way out under unconditional surrender terms. JFB asked Stalin if there was any change in Russian policy toward unconditional surrender. Stalin replied "No change."

Stalin said that unless United States and Britain had any suggestions, he would reply that nothing specific in Japanese proposal and no need for conference. Stalin said he believed Japan realized Russia was coming into the war because they could see Russian troops on border. Stalin said he would not be ready to move against Japan before August 15.

JFB had hoped Russian declaration of war against Japan would come out of this conference. Now he think United States and United Kingdom will have to issue joint statement giving Japs two weeks to surrender or face destruction. (Secret weapon will be ready by that time.) Although I knew about the atomic bomb when I wrote these notes, I dared not place it in writing in my book.

July 20

Foreign Ministers Council agreed on and London selected as meeting place. If Stalin had objected, JFB had told Eden he would pick Brussells. JFB determined to out maneuver Stalin on China. Hopes Soong will stand firm and then Russians will not go in war. Then he feels Japan will surrender before Russian goes to war and this will save China. If Russia goes in the war, he knows Stalin will take over and China will suffer.

JFB informally impressed with Truman's team of Vardeman and Vaughan. Quotes Vaughan as saying "Stalin most likable horse thief I have ever seen". JFB realizes tonight more than ever the importance of his job and the great amount of work. "This is another world to me" he said.

July 22

It is becoming more apparent that Russians have gone imperialistic and are out to extend tier sphere of influence in all directions and where-ever possible. If they maintain present demands and positions doubtful is very much will be accomplished.

July 23

After Stalin and the American dinner guests arrived, a small meek-mouse man come in very unobtrusively and the photographers did not take time to even photograph him. After he was in, someone asked who he was, and no one seemed to know. However a few days later when his meek-mild-mannered man had been elected Prime Minister of Great Britain, the photographers kicked themselves for not taking his picture, because they found they had no shots of Atlee while at Potsdam, which were good for publication.

July 24

JFB says somebody had made an awful mistake in bringing about a situation where Russia was permitted to come out of a war with the power she will have. He said England should have never permitted Hitler to rise—that the German people under a democracy would have been a far superior ally than Russia. He fears there is too much difference in the ideologies of the U.S. and U.K. to work out a long-time program of cooperation.

After Big-3 meeting today, Truman dropped over and nonchalantly told Stalin of atomic bomb. Apparently the way Truman put it was that those high explosives which they had been working on had proved successful. JFB thinks Stalin did not catch the significance. All Stalin said was "That's great, let them have it." Byrnes said that everything was fine tonight but by tomorrow he thinks the importance of what Truman told Stalin will sink in and well may it. Tests exceed expectation. Will paralyze area of 26 sq. miles. Completely wrecked steel tower 12 miles away. Statement coming out warning Japan to give up. It was that if they do not, first bomb will be dropped around the 10th of August. The terrific heat wave can be seen for 100 miles.

JFB told more about Jap peace bid by Japanese Ambassador to Russia warned his government that same thing which happened to Germany would happen to Japan if she stayed in the war. Emperor had said they would fight to the last man unless there was some modification of unconditional surrender. Stalin replied to message from Japs as previously related.

Truman has wired Chiang-Kai-Shek in response to his telegram that he (Truman) does not expect China to yield further than terms of Yalta agreement.

Hopes Soong will return to Moscow and agreement can be reached with Stalin. JFB still hoping for time, believing after atomic bomb Japan will surrender and press for claims against China.

July 26

Joint message to Japan released. This was prelude to atomic bomb, Stalin sent message about 9:30 after it had already been released. That is, turned over for publication to the press. When the President returned from the trip (Frankfurt) he had two messages handed him. One from Chiang Kai Shek authorizing him to affix his signature to the declaration to Japan and the other message from Winant stating that Churchill had been defeated.

July 28

Stalin told of another bid from Japan mediate peace. He said his answer was the same—NO. Some detected in Stalin's remarks a mild reflection on U.S. for not consulting with Russia before sending joint statement to Japan. . . .

July 31

Stalin looked immaculate in his white coat, blue trousers and gold medal on his chest. Heavy neck, strong face, twinkle in his eye. He strokes his mustache which is gray. Good set of hair laughs a lot and is almost a chain smoker. Atlee speaks firmly, but does not have the force of Churchill.

August 1

The conference ended on a high tone of harmony. Atlee began by thanking Stalin for the fine treatment they had received. Truman voiced approval of what Atlee had said and added a few words of appreciation to the other two for having him preside and said he hoped he had done a good job. Stalin responded with a few more about the President and Prime Minister. Truman then expressed the hope that the Big Three would meet again, and the next time in Washington. Stalin replied, "God willing".

Below is the agreed version of the Stalin tribute to Byrnes. At the closing session of the Big 3 conference, the Prime Minister expressed appreciation for the splendid manner in which the President had presided over the conference. After he had completed his remarks, Generalissimo Stalin said: "The Soviet Delegation wish to join in thanks expressed by the Prime Minister to the President for the way in which he has presided over this conference. "I should also like to express the thanks for the Soviet Delegation to Secretary Byrnes who has worked harder perhaps than any of us. He has brought us together in reaching so many important decisions. These sentiments, Mr. Byrnes, come from my heart."

In reply, Mr. Byrnes said: "I appreciate very much the kind statements of the Generalissimo and am glad he feels that, working with my colleagues, I have made a contribution to the success of this conference."

Generalissimo Stalin replied: "I think we all can agree this conference has been a success."

August 3

Aboard Augusta/ President, Leahy, JFB agreed Japs looking for peace. (Leahy had another report from Pacific.) President afraid they will sue for peace through Russia instead of some country like Sweden. JFB and Truman chide Leahy not to hold out news on atomic bomb. Leahy still doubtful. This was the subject of much conversation at the luncheon aboard the *Renown*. As the Justice was leaving, the King grabbed him by the arm and said, "Now if this Admiral here does not give you the right information, let me know and I will send a ship out with it."

August 6

JFB recalled how he became worried about the huge expenditure and feared repercussions because he had doubt of its working. Stimson talked to Byrnes and the Justice contented himself with writing a letter to the President suggesting he get a board of scientists to look it over and make an impartial report. "It developed that all scientists capable of investigating the project were already at work on it," JFB said.

"This goes to show how important it is to have men in key places who have the respect of the people," Truman said. "Jim, you and I know several people who, if they had been in charge of this project, it would never have succeeded, because Congress would not have had the confidence in them to permit these huge expenditures in secrecy." JFB heartily agreed.

August 10

The army picked up last night an offer by Japan to accept Potsdam surrender terms provided that it was understood the Emperor would continue to rule the state. It was decided not to awaken the President and JFB. JFB was called this morning and he rushed to the White House. Found Leahy there with President and they wanted accept Jap. proposal. Stimson came in, and he agreed it should be accepted. Snyder was going along in that direction.

JFB took different course. He pointed out that at Potsdam, the Big–3 said "unconditional surrender". Then there was an atomic bomb and no Russia in the war. "I cannot understand why now we should go further than we were willing to go at Potsdam when we had no atomic bomb, and Russia was not in the war," B said.

Leahy had a message which agreed and accepted proposal to deal with present Japanese government to maintain order on Japan. This message would have led to crucifixion of President. When JFB returned today, he said the first thing that indicated he was irked with Leahy. He said that Leahy still thought he was Secretary of State, just as he was under Roosevelt, and he had to show him differently.

Saturday August 11

At lunch, JFB told of his troubles at the White House with Leahy, and he began making plans to get MacArthur named as Supreme Commander.

August 14

Eureka—promptly at 3:00 P. M. General Marshall called and read message from Japan which was unconditional surrender.

Walter Brown was Special Assistant to Secretary of State James F. Byrnes, during the Potsdam Conference.

Editors' Note: The original typewritten Brown Diary contains several typographical errors. These have been corrected in this printing. The original document is located in the Special Collections at the Robert Muldrow Cooper Library, Clemson University, Clemson, South Carolina.

THE STIMSON DIARY:

THE SOVIETS

& THE

S–1 MASTER CARD

Monday, May 14, 1945.

I talked over with Marshall the lists of questions which the State Department had fired at me and which I enumerated in my yesterday's diary and we both decided that they were rather impractical to discuss now with anyone. I had a talk with McCloy about them. I told him to look them over and see what he thought of them; if he thought there was anything serious to answer. I told him that my own opinion was that the time now and the method now to deal with Russia was to keep our mouths shut and let our actions speak for words. The Russians will understand them better than anything else. It is a case where we have got to regain the lead and perhaps do it in a pretty rough and realistic way. They have rather taken it away from us because we have talked too much and have been too lavish with our beneficences to them. I told him this was a place where we really held all the cards. I called it a royal straight flush and we mustn't be a fool about the way we play it. They can't get along without our help and industries and we have coming into action a weapon which will be unique. Now the thing is not to get into unnecessary quarrels by talking too much and not to indicate any weakness by talking too much; let our actions speak for themselves.

Tuesday, May 15, 1945

At 9:30 we went into our meeting of the Committee of Three, Grew, Forrestal and myself being present with McCloy as recorder. Averell Harriman, the Ambassador to Russia, came with Grew; also William Phillips, formerly Under Secretary of State years ago. Forrestal brought Major Correa. We had a pretty red hot session first over the questions which Grew had propounded to us in relation to the Yalta Conference and our relations with Russia. They have been entered in the diary here so I will not repeat them. I tried to point out the difficulties which existed and I thought it premature to ask those questions; at least we were not yet in a position to answer them. The trouble is that the President has now promised apparently to meet Stalin and Churchill on the first of July and at that time these questions will become burning and it may be necessary to have it out with Russia on her relations to Manchuria and Port Arthur and various other parts of North China, and also the relations of China to us. Over any such tangled wave of problems the S-1 secret would be dominant and yet we will not know until after that time probably, until after that meeting, whether this is a weapon in our hands or not. We think it will be shortly afterwards, but it seems a terrible thing to gamble with such big stakes in diplomacy without having your master card in your hand. The best we could do today was to persuade Harriman not to go back until we had had time to think over these things a little bit harder. . . .

Sunday, July 22, 1945

At ten-forty Bundy and I again went to the British headquarters and talked to the Prime Minister and Lord Cherwell for over an hour. Churchill read Groves' report in full. He told me that he had noticed at the meeting of the Three yesterday that Truman was evidently much fortified by something that had happened and that he stood up to the Russians in a most emphatic and decisive manner, telling them as to certain demands that they absolutely could not have and that the

United States was entirely against them. He said "Now I know what happened to Truman yesterday. I couldn't understand it. When he got to the meeting after having read this report he was a changed man. He told the Russians just where they got on and off and generally bossed the whole meeting." Churchill said he now understood how this pepping up had taken place and that he felt the same way. His own attitude confirmed this admission. He now not only was not worried about giving the Russians information of the matter but was rather inclined to use it as an argument in our favor in the negotiations. The sentiment of the four of us was unanimous in thinking that it was advisable to tell the Russians at least that we were working on that subject and intended to use it when it was successfully finished.

At twelve-fifteen I called General Arnold over, showed him Harrison's two cables, showed him my answer to them and showed him Groves' report, which he read in its entirety. He told me that he agreed with me about the target which I had struck off the program. He said that it would take considerable hard work to organize the operations now that it was to move forward.

After luncheon and rest, at three-fifty we took an auto drive out into the country to the west of Babelsberg, and saw some open country and also the very battered city of Potsdam.

Source: Stimson Diary microfilm, Henry L. Stimson microfilms, Library of Congress, Manuscript Division.

THE JULY 17TH
PETITION
OF THE
MANHATTAN
SCIENTISTS

Editors' Note: The July 17th Petition is published here for the first time with a complete list of its signatories. Three weeks before atomic bombs were dropped on Hiroshima and Nagasaki the petition was circulated among scientists working in the Manhattan Project. One hundred and fifty-five members of the project signed the petition to Truman in the hope of dissuading the President from using the weapon against Japan without seriously considering "the moral responsibilities which are involved." Having originally set out to build a nuclear weapon based on fear of Germany's technical potential, a group of Manhattan Project scientists led by Leo Szilard drafted a petition to Truman arguing that Germany's defeat meant that the potential danger of an atomic threat to the Allies had been averted. They argued to Truman that the use of an atomic weapon against Japan "could not be justified" without at least giving Tokyo an opportunity to surrender once "terms which will be imposed after the war on Japan were made public in detail."

The petition's delivery to Truman and Secretary of War Stimson was deliberately delayed by General Leslie Groves, Director of the Manhattan Project, whose opposition to Szilard's efforts to persuade senior political figures against using a nuclear weapon are now well documented. According to William Lanouette, "Groves held the petition until August 1, when a telex from Tinian Island in the Pacific assured him that the A-bomb was ready for use. Having tried to reach the President, then having gone on record against use of the A-Bomb, Szilard could only await nervously the disaster . . . Groves at last forwarded Szilard's petition to Stimson's office. But still in Potsdam with Truman, Stimson would not see the petition until his return later in August. . . . In Potsdam [on July 24] . . . Secretary of War Stimson approved the final orders to drop the A-bomb 'after about 3 August'." (See "Three Attempts to Stop The Bomb" by William Lanouette, p. 99.)

A PETITION TO THE PRESIDENT OF THE UNITED STATES

July 17, 1945

Discoveries of which the people of the United States are not aware may affect the welfare of this nation in the near future. The liberation of atomic power which has been achieved places atomic bombs in the hands of the Army. It places in your hands, as Commander-in-Chief, the fateful decision whether or not to sanction the use of such bombs in the present phase of the war against Japan.

We, the undersigned scientists, have been working in the field of atomic power. Until recently we have had to fear that the United States might be attacked by atomic bombs during this war and that her only defense might lie in a counter-attack by the same means. Today, with the defeat of Germany, this danger is averted and we feel impelled to say what follows:

The war had to be brought speedily to a successful conclusion and attacks by atomic bombs may very well be an effective method of warfare. We feel, however, that such attacks on Japan could not be justified, at least not until the terms which will be imposed after the war on Japan were made public in detail and Japan were given an opportunity to surrender.

If such public announcement gave assurance to the Japanese that they could look forward to a life devoted to peaceful pursuits in their homeland and if Japan still refused to surrender our nation might then, in certain circumstances, find itself forced to resort to the use of atomic bombs. Such a step, however, ought not to be made at any time without seriously considering the moral responsibilities which are involved.

The development of atomic power will provide the nations with new means of destruction. The atomic bombs at our disposal represent only the first step in this direction, and there is almost no limit to the destructive power which will become available to the course of their future development. Thus a nation which sets the precedent of using these newly liberated forces of nature for purposes of destruction may have to bear the responsibility of opening the door to an era of devastation on an unimaginable scale.

If after the war a situation is allowed to develop in the world which permits rival powers to be in uncontrolled possession of these new means of destruction the cities of the United States as well as the cities of other nations will be in continuous danger of sudden annihilation. All the resources of the United States, moral and material, may have to be mobilized to prevent the advent of such a world situation. Its prevention is at present the solemn responsibility of the United States—singled out by virtue of her lead in the field of atomic power.

The added material strength which this lead gives to the United States brings with it the obligation of restraint and if we were to violate this obligation our moral position would be weakened in the eyes of the world and in our own eyes. It would then be more difficult for us live up to our responsibility of bringing the unloosened forces of destruction under control.

In view of the foregoing, we, the undersigned, respectfully petition: first, that you exercise your power as Commander-in-Chief to rule that the United States shall not resort to the use of atomic bombs in this war unless the terms which will be imposed upon Japan have been made public in detail and Japan knowing these terms has refused to surrender; second, that in such an event the question whether or not to use atomic bombs be decided by you in the light of the consideration presented in this petition as well as all other moral responsibilities which are involved.

The petition was signed by seventy-one scientists at the Manhattan Project's Metallurgical Laboratory (Met Lab) at the University of Chicago. The Met Lab's mission was to prepare plutonium for A-bombs. The signatories were:

[Ralph] E. Lapp	Alfred Pfanstiehl
J. J. Nickson	Hoylande D. Young
Frank Foote	Katharine Way
R. S. Mulliken	Leo A. Ohlinger
Walter Bartky	Norman Modine
W. H. Zachariasen	J. Ernest Wilkins, Jr.
E. P. Wigner	Mary Burke
Francis R. Shonka	Witfred Rall
George S. Monk	Mildred Ginsberg
John A. Simpson, Jr.	Lawrence B. Magnusson
Leo Szilard	Paul R. O'Connor
John P. Howe, Jr.	Walter J. Grundhauser
David L. Hill	[Horace] Owen France
Herbert E. Kubitschek	C. Ladd Prosser
Robert J. Maurer	Mary M. Dailey
Alexander Langsdorf, Jr.	Mariam P. Finkel
Francis Lee Friedman	Larned B. Asprey
Robert L. Purbrick	Joseph D. Teresi
Albert Wattenberg	David S. Anthony
Norman Goldstein	Truman P. Kohman
David B. Hall	D. C. Stewart
B. Roswell Russell	George Siahlo
Albert Cahn, Jr.	William P. Norris
Kenneth S. Cole	Chas. W. Hagen, Jr.
Jasper B. Jeffries	George A. Sacher
Austin M. Brues	Marietta C. Moore
Eric L. Simmons	William Rubinson
Margaret H. Rand	Edgar F. Westrum, Jr.
Robert J. Moon	Mark Fred
Marguerite N. Swift	Earl K. Hyde
William Karush	John Crawford
Robert L. Platzman	Ralph E. Telford
Geo. R. Carlson	Ellis P. Steinberg
Ethaline H. Cortelyou	Sheffield Gordon
Sherman Fried	Melvin Friedman

At the Manhattan Project's Oak Ridge facility in Tennessee, where uranium 235 was separated from uranium 238 to prepare the uranium core used in the Hiroshima bomb, a total sixty-seven scientists signed the petition.

Charles D. Coryell	D. E. Koshland, Jr.
Cecil M. Nelson	M. Creck
Paul C. Tompkins	James G. Barrick
Jack Siegel	Joseph Halperin
Ralph Livingston	Alan S. Jarrett
R. W. Stoughton	R. F. Leininger
Norman Elliot	Robert B. Scott
Joseph Khym	Kurt D. Kraus
Lionel S. Golding	John R. Dam
Nathan E. Ballou	Louis B. Wenner
Clinton R. Vanneman	Elwin H. Covey
Theodore B. Novey	Elton H. Turk
Waldo E. Cohn	Russell W'ms, Jr.
John P. McBride	Raymond R. Edwards
Earl R. Purchase	Robert A. Penneman
S. G. English	Glenn H. Jenks
Donald S. Schover	L. T. McClinton
Edward L. Brady	A. W. Adamson
Harrison S. Brown	William G. Leslie
Dwight C. Lincoln	A. R. Brosi
Howard Gest	B. H. Ketelle
Edward Shapiro	Charles W. Stanby
Edward G. Gohlmann	John A. Ghormley
A. J. Miller	J. O. Blomeke
I. E. Glendenin	L. H. Govantman
Jack K. East	C. J. Barkowski
William J. Knox	Robert L. Butenhoff
Melvin G. Bowman	J. E. Sattezaher
John P. Hunt	Gordon Johnson
F. Boldridge	Jim Kroner
Bernard J. Finkle	Stanley Rasmussen
Walton A. Rodger	D. N. Hume
W. H. Burgus	John B. Otto
R. K. Maney	

Eighteen scientists at the Clinton Laboratory in Oak Ridge stated that they "agreed in essence with the attached [Szilard] petition, but feel our attitude is more clearly expressed if its last paragraph is replaced." The last paragraph of the original draft had read: "In view of the foregoing, we, the undersigned, respectfully petition that you exercise your power as Commander-in-Chief to rule that the United States shall not, in the present phase of the war, resort to the use of atomic bombs."

The replacement they proposed read as follows: "We respectfully petition that the use of atomic bombs, particularly against cities, be sanctioned by you as Chief Executive only under the following conditions: (1) Opportunity has been given to the Japanese to surrender on terms assuring them the possibility of peaceful development in their homeland. (2) Convincing warnings have been given that a refusal to surrender will be followed by the use of a new weapon. (3) Responsibility for use of atomic bombs is shared with our allies."

L. W. Nordheim	Harry Soudak
David Saxon	Frederic Schuler
Alvin M. Weinberg	Forrest H. Murray
Edwin P. Meiners, Jr.	Raymond B. Sawyer
Louis A. Purdue	Edmond D. Cashwell
Garland M. Branch, Jr.	Harold Schweinler
E. O. Wollan	Arturo H. Suell
J. H. Rush	Richard Scatletter
Frank C. Hoyt	Lionel D. Norris, Jr.

An Oak Ridge scientist, George W. Parker, organized a counter-petition which attacked "the original Szilard petition" as a security risk, and argued that "if we can save even a handful of American lives, then let us use this weapon—now!" Parker secured the signature of one other scientist, D.S. Ballantine, to the counter-petition which also stated "we fail to see the use of the moral argument when we are considering such an immoral situation as war."

A NOTE

ON THE

JULY 17TH

PETITION

William Lanouette

ON JULY 17, 1945, the Hungarian-born physicist Leo Szilard sat in his office at the University of Chicago and bundled nine pages of a petition into a manila envelope. He then addressed it "To the President of the United States." The day before, in the New Mexico desert, the first atomic bomb had been successfully tested. Now, with this petition, Szilard and scores of his fellow Manhattan Project scientists were declaring that "moral responsibilities" should influence how the weapon they had created should be used. Earlier that spring, Szilard and a few other scientists had organized after-hours discussions about the future of the A-bomb, fearing a postwar nuclear arms race between America and Russia. General Leslie Groves, the Director of the Manhattan Project, had tried to prevent those discussions.

By July, Szilard had already made three attempts to communicate his views on the use of the bomb: first, with a letter to President Roosevelt he had drafted for Einstein's signature; second, in a May 28 meeting with President Truman's close advisor, James F. Byrnes; and third, with the June 11 recommendations of the Franck Report. All three efforts had failed. Now Szilard would make one last attempt in the form of a direct petition to President Truman. He began circulating a draft on July 1, still not knowing if—or when—the A-bomb might be tested. On July 2, Szilard sent a draft to fellow scientists in the Manhattan Project. "However small the chance might be that our petition may influence the course of events," Szilard wrote, "I personally feel that it would be a matter of importance if a large number of scientists who have worked in this field went clearly and unmistakably on record as to their opposition on moral grounds to the use of these bombs in the present phase of this war."

At Los Alamos, Szilard's friend, the Hungarian-born physicist Edward Teller, refused to sign the petition, and turned it over to Robert Oppenheimer. Teller wrote Szilard that "actual combat use might even be the best thing" to educate the public about nuclear weapons. "The accident that we worked out this dreadful thing should not give us the responsibility of having a voice in how it is to be used." Oppenheimer agreed that the scientists deserved no say in "political" decisions, but used his own position as lab director to argue for dropping the bomb on cities.

On July 4, Szilard sent petitions to the secret Manhattan Project uranium plant at Oak Ridge, Tennessee, again pleading on "moral grounds" to oppose the bomb's use. There sixty-seven scientists signed a petition urging an A-bomb demonstration. By July 6, Met Lab security agents knew that Szilard was circulating his petition and warned General Groves. The next day the Army decreed that "Groves had no objection" to the petition, provided Szilard classified it "Secret" and sent it through official channels.

On July 8, intelligence officers handed over to General Groves copies of the petition and lists of the signers. And on July 9, Groves received copies of the Szilard-Teller letters, along with an intelligence officer's warning that "Szilard might attempt to get fellow scientist[s] to stop work." Szilard had nothing so practical in mind. On July 10, he wrote a friend at Los Alamos:

> Clearly, there are more important things to do and more effective ways to influence the course of events than the circulating of a petition but I have no doubt in my own mind that from a point of view of the standing of the scientists in the eyes of the general public one or two years from now it is a good thing that a minority of scientists should have gone on record in favor of giving greater weight to moral arguments and should have exercised their right given to them by the Constitution to petition the President.

Still, by July 11, an Army intelligence officer became newly alarmed that the petition, the transmittal letter, and the names of signers "are unclassified as the Subject [Szilard] did not classify them himself." On July 12, to discredit the petition, Groves had a poll distributed to Met Lab scientists that posed five options, from military use of the bomb to no use at all. To the Army's surprise, Szilard's ideas had wide support: 127 of the 150 scientists polled (seventy-two percent) favored a demonstration. On July 13, eighteen scientists at Oak Ridge signed an amended petition that "agreed in essence" with Szilard's but favored restricted use—once Japan had been warned.

Other scientists opposed the petition outright. On July 14, Evan Young at Oak Ridge wrote his superiors that "all of us do not concur" with the petition because "it behooves us to support our brothers and buddies overseas with the best and most potent weapons it is in our power to devise, and to end this damnable confusion and strife, and to allow the world to return to peaceful pursuits as soon as possible." Saying that an A-bomb was but an "extrapolation" of fire bombing cities, he asked: "Then why do we attempt to draw the line of morality here, when it is a question of degree, not a question of kind?" Young concluded, "Therefore, with no strings attached, let the War Department use this weapon at the earliest and most expeditious moment, in whatever manner will produce optimum results in the way of shortening the war and saving American lives."

Another Oak Ridge scientist, George W. Parker, sent a similar letter on July 16 and organized a counter-petition attacking Szilard as a security risk. This counter-petition, which attracted two signers, read in part: "If we can save even a handful of American lives, then let us use this weapon—now!" It said the signers "fail to see the use of a moral argument when we are considering such an immoral situation as war," and claimed: "These sentiments, we feel, represent more truly those of the majority of Americans and particularly those who have sons and daughters in the foxholes and warships in the Pacific."

BEFORE DAWN ON JULY 16, the first A-bomb was tested at the "Trinity" site in the New Mexico desert. General Groves was elated, but a few hours later he phoned the Pentagon with a warning to "be alerted with particular vigilance on...Leo." But in Chicago, Leo was toning down his petition in order to attract more signers. The final version, dated July 17, did not call for an outright ban on the bomb, but said it should be used only after Japan received detailed surrender terms. Then the President's decision should be tempered "by all the other moral responsibilities which are involved." Szilard sealed the petition in the manila envelope and delivered it to Arthur Compton, Director of the University of Chicago Metallurgical Project. (This petition sheet was one among many items that were "cleansed" from the Enola Gay exhibit at the National Air and Space Museum.)

Szilard's cover letter states that sixty-seven Chicago scientists had signed his petition, although seventy names appear on the pages that ultimately reached the White House—and are now in the National Archives. Another eighty-five signed amended versions at Oak Ridge. In all, 155 Manhattan Project scientists signed petitions that raised moral questions about dropping A-bombs on Japan's cities, and 127 of the 150 scientists who were polled favored a demonstration of some kind. On July 17, the same day Szilard sent his petition, Oppenheimer reported to General Groves about Szilard's appeal for Los Alamos scientists to sign. And in Oak Ridge, Groves's assistant, Colonel Kenneth Nichols, telephoned the General at the Pentagon to ask: "Why not get rid of the lion?" Groves answered we "can't do that at this time." But Groves did the next best thing by negotiating with Arthur Compton for an entire week about how he should forward Szilard's petition, and it was July 24 before the package went to Nichols at Oak Ridge.

Groves knew time was running out. On July 25, in Potsdam, Germany, with the "Big Three" Allied leaders—Truman, Churchill, and Stalin—Secretary of War Stimson approved the Army order (that Groves had written) to use A-bombs "as soon as weather will permit visual bombing after about 3 August." The targets named were Hiroshima, Kokura, Nagasaki, and Niigata—all spared from fire bombing so the effects of an A-bomb would be clear.

Meanwhile, Groves's assistant, Colonel Nichols, had bundled Szilard's sealed envelope, the petition pages with eighty-five signatures from Oak Ridge, the counter-petition, the two letters supporting use of the bomb, and the poll of the scientists. But then Nichols held the package for another week, finally sending it by courier to Groves in the Pentagon on July 30. On July 31, after Groves had received a telex from Tinian Island in the Pacific that "Little Boy," the uranium bomb, was ready, he forwarded the petition to the Secretary of War's office. On August 6, the "Enola Gay" dropped a uranium bomb on Hiroshima, instantly killing 70,000 inhabitants.

The same day, Szilard tried to publicize the petition, which, on purpose, he had not classified as "Secret." On August 16, an Army intelligence officer agreed with Szilard that the petition could be declassified. Next, Szilard asked the President's secretary to concur with the petition's release, and offered Science magazine the chance to publish it—once the White House approved. But before Truman could decide, General Groves intervened, and had the petition reclassified "Secret." Szilard first mentioned the petition publicly in a speech in December

1945, but it was not described in print until Arthur Compton published his memoirs in 1956. The petition was declassified beginning in 1957, but all the versions and the letters relating to it were only released in 1961. The anthology *The Atomic Age* was the first to publish a complete copy of Szilard's petition in 1963.

Despite the shroud of military censorship, Szilard's idea that scientists become activists succeeded immediately. On September 9, 1945, physicist James Franck and sixty-four other Chicago faculty members signed a petition to President Truman urging him to share atomic secrets with other nations—in order to create an international control scheme that would curb a nuclear arms race. The next day, Franck's petition was reported widely in the newspapers, and the day after that Secretary of War Stimson argued the scientists' viewpoint at a cabinet meeting. In the spring of 1946, the United States proposed an international control plan for the atom at the United Nations, although this was never achieved.

A second result of activism within the Manhattan Project was the establishment of the Atomic Scientists of Chicago in the fall of 1945. The group formed to debate nuclear policies, to work for civilian control of atomic energy at home and international control abroad, and to "educate public opinion." Since 1945, they have published the influential Bulletin of the Atomic Scientists, a monthly that uses as a logo the "doomsday clock" ticking off the minutes to midnight—before nuclear Armageddon.

THE WORLD COURT OPINION: NUCLEAR WEAPONS AND HUMANIATARIAN LAW

Lawrence Lifschultz

... For half a century now these terrifying weapons of mass destruction have formed part of the human condition. Nuclear weapons have entered into all calculations, all scenarios, all plans. Since Hiroshima, on the morning of 6 August 1945, fear has gradually become man's first nature. His life on earth has taken on the aspect of what the Koran calls "a long nocturnal journey", like a nightmare whose end he cannot yet foresee....The very nature of this blind weapon has a destabilizing effect on humanitarian law which regulates discernment in the type of weapons used. Nuclear weapons, the ultimate evil, destabilize humanitarian law which is the law of the lesser evil. The existence of nuclear weapons is therefore a challenge to the very existence of humanitarian law... Atomic warfare and humanitarian law... appear to be mutually exclusive: the existence of the one automatically implies the non-existence of the other.

Mohammed Bedjaoui
President, International Court of Justice
July 8, 1996

IN THE COLD WAR THAT FOLLOWED THE DESTRUCTION of Hiroshima and Nagasaki, nuclear weapons became the most feared aspect of a Manichaean struggle in a divided world. Two rival superpowers—the United States and the Soviet Union—representing particular variants of modern capitalism and socialism prepared themselves for nuclear war. Within half a century of the use of the first atomic bomb, the world had become hostage to the threat of total annihilation many times over by the combined arsenal of forty thousand nuclear weapons.

The first nuclear weapon state had spawned fierce imitators who embraced the doctrine of exterminism as a method of defense. One nuclear state was unable to dissuade others not to do what it had done: its own rationales became the intrinsic logic of others. Within twenty years of Hiroshima four more states openly acquired a nuclear capability, becoming full participants in the ruling doctrine of "mutually assured destruction" and its essential corollary, "deterrence." In all these states expensive institutes were established where experts, who considered themselves perfectly rational beings, could gather and consider the "options" whereby nuclear weapons might once again be used.

Meanwhile, Israel, Pakistan, and India became "undeclared" nuclear weapon states. Their sense of nationalism and their determination to demonstrate their sovereignty led them to embrace doctrines of mass annihilation as "proof" of their parity with the Great Powers. All these states now possess the capability to conduct war which makes noncombatants the prime target of annihilation. Where conventional wars between belligerent states like India and Pakistan once resulted in military fatalities in the low thousands, the new calculus involving nuclear weapons could potentially involve the deaths of millions of civilians. In a variety of non-nuclear states, political and military elites continue to pursue the hope that one day they too might have the dubious distinction of being a member of the nuclear club.

The pursuit of nuclear weapons requires a denial of the Hiroshima experience. In fact, as Kenzaburo Oé argues, those who build nuclear weapons must first engage in an exercise of "forgetting" or refusing to know what happened to those who experienced the nuclear attacks. "Hiroshima is the prime example not of the power of atomic weapons but of the misery they cause. But we want to put that aside..." Oé writes. "[P]eople everywhere on this earth are trying to forget Hiroshima and the unspeakable tragedy perpetrated there.... Forgetting all these things, we go on living comfortably in the crazy world of the late twentieth century." [1]

The survivors of Hiroshima and Nagasaki—the *hibakusha*—went forward, so to speak, with their lives. Initially, there was simply no question of "philosophically" coming to terms with what happened or drawing some abstract "greater meaning" from the experience. What one gathers from Oé, as one does from Primo Levi's work, is how traumatized souls stumble, quite unconsciously, in search of a form of activity which might aid them against an absolute fatalism of the spirit. When posed against the immensity of the event itself, they often felt that their actions were terribly inadequate and represented failure. However, by 1964, Oé observed that a distinctive group had emerged in Hiroshima:

> They are people who take the misery inflicted upon them by the atomic bomb and convert it from a passive into an active force.... Hiroshima as a whole must exert all its energy to articulate the essential intellectual grounds for abolishing all nuclear weapons in such a way that all of the victims' dehumanizing experiences—the misery, the shame and humiliation, the meanness and degradation—may be converted into things of worth so that the human dignity of [all] the A-bomb victims may be restored....What other human means can there be for liberating the A-bombs victims from their tragic fear of a miserable death? [2]

Hiroshima and Nagasaki thus became centers of a seemingly quixotic quest. In both cities organizations were established which set out to convince the world that the survival of tens of millions of people, perhaps even hundreds of millions, could only be secured by the abolition of nuclear weapons. From both Japanese cities, small delegations traveled the world. As nuclear arsenals continued to grow, grassroots antinuclear peace movements emerged across America, Europe, and Asia seeking to educate and mobilize citizens in support of universal nuclear disarmament. The protests that these movements launched were met with the full force of the state but their continued presence generated and sustained the debate on the admissibility of nuclear weapons as legitimate means of resolving conflicts in an ostensibly civilized world.

On the fiftieth anniversary of the bombings, in small groups of two or three, the *hibakusha* turned up at city halls and churches across the United States. Frequently, town officials or local clergy were at loss to know how to respond when told that what had happened to the men and women who stood before them must never be allowed to ever again happen. Nuclear weapons had to be abolished. Many of the Americans who heard these statements had lived for years in the shadow of America's Hiroshima legend. As described in this book, the legend was a set of powerful myths which the Smithsonian Institution had been compelled to propagate. [3]

IT WAS AT THIS JUNCTURE that, in July 1996, a year after the Smithsonian exhibit was censored, the World Court took a stand in its first formal opinion on the legality of nuclear weapons. Two years earlier the United Nations General Assembly had asked the Court for an advisory opinion. The UN posed a single, yet profoundly basic, question for consideration: "Is the threat or use of nuclear weapons in any circumstance permitted under international law?" Despite efforts by four of the five nuclear weapon states to prevent any legal opinion being rendered that might somehow impinge on their freedom to exercise a "nuclear option," the Court pressed ahead and issued its advisory opinion.

For the first time, the world's preeminent judicial authority has considered the question of criminality vis-à-vis the use of a nuclear weapon and, in doing so, *it has come to the conclusion that the use of a nuclear weapon is "unlawful."* [4] It is also the Court's view that even the threat of the use of a nuclear weapon is illegal. Although there were differences concerning the implications of the right to self-defense provided by Article 51 of the UN Charter, ten of the fourteen judges hearing the case found the use or threat to use a nuclear weapon to be illegal on the basis of the existing canon of humanitarian law which governs the conduct of armed conflict.

The judges based their opinion on more than a century of treaties and conventions that are collectively known as the "Hague" and "Geneva" laws. These concern the conduct of hostilities, the protection of prisoners, protective guarantees toward non-combatants, and rights guaranteed to neutral states and their populations. The successive Hague and Geneva conventions were amplified in 1977 by the Additional Geneva Protocols and these protocols were also drawn upon to render judgment. According to Louise Doswald-Beck, "The Court listed a number of 'cardinal principles...constituting the fabric of humanitarian law,' namely, the principle of distinction, the prohibition of the use of indiscriminate weapons, the prohibition against causing unnecessary suffering to combatants, and the fact that States do not have unlimited choice of means in the weapons they use." The Court argued the following proposition in its opinion:

> The cardinal principles contained in the texts constituting the fabric of humanitarian law are the following. The first is aimed at the protection of the civilian population and civilian objects and establishes

the distinction between combatants and non-combatants; *states must never make civilians the object of attack and must consequently never use weapons that are incapable of distinguishing between civilian and military targets.* According to the second principle, it is prohibited to cause unnecessary suffering to combatants: it is accordingly prohibited to use weapons causing them such harm or uselessly aggravating their suffering. In application of that second principle, *states do not have unlimited freedom of choice of means in the weapons they use.*

The Court would likewise refer, in relation to these principles to the Martens Clause, which was first included in the Hague Convention (II) with Respect to the Laws and Customs of War on Land of 1899 and which has proved to be an effective means of addressing the rapid evolution of military technology. A modern version of that clause…reads as follows: "In cases not covered by this Protocol or by other international agreements, civilians and combatants remain under the protection and authority of the principles of international law derived from established custom, from the principles of humanity and from the dictates of public conscience." [Article I, Additional Protocol of 1977]

In conformity with the aforementioned principles, humanitarian law, at a very early stage, prohibited certain types of weapons either because of their indiscriminate effect on combatants and civilians or because of the unnecessary suffering caused to combatants, that is to say, a harm greater than that unavoidable to achieve legitimate military objectives. *If an envisaged use of weapons would not meet the requirements of humanitarian law, a threat to engage in such use would also be contrary to that law.* [6]

The Court offered "no opinion" on the question of whether the use of a nuclear weapon might be legal under specific circumstances where the very existence of a state was threatened. In the absence of an international convention banning the use of nuclear weapons under any circumstances seven judges offered "no opinion" as to "the legality or illegality of the use of nuclear weapons by a state in an extreme circumstance of self-defense, in which its very survival would be at stake." [7] The uncertainty was based in part on a scenario of aggression carried out with weapons of mass destruction. Undoubtedly, the judges asked themselves whether the threat of use of nuclear weapons is, *a priori*, an impermissible response in such a circumstance. One of the seven judges, Judge Carl-August Fleischhauer, stated that "although recourse to nuclear weapons is scarcely reconcilable with humanitarian law," threat or use of nuclear weapons might be justified in self-defense as "a last resort against an attack with nuclear, chemical or bacteriological weapons." But, he further specified, lawful exercise of the right of self-defence would require proportionality, and "[t]he margin that exists for considering that a particular threat or use of nuclear weapons could be lawful is therefore extremely narrow." [8]

Other voices among the majority of ten noted that the paradox between the right to self-defense as stated in Article 51 and the possession of a nuclear weapon for "self-defense" could be resolved by an international convention which prohibited not only the use but the possession of any nuclear weapon by any state. Under a developed and advanced regime of international control the possession, use or threat to use a nuclear weapon would evoke a sharp response from international authorities. A state in "possession" of nuclear weapons or facilities designed to construct such weapons would be declared in breach of the convention, and would expect to face harsh measures designed to irrevocably subdue any government in violation of the law.

Three of the ten judges who declared the use or threat to use nuclear weapons to be illegal dissented from the Court's ruling in one important respect. They regarded the final opinion as not sufficiently clear or forceful by leaving open the possibility that a state might justify use on the pretext or rationale of "self-defense". The dissenting justices indicated that an international convention banning nuclear weapons was not required in their view in order to declare the use of nuclear weapons unlawful whatever the circumstance. As Judge Abdul G. Koroma stated, "It is inconceivable that there is any circumstance in which their use would not violate the principles and rules of international law applicable in armed conflict and, in particular, the principles and rules of humanitarian law." [9]

Nuclear weapons were in the view of Judges Abdul Koroma, Christopher Weeramantry, and Mohamed Shahabuddeen to be considered "unlawful" regardless of the requirements of Article 51. In their opinion the exercise of "self-defense" with the use of a nuclear weapon would involve a defending state in an open violation of the cardinal principles of humanitarian law. A nuclear weapon launched against an urban center of an aggressor state by a defending state would make the defending state the source of "immeasurable suffering" to the civilian population within the territorial borders of the regime instigating the aggression. [10] The potential annihilation of millions of innocent noncombatants as a "defensive act" would be inherently unlawful, constituting a gross violation of humanitarian and other international law. Furthermore, as the Chernobyl accident demonstrated the environmental damage and subsequent deaths due to radioactivity in neutral states would violate the protections guaranteed to non-belligerent populations. Judge Weeramantry summarized this position in the following manner:

> Self-defense raises probably the most serious problem in this case….[T]he [majority of the] Court [argues that it] cannot conclude definitively whether the threat or use of nuclear weapons would be lawful or unlawful in an extreme circumstance of self-defense, in which the very survival of a state would be at stake. I have voted against this clause as I am of the view that the threat or use of nuclear weapons would not be lawful in any circumstances whatsoever, as it offends the fundamental principles of *ius in bello*. This conclusion is clear and follows inexorably from well-established principles of international law.
>
> If a nation is attacked, it is clearly entitled under the United Nations Charter to the right of self-defense. Once a nation thus enters into the domain of the *ius in bello*, the principles of humanitarian law apply to the conduct of self-defense just as they apply to the conduct of any other aspect of military operations. We must hence examine what principles of *ius in bello* apply to the use of nuclear weapons in self-defense. The first point to be noted is that the use of *force* in self-defense (which is an undoubted right) is one

thing and the use of nuclear weapons in self-defense is another. The permission granted by international law for the first does not embrace the second, which is subject to other governing principles as well.

All of the seven principles of humanitarian law discussed in this Opinion apply to the use of nuclear weapons in self-defense, just as they apply to their use in any aspect of war. Principles relating to unnecessary suffering, proportionality, discrimination, non-belligerent states, genocide, environmental damage and human rights would all be violated, no less in self-defense than in an open act of aggression. The *ius in bello* covers all use of force, whatever the reasons for resort to force. There can be no exceptions, without violating the essence of its principles....

It is necessary to reiterate here the undoubtful right of a state that is attacked to use all the weaponry available to it for the purpose of repulsing the aggressor. Yet this principle holds only so long as such weapons do not violate the fundamental rules of warfare embodied in those rules. Within these constraints, and for the purpose of repulsing the enemy, the full military power of the state that is attacked can be unleashed upon the aggressor. While this is incontrovertible, one has yet to hear an argument in any forum, or a contention in any academic literature, that a nation attacked, for example, with chemical or biological weapons is entitled to use chemical or biological weapons in self-defense, or to annihilate the aggressor's population. It is strange that the most devastating of all the weapons of mass destruction can be conceived of as offering a singular exception to this most obvious conclusion following from the bedrock principles of humanitarian law...

Self-defense, which will, as shown in the discussion of proportionality, result in all probability in all-out nuclear war, is even more likely to cause genocide than the act of launching an initial strike. If the killing of human beings, in numbers ranging from a million to a billion, does not fall within the definition of genocide, one may well ask what will. No nation can be seen as entitled to risk the destruction of civilization for its own national benefit...It seems difficult, with any due regard to the consistency that must underlie any credible legal system to contemplate that all these hard-won principles should bend aside in their course and pass the nuclear weapon by, leaving that unparalleled agency of destruction free to achieve on a magnified scale the very evils which these principles were designed to prevent. [11]

FROM OUR PERSPECTIVE OF EXAMINING THE DECISION to bomb Hiroshima and Nagasaki, the World Court's decision has retrospective meaning. It is quite obvious that during the fateful summer of 1945 the United States, as the sole power in possession of a nuclear weapon, did not face a nuclear threat from Japan. Moreover, in the summer of 1945 with the United States and its allies on the verge of victory the question "of an extreme circumstance of self-defense in which the very survival of a state would be at stake" was not even remotely an issue for any of the states in the anti-Axis alliance. The use of nuclear weapons against Hiroshima and Nagasaki unquestionably failed to distinguish between civilians and military targets, thus violating the prohibition of inflicting indiscriminate harm on civilians which the Court expressly held existed prior to the commencement of the nuclear age. Thus, in the context of the criteria set out in the World Court's opinion, the atomic bombings of Hiroshima and Nagasaki were illegal.

According to John Burroughs, an American lawyer who has written extensively on the World Court's ruling, the entire strategic doctrine by which the North Atlantic Treaty Organization (NATO) operated during the Cold War has also been called into question by the Court's advisory opinion. For several decades NATO's operational protocols maintained that a conventional attack on Western Europe by members of the Warsaw Pact would face a nuclear response. Such a nuclear response could not meet the legal requirements of proportionality and discrimination identified by the Court.[12] In November 1997, despite the World Court opinion, the United States publicly restated its position regarding the use of nuclear weapons in a document known as the Presidential Decision Directive. According to the *New York Times*, "the United States still reserves the right to be the first to use nuclear arms during a conflict, rather than vowing to use them only once attacked." [13] This policy directive reaffirms the doctrine which was at the heart of U.S. and NATO policy during the Cold War and effectively defies the World Court opinion.*

In December 1996, six months after the World Court presented its opinion, sixty generals and admirals from seventeen countries issued an unprecedented declaration. Many of these men over half a century had held the nuclear trigger in their hands with the full knowledge that the nuclear weapons states had the capability to destroy human civilization. Under various ideological justifications, they had been trained to carry out such a task with the conviction that they were honorably serving their respective countries. They knew, first hand, that on more than one occasion the use of nuclear weapons had been actively considered. Ultimately,

---

* NATO is not the only entity that has adopted a military doctrine which relies upon a nuclear response to a conventional attack. Despite being undeclared nuclear states, Israel and Pakistan have each indicated to their potential antagonists that they have the capability and the will to use nuclear weapons against the conventional forces of their opponents. In May 1990, with their respective press and citizenry completely in the dark, the governments of Pakistan and India are reported to have nearly made South Asia the first site for the use of nuclear weapons since Hiroshima and Nagasaki. In 1974 India exploded a nuclear device. This step was taken by India as a response to China's emergence as a nuclear weapons state. However, the Indian explosion, in turn, provoked Pakistan's nuclear nationalists into a competitive race to build and acquire a nuclear weapons capability.

India and Pakistan have fought three conventional wars which to one degree or another have involved the province of Kashmir. A de facto division of the province between the two countries has existed since independence. In the spring of 1990, amidst unrest and a deteriorating political situation in India's Kashmir province, Pakistan reportedly feared a major conventional assault by Indian military forces. Operating on a doctrine similar to NATO's model, Pakistani military leaders appear to have prepared themselves to launch a nuclear attack, if and when, Indian forces crossed the border between the two states. In all probability, this would have led to an Indian nuclear response. According to Richard J. Kerr, the deputy director of the C.I.A., "It was the most dangerous nuclear situation we have ever faced since I've been in the U.S. government. It may be as close as we've come to a nuclear exchange. It was far more frightening than the Cuban missile crisis." [See Seymour M. Hersh, "On the Nuclear Edge," *The New Yorker,* March 29, 1993.]

however, they concluded that their indoctrination in the belief of deterrence had prepared them for acts of mass annihilation which the World Court had now declared to be criminal in character. Their statement, in part, reads as follows:

> We, military professionals, who have devoted our lives to the national security of our countries and our peoples, are convinced that the continuing existence of nuclear weapons in the armories of nuclear powers, and the ever present threat of acquisition of these weapons by others, constitute a peril to global peace and security, and to the safety and survival of the people we are dedicated to protect.
>
> Through our variety of responsibilities and experiences with weapons, and wars in the armed forces of many nations, we have acquired an intimate and perhaps unique knowledge of the present security and insecurity of our countries and peoples. We know that nuclear weapons, though never used since Hiroshima and Nagasaki, represent a clear and present danger to the very existence of humanity. There was an immense risk of a superpower holocaust during the Cold War. At least once, civilization was on the very brink of catastrophic tragedy. That threat has now receded, but not forever—unless nuclear weapons are eliminated. [15]

The statement was signed by senior military officers, many of whom had commanded nuclear forces in the arsenals of the Soviet Union, the United States, Britain, and France. Its signatories included, General George Lee Butler (Ret.), the former commander-in-chief of all U.S. strategic nuclear forces.[16] Rear Admiral Eugene J. Carroll, Jr. (Ret.) of the U.S. Navy, who also signed the statement, stated: "Many years ago I planned a mission to destroy a relatively insignificant military target in eastern Europe. Because the target was in a major city, my bomb (small by modern standards) would have killed 600,000 human beings. The memory of that example of the utterly indiscriminate, barbarous nature of nuclear warfare is one reason that I signed the call for nuclear abolition...."[17] Admiral Carroll had concluded that "no civilized nation could ever be exonerated from crimes against humanity if it threatened or resorted to the use of nuclear explosives in warfare." [18]

Alert at last to the magnitude of the Leviathan they knew one day would not be contained, these senior military officers called upon the nations of the world to abolish nuclear weapons by specific measures. It had taken a half century but a major contingent of the world's nuclear officer corps and the World Court had arrived at the same position as the survivors of Hiroshima. In essence, they collectively affirmed the principles that Albert Einstein and Bertrand Russell had set forth in their 1955 declaration: "There lies before us, if we choose, continual progress in happiness, knowledge, and wisdom. Shall we, instead, choose death, because we cannot forget our quarrels? Remember your humanity, and forget the rest.... [I]f you cannot, there lies before you the risk of universal death." [19]

NOTES

Special thanks are due to John Burroughs for his assistance in preparing this epilogue.

1. Kenzaburo Oé, *Hiroshima Notes* (London, 1995), pp. 107-109.
2. Oé, p. 106.
3. For a discussion of the key myths that constitute this American legend, see the introduction to this volume. Lawrence Lifschultz and Kai Bird, "The Legend of Hiroshima."
4. The Court specified in its vote that "a threat or use of force by nuclear weapons that is contrary to Article 2, paragraph 4, of the United Nations Charter and that fails to meet all the requirements of Article 51, is unlawful." See the "Legality of the Threat or Use of Nuclear Weapons," *Advisory Opinion of the International Court of Justice*, transcript made available through the International Association of Lawyers Against Nuclear Arms (IALANA), Amsterdam, Netherlands, p. 36. [Emphasis added.] The full opinion, including the judges' separate statements, can be found in International Legal Materials 814, No. 4, July 1996. It is also available at the website of the International Association of Lawyers Against Nuclear Arms (IALANA). (See http://www.ddh.nl/org/ialana) All page references are to numeration listed according to the texts published at this site.
5. Louise Doswald-Beck, "International Humanitarian Law and the Advisory Opinion of the International Court of Justice on the Legality of the Threat or Use of Nuclear Weapons," *International Review of the Red Cross*, January 1, 1997, p. 37.
6. *Advisory Opinion of the International Court of Justice*, Paragraph 78. [Emphasis added.]
7. *Advisory Opinion*, Paragraph 97.
8. Judge Carl-August Fleischhauer, "Separate Opinion of Judge Fleischhauer", Paragraphs 5 and 6, IALANA Transcript.
9. "Dissenting Opinion of Judge Abdul G. Koroma," IALANA Transcript, p.16.
10. Judge Carl-August Fleischhauer stated in his opinion that the "immeasurable suffering" caused by the use of a nuclear weapon amounted to "the negation of the humanitarian considerations underlying the law applicable to armed conflict and of the principle of neutrality. The nuclear weapon cannot distinguish between civilian and military targets…The radiation released by it is unable to respect the territorial integrity of a neutral state." (See "Separate Opinion of Judge Fleischhauer", IALANA Transcript, p. 1. However, Judge Fleischhauer differed from Koroma in accepting that Article 51 could not be denied even if the right to self-defense involved a nuclear response. Fleischhauer stated, "…the denial of the recourse to the threat or use of nuclear weapons as a legal option in any circumstance could amount to a denial of self-defense itself if such recourse was the last available means by way of which the victimized state could exercise its right under Article 51 of the Charter. A finding that amounted to such a denial therefore would not, in my view, have been a correct statement of law; there is no rule in international law according to which one of the conflicting principles would prevail over the other. The fact that the attacking state itself would act in contravention of international law, would not alter the situation."
11. "Dissenting Opinion of Judge Weeramantry," IALANA Transcript, pp. 56-59.
12. Interview with John Burroughs by Lawrence Lifschultz, October 26, 1997.
13. "U.S. 'Updates' All-Out Atom War Guidelines" by Steven Lee Myers, *The New York Times*, December 8, 1997, p. A-3.
14. Joseph Gerson, *With Hiroshima Eyes* (Philadelphia, 1995). Gerson discusses in great detail a series of events ranging from the Middle East and Korea to Cuba and Vietnam where the United States either overtly or covertly threatened the use of nuclear weapons.
15. "Statement on Nuclear Weapons by International Generals and Admirals," distributed by The Stimson Center, December 5, 1996, Washington, D.C.
16. George Lee Butler, "Time to End the Age of Nukes," *The Bulletin of the Atomic Scientists*, March/April 1997.
17. Rear Admiral Eugene J. Carroll, Jr., "Down the Right Road," Letter to the Editor, *The New York Times*, December 16, 1996. In an interview prsented in a video format released by the Center for Defense Information (Washington, D.C.), Carroll notes that the "relatively insignificant" target was a rather small military depot.
18. Letter by Rear Admiral Carroll to Lawrence Lifschultz, dated August 29, 1997.
19. "The Peril of Univeral Death" by Albert Einstein and Bertrand Russell, *Hiroshima's Shadow*, p. 487.

Gar Alperovitz's most recent book is *The Decision to Use the Atomic Bomb and the Architecture of an American Myth* (New York, July 1995). Among his other publications are a new edition of *Atomic Diplomacy: Hiroshima and Potsdam* (originally published in 1965), *Rebuilding America* (with Geoffrey Faux), *Strategy and Program*, and *Cold War Essays*. Alperovitz is currently President of the National Center for Economic and Security Alternatives.

Barton J. Bernstein is professor of history at Stanford University, where he co-directs the International Relations Program and the International Policy Studies Program. He writes on nuclear history, Cold War policies, and science and technology policy, including medical issues. He has published *The Atomic Bomb: The Critical Issues* (1976), among other volumes, and has recently published a long essay entitled, "The Struggle Over History: Defining the Hiroshima Narrative," in *Judgment at the Smithsonian: The Bombing of Hiroshima and Nagasaki*, ed. by Philip Nobile, (New York, 1995).

P. M. S. Blackett was a 1948 winner of the Nobel Prize in physics. He was a professor of physics at Manchester University and until 1948, he served on Britain's Advisory Committee on Atomic Energy. In 1947, he received the American Medal of Merit, the highest military honor given by the U.S. government to civilians. He is the author of *Fear, War, and the Bomb: Military and Political Consequences of Atomic Energy* (New York, 1948/49).

Paul Boyer is Merle Curti Professor of History and director of the Institute for Research in the Humanities at the University of Wisconsin-Madison. His books include *By Bomb's Early Light: American Thought and Culture at the Dawn of the Atomic Age* (1984; reissued with a new introduction by the author in 1994).

Wilfred Burchett (1911-1983) was an Australian combat journalist who reported from the battlefields of World War II, the Korean War, and the Indochina wars. He is the author of several books, including *Shadows of Hiroshima* (London, 1983).

Albert Camus (1913-1960) was a French novelist, essayist, and dramatist. During World War II he was active in the French Resistance and was editor of *Combat*. The author of many works which develop existentialist themes, Camus was awarded the 1957 Nobel Prize in literature.

Tony Capaccio is the editor of *Defense Week*, a defense journal based in Washington, D.C. He has covered the military for a decade and is a former staff associate of columnist Jack Anderson.

Norman Cousins (1915-1990) was an editor of *Saturday Review* from 1942–1971. An essayist and lecturer, Cousins was co-chair of the Citizens' Committee for a Nuclear Test Ban Treaty, Honorary President of the United World Federalists and the recipient of numerous public service awards. He was the author of many books, including *Modern Man is Obsolete*, *In God We Trust*, and *In Present Tense*.

John W. Dower, is Henry Luce Professor of History and International Cooperation at the Massachusetts Institute of Technology. He is the author of *War Without Mercy: Race & Power in the Pacific War* (New York, 1986), *Empire and Aftermath: Yoshida Shigeru and the Japanese Experience, 1878-1954*, *The Elements of Japanese Design*, and co-editor of *The Hiroshima Murals: The Art of Iri Maruki and Toshi Maruki*. Most recently, he published *Japan in War and Peace: Selected Essays* (1994).

Albert Einstein (1879-1955), a German-born American physicist and Nobel laureate, is best known as the creator of the special and general rules of relativity and for his hypothesis concerning the particle nature of light. After the war, Einstein was active in the cause of international disarmament.

Paul Fussell is Professor Emeritus of English at the University of Pennsylvania and the author of *Thank God for the Atom Bomb And Other Essays* (New York, 1988) and numerous other books. His book *The Great War and Modern Memory* won the National Book Award in 1976 as well as the National Book Critics Circle Award.

Mahatma Gandhi (1869-1948) was a leading figure in India's national movement for independence. He consistently advocated non-violence as a philosophy for political actions, and more generally, as a way of living.

Stanley Goldberg (1934-1996) was a historian of science (B.S., Physics, Antioch College; Phd., Harvard University) and a consultant to the Smithsonian Institution. He was the author of *Understanding Relativity: Origins and Impact of a Scientific Revolution* (Boston, 1984) and numerous articles on the history of late nineteenth and early twentieth century physics and its relationship to changing cultural fashions and values. At the time of his death, he was working on a biography of General Leslie Groves, a project which will be completed by Robert Standish Norris and published by Steerforth Press.

Adam Goodheart is a senior editor at *Civilization* magazine, where he writes the column "Lost Arts." His articles have also appeared in the *Washington Post*, the *New York Times*, *Playboy*, the *Utne Reader* and other publications.

Tamiki Hara (1905-1951) was born in Hiroshima and graduated from the English Department of Keio University. A poet, he survived the atomic bombing at Hiroshima and, in 1947, published the short story, "Summer Flower," which won the first Takitaro Minakami Prize. According to Kenzaburo Oé, "During the Korean War, when it was rumored that atomic bombs might again be used, [Hara] committed suicide."

Dr. Shuntaro Hida is the author of "The Day Hiroshima Disappeared" which has appeared in Japanese, French, and German. The excerpt published here is the first translation that has appeared in English. Since the war, Dr. Hida has continued working with survivors of the nuclear bombing and pioneered research on the long-term effects of radiation.

William Lanouette, a writer who has specialized in atomic energy for more than twenty-five years, is the author of *Genius in the Shadows: A Biography of Leo Szilard, The Man Behind the Bomb* (New York, 1993; Chicago, 1994). Lanouette has served on the staffs of *Newsweek, The National Observer,* and *National Journal,* and was most recently the Washington Correspondent for the *Bulletin of the Atomic Scientists.*

David Lawrence founded and edited *United States News* in 1933 which later changed its name to *U.S. News and World Report.* Lawrence wrote numerous books, including *True Story of Woodrow Wilson, Beyond the New Deal,* and *Stumbling Into Socialism.*

Dwight Macdonald (1906–1982) was a staff writer for *Fortune* magazine (1929–36), associate editor of *Partisan Review* (1937–43), editor and publisher of *Politics* (1944–49), and a staff writer for the *New Yorker* (1951–71). Macdonald was the author of numerous essays and books, including *The Root Is the Man, The Ford Foundation: The Men and the Millions,* and *Against the Grain: Essays on the Effects of Mass Culture.*

Mary McCarthy (1912–1989) was an editor of *Partisan Review* (1937–38), a drama critic, teacher and novelist. Her books include *The Oasis, The Groves of Academe, Memories of a Catholic Girlhood, The Group,* and *Vietnam;* these and her many other books and magazine articles won her high acclaim as a critic, essayist and novelist.

Robert L. Messer, Associate Professor of History at the University of Illinois at Chicago, is author of *The End of an Alliance: James F. Byrnes, Roosevelt, Truman and the Origins of the Cold War.* For nearly twenty years he has written, lectured and otherwise actively participated in the on-going public debate on the history and legacy of the atomic bombings of Hiroshima and Nagasaki.

Uday Mohan is a graduate student in the history department at American University. He is writing a thesis on how the United States media has represented the atomic bombing of Hiroshima since 1945.

Felix M. Morley (1894–1982) was a journalist, author and educator with Quaker roots and a lifelong commitment to international peace. During World War I he served on a Quaker-sponsored ambulance train behind the British front in France. In the 1920s he oversaw publications and public information for the League of Nations in Geneva, Switzerland. From 1933–40 he was editor of the *Washington Post.* During World War II, while president of his alma mater, Haverford College, he helped found and was first editor of *Human Events,* the *Washington News* and *Opinion Weekly.* Morley's later books included *The Power in the People, Freedom and Federalism* and his 1979 memoir, *For the Record.*

Lewis Mumford (1895–1990) was an American social philosopher, historian, and urban planner. He was editor of a number of publications, including the *Sociological Review* (London, 1920) and an annual anthology of American writing, *The American Caravan* (1927–1936). He was elected to the American Academy of Arts and Letters in 1955 and received the United States Presidential Medal of Freedom in 1964. His works include *The Culture of Cities* (1938), *Condition of Man* (1944), *The City in History* (1961), *Interpretations and Forecasts* (1973), and *Sketches from Life* (1982).

A.J. Muste (1885–1967) was a revolutionary pacifist, a founder of the American Workers Party, a leader of the Fellowship of Reconciliation, and a contributing editor of *Dissent* magazine.

Reinhold Niebuhr (1892–1971) graduated from Yale Divinity School in 1914 and was a pastor in Detroit from 1915–28. Thereafter he taught at Union Theological Seminary and wrote numerous books and essays, including *Leaves from the Notebook of a Tamed Cynic*, *Moral Man and Immoral Society*, *An Interpretation of Christian Ethics*, and *Children of Darkness*. He was a founding member, in 1947, of Americans for Democratic Action (A.D.A.) and a long-time Contributing Editor of *Christian Century*.

Kenzaburo Oé, born in 1935, has published about forty novels, books of short stories, critical and political essays and was awarded the Nobel Prize for Literature in 1994.

John Rawls is University Professor Emeritus at Harvard University where he taught for 34 years.

Joseph Rotblat won the 1995 Nobel Peace Prize. He is Emeritus Professor of Physics at the University of London, St. Bartholomew's Hospital Medical College. A founder of the Pugwash Conference on Science and World Affairs, he was its secretary general for seventeen years.

Bertrand Russell (1872–1970) was a British philosopher, mathematician, and Nobel laureate, whose emphasis on logical analysis influenced the course of twentieth-century philosophy. He was a pacifist, an advocate of social justice, and a proponent of nuclear disarmament.

Ronald E. Santoni holds the Maria Theresa Barney Chair of Philosophy at Denison University in Ohio. In addition to his recently published work on Sartre, *Bad Faith, Good Faith* and *Authenticity in Sartre's Early Philosophy* (Philadelphia, 1995), he is co-editor of *Social and Political Philosophy*, editor of *Religious Language and the Problem of Religious Knowledge*, and contributor to numerous books and journals. He is currently President of Concerned Philosphers for Peace.

Murray Sayle, an Australian, lives in Japan.

Mark Selden, Binghamton and Cornell Universities. He is co-editor with Laura Hein of *Living with the Bomb. American and Japanese Cultural Conflicts in the Nuclear Age*.

Martin J. Sherwin, professor of history at Tufts University, is the author of *A World Destroyed: The Atomic Bomb and the Grand Alliance* (Knopf/Vintage, 1976/1987). The author of numerous journal articles, he is currently writing a biography of J. Robert Oppenheimer. In 1995, he was co-chair with Kai Bird of the Historians' Committee for Open Debate on Hiroshima.

Edgar Raymond Smothers (1932–1970) was a Jesuit Priest and scholar whose articles were published in numerous journals including the *Harvard Theological Review, Catholic Biblical Quarterly, Theological Studies,* and *America.*

Hideko Tamura Snider is the author of *One Sunny Day* (Chicago, 1996). A child in Hiroshima when the city was destroyed in 1945 by an atomic bomb, she came to the United States in 1952 after finishing high school. She is a therapist in private practice and a part-time social worker in the Radiation Oncology Department at the University of Chicago Hospital.

Henry L. Stimson (1867–1950) was Governor General of the Philippines, Secretary of War for President William Howard Taft (1911–13), Secretary of State for President Herbert Hoover (1929–33) and Secretary of War for President Franklin D. Roosevelt (1940–45). He co-authored with McGeorge Bundy a memoir, *On Active Service in Peace and War* (New York, 1948).

Norman Thomas (1884–1968) graduated from Princeton University in 1905 and received a divinity degree from Union Theological Seminary in 1911. Ordained in the Presbyterian Church in 1911, Thomas was the pastor for several churches in New York City until he became the associate editor of *The Nation* in 1921–22. The following year, he became the director of the League for Industrial Democracy. He was the Socialist Party's candidate for governor of New York in 1924, and its presidential candidate in 1928, 1932 and 1936. He was the author of numerous books, including *The Conscientious Objector in America, America's Way Out: A Program for Democracy,* and *War: No Profit, No Glory.*

Sanho K. Tree is a Research Associate at the Institute for Policy Studies. From 1989 to 1995 he was the archival research director for historian Gar Alperovitz's book *The Decision to Use the Atomic Bomb and the Architecture of an American Myth.* He was also Research Director for the Historians' Committee for Open Debate on Hiroshima.

Mike Wallace teaches at John Jay College of the City University of New York. The full text of his essay, "The Battle of The Enola Gay," appears in *Mickey Mouse History and Other Essays on American Memory* (Philadelphia, 1996).

Michael Yavenditti is a professor at Alma College, Michigan. His articles have appeared in *Film & History, The Historian,* and *Mid-America.*

EDITORS

Kai Bird is the author of *The Chairman: John J. McCloy, The Making of the American Establishment* (New York, 1992). A Contributing Editor of *The Nation*, he has written essays and books reviews for *Foreign Policy, The Washington Post Book World, Tikkun magazine, Diplomatic History* and numerous other publications. He is currently completing a biography of William and McGeorge Bundy. In 1995, he was co-chair with Martin Sherwin of the Historians' Committee for Open Debate on Hiroshima.

Lawrence Lifschultz has been a South Asia correspondent of the *Far Eastern Economic Review*. He has also written extensively on Asian and European affairs for *The Guardian* (London), *Le Monde Diplomatique*, the BBC and *The Nation*. He is co-editor with Rabia Ali of *Why Bosnia? Writings on the Balkan War* (Stony Creek, CT, 1993) and is the author of the forthcoming volume *The Economic Foundations of a Modern Imperium: the Industrial Development of the United States from Civil War to World War*.

SELECTED BIBLIOGRAPHY

Allen, Thomas B. and Norman Polmar. *Code-Name Downfall: The Secret Plan to Invade Japan—And Why Truman Dropped the Bomb.* New York: Simon & Schuster, 1995.

Alperovitz, Gar. *The Decision to Use the Atomic Bomb.* New York: Alfred A. Knopf, 1995.

Alperovitz, Gar. *Atomic Diplomacy: Hiroshima and Potsdam,* expanded and updated. New York: Penguin, 1985.

Bernstein, Barton J., ed. *The Atomic Bomb: The Critical Issues.* Boston: Little, Brown and Co., 1976.

Bird, Kai. Chapter 12, "Hiroshima," *The Chairman: John J. McCloy, the Making of the American Establishment.* New York: Simon & Schuster, 1992.

Bosworth, R.J.B. *Explaining Auschwitz & Hiroshima.* New York: Routledge, 1993.

Boyer, Paul. *By the Bomb's Early Light.* New York: Pantheon, 1985.

Braw, Monica. *The Atomic Bomb Suppressed: American Censorship in Occupied Japan.* Armonk, New York: M.E. Sharpe, 1991.

Bundy, McGeorge. *Danger and Survival: Choices about the Bomb in the First Fifty Years.* New York: Random House, 1988.

Burchett, Wilfred. *Shadows of Hiroshima.* London: Verso, 1983.

Dower, John. War *Without Mercy: Race & Power in the Pacific War.* New York: Pantheon, 1986.

Drea, Edward J. *MacArthur's Ultra: Codebreaking and the War Against Japan, 1942-1945.* Lawrence, Kansas: University Press of Kansas, 1992.

Eisenhower, Dwight D. *The White House Years: Mandate for Change, 1953-1956.* Garden City, New York: Doubleday, 1963.

Feifer, George. Tennozan: *The Battle of Okinawa and the Atomic Bomb.* New York: Ticknor & Fields, 1992.

Feis, Herbert. *The Atomic Bomb and the End of World War II.* Princeton: Princeton University Press, 1966.

Ferrell, Robert H. *Harry S. Truman: A Life.* Columbia, Missouri: University of Missouri Press, 1994.

Fussell, Paul. Chapter 1, "Thank God for the Atom Bomb", in *Thank God for the Atom Bomb and Other Essays.* New York:, 1988.

Gerson, Joseph. *With Hiroshima Eyes: Atomic War, Nuclear Extortion and Moral Imagination.* Philadelphia: New Society Publishers, 1995.

Giovannitti, Len and Fred Freed. *The Decision to Drop the Bomb.* New York: Coward-McCann, 1965.

Harwit, Martin. *An Exhibit Denied: Lobbying the History of the Enola Gay.* New York: Springer-Verlag, 1996.

Hershberg, James G. *James B. Conant: Harvard to Hiroshima and the Making of the Nuclear Age.* New York: Alfred A. Knopf, 1993.

Herken, Gregg. *The Winning Weapon: The Atomic Bomb in the Cold War, 1945-50.* New York: Alfred Knopf; Princeton: Princeton University Press, 1981 and 1988 (new preface).

Hersey, John. *Hiroshima.* New York: Vintage Books, 1985.

Hogan, Michael, ed. *Hiroshima in History and Memory.* New York: Cambridge University Press, 1996.

Holloway, David. *Stalin and the Bomb: The Soviet Union and Atomic Energy, 1939-1956.* New Haven: Yale University Press, 1994.

Iriye, Akira. *Power and Culture: The Japanese-American War, 1941-1945.* Cambridge: Harvard University Press, 1981.

Jones, Vincent C. *Manhattan, the Army and the Atomic Bomb.* Washington, D.C.: Center of Military History, U.S. Army, 1985.

Lanouette, William with Bela Szilard. *Genius in the Shadows: A Biography of Leo Szilard, the Man Behind the Bomb.* New York: Charles Scribner's Sons, 1992.

Leahy, William. *I Was There: The Personal Story of the Chief of Staff to Presidents Roosevelt and Truman, based on His Notes and Diaries Made at the Time.* New York: Whittlesey House, 1950.

Leffler, Melvyn P. *A Preponderance of Power: National Security, the Truman Administration, and the Cold War.* Stanford: Stanford University Press, 1992.

Lifton, Robert Jay and Greg Mitchell. *Hiroshima In America: Fifty Years of Denial.* New York: G.P. Putnam, 1995.

Linenthal, Edward Tabor. "Pearl Harbor." *In Sacred Ground: Americans and their Battlefields.* Urbana: University of Illinois Press, 1993. 2nd ed.

Linenthal, Edward T. and Tom Engelhardt, eds. *History Wars: The Enola Gay and Other Battlers for the American Past.* New York: Metropolitan Books, Henry Holt & Co., 1996.

McCullough, David. *Truman.* New York: Simon & Schuster, 1992.

Maddox, Robert James. *The New Left and the Origins of the Cold War.* Princeton: Princeton University Press, 1973.

Messer, Robert L. *The End of an Alliance: James F. Byrnes, Roosevelt, Truman and the Origins of the Cold War.* Chapel Hill: University of North Carolina Press, 1982.

Muresianu, John. *War of Ideas: American Intellectuals and the World Crisis, 1938-1945.* New York: Garland, 1988.

Nobile, Philip. *Judgment at the Smithsonian.* New York: Marlowe & Co., 1995.

Novick, Peter. *That Noble Dream: The "Objectivity Question" and the American Historical Profession.* Cambridge: Cambridge University Press, 1988.

Piehler, G. Kurt. *Remembering War the American Way.* Washington, D.C.: Smithsonian, 1995.

Rhodes, Richard. *The Making of the Atomic Bomb.* New York: Simon & Schuster, 1986.

Robertson, David. *Sly and Able: A Political Biography of James F. Byrnes.* New York: W.W. Norton, 1994.

Shaheen, Jack G. and Richard Taylor. "The Beginning or the End." In *Nuclear War Films.* Carbondale: Southern Illinois University Press, 1978.

Sherry, Michael. *The Rise of American Air Power: The Creation of Armageddon.* New Haven: Yale University Press, 1987.

Sherwin, Martin. *A World Destroyed: Hiroshima and the Origins of the Arms Race,* rev. ed. New York: Alfred Knopf, 1987.

Shinobu, Seizaburo, *Seidan no Rekishigaku .* (Historical Meaning of the Emperor's Majestic Decision), Tokyo: Keiso Shobo, 1992.

Sigal, Leon. *Fighting to a Finish: The Politics of War Termination in the United States and Japan.* Ithaca: Cornell University Press, 1988.

Skates, John Ray. *The Invasion of Japan: Alternative to the Bomb.* Columbia, SC: University of South Carolina Press, 1994.

Snider, Hideko Tamura. *One Sunny Day: A Child's Memories of Hiroshima.* Chicago: Open Court, 1996.

Spector, Ronald H. Eagle *Against the Sun: The American War With Japan.* New York: Vintage, 1985.

Stoff, Michael, Jonathan Fanton, and R. Hal Williams. *The Manhattan Project: A Documentary Introduction to the Atomic Age.* Philadelphia: Temple University Press, 1991.

Takaki, Ronald. *Hiroshima: Why America Dropped the Bomb.* Boston: Little, Brown & Co., 1995.

Treat, John Wittier. *Writing Ground Zero: Japanese Literature and the Atomic Bomb.* Chicago: University of Chicago Press, 1995.

Truman, Harry S. *Off the Record: The Private Papers of Harry S. Truman,* ed. Robert H. Ferrell. New York: Harper & Row, 1980; Penguin, 1982.

Udall, Stewart L. *The Myths of August,* New York: Pantheon Books, 1994.

Walzer, Michael. *Just and Unjust Wars: A Moral Argument with Historical Illustrations.* New York: Basic Books, 1977.

Walker, Samuel J. *Prompt and Utter Destructon: Truman and the Use of Atomic Bokmbs Against Japan.* Chapel Hill: University of North Carolina Press, 1997.

Weart, Spencer. *Nuclear fear: A History of Images.* Cambridge, Mass.: Harvard University Press, 1988.

Weinberg, Gerhard L. *A World At Arms: A Global History of World War II.* New York: Cambridge University Press, 1994.

Winkler, Allan. *Life Under a Cloud: American Anxiety about the Atom.* New York: Oxford, 1993.

Wyden, Peter. *Day One: Before Hiroshima and After.* New York: Simon & Schuster, 1984.

ACKNOWLEDGEMENTS

Our thanks to the following authors and publications for permission to reproduce their work in this volume. The editors and many of our contributors have asked that their royalties for this book be donated to the Hiroshima Memorial Peace Museum, the Nagasaki Atomic Bomb Museum, and the Historian's Committee for an Open Debate on Hiroshima. Pamphleteer's Press is supporting this effort.

"Beyond the Smithsonian Flap" by Gar Alperovitz first appeared in the *Washington Post,* 16 October 1994.

" Enola Gay: A New Consensus" by Gar Alperovitz first appeared in the *Washington Post,* 4 February 1995.

"Historians Reassess: Did we Need to Drop the Bomb?" by Gar Alperovitz is based on "Did We Need to Drop the Bomb? A Historian Weighs the Evidence" *Technology Review* (August/September 1990) and "Historian's Reassess," *Foreign Policy 99* (September 1995), copyright 1995 by the Carnegie Endowment for International Peace.

"Hiroshima, Rewritten" by Barton Bernstein. First appeared in the *New York Times,* 31 January 1995.

"A Postwar Myth: 500,000 U.S. Lives Saved" by Barton Bernstein first appeared in *The Bulletin of the Atomic Scientists,* June 1986. Copyright 1986 by the Educational Foundation for Nuclear Science. Minor revisions have been made to the version printed in this volume.

"Seizing the Contested Terrain of Early Nuclear History" by Barton Bernstein first appeared in *Diplomatic History,* Spring 1995. Minor revisions have been made to the version printed in this volume.

"The Curators Cave In" by Kai Bird first appeared in the *New York Times,* 9 October 1994.

"Enola Gay: Politically Correct" by Kai Bird first appeared in the *Washington Post,* 4 February 1995.

The Bissell Memo: Prospects for Japan's Surrender by Major General Clayton Bissell, Assistant Chief of Staff, The War Department, Military Intelligence Division. Bissell Papers, 7 July, 1945. ID #926728, box 74. Assistant Chief of Staff for Intelligence Papers, Record Group 319, National Archives.

The Decision to Drop the Bomb by P.M.S. Blackett was originally published in *Fear, War and the Bomb: Military and Political Consequences of Atomic Energy* by P.M.S. Blackett published by McGraw Hill Book Company (1947).

"Victory for What? The Voice of the Minority" by Paul Boyer first appeared in *By the Bomb's Early Light: American Thought and Culture at the Dawn of the Atomic Age,* Pantheon Books, (1984) and a new edition with a new introduction by the author, University of North Carolina Press (1994).

"The Brown Diary: August 3rd Byrnes Acknowledges Japan 'Looking for Peace.'" July 1945. Mss 90 James F. Byrnes Collection, folder 602, transcriptions from the Walter Brown Journal. Published with the permission of Special Collections, Clemson University Libraries, Clemson, South Carolina. NOTE: Byrnes had the journal transcribed, possibly by U.S. Naval Intelligence.

"The First Nuclear War" by Wilfred Burchett first appeared in *Shadows of Hiroshima,* Verso (1983).

"After Hiroshima: Between Hell and Reason" by Albert Camus first appeared in *Combat,* 8 August 1945. © Editions Gallimard, Paris, 1950. Translated by Ronald E. Santoni in *Philosophy Today,* Spring 1988.

How the U.S. Press Missed the Target by Tony Capaccio and Uday Mohan first appeared as *Missing the Target* in *American Journalism Review,* July/August 1995.

"The Literacy of Survival" by Norman Cousins first appeared in *The Saturday Review of Literature,* September 1946.

"How a Genuine Democracy Should Celebrate Its Past" by John Dower first appeared in *The Chronicle of Higher Education,* 16 June 1995.

"Unconditional Surrender at the Smithsonian" by John Dower first appeared in *Technology Review,* August/September 1995, as "Politics of Memory."

"The Horror and The Shame" by the Editors of *Commonweal* first appeared in *Commonweal*, 24 August 1945 (vol. XLII, No 19). copyright *Commonweal*.

"Nothing But Nihilism" by the Editors of *Catholic World* first appeared in *Catholic World*, September 1945. Copyright Paulist Press.

"Atomic Warfare and the Christian Faith" from a report of the Federal Council of Churches, 1946. Copyright the National Council of Churches of Christ in the U.S.A.

"The Forrestal Diary: Japanese Peace Feelers" by James V. Forrestal, Secretary of the Navy, from a memorandum of 19 June; 13, 15, 24, 26 July 1945. James V. Forrestal Diaries, Box No.1, Vol. 2. Seeley G. Mudd Manuscript Library, Department of Rare Books and Special Collections, Princeton University Libraries.

"The Forrestal Diary: McCloy's Dissent on the Emperor & Prior Warning" by James F. Forrestal, Secretary of the Navy, from a memorandum of 8 March 1947. *James V. Forrestal Diaries*, Box No. 3, Vol. 6. Seeley G. Mudd Manuscript Library, Department of Rare Books and Special Collections, Princeton University Libraries.

"Thank God for the Atom Bomb" by Paul Fussell first appeared in *The New Republic*, 26 August 1991. Copyright 1988 by Paul Fussell.

"Racing to the Finish" by Stanley Goldberg. A portion of this essay was originally published under this title in the *Journal of American-East Asian Relations*, Vol. 4, No. 2 (Summer 1995). Copyright 1995 by Imprint Publications. Reproduced by permission of the publisher. Another portion of this essay was published as "Groves Takes the Reins", and first appeared in *The Bulletin of the Atomic Scientists*. December 1992. Copyright 1992 by the Educational Foundation for Nuclear Science.

"The Smithsonian Suffers Legionnaire's Disease" by Stanley Goldberg first appeared in *The Bulletin of the Atomic Scientists*, May 1995. Copyright 1995 by the Educational Foundation for Nuclear Science.

"The Invasion that Never Was" by Adam Goodheart first appeared in *Civilization*, January/February 1995. Copyright Adam Goodheart, 1995.

"The Grew Memo: Accept Emperor as Post-War Constitutional Monarch" by Joseph Grew. From a memorandum of 28 May 1945. First published in *Turbulent Era*, Volume II. Republished with the permission of the Houghton Library, Harvard University.

"Summer Flower" by Tamiki Hara first appeared in *The Crazy Iris and Other Stories of the Atomic Aftermath* edited by Kenzaburo Oé, published by Grove Press 1985.

"The Enola Gay: A Nation's and a Museum's Dilemma" by Martin Harwit first appeared in the *Washington Post*, 7 August 1994. Copyright the *Washington Post*.

"The Day Hiroshima Disappeared" by Shuntara Hida was first published as "Under the Mushroom Shaped Cloud in Hiroshima" in *The Day Hiroshima Disappeared*, 1982. Reprinted with permission from the author.

"Truman was Right in 1945" by Alfred R. Hunt first appeared in the *Wall Street Journal*, 8 August 1985. Reprinted with permission of the *Wall Street Journal*, copyright 1985, Dow Jones & Company, Inc. All rights reserved.

"World War II Revisited" by Charles Krauthammer first appeared in the *Washington Post*, 19 August 1994. Copyright the *Washington Post*.

"Three Attempts to Stop the Bomb" by William Lanouette first appeared in *Genius in the Shadows: A Biography of Leo Szilard* by William Lanouette with Bela Silard. Reprinted with the permission of Scribner, an imprint of Simon & Schuster. Copyright 1992 William Lanouette.

"What Hath Man Wrought" by David Lawrence first appeared in *U.S. News and World Report*, 17 August 1945.

"The Leahy Diary: Prospect of a Negotiated Surrender". An entry from the *Diaries of William D. Leahy*, Chief of Staff to the President and Member of the Joint Chiefs of Staff, Leahy Diary, 18 June 1945. William D. Leahy Papers, Library of Congress, Manuscript Division.

"The 'Hiroshima' New Yorker" by Mary McCarthy first appeared in *politics*, vol. 3, #10, November 1946. Reprinted with permission of the Mary McCarthy Literary Trust.

"The McCloy Diary: General Marshall Argues Restrict First Use to Military Target" by John J. McCloy. From a Memorandum of Conversation between General Marshall, Secretary Stimson, and Assistant Secretary of War John J. McCloy, in John J. McCloy Papers (Box DY1, Folder 17), Amherst College Archives and Special Collections, Amherst, MA.

"The McCloy Diary: Warning, Surrender & Truman's 'Big Red Apple'" by John J. McCloy. Exerpts from diary entries of 17, 23, 24, July 1945 in John J. McCloy Papers, (Box DY1, Folder 18) Amherst College Archives and Special Collections, Amherst, MA.

"The Decline to Barbarism" by Dwight Macdonald first appeared as "The Bomb" in *politics*, September 1945.

"The Marshall Memo: Change the Terms of Unconditional Surrender" by George C. Marshall. Source: From George C. Marshall to Stimson, "ABC 337 (11 January 45) Sec 1-A" Entry 421, Record Group 165, National Archives. Reprinted with permission of the George C. Marshall Library, Lexington, Virginia.

"New Evidence on Truman's Decision" by Robert L. Messer first appeared in *The Bulletin of the Atomic Scientist*, August 1985. Copyright 1985 by the Educational Foundation for Nuclear Science.

"The Construction of Conventional Wisdom" by Uday Mohan and Sanho Tree. Originally published in the *Journal of American-East Asian Relations*, vol. 4, No.2, (Summer 1985). Copyright 1995 by Imprint Publications. Reproduced by permission of the publisher.

"The Return to Nothingness" by Felix Morley first appeared in *Human Events*, 29 August, 1945. Copyright *Human Events*, 1945.

"Gentlemen, Are You Mad?" by Lewis Mumford first appeared in the 2 March 1946 issue of *The Saturday Review of Literature*.

"Has It Come to This?" by A.J. Muste first appeared in *Not By Might* published by Harper & Brothers Publishers, 1947.

"What New Consensus?" by Robert P. Newman first appeared in the *Washington Post*, 30 November 1994. Copyright the *Washington Post*.

"The Smithsonian and the Bomb", an editorial in the *New York Times* first appeared in the *New York Times*, 5 September 1994. Copyright the *New York Times*.

"Our Relations to Japan" by Reinhold Niebuhr first appeared in *Christianity and Crisis*, 17 September 1945.

"The Unsurrendered People" by Kenzaburo Oé first appeared in *Hiroshima Notes*, New York, London: Marion Boyars Publishers (1995).

"Fifty Years after Hiroshima" by John Rawls first appeared in *Dissent*, Summer 1995.

"The Revisionists' Agenda" by Stephen S. Rosenfeld first appeared in the *Washington Post*, 4 August 1995. Copyright the *Washington Post*.

"Leaving the Bomb Project" by Joseph Rotblat first appeared in *The Bulletin of the Atomic Scientists*, August 1985. Copyright 1985 by the Educational Foundation for Nuclear Science.

"A Note on Between Hell and Reason" by Ronald E. Santoni first appeared in the *Concerned Philosophers for Peace Newsletter*, October 1987 and in *Philosophy Today*, Spring 1988. Reproduced by permission of Ronald E. Santoni.

"Did the Bomb End the War?" by Murray Sayle originally appeared as "Letter from Hiroshima: Did the Bomb End the War?" in *The New Yorker*, 31 July 1995. Copyright Murray Sayle, 1995. All rights reserved. Reproduced by permission of Murray Sayle and *The New Yorker*.

"The Logic of Mass Destruction" by Mark Selden originally appeared as "Before the Bomb: the "Good War," Air Power and the Logic of Mass Destruction" in *Contention*, vol.5, #1, Fall 1995.

"Hiroshima & Modern Memory" by Martin Sherwin first appeared in *The Nation*, 10 October 1981.

"Memory, Myth and History" by Martin Sherwin originally appeared as "Hiroshima as Politics and History" in *The Journal of American History* 82 (December 1995), 1085-93.

"An Opinion on Hiroshima" by Edgar R. Smothers, S.J. first appeared in *America*, 5 July 1947. Reprinted with permission of America Press, Inc., 106 West 56th Street, New York, N.Y. 10019. Copyright 1947. All Rights Reserved.

"Hiroshima Memories" by Hideko Tamura Snider adapted from a longer work, *One Sunny Day*, Chicago: Open Court, 1996. First appeared in *The Bulletin of the Atomic Scientists*. Copyright 1985, 86, 92, 95 by the Educational Foundation for Nuclear Science.

"The Decision to Drop the Bomb" by Henry Stimson first appeared in *Harper's Magazine*. February 1947. Copyright 1947 by *Harper's Magazine*. All rights reserved. Reproduced from the February issue by special permission.

"The Stimson Diary: The Soviets & the S-1 Master Card" by Henry Stimson. Memo to President Truman, 2 July 1945. Henry L. Stimson Papers, Manuscripts and Archives, Yale University Library.

"The Stimson Memo: Prior Warning with 'Ample Time'" by Henry L. Stimson, Secretary of War to President Truman, 14 May 1945. Papers of Naval Aide, Harry S. Truman Library, Independence, Missouri.

"The July 17th Petition of Manhattan Scientists to Truman" by Leo Szilard & Colleagues, National Archives, Record Group 77, Harrison-Bundy Files, Box 153, Folder 76. Also appeared in *The Atomic Age*, edited by